This book is to be returned on or before the last date stamped below.

11.4.16

WITHDRAWN

D1429424

Praise for the first edition

"Health psychology has developed rapidly as a discipline over the past 25 years and this book gives a very valuable contemporary view of the area. The editors and authors are world experts in their fields and they offer a well-organised overview of the empirical evidence, theoretical approaches and opportunities for intervention in behaviour relevant to health, illness and healthcare."

—**Professor Marie Johnston**, School of Psychology,
University of Aberdeen

"*Health Psychology* offers a well-structured, state-of-the-art overview of the major theoretical, empirical and practical issues, written by leading international experts. It is an indispensable companion for students, researchers and practitioners. *Health Psychology* is an essential volume that moves the field another step ahead."

—**Wilmar Schaufeli**, PhD, Director of the Research Institute
Psychology & Health, Utrecht University

"Written by a team of internationally known writers and researchers in the field, this book stands out from other textbooks of health psychology. The opening chapter alone ought to be mandatory reading for anyone contemplating health psychology as a career and those in related professions, while the ensuing chapters give new interest to the major issues in current mainstream health psychology. This is a timely and welcome contribution to the discipline."

—**Sandra Horn**, School of Psychology,
University of Southampton

"This volume constitutes a major step forward in the development of health psychology as a science and as a professional discipline by giving an up-to-date and thorough overview of the field, often with a refreshing European flavour. It offers a number of useful features like mentioning key studies for a certain area and proposing 'discussion points'."

—**Professor Dr Jan Vinck**, Limburgs
Universitair Centrum, Belgium

"This comprehensive collection provides an authoritative overview of current thinking in health psychology research. A team of leading and predominantly European researchers map out the state of the science in an accessible and informative style."

—**Professor Charles Abraham**, Department of Psychology,
University of Sussex

"*Health Psychology* is another very good textbook that has much to offer those with an interest in health psychology …The content is densely packed, but the 'Chapter Outline' and 'Key Concepts' at the beginning of each chapter ensure that finding particular information is quick and easy …The book has a contemporary feel to it, referring to up-to-date studies and ideas. Many of the chapters are thoughtful and critical, and often acknowledge current difficulties and shortcomings."

—**Emma Dures**, University of the West of England, *Psychology,
Health and Medicine*, February 2005, 10(1): 122–124

Health Psychology

SECOND EDITION

Edited by David French, Kavita Vedhara,
Ad A. Kaptein and John Weinman

This edition first published 2010 by the British Psychological Society and Blackwell Publishing Ltd
© 2010 Blackwell Publishing Ltd

BPS Blackwell is an imprint of Blackwell Publishing, which was acquired by John Wiley & Sons in February 2007. Blackwell's publishing program has been merged with Wiley's global Scientific, Technical, and Medical business to form Wiley-Blackwell.

Registered Office
John Wiley & Sons Ltd, The Atrium, Southern Gate, Chichester, West Sussex, PO19 8SQ, UK

Editorial Offices
350 Main Street, Malden, MA 02148-5020, USA
9600 Garsington Road, Oxford, OX4 2DQ, UK
The Atrium, Southern Gate, Chichester, West Sussex, PO19 8SQ, UK

For details of our global editorial offices, for customer services, and for information about how to apply for permission to reuse the copyright material in this book please see our website at www.wiley.com/wiley-blackwell.

The right of David French, Kavita Vedhara, Ad A. Kaptein & John Weinman to be identified as the author of this work has been asserted in accordance with the UK Copyright, Designs and Patents Act 1988.

Wiley also publishes its books in a variety of electronic formats. Some content that appears in print may not be available in electronic books.

Designations used by companies to distinguish their products are often claimed as trademarks. All brand names and product names used in this book are trade names, service marks, trademarks or registered trademarks of their respective owners. The publisher is not associated with any product or vendor mentioned in this book. This publication is designed to provide accurate and authoritative information in regard to the subject matter covered. It is sold on the understanding that the publisher is not engaged in rendering professional services. If professional advice or other expert assistance is required, the services of a competent professional should be sought.

Library of Congress Cataloging-in-Publication Data

Health psychology / edited by David French ... [et al.]. – 2nd ed.
    p. ; cm.
  Includes bibliographical references and index.
  ISBN 978-1-4051-9461-7 (plpc : alk. paper) – ISBN 978-1-4051-9460-0 (pbk. : alk. paper)
1. Clinical health psychology.   I. French, David (David P.)   II. British Psychological Society.
  [DNLM: 1. Psychology, Clinical. WM 105 H3342 2010]
  R726.7.H433 2010
  616.001′9–dc22

                                                  2010011918

A catalogue record for this book is available from the British Library.

Set in 10/12pt Bembo by SPi Publisher Services, Pondicherry, India

The British Psychological Society's free Research Digest e-mail service rounds up the latest research and relates it to your syllabus in a user-friendly way. To subscribe go to www.researchdigest.org.uk or send a blank e-mail to subscribe-rd@lists.bps.org.uk.

1   2010

Contents

List of Contributors

Charles Abraham
Department of Psychology, University of Sussex, Falmer, Brighton, BN1 9QG, UK

Emily Arden-Close
Department of Psychology, The University of Sheffield, Western Bank, Sheffield, S10 2TN, UK

Robert Aunger
Disease Control and Vector Biology Unit, London School of Hygiene & Tropical Medicine, Keppel Street, London, WC1E 7HT, UK

Stuart J.H. Biddle
School of Sport and Exercise Sciences, Loughborough University, Loughborough, Leicestershire, LE11 3TU, UK

Kate Brain
Institute of Medical Genetics, School of Medicine, Cardiff University, Heath Park, Cardiff, CF14 4XN, UK

Elizabeth Broadbent
Department of Psychological Medicine, Faculty of Medical and Health Sciences, School of Medicine, The University of Auckland, Private Bag 92019, Auckland, New Zealand

Jos F. Brosschot
Department of Psychology, University of Leiden, 2300 RB Leiden, The Netherlands

Chris Bundy
School of Psychological Sciences, The University of Manchester, Coupland Building, Oxford Road, Manchester, M13 9PL, UK

Linda D. Cameron
Department of Psychology, The University of Auckland, Building 734, Room 33, Tamaki Campus, Auckland, New Zealand

Jane Clatworthy
Department of Practice and Policy, School of Pharmacy, University of London, 29-39 Brunswick Square, London, WC1N 1AX, UK

Andrea Croom
Division of Psychology, Department of Psychiatry, University of Texas Southwestern Medical Center, 5323 Harry Hines Boulevard, Dallas, TX 75390-9044, USA

Jason Dahn
Department of Psychology and Sylvester Comprehensive Cancer Center, College of Arts & Sciences, University of Miami, Coral Gables, Florida 33124, USA

H. Clare Daniel
The Pain Management Centre, The National Hospital for Neurology and Neurosurgery, University College London Hospitals NHS Foundation Trust, Queen Square, London, WC1N 3BG, UK

Diane Dixon
Department of Psychology, University of Strathclyde, Graham Hills Building, 40 George Street, Glasgow G1 1QE, UK

Linda M. Drew
Division of Psychology, Department of Psychiatry, University of Texas Southwestern Medical Center, 5323 Harry Hines Boulevard, Dallas, TX 75390-9044, USA

Christine Eiser
Department of Psychology, The University of Sheffield, Western Bank, Sheffield, S10 2TN, UK

Kelly B. Filipkowski
Department of Psychology, Syracuse University, 402 Huntington Hall, Syracuse, NY 13244-2340, USA

Jill Francis
Health Services Research Unit, University of Aberdeen, 3rd Floor, Health Sciences Building, Foresterhill, Aberdeen, AB25 2ZD, UK

Benjamin Gardner
Health Behaviour Research Centre, Department of Epidemiology and Public Health, University College London, 1–19 Torrington Place, London, WC1E 6BT, UK

Sue Hall
Department of Palliative Care, Policy and Rehabilitation, King's College London, Denmark Hill Campus, Cutcombe Road, London, SE5 9RJ, UK

Richard Hammersley
Department of Psychology, Glasgow Caledonian University, 70 Cowcaddens Road, Glasgow, G4 0BA, UK

Madeline Hernandez
Department of Psychology, College of Arts & Sciences, University of Miami, Coral Gables, Florida 33124, USA

Rob Horne
Department of Practice and Policy, School of Pharmacy, University of London, 29-39 Brunswick Square, London, WC1N 1AX, UK

Myra S. Hunter
Department of Health Psychology, Institute of Psychiatry, Fifth Floor, Thomas Guy House, Guys Hospital, London, SE1 9RT, UK

Marie Johnston
Institute of Applied Health Sciences, University of Aberdeen Medical School, Polwarth Building, Aberdeen AB25 2ZD, UK

Nina Knoll
Institute for Medical Psychology, Charité – Universitätsmedizin Berlin, Luisenstraße 57, 10117 Berlin, Germany

Patricia Loft
Department of Psychological Medicine, Faculty of Medical and Health Sciences, School of Medicine, The University of Auckland, Private Bag 92019, Auckland, New Zealand

Hannah McGee
Department of Psychology, Division of Population Health Sciences, Royal College of Surgeons in Ireland, 120 St Stephens Green, Dublin 2, Republic of Ireland

Rona Moss-Morris
School of Psychology, Shackleton Building, University of Southampton, Highfield, Southampton, SO17 1BJ, UK

Jane Ogden
Department of Psychology, The University of Surrey, Guildford, Surrey, GU2 7XH, UK

Jeffrey T. Parsons
Center for HIV/AIDS Educational Studies and Training (CHEST), Hunter College and Graduate Center of the City University of New York (CUNY), 695 Park Avenue, Room 611N, New York, NY 10065, USA

Sheila Payne
Division of Health Research, School of Health and Medicine, Lancaster University, Bowland Tower Easter, Lancaster, LA1 4YW, UK

Frank Penedo
Department of Psychology and Sylvester Comprehensive Cancer Center, College of Arts & Sciences, University of Miami, Coral Gables, Florida 33124, USA

Lena Ring
Department of Pharmacy, Uppsala University, Box 580, 751 23 Uppsala, Sweden

Magdalene Rosairo
Department of Health Psychology, Institute of Psychiatry, Fifth Floor, Thomas Guy House, Guys Hospital, London, SE1 9RT, UK

Suzanne E. Scott
Department of Oral Health Services Research & Dental Public Health, Dental Institute, King's College London, Caldecot Road, London, SE5 9RW, UK

Ralf Schwarzer
Health Psychology, Freie Universität Berlin, Habelschwerdter Allee 45, 14195 Berlin, Germany

Lion Shahab
Cancer Research UK Health Behaviour Research Centre, Department of Epidemiology and Public Health, University College London, 1-19 Torrington Place, London, WC1E 6BT, UK

Andrew Steptoe
Psychobiology Group, Department of Epidemiology and Public Health, University College London, 1–19 Torrington Place, London, WC1E 6BT, UK

Kim G. Smolderen
Centre of Research on Psychology in Somatic Diseases, Department of Medical Psychology, Tilburg University, Room P610, PO Box 90153, 5000 LE Tilburg, The Netherlands

Joshua M. Smyth
Department of Psychology, Syracuse University, 402 Huntington Hall, Syracuse, NY 13244-2340, USA

Falko F. Sniehotta
Fuse – the Centre for Translational Research in Public Health, William Leech Building, Framlington Place, Newcastle University, Newcastle upon Tyne, NE2 4HH, UK

Stephen Sutton
Institute of Public Health, University of Cambridge, Forvie Site, Robinson Way, Cambridge, CB2 0SR, UK

Julian F. Thayer
Department of Psychology, The Ohio State University, 133 Psychology Building, 1835 Neil Avenue, Columbus, OH 43210, USA

Ayse K. Uskul
Department of Psychology, University of Essex, Colchester CO4 3SQ, UK

Ad Vingerhoets
Room P206, PO Box 90153, 5000 LE Tilburg, The Netherlands

Jane Wardle
Health Behaviour Research Centre, Department of Epidemiology and Public Health, University College London, 1–19 Torrington Place, London, WC1E 6BT, UK

Alison J. Wearden
School of Psychological Sciences, The University of Manchester, Coupland Building, Oxford Road, Manchester, M13 9PL, UK

Brooke E. Wells
Center for HIV/AIDS Educational Studies and Training (CHEST), 250 W. 26th Street, Suite 300, New York, NY 10001, USA

Robert West
Cancer Research UK Health Behaviour Research Centre, Department of Epidemiology and Public Health, University College London, 1-19 Torrington Place, London, WC1E 6BT, UK

Deborah J. Wiebe
Division of Psychology, Department of Psychiatry, University of Texas Southwestern Medical Center, 5323 Harry Hines Boulevard, Dallas, TX 75390-9044, USA

Amanda C. de C. Williams
Research Department of Clinical, Educational & Health Psychology, University College London, Gower Street, London, WC1E 6BT, UK

Alison J. Wright
Division of Health & Social Care Research, King's College London, 42 Weston Street, London, SE1 3QD, UK

1

Health Psychology

Introduction to Second Edition

David P. French, Kavita Vedhara, Ad A. Kaptein and John Weinman

Health psychology is concerned with the study of psychological processes in health, illness and health care, and this book has been structured to provide an authoritative overview of the field. Later in this introduction we will outline some of the key issues and areas within health psychology but, before that, we would like to summarise the changes to the book since the first edition.

The first edition of this book was published in 2004 and was very well received by the health psychology community. In 2008, we obtained very constructive feedback on the first edition and this has been used as the basis for planning the second edition. The most important feedback concerned the generally high quality of the chapters, all of which were written by subject experts. However, our attention was also drawn to the fact that some key topics were either missing or only partially covered. In particular it was recommended that the book needed to provide a good quality coverage of all the key areas and topics listed in syllabus recommendations for masters degree-level health psychology programmes, such as those provided by the British Psychological Society (Division of Health Psychology Training Committee, 2008). Thus, in this edition, we have not only continued to ensure that all the chapters are written by subject experts but we have also substantially extended the scope of the book by adding many new chapters, which has resulted in a very comprehensive coverage of the key areas. In particular, there is greater coverage of specific health behaviours, health-behaviour models and processes, individual and contextual factors, and underlying psychobiological processes. Since the

book has now grown considerably in size and breadth of coverage, the original editors were really pleased to be joined by David French and Kavita Vedhara as co-editors for this edition in order to extend the scope and expertise of the editorial team.

In order to achieve all this, we have added 20 entirely new chapters as well as changing a number of existing chapters. In addition to providing a general overview of the role of behaviour in health (Steptoe *et al.*, Chapter 2), we now have included specific chapters focusing on the key behaviours which have significant influences on health and well-being. Thus we now include separate chapters on smoking (Shahab & West, Chapter 3), physical activity (Biddle, Chapter 4), eating behaviour (Odgen, Chapter 5), alcohol and drug use (Hammersley, Chapter 6) and sexual health and behaviour (Parsons & Wells, Chapter 7), all of which now ensures that the book has a really comprehensive coverage of those health-related behaviours that make a major contribution to public health.

The first edition had a single, general chapter which covered the social-cognition models used to explain variation in health-related behaviours. We have now split this material into three chapters, to reflect the advances in knowledge brought about largely by the rapid increase in quality and quantity of intervention studies using these models. We have included a chapter on risk perception (Wright, Chapter 9), which also covers research on the effectiveness of different approaches to risk communication in changing health-related behaviour, in addition to chapters on changing health-related behaviours using both stage models (Sniehotta & Aunger, Chapter 11), and non-stage or 'continuum' models such as the theory of planned behaviour (Sutton, Chapter 10). Extending this theme of applying theory to intervention, another of the new chapters deals with general issues in health behaviour interventions (Abraham, Chapter 8). The inclusion of this topic reflects the increasing concern of health psychology with the development of theory-based interventions, which aim to ensure not only that behaviour-change interventions are based on a sound theoretical understanding of the determinants of the behaviour but also make it possible to understand how and why such interventions succeed or fail.

A similar logic also applies to another new chapter, namely the one on health care professional behaviour (Francis & Johnston, Chapter 15), which describes the ways in which health psychologists are using psychological theories to both understand and influence key clinical behaviours. This new chapter has effectively replaced the one on communication in health care in the first edition, partly because the editorial team felt that no substantive recent developments had taken place in medical communication research but mainly because we felt that the contribution of health psychology to understanding and improving the clinical behaviour of health-care professionals represents an exciting and new extension of the discipline. Just as it is recognised that many patients do not follow medical advice or treatment, we now realise that health-care professionals often fail to adopt recommended evidence-based new clinical practices. The widespread patterns of treatment non-adherence has generated considerable research not only into understanding the reasons for this but also into testing the efficacy of interventions to remedy non-adherence, and this work is included in yet another new chapter (Horne & Clatworthy, Chapter 14). Another area of developing medical practice, where there are important psychological issues to consider, is that of screening and prevention. Thus we have included a new chapter which describes some of the emotional, cognitive and behavioural consequences associated with undergoing screening (Brain, Chapter 17).

Whereas the first edition had a single chapter on pain and symptom perception, we have now divided these topics in order to do justice to each. Thus, while the new chapter on symptom perception and help seeking (Scott, Chapter 13) focuses on the important links between the processes involved in detecting symptoms and the decision to seek help, the revised pain chapter covers the key conceptual and clinical issues in pain, perception, cognition and behaviour (Daniel & Williams, Chapter 24).

As well as recognising the importance of stress, stress-related emotions and associated physiological processes in health outcome (Thayer & Brosschot, Chapter 19) and in hospitalisation and medical procedures (Smolderen & Vingerhoets, Chapter 18), we also thought that it was important to introduce a new chapter giving an overview of psychoneuroimmunology (Broadbent & Loft, Chapter 20) since this field provides insights into some of the key pathways and mechanisms through which psychological states can influence physiological processes and disease outcomes. Following this, we now have new authors and a new approach to the chapter on coping with stress (Smyth & Filipkowski, Chapter 21) and an updated chapter, which overviews the influence of social support on health and illness (Schwarzer & Knoll, Chapter 22). The chapters on illness cognition and behaviour (Cameron & Moss-Morris, Chapter 12) and quality of life (McGee & Ring, Chapter 26) have also been updated to reflect new developments in these areas. Also updated and considerably revised because of the inclusion of new authors and new research in the field is the chapter on psychological interventions in chronic illness (Wearden & Bundy, Chapter 16).

The final way in which this edition has been influenced by the British Psychological Society's recommended curriculum for health psychology is reflected in the inclusion of a number of new chapters focusing on both individual and contextual factors which can influence psychological processes in health and illness. Thus we now include an overview of the ways in which personality factors can influence health and illness-related behaviour (Wiebe et al., Chapter 23). We have also recognised the importance of a life-span perspective in health psychology by the introduction of new separate chapters on developmental and family influences (Arden-Close & Eiser, Chapter 29) and ageing and health (Penedo et al., Chapter 30). In addition, new chapters on social-cultural perspectives (Uskul, Chapter 27) and gender influences on health (Hunter & Rosairo, Chapter 28) provide coverage of the considerable influence of these two major social/contextual factors in health and illness behaviour. Moreover, we have included new chapters that recognise the actual and potential input which health psychologists can contribute to understanding of the nature of disability (Dixon & Johnston, Chapter 25) and to the needs of patients at the end of life (Hall & Payne, Chapter 31).

The addition of so many high-quality new chapters together with the updating and development of existing chapters has ensured that this volume, quite uniquely, now provides an expert-based coverage of the breadth of content recommended for masters level degree courses in health psychology (e.g. Division of Health Psychology Training Committee, 2008). The only areas of such courses we do not attempt to cover relate to generic issues of methodology and research, which already have numerous excellent books devoted to them (e.g. Field, 2009; Smith, 2003), as well as book chapters which focus on these same issues in a health psychology context (French *et al.*, 2004; Johnston *et al.*, 2004; Sutton & French, 2004). The remainder of this introductory chapter includes an overview of the context and nature of health psychology research and practice.

Health Psychology in Context

Health and illness have long been the object of scientific and clinical interest for psychologists. Health psychology was first used in a book title in 1979 (Stone, Cohen & Adler). Over 30 years on, one would need a large bookcase to hold all the books that have 'health psychology' in their titles or that belong to the category of health psychology. The year 1979 was important for the formal establishment of the subdiscipline. The book by Stone *et al.* (1979) was published, and in September 1979, Matarazzo presented his presidential address to the Division of Health Psychology at an APA meeting. The title of his address was 'Behavioral Health and Behavioral Medicine – Frontiers for a New Health Psychology' (Matarazzo, 1980). He defined health psychology as 'the aggregate of the specific educational, scientific, and professional contributions of the discipline of psychology to the promotion and maintenance of health, the prevention and treatment of illness, and the identification of

Figure 1.1 Health psychology and related disciplines

etiologic and diagnostic correlates of health, illness, and related dysfunction' (p. 815). In the 1982 definition, the following text was added: '… and to the analysis and improvement of the health care system and health policy formation' (Matarazzo, 1982, p. 4).

Health psychology is sometimes confused with a number of related disciplines (Weinman & Petrie, 2009). Figure 1.1 summarises the position of health psychology and those disciplines in a grid with 'psychology–medicine' on the *x*-axis, and 'mental disorders–physical disorders' on the *y*-axis (Kaptein & Weinman, 2004, pp. 4–6). Of course, separating 'mental problems' from 'physical disorders' is artificial, and the allocation of the different disciplines into their positions in the four quadrants may be somewhat forced. The quadrant with 'psychology' and 'physical disorders' constitutes health psychology. As we will discuss in detail in the next section, in health psychology, psychological theories and methods are applied in order to examine how to ensure that people stay healthy or achieve better adaptation to or recovery from illness.

Clinical psychology focuses on patients, or clients, with mental health problems (e.g. phobias, anxiety disorders, depression, substance abuse). The theoretical models and interventions that clinical psychologists apply to clients with these problems have been shown to be applicable to patients with chronic physical health problems (White, 2001). This has encouraged clinicians and researchers to apply these models to individuals with physical health problems as well. In this sense, health psychology and behavioural medicine were influenced and shaped by clinical psychology, and there are now many clinical psychologists who work in the area of clinical health psychology (e.g. Bennett Johnson *et al.*, 2002; Kennedy, 2007; Newman *et al.*, 2009).

Psychiatry also focuses on patients with mental health problems. Psychiatrists mainly adopt a biomedical approach to patients with such disorders, applying medication and medical treatment. Currently, psychiatry appears to be dominated by biomedical, genetic and molecular approaches but, within psychiatry, there are practitioners who make use of psychological treatments, either on their own or more commonly in conjunction with medical approaches.

Behavioural medicine, liaison psychiatry and *medical psychology* are in the quadrant 'physical disorders' and 'medicine'. These three fields all focus on physical disorders and diseases, although there are differences in their emphasis and theoretical background. Behavioural medicine is defined as 'the interdisciplinary field concerned with the development and integration of behavioural, psychosocial, and biomedical science, knowledge and techniques, relevant to the understanding of health and illness, and the application of this knowledge and these techniques to prevention, diagnosis, treatment and rehabilitation' (Outlook SBM, 1995, p. 1). Central to behavioural medicine is its interdisciplinary nature, and the emphasis on integration of behavioural and biomedical knowledge. In addition, although behavioural medicine also incorporates (primary) prevention, just like health psychology, behavioural medicine's emphasis is more on treatment and rehabilitation. A comparison of the content of the major journals in behavioural medicine (*Annals of Behavioral Medicine, Behavioral Medicine, International Journal of Behavioral Medicine, Journal of Behavioral Medicine*) with the major journals in health psychology (*Health Psychology, British Journal of Health Psychology, Psychology & Health*) easily demonstrates this point.

Liaison psychiatry is a subspecialty within psychiatry, focusing on patients in a medical setting whose responses to illness – for medical or psychological reasons – lead to problems for the patient and/or the medical staff. Although liaison psychiatry and health psychology have developed over a similar period of time with a number of overlapping interests and concerns, there are some important differences between the two fields. Whereas liaison psychiatry has its major focus on patients with physical health problems and who are experiencing psychological difficulties, health psychology has a much broader remit since it is concerned with all behaviours which influence health and illness in all individuals. Thus, while health psychology has focused on the development of theoretically based explanations and interventions for health-related and illness-related behaviours, liaison psychiatry has been concerned primarily with the diagnosis and treatment of people with either unexplained symptoms or with psychiatric disorders occurring in the context of a physical health problem.

Medical psychology is an older term which was used for describing the disciplinary area for psychologists who worked in medical settings (medical schools and hospitals), and who diagnosed and managed patients with physical health problems and were often involved with teaching and training of medical students and staff about psychology as applied to health and illness. However, this term is used much less frequently now, as most psychologists working in these contexts tend to be called health or clinical health psychologists.

Health Psychology and its Four Fields

We now move on from defining and demarcating scientific disciplines to illustrations of the four core elements of health psychology. The *first* element of health psychology, given Matarazzo's definition, is the promotion and maintenance of health. Studies in this area are aimed at healthy individuals and identifying where health psychology is instrumental in achieving this aim. Wardle (2000) has labelled this 'public health psychology', and has outlined various areas where health psychology can play a role.

Kaplan (2000) pointed out how 'promotion and maintenance of health' have very different connotations in medicine and (health) psychology. Prevention in the medical context pertains to 'identifying an existing disease at an early stage and eliminating the problem before it gets out of control', while prevention in behavioural models pertains to 'maneuvers that reduce the chances that a health problem will ever develop' (p. 382). Physicians and others working with a medical model of health and illness often define activities that scientists and clinicians who work in a behavioural model would call 'secondary prevention' as 'primary prevention'. This is a matter that is not only limited to a semantic issue, or to confusion in medical students and behavioural-science teachers when they teach about prevention. As Kaplan (2000) emphasises, 'Secondary prevention is typically based on a traditional biomedical model that requires the diagnosis and treatment of an existing condition and that usually involves one or more of the following: medical diagnosis, surgery, or use of medications. Primary prevention is usually based on a behavioral rather than a disease model. Diagnosis plays a lesser role because there is no disease to diagnose. Intervention is typically behavioral and might include exercise, dietary change, or the avoidance or reduction of alcohol use. Interventions might also include public policy changes' (p. 383). However, in the context of secondary prevention, reduction of disease risk or progression may be achieved by behaviour changes, either to promote increased physical activity or improved dietary choice or to reduce the risks associated with smoking, alcohol and drug use, and certain sexual behaviours.

The *second* element, prevention and treatment of illness, has some overlap with the first area, but more obviously focuses on people who have been identified to be at risk for disease (e.g. those who have been screened to be at risk for coronary heart disease or stroke from blood pressure screening, or for colorectal, cervical or breast cancer as the result of screening programmes involving testing for faecal occult blood, the cervical smear test and mammography, respectively). Here the aim is to detect risk or early signs of disease at an early enough stage in order to eliminate or slow down its development. Although this approach is often thought of as primarily biomedical, it may also involve key behavioural factors. Thus there is now considerable evidence of the importance of psychological factors in the uptake (Cooke & French, 2008; Jepson *et al.*, 2000) and impact of screening (Brain, Chapter 17). Moreover, if risks are identified then subsequent prevention is often achieved through behavioural changes and/or medical options, such as anti-hypertensive or lipid lowering medication, which also involve a major behavioural component (i.e. adherence to the treatment).

Health psychologists have an excellent track record when it comes to psychological interventions in people who are ill. There are now many studies, as well as systematic reviews (including Cochrane reviews), and meta-analyses of psychological interventions aimed at improving either disease or disease-related outcomes, such as depression or quality of life, across a wide range of physical health problems (see Kennedy, 2007; Newman *et al.*, 2009).

If we consider three of the major physical illnesses and some of the best intervention studies from a (clinical) health psychology point of view, a number of important papers illustrate what the field has to offer. Linden *et al.* (1996), in a meta-analysis of behavioural interventions in cardiovascular disease, conclude, 'The addition of psychosocial treatments to standard cardiac rehabilitation regimens reduces mortality and morbidity, psychological distress, and some biological risk factors' (p. 745). In the area of cancer, Rehse and Pukrop (2003) and Meyer and Mark (1995) present two meta-analyses on the effects of psychosocial interventions on 'quality of life' and other major outcome measures. The conclusions by Meyer and Mark are of the utmost importance: 'it would be an inefficient use of research resources to conduct more studies … to ask the simple question: Is there an effect of behavioural, educational, social support, and non-behavioural counselling and therapy interventions on the emotional adjustment, Functional adjustment, and treatment-and disease-related symptoms of cancer patients? These interventions have a consistent beneficial effect on all three areas' (p. 106). In the area of the third leading cause of death in developed societies, chronic obstructive pulmonary disease (COPD), Lacasse *et al.* (2003) in a Cochrane review conclude that psychosocial interventions 'relieve dyspnea and fatigue, and enhance patients' sense of control over their condition. These improvements are moderately large and clinically significant' (p. 1; see also Kaptein & Creer, 2002). However, not all such reviews are so positive in their conclusions and there are a number of areas where there is not yet consistent evidence of positive outcomes from psychological intervention (e.g. Yorke *et al.*, 2006).

Two further issues deserve discussion. The first has to do with the kind of outcome measures which health psychologists choose as dependent variables in the intervention studies examining effects of psychological or psychosocial treatment on various conditions. As outlined by Kaplan (1990) in his important paper 'Behavior as the Central Outcome in Health Care', choosing observable outcome measures which make sense in the real world is his preferred type of dependent variable. It is important to consider Kaplan's views when planning a study, or when studying the research literature in health psychology. All too often, health psychologists fall victim to the trap of examining associations between two self-report measures, and so it is no surprise to find high correlations between self-reports of, for example, life events and physical symptoms. Self-reports are susceptible to a variety of biases and it is equally important to try and predict more 'objective' indicators, such as survival, resumption of work and social activities (Petrie *et al.*, 2002). Secondly, various authors, health psychologists themselves, increasingly publish critical papers on a number of major issues in health psychology. For example, Ogden (2003) has critically reviewed the social cognition theories developed in the health psychology domain, and concluded that 'If social cognition models are to be given the status of theories, then it is recommended that the critical eye that psychologists place on other areas of research also be cast on this one' (p. 427). Similarly, Salmon and Hall (2003) have critically reviewed one of the pet concepts of health psychologists ('patient empowerment and control'). These papers illustrate the coming of age of health psychology: the area is being criticised by scientists who contribute to the further development of health psychology.

The *third* element of health psychology in Matarazzo's definition is 'etiologic and diagnostic correlates of health and illness'. Illustrations of these two topics can be found in almost any recent issue of a health psychology journal. Appels' work on 'vital exhaustion' as a contributor to the incidence of myocardial infarction is a good example of the role of a psychological factor in the aetiology of a major illness (van Diest *et al.*, 2002). With this type of research, the use of appropriate designs and well-chosen samples is crucial. Thus health psychology research has needed to make use of longitudinal, case-control and quasi-experimental designs in order to establish the role of psychological factors in the aetiological process.

The *fourth* and final element is 'health care system and health policy'. Health psychology research aiming at examining or changing the health-care system and/or health policy is rather scarce. However, there are interesting studies which have examined the impact of different types of health-care environment on patient well-being and recovery (e.g. Devlin & Arnell, 2003), and there is growing interest in examining the role of psychological factors in explaining variation in health-care professional behaviour, particularly in the adoption of evidence-based approaches to investigation and treatment (see Chapter 15, this volume).

Types of Health Psychology Research

As in every other area of psychology, there are very different types of research conducted within health psychology. A broad distinction can be made between three broad categories of study, namely those which are descriptive, predictive or intervention-based.

At the most basic level are the descriptive studies, which represent a very useful first step in research since they provide accounts of the nature and range of key behaviours or other psychological processes. For example, descriptions of the levels of engagement in different health behaviours such as daily physical activity or dietary intake (see Chapter 2, this volume), or of the ways in which people cope with stressors, including major health problems (see Chapter 21, this volume) provide an important database for the discipline.

Typically, *predictive studies* will involve either the development or application of psychological theories. A large number of theories have been developed for explaining variations in health- and illness-related behaviour, and these continue to be refined in order to improve their predictive power. Some have been borrowed from other areas of psychology, particularly from social psychology, and applied to the explanation of different health behaviours whereas others have been developed specifically within the context of health psychology research and both have been shown to be valuable. In a discussion of general and health-specific models of self regulation, Cameron and Leventhal (2003) point to the important interchange between general and health-specific models, and the potential that this can offer for enhancing the flow of information between the fields of social cognition and personality and health psychologies. In this way health psychology research can effectively inform the development of theory in these other fields; and so the fields can develop in synchrony.

Despite the importance of descriptive and predictive studies for establishing the empirical and theoretical basis of health psychology, a more definitive test of theory needs to involve experimental or quasi-experimental methodologies. Increasing levels of confidence in explaining health and illness behaviour can be gained from studies in which independent variables (e.g. arousal, emotion, knowledge, beliefs, etc.) are experimentally manipulated in order to see whether this results in predicted/hypothesised changes in behaviour or other outcomes, including health. This can be achieved using laboratory-type experimental methods where tight control can be exercised over the manipulation of independent variables and where dependent variables can be observed and/or measured with precision. For example, psycho-physiological studies have been conducted to establish relations between such factors as stressors and both physiological (e.g. blood pressure, salivary control, immune function) and psychological outcomes (e.g. mood, information processing). Similarly there is increasing use of analogue or vignette studies, which not only allow the researcher to investigate how individuals respond to imagined scenarios (e.g. being provided with a genetic test result – Wright *et al.*, 2006) but also to see how responses are affected by the manipulation of specific variables, such as the type of information presented or the way in which it is framed.

In the longer term, the most valuable types of experimental or quasi-experimental study in health psychology will be those involving interventions based on the findings from earlier predictive studies, which were based in turn on relevant theory. For example, building on the evidence that illness and treatment beliefs predict differences in illness-related behaviour, there are now a small but growing number of intervention studies designed to modify beliefs as a basis for changing behaviour and related outcomes (see Broadbent *et al.*, 2009; French *et al.*, 2008, Karamanidou *et al.*, 2008; Petrie *et al.*, 2002;). These not only provide a test of the intervention but can also allow the researcher to develop and refine the underlying theory.

Another important distinction in health psychology research is between the use of qualitative and quantitative research methods, which can differ considerably in their approach and function. Quantitative approaches typically involve the use of methods for measuring and/or manipulating variables, and for defining relationships between them in order to describe processes, test hypotheses or examine the impact of an intervention. In contrast, qualitative research is often more concerned with understanding the meaning of experience or situations as they are interpreted by the individuals participating in a study.

Traditionally, psychology research, and health psychology research in particular, have relied more on theory-based quantitative methods, but there is increasing use of qualitative methods for guiding research and developing theory (e.g. Yardley, 2000). There is not space here to discuss the assumptions underlying qualitative research or to map out the range of approaches that can be used for data collection or analysis. Nevertheless it is important to note that many methods exist, including interview, focus groups and observational methods, and these typically but not exclusively involve the use of audio or video recording for the collection of data. Most commonly, qualitative research involves the use of in-depth interviews or focus group discussions to generate data, which then can be analysed in a range of ways, and vary in their level of imposed structure and their underlying assumptions.

The qualitative/quantitative distinction is sometimes presented or perceived as a competitive, either–or issue, and this is both absurd and pointless. Both qualitative and quantitative research encompasses several variations in terms of intent and underlying assumptions, and researchers need to be clear about the overall aims of their research in order to select the appropriate method (see French *et al.*, 2004).

Journals in Health Psychology

A growing number of journals focusing on health psychology have been established in the past 10 to 20 years, helping the field to develop. *Health Psychology* is the subdiscipline-linked journal with the highest impact factor score of journals in the specific health psychology area. The other key journals include

Psychology & Health, British Journal of Health Psychology, Journal of Health Psychology and *Psychology, Health & Medicine*. In addition, health psychologists publish papers in journals with a more or less explicit multi-disciplinary focus such as *Journal of Psychosomatic Research, Psychosomatic Medicine, Social Science & Medicine, Behavioral Medicine, Patient Education and Counseling, Quality of Life Research*, or in general psychology or medical journals (e.g. *Psychological Bulletin, Lancet, Archives of Internal Medicine*). Some non-English-language national journals publish important health psychology papers as well. These include *Zeitschrift für Gesundheitspsychologie* (*Journal of Health Psychology*) in Germany, and *Psychologie & Gezondheid* (*Psychology & Health*) in the Netherlands.

In addition to the specific journals, there are now a number of volumes, which have brought together collections of key papers in health psychology. The most comprehensive of these is a four-volume set of key and classic papers, which cover all the major areas outlined by Matarazzo and were selected on the basis of their recommendation by a wide group of health psychologists from a number of countries (Weinman *et al.*, 2007).

Health Psychology – Discipline or Profession?

In recent years, health psychology has developed strongly as a discipline, but there is still uncertainty about the nature of the professional roles and training needs of health psychology practitioners. One important step in this process was the publication of *Health Psychology: A Discipline and a Profession* (Stone *et al.*, 1987), a collection of papers from a conference which brought together leading US health psychologists in a discussion of training-related issues. The contributors attempted to define the knowledge and skills base of health psychology, as well as identify the contexts where these could be applied. This early volume is therefore something of a landmark in the attempt to map out the disciplinary and professional basis of health psychology.

Earlier in this chapter we outlined the emergent knowledge base of health psychology, and we also referred to the many textbooks and journals devoted to the discipline which provide strong evidence of its scope

and quality. The professional development of health psychology has inevitably taken longer, but this is now clearly beginning to happen in many countries. Textbooks in clinical health psychology (e.g. Bennett Johnson *et al.*, 2002) and on psychological interventions in healthcare (e.g. Kennedy, 2007) provide clear indications of the ways in which health psychology approaches can be applied in preventive or clinical settings. Despite this, there is still a lack of consensus as to the best way to train psychology graduates for the professional roles which are now recognised within health psychology.

One example of a training model is the tripartite approach to professional training in health psychology which originated in the UK, with its view of professional practice in terms of research, teaching and training, and consultancy, and this has been mapped out and developed by Michie and Abraham (2004). In addition to these three core areas of professional practice, there are a range of other roles involving interventions at all sorts of levels from delivering primary prevention to providing support and behaviour change initiatives in people with major health problems, as we have outlined earlier in this chapter.

Within Europe there have been attempts to define the core areas of training for professional health psychology, and some common themes are emerging (Marks *et al.*, 1998; McIntyre *et al.*, 2004). As the key aims and methods of professional training in health psychology are mapped out, and as professional roles emerge, there will be a greater understanding of what health psychologists can and should be doing to improve health and health care.

In this book, we have been fortunate in obtaining very high-level contributions on the main areas of health psychology from major experts in the field. In addition to providing current, critical overviews of these key areas, many have also provided excellent examples of the wide range of professional roles which are possible for health psychologists. Over the next few years, there will need to be further development and agreement about the content and best methods for implementing professional health psychology training. As health psychologists branch out and apply their knowledge and skills more widely to the improvement of health and health care, this will provide an excellent real-world test of the adequacy and applicability of their knowledge and theoretical base. Inevitably the result is that we will become more aware of the gaps in the knowledge base as well as the limitations in the explanatory value and relevance of current theories. This, in turn, will provide the impetus for further work incorporating refinements in research methods and theoretical models, in the continuing attempts to improve our understanding of the role of psychological factors in health, illness and health care. Although health psychology is still in its relative infancy, it is now being recognised by governmental and funding bodies as a core discipline in health-related research, along with, for example, health economics, epidemiology. We very much hope that the second edition of this book provides a comprehensive and representative account of the progress in the discipline and serves as a foundation for the development of professional roles and training.

Discussion Points

1 Summarise the reasons underlying the emergence of health psychology, and relate these to the limitations of a narrowly biomedical view of health and health care.

2 In a few sentences write how the disciplines in Figure 1.1 would conceptualise myocardial infarction, how each of the disciplines would go about reducing distress in patients with myocardial infarction, and which theoretical approach each discipline would be using.

3 Find out what the most important journals are respectively for the six disciplines (Figure 1.1), based on SSCI and SCI impact.

4 Find, study and critically review an empirical paper on what health psychologists would designate 'primary prevention'. Find, study and critically review an empirical paper on what physicians would designate 'primary prevention'. Analyse similarities and differences.

5 Design the outline, by giving chapter titles, of a book that introduces health psychology to (a) undergraduate psychology students; (b) graduate psychology students; (c) medical students.

References

Bennett Johnson, S., Perry, N.W. & Rozensky, R.H. (Eds.) (2002). *Handbook of clinical health psychology*. Washington, DC: American Psychological Association.

Broadbent, E., Ellis, C., Thomas, J., Gamble, G. & Petrie, K. (2009). Further development of an illness perception intervention for myocardial infarction patients: A randomized controlled trial. *Journal of Psychosomatic Research, 67,* 17–23.

Cameron, L.D. & Leventhal, H. (2003). Self-regulation, health, and illness: An overview. In L.D. Cameron & H. Leventhal (Eds.) *The self-regulation of health and illness behaviour* (pp. 1–13). London: Routledge.

Cooke, R. & French, D.P. (2008). How well do the theory of reasoned action and theory of planned behaviour predict intentions and attendance at screening programmes? A meta-analysis. *Psychology & Health, 23,* 745–765.

Devlin, A.S. & Arnell, A.B. (2003). Health care environments and patient outcomes. *Environment and Behaviour, 35,* 665–694.

Division of Health Psychology Training Committee (2008). *Criteria for the accreditation of MSc programmes in health psychology*. Leicester: British Psychological Society.

Field, A.P. (2009). *Discovering statistics using SPSS: and sex and drugs and rock 'n' roll* (3rd edn). London: Sage.

French, D.P., Yardley, L. & Sutton, S.R. (2004). Research methods in health psychology. In S. Sutton, A. Baum & M. Johnston (Eds.) *The Sage handbook of health psychology* (pp. 262–287). London: Sage.

French, D.P., Wade, A.N., Yudkin, P., Neil, H.A.W., Kinmonth, A.L. & Farmer, A.J. (2008). Self-monitoring of blood glucose changed non-insulin treated type 2 diabetes patients' beliefs about diabetes and self-monitoring in a randomised trial. *Diabetic Medicine, 25,* 1218–1228.

Jepson, R., Clegg, A., Forbes, C., Lewis, R., Sowden, A. & Kleijnen, J. (2000). The determinants of screening uptake and interventions for increasing uptake: A systematic review. *Health Technology Assessment,* 4(14).

Johnston, M., French, D.P., Bonetti, D. & Johnston, D.W. (2004). Assessment and measurement in health psychology. In S. Sutton, A. Baum & M. Johnston (Eds.) *The Sage handbook of health psychology* (pp. 288–323). London: Sage.

Kaplan, R.M. (1990). Behavior as the central outcome in health care. *American Psychologist, 45*, 1211–1220.

Kaplan, R.M. (2000). Two pathways to prevention. *American Psychologist, 55*, 382–396.

Kaptein, A.A. & Creer, T.L. (Eds.) (2002). *Respiratory disorders and behavioral medicine*. London: Martin Dunitz.

Kaptein, A.A. & Weinman, J. (2004). Health psychology: some introductory remarks. In A.A. Kaptein & J. Weinman (Eds.) *Health Psychology* (pp. 3–18). Oxford: British Psychological Society and Blackwell Publishing Ltd.

Karamanidou, C., Weinman, J. & Horne, R. (2008). Improving haemodialysis patients' understanding of phosphate-binding medication: A pilot study of a psycho-educational intervention designed to change patients' perceptions of the problem and treatment. *British Journal of Health Psychology, 31*, 205–214.

Kennedy, P. (Ed.) (2007). *Psychological management of physical disabilities. A practitioner's guide*. London: Routledge.

Lacasse, Y., Brosseau, L., Milne, S., Martin, S., Wong, E., Guyatt, G.H., Goldstein, R.S. & White, J. (2003). Pulmonary rehabilitation for chronic obstructive pulmonary disease (Cochrane Review). In *The Cochrane Library*, Issue 3. Oxford: Update.

Linden, W., Stossel, C. & Maurice, J. (1996). Psychosocial interventions for patients with coronary artery disease: A meta-analysis. *Archives of Internal Medicine, 156*, 745–752.

Marks, D., Brucher-Albers, C., Donker, F., Jepsen, Z., Rodriguez-Marin, J., Sidot, S. & Backman, B. (1998). Health psychology 2000: The development of professional health psychology. *Journal of Health Psychology, 3*, 149–160.

Matarazzo, J.D. (1980). Behavioral health and behavioral medicine: Frontiers for a new health psychology. *American Psychologist, 35*, 807–817.

Matarazzo, J.D. (1982). Behavioral health's challenge to academic, scientific, and professional psychology. *American Psychologist, 37*, 1–14.

McIntyre, T., Folkman, S., Paxton, S.J., McGee, H., deRidder, D., & Schreurs, K. (2004). Training models: International commentaries. In S. Michie & C. Abraham (Eds.) *Health psychology in practice* (pp. 46–62). Oxford: Blackwell.

Meyer, T.J. & Mark, M.M. (1995). Effects of psychosocial interventions with adult cancer patients: A meta-analysis of randomized experiments. *Health Psychology, 14*, 101–108.

Michie, S. & Abraham, C. (Eds.) (2004). *Health psychology in practice*. Oxford: Blackwell.

Newman, S., Steed, L. & Mulligan, K. (Eds.) (2009). *Chronic physical illness: Self-management and behavioural interventions*. Milton Keynes: Open University Press.

Ogden, J. (2003). Some problems with social cognition models: A pragmatic and conceptual analysis. *Health Psychology, 22*, 424–428.

Outlook Society of Behavioral Medicine (1995). President's message (1). Knoxville, TN: SBM.

Petrie, K.P., Cameron, L.D., Ellis, C.J., Buick, D. & Weinman, J. (2002). Changing illness perceptions after myocardial infarction: An early intervention randomized controlled trial. *Psychosomatic Medicine, 64*, 580–586.

Rehse, B. & Pukrop, R. (2003). Effects of psychosocial interventions on quality of life in adult cancer patients: Meta-analysis of 37 published controlled outcome studies. *Patient Education and Counseling, 50*, 179–186.

Salmon, P. & Hall, G.M. (2003). Patient empowerment and control: A psychological discourse in the service of medicine. *Social Science & Medicine, 57*, 1969–1980.

Smith, J. (Ed.) (2003). *Qualitative psychology: a practical guide to research methods*. London: Sage.

Stone, G.C., Cohen, F. & Adler, N.E. (Eds.) (1979). *Health psychology – A handbook*. San Francisco: Jossey-Bass.

Stone, G.C., Weiss, S.M., Matarazzo, J.D., Miller, N. E., Rodin, J., Belar, C.D. et al. (1987). *Health psychology: a discipline and a profession*. Chicago: University of Chicago Press.

Sutton, S. & French, D.P. (2004). Planning research: Design, sample, measures. In S. Michie & C. Abraham (Eds.) *Health psychology in practice* (pp. 83–103). Oxford: BPS Blackwell.

Van Diest, R., Hamulyak, K., Kop, W.J., van Zandvoort, C. & Appels, A. (2002). Diurnal variations in coagulation and fibrinolysis in vital exhaustion. *Psychosomatic Medicine, 64*, 787–792.

Wardle, J. (2000). Editorial. Public health psychology: Expanding the horizons of health psychology. *British Journal of Health Psychology, 5*, 329–336.

Weinman, J., Johnston, M. & Molloy, G. (Eds.) (2007). *Health psychology*. London: Sage.

Weinman, J. & Petrie, K.J. (2009). Health psychology. In M.G. Gelder, N.C. Andreasen, J.J. Lopez-Ibor Jr. & J.R. Geddes (Eds.) *New Oxford textbook of psychiatry* (2nd edn, pp. 1135–1143). Oxford: Oxford University Press.

White, C.A. (2001). *Cognitive behaviour therapy for chronic medical problems*. Chichester: Wiley.

Wright, A.J., French, D.P., Weinman, J. & Marteau, T.M. (2006). Can genetic risk information enhance motivation for smoking cessation? An analogue study. *Health Psychology, 25*, 740–752.

Yardley, L. (2000). Dilemmas in qualitative health research. *Psychology & Health, 15*, 215–218.

Yorke, J., Fleming, S.L. & Shuldham, C.M. (2006). Psychological interventions for adults with asthma. *Cochrane Database of Systematic Reviews*, Issue 1, CD No. CD002982.

Part I

Health-Related Behaviour

2

The Role of Behaviour in Health

Andrew Steptoe, Benjamin Gardner
and Jane Wardle

Chapter Outline

Understanding the determinants of health behaviour and identifying more effective methods of promoting behaviour change and healthier lifestyles are two of the central issues in health psychology. This chapter focuses on what we mean by health behaviours, how they are related to disease and disability, and how they are patterned in the population. The chapter begins with an outline of why health behaviours are important for public health, including a summary of the development of the health behaviour concept and definitions of health behaviour. The chapter then discusses several major health behaviours, including diet, physical activity, tobacco use, alcohol consumption, cancer screening, sexual behaviour and hazardous driving behaviour. In each case, we describe the associations with disease, the prevalence of the behaviours in various countries of the developed world and how the behaviours are patterned in relation to gender and socioeconomic status. The chapter concludes with a description of the range of influences on health behaviour, ranging from sociocultural and economic factors to aspects of the individual's health and biology.

Key Concepts

AIDS/HIV
Alameda county study
Alcohol consumption
Attributable risk
Cancer screening
Carcinogenesis
Chronic disease
Drinking and driving
Driving speed
Family determinants
Food choice
Health-service provision
Human papillomavirus
Leading causes of death
Legislation
Measurement of behaviour
Obesity
Physical activity
Preventive health
  behaviours
Sexually transmitted
  disease
Socioeconomic status
Standardised death rate
Tobacco epidemic

Introduction

What causes most death and disability? Table 2.1 summarises the main causes of death in the 49 countries of Europe averaged together, and in the UK and Germany. Cardiovascular diseases and cancer are by far the most common causes of death, together accounting for 64 per cent of male and 71 per cent of female deaths. The most frequent individual diagnosis is coronary heart disease in men and women, but stroke, lung cancer and breast cancer are also very common, while a significant proportion of people die from respiratory diseases such as chronic obstructive pulmonary disease. The other leading causes are accidents and unintentional injury, coming from incidents such as road traffic accidents, injury in the home and accidental poisoning. Death rates from cancer are somewhat higher in both the UK and Germany compared with the rest of Europe, while cardiovascular deaths are less frequent. The pattern is similar in the USA, where recent figures indicate that 32 per cent of men and 32 per cent of women died from cardiovascular disease, and 24 per cent and 23 per cent respectively from cancer (National Center for Health Statistics, 2009).

Of course, everybody must die of something, so these medical conditions may cause most deaths because they are diseases of old age. If this were so, we would expect them to cause high proportions of deaths among elderly people and low proportions of deaths among young people. Table 2.2, which summarises causes of death in the UK across adult age groups, shows that this is not the case. While the percentage of deaths caused by cardiovascular disease peaks in the over 75s, a quarter of deaths in middle age (45–54 years) are attributable to cardiovascular disease. A quarter of deaths among young to middle-aged adults (35–44 years) are cancer-related and cancer is the most common cause of death in women between 45 and 64 years. Similarly in the USA, the leading causes of death in 45–64 year olds are cancers (33 per cent) followed by stroke and diseases of the heart (26 per cent; National Center for Health Statistics, 2009).

The figures in Table 2.2 describe the relative importance of different causes of death, and not absolute rates. The 'standardised death rate', shown on the left of the table, indicates how many people died in each category. Unsurprisingly, fewer young adults died overall, so the absolute number of deaths in younger groups is smaller than in older cohorts; but nevertheless, these comparisons show the stable influence of the common causes of death across the lifespan.

Efforts to improve health in the developed world must tackle this set of health problems, and doing so requires understanding their causes. There are well-documented links between mortality and its common causes, and socioeconomic status (SES). People from more deprived social backgrounds and those with lower prestige jobs tend to die younger and suffer from more chronic medical conditions and psychiatric problems. Measurement of SES is complicated, but common markers include occupation, income, educational attainment and scales of material deprivation. Figure 2.1 shows rates of deaths attributable to cardiovascular disease and cancer among men in the UK using occupational class as the index of SES (White et al., 2008). The bar on the far left relates to people of the highest SES (those in higher managerial positions), and the bar on the far right the lowest (those in routine or manual employment). The figure shows an orderly increase in deaths attributable to these two health problems with decreasing SES, so that the least privileged people are nearly three times more likely to die of cardiovascular disease, and twice as likely to die of cancer, than are the most privileged. This classification excludes people who have been unemployed for more than a year or never worked, who are likely to have higher morbidity and mortality than those currently or recently in employment (Gardner & Oswald, 2004). Similar patterns have been revealed using other indicators of SES, each of which demonstrate that those lower down the social ladder face greater challenges to health.

SES *predicts* but does not *explain* health outcomes. The underlying causes of this relationship must be identified if campaigns to improve health and reduce inequalities are to be successful. Over the past half century, it has been realised that behaviours, such as smoking, dietary choice, alcohol consumption and regular physical activity, play an important role in health outcomes (Adler et al., 1999). Behavioural

Table 2.1 Percentage of deaths from major causes in Europe and the UK

	Europe[a]		United Kingdom[b]		Germany[c]
	Men	Women	Men	Women	
All cardiovascular diseases	43%	54%	35%	34%	47%
Coronary heart disease	21%	22%	19%	14%	21%
Stroke	11%	17%	8%	11%	10%
Other cardiovascular	11%	15%	8%	9%	16%
All cancers	21%	17%	29%	26%	27%
Lung cancer	6%	2%	7%	5%	5%
Breast cancer		3%		4%	2%
Colorectal cancer	2%	2%	3%	3%	4%
Other cancers	13%	10%	19%	14%	16%
Respiratory diseases	7%	6%	13%	14%	6%
Accidents and injuries	12%	5%	5%	3%	4%
Other causes	**17%**	**18%**	**18%**	**23%**	**16%**

[a] European data from across all 48 countries of Europe, latest available year. From Allender, S., Peto, V., Scarborough, P., Kaur, A. & Rayner, M. (2008a). *Coronary heart disease statistics*. London: British Heart Foundation.
[b] Figures from 2006. From Allender, S., Scarborough, P., Peto, V., Rayner, M., Leal, J., Luengo-Fernandez, R. & Gray, A. (2008b). *European cardiovascular disease statistics*. Brussels: European Heart Network.
[c] Men and women combined. World Health Organization figures from 2002.

Table 2.2 Percentage of UK deaths attributable to cardiovascular disease and cancer, 2007

	Standardised death rate per 1,000,000		All cardiovascular diseases		All cancers	
Age	Men	Women	Men	Women	Men	Women
25–34 years	894	390	9%	11%	11%	26%
35–44 years	1,537	916	20%	14%	18%	41%
45–54 years	3,422	2,273	29%	16%	30%	51%
55–64 years	8,743	5,561	31%	18%	41%	54%
65–74 years	22,489	14,478	33%	27%	41%	44%
75–84 years	62,822	44,943	37%	36%	31%	14%
85+ years	160,996	143,587	38%	39%	20%	13%

Source: National Statistics/ Defra (2008). *Family food: A report on the 2007 Expenditure and Food Survey*. London: The Stationery Office. © Crown Copyright material reproduced with the permission of the Controller HMSO.

factors are estimated to account for half of the premature death from the 10 leading causes (Gruman & Follick, 1998). For example, although many factors are involved in the development of cardiovascular disease, cancers and chronic respiratory diseases, it is recognised that healthier lifestyles are key to reducing the incidence of these conditions, while early detection through screening and other medical assessments can improve outcomes. Health behaviours make a widespread contribution to social inequalities in health;

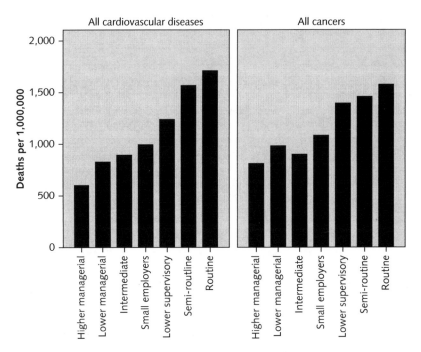

Figure 2.1   The relationship between occupational social class and age-adjusted deaths attributed to cardiovascular diseases or cancer among men aged 25–64 in England and Wales. Occupational social class is measured using the National Statistics Socioeconomic Classification (NS-SEC)

Source: White, C., Edgar, G. & Siegler, V. (2008). Social inequalities in male mortality for selected causes of death by the National Statistics Socioeconomic Classification, England and Wales, 2001–03. *Health Statistics Quarterly, 38,* 19–32. © Crown Copyright material reproduced with the permission of the Controller HMSO.

as will be seen later in the chapter, people from less privileged backgrounds tend to smoke and drink more, eat less fruit and vegetables, and take less exercise than do those in higher socioeconomic positions.

The Development of the Health Behaviour Concept

The modern concept of health behaviour can be dated back to the pioneering research of the epidemiologist Sir Richard Doll, whose study of thousands of British doctors began in the 1950s and identified smoking as a major precursor of premature mortality (Doll & Hill, 1964). Since then, numerous epidemiological and laboratory studies have investigated dietary choices, alcohol consumption, patterns of physical exercise, sexual behaviour and safety practices in relation to specific health outcomes. The notion that health behaviours might cluster into a healthy lifestyle owes its scientific foundation to the Alameda County Study. This investigation of just under 7,000 adults living in Alameda County, California, began in 1965 with a postal questionnaire, followed by regular surveys of death and illness. When the factors measured at baseline were analysed against later mortality, seven aspects of lifestyle predicted mortality: not being physically active; smoking; sleeping for either short (less than 7 hours) or long (more than 8 hours) periods nightly; skipping breakfast; eating snacks between meals; regularly drinking more than 5 units of alcohol at one session; and being either overweight or underweight (Belloc, 1973). Importantly, the more positive health habits that people reported, the lower their risk of death. These same behaviours were also related to future disability (Breslow & Enstrom, 1980).

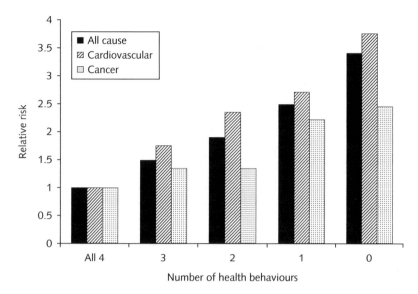

Figure 2.2   The relative risk of death over an average of 11 years in men and women aged 45–79 years, classified according to the number of healthy behaviours (not smoking, physical activity, moderate alcohol consumption and eating fruit and vegetables). Results are presented as relative risks with participants with all four healthy behaviours as the reference group, and are adjusted for age, gender and body mass index

Source: Khaw, K.T., Wareham, N., Bingham, S., Welch, A., Luben, R. & Day, N. (2008). Combined impact of health behaviours and mortality in men and women: the EPIC-Norfolk prospective population study. *PLoS Medicine, 5,* e12. Covered by the Creative Commons Attribution license.

A more modern version of this concept of healthy lifestyle was recently documented in a much larger study of men and women in England. Khaw *et al.* (2008) analysed data from the EPIC-Norfolk Study, a longitudinal study of 20,244 men and women without known cardiovascular disease or cancer when they were first surveyed (age 45–79). Over an average follow-up period of 11 years, deaths were inversely associated with four health behaviours: not smoking; being physically active; drinking moderately; and eating five or more servings of fruit and vegetables per day. As can be seen in Figure 2.2, the fewer of these positive behaviours that were performed, the greater the risk of deaths from 'all causes', cardiovascular disease and cancer. Work of this kind has stimulated researchers to look beyond individual risk factors for individual illnesses, and think of health behaviour as a broader construct. Health-related behaviours have a range of effects that are not limited to a single disease endpoint, and different behaviours may have common determinants.

The Definition of Health Behaviour

There are two broad types of health behaviour: those that increase risk and those that promote health. Health risk behaviour can be defined as *any activity undertaken by people with a frequency or intensity that increases risk of disease or injury*. Common health risk behaviours include cigarette smoking, taking narcotic drugs, excessive alcohol consumption, eating large amounts of high-fat foods, some sexual behaviours and drink driving. Our definition indicates that the amount or 'dose' of the behaviour may be important. This is not the case for most behaviours, but there are instances in which moderate levels may be beneficial; as will be seen later in the chapter, there is evidence that moderate alcohol consumption is associated with more favourable health outcomes than either heavy drinking or complete abstinence.

The definition of positive health behaviour is more controversial. The first to attempt a formal definition were Kasl and Cobb (1966) who stated that health behaviour was 'any activity undertaken by a person believing himself to be healthy for the purpose of preventing disease or detecting it at an asymptomatic stage'. This definition is orientated towards detection and prevention of disease by healthy individuals, and does not include actions by people who are already ill. However, much health behaviour is carried out by people with a diagnosed condition, and is aimed at delaying the further progression of the disorder. Kasl and Cobb's definition also regarded a health behaviour as one that is consciously carried out for health-enhancing purposes. But both positive and risk health behaviours are important regardless of whether the individual carries out the activity for health reasons. Exercising on most days would be regarded as a positive health behaviour, whether the person does this for health reasons, or because they are sports fans, play in teams, enjoy the social aspects or are trying to look good. We would therefore define positive health behaviours as *activities that may help to prevent disease, detect disease and disability at an early stage, promote and enhance health, or protect from risk of injury*. Common positive health behaviours include regular physical exercise, fruit and vegetable intake, using sunscreen, using a seatbelt, driving sensibly and taking advantage of medical and dental screening opportunities.

Several general points emerge from these definitions of health behaviour.

1   The concept of health behaviour is fluid, and activities that are included can change as medical knowledge develops. In the 1950s in Britain, children were encouraged to eat the fat on meat, and refusal to do so was considered a sign of fussy eating. The use of a condom when having sex with a person whose sexual history is unknown only emerged as a preventive health behaviour within the past 25 years. It is also likely that there are other activities that people do now without a moment's thought that may turn out to have adverse health effects.

2   Health behaviours are not uniformly important, but vary in their influence across time and across different populations. In the developing world, hand washing is among the most important health behaviours because of its impact on the spread of infection, but it is less significant in developed countries except in health professionals. Obesity, which is not itself a health behaviour but is strongly determined by excessive energy intake coupled with lack of physical activity, was a rare clinical phenomenon 50 years ago, but has now become a public health scourge.

3   The strength of the evidence relating behaviours with health outcome is extremely variable. Some findings have emerged from case-control studies, comparing people who do and do not have an illness, while others are backed by prospective epidemiological research, studies of trends over time, or experimental research on the biological mechanisms through which the behaviour could affect the disease process. A basic principle of research is that association is not the same as cause. An association between a behaviour and a health outcome may be a chance occurrence, or due to some third underlying factor that is related both to the behaviour and the illness. It is essential that results are replicated with different samples, and that there is some understanding of the biological mechanisms responsible, before we can be more confident about health behaviours. In an ideal world, this would be followed up with experimental studies that modify the health behaviour and demonstrate positive effects on health outcomes. We need to be certain that any health education advice is based on sound scientific data, otherwise there is a danger that we reinforce the sceptical public's view that scientists can't make up their minds, and say something is dangerous one day and safe the next.

4   Our definitions of health behaviour recognise that these activities may be done for non-health reasons. Some healthy habits such as tooth-brushing and limiting fat in the diet may be driven by non-health motives like concern for appearance. This means that health motives may be relatively unimportant in some cases; raising the possibility that programmes of health behaviour change that focus only on providing health knowledge or changing health-related attitudes would lose out on some other motivational routes. Health psychologists need to view behaviour in a broad context, and recognise that health motivations and cognitions

are part of a wider set of influences on health behaviour. A summary of these wider influences is provided later in the chapter.

Important Health Behaviours in the Modern World

The next sections of this chapter provide information about the main health risk and positive health behaviours that are relevant to the population at large. Some of these behaviours are described in further detail in Chapters 3–7 of this book, so this chapter provides broader information about the social epidemiology of health behaviours. A number of other important health behaviours, including sunscreen use, sleep patterns, drug use, dental health behaviour and breast self-examination are not discussed in the interests of space.

It is helpful to put the evidence about the importance of behaviours for health into the broader context of the causes of death and disease. Health policy researchers have carried out sophisticated statistical modelling analyses to work out the amount of death and disease attributable to lifestyle factors. These models use data from aetiological studies of disease, aggregating effects across different conditions. For instance, instead of calculating the impact of smoking just on lung cancer, its influence on all cancers, heart disease, stroke, lung diseases and other problems can be added together. An impression of the combined risk attributable to different lifestyle factors is summarised in Table 2.3, from a recent investigation of deaths in the USA (Danaei et al., 2009). It can be seen that 21 per cent of male and 18 per cent of female deaths can be attributed to tobacco. Total energy intake (a determinant of overweight) and different dietary components together account for nearly 20 per cent of deaths, while physical activity is important not only for its influence on body weight, but independently as well. Analyses of this kind make a strong case for the critical role played by behaviours in health and the prevention of disease and premature death.

Health behaviours take place within a social context, which may influence the impact that interventions can have on changing behaviour. We next discuss the main health risk and positive health behaviours

and how they are distributed in the population, focusing on sex differences and variations by age and socioeconomic status.

Diet

Food has always been of fundamental importance for health, both in getting enough food to provide for energy needs, and getting the right balance of foods to meet nutrient requirements. The modern food supply, combined with an increasingly sedentary lifestyle, has led to an epidemic of overconsumption, not only of energy, but also of fat, sugar and salt. In parallel, high-fibre, nutrient-rich, plant-based foods such as vegetables and fruits are underconsumed. Declines in diet quality and levels of physical activity have together led to epidemic increases in obesity in both adults and children.

Fat intake Saturated fat intake is directly associated with serum cholesterol levels, which in turn are strongly and linearly related to risk of atherosclerosis and heart disease. While we know that heart disease is a multi-factorial condition, a high-fat diet appears to be the necessary condition for its development. In areas like rural China where fat intake is very low, population cholesterol levels are well below the typical values found in the West and heart disease is extremely rare (Campbell et al., 1998).

Fat is the most energy-dense of the macronutrients, and so fat intake is strongly linked to weight gain. Higher fat diets promote weight gain in rats. Human studies show that low-fat diets are almost always associated with some weight loss, because without significant amounts of fat in the diet it is much more difficult to sustain high energy intake (Astrup, 2001).

US guidelines suggest that adults and children should derive at most 35 per cent of energy (calories) from fat, and there are similar guidelines elsewhere in the world (US Department of Health and Human Services, 2005; World Health Organization, 2003). Only people who are highly physically active and have diets rich in fruits, vegetables and grain are likely to be able to consume 35 per cent of fat in their diet without damaging their health. Most people require a lesser proportion of fat to stay healthy.

Table 2.3   Deaths from all causes attributable to lifestyle factors (2005)

	Men		Women		Both sexes	
	N deaths	%	N deaths	%	N deaths	%
Tobacco	248,000	20.7	219,000	17.5	467,000	19.1
Overweight/obesity	114,000	9.5	102,000	8.2	216,000	8.8
Physical inactivity	88,000	7.3	103,000	8.2	191,000	7.8
High LDL cholesterol[a]	60,000	5.0	53,000	4.2	113,000	4.6
High dietary salt	49,000	4.1	54,000	4.3	102,000	4.2
Alcohol use	45,000	3.8	20,000	1.6	64,000	2.6
Low fruit and vegetable intake	33,000	2.8	24,000	1.9	58,000	2.4

[a] LXDL (low density lipoprotein) cholesterol is strongly influenced by dietary fat consumption.
Source: Danaei, G. *et al.* (2009). The preventable causes of death in the United States: Comparative risk assessment of dietary, lifestyle, and metabolic risk factors. *PLoS Med, 6*, e1000058. Covered by Creative Commons Attribution License.

Figure 2.3 shows that average fat consumption per person is well above recommended levels in many European countries. However, the use of lower-fat versions of foods (e.g. semi-skimmed rather than full-fat milk) has become one of the most commonly reported health behaviours. For example, more than 50 per cent of adults in the UK say that they try to limit fatty foods in their diet (Wardle & Griffith, 2001).

Women tend to consume more lower-fat foods than men, which appears to be primarily due to their greater use of deliberate weight control strategies and their greater concern about diet and health. But epidemiological data have not found striking sex differences or SES differences in fat intake (Gregory *et al.*, 1990); this may be because some luxury foods are high in fat or because of substitution of monounsaturated for polyunsaturated fats.

Fruit and vegetable intake   Fruits and vegetables are nutrient-rich foods that are also low in energy density. Fruit and vegetable consumption has been linked with low rates of the development of heart disease and many cancers in a number of large-scale studies (Marmot *et al.*, 2007; Ness & Powles, 1997; Peto, 2001). On the basis of epidemiological research the World Health Organization has recommended an intake of at least 400 g of fruit and vegetables a day. This has been translated in many countries into five servings a day (at least three of vegetables and two of fruit).

The average intake in most countries is well below the recommended level. A recent survey suggested that adults in the UK consume an average of 3.8 portions per day, with fewer than 30 per cent eating five or more servings (Craig & Shelton, 2008). Surveys in the USA indicate that only 25 per cent of adults eat five or more servings a day (Blanck *et al.*, 2008). As shown in the lower panel of Figure 2.3, southern European countries (e.g. Greece, Portugal), where fruits and vegetables are plentiful, cheap and an established element of the normal meal, tend to have higher consumption than northern European countries – although there is a fear that the spread of the 'fast food' culture, processed meals and fat-based desserts, will erode this advantage.

Women tend to eat more fruit and vegetables than men (Hoare *et al.*, 2004), partly due to their greater investment in healthy dietary choices. Households with children eat less fruit and vegetables than adult households, suggesting that children's reluctance to eat these foods could influence the family meal patterns (Ministry of Agriculture, Food and Fisheries, 2000). Low socioeconomic status groups tend to buy strikingly less fruit and vegetables than high status groups (National Statistics/Defra, 2008). Limited intake of fruit and vegetables may be one reason why less privileged groups are at greater disease risk.

Fat consumption

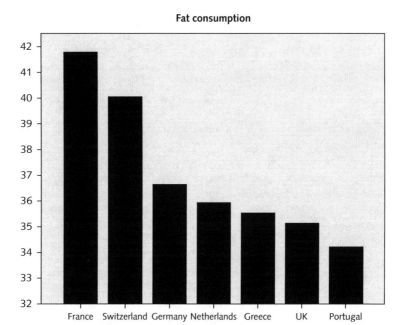

Fruit and vegetables

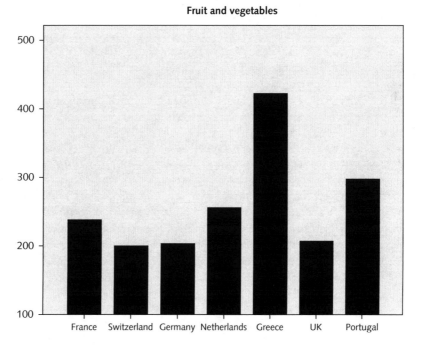

Figure 2.3 Percentage energy derived from fat (upper panel), and availability of fruit and vegetables (kg per person per year) in selected countries in 2003

Source: World Health Organization (2009). European Health for All Database. Copenhagen: World Health Organization. Retrieved 23 June 2009 from http://www.euro.who.int/hfadb. Reprinted with permission.

Physical activity

Regular physical activity has a wide range of positive effects on health. Since obesity arises from an imbalance between energy intake (food) and energy expenditure (activity), physical activity may also help to prevent weight gain and obesity. Physical inactivity is related to premature mortality, particularly death from coronary heart disease. It has been estimated that sedentary adults are twice as likely to develop premature heart disease than active adults; an effect that remains significant, after controlling statistically for other factors. The mechanism underlying this effect is probably a combination of influences on the major risk factors for heart disease, including body weight, high blood pressure, blood cholesterol levels and diabetes. Physically active people are also at lower risk of cancer, and activity contributes to the maintenance of bone mass and bone mineral density, which is thought to reduce the risk in older people of falling and suffering from fractures. In addition, physically active people report more positive mood profiles than the sedentary, feeling less tense, anxious and depressed, and have a greater capacity to cope with stress.

Many countries recommend that adults engage in at least 30 minutes of moderate or vigorous physical activity on at least five days a week, and children are advised to take 60 or more minutes of moderate or vigorous activity daily. Levels of physical activity decline throughout the life course: in England, 52 per cent of men and 36 per cent of women aged 25–34 years are active at recommended levels, decreasing to 35 per cent men and 27 per cent of women aged 55–64 years (NHS, 2009). At the other extreme, 19 per cent of men and 27 per cent of women aged 25–34 engage in little or no moderate physical activity each week, increasing to 37 per cent and 38 per cent respectively at 55–64 years (NHS, 2009).

There are considerable cross-national differences in activity levels: among 15-year-old students for example, the proportions exercising for one or more hours daily range from 29 per cent of girls and 46 per cent of boys in Slovakia, to 14 per cent of girls and 34 per cent of boys in the USA, and 9 per cent of girls and 18 per cent of boys in England (Currie et al., 2008).

Men tend to be more physically active than women. This is one of the few health behaviours in which men have an advantage, but the difference appears unrelated to health concerns. Rather, men participate in sporting activities more than women, and are also more likely to have active manual jobs. As far as leisure time physical activities are concerned, there is a social gradient in both men and women, with people of higher socioeconomic status being more physically active (Martinez-Gonzales et al., 2001).

Tobacco use

The burden of disease attributable to smoking in developed countries is greater than for any other health behaviour. Cigarette smoking leads to increased risk of coronary heart disease, lung cancer, and cancers of the larynx, oesophagus, mouth, bladder and cervix. Other problems related to tobacco use include stroke, vascular disease in the legs, and chronic obstructive pulmonary diseases such as bronchitis and emphysema. Smokers tend to have poorer psychological well-being and more depressive symptoms and psychiatric problems than non-smokers. Smoking also causes a number of pregnancy complications, including detached placenta, bleeding, premature delivery and low birth weight.

Several different biological mechanisms are responsible for the impact of smoking on health. Tobacco smoke contains about 4000 chemicals, at least 40 of which are carcinogenic. These lead to mutations in the cells of different tissues, some of which proliferate clonally in an uncontrolled fashion. The effects of smoking on cardiovascular disease are due in part to damage done to the vascular endothelium, the single layer of cells lining blood vessels. The impact of smoking on pregnancy outcomes results from changes in blood flow and supply of nutrients from the mother to the foetus, leading to growth retardation.

Many of the adverse health effects are reversible. Although timing varies, for many conditions the increased risk associated with smoking disappears after a short period, although cancer risks merely stop increasing. Preventing people from starting smoking and intervening to encourage smokers to stop are therefore equally important targets for health psychology.

Across the world, around 35 per cent of men and 22 per cent of women in developed countries smoke, although rates are a lot lower in some countries and the sex difference is also narrowing (Mackay &

Eriksen, 2002). The proportion of smokers in a range of developed countries, as derived from self-report surveys, is summarised in Table 2.4. Smoking is typically less prevalent among women than men, though

Table 2.4 Smoking in the adult population and in 15-year-old children

	Adult population[1]		15 year olds[2]	
	Men	Women	Boys	Girls
Australia	21%	18%	—[3]	—[3]
England	28%	26%	16%	20%
Germany	39%	31%	26%	29%
Greece	47%	29%	9%	11%
The Netherlands	32%	25%	19%	20%
Sweden	17%	20%	6%	14%
USA	26%	21%	12%	8%

All percentages refer to the proportion of people smoking at least one cigarette a day.
[1] Latest available year. From Shafey, O., Dolwick, S. & Guindon, G.E. (2003). *Tobacco control country profiles* (2nd edn). Atlanta, GA: American Cancer Society.
[2] Data from Currie, C. *et al.* (2004). *Young people's health in context. Health behaviour in school-aged children (HSBC) study: International report from the 2001/2002 survey.* Copenhagen: World Health Organization.
[3] No data available

the size of the gender discrepancy varies across countries. Smoking rates have levelled off or declined over the past 25 years in many countries, but rates in young people have not shown as strong a decrease. As Table 2.4 shows, the proportion of 15 year olds who smoke regularly is rather high. This is significant because people who start smoking when they are young are more likely to smoke heavily and become more nicotine-dependent. A new generation of heavier smokers may therefore be emerging.

One of the strongest influences on smoking in the developed world is socioeconomic position. Figure 2.4 shows the pattern of cigarette smoking in the UK in adults classified on two socioeconomic indices: occupational class and educational attainment (Jarvis & Wardle, 1999). Odds ratios are presented so that the figure shows the likelihood that someone will smoke in each socioeconomic position, compared with the reference rate of 1 in the highest occupational group, or most educated group. For both criteria, smoking increases with decreasing socioeconomic status, so that less privileged people are much more likely to smoke. This pattern is due partly to higher rates of starting smoking in lower status groups, and to higher rates of stopping smoking in the better-off sectors of the population.

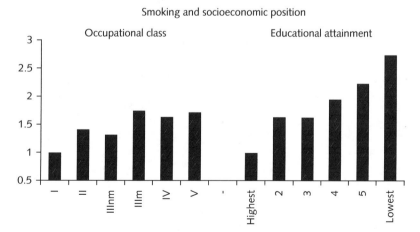

Figure 2.4 The relationship between socioeconomic status as defined by occupational social class (left panel) and educational attainment (right panel) in the UK. Values represent odds ratios, with Class 1 and the highest educational group as the reference categories. Nm = non-manual, m = manual

Source: Jarvis, M.J. & Wardle, J. (1999). Social patterning of individual health behaviours: The case of cigarette smoking. In M.G. Marmot & R.G. Wilkinson (Eds.) *Social determinants of health* (pp. 240–255). Oxford: Oxford University Press. Reproduced with permission of Oxford University Press.

Sexual behaviour

The HIV/AIDS epidemic has transformed the impact of sexual behaviour on health. Before infection with human immunodeficiency virus (HIV) was identified in 1981, the most serious sexually transmitted disease had been syphilis, and this had largely been eliminated with antibiotics. Global rates of infection with HIV/AIDS have stabilised in recent years, but remain high (UNAIDS, 2008). More than 33 million people live with HIV/AIDS, an estimated 22 million of whom live in sub-Saharan Africa, compared with 1.2 million in North America and 800,000 in Western and Central Europe.

Other unpleasant but not life-threatening conditions such as gonorrhoea and genital herpes are highly prevalent sexually transmitted diseases. Sexually transmitted infections are more common in teenagers and young adults than in older groups. Sexual behaviour can also spread viruses linked with cancer risk: hepatitis B is sexually transmitted and is linked with liver cancer, and, as noted later in this chapter, types of human papillomavirus (HPV) are responsible for cervical cancer.

Various sexual behaviours can pose a health risk, such as early age of first intercourse, multiple sexual partners, the failure to use condoms and anal intercourse. Information about risky sexual behaviours is available in national surveys from many countries. In a survey in the UK undertaken between 1999 and 2001, for example, 15 per cent of men and 9 per cent of women in the age range 16–44 years reported having had at least one sexual partner other than their regular partner in the past 12 months (Johnson et al., 2001). Additionally, 67 per cent of sexually active males and 76 per cent of females with two or more sexual partners in the past year reported not consistently using condoms during sex (Johnson et al., 2001).

In high-risk groups, unsafe sexual practices are common. One survey found that 20 per cent of HIV-positive gay and bisexual men had recently had unprotected anal intercourse with a partner of negative or unknown HIV status (Elford et al., 2007). A study of HIV positive women reported that more than 40 per cent had engaged in unprotected vaginal intercourse, and 10 per cent in unprotected anal intercourse, in the previous six months (Kalichman, 1999). The occurrence of risky sexual behaviour is particularly high among intravenous drug users, homeless people and others at the margins of society.

Alcohol

The health risks of alcohol can be divided into problems that result from excessive intake such as alcohol dependence, foetal alcohol syndrome and alcoholic liver cirrhosis, and illnesses in which alcohol is one of a number of important causal factors. The latter include risk of high blood pressure, cardiac arrhythmias, and cancers of the mouth, throat, colon and rectum. The mechanisms responsible for some of these effects are beginning to be understood. For example, ethanol is broken down by cells and bacteria in the mouth and digestive system to create a potent carcinogen called acetaldehyde. Alcohol also contributes in a crucial way to road traffic accidents and domestic violence, and is associated with problems like sexually transmitted disease.

Assessing the health impact of alcohol is complicated for two reasons. Firstly, many adverse effects depend not only on how much is drunk overall, but also on the pattern of consumption. Binge drinking has particular health risks; drinking heavily on just two nights a week may lead to worse health outcomes than drinking the same total amount evenly over all seven days of the week. Secondly, there appears to be a U-shaped relationship between alcohol use and mortality in the United States and Western Europe (Marmot, 2001). The explanation of this pattern is still controversial, but it may be due to a protective effect of moderate intake on coronary heart disease. In addition to health impact, alcohol abuse causes immense social harm, and it has been estimated that the costs associated with alcohol amount to more than one per cent of the gross national product in high and middle income countries (Rehm et al., 2009).

Estimating the amount of alcoholic beverages drunk in different countries is not easy, because there are variations in the preferred type of beverage – beer, wine or spirits – and in some cultures the amount of home brewing and illicit production is high. Table 2.5 summarises data from the USA and various European countries (World Health Organization, 2004). There are wide variations even between these few countries,

Table 2.5 Alcohol consumption in the adult population and in 15 year olds

| | Total population | | | 15 year olds[3] | |
| | Per capita consumption[1] | Heavy drinkers[2] | | Boys | Girls |
		Male	Female		
Austria	12.6 L	17%	7%	36%	33%
Finland	10.4 L	6%	3%	18%	15%
France	13.5 L	17%	8%	23%	11%
Germany	12.9 L	11%	11%	46%	33%
Italy	9.1 L	10%	2%	48%	28%
United Kingdom[4]	10.4 L	39%	42%	56%	49%
USA	8.5 L	6%	5%	21%	11%

[1] Per capita consumption in litres of pure alcohol in adults aged 15 or older in latest available year.
[2] Typically defined as percentage of adult male drinkers drinking 40 g or more of pure alcohol per day and adult female drinkers drinking 20 g or more pure alcohol per day. From World Health Organization (2004). *Global status report on alcohol 2004*. Geneva: World Health Organization.
[3] 15-year-old children who report drinking beer, wine or spirits at least weekly. Currie, C. *et al.* (2004). *Young people's health in context. Health behaviour in school-aged children (HSBC) study: International report from the 2001/2002 survey*. Copenhagen: World Health Organization.
[4] Data for 15 year olds refers to England only.

with the highest *per capita* consumption in France and the lowest in the USA. While it is likely that countries with a higher overall consumption level will have more problem drinkers, overall consumption statistics can mask patterns of heavy drinking. In the UK and Finland, 10 litres of alcohol *per capita* are consumed in total, yet 40 per cent of UK drinkers drink to excess on an average day, compared to around 5 per cent of Finnish drinkers.

Alcohol consumption is more common in men than women, though the gap is smaller in developed countries than in the developing world. This pattern begins early in life, with more male than female adolescents being regular drinkers. The age at which people start drinking predicts the likelihood of later problems. As can be seen in Table 2.5, around half of 15-year-old boys in Germany, Italy and England drink at least once a week.

There is good evidence that heavy alcohol consumption is more common in lower SES groups, particularly among men. Deaths from diseases caused by alcohol show a clear social gradient, with higher rates in less privileged groups. This is illustrated in Figure 2.5 with the death rate by social class from

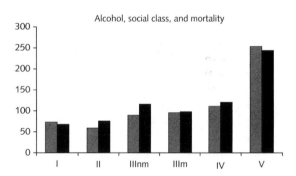

Figure 2.5 Standardised mortality ratio (SMR) by social class for alcohol dependence syndrome (hatched bars) and chronic liver disease and cirrhosis (solid bars) for men aged 20–64 in England and Wales (1991–3). Social class ranges from professional (I) to unskilled manual (V). The SMR is the death rate standardised to an average of 100 for the population, so values less than 100 indicate better than average, while values over 100 are worse than average
Source: Drever, F. & Whitehead, M. (Eds.) (1997). *Health inequalities*. London: The Stationery Office. © Crown Copyright material reproduced with the permission of the Controller HMSO.

two causes: alcohol dependent syndrome, and chronic liver disease and cirrhosis. Rates increase with lower occupational position, but the slope is comparatively small until the lowest stratum (that of unskilled manual workers) is reached. There is rather less of a social gradient in moderate than in heavy alcohol consumption.

Cancer screening

Cancer is a multi-stage process, involving a sequence of probably 4–6 mutations in the cells before they develop their full damaging and invasive potential. The purpose of screening is to detect abnormalities before the disease process is clinically manifest. Its value in cancer comes from detecting malignant or even pre-malignant transformations, at a stage before there is significant invasion to surrounding tissues or metastases (migration of cancer cells to other regions of the body through the lymphatic or blood system to set up secondary cancers at the new sites). Each cancer has a different developmental process and medical technology has developed strategies for identifying the earliest stages better for some cancers than others. In colorectal cancer, the early abnormalities (adenomatous polyps) can be visualised directly during sigmoidoscopic examination and removed quickly and easily, thereby entirely eliminating the risk of further malignant transformation at that site (UK Flexible Sigmoidoscopy Screening Trial Investigators, 2002). Cervical cancer also has an established pre-malignant stage, and tests for the viral causal agent (human papillomavirus or HPV) and the use of Papanicolaou (Pap) smears have both been linked with reduced mortality (Cuzick et al., 2000; Sasieni & Adams, 1999).

For some other cancers (e.g. breast and prostate cancer), techniques are not yet available to detect a pre-malignant stage, so screening aims to identify the area of cell proliferation before the cells have mutated to their metastasising form. In these cases, surgical treatment is likely to be required whenever any abnormality is detected. The benefit of screening in these cases depends on availability of treatments which are either more effective at that early stage, or offer equivalent benefit with less associated toxicity.

Some cancers are known to develop more readily in individuals who have inherited specific mutations from one of their parents (e.g. BRCA1 for breast cancer; HNPCC for colorectal cancer). Advances in genetic technologies are making it feasible to screen for these mutations, either by testing for the risky polymorphisms in the individual's DNA or, where the gene is not yet cloned, testing for susceptibility by comparing the DNA of the individual to be tested with that of affected and unaffected relatives. Individuals with the susceptible genotype can be offered frequent surveillance to give the maximum chance of detecting cancer at the earliest possible stage. Higher risk individuals should take steps to avoid exposure to aspects of the environment that increase cancer risk (e.g. tobacco) and consider chemoprevention (e.g. tamoxifen for women at higher risk of breast cancer) or, in cases where the risk is even higher, prophylactic surgery to reduce the likelihood of the malignant transformations starting in the at-risk organs.

The value of screening to public health depends on two related factors. Firstly, the benefits of screening for reducing mortality must outweigh treatment costs. In this respect, evidence supports the value of screening in reducing cervical cancer mortality (Peto et al., 2004), colorectal cancer mortality (Atkin & Northover, 2003) and breast cancer mortality (Smith et al., 2004). There is controversy about the costs and benefits of other forms of cancer screening, especially prostate screening (Moore et al., 2009). Secondly, high screening uptake rates among the at-risk population are needed to achieve the most benefits. Most developed countries have public education campaigns which advise on screening regimens. Some countries such as the UK record participation and send invitations to individuals when their screening is due, which tends to result in good attendance rates across the board. Other countries (e.g. the USA) publicise screening recommendations and providers are encouraged to recommend screening, but individuals must make their own arrangements.

By reputation, men are less willing than women to involve themselves with medical care. Research into colorectal cancer (one of the few cancers screened for in both men and women) documents tendencies for women to attend screening more than men (McQueen et al., 2006; Weller et al., 2009).

Additionally, there is evidence that groups with lower income, lower levels of education and from

Table 2.6 Hazardous driving behaviours in European populations

	Driving over the speed limit		Drink driving[1]	Seatbelt use[2]
	Motorways	Urban areas		
Germany	20%	7%	2.4%	84%
Greece	40%	6%	7.9%	36%
Hungary	16%	12%	1.3%	52%
Italy	24%	12%	7.3%	35%
The Netherlands	31%	7%	1.9%	77%
Spain	37%	11%	7.2%	43%
United Kingdom	26%	4%	0.6%	91%

[1] Driving after drinking over the legal limit at least once in the past week.
[2] Always wearing a seatbelt in urban areas.
Source: Data from 2002–03. Social Attitudes to Road Traffic Risk in Europe (2004). *European drivers and road risk: Report on principal analyses.* Retrieved 23 June 2009 from http://sartre.inrets.fr/documents-pdf/repS3V1E.pdf.

more deprived backgrounds are less likely to participate in screening (Breen *et al.*, 2001; McCaffery *et al.*, 2002; Von Wagner *et al.*, in press). The fact that SES differences in participation are observed even where screening is free to all suggests that the barriers are not only financial. In general, public attitudes towards screening are positive; most people accept the view that earlier detection is likely to lead to a better outcome. Individually, however, there are variations in the perception of the value of, or need for, screening. Attitudinal factors associated with non-attendance include feeling healthy and not in need of medical checks (demonstrating the failure of the message that screening is to pick up problems *before* symptoms develop), being frightened of cancer, and being embarrassed about the test procedure (Wardle *et al.*, 2000). Factors such as fear of cancer and concerns about the test procedure may lie behind the socioeconomic differences in attendance.

Hazardous driving behaviour

Road traffic injuries are the second-leading cause of death for children and young adults worldwide (Peden *et al.*, 2004). In the USA in 2007, for example, around 41,000 people were killed and 2,500,000 injured in road accidents (National Highway Traffic Safety Administration, 2009). Three behaviours are particularly important in increasing the risk of the vehicle

crashes and injury: drink driving, not using a seatbelt and driving too fast. Alcohol was implicated in 32 per cent of fatal crashes in the USA in 2007 (National Highway Traffic Safety Administration, 2009). The problem is particularly marked among the young, since drivers aged 21–24 have the highest intoxication rates. The risk of involvement in fatal crashes rises with blood alcohol concentration in all age groups, but the slope is steepest in the young (Zador *et al.*, 2000).

Seatbelts are estimated to be 60 per cent effective in reducing road accident mortality (Cummings *et al.*, 2003), and so are one of the most important means of reducing injury. In contrast, speeding is one of the most important factors contributing to crashes. Again in the USA, speeding is the primary cause of 22 per cent of all fatal crashes, and over half a million people receive injuries in speeding-related crashes per year. Of all drivers involved in fatal crashes, young men are the most likely to be speeding. The speed a vehicle is travelling on impact determines the severity of injury in pedestrians. It has been estimated that 5 per cent of pedestrians hit at 20 miles per hour are killed, increasing to 85 per cent of those hit at 40 miles per hour (World Health Organization, 2001).

Table 2.6 summarises data from seven European countries and shows that a significant proportion of drivers in these countries disobey speed limits, have driven after drinking too much over the past week, and do not regularly use seatbelts when sitting in the front of a vehicle. The figures were collected by self-report, so probably underestimate the extent of hazardous behaviour. Nonetheless, large differences between countries are evident. In the UK and Germany, the vast majority of respondents reported using seatbelts, compared with the minority in Italy and Greece. High rates of disobeying speed limits were found in Spain and Greece, and in these countries the prevalence of drink driving was also greatest.

Hazardous driver behaviours are far more common in men than women. They are also typically associated with age and socioeconomic status, such that older drivers and those of higher social status tend to be safer in their behaviour.

Determinants of Health Behaviour

Psychological influences on health behaviours are discussed in Chapters 8–11 of the present book. However, it is important to appreciate the broader cultural and social context, not only for a fuller understanding of why people act in the way they do, but because non-psychological factors may limit the impact that interventions can have on changing behaviour. The broader determinants also remind us that most people do not carry out positive health practices or indulge in risk behaviours primarily for health reasons, or often even for conscious reasons at all. In this section, we therefore summarise the wider determinants of health behaviour, beginning with the broadest national and even international factors, narrowing down to issues that are influential within the individual.

Sociocultural and national factors

One reason that there are wide variations in the frequency of different positive and risk behaviours is national, cultural and religious tradition. Most countries have a distinctive cuisine, with preferences for particular foods, and methods of preparation. Some religions and cultures disapprove of alcohol and smoking, while others proscribe the eating of meat from particular animals. Cultural factors also affect the behaviour of young adults prior to marriage, and place limits on sexual expression.

Legislative factors

Several health-compromising behaviours are affected by laws. In many countries, for example, it is illegal to sell tobacco to children. While this does not prevent children from smoking, the difficulty of obtaining cigarettes may affect smoking rates. Laws also govern the purchasing of alcohol, while various drugs and sexual practices may be outlawed. There is good evidence that laws concerning drink driving and seatbelt use have an impact on these behaviours (DeJong & Hingson, 1998). The method of law enforcement is also relevant. Laws concerning selling alcohol to minors have little deterrent effect if they are not constantly monitored. In the case of driving, primary enforcement, when police officers are allowed to stop a vehicle solely for something like a seatbelt violation, has substantially greater effects than secondary enforcement, when a violation can only be cited after the vehicle has been stopped for another suspected misdemeanour (Dinh-Zarr et al., 2001). Laws concerning the fitting of seatbelts to cars, or the presence of physical education within the school curriculum, again influence the occurrence of the behaviour. Laws on smoking in public places have also been shown to influence smoking rates.

Macroeconomics

Many health behaviours cost money. Cigarettes, alcohol, food, exercise facilities and access to health care in some countries have to be purchased. Economic factors such as the buoyancy of the economy and availability of disposable income, together with taxes on tobacco and alcohol, have perceptible effects on behaviour.

Systems of provision and services

Some health behaviours are dependent on the availability of goods and services. If manufacturers do not make palatable low-fat foods, and these are not stocked in retail outlets, then people are not likely to eat them. If people live in dense, urban environments without sport and leisure facilities or where there are no walkable routes, their physical activity levels will suffer. There has been a striking increase in the availability of high protection sunscreen in many countries over recent years, which has a direct association with protection from damaging sun exposure. The provision of smoke-free environments reduces smoking levels, and may help deter a proportion of smokers altogether.

Health-service provision

Many of the methods that people use to prevent disease depend on the availability of appropriate health services. Even if they want to, people cannot get screened for cancer if there are no facilities and cannot have their teeth checked if they have no access to dental services. Similar factors apply to immunisation programmes and health checks for markers like blood pressure and cholesterol.

Sociodemographic factors

As we have illustrated at several points in this chapter, health behaviours are strongly associated with age, sex and socioeconomic status.

Health status

The ability to carry out many health behaviours is affected by personal health, while illness may provide additional motivation for behaviour change. For example, many people with disabilities or chronic lung disease are limited in the physical exercise they can carry out. People with diabetes and other metabolic disorders may have particular dietary requirements. The effectiveness of medications taken by people with HIV can be affected by alcohol and diet. Diagnosis with a condition like coronary heart disease or noninsulin dependent diabetes may provide the stimulus for weight reduction through dietary change and physical exercise.

Social and family factors

Health behaviours are strongly affected by peer group influences, family habits and social networks (Baranowski, 1997). Family habits have a strong impact on food choice, cigarette smoking, alcohol consumption and physical exercise habits. For example, children of adults who smoke are more likely to become smokers (Biglan et al., 1995). Health behaviours have been successfully modified through social support interventions, as in the studies involving supportive lay health advisors to encourage breast cancer screening among rural African American women (Earp et al., 2002). Recent observations of social clustering of weight have added a new dimension to the understanding of social influence (Christakis & Fowler, 2007).

Psychological factors

These are detailed in Chapters 8–11.

Biological factors

Finally, it should be emphasised that some health behaviours are determined in part by biological factors. Factors such as nicotine and opiate dependence are strong determinants of smoking and drug use, respectively. Dietary choice may be influenced in part by the metabolic or psychological effects of particular nutrients, while alcohol has an important reciprocal relationship with biological stress responses (Sayette, 1993). There is also increasing interest in investigating the impact of genetic factors on health-related behaviours, with evidence from twin studies that there is a heritable component to smoking initiation and nicotine addiction, as well as to body weight and obesity (Plomin et al., 2000).

Summary and Conclusions

Health behaviours are a central topic in health psychology. A wide range of everyday activities are relevant to health risk and health promotion. The occurrence of health behaviours varies systematically in relation to culture, gender, age and socioeconomic status. Health behaviours are determined by a range of personal and sociocultural factors, and need to be understood within the broad context of people's lives.

Discussion Points

1   How do we know whether an activity is a 'health behaviour'?
2   What is the best way to inform the public about health behaviours?
3   Why is low socioeconomic status associated with less healthy behaviours?
4   Is there such a thing as a 'healthy lifestyle'?
5   Should the way people drive really be described as health behaviour?
6   Are health risk behaviours such as smoking a matter of free choice?
7   Should we legislate against health risk behaviours?

Further Reading

Christakis, N.A. & Fowler, J.H. (2008). The collective dynamics of smoking in a large social network. *New England Journal of Medicine, 358*, 2249–2258.

Cummings, K.M., Fong, G.T. & Borland, R. (2009). Environmental influences on tobacco use: Evidence from societal and community influences on tobacco use and dependence. *Annual Review of Clinical Psychology, 5*, 433–458.

DeJong, W. & Hingson, R. (1998). Strategies to reduce driving under the influence of alcohol. *Annual Review of Public Health, 19*, 359–378.

Glanz, K., Rimer, B.K. & Viswanath, K. (2008). *Health behavior and health education: theory, research and practice* (4th edn). New York: Jossey-Bass.

Harris, J.L., Pomeranz, J.L., Lobstein, T. & Brownell, K.D. (2009). A crisis in the marketplace: How food marketing contributes to childhood obesity and what can be done. *Annual Review of Public Health, 30*, 211–225.

Institute of Medicine. (2001). *Health and behavior: The interplay of biological, behavioral, and societal influences*. Washington, DC: National Academy of Sciences.

Rehm, J., Mathers, C., Popova, S., Thavorncharoensap, M., Teerawattananon, Y. & Patra, J. (2009). Global burden of disease and injury and economic cost attributable to alcohol use and alcohol-use disorders. *Lancet, 373*, 2223–2233.

Wang, Y. & Lobstein, T. (2006). Worldwide trends in childhood overweight and obesity. *International Journal of Pediatric Obesity, 1*, 11–25.

References

Adler, N.E., Marmot, M., McEwen, B.S., & Stewart, J. (Eds.) (1999). *Socioeconomic status and health in industrial nations: Social, psychological and biological pathways* (Vol. 896). New York: New York Academy of Sciences.

Allender, S., Peto, V., Scarborough, P., Kaur, A. & Rayner, M. (2008a). *Coronary heart disease statistics*. London: British Heart Foundation.

Allender, S., Scarborough, P., Peto, V., Rayner, M., Leal, J., Luengo-Fernandez, R. & Gray, A. (2008b). *European cardiovascular disease statistics*. Brussels: European Heart Network.

Astrup, A. (2001). The role of dietary fat in the prevention and treatment of obesity. Efficacy and safety of low-fat diets. *International Journal of Obesity, 25*, S46–S50.

Atkin, W.S. & Northover, J.M.A. (2003) Population-based endoscopic screening for colorectal cancer. *Gut, 52*, 321–322.

Baranowski, T. (1997). Families and health actions. In D.S. Gochman (Ed.) *Handbook of health behavior research, vol. 1:*

personal and social determinants (pp. 179–206). New York: Plenum.

Belloc, N.B. (1973). Relationship of health practices and mortality. *Preventive Medicine, 2*, 67–81.

Biglan, A., Duncan, T.E., Ary, D.V. & Smolkowski, K. (1995). Peer and parental influences on adolescent tobacco use. *Journal of Behavioral Medicine, 18*, 315–330.

Blanck, H.M., Gillespie, C., Kimmons, J.E., Seymour, J.D. & Serdula, M.K. (2008). Trends in fruit and vegetable consumption among U.S. men and women, 1994–2005. *Preventing chronic disease: public health research, practice, and policy, 5*. Retrieved 12 June 2009 from http://www.cdc.gov/pcd/issues/2008/apr/07_0049.htm.

Breen, N., Wagener, D.K., Brown, M.L., Davis, W.W. & Ballard-Barbash, R. (2001). Progress in cancer screening over a decade: Results of cancer screening from the 1987, 1992, and 1998 National Health Interview Surveys. *Journal of the National Cancer Institute, 93*, 1704–1713.

Breslow, L. & Enstrom, J. E. (1980). Persistence of health habits and their relationship to mortality. *Preventive Medicine, 9*, 469–483.

Campbell, T.C., Parpia, B. & Chen, J. (1998). Diet, lifestyle, and the etiology of coronary artery disease: The Cornell China study. *American Journal of Cardiology, 82*, 18T–21T.

Christakis, N.A. & Fowler, J. H. (2007). The spread of obesity in a large social network over 32 years. *New England Journal of Medicine, 357*, 370–379.

Craig, R. & Shelton, N. (Eds.) (2008). *Health Survey for England 2007: Latest trends*. London: NHS Information Centre.

Cummings, P., Wells, J.D. & Rivara, F.P. (2003). Estimating seat belt effectiveness using matched-pair cohort methods. *Accident Analysis & Prevention, 35*, 143–149.

Currie, C., Gabhainn, S.N., Godeau, E., Roberts, C., Smith, R., Currie, D. et al. (2008). *Inequalities in young people's health*. Copenhagen: World Health Organization.

Currie, C., Roberts, C., Morgan, A., Smith, R., Settertobulte, W., Samdal, O. & Rasmussen, V.B. (2004). *Young people's health in context. Health behaviour in school-aged children (HSBC) study: International report from the 2001/2002 survey*. Copenhagen: World Health Organization.

Cuzick, J., Sasieni, P., Davies, P., Adams, J., Normand, C., Frater, A. et al. (2000). A systematic review of the role of human papillomavirus (HPV) testing within a cervical screening programme: Summary and conclusions. *British Journal of Cancer, 83*, 561–565.

Danaei, G., Ding, E.L., Mozaffarian, D., Taylor, B., Rehm, J., Murray, C.J. & Ezzati, M. (2009). The preventable causes of death in the United States: Comparative risk assessment of dietary, lifestyle, and metabolic risk factors. *PLoS Medicine, 6*, e1000058.

DeJong, W. & Hingson, R. (1998). Strategies to reduce driving under the influence of alcohol. *Annual Review of Public Health, 19*, 359–378.

Dinh-Zarr, T.B., Sleet, D.A., Shults, R.A., Zaza, S., Elder, R.W., Nichols, J.L. et al. (2001). Reviews of evidence regarding interventions to increase the use of safety belts. *American Journal of Preventive Medicine, 21*, 48–65.

Doll, R. & Hill, A.B. (1964). Mortality in relation to smoking: Ten years' observations of British doctors. *British Medical Journal, i*, 1399–1414, 1460–1497.

Drever, F. & Whitehead, M. (Eds.). (1997). *Health inequalities*. London: The Stationery Office.

Earp, J.A., Eng, E., O'Malley, M.S., Altpeter, M., Rauscher, G., Mayne, L. et al. (2002). Increasing use of mammography among older, rural African American women: Results from a community trial. *American Journal of Public Health, 92*, 646–654.

Elford, J., Ibrahim, F., Bukutu, C. & Anderson, J. (2007). Sexual behaviour of people living with HIV in London: Implications for HIV transmission. *AIDS, 21*, S63–S70.

Gardner, J. & Oswald, A. (2004). How is mortality affected by money, marriage, and stress? *Journal of Health Economics, 23*, 1181–1207.

Gregory, J., Foster, K., Tyler, H. & Wiseman, M. (1990). *The Dietary and Nutritional Survey of British Adults. A survey of the dietary behaviour, nutritional status and blood pressure of adults aged 16–64 living in Great Britain*. London: The Stationery Office.

Gruman, J. & Follick, M. (Eds.) (1998). *Putting evidence into practice: The OBSSR report of the working group on the integration of effective behavioral treatments into clinical care*. Bethesda, MD: Office of Behavioral and Social Sciences Research, NIH.

Hoare, J., Henderson, L., Bates, C.J., Prentice, A., Birch, M., Swan, G. & Farron, M. (2004). *The National Diet and Nutrition Survey: Adults aged 19 to 64 years*. London: The Stationery Office.

Jarvis, M.J. & Wardle, J. (1999). Social patterning of individual health behaviours: The case of cigarette smoking. In M.G. Marmot & R.G. Wilkinson (Eds.) *Social determinants of health* (pp. 240–255). Oxford: Oxford University Press.

Johnson, A.M., Mercer, C.H., Erens, B., Copas, A.J., McManus, S., Wellings, K. et al. (2001) Sexual behaviour in Britain: Partnerships, practices, and HIV risk behaviours. *Lancet, 358*, 1835–1842.

Kalichman, S.C. (1999). Psychological and social correlates of high-risk sexual behaviour among men and women living with HIV/AIDS. *AIDS Care, 11*, 415–427.

Kasl, S.V. & Cobb, S. (1966). Health behavior, illness behavior, and sick role behavior. I. Health and illness behavior. *Archives of Environmental Health, 12*, 246–266.

Khaw, K.T., Wareham, N., Bingham, S., Welch, A., Luben, R. & Day, N. (2008). Combined impact of health behaviours and mortality in men and women: The EPIC-Norfolk prospective population study. *PLoS Medicine, 5*, e12.

Mackay, J. & Eriksen, M. (2002). *The Tobacco Atlas*. Geneva: World Health Organization.

Marmot, M.G. (2001). Alcohol and coronary heart disease. *International Journal of Epidemiology, 30*, 724–729.

Marmot, M., Atinmo, T., Byers, T., Chen, J., Hirohata, T., Jackson, A. et al. (2007). *Food, nutrition, physical activity, and the prevention of cancer: A global perspective*. Washington, DC: American Institute for Cancer Research.

Martinez-Gonzales, M.A., Varo, J.J., Santos, J.L., De Irala, J., Gibney, M., Kearney, J. & Martinez, J.A. (2001). Prevalence of physical activity during leisure time in the European Union. *Medicine & Science in Sports & Exercise, 33*, 1142–1146.

McCaffery, K., Wardle, J., Nadel, M. & Atkin, W. (2002). Sociodemographic variation in participation in flexible sigmoidoscopy screening for colorectal cancer. *Journal of Medical Screening, 9*, 104–108.

McQueen, A., Vernon, S.W., Meissner, H.I., Klabunde, C.N. & Rakowski, W. (2006). Are there gender differences in colorectal cancer test use prevalence and correlates? *Cancer Epidemiology Biomarkers & Prevention, 15*, 782–791.

Ministry of Agriculture, Food and Fisheries. (2000). *National Food Survey 1999*. London: The Stationery Office.

Moore, A.L., Dimitropoulou, P., Lane, A., Powell, P. H., Greenberg, D.C., Brown, C.H. *et al.* (2009). Population-based prostate-specific antigen testing in the UK leads to a stage migration of prostate cancer. *British Journal of Urology, 104*, 1592–1598.

National Center for Health Statistics. (2009). *Health, United States, 2008*. Hyattsville, MD: National Center for Health Statistics.

National Highway Traffic Safety Administration. (2009). *Traffic safety facts 2007 data: Overview*. Retrieved 23 June 2009 from http://www-nrd.nhtsa.dot.gov/Pubs/TSF2007FE.PDF.

National Statistics/Defra. (2008). *Family food: A report on the 2007 expenditure and food survey*. London: The Stationery Office.

Ness, A.R. & Powles, J.W. (1997). Fruit and vegetables, and cardiovascular disease: A review. *International Journal of Epidemiology, 26*, 1–13.

NHS Information Centre (2009). *Statistics on obesity, physical activity and diet: England, February 2009*. Retrieved 7 July 2009 from http://www.ic.nhs.uk/webfiles/publications/opan09/OPAD per cent20Feb per cent202009 per cent-20final.pdf.

Peden, M., Scurfield, R., Sleet, D., Mohan, D., Hyder, A.A., Jarawan, E. & Mathers, C. (2004). *World report on road traffic injury prevention*. Geneva: World Health Organization.

Peto, J. (2001). Cancer epidemiology in the last century and the next decade. *Nature, 411*, 390–395.

Peto, J., Gilham, C., Fletcher, O. & Matthews, F.E. (2004). The cervical cancer epidemic that screening has prevented in the UK. *Lancet, 9430*, 249–256.

Plomin, R., DeFries, J.C., McClearn, G.E. & McGuffin, P. (2000). *Behavioral genetics* (4th edn). New York: W.H. Freeman.

Rehm, J., Mathers, C., Popova, S., Thavorncharoensap, M., Teerawattananon, Y., & Patra, J. (2009). Global burden of disease and injury and economic cost attributable to alcohol use and alcohol-use disorders. *Lancet, 373*, 2223–2233.

Sasieni, P. & Adams, J. (1999). Effect of screening on cervical cancer mortality in England and Wales: Analysis of trends with an age period cohort model. *British Medical Journal, 318*, 1244–1245.

Sayette, M.A. (1993). An appraisal-disruption model of alcohol's effects on stress responses in social drinkers. *Psychological Bulletin, 114*, 459–476.

Shafey, O., Dolwick, S. & Guindon, G.E. (2003). *Tobacco control country profiles* (2nd edn). Atlanta, GA: American Cancer Society.

Smith, R.A., Cokkinides, V. & Eyre, H.J. (2004). American Cancer Society guidelines for the early detection of cancer, 2004. *CA: A Cancer Journal for Clinicians, 54*, 41–52.

Social Attitudes to Road Traffic Risk in Europe (2004). *European drivers and road risk: Report on principal analyses*. Retrieved 23 June 2009 from http://sartre.inrets.fr/documents-pdf/repS3V1E.pdf.

UK Flexible Sigmoidoscopy Screening Trial Investigators. (2002). Single flexible sigmoidoscopy screening to prevent colorectal cancer: baseline findings of a UK multicentre randomised trial. *Lancet, 359*, 1291–1300.

UNAIDS (2008). *2008 Report on the global AIDS epidemic*. Retrieved 23 June 2009 from http://www.unaids.org/en/KnowledgeCentre/HIVData/GlobalReport/2008/2008_Global_report.asp.

US Department of Health and Human Services (2005). *Dietary guidelines for Americans* (6th edn). Washington, DC: US Government Printing Office.

von Wagner, C., Good, A., Wright, D., Rachet, B., Obichere, A., Bloom, S. & Wardle, J. (in press). Inequalities in colorectal screening participation in London in the first round of the national screening programme. *British Journal of Cancer*.

Wardle, J. & Griffith, J. (2001). Socioeconomic status and weight control practices in British adults. *Journal of Epidemiology & Community Health, 55*, 185–190.

Wardle, J., Sutton, S., Williamson, S., Taylor, T., McCaffery, K., Cuzick, J. *et al.* (2000). Psychosocial influences on older adults' interest in participating in bowel cancer screening. *Preventive Medicine, 31*, 323–334.

Weller, D.P., Patnick, J., McIntosh, H.M. & Dietrich, A.J. (2009) Uptake in cancer screening programmes. *Lancet Oncology, 10*, 693–699.

White, C., Edgar, G. & Siegler, V. (2008). Social inequalities in male mortality for selected causes of death by the National Statistics Socioeconomic Classification, England and Wales, 2001–03. *Health Statistics Quarterly, 38*, 19–32.

World Health Organization (2001). *A 5-year WHO strategy for road traffic injury prevention*. Geneva: World Health Organization.

World Health Organization (2003). *Diet, nutrition and the prevention of chronic diseases*. Geneva: World Health Organization.

World Health Organization (2004). *Global status report on alcohol 2004*. Geneva: World Health Organization.

World Health Organization (2009). *European health for all database*. Copenhagen: World Health Organization. Retrieved 23 June 2009 from http://www.euro.who.int/hfadb.

Zador, P.L., Krawchuk, S.A. & Voas, R.B. (2000). Alcohol-related relative risk of driver fatalities and driver involvement in fatal crashes in relation to driver age and gender: An update using 1996 data. *Journal of Studies in Alcohol, 61*, 387–395.

3

Smoking

Lion Shahab and Robert West

Chapter Outline

The history of the tobacco plant, which originated in the Americas, goes back over 2000 years being first used by indigenous populations in ritualistic ceremonies and for its stimulant properties (Corti, 1931). With the discovery of America, tobacco became available in Europe, and in the 16th and 17th centuries was initially smoked in pipes, then used as snuff (ground into fine powder and sniffed into the nose) and by the 19th century also smoked as cigars (Royal College of Physicians, 2000). However, it was not until the invention of the manufactured cigarette, in the latter part of the 19th century, that smoking became a mass phenomenon. Smoking cigarettes is by far the most common and arguably dangerous form of tobacco use today (Shahab, 2008); worldwide there are over 1.3 billion smokers (Mackay *et al.*, 2006) and smoking was estimated to claim at least 5 million lives in 2000 alone (Ezzati & Lopez, 2003).

This chapter outlines who smokes and why people smoke at all. In addition to describing the financial and health implications arising from tobacco use, this chapter will provide an overview of the best treatment currently available for tobacco dependence and what health professionals can do to help smokers achieve abstinence.

Key Concepts

Addiction
Dependence
Nicotine
Smoking
Tobacco use

Who Smokes

In the developed world, tobacco use prevalence peaked in the mid-20th century and has steadily decreased ever since. This is in contrast to most developing nations or nations in transition where prevalence has been increasing over the latter part of the 20th century such that the vast majority of smokers now live in the developing world (World Health Organization, 1997). Given changes in the population composition and the relaxation in the attitude towards smoking among women, it is predicted that despite the fall in smoking prevalence in many Western countries, there will be at least 400 million more smokers worldwide in a decade (Guindon & Boisclair, 2003).

Smoking is generally more common among men than women; globally four out of five smokers are male (Shafey et al., 2003). However, the gender gap has been much reduced in the developed world, and in some countries (e.g. Australia) male and female smoking rates are virtually identical (Mackay et al., 2006). This is in contrast to the developing world, where female smoking prevalence is still lower, mostly due to social and cultural stigma attached to smoking among women (Mackay & Amos, 2003), but this is likely to change with shifts in attitudes and marketing by tobacco companies in these countries (Shafey et al., 2003).

Tobacco use starts early; most current smokers will have initiated the habit before the age of 18 (The Global Youth Tobacco Survey Collaborative Group, 2002). Whilst smoking rates among adolescents are declining in some countries, they stagnate and may even be increasing in others (Shafey et al., 2003). Across the human life-span, smoking prevalence takes a bell-shaped form; that is, smoking rates are low in both young and old age and peak somewhere before middle-age (Pomerleau et al., 2004). The reason for this pattern is two-fold: following smoking initiation due to peer pressure and other environmental influences, less dependent smokers start to stop smoking as they grow older, while more dependent smokers continue to smoke and as a consequence start to die prematurely from middle age onwards.

Within a given country, there will be differences in smoking patterns associated with different ethnic groups. In the UK, for instance, smoking prevalence among minority ethnic groups is somewhat lower than among the UK population as a whole (Goddard, 2006). However, ethnic minority groups also display stronger gender biases for smoking. In the US, smoking prevalence in the Asian community among men is three times higher, and in the Hispanic community two times higher, than among women, while gender differences in smoking rates are less pronounced in people with other ethnic backgrounds (Rock et al., 2007).

Although smoking is strongly associated with various markers of socioeconomic status (SES), the direction of this relationship is variable. In countries with weaker tobacco control measures where less is known about the health consequences of smoking, cigarette consumption is mostly determined by income, leading to a positive correlation between smoking and SES (Lopez et al., 1994). By contrast, in countries with strong tobacco control policies and high awareness of the negative consequences of smoking, smokers that are better off are more likely to successfully stop smoking than more deprived smokers resulting in a negative relationship between smoking and SES (Jarvis & Wardle, 2005). This is most likely due to deprived smokers lacking sufficient financial, emotional and environmental resources to aid smoking cessation (Kotz & West, 2009).

A factor often overlooked is the strong association of tobacco use with mental disorders. Smoking prevalence is much higher among people with any mental illness including psychotic, panic, generalised anxiety and obsessive-compulsive disorders, phobias, depression and even eating disorders (West & Jarvis, 2005). The relationship between smoking prevalence and mental disorders appears to be even stronger in institutionalised individuals and particularly pronounced in schizophrenics of whom 80 per cent smoke as inpatients, possibly due to self-medication with nicotine in order to lessen symptoms and side effects of neuroleptic medication (Smith et al., 2002).

Why People Smoke

The main challenge for theories of addiction is to explain why people smoke despite being aware of the negative consequences of their behaviour and how this happens at the individual and societal level. Theories of addiction may focus on general processes and on conceptualising addiction in broad social, biological or psychological terms; they may focus on how particular stimuli become addictive, on individual susceptibility, on environmental factors or on recovery and relapse (West, 2001). The ultimate aim of any such theory, however, is to provide a coherent, consistent, parsimonious and true picture of why people smoke in order to suggest possible mechanisms that can be used to help smokers stop.

While different theories emphasise different aspects of human behaviour to explain why people smoke, they can be broadly construed as either cognitive (within direct control of the user) or non-cognitive (outside direct control of the user) theories (Cummings, 1997). For instance, rational choice theories such as the theory of rational addiction (Becker & Murphy, 1988) would argue that smokers engage in a cost-benefit analysis and willingly chose to smoke because they accept the adverse outcomes in exchange for the perceived benefits of smoking. By contrast, theories of irrational choice such as affect heuristic theory (Finucane et al., 2000) would argue that people do not rationally choose to smoke but rather are guided by emotions associated with the choice and that emotions influence any cost-benefit judgement. Indeed, studies evaluating cognitive processing in smokers show that they have cognitive biases and pre-attentively evaluate drug cues, which is likely to skew somato-visceral, behavioural and cognitive responses of smokers (Ryan, 2002).

Other theories suggest that addiction results from disruption of impulse and self-control. The disease model of addiction (Jellinek, 1960) would thus argue that smoking is a medical disorder (likely to be mediated by genetic vulnerability) that leads to loss of control due to abnormalities caused by smoking, whereas Cloninger's tri-dimensional personality theory (Cloninger, 1987) would argue that pre-existing psychological patterns (in terms of harm avoidance, novelty seeking and reward dependence) predispose towards addictive behaviours. All of these theories provide important insights into why people smoke but are necessarily limited by focusing on a narrow aspect of a complex behaviour. For an attempt to unify existing theories and provide a synthetic theory

of addiction, the interested reader is referred to the PRIME theory of addiction (West, 2006a).

Arguably, the most accepted and parsimonious theory of why people smoke derives from the social learning perspective that sees smoking as an acquired habit, learned through classical and operant conditioning and observational learning. But what drives conditioning? The clue lies in the fact that the range of tobacco products available have one element in common crucial to the development of dependence: nicotine, an alkaloid that affects brain neurochemistry (Jarvis, 2004). The exact mechanism by which nicotine creates dependence is not clear and the addictive effects may be enhanced by additives to tobacco other than nicotine such as ammonia (Henningfield et al., 2004).

The reason why the use of cigarettes is more prevalent than the use of other forms of tobacco is likely due to its design as a particularly efficient nicotine delivery device. After a puff on a cigarette, nicotine is very rapidly absorbed into the blood stream through the alveoli in the lung and takes less than 20 seconds to reach the brain (Henningfield et al., 1993). The design of cigarettes means that smokers have 'fingertip control' over the dose of nicotine they ingest by adjusting the intensity and frequency of puffing to suit their personal preferences (Russell & Feyerabend, 1978).

The addictive potential of cigarettes is high and even just smoking a single cigarette may be enough to predispose someone to become a smoker much later in life (Fidler et al., 2006). Observational learning and modelling (e.g. seeing parents and friends smoke), curiosity, desire to enact or convey a particular identity, beliefs about positive effects of smoking on mood and weight control can all play some role in starting to smoke. With repeated use, classical and operant conditioning leads to dependence on nicotine as smoking is positively and negatively reinforced and abstinence punished (West & Shiffman, 2007).

Positive reinforcement occurs as nicotine activates nicotinic acetylcholine receptors found in the meso-corticolimbic reward pathway (Gotti et al., 1997), which results in the release of dopamine, a reward neurotransmitter, in the nucleus accumbens shell and other areas that are associated with hedonic emotional effects (Watkins et al., 2000). At doses around 60 mg nicotine is lethal, but smokers usually absorb no more than 2 mg per cigarette, which is rapidly metabolised with a plasma half life of approximately 90 minutes (Benowitz & Jacob, 1984). In novice users, nicotine will typically cause nausea as well as symptoms of activation of the autonomic nervous system such as tremors and sweating. It also causes dizziness and what is for some people a mildly pleasant 'buzz' (West & Hardy, 2007). After a couple of weeks, chronic tolerance develops but only to the unpleasant side effects not to the positive subjective experience of smoking. This means that a long-term smoker normally needs the same dose to obtain sought-after effects as a novice smoker.

Negative reinforcement is the result of changes in the dopaminergic system following chronic exposure to nicotine that reduce dopamine release and increase levels of corticotropin-releasing factor during phases of abstinence (Watkins et al., 2000). These changes contribute to unpleasant withdrawal symptoms such as poor concentration, irritability, restlessness and depression, which smokers learn to avoid by smoking (West & Shiffman, 2007). The presence of secondary sensory and behavioural as well as environmental cues (the lighting of a cigarette, ensuing sensation and stimulation in the mouth and throat, sitting in the pub) become associated with smoking and thus can act to reinforce it (Rose et al., 1993) and there are various sociocultural factors (e.g. peer smoking, general acceptance of smoking) that have an influence over the expression of the behaviour (Tyas & Pederson, 1998).

It is important to remember that nicotine can influence various levels of the motivational system (plans, evaluations, motives and impulses) thereby creating dependence in interaction with psychological, social and environmental factors (cf. West, 2006a). Thus, once they have started to smoke, there are many reasons smokers cite to explain why they continue to do so (McEwen et al., 2008). For instance, smokers report that they enjoy smoking and that it helps them cope with stress. They also believe it helps with weight control and aids concentration. Interestingly, there is little objective evidence that supports the existence of these beneficial effects of smoking (West & Hardy, 2007).

Considering the addictive nature of nicotine, which has been likened to that of Class A drugs such as heroin and cocaine (Centers for Disease Control and Prevention, 1988), and the continued wide-spread acceptance of the habit (Mackay et al., 2006), it is not surprising that tobacco dependence has arguably become the most prevalent and devastating form of any drug addiction in modern times (Shahab, 2008).

The Effects of Smoking and the Benefits of Stopping

Tobacco use kills more people than HIV, illicit drugs and alcohol combined (Ezzati et al., 2002) and is thought to have killed in excess of 100 million people worldwide during the last century alone (Mackay et al., 2006). The damaging effects of tobacco use arise from the ingestion of a dangerous mix of noxious and toxic compounds including 60 known human carcinogens that constitute tobacco smoke (International Agency for Research on Cancer, 2004). However, nicotine itself is not carcinogenic.

These toxins cause a range of diseases and disorders. Most smoking-related deaths worldwide are due to lung cancer, chronic obstructive pulmonary disease (COPD) and cardiovascular disease (CVD). Together these account for 70 per cent of all smoking-related deaths (Ezzati & Lopez, 2004). In turn, it is estimated that up to 70 per cent of COPD-related deaths, 20–40 per cent of all cancer deaths, and around 20 per cent of CVD-related deaths are caused by smoking (Jarvis, 2003). However, in addition to its major impact on global mortality, tobacco use also results in a great number of morbidities. In fact, there are about 20 smokers suffering from comorbid, disabling diseases, most commonly respiratory or cardiovascular diseases or cancer, to every one smoker who dies in a given year (Hyland et al., 2003). A number of other non-fatal diseases for which tobacco use is a known or probable cause or exacerbating factor are provided in Table 3.1.

In addition to its effects on physical health, smoking has also been shown to impact mental health. Smokers are nearly twice as likely as non-smokers to show signs of mental illness irrespective of the exact type of disorder (Farrell et al., 2001). While the evidence suggests a causal link from mental disorders to smoking, there is also evidence that smoking may

Table 3.1 Disorders and diseases linked to tobacco use

Smoking

Cancer of the lung	COPD[1]	Infertility
Cancer of the larynx	Pneumonia	Spontaneous abortion
Cancers of the oral cavity	Asthma attacks	Stillbirth
Cancer of the nasopharynx	Coronary heart disease	Low birth weight
Cancer of the oropharynx[3]	Aortic aneurism	Conduct disorder[2]
Cancer of the oesophagus	Cerebrovascular disease	SIDS[4]
Cancer of the liver	Peripheral vascular disease	Low back pain
Cancer of the cervix	Vascular dementia	Osteoporosis
Cancer of the pancreas	Periodontitis	Tuberculosis
Cancer of the stomach	Macular degeneration	Type II diabetes
Cancer of the bladder	Cataract	Peptic ulcer disease
Leukaemia	Hearing loss	Surgical complications

Smokeless tobacco use[5]
Cancer of the oral cavity

[1] Chronic obstructive pulmonary disease; [2] In offspring of women who smoked during pregnancy; [3] And hypopharynx; [4] Sudden infant death syndrome; [5] These vary greatly in concentrations of carcinogens and therefore risk.
Source: Adapted from West, R. (2006). Tobacco control: present and future. *British Medical Bulletin*, 77, 123–136.

increase susceptibility to develop mental illnesses (West & Jarvis, 2005). For instance, it has been observed that smoking in adolescents precedes the onset of anxiety disorders and depression (Brown *et al.*, 1996), possibly due to the effects of nicotine on mood and interactions with monoamine neurotransmitters or due to common, genetic mechanisms that increase susceptibility to both smoking and mental disorders (Isensee *et al.*, 2003).

Both the duration of tobacco use and the amount used influence the likelihood of disease occurrence, though duration of use has a greater impact (Jarvis, 2003). A life-long smoker's life expectancy is cut short by about 10 years on average (Doll *et al.*, 2004); more than one in two continuing smokers eventually dies from smoking cigarettes (*Doll et al.*, 2004; Thun *et al.*, 1995). Importantly, smokers do not avoid 'old age' by smoking, they just age more quickly and develop diseases of non-smokers at a much younger age (Stovring *et al.*, 2004). Risk of tobacco use is primarily conferred by carcinogens contained in smoke, thus the use of tobacco that involves combustion (i.e. cigars, pipes and cigarettes) is particularly dangerous. By contrast, use of tobacco that does not involve combustion

(i.e. smokeless forms of tobacco such as snuff, chewing or dipping tobacco) is less risky. While these still carry risk, in particular of head and neck cancers, some smokeless forms such as Swedish snus appear to have very low levels of carcinogens and consequently carry relatively minimal, long-term health risks (Foulds *et al.*, 2003).

The public health implications of tobacco use (in particular smoking) are exacerbated by an important component; namely, its impact on those who do not use tobacco themselves but who are exposed to tobacco carcinogens. There is persuasive evidence of the consequences of passive smoking: non-smokers living with smokers have an excess risk of 15 per cent to suffer smoking-related diseases (Hill *et al.*, 2004) and are more likely to develop lung cancer, stroke and ischemic heart disease (USDHHS, 2004). Epidemiological studies from the UK suggest that secondhand tobacco smoke may cause up to 1 in 10 of smoking-related deaths per year (Jamrozik, 2005). Moreover, children born to mothers who smoke during pregnancy are both more likely to die from cot death and to experience serious and at times rather insidious health and social consequences later on in life after controlling for putative confounding factors. They are not only more likely to have a low birth weight, cognitive impairment and attention deficit disorder but are also more predisposed to becoming delinquent (DiFranza *et al.*, 2004). Altogether, the health effects of smoking provide grim reading and if current trends continue, smoking-related deaths are estimated to reach 10 million per year by 2020 (Mackay *et al.*, 2006).

Smoking and tobacco use also have substantial financial implications for individuals and society through their impact on health care, loss of productivity through absenteeism, fires caused by smoking, diversion of agricultural land and environmental damage. As an example, the total cost of tobacco use to the US, is thought to be near US$200 billion per year (Centers for Disease Control and Prevention, 2007), and smoking-related fires cause worldwide damage of around US$27 billion each year (Mackay *et al.*, 2006). Each pack of cigarettes costs society and individual smokers close to $40 when combining actual price with additionally incurred costs (Sloan *et al.*, 2004). It makes up a large proportion of total household spending, especially in developing countries and increases personal poverty (World Health Organization, 2004). As tobacco use consumes around 2 per cent of GDP globally, it is therefore likely that smokers still incur net costs to society even when the taxation on tobacco products and a shorter lifespan of smokers are taken into account in economic models (Lightwood *et al.*, 2000).

The health benefits of smoking cessation are beyond doubt; there are immediate positive effects by slowing lung function decline, post-operative complications and halting the occurrence and further progress of heart disease (USDHHS, 1990). Stopping smoking has profound effects on the subsequent risk to develop smoking-related diseases such as lung cancer, cutting the risk of contracting it by half (Peto *et al.*, 2000). Smoking cessation improves reproductive health (Peate, 2005), and there is evidence that quitting smoking may improve mental health (Mino *et al.*, 2000) and increase happiness levels (Shahab & West, 2009).

However, the earlier a smoker quits the habit, the greater the benefits obtained. If smokers stop before the age of 35, they have a near normal life expectancy (Doll *et al.*, 2004). Indeed, around 90 per cent of excess mortality due to smoking can be avoided if smokers

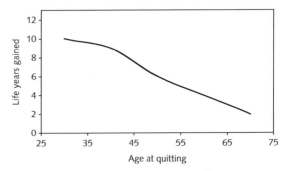

Figure 3.1 Life years saved by age of quitting
Source: Data from Doll, R., Peto, R., Boreham, J. & Sutherland, I. (2004). Mortality in relation to smoking: 50 years' observations on male British doctors. *British Medical Journal, 328,* 1519–1528.

stopped before middle age at around 30 years of age (Peto *et al.*, 2000). Since the risk of lung cancer and lung-function decline stabilises at the time of cessation but does not improve (Anthonisen *et al.*,1994; Doll *et al.*, 2004), early smoking cessation is therefore imperative in order to regain life years that would be potentially lost to smoking (see Figure 3.1).

Yet, stopping smoking at any age is beneficial to a person's health, even if smokers have begun to develop smoking-related diseases (Taylor Jr. *et al.*, 2002). Smoking cessation also benefits non-smokers who would usually be exposed to second-hand smoke. Thus partners of ex-smokers are less likely to develop cancer than non-smokers living with smokers, and babies born to mothers who stopped smoking during pregnancy are healthier than babies of full-term smoking mothers (National Cancer Institute, 1999). In addition, as people who quit smoking stop spending money on cigarettes, they also financially benefit from cessation. This is particularly true for poorer smokers in developing nations, who would usually divert money that should be spent on vital necessities to buy tobacco products (World Health Organization, 2004).

How to Assess Smokers and Help Them Stop

The psychological and behavioural consequences of smoking are important for the assessment of tobacco-related disorders. Although generic substance

Table 3.2 Fagerström test for nicotine dependence

Question	Score*
(1) How soon after you wake up do you smoke your first cigarette?[#]	After 60 minutes (0) 31–60 minutes (1) 6–30 minutes (2) Within 5 minutes (3)
(2) Do you find it difficult to refrain from smoking in places where it is forbidden?	No (0) Yes (1)
(3) Which cigarette would you hate most to give up?	First in the morning (1) Any other (0)
(4) How many cigarettes per day do you smoke?[#]	10 or less (0) 11–20 (1) 21–30 (2) 31 or more (3)
(5) Do you smoke more frequently during the first hours after awakening than during the rest of the day?	No (0) Yes (1)
(6) Do you smoke even if you are so ill that you are in bed most of the day?	No (0) Yes (1)

* 0–2 Very low dependence; 3–4 Low dependence; 5 Medium dependence; 6–7 High dependence; 8–10 Very high dependence; [#] Used for Heaviness of Smoking Index (HSI).
Source: Adapted from Heatherton, T.F., Kozlowski, L.T., Frecker, R.C. & Fagerström, K.O. (1991). The Fagerström test for nicotine dependence: A revision of the Fagerström tolerance questionnaire. *British Journal of Addiction, 86*, 1119–1127.

dependence can be measured following criteria from DSM-IV and ICD10, these do not differentiate well between smokers (Woody *et al.*, 1993). Classifying smokers along a continuum of dependence in a convenient manner, the Fagerström Test of Nicotine Dependence (FTND; Heatherton *et al.*, 1991) is probably the most ubiquitously used tool to assess nicotine dependence. It scores smokers on a scale from 0–10 based on six questions (Table 3.2).

The FTND has good reliability and validity and predicts a smoker's ability to stop smoking and is a good correlate of biochemical measures of dependence (e.g. Breslau & Johnson, 2000). The Heaviness of Smoking Index, a shorter version of the FTND, makes use of only two questions of the FTND (see Table 3.2) and has also proven reliability and validity (John *et al.*, 2004). There are also various other multidimensional instruments to assess nicotine dependence used to a lesser degree such as the Nicotine Dependence Syndrome Scale (Shiffman *et al.*, 2004).

As an alternative to questionnaires, biochemical markers can provide an objective measure of cigarette consumption and dependence. The most commonly used biomarkers are expired air carbon monoxide, easily and cheaply measured with commercially available breathalysers, which is a relatively good marker of smoke exposure, and cotinine, a metabolite of nicotine measured in plasma, saliva and urine, which is more expensive but has better sensitivity and specificity and can be detected for longer (Benowitz *et al.*, 2002).

The overall aim of smoking cessation interventions is very simple: to ensure that the motivation not to smoke is higher than the motivation to smoke at all times when the opportunity to smoke exists. However, as described above, dependence on cigarettes is a complex phenomenon, which is determined by a smoker's internal (e.g. physical addiction to nicotine) as well as external (e.g. cultural expectation, peer pressure, smoking cues) environment and the process of smoking cessation is equally complex as the factors that trigger a quit attempt are likely to be different from those that maintain it (Vangeli & West, 2008). Treatment therefore needs to focus on these different aspects. One way to conceptualise existing approaches in tobacco control is in terms of their implementation at the individual or population level and the focus on smokers' internal and external environments with the ultimate aim to increase quit attempts and sustain abstinence (Figure 3.2).

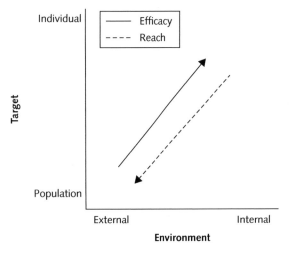

Figure 3.2   Taxonomy of tobacco control approaches

The range of effective measures that target the whole population of smokers to trigger a quit attempt primarily focus on a smoker's external environment and include changes in legislation and policy (tax increases, reduction of smuggling, smoking bans, introduction of warning labels), increasing public awareness (mass media campaigns, dissemination of research findings) and provision of brief advice to stop smoking from health professionals.

While population approaches have wide reach, they tend to be cursory and not intensive and consequently result in low cessation rates, e.g. even the most committed mass media campaigns rarely increase smoking cessation rates by more than 2 per cent, if at all (Hopkins *et al.*, 2001). This is because the initial push towards cessation is rarely enough to lead to long-term abstinence. As Figure 3.3 shows, most smokers relapse within one week of the start of unaided quit attempts and relapse risk becomes low only after 12 weeks of abstinence (Hughes *et al.*, 2004).

For this reason, treatments supporting an individual smoker through the first and toughest stages of smoking cessation are required. These tend to focus on a

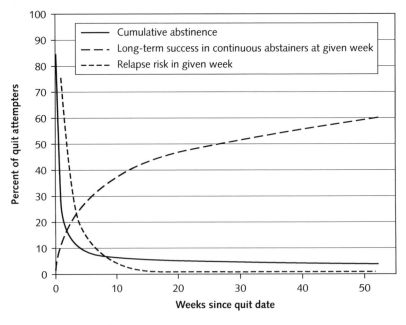

Figure 3.3   Relapse curves during smoking cessation
Source: Adapted from West, R. & Stapleton, J. (2008). Clinical and public health significance of treatments to aid smoking cessation. *European Respiratory Review, 17,* 199–204.

Table 3.3 Effectiveness of individual level smoking cessation treatments

Treatment	Comparison	Approximate increase in cessation rate at 6 months
Nicotine replacement therapy (all forms 8–12 weeks) without behavioural support	Placebo	5%
Nicotine replacement therapy (all forms 8–12 weeks) with behavioural support	Placebo with behavioural support	10%
Bupropion (300 mg bid 8 weeks) with behavioural support	Placebo with behavioural support	10%
Nortriptyline (1.5 mg bid 8 weeks) with behavioural support	Placebo with behavioural support	10%
Varenicline (1.5 mg bid 12 weeks) with behavioural support	Placebo with behavioural support	15%
Self-help material	No support or placebo material	1%
Face-to-face behavioural support from a specialist (4–8 weeks)	Brief advice or written materials	5%
Telephone-based behavioural support (4–8 weeks)	Brief advice or written materials	5%
Combination of behavioural support and medication	Quitting without help	10–20%

Source: Adapted from West, R. & Stapleton, J. (2008). Clinical and public health significance of treatments to aid smoking cessation. *European Respiratory Review, 17*, 199–204.

smoker's internal environment by using pharmacotherapy to reduced motivation to smoke and behavioural support to increase motivation not to smoke, ensure appropriate use of pharmacotherapy and enhance self-regulatory capacity. As these interventions tend to be more intensive, smoking cessation rates are higher but their reach is lower (Figure 3.2). While the efficacy of interventions varies somewhat (Table 3.3), overall, they are highly cost-effective compared with other life-saving medical treatments (West & Hardy, 2007).

Pharmacotherapy is very effective and the number of available products to aid smoking cessation now is greater than ever. There is a range of nicotine replacement therapies (NRT) of comparative efficacy (lozenge, gum, patch, spray, inhaler and sublingual tablets) that replace nicotine in the body to reduce craving and withdrawal symptoms. Non-nicotine pharmacotherapy includes the anti-depressants bupropion and nortriptyline. Varenicline, a selective partial antagonist of nicotinic alpha4–beta2 receptors, is the latest addition to this array of products and has been shown to be highly effective. A new and potentially very promising treatment that is being developed is a nicotine vaccine to stop nicotine from crossing the blood–

brain barrier thus preventing its pharmacological effects (Hatsukami, *et al.*, 2005).

Similar to pharmacotherapy, there is an equally varied range of psychological interventions that include telephone counselling, self-help interventions, social support provision, aversive smoking, hypnotherapy and face-to-face behavioural counselling. Of these, only self-help interventions, telephone and face-to-face group or individual behavioural counselling have been proven to be effective in randomised controlled trials (Shahab & Fidler, 2010) increasing cessation rates by between 1–10 per cent (Table 3.3). Surprisingly, little is known about what makes psychological interventions effective. However, practical and intra-treatment social support, multiple sessions of treatment, tailoring of information and appropriate training of counsellors are considered important elements (USDHHS, 2008; West *et al.*, 2000). Whilst self-help interventions, which involve the provision of written material, quit kits or audiotapes, have only a small effect, they are cheap and have the potential to reach large populations. Interactive, online smoking cessation interventions are particularly promising in this regard as they appear to be able to bridge the gap between reach and efficacy and can provide highly individualised and intensive interventions to a large number of people (Shahab & McEwen, 2009).

Some smokers may find it impossible to stop smoking completely. For this reason, various harm reduction methods (e.g. use of smokeless forms of tobacco; cutting down consumption while using NRT; long-term use of NRT) have been proposed to aid these smokers (Stratton *et al.*, 2001). While there is no evidence that cutting down cigarette consumption in itself is beneficial in terms of health risks (Adda & Cornaglia, 2006), most likely because smokers tend to compensate by smoking fewer cigarettes more intensely (Hurt *et al.*, 2000), there is some evidence that concurrent use of NRT while cutting down may help smokers stop completely (Wennike *et al.*, 2003). Although the long-term benefits of harm reduction methods have yet to be evaluated (Hatsukami *et al.*, 2004), harm reduction is likely to be particularly helpful for highly addicted smokers and, as shown for Swedish snus, can result in real public health benefits (Ramstrom & Foulds, 2006).

The combination of pharmacotherapy with behavioural counselling to support complete cessation yields the highest success rates (Table 3.3) and therefore should be the treatment of choice for any smoker trying to stop. Indeed, common sense and current evidence suggest that the most successful strategies to help people stop smoking involve multiple approaches implemented in tandem within a comprehensive tobacco control scheme (World Health Organization, 1998).

The Role of Health Professionals

Health psychologists and other health professionals have a two-fold task in reducing the burden of tobacco use and increasing smoking cessation. First, through frequent contact with smokers in the health setting, they are in a unique environment to encourage smokers to make quit attempts by using evidence of early warning signs of smoking-related diseases to appeal to smokers' health concerns. Although routinely delivered brief quit advice increases cessation rates by only around 2 per cent (Lancaster & Stead, 2004), it can have a large impact at the population level given the number of smokers seen by health professionals each year.

Second, health psychologist can provide more intensive support to people who have decided to stop smoking to turn smokers into long-term abstainers. Health psychologists in the UK and other countries are trained and employed as smoking cessation counsellors and are provided with a unique skill-set to help smokers maximise their chances of cessation. As no particular theoretical approach appears to be superior, the general model focuses on providing both practical and emotional support, advice on how to cope with difficult situations, minimise the desire to smoke and using health-related, financial, social and aesthetic motivational arguments to strengthen a smoker's motivation to stay abstinent. However, while the theoretical underpinning of behavioural support may be indeterminate, there is unequivocal support which medications are effective for smoking cessation and which are not. The use of pharmacotherapy provides smokers with their best chance of stopping smoking and overcoming the early critical period of smoking cessation without relapsing. Health psychologists and other health professionals therefore have a crucial role in ensuring that smokers attempting to stop are adequately informed about the importance of pharmacotherapy for a successful quit attempt, and are provided with access to and are educated about the correct use of medication. This is especially important given the fact that some health professionals still refuse to provide medication to patients who want to stop smoking and would like to have pharmacological support (Vogt *et al.*, 2006).

The role of health professionals in smoking cessation treatment has been formalised in various guidelines (e.g. Graham *et al.*, 2007; NICE, 2008; Rabe *et al.*, 2007; USDHHS, 2008; West *et al.*, 2000) and is endorsed by relevant professional bodies. Thus doctors in primary care are provided with financial incentives to ensure that they regularly check whether their patients smoke and advise smokers to make a quit attempt, ideally using the best treatment available, i.e. a combination of psychological support and medication (BMA, 2003). In addition, a dedicated smoking cessation service has been set up in the UK that provides state-of-the-art support to nearly 700,000 smokers yearly who would like to stop smoking (Department of Health, 2008). It is hoped that this model of health professionals providing committed and effective treatment to smokers who want to stop smoking can be exported to many more countries following the ratification of the world's first public health treaty in 2004, the Framework Convention on Tobacco Control, which supports the inclusion of smoking cessation programmes in national health plans (Wipfli *et al.*, 2004).

Discussion Points

1 Discuss the contribution of smoking to health inequalities.
2 Is smoking more than an addiction to nicotine?
3 Given the consequences of smoking, should the sale of tobacco be banned?
4 What do you think constitutes a maximally effective intervention to reduce national smoking prevalence? What would be key components of the intervention and why?
5 How can health professionals be encouraged to take a greater role in promoting smoking cessation?

Further Reading

McEwen, A., Hajek, P., McRobbie, H. & West, R. (2006). *Manual of smoking cessation*. Oxford: Blackwell Publishing.

West, R. & Shahab, L. (2010). Smoking cessation interventions. In A. Killoran & M. Kelly (Eds.) *Evidence-based public health*. Oxford: Oxford University Press.

West, R. & Shiffman, S. (2007). *Fast facts: Smoking cessation* (2nd edn). Oxford: Health Press.

References

Adda, J. & Cornaglia, F. (2006). Taxes, cigarette consumption, and smoking intensity. *American Economic Review, 96*, 1013–1028.

Anthonisen, N.R., Connett, J.E., Kiley, J.P., Altose, M.D., Bailey, W.C., Buist, A.S. *et al.* (1994). Effects of smoking intervention and the use of an inhaled anticholinergic bronchodilator on the rate of decline of FEV1. The Lung Health Study. *Journal of the American Medical Association, 272*, 1497–1505.

Becker, G.S. & Murphy, K.M. (1988). A theory of rational addiction. *Journal of Political Economy, 96*, 675–700.

Benowitz, N.L. & Jacob, P.I. (1984). Daily intake of nicotine during cigarette smoking. *Clinical Pharmacology & Therapeutics, 35*, 499–504.

Benowitz, N.L., Jacob, P., III, Ahijevych, K., Jarvis, M.J., Hall, S., LeHouezec, J. *et al.* (2002). Biochemical verification of tobacco use and cessation. *Nicotine & Tobacco Research, 4*, 149–159.

BMA (2003). *The New GMS contract 2003: Investing in general practice*. London: NHS Confederation.

Breslau, N. & Johnson, E.O. (2000). Predicting smoking cessation and major depression in nicotine-dependent smokers. *American Journal of Public Health, 90*, 1122–1127.

Brown, R.A., Lewinsohn, P.M., Seeley, J.R. & Wagner, E.F. (1996). Cigarette smoking, major depression, and other psychiatric disorders among adolescents. *Journal of the American Academy of Child & Adolescent Psychiatry, 35*, 1602–1610.

Centers for Disease Control and Prevention (1988). *The health consequences of smoking. Nicotine: A report of the Surgeon General*. Rockville, MD: US Department of Health and Human Services.

Centers for Disease Control and Prevention (2007). *Best practices for comprehensive tobacco control programs – 2007*. Atlanta, GA: US Department of Health and Human Services.

Cloninger, C.R. (1987). A systematic method for clinical description and classification of personality variants. A proposal. *Archives of General Psychiatry, 44*, 573–588.

Corti, E. (1931). *A history of smoking*. London: George G. Harrap.

Cummings, K. (1997). Health policy and smoking and tobacco use. In D. Gochman (Ed.) *Handbook of health behavior research IV* (pp. 231–252). New York: Plenum Press.

Department of Health (2008). *Statistics on NHS Stop Smoking Services in England, April 2007 to March 2008*. Leeds: Information Centre for Health and Social Care.

DiFranza, J.R., Aligne, C.A. & Weitzman, M. (2004). Prenatal and postnatal environmental tobacco smoke exposure and children's health. *Pediatrics, 113*, 1007–1015.

Doll, R., Peto, R., Boreham, J. & Sutherland, I. (2004). Mortality in relation to smoking: 50 years' observations on male British doctors. *British Medical Journal, 328*, 1519–1528.

Ezzati, M. & Lopez, A.D. (2003). Estimates of global mortality attributable to smoking in 2000. *Lancet, 362*, 847–852.

Ezzati, M. & Lopez, A.D. (2004). Regional, disease specific patterns of smoking-attributable mortality in 2000. *Tobacco Control, 13*, 388–395.

Ezzati, M., Lopez, A.D., Rodgers, A., Vander, H.S. & Murray, C.J. (2002). Selected major risk factors and global and regional burden of disease. *Lancet, 360*, 1347–1360.

Farrell, M., Howes, S., Bebbington, P., Brugha, T., Jenkins, R., Lewis, G. *et al.* (2001). Nicotine, alcohol and drug dependence and psychiatric comorbidity. Results of a national household survey. *British Journal of Psychiatry, 179*, 432–437.

Fidler, J.A., Wardle, J., Brodersen, N.H., Jarvis, M.J. & West, R. (2006). Vulnerability to smoking after trying a single cigarette can lie dormant for three years or more. *Tobacco Control, 15*, 205–209.

Finucane, M.L., Alhakami, A., Slovic, P. & Johnson, S.M. (2000). The affect heuristic in judgments of risks and benefits. *Journal of Behavioral Decision Making, 13*, 1–17.

Foulds, J., Ramstrom, L., Burke, M. & Fagerström, K. (2003). Effect of smokeless tobacco (snus) on smoking and public health in Sweden. *Tobacco Control, 12*, 349–359.

Goddard, E. (2006). *General household survey: Smoking and drinking among adults, 2005*. London: Office of National Statistics.

Gotti, C., Fornasari, D. & Clementi, F. (1997). Human neuronal nicotinic receptors. *Progress in Neurobiology, 53*, 199–237.

Graham, I., Atar, D., Borch-Johnsen, K., Boysen, G., Burell, G., Cifkova, R. *et al.* (2007). European guidelines on cardiovascular disease prevention in clinical practice: Executive summary. *Atherosclerosis, 194*, 1–45.

Guindon, G. & Boisclair, D. (2003). *Past, current and future trends in tobacco use*. Washington, DC: International Bank for Reconstruction and Development/World Bank.

Hatsukami, D.K., Henningfield, J.E. & Kotlyar, M. (2004). Harm reduction approaches to reducing tobacco-related mortality. *Annual Review of Public Health, 25*, 377–395.

Hatsukami, D.K., Rennard, S., Jorenby, D., Fiore, M., Koopmeiners, J., de Vos, A. *et al.* (2005). Safety and immunogenicity of a nicotine conjugate vaccine in current smokers. *Clinical Pharmacology & Therapeutics, 78*, 456–467.

Heatherton, T.F., Kozlowski, L.T., Frecker, R.C. & Fagerström, K.O. (1991). The Fagerström test for nicotine dependence: A revision of the Fagerström tolerance questionnaire. *British Journal of Addiction, 86*, 1119–1127.

Henningfield, J., Pankow, J., & Garrett, B. (2004). Ammonia and other chemical base tobacco additives and cigarette nicotine delivery: Issues and research needs. *Nicotine & Tobacco Research, 6*, 199–205.

Henningfield, J.E., Stapleton, J.M., Benowitz, N.L., Grayson, R.F. & London, E.D. (1993). Higher levels of nicotine in arterial than in venous blood after cigarette smoking. *Drug and Alcohol Dependence, 33*, 23–29.

Hill, S., Blakely, T., Kawachi, I. & Woodward, A. (2004). Mortality among 'never smokers' living with smokers: Two cohort studies, 1981–4 and 1996–9. *British Medical Journal, 328*, 988–989.

Hopkins, D.P., Briss, P.A., Ricard, C.J., Husten, C.G., Carande-Kulis, V.G., Fielding, J.E. *et al.* (2001). Reviews of evidence regarding interventions to reduce tobacco use and exposure to environmental tobacco smoke. *American Journal of Preventive Medicine, 20*, 16–66.

Hughes, J.R., Keely, J. & Naud, S. (2004). Shape of the relapse curve and long-term abstinence among untreated smokers. *Addiction, 9*, 29–38.

Hurt, R.D., Croghan, G.A., Wolter, T.D., Croghan, I.T., Offord, K.P., Williams, G.M. *et al.* (2000). Does smoking reduction result in reduction of biomarkers associated with harm? A pilot study using a nicotine inhaler. *Nicotine & Tobacco Research, 2*, 327–336.

Hyland, A., Vena, C., Bauer, J., Li, Q., Giovino, G., Yang, J. *et al.* (2003). Cigarette smoking-attributable morbidity – United States 2000. *Morbidity and Mortality Weekly Report, 52*, 824–844.

International Agency for Research on Cancer (2004). Tobacco smoke and involuntary smoking. In *IARC monographs on the evaluation of carcinogenic risks to humans. Vol. 83* (pp. 973–991). Lyon: IARC.

Isensee, B., Wittchen, H.U., Stein, M.B., Hofler, M. & Lieb, R. (2003). Smoking increases the risk of panic: Findings from a prospective community study. *Archives of General Psychiatry, 60*, 692–700.

Jamrozik, K. (2005). Estimate of deaths attributable to passive smoking among UK adults: Database analysis. *British Medical Journal, 330*, 812–816.

Jarvis, M.J. (2003). Epidemiology of cigarette smoking and cessation. *Journal of Clinical Psychiatry Monograph, 18*, 6–11.

Jarvis, M.J. (2004). Why people smoke. *British Medical Journal, 328*, 277–279.

Jarvis, M.J. & Wardle, J. (2005). Social patterning of individual health behaviours: The case of cigarette smoking. In M. Marmot & R. Wilkinson (Eds.) *Social determinants of health* (2nd edn, pp. 224–237). New York: Oxford University Press.

Jellinek, E. (1960). *The disease concept of alcoholism*. New Brunswick, NJ: Hillhouse Press.

John, U., Meyer, C., Schumann, A., Hapke, U., Rumpf, H.J., Adam, C. *et al.* (2004). A short form of the Fagerström test for nicotine dependence and the heaviness of smoking index in two adult population samples. *Addictive Behaviors, 29*, 1207–1212.

Kotz, D. & West, R. (2009). Explaining the social gradient in smoking cessation: It's not in the trying, but in the succeeding. *Tobacco Control, 18*, 43–46.

Lancaster, T. & Stead, L. (2004). Physician advice for smoking cessation. *Cochrane Database of Systematic Reviews (Online)*. CD000165.

Lightwood, J., Collins, D., Lapsley, H. & Novotny, T. (2000). Estimating the cost of tobacco use. In P. Jha & F. Chaloupka (Eds.) *Tobacco control in developing countries* (pp. 63–103). Oxford: Oxford University Press.

Lopez, A., Collishaw, N. & Piha, T. (1994). A descriptive model of the cigarette epidemic in developed countries. *Tobacco Control, 3*, 242–247.

Mackay, J., Eriksen, M. & Shafey, O. (2006). *The tobacco atlas* (2nd edn). Atlanta: American Cancer Society.

Mackay, J. & Amos, A. (2003). Women and tobacco. *Respirology, 8*, 123–130.

McEwen, A., West, R. & McRobbie, H. (2008). Motives for smoking and their correlates in clients attending Stop Smoking treatment services. *Nicotine & Tobacco Research, 10*, 843–850.

Mino, Y., Shigemi, J., Otsu, T., Tsuda, T. & Babazono, A. (2000). Does smoking cessation improve mental health? *Psychiatry and Clinical Neurosciences, 54*, 169–172.

National Cancer Institute (1999). *Health effects of exposure to environmental tobacco smoke: The report of the California Environmental Protection Agency. Smoking and tobacco monograph no.10.* (99-4645 ed.). Bethesda, MD: National Institutes of Health.

NICE (2008). *Smoking cessation services in primary care, pharmacies, local authorities and workplaces, particularly for manual working groups, pregnant women and hard to reach communities* (Rep. No. NICE public health guidance 10). London: National Institute for Health & Clinical Excellence.

Peate, I. (2005). The effects of smoking on the reproductive health of men. *British Journal of Nursing, 14*, 362–366.

Peto, R., Darby, S., Deo, H., Silcocks, P., Whitley, E. & Doll, R. (2000). Smoking, smoking cessation, and lung cancer in the UK since 1950: Combination of national statistics with two case-control studies. *British Medical Journal, 321*, 323–329.

Pomerleau, J., Gilmore, A., McKee, M., Rose, R., & Haerpfer, C.W. (2004). Determinants of smoking in eight countries of the former Soviet Union: Results from the living conditions, lifestyles and health study. *Addiction, 99*, 1577–1585.

Rabe, K.F., Hurd, S., Anzueto, A., Barnes, P.J., Buist, S.A., Calverley, P. *et al.* (2007). Global strategy for the diagnosis, management, and prevention of chronic obstructive pulmonary disease – GOLD executive summary. *American Journal of Respiratory and Critical Care Medicine, 176*, 532–555.

Ramstrom, L.M. & Foulds, J. (2006). Role of snus in initiation and cessation of tobacco smoking in Sweden. *Tobacco Control, 15*, 210–214.

Rock, V., Malarcher, A., Kahende, J., Asman, K., Husten, C. & Caraballo, R. (2007). Cigarette smoking among adults – United States, 2006. *Morbidity and Mortality Weekly Report, 56*, 1157–1161.

Rose, J.E., Behm, F.M. & Levin, E.D. (1993). Role of nicotine dose and sensory cues in the regulation of smoke intake. *Pharmacology Biochemistry & Behavior, 44*, 891–900.

Royal College of Physicians (2000). *Nicotine addiction in Britain. A report of the Tobacco Advisory Group of the Royal College of Physicians.* London: Royal College of Physicians of London.

Russell, M.A.H. & Feyerabend, C. (1978). Cigarette-smoking – dependence on high-nicotine boli. *Drug Metabolism Reviews, 8*, 29–57.

Ryan, F. (2002). Detected, selected, and sometimes neglected: Cognitive processing of cues in addiction. *Experimental and Clinical Psychopharmacology, 10*, 67–76.

Shafey, O., Dolwick, S. & Guindon, G. (2003). *Tobacco control country profile 2003.* Atlanta, GA: American Cancer Society.

Shahab, L. (2008). The epidemiology of smoking: a growing concern. In M. Miravitlles (Ed.) *Hot topics in respiratory medicine* (Issue 8, pp. 7–14). Modena: FB Communications.

Shahab, L. & Fidler, J. (2010). Tobacco-related disorders. In P. Sturmey & M. Hersen (Eds.) *Handbook of evidence-based practice in clinical psychology, vol. II: Adult disorders.* New York: Wiley.

Shahab, L. & McEwen, A. (2009). Online support for smoking cessation: a systematic review of the literature. *Addiction, 104*, 1792–1804.

Shahab, L. & West, R. (2009). Do ex-smokers report feeling happier following cessation? Evidence from a cross-sectional survey. *Nicotine & Tobacco Research, 11*, 553–557.

Shiffman, S., Waters, A. & Hickcox, M. (2004). The nicotine dependence syndrome scale: A multidimensional measure of nicotine dependence. *Nicotine & Tobacco Research, 6*, 327–348.

Sloan, F.A., Ostermann, J. & Picone, G. (2004). *The price of smoking.* Cambridge, MA: Massachusetts Institute of Technology.

Smith, R.C., Singh, A., Infante, M., Khandat, A. & Kloos, A. (2002). Effects of cigarette smoking and nicotine nasal spray on psychiatric symptoms and cognition in schizophrenia. *Neuropsychopharmacology, 27*, 479–497.

Stovring, N., Avlund, K., Schultz-Larsen, K. & Schroll, M. (2004). The cumulative effect of smoking at age 50, 60, and 70 on functional ability at age 75. *Scandinavian Journal of Public Health, 32*, 296–302.

Stratton, S., Shetty, P., Wallace, R. & Bondurant, S. (2001). *Clearing the smoke: Addressing the science base for tobacco harm reduction.* Washington, DC: National Academy Press.

Taylor, D.H., Jr., Hasselblad, V., Henley, S.J., Thun, M.J. & Sloan, F.A. (2002). Benefits of smoking cessation for longevity. *American Journal of Public Health, 92*, 990–996.

The Global Youth Tobacco Survey Collaborative Group (2002). Tobacco use among youth: A cross-country comparison. *Tobacco Control, 11*, 252–270.

Thun, M.J., Day-Lally, C.A., Calle, E.E., Flanders, W.D. & Heath, C.W. Jr. (1995). Excess mortality among cigarette smokers: Changes in a 20-year interval. *American Journal of Public Health, 85*, 1223–1230.

Tyas, S.L. & Pederson, L.L. (1998). Psychosocial factors related to adolescent smoking: A critical review of the literature. *Tobacco Control, 7*, 409–420.

USDHHS (1990). *The health benefits of smoking cessation: A report of the Surgeon General.* Rockville, MD: US Department of Health and Human Services.

USDHHS (2004). *The health consequences of smoking: A report of the Surgeon General.* Atlanta, GA: US Department of Health and Human Services.

USDHHS (2008). *Clinical practical guidelines. Treating tobacco use and dependence – 2008 update.* Rockville, MD: US Department of Health and Human Services.

Vangeli, E. & West, R. (2008). Sociodemographic differences in triggers to quit smoking: Findings from a national survey. *Tobacco Control, 17*, 410–415.

Vogt, F., Hall, S. & Marteau, T. M. (2006). General practitioners' beliefs about effectiveness and intentions to prescribe smoking cessation medications: qualitative and quantitative studies. *BMC Public Health, 6*, 277.

Watkins, S.S., Koob, G.F. & Markou, A. (2000). Neural mechanisms underlying nicotine addiction: Acute positive reinforcement and withdrawal. *Nicotine & Tobacco Research, 2*, 19–37.

Wennike, P., Danielsson, T., Landfeldt, B., Westin, A. & Tonnesen, P. (2003). Smoking reduction promotes smoking cessation: Results from a double blind, randomized, placebo-controlled trial of nicotine gum with 2-year follow-up. *Addiction, 98*, 1395–1402.

West, R. (2001). Theories of addiction. *Addiction, 96*, 3–13.

West, R. (2006a). *Theory of addiction.* Oxford: Blackwell Publishing Ltd.

West, R. (2006b). Tobacco control: present and future. *British Medical Bulletin, 77*, 123–136.

West, R. & Hardy, A. (2007). Tobacco use. In S. Ayers, A. Baum, C. McManus, S. Newman, K. Wallston, J. Weinman, & West R (Eds.), *Cambridge Handbook of Psychology, Health and Medicine* (pp. 908–912). New York: Cambridge University Press.

West, R. & Jarvis, M.J. (2005). Tobacco smoking and mental disorder. *International Journal of Psychiatry and Behavioral Sciences, 15*, 10–17.

West, R., McNeill, A. & Raw, M. (2000). Smoking cessation guidelines for health professionals: An update. Health Education Authority. *Thorax, 55*, 987–999.

West, R. & Shiffman, S. (2007). *Fast facts: Smoking cessation.* (2nd edn). Oxford: Health Press.

West, R. & Stapleton, J. (2008). Clinical and public health significance of treatments to aid smoking cessation. *European Respiratory Review, 17*, 199–204.

World Health Organization (1997). *Tobacco or health: a global status report.* Geneva: World Health Organization.

World Health Organization (1998). *Guideline for controlling and monitoring the tobacco epidemic.* Geneva: World Health Organization.

World Health Organization (2004). Tobacco increases the poverty of individuals and families. http://www.who.int/tobacco/communications/events/wntd/2004/tobaccofacts_families/en/print.html.

Wipfli, H., Stillman, F., Tamplin, S., da Costa e Silva, V.L., Yach, D. & Samet, J. (2004). Achieving the framework convention on tobacco control's potential by investing in national capacity. *Tobacco Control, 13*, 433–437.

Woody, G.E., Cottler, L.B. & Cacciola, J. (1993). Severity of dependence: Data from the DSM-IV field trials. *Addiction, 88*, 1573–1579.

4

Physical Activity

Stuart J.H. Biddle

Chapter Outline

Physical activity is a very important health behaviour. In this chapter, physical activity is defined, the key health benefits are briefly highlighted and the evidence concerning interventions to increase physical activity is summarised. Such interventions include those aimed at individuals and small groups, communities (schools and worksites) and the population at large via mass media. Moreover, consideration is given to the use of new technologies in behaviour change. Commentary is provided on preventing declines in physical activity.

Key Concepts

Correlates
Exercise
Interventions
Physical activity
Sedentary behaviour
Tracking

Introduction

People in industrialised countries now adopt lifestyles that were quite unknown until very recently in respect of human evolution. From early beginnings of the hunter-gatherer through to active manual employment or substantial energy expenditure in home-based chores and active forms of transport, to the industrial-technological 'obesogenic' and 'slothogenic' society of today, human lifestyles have clearly changed. Such changes in lifestyle that reflect low levels of habitual physical activity are associated with significant health problems. 'Hypokinetic diseases', or health problems caused by, or related to, a lack of physical activity were identified in ancient societies, and documented systematically over the past half century (Hardman & Stensel, 2009). Such hypokinetic problems can include poor mental health, coronary heart disease (CHD), obesity, low back pain, osteoporosis, hypertension, diabetes and some cancers. The UK government's Chief Medical Officer (CMO) states that 'there are few public health initiatives that have a greater potential for improving health and well-being than increasing the activity levels of the population' (Department of Health, 2004). The evidence linking physical activity patterns with such health measures is increasing rapidly and reflects the growing importance of physical activity as a key public health issue. Although the media focus on obesity is obvious, physical activity affects more than energy balance.

What is Physical Activity?

Caspersen et al. (1985) defined physical activity as any movement of the body produced by the skeletal muscles that results in energy expenditure. As far as health outcomes are concerned, the energy expenditure is usually required to be well above resting levels. It is important to note that there are many forms of physical activity. These can include structured exercise and sport, as well as active forms of transport (e.g. walking to work), recreational play (e.g. street games), physical education in schools and other physical activity opportunities, such as stair climbing.

'Exercise' is a subcomponent of physical activity that requires 'planned, structured and repetitive bodily movement' (Caspersen et al., 1985, p. 127), often with the intent of maintaining or improving physical fitness. Sport is a sub-component of exercise whereby the activity is rule governed, structured, competitive and involves gross motor movement characterised by physical strategy, prowess and chance (Rejeski & Brawley, 1988). This rules out sedentary games such as chess and bridge, but can include darts or snooker, even though they have little or no physical health benefits. The distinction between physical activity, exercise and sport is important for health psychologists because they reflect different, though overlapping, classes of behaviour.

Finally, it is important to note that there is an increasing recognition of the importance of reducing 'sedentary behaviour' in addition to increasing physical activity (Pate et al., 2008). Sedentary behaviour could be operationally defined as primarily sitting-based behaviours, such as television viewing, computer use and motorised transport. Research is beginning to show that we spend large amounts of time being sedentary and that this may have significant deleterious effects on our health, including increased risk of obesity and diabetes (Hamilton et al., 2008). It should be noted that 'sedentary behaviours' are specific behaviours in their own right and not simply a reflection of lack of physical activity. For example, excessive television viewing in adults has been shown to be associated with greater levels of overweight and obesity even in those who have 'adequate' levels of physical activity (Sugiyama et al., 2008). Relationships are less clear in young people (Stensel et al., 2008). The level and strength of evidence for a relationship between physical activity and a range of important physical and psychological health outcomes are shown in Table 4.1.

Physical Activity Guidelines: How much is enough?

With any health behaviour, the question is often posed concerning what levels are 'healthy', 'unhealthy' or 'appropriate'. Guidelines concerning how much physical activity should be recommended for public health are, unsurprisingly, contentious. The main recommendations for young people and adults are stated in Table 4.2, including updated recommendations from the United States.

Table 4.1 Level of strength of evidence for a relationship between physical activity and health outcomes reported in the CMO's report

Condition	Preventive effects			Therapeutic effects	
	Level of evidence[a]	Strength of effect	Evidence of a dose–response relationship	Level of evidence[a]	Strength of effect
Cardiovascular disease:					
Coronary heart disease	High	Strong	Yes	Medium	Moderate
Stroke: occlusive	High	Moderate		Low	Weak
Stroke: haemorrhagic	Medium	Weak		Low	Weak
Peripheral vascular disease	No/ insufficient data			Medium	Moderate
Obesity and overweight	Medium	Moderate		Medium	Moderate
Type 2 diabetes	High	Strong	Yes	Medium	Weak
Musculoskeletal disorders:					
Osteoporosis	High	Strong		Medium	Weak
Osteoarthritis	No/ insufficient data			Medium	Moderate
Lower back pain	Medium	Weak		High	Moderate
Psychological well-being and mental illness:					
Clinical depression	Low	Weak		Medium	Moderate
Other mental illness	No/ insufficient data			Low	Weak
Mental well-being				Medium	Moderate
Mental function	Low	Moderate		Low	Weak
Social well-being	No/ insufficient data			Low	Weak
Cancer:					
Overall	Medium	Moderate	Yes	No/ insufficient data	
Colon	High	Strong	Yes	No/ insufficient data	
Rectal	Medium	No effect		No/ insufficient data	
Breast	High	Moderate	Yes	No/ insufficient data	
Lung	Low	Moderate		No/ insufficient data	
Prostate	Medium	Equivocal		No/ insufficient data	
Endometrial	Low	Weak	Yes	No/ insufficient data	
Others	Low	Equivocal		No/ insufficient data	

[a] Volume and quality of data.

Source: Department of Health (2004). *At least five a week: Evidence on the impact of physical activity and its relationship to health. A report from the Chief Medical Officer*. London: Department of Health. © Crown Copyright material reproduced with the permission of the Controller HMSO.

Interventions to Increase Physical Activity

Health psychologists are interested in understanding and changing behaviour. Those focusing on physical activity need to have knowledge concerning the factors associated with physical activity, including variables that may be inhibiting participation. Such factors are often labelled 'correlates' or 'determinants' of physical activity (Biddle & Mutrie, 2008). These factors

Table 4.2 Guidelines for physical activity for young people and adults

Focus	Guidelines
Young people (Department of Health, 2004)	Children and young people should achieve a total of at least 60 minutes of at least moderate intensity physical activity each day. At least twice per week this should include activities to improve bone health, muscle strength and flexibility
Adults (UK) (Department of Health, 2004)	Adults should achieve a total of at least 30 minutes a day of at least moderate intensity physical activity on 5 or more days of the week
Adults up to aged 65 years (USA) (Haskell *et al.*, 2007)	Do moderately intense aerobic physical activity for 30 minutes a day, 5 days a week *Or* Do vigorously intense aerobic physical activity 20 minutes a day, 3 days a week *And* Do 8 to 10 strength-training exercises, 8 to 12 repetitions of each exercise twice a week

affect, or are thought to affect, participation in physical activity. With the identification of correlates of behaviour, interventions to change physical activity can be tested and should be based on sound theoretical foundations. Therefore, there are three key issues for health psychologists to consider:

- What are the key psychological and non-psychological correlates that might act as mediators of successful physical activity behaviour change? That is, what correlates can be changed in order to affect physical activity?
- What are the key psychological and non-psychological correlates that might act as moderators of successful physical activity behaviour change? That is, what correlates might differentially affect the success of the intervention?
- What appropriate psychological, non-psychological or multidisciplinary theories are appropriate to underpin the intervention? (Space does not allow for discussion concerning psychological theories, and some are covered elsewhere in this book.)

Non-psychological correlates might include those that are demographic, biological, social, cultural or environmental. Moreover, interventions can take place at different levels, with targeting possible at the level

of the individual (e.g. counselling), small group (e.g. exercise class), community (including specified settings, such as schools or worksites) or whole populations (e.g. via mass media).

Interventions: individuals and small groups

Hillsdon and Thorogood (1996) conducted a systematic review of intervention strategies for the promotion of physical activity. Their conclusions suggested that individual interventions that do not require attendance at a facility, such as walking, are likely to be most successful and that regular follow-up improves adherence. Kahn *et al.* (2002) conducted a comprehensive systematic review of interventions to promote physical activity and concluded that there was strong evidence that strengthening local support networks through buddy systems, walking groups and exercise contracts increased physical activity. There was also strong evidence that personalised health behaviour-change programmes, tailored to an individual's specific stage of behaviour or interest, were effective in increasing physical activity. Activities such as goal setting, social support schemes, self-reward schemes, relapse prevention and active living approaches to physical activity promotion were viewed as particularly effective.

Self-monitoring is often recommended as an individual tool to help behaviour change. With greater accessibility to 'objective' measures of physical activity, such as pedometers, this method is now widely practised. Modern pedometers are cheap to manufacture and they have been used by some large food companies as free gifts. The notion that 10,000 steps a day are required for health has been promoted. For example, a large-scale community campaign in the town of Rockhampton in Australia employed widespread media advertising, harnessed support from health services and attempted policy and environmental change to engage the public in a '10,000 steps' campaign. Evaluations of such complex community interventions are not straightforward but results suggest that there was a 1 per cent increase in the proportion of Rockhampton residents who were sufficiently active for health benefit as a result of this campaign (Brown et al., 2006). Residents in a comparison town showed a 7 per cent decline in activity over the same time period, suggesting that there may be a secular trend for decreased activity and that the campaign may have halted this decline in Rockhampton.

A systematic review of 32 studies (Tudor-Locke et al., 2001) showed that the 10,000-step goal may be too low for children and too high for sedentary individuals and individuals with chronic illness. Recent data from Marshall et al. (2009) led to the recommendation that adults are encouraged to walk a minimum of 3000 steps in 30 minutes on 5 days of the week or three bouts of 1000 steps in 10 minutes each day. However, pedometer counts will register all steps, and not just those undertaken over discrete walking bouts.

Studies have shown that the presence of a pedometer alone (Rooney et al., 2003), or feedback from a pedometer, can increase walking steps (Stovitz et al., 2005). Other studies have shown less positive results. Pedometers are currently being employed as a means to promote walking, with indications of some success (Bravata et al., 2007). The evidence base for pedometers increasing physical activity is weak at this point and the National Institute for Health and Clinical Excellence (NICE) (2006) has recommended that there is insufficient evidence to recommend the use of pedometers. Clearly there is a need to increase this evidence base.

Breckon and colleagues (2008) conducted a review of 26 studies investigating individual face-to-face physical activity counselling in primary care settings. Specifically, they sought to examine what theory underpinned the counselling intervention and the level of treatment fidelity applied throughout the counselling. For fidelity, they examined five aspects, including the design of the intervention, the training of the 'counsellor', the fidelity of delivery, 'receipt' of the intervention (is it understood by the client/patient?) and enactment (application of the treatment by the client). Results showed that the trans-theoretical model (TTM) was the dominant theory used but reporting was mixed concerning other parameters of the interventions. This makes it difficult to replicate studies and to assess how or why behaviour change was successful or unsuccessful. For example, few studies described the training or background of the counsellor, the frequency or duration of the intervention or treatment fidelity. Results overall showed largely positive effects on behavioural or physiological outcome measures.

One individual-based approach for health behaviour change is counselling or personal consultation. Loughlan and Mutrie (1995) offered guidelines about using a person-centred exercise consultation approach to increasing activity levels. These guidelines were based on the available knowledge of what assists people in making physical activity behaviour change. The person doing the consultation must have excellent communication and reflective listening skills, and empathy for the people who are seeking help. Exercise consultants must also have good knowledge about physical activity for general and clinical populations, including the current activity recommendations and any contraindications for particular groups. Finally, exercise consultants must understand the various theories of behaviour change and the various factors that will influence whether or not a person will succeed in becoming more active.

'Motivational interviewing' (MI) has become a popular approach in health behaviour change (Miller & Rollnick, 2002) and has now been applied to physical activity, often using the TTM as its foundation (Breckon et al., 2008). Evidence from a systematic review of intervention trials suggests that it can be effective in bringing about meaningful change in health outcomes (Rubak et al., 2005).

Interventions in the community

For physical activity to have a significant effect on public health, interventions aimed at communities and mass populations must be used in addition to those aimed at individuals or small groups. Kahn et al. (2002) found strong evidence that the use of large-scale, high visibility, multi-strand community-wide campaigns that used a range of methods was effective in increasing physical activity. The community-wide campaigns reviewed tended to address a range of risk factors, not only physical activity. They often had strong communication and education elements and were directed at wide-ranging audiences. In addition, they were likely to involve social support across a range of settings. Kahn et al.'s review included 10 studies with interventions ranging from six weeks to six months in duration. The median net increase in the proportion of people being active was 4.2 per cent and two of the 10 studies showed median net increase in energy expenditure of 16.3 per cent. It was concluded that such interventions are likely to be effective across diverse settings and groups but that interventions should be adapted to specific target populations. In this section, interventions that have targeted the important community settings of schools and workplaces are reviewed. Later, interventions through mass media and new technologies will be discussed.

Schools   Interest in how schools promote physical activity is longstanding with estimates that over one-third of children's physical activity will occur at schools (Stratton et al., 2008). A central part of a school that is identified with the promotion of physical activity is physical education (PE). Studies vary from extensive increases in time, such as through daily PE interventions, to relatively minor changes in emphasis in existing curriculum time (Almond & Harris, 1998). Two comprehensive reviews have addressed physical activity interventions in schools (Kahn et al., 2002; Stone et al., 1998). Kahn et al. found 13 studies suitable for review that addressed the issue of increasing time spent in PE lessons in moderate-to-vigorous activity.

Results showed (a) consistent increases in physical activity in lessons when such changes were targeted, e.g. through modified activities, or changing the length or frequency of PE classes, and (b) no evidence for harming academic achievement when increasing time allocated to PE.

Overall, Kahn et al. (2002) concluded 'there is strong evidence that school-based PE is effective in increasing levels of physical activity and improving physical fitness' (p. 81). An earlier review by Stone et al. (1998) concluded that the strongest evidence base was for those in the later years of primary school and for changes to the school environment. Moreover, they found inconsistent evidence for changes in physical activity outside of school. In other words, some interventions designed to increase activity in PE lessons had a positive effect on activity elsewhere, whereas other studies either showed no effect or a decrease in activity. A more recent review by van Sluijs et al. (2007) concluded that interventions designed to increase physical activity and conducted in schools were inconclusive for both children and adolescents, although the results were much more positive when a community or family element was added for adolescents.

There are a number of studies that have addressed the issue of decreasing sedentary behaviour rather than increasing physical activity itself (Biddle & Gorely, 2005). Some are laboratory based while others have used educational interventions, including the school classroom (Gortmaker et al., 1999; Robinson, 1999). Kahn et al. (2002), in reviewing three studies where reductions in television viewing and video game playing were targeted, concluded that there was insufficient evidence to suggest that such strategies increased physical activity, thus being consistent with meta-analytic data from Marshall et al. (2004).

Promoting walking or cycling to school has a number of advantages, including a large potential population (Faulkner et al., 2009). However, there are very few studies providing guidance on the motivational influences of walking to school. Travelling to school by foot is likely to be strongly influenced by social-environmental, rather than just psychological factors, although the social psychology of the parent may be important. The key social-environmental factors appear to be work patterns of the parents, convenience of driving children to school prior to going on to work, proximity of school to home and degree of parental consent to allow children to travel independently to school.

Finally, the context of the school break time is an important one for physical activity in schools. A brief review of studies indicates that environmental changes to the school playground, or the introduction of extra equipment, can enhance activity levels (Stratton et al., 2008).

Worksites The workplace is an important location for health promotion because it can involve large numbers of people who can be reached with relative ease and regularity. When combined with interventions in schools, a very large proportion of the population can be targeted. Subjective reports often suggest favourable changes in productivity and absenteeism with the introduction of a worksite health promotion programme, however, review-level data provide less grounds for optimism (Proper et al., 2002). Moreover, a meta-analytic review has suggested that worksite interventions have yet to demonstrate improvements in physical activity or fitness (Dishman et al., 1998). Forty-five effect sizes were obtained from 26 studies. The average effect was no more than one-quarter of a standard deviation. Similarly, environmental changes in the workplace (e.g. provision of facilities) have not been shown to be effective in changing levels of physical activity, although study designs are generally weak (Engbers et al., 2005).

While better designed workplace interventions are developed, the worksite may also be a useful location for physical activity behaviour change through the use of physically active travel. Actively commuting to work has several advantages as an intervention strategy. First, many adults commute to work on most days of the week, thus providing a very large group of people to target. Second, the time allocated to work travel is clearly identifiable in the routine of the typical day and week, thus making it more amenable to targeting.

Systematic encouragement of cycling and the development of cycle lanes have met with limited success in the UK, with rates of cycling still low compared to some other European countries. Even in a UK city where cycle lanes were provided, but were not separate from traffic, participants tended to not want to cycle and opted instead to walk (Mutrie et al., 2002). City planners ideally want a modal shift from people using cars to people using public transport and actively commuting. However, as Ogilvie and colleagues established in a systematic review of 22 intervention studies, in which shifting participants to more active means of transport was a goal, there was no evidence that publicity campaigns, engineering measures and other interventions are effective (Ogilvie et al., 2004). Recent guidance from NICE suggested there was insufficient evidence to recommend the use of cycling schemes to promote physical activity (National Institute for Health and Clinical Excellence, 2006).

Interventions for the whole population: mass media

Interventions can be delivered at various levels. The 'highest' or most abstract level is through targeting the whole population via mass media. Much of this is based on the premise that mass media messages will at least change 'attitude' and maybe even behaviour. Unfortunately, often campaigns have been based on a simplistic and atheoretical understanding of the nature of attitude and its relationship with behaviour or on the meaning of messages (Finlay & Faulkner, 2005). Many physical activity campaigns have simply listed the potential positive outcomes that may accrue from participation, such as weight loss, improved aerobic fitness and an improved figure/physique. McGuire's (1969) well-known sequence of cognitive responses, or 'chain of persuasion', suggests that for a message to influence behaviour, it must involve message exposure, attention, comprehension, yielding (where the recipient is persuaded by the content of the message), retention, retrieval, decision to act, and acting in accordance with the message itself. Meeting all of these stages suggests that it is not easy to move from mass media message to behaviour.

A 'social marketing' approach to community physical activity promotion has been advocated and this is consistent with some of the notions discussed. Donovan and Owen (1994) define social marketing as 'the applications of the principles and methods of marketing to the achievement of socially desirable goals' (p. 250). Drawing on McGuire's 'chain of persuasion', Donovan and Owen propose that mass media advertising may work best in the early stages of this chain (e.g. exposure, attention, comprehension) rather than at the level of behaviour change. This may account for the observation that mass media campaigns are not that successful at behaviour change (Redman et al., 1990).

The most extensive review of the impact of mass media on physical activity was conducted by Marcus et al. (1998). They located 28 studies, including experimental and quasi-experimental designs. They concluded that the recall of messages was high, but little impact was detected on physical activity itself, a conclusion also reached in a more recent review (Finlay & Faulkner, 2005). A more optimistic conclusion about mass media campaigns in health more generally was made by Noar (2006), although this was based on the recommendation that mass media campaigns be targeted and well executed. Indeed, the VERB campaign in the United States is consistent with this and was designed to raise physical activity levels in children. The campaign showed success and is now well documented (Collins & Wechsler, 2008).

Kahn et al. (2002) concluded that there was insufficient evidence that mass media campaigns, when used alone, effectively changed physical activity. National agencies tasked with the promotion of physical activity and the need to raise the public's awareness are now faced with a dilemma about whether or not to spend money on mass media campaigns. It may not be realistic for the aim of a mass media campaign to be behaviour change, which seems hard to achieve, by contrast with awareness raising (Cavill & Bauman, 2004). For example, a television advertisement featuring the captain of the Scotland rugby team produced very high levels of awareness of the message that walking was a good form of exercise. Seventy per cent of the participants in the evaluation said that they were aware of the advert one month after it had been televised, but the advert did not produce any discernible changes in behaviour (Wimbush et al., 1997). In England, a three-year evaluation of the national 'Active for Life' campaign was conducted (Hillsdon et al., 2001). The evaluation showed that 6–8 months after

the main advertising on television 38 per cent were aware of the campaign. There was a small increase (3.7 per cent) in the percentage of the cohort who knew that 30 minutes of activity was the recommended daily minimum, but there was no overall increase in physical activity.

Interventions using new technologies

The very rapid developments being witnessed in communication technologies suggests that using such methods to promote physical activity must be very recent. While it is true that data were sparse until recently, Dirkin (1994) highlighted pertinent issues over a decade and a half ago (a long time in respect of current technological advances). In addition to the technological developments in measuring physical activity, and the role that such devices might play in motivating behaviour, physical activity can also be promoted via mobile and other phones, as well as via the internet.

Fjeldsoe and colleagues (2009) reviewed research concerning the use of mobile phones for text (SMS) messages designed for health behaviour change. This type of intervention has very wide population reach due to the high ownership of such phones over the past few years. In addition, the authors claimed that messages can be tailored and delivered instantly. The review analysed 14 studies across diverse health behaviours. Positive behaviour change outcomes were seen in all but one study. This now needs extending to physical activity research.

Eakin et al. (2007) reviewed interventions designed to change physical activity and nutrition that used telephone delivery. Of the 16 studies on physical activity, 11 reported positive outcomes, with effect sizes calculated from eight studies. These effects ranged from small to large. Moreover, all six studies that assessed physical activity over six months showed sustainability of the positive effects. Most of the studies in the review also used adjunct intervention methods, such as printed materials. However, the review suggests that the telephone can be an effective method for delivering physical activity behaviour change.

Interventions to increase physical activity delivered via a website were reviewed by Vandelanotte et al. (2007). Fifteen studies were reviewed, with increases in physical activity being reported in eight. Outcomes were better when interventions had more than five contacts with participants and when the time to follow-up was less than six months. This may reflect the nature of internet use whereby excessive contact may be seen as intrusive or simply a time barrier.

Prevention

In addition to changing physical activity in an already inactive population (Biddle & Mutrie, 2008), agencies are interested in preventing declines in physical activity, such as those seen during adolescence and across the adult age span (Sallis, 2000). Preventive measures may need to focus on two key elements: (a) young people (to sustain quite high levels of physical activity seen in childhood); and (b) the environment.

The assumption that active children become active adults suggests that little needs to be done to prevent declines in physical activity. The most comprehensive review on physical activity 'tracking' by age was conducted by Malina (1996). He concluded that the magnitude of tracking during adolescence and into adulthood is 'low to moderate'. Telama et al. (2005), reporting 21 years of follow-up data from the 'Cardiovascular risk in young Finns' longitudinal study, showed correlations between measures of physical activity for 9-, 12-, 15-, 18- and 21-year follow-ups. These declined with time, as expected, and generally were low to moderate in strength, although some association was still evident after 21 years.

Pate et al. (1999) have reported tracking data for rural, predominantly African American children over a three-year time period using self-report measures. Stability was low to moderate for vigorous physical activity (r = 0.36) and moderate to vigorous physical activity (0.24), but slightly higher for television viewing (0.41). This suggests that some sedentary behaviours might track better than physical activity (Biddle et al., 2004) although more data are required.

Evidence on the stability of physical activity across the life span therefore suggests that the relationship between physical activity in childhood or adolescence with that in adulthood is small. Research into tracking must account for the quality of childhood experiences in physical activity as well as the changes in activity levels during childhood, adolescence and adulthood (Cavill & Biddle, 2003).

Environmental influences have now been recognised as being of importance in many health fields. For example, environments that promote sedentary behaviour, while at the same time making it easy to buy food with high fat content, have been labelled 'obesogenic' (Egger & Swinburn, 1997). Considerations of how the environment might influence physical activity could include seasonal variation in the amount of daylight and pleasant weather for being active, easy access to facilities or places to be active, and the design of neighbourhoods that promote or inhibit walking and cycling as means of transport.

A systematic review has been reported on the environmental factors that might influence physical activity for adults (Humpel et al., 2002). The researchers identified 19 studies that examined the relationship between attributes of the physical environment and physical activity and there were associations with physical activity for ease of access to facilities, having places near by to be active, and perceived positive aesthetics of the local area (such as enjoyable scenery). Weather and safety did not show an association. This suggests that some features of the environment may be important in the prevention of declines in physical activity. Guidance is now available on how best to promote physical activity through the natural and built environment (National Institute for Health and Clinical Excellence, 2008).

Conclusion

Physical activity is an important health behaviour with numerous health benefits. Health psychologists need to understand the nature of different physically active behaviours and how best to promote changes in these behaviours. Moreover, sedentary behaviours require further study.

Discussion Points

1   In addition to psychological correlates of physical activity, what additional influences might be affecting how active we are in contemporary society?
2   Why might a tool such as a pedometer help people to walk more?
3   How might physical activity be increased in schools?
4   Does the worksite have a role to play in promoting physical activity at work? If so, how and why?
5   Speculate on how new technologies could be used to promote physical activity and decrease sedentary behaviour.
6   Should we expect physical activity to 'track' well from childhood to adulthood?

Further Reading

Biddle, S.J.H. & Mutrie, N. (2008). *Psychology of physical activity: Determinants, well-being and interventions* (2nd edn). London: Routledge.

Bouchard, C. (Ed.) (2000). *Physical activity and obesity*. Champaign, IL: Human Kinetics.

Department of Health (2004). *At least five a week: Evidence on the impact of physical activity and its relationship to health. A report from the Chief Medical Officer.* London: Department of Health.

Dishman, R.K., Washburn, R.A. & Heath, G.W. (2004). *Physical activity epidemiology*. Champaign, IL: Human Kinetics.

Hardman, A.E. & Stensel, D.J. (2009). *Physical activity and health: The evidence explained* (2nd edn). London: Routledge.

Sallis, J.F. & Owen, N. (1999). *Physical activity and behavioral medicine*. Thousand Oaks, CA: Sage.

Smith, A.L. & Biddle, S.J.H. (Eds.) (2008). *Youth physical activity and sedentary behavior: Challenges and solutions*. Champaign, IL: Human Kinetics.

References

Almond, L. & Harris, J. (1998). Interventions to promote health-related physical education. In S.J.H. Biddle, N. Cavill & J.F. Sallis (Eds.) *Young and active? Young people and health-enhancing physical activity: Evidence and implications* (pp. 133–149). London: Health Education Authority.

Biddle, S.J.H. & Gorely, T. (2005). Couch kids: Myth or reality? *The Psychologist, 18*(5), 276–279.

Biddle, S.J.H., Gorely, T. & Stensel, D.J. (2004). Health-enhancing physical activity and sedentary behaviour in children and adolescents. *Journal of Sports Sciences, 22,* 679–701.

Biddle, S.J.H. & Mutrie, N. (2008). *Psychology of physical activity: Determinants, well-being and interventions* (2nd edn). London: Routledge.

Bravata, D.M., Smith-Spangler, C., Sundaram, V., Gienger, A.L., Lin, N., Lewis, R. *et al.* (2007). Using pedometers to increase physical activity and improve health: A systematic review. *Journal of the American Medical Association, 298*(19), 2296–2304.

Breckon, J.D., Johnston, L.H. & Hutchinson, A. (2008). Physical activity counseling content and competency: A systematic review. *Journal of Physical Activity and Health, 5,* 398–417.

Brown, W.J., Mummery, K., Eakin, E. & Schofield, G. (2006). 10,000 steps Rockhampton: Evaluation of a whole community approach to improving population levels of physical activity. *Journal of Physical Activity and Health, 3,* 1–14.

Caspersen, C.J., Powell, K.E. & Christenson, G.M. (1985). Physical activity, exercise and physical fitness: Definitions and distinctions for health-related research. *Public Health Reports, 100,* 126–131.

Cavill, N. & Bauman, A. (2004). Changing the way people think about health-enhancing physical activity: Do mass media campaigns have a role? *Journal of Sports Sciences, 22*(8), 771–790.

Cavill, N. & Biddle, S. (2003). The determinants of young people's participation in physical activity, and investigation of tracking of physical activity from youth to adulthood. In A. Giles (Ed.) *A lifecourse approach to coronary heart disease prevention: Scientific and policy review* (pp. 179–197). London: The Stationery Office.

Collins, J.L. & Wechsler, H. (2008). The VERB Campaign. *American Journal of Preventive Medicine, 34*(6, Supplement 1), S171–S172.

Department of Health (2004). *At least five a week: Evidence on the impact of physical activity and its relationship to health. A report from the Chief Medical Officer.* London: Department of Health.

Dirkin, G. (1994). Technological supports for sustaining exercise. In R.K. Dishman (Ed.) *Advances in exercise adherence* (pp. 237–247). Champaign, IL: Human Kinetics.

Dishman, R.K., Oldenburg, B., O'Neal, H. & Shephard, R.J. (1998). Worksite physical activity interventions. *American Journal of Preventive Medicine, 15*, 344–361.

Donovan, R.J. & Owen, N. (1994). Social marketing and population interventions. In R.K. Dishman (Ed.) *Advances in exercise adherence* (pp. 249–290). Champaign, IL: Human Kinetics.

Eakin, E.G., Lawler, S.P., Vandelanotte, C. & Owen, N. (2007). Telephone interventions for physical activity and dietary behavior change: A systematic review. *American Journal of Preventive Medicine, 32*(5), 419–434.

Egger, G. & Swinburn, B. (1997). An 'ecological' approach to the obesity pandemic. *British Medical Journal, 315*, 477–480.

Engbers, L.H., van Poppel, M.N.M., Chin, A., Paw, M.J. & Van Mechelen, W. (2005). Worksite health promotion programs with environmental changes: A systematic review. *American Journal of Preventive Medicine, 29*, 61–70.

Faulkner, G.E.J., Buliung, R.N., Flora, P.K. & Fusco, C. (2009). Active school transport, physical activity levels and body weight of children and youth: A systematic review. *Preventive Medicine, 48*(1), 3–8.

Finlay, S.-J. & Faulkner, G.E. (2005). Physical activity promotion through mass media: Inception, production, transmission and consumption *Preventive Medicine, 40*, 121–130.

Fjeldsoe, B.S., Marshall, A.L. & Miller, Y.D. (2009). Behavior change interventions delivered by mobile telephone short-message service. *American Journal of Preventive Medicine, 36*(2), 165–173.

Gortmaker, S.L., Peterson, K.E., Wiecha, J., Sobol, A.M., Dixit, S., Fox, M.K. *et al.* (1999). Reducing obesity via a school-based interdisciplinary intervention among youth: Planet Health. *Archives of Pediatric & Adolescent Medicine, 153*, 409–418.

Hamilton, M.T., Healy, G.N., Dunstan, D.W., Zderic, T.W. & Owen, N. (2008). Too little exercise and too much sitting: Inactivity physiology and the need for new recommendations on sedentary behavior. *Current Cardiovascular Risk Reports, 2*, 292–298.

Hardman, A.E. & Stensel, D.J. (2009). *Physical activity and health: The evidence explained* (2nd edn). London: Routledge.

Haskell, W.L., Lee, I.M., Pate, R.R., Powell, K.E., Blair, S.N., Franklin, B.A. *et al.* (2007). Physical activity and public health: Updated recommendation for adults from the American College of Sports Medicine and the American Heart Association. *Medicine &d Science in Sports* Exercise, 39*(8), 1423–1434.

Hillsdon, M., Cavill, N., Nanchahal, K., Diamond, A. & White, I.R. (2001). National level promotion of physical activity: Results from England's *ACTIVE* for LIFE campaign. *Journal of Epidemiology & Community Health, 55*, 755–761.

Hillsdon, M. & Thorogood, M. (1996). A systematic review of physical activity promotion strategies. *British Journal of Sports Medicine, 30*, 84–89.

Humpel, N., Owen, N. & Leslie, E. (2002). Environmental factors associated with adults' participation in physical activity: A review. *American Journal of Preventive Medicine, 22*(3), 188–199.

Kahn, E.B., Ramsey, L.T., Brownson, R.C., Heath, G.W., Howze, E.H., Powell, K.E. *et al.* (2002). The effectiveness of interventions to increase physical activity: A systematic review. *American Journal of Preventive Medicine, 22*(4S), 73–107.

Loughlan, C. & Mutrie, N. (1995). Conducting an exercise consultation: Guidelines for health professionals. *Journal of the Institute of Health Education, 33*(3), 78–82.

Malina, R.M. (1996). Tracking of physical activity and physical fitness across the lifespan. *Research Quarterly for Exercise and Sport, 67*(3), S48–S57.

Marcus, B.H., Owen, N., Forsyth, L.H., Cavill, N. & Fridinger, F. (1998). Physical activity interventions using mass media, print media, and information technology. *American Journal of Preventive Medicine, 15*, 362–378.

Marshall, S.J., Biddle, S.J.H., Gorely, T., Cameron, N. & Murdey, I. (2004). Relationships between media use, body fatness and physical activity in children and youth: A meta-analysis. *International Journal of Obesity, 28*, 1238–1246.

Marshall, S.J., Levy, S.S., Tudor-Locke, C.E., Kolkhorst, F.W., Wooten, K.M., Ji, M. *et al.* (2009). Translating physical activity recommendations into a pedometer-based step goal: 3000 steps in 30 minutes. *American Journal of Preventive Medicine, 36*(5), 410–415.

McGuire, W.J. (1969). The nature of attitudes and attitude change. In G. Lindzey & E. Aronson (Eds.) *Handbook of social psychology: Vol. III* (pp. 136–314). Reading, MA: Addison-Wesley.

Miller, W.R. & Rollnick, S. (2002). *Motivational interviewing: Preparing people for change.* New York: Guilford Press.

Mutrie, N., Carney, C., Blamey, A., Crawford, F., Aitchison, T. & Whitelaw, A. (2002). 'Walk in to work out': A randomised controlled trial of self help intervention to promote active commuting. *Journal of Epidemiology & Community Health, 56*, 407–412.

National Institute for Health and Clinical Excellence (2006). *Four commonly used methods to increase physical activity: Brief interventions in primary care, exercise referral schemes, pedometers and community-based exercise programmes for walking and cycling.* London: National Institute for Health and Clinical Excellence.

58   STUART J.H. BIDDLE

National Institute for Health and Clinical Excellence (2008). *Promoting and creating built and natural environments that encourage and support physical activity*. London: National Institute for Health and Clinical Excellence.

Noar, S.M. (2006). A 10-year retrospective of research in health mass media campaigns: Where do we go from here? *Journal of Health Communication, 11*, 21–42.

Ogilvie, D., Egan, M., Hamilton, V. & Petticrew, M. (2004). Promoting walking and cycling as an alternative to using cars: Systematic review. *British Medical Journal, 329*, 763–766.

Pate, R.R., O'Neill, J.R. & Lobelo, F. (2008). The evolving definition of 'sedentary'. *Exercise and Sport Sciences Reviews, 36*(4), 173–178.

Pate, R.R., Trost, S.G., Dowda, M., Ott, A.E., Ward, D.S., Saunders, R. *et al.* (1999). Tracking of physical activity, physical inactivity, and health-related physical fitness in rural youth. *Pediatric Exercise Science, 11*, 364–376.

Proper, K.I., Staal, B.J., Hildebrandt, V.H., van der Beek, A.J. & van Mechelen, W. (2002). Effectiveness of physical outcome programs at worksites with respect to work-related outcomes. *Scandinavian Journal of Work and Environmental Health, 28*(2), 78–84.

Redman, S., Spencer, E.A. & Sanson-Fisher, R.W. (1990). The role of mass media in changing health-related behaviour: A critical appraisal of two models. *Health Promotion International, 5*, 85–101.

Rejeski, W.J. & Brawley, L.R. (1988). Defining the boundaries of sport psychology. *The Sport Psychologist, 2*, 231–242.

Robinson, T.N. (1999). Reducing children's television viewing to prevent obesity: A randomized controlled trial. *Journal of the American Medical Association, 282*(16), 1561–1567.

Rooney, B., Smalley, K., Larson, J. & Havens, S. (2003). Is knowing enough? Increasing physical activity by wearing a pedometer. *Wisconsin Medical Journal, 102*(4), 31–36.

Rubak, S., Sandbaek, A., Lauritzen, T. & Christensen, B. (2005). Motivational interviewing: A systematic review and meta-analysis. *British Journal of General Practice, 55*, 305–312.

Sallis, J.F. (2000). Age-related decline in physical activity: A synthesis of human and animal studies. *Medicine & Science in Sports & Exercise, 32*, 1598–1600.

Stensel, D.J., Gorely, T. & Biddle, S.J.H. (2008). Youth health outcomes. In A.L. Smith & S.J.H. Biddle (Eds.) *Youth physical activity and sedentary behavior: Challenges and solutions* (pp. 31–57). Champaign, IL: Human Kinetics.

Stone, E.J., McKenzie, T.L., Welk, G.J. & Booth, M.L. (1998). Effects of physical activity interventions in youth: Review and synthesis. *American Journal of Preventive Medicine, 15*, 298–315.

Stovitz, S., VanWormer, J., Center, B. & Bremer, K. (2005). Pedometers as a means to increase ambulatory activity for patients seen at a family medicine clinic. *Journal of the American Board of Family Practice, 18*, 335–343.

Stratton, G., Fairclough, S.J. & Ridgers, N.D. (2008). Physical activity levels during the school day. In A.L. Smith & S.J.H. Biddle (Eds.) *Youth physical activity and sedentary behavior: Challenges and solutions* (pp. 321–350). Champaign, IL: Human Kinetics.

Sugiyama, T., Healy, G.N., Dunstan, D.W., Salmon, J. & Owen, N. (2008). Joint associations of multiple leisure-time sedentary behaviours and physical activity with obesity in Australian adults. *International Journal of Behavioral Nutrition and Physical Activity, 5*.

Telama, R., Yang, X., Viikari, J., Valimaki, I., Wanne, O. & Raitakari, O. (2005). Physical activity from childhood to adulthood: A 21-year tracking study. *American Journal of Preventive Medicine, 28*(3), 267–273.

Tudor-Locke, C., Ainsworth, B.E., & Popkin, B.M. (2001). Active commuting to school: An overlooked source of children's physical activity? *Sports Medicine, 31*, 309–313.

van Sluijs, E.M.F., McMinn, A.M. & Griffin, S. J. (2007). Effectiveness of interventions to promote physical activity in children and adolescents: Systematic review of controlled trials. *British Medical Journal, 335*, 703–707.

Vandelanotte, C., Spathonis, K.M., Eakin, E.G. & Owen, N. (2007). Website-delivered physical activity interventions: A review of the literature. *American Journal of Preventive Medicine, 33*(1), 54–64.

Wimbush, E., Macgregor, A. & Fraser, E. (1997). Impacts of a mass media campaign on walking in Scotland. *Health Promotion International, 13*, 45–53.

5

Eating Behaviour

Jane Ogden

Chapter Outline

This chapter describes three main psychological perspectives to understanding eating behaviour. First it examines developmental models of food choice which focus on exposure, social learning and associative learning. Second, it examines research which has drawn upon cognitive theories and social cognition models. Finally it examines the weight concern model of eating behaviour which focuses on the impact of dieting. Throughout the chapter, each perspective will be illustrated with interventions that have both been informed by, and have themselves informed, each theoretical approach.

Key Concepts

Ambivalence
Associative learning
Cognitive models
Denial
Dieting
Exposure
Parental control
Restraint theory
Social learning
Thought suppression

Developmental Models of Eating Behaviour

A developmental approach to eating behaviour focuses on the development of food preferences in childhood and emphasises the importance of learning and experience. Birch, who has extensively studied eating behaviour, described a developmental systems perspective (e.g. Birch, 1999). Central concepts in this perspective are exposure, social learning and associative learning, and details of these concepts are elaborated below.

Exposure

Human beings need to consume a variety of foods in order to have a balanced diet, and yet can sometimes show a fear and avoidance of novel foodstuffs, known as 'neophobia'. This has been called the 'omnivore's paradox' (Rozin, 1976). Young children will show neophobic responses to food but must come to accept and eat foods which may originally appear as threatening. Research has shown that mere exposure to novel foods can change children's preferences. For example, Birch and Marlin (1982) gave two-year-old children novel foods over a six-week period. One food was presented 20 times, one 10 times, one 5 times, while one remained novel. The results showed a direct relationship between exposure and food preference, and indicated that a minimum of about 8 to 10 exposures was necessary before preferences began to shift significantly. However, research also indicates that the impact of exposure to new foods is accumulative, whereby as more new foods are added to a diet they take less exposures before they become acceptable (Williams et al., 2008). Wardle et al. (2003) carried out an intervention study which involved identifying a least preferred vegetable in children aged 2–6 years then assigning them to one of three groups: exposure, information or control. The results showed that after 14 days those in the exposure group (involving daily exposure to the vegetable) ate more of the vegetable in a taste test and reported higher ratings of liking and ranking compared to the other two groups. Similarly research indicates that children can identify and are willing to taste vegetables if purchased by their parents (Busick et al., 2008). Simple exposure can therefore change intake and preference.

Neophobia has been shown to be greater in males than females (both adults and children), to run in families (Hursti & Sjoden, 1997) and to be minimal in infants who are being weaned onto solid foods but greater in toddlers and pre-school children (Birch et al., 1998). At times neophobia persists and is sometimes called being a 'picky eater' or a 'fussy eater' and can be measured using a neophobia questionnaire (MacNicol et al., 2003). This is considered the avoidance of a variety of foods even when these foods are familiar (Dovey et al., 2008).

Social learning

Social learning describes the impact of observing other people's behaviour on one's own behaviour and is sometimes referred to as 'modelling' or 'observational learning' (Bandura, 1977). This has been explored in terms of the role of peers, parents and the media.

Peers   An early study explored the impact of 'social suggestion' on children's food choices, arranging to have children observe a series of role models making food choices different from their own (Duncker, 1938). The models chosen were other children, an unknown adult and a fictional hero. The results showed a change in the child's food preference if the model was an older child, a friend or the fictional hero. The unknown adult had no impact on food preferences. In another study, peer modelling was used to change children's preference for vegetables (Birch, 1980). The target children were placed at lunch for four consecutive days next to other children who preferred a different vegetable (peas vs. carrots). By the end of the study the children showed a shift in their vegetable preference which persisted at a follow-up assessment several weeks later. Similarly, Salvy et al. (2008) asked children to play a sorting task whilst exposed to cookies either on their own, with an unfamiliar peer or a sibling and reported that the consumption of cookies was highest in those sat with their sibling. However, children do not just eat when others are eating but are influenced by what others are eating. For example, Addessi et al. (2005) sat children next to either an adult who was not eating or eating a food of the same colour as a novel food or eating a food of a different colour to the novel food. The results showed that the children were more likely to consume the novel food when the adult was in the same colour food condition. The impact of social learning has also been shown in an intervention study designed to change children's eating behaviour using video-based peer modelling (Lowe et al., 1998). This series of studies used video material of 'food dudes' – older children enthusiastically consuming refused food – which was shown to children with a history of food refusal. The results showed that exposure to the 'food dudes' significantly changed the children's food preferences and specifically increased their consumption of fruit and vegetables.

Parents   Parental behaviour is also central to social learning. For example, adolescents are more likely to eat breakfast if their parents do (Pearson *et al., 2009*). Emotional eating, which is defined as eating in response to emotions such as boredom, unhappiness and stress, is concordant between adolescents and their parents (Snoek *et al., 2007*). Further, Olivera *et al.* (1992) reported a correlation between mothers' and children's food intakes for most nutrients in preschool children, and suggested targeting parents to try to improve children's diets. Likewise, Contento *et al.* (1993) found a relationship between mothers' health motivation and the quality of children's diets. Parental behaviour and attitudes are therefore generally found to be central to the process of social learning.

There is, however, some evidence that mothers and children are not always in line with each other. For example, Wardle (1995) reported that mothers rated health as more important for their children than for themselves. Alderson and Ogden (1999) similarly reported that whereas mothers were more motivated by calories, cost, time and availability for themselves, they rated nutrition and long-term health as more important for their children. In addition, mothers may also differentiate between themselves and their children in their choices of food. For example, Alderson and Ogden (1999) indicated that mothers fed their children more of the less healthy dairy products, breads, cereals and potatoes, and fewer of the healthy equivalents to these foods, than they ate themselves. For example whereas they might feed their children chips they would report eating jacket potatoes and whereas they would consume low-fat cheese their children would have full-fat cheese. Furthermore, this differentiation was greater in dieting mothers, suggesting that mothers who restrain their own food intake may feed their children more of the foods that they are denying themselves.

The media   The role of social learning is also shown by the impact of television and food advertising. Radnitz *et al.* (2009) analysed the nutritional content of food on the television aimed at children under five and showed that unhealthy foods were given almost twice as much air time and were shown as being valued significantly more than healthy foods. This indicates that children are being exposed to media information from which they may learn unhealthy food preferences or eating behaviour. The impact of the media has been shown by responses to high-profile diets or food scares. For example, after Eyton's *The F-Plan Diet,* which recommended a high fibre diet, was launched with a great deal of media attention in 1982, sales of bran-based cereals rose by 30 per cent, whole-wheat bread by 10 per cent, whole-wheat pasta by 70 per cent and baked beans by 8 per cent. Similarly, when Edwina Currie, then junior health minister in the UK, said on television in December 1988 that 'most of the egg production in this country, sadly, is now infected with salmonella', egg sales fell by 50 per cent and by 1989 were still only at 75 per cent of their previous levels (Mintel, 1990). Likewise, massive publicity about the health risks of beef in the UK between May and August 1990 resulted in a 20 per cent reduction in beef sales.

Halford *et al.* (2004) used an experimental design to evaluate the impact of exposure to food-related adverts. Lean, overweight and obese children were shown a series of food and non-food-related adverts and their snack food intake was then measured in a controlled environment. The results showed that overall the obese children recognised more of the food adverts than the other children and that the degree of recognition correlated with the amount of food consumed. Furthermore, all children ate more after exposure to the food adverts than the non-food adverts. Similarly, King and Hill (2008) showed adverts for healthy or less healthy foods to children and measured their hunger, food choice and product recall. No effects were found for hunger or food choice but children could remember more of the less healthy than the healthy foods.

Associative learning

Associative learning refers to the impact of contingent factors on behaviour. At times these contingent factors can be considered reinforcers, in line with operant conditioning. In terms of food choice, research has explored the impact of pairing food cues with aspects of the environment. In particular, in some studies food has been paired with a reward and in other studies food has been used as the reward.

Rewarding food choice   Some research has examined the effect of rewarding food choice, as in 'If you eat your vegetables I will be pleased with you'. For example, Birch *et al.* (1980) gave children food in association with positive adult attention compared with more neutral situations. This was shown to increase food preference. Similarly, Barthomeuf *et al.* (2007) explored whether the emotion expressed on people's faces could influence food preferences. Men and women were exposed to a series of pictures of liked or disliked foods, either portrayed on their own or accompanied by people eating them and expressing one of three emotions: disgust, pleasure or neutrality. The results showed that the expression of the eater influenced ratings of preference but this depended not only on the expression used but also on the food category. In particular, the desire to eat a disliked food increased if the person pictured eating it was expressing pleasure but this emotion had no effect on the desire to eat a liked food. Further the desire to eat a liked food decreased if the eater was expressing disgust or was being neutral but these emotions had no effect on a disliked food. Therefore pairing a food with emotion can change the preference for that food, but this is influenced both by the emotion and the person's prior food preferences.

Food as the reward   Other research has explored the impact of using food as a reward. For these studies, gaining access to the food is contingent upon another behaviour, as in 'If you are well behaved you can have a cookie'. Birch *et al.* (1980) presented children with

foods either as a reward, as a snack, or in a non-social situation (the control). The results showed that food acceptance increased if the foods were presented as a reward, but that the more neutral conditions had no effect. This suggests that using food as a reward increases the preference for that food.

The relationship between food and rewards, however, appears to be more complicated than this. In one study, children were offered their preferred fruit juice as a means to be allowed to play in an attractive play area (Birch *et al.*, 1982). The results showed that using the juice as a means to get the reward reduced the preference for the juice. Similarly, Lepper *et al.* (1982) told children stories about children eating imaginary foods called 'hupe' and 'hule,' in which the child in the story could only eat one if they had finished the other. The results showed that the food which was used to get the reward became the least preferred one, and this has been supported by similar studies (Birch *et al.*, 1984; Newman & Taylor, 1992). These examples are analogous to saying 'If you eat your vegetables you can eat your dessert'. Although parents use this approach to encourage their children to eat vegetables, the evidence indicates that this may be increasing their children's preference for pudding even further, as pairing two foods results in the 'reward' food being seen as more positive than the 'access' food. As Birch (1999) concluded, 'Although these practices can induce children to eat more vegetables in the short run, evidence from our research suggests that in the long run parental control attempts may have negative effects on the quality of children's diets by reducing their preferences for those foods' (p. 51).

Not all researchers, however, agree with this conclusion. Dowey (1996) reviewed the literature examining food and rewards and argued that the conflicting evidence may relate to methodological differences between studies. He further proposed that studies designed to change food preference should be conducted in real-life situations, should measure outcomes over time and not just at one time-point, should involve clear instructions to the children, and should measure actual food intake, not just the child's stated preference. The 'food dudes' intervention study described above incorporated these methodological considerations into its design (Lowe *et al.*, 1998). It concluded that food preferences could be improved by offering rewards for food consumption as long as the 'symbolic context' of reward delivery was positive and did not indicate that 'eating the target foods was a low value activity' (p. 78). As long as the child cannot think 'I am being offered a reward to eat my vegetables, therefore vegetables must be an intrinsically negative thing', then rewards may work. One intervention introduced a 'Kid's choice' school lunch programme whereby children were given tokens for eating fruit or vegetables which could be later traded in for prizes. The results showed that preference and consumption increased two weeks after the programme had started (Hendy et al., 2005). However, by seven months when the programme had finished levels had returned to baseline. Rewarding food choice seems to improve food preferences although this may not persist when the rewards are removed.

Food and control The associations between food and rewards highlight a role for parental control over eating behaviour. Some research has addressed the impact of control as studies indicate that parents often believe that restricting access to food and forbidding their children to eat food are good strategies to improve food preferences (Casey & Rozin, 1989; Moore et al., 2007). Birch (1999) reviewed the evidence for the impact of imposing any form of parental control over food intake and argued that it is not only the use of foods as rewards which can have a negative effect on children's food preferences but also attempts to limit a child's access to foods. She concluded from her review that 'child feeding strategies that restrict children's access to snack foods actually make the restricted foods more attractive' (Birch, 1999, p. 11). For example, Jansen et al. (2007) allocated parents to either the prohibition or the no prohibition group, which differed in terms of whether they were asked to forbid or not forbid the consumption of target foods. The results showed that prohibition resulted in a greater desire for the target food and a greater consumption of this food compared to other foods. Similarly, when food is made freely available research indicates that children will choose more of the restricted than the unrestricted foods particularly when the mother is not present (Fisher & Birch, 1999; Fisher et al., 2000). From this perspective parental control would seem to have a detrimental

impact upon a child's eating behaviour. In contrast, however, some studies suggest that parental control may actually reduce weight and improve eating behaviour. For example Wardle et al. (2002) suggested that 'lack of control of food intake [rather than higher control] might contribute to the emergence of differences in weight' (p. 453). Similarly, Brown and Ogden (2004) reported that greater parental control was associated with higher intakes of healthy snack foods.

In part these contradictory results may reflect the contradictory nature of parental control with parental control being a more complex construct than acknowledged by any of the existing measures. Ogden et al. (2006) explored this possibility and examined the effect of differentiating between 'overt control' which can be detected by the child (e.g. being firm about how much your child should eat) and 'covert control' which cannot be detected by the child (e.g. not buying unhealthy foods). The results showed that these different forms of control did differently predict snack food intake and that whilst higher covert control was related to decreased intake of unhealthy snacks, higher overt control predicted an increased intake of healthy snacks. Similar results were also found in another sample of parents with small children (Brown et al., 2008) indicating that whilst some forms of control may well be detrimental to a child's diet, others may be beneficial. In particular controlling the child's environment in terms of what food is brought into the house or which cafés and restaurants they visit may encourage healthy eating without having the rebound effect of more obvious forms of control. The role of covert control is further supported by evidence that children eat according to the amount on their plate and that the best predictor of the amount consumed is the amount served suggesting that parents can successfully control their children's diets (Mrdjenovic & Levitsky, 2005).

A developmental model of food choice therefore emphasises learning with a focus on exposure, social learning and associative learning. It also highlights the role of control and how this can influence food intake. This has implications for interventions designed to change food intake. In particular the research informed by a developmental model would suggest that in terms of exposure techniques eating behaviour could be improved by limiting access to unhealthy foods and increasing a population's familiarity with more healthy ways of eating. In line with social learning approaches children could be encouraged to eat more healthily by watching their peers and parents doing so. Therefore interventions should target parents to model healthy eating and target schools to encourage children who have more unhealthy food preferences to be exposed to those children who eat the foods that they avoid. Furthermore sources of media information such as the internet and television could be used to present images of children and parents eating healthily in ways that makes them attractive and powerful role models. Associative learning techniques can also be used to inform interventions and the research indicates that whilst rewarding healthy eating can promote an improved diet, using food as a reward for eating other foods may be detrimental. Thus healthy eating needs to be paired with reinforcements such as parental pleasure, peer approval and enjoyment whilst avoiding making 'treat' foods seems even more enjoyable by using them as rewards. Finally, research from a developmental perspective highlights the important role of control which pervades all models of eating behaviour and indicates that whilst interventions to promote healthy eating may involve controlling access to unhealthier foods this needs to be managed in such a way that the foods being controlled are not simultaneously embedded with meanings relating to 'pleasure', treat' or 'forbidden'. This last point illustrates the dilemma that faces any attempts to promote healthy eating: the needs to reinforce and encourage the consumption of a healthier diet without making unhealthier foods even more attractive.

Cognitive Models of Eating Behaviour

A cognitive approach to food choice focuses on an individual's cognitions and has explored the extent to which cognitions predict and explain behaviour. Most research using a cognitive approach has drawn on social cognition models including the health belief model (HBM: Becker & Rosenstock, 1984), the protection motivation theory (PMT: Rogers, 1985), the theory of reasoned action (TRA: Fishbein & Ajzen, 1975), the theory of planned behaviour (TPB: Ajzen,

1985) and the health action process approach (HAPA: Schwarzer, 1992). These models vary in terms of whether they use behavioural intentions or actual behaviour as their outcome variable and the combination of cognitions that they include. The models have been applied to eating behaviour both as a means to predict food choice and as central to interventions to change food choice. This chapter will focus on research using the TRA and TPB, as these have most commonly been applied to aspects of food choice.

Some studies have used the TRA and the TPB to explore the cognitive predictors of actual behaviour. For example, Shepherd and Stockley (1985) used the TRA to predict fat intake, and reported it was more strongly predicted by attitude than by subjective norms. Similarly, attitude has also been found to be the best predictor of table salt use (Shepherd & Farleigh, 1986), eating in fast-food restaurants (Axelson et al., 1983), the frequency of consuming low-fat milk (Shepherd, 1988), and healthy eating conceptualised as high levels of fibre and fruit and vegetables and low levels of fat (Povey et al., 2000). Research has also pointed to the role of perceived behavioural control in predicting behaviour, particularly in relation to weight loss (Schifter & Ajzen, 1985) and healthy eating (Povey et al., 2000). The social-norms component of these models has consistently failed to predict eating behaviour.

Some studies have explored the impact of adding extra variables to the standard framework described within the social cognition models. For example, Shepherd and Stockley (1987) examined the predictors of fat intake and included a measure of nutritional knowledge, but found that this was not associated with either their measure of attitudes or their participants' behaviour. Povey et al. (2000) included additional measures of descriptive norms (e.g. 'To what extent do you think the following groups eat a healthy diet?'), and of perceived social support (e.g. 'To what extent do you think the following groups would be supportive if you tried to eat a healthy diet?') but found that these variables did not add anything to the core cognitions of the TPB.

Studies have also explored the role of ambivalence in predicting behaviour (Thompson et al., 1995) and this has been applied to food choice (Sparks et al., 2001). Ambivalence has been defined in a variety of different ways. For example, Breckler (1994) defined it as 'a conflict aroused by competing evaluative predispositions', and Emmons (1996) defined it as 'an approach–avoidance conflict – wanting but at the same time not wanting the same goal object'. Central to all definitions of ambivalence is the simultaneous presence of both positive and negative values which seems particularly pertinent to food choice, as individuals may hold contradictory attitudes towards foods in terms such as 'tasty', 'healthy', 'fattening' and 'a treat'. Sparks *et al.* (2001) incorporated the concept of ambivalence into the TPB and assessed whether it predicted meat or chocolate consumption. Participants were 325 volunteers who completed a questionnaire, including a measure of ambivalence assessed in terms of the mean of both positive and negative evaluations (e.g. 'How positive is chocolate?' and 'How negative is chocolate?') and then subtracting this mean from the absolute difference between the two evaluations (i.e. 'total positive minus total negative'). This computation provides a score which reflects the balance between positive and negative feelings. In line with previous TPB studies, the results showed that attitudes per se were the best predictor of the intention to consume both meat and chocolate. The results also showed that the relationship between attitude and intention was weaker in those participants with higher ambivalence. This implies that holding both positive and negative attitudes to a food makes it less likely that the overall attitude will be translated into an intention to eat it.

Research has also highlighted the importance of past behaviour and habit in predicting a number of different aspects of eating including seafood consumption and the intake of sweetened drinks (e.g. Honkansen *et al.*, 2005; Kremers *et al.*, 2007). In line with research using social cognition models in other health-related areas, research into eating behaviour has also added implementation intentions as a means to change dietary behaviour which relate to the specific 'where' and 'when' a particular behaviour will occur. For example, Armitage (2004) asked 264 participants recruited from a workplace in northern England to rate their motivation to eat a low-fat diet before being randomly allocated to either the implementation condition or the control condition. Those in the implementation condition were asked to describe a plan to eat a low-fat diet for the next month and to formulate their plans in as much detail as possible. Their food intake was measured using a food frequency questionnaire after one month. The results showed that this simple intervention resulted in a significant decrease in the proportion of energy derived from fat which could not be explained by baseline differences in motivations indicating that implementation intentions had changed subsequent behaviour.

A cognitive model of eating behaviour therefore emphasises the ways in which an individual's beliefs predict their behaviour. This framework has been used to inform interventions designed to change what people eat. In particular, it indicates that cognitions may relate to food intake and that changing these cognitions could result in changes in the ways in which people eat. For example, interventions could use structure approaches such as cognitive behavioural therapy, relapse prevention or counselling to change beliefs or could offer information in the form of websites or leaflets. To date, much research focusing on a cognitive perspective has limited its focus to those cognitions described by specified models. Food, however, is embedded with a multitude of meanings relating to emotions, social relationships, communication, power and identity. These meanings will be considered below in the context of a weight concern model of eating behaviour.

A Weight Concern Model of Eating Behaviour

A developmental model emphasises learning and a cognitive model emphasises beliefs in determining eating behaviour. A weight concern model incorporates both these dimensions but highlights the impact that the meanings and roles of food have on eating behaviour. This array of meanings was described eloquently by Todhunter (1973):

> Food is prestige, status and wealth ... It is ... an expression of hospitality, friendship, affection, neighbourliness, comfort.... Most of all it is tradition. There are Sunday foods and weekday foods, family foods and guest foods; foods with magical properties and health and disease foods (p. 301).

These meanings influence the ways in which people eat and can lead to body dissatisfaction and dieting. In the late 1970s, a new theory of eating behaviour known as 'restraint theory' emerged, which emphasised the importance of dieting and suggested that restrained eating (attempting to eat less) might be a better predictor of food intake than weight per se (Herman & Mack, 1975; Hibscher & Herman, 1977). Restrained eating has become increasingly synonymous with dieting, and restraint theory was developed as a framework to explore this behaviour. Some studies inspired by restraint theory suggest that dieters eat the same as unrestrained eaters (e.g. Sysko et al., 2007) or less than unrestrained eaters (e.g. Kirkley et al., 1988; Laessle et al., 1989; Thompson et al., 1988). Most studies following a restraint theory perspective have argued that although imposing cognitive restraint on food intake may result in dieters eating less or the same as non-dieters, restraint can also lead to episodes of overeating.

Restrained eating and overeating

Restraint theory argues that restrained eating results in both under- and overeating, and the first study illustrating overeating in dieters used a preload/taste-test paradigm (Herman & Mack, 1975) and involved giving subjects either a high-calorie preload (e.g. a high-calorie milkshake, a chocolate bar) or a low-calorie preload (e.g. water, a cracker). After eating/drinking the preload, subjects are asked to take part in a taste test. Subjects are asked to rate a series of different foods (e.g. cookies, snacks, ice cream) for a variety of different qualities such as saltiness, sweetness and preference. The subjects are left alone for a set period of time to rate the foods and then the amount they have eaten is weighed (the subjects do not know that this will happen). The aim of the preload/taste-test method is to measure food intake in a controlled environment (the laboratory) and to examine the effect of preloading on eating behaviour. The results from this first study indicated that whereas the non-dieters showed compensatory regulatory behaviour, and ate less after the high-calorie preload, the dieters consumed more in the taste test if they had had the high-calorie preload than the low-calorie preload.

The Herman and Mack (1975) study illustrated overeating in response to a high-calorie preload. Research suggests that overeating may also be triggered by lowered mood, preloads believed to be high in calorie, a need to escape from self-awareness, smoking abstinence and food cues (e.g. Fedoroff et al., 1997; Heatherton & Baumeister, 1991; Herman & Mack, 1975; Mills & Palandra, 2008; Ogden, 1994; Spencer & Fremouw, 1979). Further research has also shown that restrained eaters often eat more per se. For example, Ruderman and Wilson (1979) used a preload/taste-test procedure and reported that restrained eaters consumed significantly more food than the unrestrained eaters, irrespective of preload size. Similarly, Klesges et al. (1992) examined the eating behaviour of 141 men and 146 women and indicated that although restrained eaters ingested significantly fewer calories overall than unrestrained eaters, they were consuming a higher amount of fat. Several terms have been used to describe the overeating found in restrained eaters. 'Counter-regulation' refers to the relative overeating shown following a high-calorie preload compared to a low-calorie one. The term 'disinhibition' has been defined as 'eating more as a result of the loosening of restraints in response to emotional distress, intoxication or preloading' (Polivy & Herman, 1989, p. 342), and 'The what the hell effect' (Herman & Polivy, 1984) has been used to characterise overeating following a period of attempted undereating. The recognition of overeating in dieters and the development of restraint theory paved the way for a wealth of research examining when and why dieters sometimes overeat, and the role of restraint in this behaviour.

The causal analysis of overeating

The causal analysis of eating behaviour was first described by Herman and Polivy (Herman & Mack, 1975; Herman & Polivy, 1980, 1988; Polivy & Herman, 1985). They suggested that dieting and bingeing were causally linked, and that 'restraint not only precedes overeating but contributes to it causally' (Herman & Polivy, 1988, p. 33). This suggests that attempting not to eat, paradoxically, increases the probability of overeating, the specific behaviour dieters are attempting to avoid. The causal analysis of restraint represented a new approach to eating behaviour, and the prediction that restraint actually caused overeating was an interesting reappraisal of the situation. Wardle further developed this analysis (Wardle, 1980), and Wardle and Beales (1988) experimentally tested the causal analysis of overeating. They randomly assigned 27 obese women to either a diet group, an exercise group or a no-treatment control group for seven weeks. At weeks 4 and 6 all subjects took part in a laboratory session designed to assess their food intake. The results showed that subjects in the diet condition ate more than both the exercise and the control group, supporting a causal link between dieting and overeating. From this analysis, the overeating shown by dieters is actually caused by attempts at dieting.

Mood modification

Dieters overeat in response to lowered mood, and researchers have argued that disinhibitory behaviour enables the individual to mask their negative mood with the temporary heightened mood caused by eating. This has been called the 'masking hypothesis', and has been tested by empirical studies. For example, Polivy and Herman (1999) told female subjects that they had either passed or failed a cognitive task and then gave them food either in small controlled amounts or were allowed as much as they wanted. The results in part supported the masking hypothesis as the dieters who ate freely attributed more of their distress to their eating behaviour than to the task failure. The authors argued that dieters may overeat as a way of shifting responsibility for their negative mood from uncontrollable aspects of their lives to their eating behaviour. This mood modification theory of overeating has been further supported by research indicating that dieters eat more than non-dieters when anxious, regardless of the palatability of the food (Polivy et al., 1994). Overeating is therefore functional for dieters as it masks dysphoria, and this function is not influenced by the sensory aspects of eating.

The role of denial

Cognitive research illustrates that thought suppression and thought control can have the paradoxical effect of making the thoughts that the individual is trying to suppress more salient (Wenzlaff & Wegner, 2000). This has been called the 'theory of ironic processes of mental control' (Wegner, 1994) and describes a rebound effect that is shown for both thoughts and behaviours. For example, in an early study participants were asked to try not to think of a white bear but to ring a bell if they did (Wegner et al., 1987). The results showed that those who were trying not to think about the bear thought about the bear more frequently than those who were told to think about it. Similar results have been found for thinking about sex (Wegner et al., 1999), thinking about mood (Wegner et al., 1993) and thinking about a stigma (Smart & Wegner, 1999). A decision not to eat specific foods or to eat less is central to the dieter's cognitive set. This results in a similar state of denial and attempted thought suppression, and dieters have been shown to see food in terms of 'forbiddenness' (e.g. King et al., 1987) and to show a preoccupation with the food that they are trying to deny themselves (Fletcher et al., 2007; Grilo et al., 1989; Ogden, 1995). Furthermore dieters have been shown to hold more negative views about high-calorie food when measured explicitly and more positive views when measured implicitly, reflecting their conflicts around what they want to eat and what they feel they should want to eat (Hoefling & Strack, 2008). Some research has explored rebound effects following thought suppression for both subsequent thoughts and actual eating behaviour. For example, Soetens et al. (2006) directly related the theory of thought suppression to eating behaviour and used an experimental design to explore the impact of trying to suppress eating-related thoughts on subsequent thoughts about eating. The results showed that disinhibited restrained eaters (i.e. those who try to eat less but often overeat) used more thought suppression than the other groups. Further, this group also showed a rebound effect following a thought suppression task about food. This means that restrained eaters who tend to overeat try to suppress thoughts about food more often, but if they do, then think about food more often afterwards. Soetens and Braet (2006) reported a similar rebound effect for obese high restrained eaters and food-related thoughts and Erskine (2008) reported a rebound effect for the consumption of chocolate with both men and women consuming more chocolate in a taste test if they had previously been asked to suppress thoughts about eating chocolate.

If suppressing thoughts makes you think about things more then the reverse should also be the case. In line with this approach some research has explored the effectiveness of a cue exposure procedure whereby dieters have been exposed to foods that are forbidden as a means to counteract the impact of thought suppression (e.g. Soetens *et al.*, 2008; Van Gucht *et al.*, 2008). Results from these studies have been promising and have shown a reduction in a number of measures including chocolate craving, food intake and saliva secretion after cue exposure. It is possible, therefore, that the decision to diet and to not eat undermines any attempts at weight loss. As soon as food is denied it becomes forbidden and therefore desired and therefore more of it is eaten. Exposure to these forbidden foods may, however, be a useful strategy to reduce food intake in the longer term.

In summary, food is embedded with many meanings relating to emotions, social interaction, communication and aspects of self identity. At times this can result in body dissatisfaction and a desire to lose weight. A weight concern approach to eating behaviour emphasises the impact of dieting on food intake and draws upon restraint theory which argues that dieting is linked with overeating. Studies which have used either experimental or descriptive methodologies have implications for understanding when interventions designed to promote eating less and subsequent weight loss are effective. In particular, research indicates that if interventions designed to promote dietary change and weight loss are to be successful then whilst encouraging a reduction in food intake they must avoid feelings of denial and attempt to re-establish new healthier eating habits which can be sustained in the longer term without making older habits appear more attractive. Thus, as food is already embedded with many meanings, and whilst these meanings can promote overeating, any attempts to encourage eating less or

differently must avoid simultaneously enhancing those meanings relating to overeating or eating unhealthily.

Conclusion

There are many different approaches to understanding food choice. This chapter has focused on three overarching theories. First it has described a developmental perspective which emphasises the impact of learning though exposure, social learning and associative learning. This approach highlights the role of important others, cues and associations in the development of food preferences, and draws on the central tenets of learning theory. Secondly it has described a cognitive approach to food choice which emphasises food choice as the end-product of a series of interacting cognitions. Finally it has described a weight control approach with its emphasis on dietary restraint. Each of these perspectives has been informed by and has itself informed interventions and has implications for the development of future methods for bringing about successful changes in food intake. Cutting across these three perspectives are two core components which are central to any attempts to intervene and change eating behaviour. First are the meanings associated with food which are learned through our childhood experiences and reflected in our adult cognitions. These meanings influence the ways in which we think about food, our food preferences and the ways we eat. Second is the issue of control and denial which arises when any attempts are made to limit access to unhealthy foods or influence the amount or content of what we eat. Successful interventions to change eating behaviour have to address both these components and facilitate behaviour change through imposing some degree of control whilst not simultaneously enhancing those meanings associated with food which encourage overeating. This is the dilemma facing any attempt at behavioural intervention. It explains why changing eating behaviour is problematic, why weight loss attempts are only occasionally successful and why interventions targeting the individual need the support from policy makers and industry to create a structure in which individual choices about healthy eating are supported and not undermined by the environment in which they take place.

Discussion Points

1 To what extent are our food preferences influenced by learning?
2 How can psychological theories explain cross-cultural differences in food preferences?
3 How should parents encourage their children to eat healthily?
4 Why is childhood obesity on the increase?
5 How can psychological theories inform weight loss interventions?
6 How do some people manage to change their eating behaviour for the longer term?

Further Reading

Armitage, C.J. (2004). Evidence that implementation intentions reduce dietary fat intake: A randomized trial. *Health Psychology, 23*, 319–323.

Birch, L.L. (1999). Development of food preferences. *Annual Review of Nutrition, 19*, 41–62.

Conner, M. & Armitage, C.J. (2002). *The social psychology of food*. Buckingham: Open University Press.

Hendy, H.M., Williams, K.E. & Camise, T.S. (2005) 'Kid's Choice' school lunch program increases children's fruit and vegetable acceptance. *Appetite, 45*, 250–263.

Lepper, M., Sagotsky, G., Dafoe, J.L. & Greene, D. (1982). Consequences of superfluous social constraints: Effects on young children's social inferences and subsequent intrinsic interest. *Journal of Personality and Social Psychology, 42*, 51–65.

Ogden, J. (2009). *The psychology of eating: From healthy to disordered behaviour* (2nd edn). Oxford: Wiley-Blackwell.

Ogden, J. & Hills, L. (2008). Understanding sustained changes in behaviour: The role of life events and the process of reinvention. *Health: An International Journal, 12*, 419–437.

Wardle, J., Cooke, L.J., Gibson, E.L., Sapochnik, M., Sheiham, A. & Lawson, M. (2003). Increasing children's acceptance of vegetables: A randomized trial of parent-led exposure. *Appetite, 40*, 155–162.

References

Ajzen, I. (1985). From intention to actions: A theory of planned behavior. In J. Kuhl & J. Beckman (Eds.) *Action-control: From cognition to behavior* (pp. 11–39). Heidelberg: Springer.

Alderson, T. & Ogden, J. (1999). What mothers feed their children and why. *Health Education Research: Theory and Practice, 14*, 717–727.

Addessi, E., Galloway, A.T., Visalberghi, E. & Birch, L.L. (2005). Specific social influences on the acceptance of novel foods in 2–5-year-old children. *Appetite, 45*, 264–271.

Armitage, C.J. (2004). Evidence that implementation intentions reduce dietary fat intake: A randomized trial. *Health Psychology, 23*, 319–323.

Axelson, M.L., Brinberg, D. & Durand, J.H. (1983). Eating at a fast-food restaurant: A social-psychological analysis. *Journal of Nutrition Education, 15*, 94–98.

Bandura, A. (1977). Self efficacy: Toward a unifying theory of behavior change. *Psychological Review, 84*, 191–215.

Barthomeuf, L., Rousset, S. & Droit-Volet, S. (2007). Emotion and food: Do the emotions expressed on other people's faces affect the desire to eat liked and disliked food products? *Appetite, 48*, 211–217.

Becker, M.H. & Rosenstock, I.M. (1984). Compliance with medical advice. In A. Steptoe & A. Mathews (Eds.) *Health care and human behaviour*. London: Academic Press.

Birch, L.L. (1980) Effects of peer models' food choices and eating behaviors on preschoolers' food preferences. *Child Development, 51*, 489–496.

Birch, L.L. (1999). Development of food preferences. *Annual Review of Nutrition, 19*, 41–62.

Birch, L.L., Birch, D., Marlin, D. & Kramer, L. (1982). Effects of instrumental eating on children's food preferences. *Appetite, 3*, 125–134.

Birch, L.L., Gunder, L., Grimm-Thomas, K. & Laing, D.G. (1998). Infants' consumption of a new food enhances acceptance of similar foods. *Appetite, 30*, 283–295.

Birch, L.L. & Marlin, D.W. (1982). I don't like it; I never tried it: Effects of exposure on two-year-old children's food preferences. *Appetite, 23*, 353–360.

Birch, L.L., Marlin, D. & Rotter, J. (1984). Eating as the 'means' activity in a contingency: Effects on young children's food preference. *Child Development, 55,* 431–439.

Birch, L.L., Zimmerman, S. & Hind, H. (1980). The influence of social affective context on preschool children's food preferences. *Child Development, 51,* 856–861.

Breckler, S.J. (1994). A comparison of numerical indexes for measuring attitude ambivalence. *Educational and Psychological Measurement, 54,* 350–365.

Brown, J. & Ogden, J. (2004). Children's eating attitudes and behaviour: A study of the modelling and control theories of parental influence. *Health Education Research: Theory and Practice, 19,* 261–271.

Brown, K., Ogden, J., Gibson, L. & Vogele, C. (2008). The role of parental control practices in explaining children's diet and BMI. *Appetite, 50,* 252–259.

Busick, D.B., Brooks, J., Pernecky, S., Dawson, R. & Petzoldt, J. (2008). Parent food purchases as a measure of exposure and preschool-aged children's willingness to identify and taste fruit and vegetables. *Appetite, 51,* 468–473.

Casey, R.M. & Rozin, P. (1989). Changing children's food preferences: Parents' opinions. *Appetite, 12,* 171–182.

Contento, I.R., Basch, C., Shea, S., Gutin, B., Zybert, P., Michela, J.L. & Rips, J. (1993). Relationship of mothers' food choice criteria to food intake of pre-school children: Identification of family subgroups. *Health Education Quarterly, 20,* 243–259.

Dovey, T.M., Staples, P.A., Gibson, E.L. & Halford, J.C. (2008) Food neophobia and 'picky/fussy' eating in children: A review. *Appetite, 50,* 181–193.

Dowey, A.J. (1996). *Psychological determinants of children's food preferences.* Unpublished PhD dissertation, University of Wales, Bangor.

Duncker, K. (1938). Experimental modification of children's food preferences through social suggestion. *Journal of Abnormal Social Psychology, 33,* 489–507.

Emmons, R.A. (1996). Strivings and feeling: Personal goals and subjective well-being. In P.M. Gollwitzer & J.A. Bargh (Eds.) *The psychology of action: Linking cognition and motivation to behavior* (pp. 313–337). New York: Guilford Press.

Erskine, J.A. (2008). Resistance can be futile: Investigating behavioural rebound. *Appetite, 50,* 415–421.

Fedoroff, I.C., Polivy, J. & Herman, C.P. (1997). The effect of pre-exposure to food cues on the eating behavior of restrained and unrestrained eaters. *Appetite, 28,* 33–47.

Fishbein, M. & Ajzen, I. (1975). *Belief, attitude, intention, and behavior: An introduction to theory and research.* Reading, MA: Addison-Wesley.

Fisher, J.O. & Birch, L.L. (1999). Restricting access to a palatable food affects children's behavioral response, food selection and intake. *American Journal of Clinical Nutrition, 69,* 1264–1272.

Fisher, J.O., Birch, L.L., Smiciklas-Wright, H. & Piocciano, M.F. (2000). Breastfeeding through the first year predicts maternal control in feeding and subsequent toddler energy intakes. *Journal of the American Dietetic Association, 100,* 641–646.

Fletcher, B., Pine, K.J., Woodbridge, Z. & Nash. A. (2007). How visual images of chocolate affect the craving and guilt of female dieters. *Appetite, 48,* 211–217.

Grilo, C.M., Shiffman, S. & Wing, R.R. (1989). Relapse crisis and coping among dieters. *Journal of Consulting and Clinical Psychology, 57,* 488–495.

Halford, J.C., Gillespie, J., Brown, V., Pontin, E.E. & Dovey, T.M. (2004). Effect of television advertisements for foods on food consumption in children. *Appetite, 42,* 221–225.

Heatherton, T.F. & Baumeister, R.F. (1991). Binge eating as an escape from self awareness. *Psychological Bulletin, 110,* 86–108.

Hendy, H.M., Williams, K.E. & Camise, T.S. (2005). 'Kid's Choice' school lunch program increases children's fruit and vegetable acceptance. *Appetite, 45,* 250–263.

Herman, C.P. & Mack, D. (1975). Restrained and unrestrained eating. *Journal of Personality, 43,* 646–660.

Herman, C.P. & Polivy, J. (1980). Restrained eating. In A.J. Stunkard (Ed.) *Obesity* (pp. 208–225). Philadelphia: W.B. Saunders.

Herman, C.P. & Polivy, J.A. (1984). A boundary model for the regulation of eating. In A.J. Stunkard & E. Stellar (Eds.) *Eating and its disorders* (pp. 141–156). New York: Raven Press.

Herman, C.P. & Polivy, J.A. (1988). Restraint and excess in dieters and bulimics. In K.M. Pirke & D. Ploog (Eds.) *The psychobiology of bulimia.* Berlin: Springer-Verlag.

Hibscher, J.A. & Herman, C.P. (1977). Obesity, dieting, and the expression of 'obese' characteristics. *Journal of Comparative Physiological Psychology, 91,* 374–380.

Hoefling, A. & Strack, F. (2008). The tempting effect of forbidden foods: High calorie content evokes conflicting implicit and explicit evaluation in restrained eaters. *Appetite, 51,* 681–689.

Honkansen, P., Olsen, S.O. & Verplanken, B. (2005) Intention to consume seafood: The importance of habit. *Appetite, 45,* 161–168.

Hursti, U.K.K. & Sjoden, P.O. (1997). Food and general neophobia and their relationship with self-reported food choice: Familial resemblance in Swedish families with children of ages 7–17 years. *Appetite, 29,* 89–103.

Jansen, E., Mulkens, S. & Jansen, A. (2007). Do not eat the red food! Prohibition of snacks leads to their relatively higher consumption in children. *Appetite, 49,* 572–577.

King, G.A., Herman, C.P. & Polivy, J. (1987). Food perception in dieters and non-dieters. *Appetite, 8*, 147–158.

King, L. & Hill, A.J. (2008). Magazine adverts for healthy and less healthy foods: Effects on recall but not hunger or food choice by pre-adolescent children. *Appetite, 51*, 194–197.

Kirkley, B.G., Burge, J.C. & Ammerman, M.P.H. (1988). Dietary restraint, binge eating and dietary behaviour patterns. *International Journal of Eating Disorders, 7*, 771–778.

Klesges, R.C., Isbell, T.R. & Klesges, L.M. (1992). Relationship between dietary restraint, energy intake, physical activity, and body weight: A prospective analysis. *Journal of Abnormal Psychology, 101*, 668–674.

Kremers, S.P., van der Horst, K. & Brug, J. (2007). Adolescent screen-viewing behaviour is associated with consumption of sugar-sweetened beverages: The role of habit strength and perceived parental norms. *Appetite, 48*, 345–350.

Laessle, R.G., Tuschl, R.J., Kotthaus, B.C. & Pirke, K.M. (1989). Behavioural and biological correlates of dietary restraint in normal life. *Appetite, 12*, 83–94.

Lepper, M., Sagotsky, G., Dafoe, J.L. & Greene, D. (1982). Consequences of superfluous social constraints: Effects on young children's social inferences and subsequent intrinsic interest. *Journal of Personality and Social Psychology, 42*, 51–65.

Lowe, C.F., Dowey, A. & Horne, P. (1998). Changing what children eat. In A. Murcott (Ed.) *The nation's diet: The social science of food choice* (pp. 57–80). London: Longman.

MacNicol, S.A.M., Murray, S.M. & Austin, E.J. (2003). Relationships between personality, attitudes and dietary behaviour in a group of Scottish adolescents. *Personality and Individual Differences, 35*, 1753–1764.

Mills, J.S. & Palandra, A. (2008). Perceived caloric content of a preload and disinhibition among restrained eaters. *Appetite, 50*, 240–245.

Moore, S.N., Tapper, K. & Murphy, S. (2007). Feeding strategies used by mothers of 3–5-year-old children. *Appetite, 49*, 704–707.

Mintel (1990). *Eggs. Market intelligence.* London: Mintel.

Mrdjenovic, G. & Levitsky, D.A. (2005). Children eat what they are served: The imprecise regulation of energy intake. *Appetite, 44*, 273–282.

Newman, J. & Taylor, A. (1992). Effect of a means-end contingency on young children's food preferences. *Journal of Experimental Psychology, 64*, 200–216.

Ogden, J. (1994). The effects of smoking cessation, restrained eating, and motivational states on food intake in the laboratory. *Health Psychology, 13*, 114–121.

Ogden, J. (1995). Cognitive and motivational consequence of dieting. *European Eating Disorders Review, 24*, 228–241.

Ogden, J., Reynolds, R. & Smith, A. (2006). Expanding the concept of parental control: A role for overt and covert control in children's snacking behaviour. *Appetite, 47*, 100–106.

Olivera, S.A., Ellison, R.C., Moore, L.L., Gillman, M.W., Garrahie, E.J. & Singer, M.R. (1992) Parent–child relationships in nutrient intake: The Framingham Children's Study. *American Journal of Clinical Nutrition*, 56, 593–598.

Pearson, N., Biddle, S.J. & Gorely, T. (2009). Family correlates of breakfast consumption among children and adolescents: A systematic review. *Appetite, 52*, 1–7.

Polivy, J. & Herman, C.P. (1985). Dieting and bingeing. A causal analysis. *American Psychologist, 40*, 193–201.

Polivy, J.A. & Herman, C.P. (1989). Dietary restraint and binge eating: A response to Charnock. *British Journal of Clinical Psychology, 28*, 341–343.

Polivy, J. & Herman, C.P. (1999). Distress and eating: Why do dieters overeat? *International Journal of Eating Disorders, 26*, 153–164.

Polivy, J., Herman, C.P. & McFarlane, T. (1994). Effects of anxiety on eating: Does palatability moderate distress-induced overeating in dieters? *Journal of Abnormal Psychology, 103*, 505–510.

Povey, R., Conner, M., Sparks, P., James, R. & Shepherd, R. (2000). The theory of planned behaviour and healthy eating: Examining additive and moderating effects of social influence variables. *Psychology & Health, 14*, 991–1006.

Radnitz, C., Byrne, S., Goldman, R., Sparks, M., Gantshar, M. & Tung, K. (2009). Food cues in children's television programs. *Appetite, 52*, 230–233.

Rogers, R.W. (1985). Attitude change and information integration in fear appeals. *Psychological Reports, 56*, 179–182.

Rozin, P. (1976). The selection of foods by rats, humans, and other animals. In J. Rosenblatt, R.A. Hinde, C. Beer & E. Shaw (Eds.) *Advances in the study of behavior* (vol. 6, pp. 21–67). New York: Academic Press.

Ruderman, A.J. & Wilson, G.T. (1979). Weight, restraint, cognitions and counter-regulation. *Behaviour Research and Therapy, 17*, 581–590.

Salvy, S.J., Vartanian, L.R., Coelho, J.S., Jarrin, D. & Pliner, P.P. (2008). The role of familiarity on modeling of eating and food consumption in children. *Appetite, 50*, 514–518.

Schifter, D.A. & Ajzen, I. (1985). Intention, perceived control, and weight loss: An application of the theory of planned behavior. *Journal of Personality and Social Psychology, 49*, 843–851.

Schwarzer, R. (1992). Self efficacy in the adoption and maintenance of health behaviours: Theoretical approaches and a new model. In R. Schwarzer (Ed.) *Self efficacy: Thought control of action* (pp. 217–243). Washington, DC: Hemisphere.

Shepherd, R. (1988). Belief structure in relation to low-fat milk consumption. *Journal of Human Nutrition and Dietetics, 1*, 421–428.

Shepherd, R. & Farleigh, C.A. (1986). Attitudes and personality related to salt intake. *Appetite, 7*, 343–354.

Shepherd, R. & Stockley, L. (1985). Fat consumption and attitudes towards food with a high fat content. *Human Nutrition: Applied Nutrition, 39A,* 431–442.

Shepherd, R. & Stockley, L. (1987). Nutrition knowledge, attitudes, and fat consumption. *Journal of the American Dietetic Association, 87,* 615–619.

Smart, L. & Wegner, D.M. (1999). Covering up what can't be seen: Concealable stigma and mental control. *Journal of Personality and Social Psychology, 77,* 474–486.

Snoek, H.M., Engels, R.C., Janssens, J.M. & van Strien, T. (2007). Parental behaviour and adolescents' emotional eating. *Appetite, 49,* 223–230.

Soetens, B. & Braet, C. (2006). 'The weight of thought': Food-related thought suppression in obese and normal-weight youngsters. *Appetite, 46,* 309–317.

Soetens, B., Braet, C., Dejonckheere, P. & Roets, A. (2006). When suppression backfires: The ironic effects of suppressing eating related thoughts. *Journal of Health Psychology, 11,* 655–668.

Soetens, B., Braet, C., Van Vlierberghe, L. & Roets, A. (2008). Resisting temptation: Effects of exposure to a forbidden food on eating behaviour. *Appetite, 51,* 202–205.

Sysko, R., Walsh, T.B. & Wilson, G.T. (2007). Expectancies, dietary restraint, and test meal intake among undergraduate women. *Appetite, 49,* 30–37.

Sparks, P., Conner, M., James, R., Shepherd, R. & Povey, R. (2001). Ambivalence about health-related behaviours: An exploration in the domain of food choice. *British Journal of Health Psychology, 6,* 53–68.

Spencer, J.A. & Fremouw, M.J. (1979). Binge eating as a function of restraint and weight classification. *Journal of Abnormal Psychology, 88,* 262–267.

Thompson, J.P., Palmer, R.L. & Petersen, S.A. (1988). Is there a metabolic component to counterregulation? *International Journal of Eating Disorders, 7,* 307–319.

Thompson, M., Zanna, M. & Griffin, D. (1995). Let's not be indifferent about (attitudinal) ambivalence. In R.E. Perry & J.A. Krosnick (Eds.) *Attitude strength: Antecedents and consequences* (pp. 361–86). Hillsdale, NJ: Erlbaum,

Todhunter, E.N. (1973). Food habits, food faddism and nutrition. In M. Rechcigl (Ed.) *Food, nutrition and health: World review of nutrition and dietetics* (vol. 16, pp. 186–317). Basel: Karger.

Van Gucht, D., Vansteenwegen, D., Beckers, T., Hermans, D., Baeyens, E. & van den Bergh, O. (2008). Repeated cue exposure effects on subjective and physiological indices of chocolate craving. *Appetite, 50,* 19–24.

Wardle, J. (1980). Dietary restraint and binge eating. *Behaviour Analysis and Modification, 4,* 201–209.

Wardle, J. (1995). Parental influences on children's diets. *Proceedings of the Nutrition Society, 54,* 747–758.

Wardle, J. & Beales, S. (1988). Control and loss of control over eating: An experimental investigation. *Journal of Abnormal Psychology, 97,* 35–40.

Wardle, J., Cooke, L.J., Gibson, E.L., Sapochnik, M., Sheiham, A. & Lawson, M. (2003). Increasing children's acceptance of vegetables: A randomized trial of parent-led exposure. *Appetite, 40,* 155–162.

Wardle, J., Sanderson, S., Guthrie, C.A., Rapoport, L. & Plomin, R. (2002). Parental feeding style and the inter-generational transmission of obesity risk. *Obesity Research, 10,* 453–462.

Wegner, D.M. (1994). Ironic processes of mental control. *Psychological Review, 101,* 34–52.

Wegner, D.M., Erber, R. & Zanakos, S. (1993). Ironic processes in the mental control of mood and mood related thought. *Journal of Personality and Social Psychology, 65,* 1093–1094.

Wegner, D.M., Schneider, D.J., Cater, S.R. III & White, T.L. (1987). Paradoxical effects of thought suppression. *Journal of Personality and Social Psychology, 53,* 5–13.

Wegner, D.M., Shortt, J.W., Blake, A.W. & Page, M.S. (1999). The suppression of exciting thoughts. *Journal of Personality and Social Psychology, 58,* 409–418.

Wenzlaff, R.M. & Wegner, D.M. (2000). Thought suppression. *Annual Review of Psychology, 51,* 59–91.

Williams, K.E., Paul, C., Pizzo, B. & Riegel, K. (2008). Practice does make perfect: A longitudinal look at repeated taste exposure. *Appetite, 51,* 739–742.

6

Alcohol and Drug Use

Richard Hammersley

Chapter Outline

Alcohol and drugs are major causes of preventable morbidity and mortality. Posing drugs and alcohol issues as problems of addiction is not sufficient, because not all users with related health problems are substance dependent, while problems such as binge drinking, cannabis and ecstasy use barely fit the dependence model at all. Moreover, conceptualising drug problems as 'addiction' can lead to unhelpful social exclusion, disempowerment and stereotyping of users, to complacency about the harms of population substance use and to a search for biological cures for the disorders, rather than enhanced psychosocial and political interventions for these problems. Interventions often use psychological techniques pertinent to health psychology. Health psychology could focus more on alcohol and drugs because its models predict such behaviours. Health psychologists will come to play a bigger role in drug and alcohol problems, as practitioner-scientists with skills at facilitating lifestyle changes, enhancing people's cognitive and emotional coping and providing input to health policy and planning.

Key Concepts

Addictions
Alcohol
Dependence
Drugs
Health behaviour models
Measurement of use
   prevalence
Morbidity
Mortality
Problem drug use
Role of health
   psychologists
Social and political
   construction

Psychosocial Epidemiology of Alcohol and Drugs

Across Europe 55 million adults are estimated to drink at harmful levels and alcohol is responsible for some 195,000 deaths per year, the third largest cause of early death and illness behind tobacco and high blood pressure; itself causable by alcohol consumption (Mukamal, 2004). The European Commission estimates that one-quarter of deaths of men aged 15–29 and 1 in 10 female deaths in the same age range are due to alcohol (European Commission, 2006). Harms of alcohol include risks of cardiovascular diseases, cancers, liver disease and obesity, traffic and other accidents, being the victim or perpetrator of violence, engaging in or being exposed to hazardous behaviours such as unsafe sex (or even swimming with crocodiles; Martinac & Measham, 2008) and mental health, with depression and suicide often involving alcohol abuse (Norstrom & Ramstedt, 2005). Despite some evidence that 1–2 drinks a day have health benefits, the statistics show that drinking this amount is unusual and a safe message for all drinkers is to drink less.

Of adult Europeans, 22 per cent have tried cannabis, 3.6 per cent cocaine, 2.8 per cent ecstasy and 3.3 per cent amphetamines. Use of opioids such as heroin is too rare to record accurately in general population surveys. Problematic opioid use occurs at rates of between 1 in 1000 and 6 in 1000 of population and drug-related deaths accounted for 3.5 per cent of deaths amongst 15–39 year olds, mostly involving opioids (EMCDDA, 2009).

Recent use is measured more variably. In the UK, which leads Europe on drug use, the British Crime Survey (Hoare & Flatley, 2008) found that in 2007–8 some 36 per cent of 16–59 year olds had tried at least one illegal drug during their lives. In the preceding year, 7.4 per cent admitted using cannabis, 2.3 per cent cocaine, 1.5 per cent ecstasy, 1 per cent amphetamines, 0.6 per cent hallucinogens and 0.2 per cent heroin. So, past year drug use is relatively rare, but some drug use in a modern person's lifetime is relatively common.

One difficulty in the study of substance use lies in estimating true prevalence, frequency and quantity. Problems include that the activities: are illegal and hence misrepresented and under-reported; involve consuming substances of unknown potency and content; are often habitual and cognitively impairing, hence ill-remembered; involve answering survey questions that classify substance-using behaviours in different ways (Hammersley, 1994). There are also many other technical difficulties and the validity of even the British Crime Survey is debated (e.g. MacDonald & Pudney, 2000). The operational resolution of these issues is complex and determines the outcome of research (e.g. Collins et al., 1983). Yet only in alcohol research (e.g., Fillmore et al., 1994) is there some agreement about the most appropriate means of assessing 'use' and 'dependence'. Even for alcohol, a number of alternative questionnaire assessments of alcohol problems or alcohol dependence exist and compete.

Turning to understanding the contribution of substance use to diseases, the blood-borne diseases that can be transmitted by unhygienic drug injecting fit conventional physical disease epidemiology, so does liver cirrhosis. For cardiovascular diseases and cancers, substance use is just one of a number of contributing factors and it is not straightforward to disentangle the various causal contributions, particularly as the different health-related behaviours are correlated in complex ways: obesity, alcohol intake, smoking, lack of exercise, other drug use. For example, to estimate the contribution of alcohol to cancer it is necessary to control for tobacco use by alcohol drinkers. People often smoke most when drunk and, inconveniently, this will tend to make their recall of intake even less accurate than usual. For such reasons, it is often not straightforward to identify the health risks of a specific substance. 'Psychosocial epidemiology' wrestles with such problems, usually accepting definitive answers are elusive, if not methodologically impossible.

Nonetheless, some of the drug-related harms are worrying. The harms of cannabis are unclear, but it is of concern that cannabis is often high potency and taken with alcohol (Hammersley et al., 2003). It is also of concern that many people under 17 use cannabis heavily (Miller & Plant, 2002), and that in the UK people tend to smoke cannabis mixed with tobacco and use tobacco alone when cannabis is in short supply (Amos et al., 2004). Furthermore, alcohol and cannabis together have the potential to replace heroin and cocaine as the 'drugs of choice' amongst socially excluded youth. Finally, the complex neuropsychological effects of cannabis may raise people's risks of schizophrenia, assuming they were vulnerable to this disorder (Cohen *et al.*, 2008).

Ecstasy use is occasionally linked to sudden death, with hyperthermia being one important factor (Schifano *et al.*, 2006), yet this is rare relative to the number of incidents of use. Ecstasy may also be linked to temporary depression and verbal memory deficits, as well as perhaps longer-lasting deficits, but it is unclear whether or not the magnitude of these effects are of clinical concern (Bedi & Redman, 2008; de Sola LLopis *et al.*, 2008; Durdle *et al.*, 2008; Guillot & Greenway, 2006).

There are also considerable harms related to drug injecting, including blood-borne infections (Monto *et al.*, 2008) and abscesses, necrosis and infarctions due to tissue damage at injection sites (Murray-Lillibridge *et al.*, 2006). There are also cases of mental health problems triggered by or linked to use of various substances. Hammersley (2008) provides a more comprehensive summary of the harms of specific drugs. However, the largest source of drug-related harms lies, in a more complex way, with the nature of drug dependence or 'problem drug use'.

More than Addiction

Drugs and alcohol problems are often posed as problems of addiction, but this way of conceptualising them is increasingly criticised. Addiction is a type of psychiatric problem that belongs to individual people and is largely caused by genetic, developmental, psychological and social abnormalities. At the extreme, substance use problems are conceptualised as diseases, or at least biologically determined disorders (e.g. National Institute on Drug Abuse, 2006). There are people who use substances in extreme ways and fit criteria for dependence, but this does not prove that the causation of their problems is primarily biological. People's environments and life histories, their learning encounters with specific substances and their individual neurobiology interact to cause dependence in complex ways (e.g. Orford, 2001; West, 2006). The

descriptive phrase 'problem drug user' has been coined in the UK to avoid some of these issues.

Successful interventions for substance dependence tend to be psychological, including cognitive behavioural therapy (Beck *et al.*, 1993; Young, 1999), motivational interviewing (Miller & Rollnick, 1991) or systemic therapy (Liddle & Dakof, 1995). Neuropsychopharmacological interventions are still only adjuncts to therapeutic talk. Without additional psychological input substitute prescribing is considerably less effective (Seivewright, 2000).

Some people have great difficulty quitting drugs or alcohol, but it is common to change with little or no professional assistance (Granfield & Cloud, 1999), or with some support from self-help organisations (Kyrouz & Humphreys, 1997). Those with less severe problems tend to have better outcomes (e.g. Allen *et al.*, 1999). Clinical thinking on drug problems can be exaggerated because clinicians see people who have not successfully self-controlled their problems. Substance use in non-clinical populations can be more moderate and controlled, but some people can use 'addictive' drugs for extended periods without becoming addicted. Many heavy drinkers drink unobtrusively, to the detriment of their health, but without clear-cut dependence (Harthey *et al.*, 2003). There are also unobtrusive heroin users (Dalgarno & Shewan, 2005) and cocaine users (Ditton & Hammersley, 1996). Research outside the clinic has not supported the idea that after a certain duration and intensity of use addiction is the inevitable result of biological changes wrought by the drug.

For a wide range of drugs including alcohol, cannabis, cocaine, heroin and ecstasy, about 1 in 10 users show signs of dependence (see Hammersley, 2008, p. 174), leaving 9 in 10 who do not. That majority is not immune to health and social problems related to substance use. For example, the majority of people in Europe who drink alcohol at all report drinking more than current UK health guidelines (Anderson & Baumberg, 2006). Cannabis, under-researched in the 1980s and 1990s, now appears to pose health risks for nondependent users, most notably the health risks of smoking (Amos *et al.*, 2004). Long-term cannabis users conform neither to stereotypes of the addict, nor to stereotypes of cannabis being harmless, or even beneficial, to the user (Coggans *et al.*, 2004). For the so-called 'hard' drugs including heroin and cocaine, the standard view assumes that their normative forms of use are either mere experimentation or a rapid progress into addiction, with daily heavy use. In reality, many users of hard drugs have long-standing patterns of use over years that do not slide into dependence, or fit criteria for misuse, yet are not necessarily problem-free (Shewan & Dalgarno, 2005). Across the lifespan, a person can use alcohol and drugs in varied ways, with varied health-related consequences, which do not necessarily cease when addiction stops. So drug and alcohol problems are not only problems of addiction.

For example, ex-drug injectors may have hepatitis C and compromise their liver function further by 'normal' heavy drinking (Monto et al., 2008), which is dangerous and unwise but not, of itself, an 'alcohol problem'. Indeed, in one sense, 'merely' drinking alcohol and smoking tobacco and cannabis may seem a successful outcome compared to what went before. On the other hand, a person's identity as a former injector does not really justify neglecting their current health risks.

Health Psychology, Psychiatry, Public Health and Clinical Psychology

The standard thinking, particularly in policy documents, is that substance users can be divided into a majority who only use and a minority of problem users (e.g. HM Government, 2008). The majority need to be legislated, taxed, educated, socialised, or cajoled into temperate, safer, patterns of use, while the minority need intensive specialist treatment. These divide neatly into public and mental health problems. In the UK, only a small number of practising clinical psychologists work on substance use problems (e.g., Orford, 2001; Miller & Heather, 1998; Velleman, 2001) and much psychiatry is biologically oriented. The theories and emerging practices of health psychology offer a useful alternative way of understanding and tackling drug and alcohol problems. Tobacco smoking is clearly a central health psychology issue, but the sub-discipline has focused less on alcohol and drugs. For example, only 2 per cent of papers in health psychology journals are about drugs or alcohol (based on

papers published in Health Psychology, Psychology & Health, Journal of Health Psychology and British Journal of Health Psychology 1984–2008). There is potential for more attention to substance use as a major class of health behaviour that would benefit from increased psychological understanding.

Over the past 15 years, one challenge to the standard view has been increased concern over forms of substance use that seem problematic but do not involve users who fit diagnostic criteria for abuse or dependence. First, so-called 'binge drinking', better referred to as 'heavy episodic drinking', or 'extreme drinking' (Martinic & Measham, 2008). Second, heavy cannabis use, where long-term users can fit some criteria for dependence, but without subjective distress or help-seeking (Coggans et al., 2004). Third, use of ecstasy. Showing that it is less dangerous than horse riding (Nutt, 2009) recently got the chair of the UK Advisory Council on the Misuse of Drugs into political trouble (The Guardian, 2009), illustrating the value-laden nature of risk assessments about drugs. Fourth, use of ketamine, dangerous but not addictive (Griffin et al., 2008). The diversity of these patterns of use and the associated problems illustrates the complexities of substance use, perhaps better framed as health-related behaviour rather than dependence or compulsion.

Previous critiques of the standard view of substance use problems tended to originate in sociology and social policy. Critiques tend to point out that problems of addiction are socially constructed, are often correlated with poverty and deprivation, and that the substance using habits of the poor and socially excluded tend to be constructed as social and personal problems meriting intensive interventions, whereas the identical, or very similar, behaviours of more included and affluent citizens are constructed as normal, understandable and meriting lighter interventions (see Hammersley, 2008; RSA, 2007). For example, in Scotland young people drinking red wine al fresco in a park are policed differently depending on their clothing and, indeed, the brand of wine being drunk (Galloway et al., 2007).

The social construction of drug and alcohol problems has more serious consequences. Drug injectors who share equipment are extremely prone to life-threatening blood-borne infections including hepatitis

B and C, as well as HIV (Monto *et al.*, 2008). Their lives can be protected by measures such as making sterile injecting equipment available and providing vaccination against hepatitis. The stigma of drug injecting is such that in the recent past drug injectors have often been denied these health-protecting measures on the rather twisted logic that protecting their health was 'encouraging them' to use drugs (Drucker & Clear, 1999). On this reasoning, quality controlling alcoholic drinks, rather than letting them contain poisons, 'encourages' excess drinking (it does, but …).

In short, stereotyping of problems tends to exaggerate and demonise the already severe problems of illicit drug use, whilst creating complacency about alcohol use, particularly high intake with little fuss. Existing laws are based in part on quirks of history, panic and precedent (Bean, 2004). Unfortunately, human risk management behaviour is not as simple as avoiding risky activities and seeking out safe ones. For instance, Adams (1995) gives evidence that wearing seat belts makes people drive their cars more dangerously because they feel safer. He offers the thought experiment of how people would drive should steering wheels have large, sharp spikes in their centres, rather than airbags.

Conversely, people tend to do less of activities perceived to be dangerous, until those activities begin to be perceived as safe, because the actual dangers now rarely occur. For example, Adams (1995) shows that streets seem safer only because parental fear has stopped children using the streets so much. This can lead to cycles of risk and of risk perception. Also, affluent societies tend to have become more and more averse to risk over the past 50 years (Bauman, 2006; Ericson, 2006). Events previously conceptualised as unavoidable accidents or misfortunes are now subject to prevention. People tend to choose 'safe' activities rather than 'dangerous' ones, when such choices are available. Consequently, highlighting the very real dangers of drugs during the 1990s may have driven young nascent substance users into the welcoming arms of the alcohol industry (Forsyth, 2007). Current growing policy concerns about alcohol could lead to its stricter control and drive intoxicant seekers elsewhere.

Measures limiting the population's exposure to alcohol can reduce the adverse impact of alcohol intake in the population (see Anderson & Baumberg, 2006), although they are unpopular with the alcohol industry and with consumers. Measures with some evidence of success include: raising and keeping high the price of alcohol through taxation (the real price of alcohol has fallen over the past 30 years in the UK); limiting the number of alcohol sales outlets, and their opening hours; restricting the advertising and promotion of alcohol; and making alcohol less accessible to young people by raising drinking ages (Anderson & Baumberg, 2006; Rasitrick *et al.*, 1999). It is not known whether increased repression of alcohol leads to increased use of illegal drugs at the population level, or whether this matters for health, because at the population level the health effects of alcohol are so bad. A key challenge for healthier nations will be to reduce people's general thirst for intoxication.

The Psychological Level

Relatively little work conceptualises substance use at the psychological level, where people's cognitions and emotions influence their behaviour. The psychological level includes beliefs, thoughts, habits, knowledge, outcome expectancies, social representations, emotions and moods. It is also at this level that the person develops across the lifespan and it is where psychological interventions take effect.

There is commonly comorbidity between substance dependence and other mental health problems (Farrell *et al.*, 2001). Moreover, relatively moderate substance use by people with serious mental health problems can worsen their problems by interfering with the action of medication, by leading to markedly unusual and inappropriate behaviour, by leading to an avoidance of treatment and a diminution of effective coping strategies, or by placing the person in risky social and legal situations where they will struggle to cope.

Similarly, it is widely, and probably correctly, assumed that substance use is of more concern when the user is a younger teenager. It is increasingly plausible that alcohol, cannabis and other drugs have particularly adverse effects on brains that are still developing (Coalition for Juvenile Justice, 2006). Psychological therapies have also evolved brief and self-help versions appropriate for people with relatively minor substance use problems (Dunn et al., 2001), including younger people who do not yet meet criteria for dependence, and may never do so.

Moreover, it is at the psychological level that people's beliefs, attitudes, norms and expectations about substance use (and life in general) need to be changed in order to reduce substance use. For, along with overeating and physical inactivity, substance use (including tobacco and alcohol) is the major outstanding cause of physical morbidity and mortality in the developed world (e.g. Bertakis & Azari, 2004). It is also worth remembering that substance use is often entangled in a host of other physical and mental health problems, from accidents and violence, through a wide range of internal medical conditions, across non-concordance with medication and medical advice, to many common mental health problems and inherited and acquired disorders of attention, memory and planning, such as dyslexia and ADHD. All this offers a substantial and challenging terrain for future health psychology work.

Cannabis and Alcohol Compared

Some policy makers and media have latched on to concerns about cannabis and psychosis. In the UK decisions to reclassify cannabis as a class C drug (in 2004), then changing it back to a more serious class B drug (in 2009), were not based on good evidence, or expert consensus. Quite basic questions about cannabis use cannot be answered because the research has not been conducted: Is marijuana higher in THC content more dangerous, or do different mixes of cannabinoids have different effects? What do people actually smoke, how do they smoke and how often do they smoke? What are the psychological effects of smoking tobacco–cannabis mixtures as opposed to cannabis only? To what extent is youthful cannabis use a marker for other problems (and sometimes heavy use of other substances) rather than a cause of problems? These kinds of deficiencies in the evidence base apply also to our understanding of other illicit drugs.

In contrast to cannabis, controls on alcohol are not generally increased despite evidence that it is linked to problems including Korsakoff's dementia, suicide and

depression, because it is known that additional causal factors beyond alcohol use explain such problems. Illegal drugs are treated very differently. It might have been better to encourage cannabis users to smoke less than to make their behaviour uniformly more illegal. One challenge for health psychology is to work out ways of tackling substance use in nuanced and considered ways.

Survey work on alcohol is more advanced internationally, both in terms of specialised surveys and questions on alcohol integrated into more general surveys. One good practice is to use alcohol diaries where possible to estimate intake, rather than simple survey questions (e.g., Stockwell et al., 2004); this is rarely attempted with other drugs. A common finding is substantial under-reporting of alcohol consumption, where it can be matched to more objective measures such as excise figures (Stockwell et al., 2004). That the population does not remember, or choose to realise or admit, drinking a third or more of the alcohol sold wholesale should not be passed over as a minor measurement problem, but perhaps challenges the usefulness of survey questionnaires as methods of eliciting accurate reports of substance using behaviour. Certainly, it stretches the concept of sampling 'error' beyond its natural limit. Numerating things in ways that are inaccurate to the point of being wrong may simply give a spurious air of science to what is essentially guesswork.

Despite these problems, surveys of alcohol consumption have enabled progress in understanding what affects drinking. With opposition from the alcohol industry, who locate alcohol harms in a problematic minority of drinkers, it is now clear alcohol harm at the population level is largely a function of intake, which is in turn a function of population-level parameters including the price of alcohol, how available it is and cultural norms about appropriate and inappropriate drinking (see Rasitrick et al., 1999). The recognition that alcohol is hazardous for health has sometimes led to changed cultural norms, e.g. reduced wine drinking in France, reductions in drunk driving in the UK. In the UK, alcohol intake appears to have increased across the last 50 years or so, although it has not yet returned to the high levels found pre-1900 (Barr, 1995).

Some progress has been made in understanding how individuals decide to drink, or engage in other health behaviours. Less is understood about how societies form and change social norms about drinking. On the media, television and film generally portray a large number of drinking episodes that have no consequences (e.g., Mathios *et al.*, 1998). It is not clear how these impact viewers' drinking behaviour. Media portrayals of drugs have been equally unhelpful (e.g., Orcutt & Turner, 1993).

The legality of alcohol makes it far easier to study and more feasible to gather data on price, marketing etc., which allows examination of the economics of substance use. Doing the same thing with an illegal market is beset with problems (see Godfrey *et al.*, 2001). In short, there is potential for applying the knowledge of drinking to understanding of drug use. There is also potential for applying understandings of health behaviours more widely to the domain of substance use.

Health Psychology Theories and Substance Use

West (2006) reviewed some 30 theories of addiction and found them often so diverse as to defy comparison. A leading expert in tobacco smoking, he also the author of PRIME theory, which proposes that addiction is fundamentally a problem of motivation. One challenge, then, is to understand and model motivation. Hammersley and Reid (2009) have developed a theory of how ingesting a drug or foodstuff can influence mood. Interestingly, this involved reconceptualising 'mood' as something more transient and fragile than had been commonly supposed. Theories in wide use in health psychology, discussed elsewhere in this book, are also relevant to substance use. It is worth noting that the transtheoretical model has largely failed as an account of behaviour change, although many practitioners continue to find it descriptively appealing (see West, 2006). The theory of planned behaviour has been used to predict substance use and there is considerable potential to use wider models of social cognition as well (Conner & Norman, 2005).

One important component of social cognitive models may be people's perceived norms for substance use (Perkins *et al.*, 2005). Substances and patterns of use that are more widely publicised and discussed tend to be regarded as more typical than they really are. Moreover, heavier substance users tend to mingle with other users and come to think that relatively heavy use is more normal than it is. Consequently, people tend to believe drug and alcohol use is more common than it really is, which trivialises their own unhealthy behaviour. One implication is that huge publicity about drug and alcohol problems may raise people's perceived norms, increasing use, even although most of the coverage is intended to warn and deter.

Also promising are theories involving outcome expectancies – what people anticipate or believe will happen after doing something – which can quite strongly predict alcohol use, and the decision to quit or moderate drinking (Jones *et al.*, 2001). Another line of research looks at attentional and memory biases correlated with substance use, although how these relate to use is unclear (Hogarth *et al.*, 2008). This segues into the clinical treatment of substance use problems.

Theoretically, psychological therapies assume that people's thoughts create and sustain their problematic use of drugs and alcohol. It used to be assumed that addicts were literally compelled to consume their drugs, but there is much evidence to the contrary. The most striking evidence is that people who have consumed opiates long and heavily enough to be physiologically dependent nonetheless quit if their circumstances change and they do not think of themselves as 'addicts'. This applied to soldier addicts returning from Vietnam where heroin had been widely available (Robins *et al.*, 2000) and it applies also to patients receiving morphine for pain in hospital (Nicholson, 2003). Logically, then, physiological dependence is not enough to create long-standing problems with a drug.

Contribution of the Health Psychologist

In the contemporary health and social care setting, numerate, yet interpersonally skilled, health-care professionals such as health psychologists can bring many things to drug and alcohol issues. One is a scientific, numerate and rational approach to the problems. These problems are complex and beset with measurement issues, artefacts, spurious relationships, reporting errors, plain old lying, motivated misrepresentation of information and difficulties in discriminating between different qualities of evidence and information. Clinically, there is a need for more applied research and reflective practice of the kinds that health psychologists are competent to conduct.

Part of the scientific attitude is to be temperate, compassionate and understanding about substance use problems. Set in a social context (e.g., Hammersley, 2008), we are all substance users. Exaggerating, stereotyping and stigmatising the problems have not been productive. Patient perspectives and patient understandings are a core part of health psychology that could be better applied to substance use problems.

Another useful thing is to be drug and alcohol minded in navigating the psychology of health issues. Many superficially unrelated problems turn out to have substance use as a component. Examples are as diverse as accidents in the home, relapse amongst chronic mental health patients, depression and obesity. People with physical or mental health problems often need also to address their alcohol and drug use.

Whatever the presenting problem, it is worth considering substance use, if only to rule it out.

It is also important to advocate the psychological, or cognitive, level in the causation substance use patterns, rather than assuming it is predominantly a matter of biology, or of culture. Even in a society like ours that covertly values frequent intoxication, people are not compelled to excess. Health behaviours involve personal choice, sometimes dysfunctional cognitions and sensible moderation. So far, explanations that involve involuntary compulsion by biology or social forces have been less helpful. Making everyone more psychologically minded can help to improve policies and practices in this area.

Health psychologists already play an important role in prevention. The trickiest thing is deciding what one is trying to prevent regarding substance use, for lifetime complete temperance is highly improbable (Hammersley, 2008). Increasingly, prevention work is moving towards the addressing of entire lifestyles, rather than focusing narrowly on drugs or substances. Unhealthy habits, excess and the management of mood by consumption are generic issues. In the future, health psychologists will also play a growing role in individual interventions for substance use. Hopefully, the future will see less stigmatisation and more integration of substance use issues into everyday health care.

Discussion Points

1   On drugs, how useful would it be to study the health beliefs of policy makers, as well as patients?
2   How can biological and psychological understandings of substance dependence be integrated?

3   How might health psychologists best contribute to managing drug and alcohol problems?

Further Reading

Anderson, P. & Baumberg, B. (2006). *Alcohol in Europe: A public health perspective*. Brussels: European Commission. Retrieved 15 May 2007 from http://ec.europa.eu/health-eu/news_alcoholineurope_en.htm.

Miller, W.R. & Heather, N. (1998). *Treating addictive behaviors*. New York: Plenum.

Orford, J. (2001). *Excessive appetites: A psychological view of the addictions* (2nd edn). Chichester: Wiley.

RSA (2007). *Drugs – facing facts: The report of the RSA Commission on Illegal Drugs, Communities and Public Policy*. London: Royal Society for the Encouragement of Arts, Manufactures and Commerce.

Velleman, R.D.B. (2001). *Counselling for alcohol problems* (2nd edn). London: Free Association Books.

West, R. (2006). *Theory of addiction*. Oxford: Blackwell.

References

Adams, J. (1995) *Risk*. London: Routledge.

Allen, J.P., Mattson, M.E., Miller, W.R., Tonigan, J.S., Connors, G.J., Rychtarik, R.G. *et al.* (1999). Summary of Project MATCH. *Addiction, 94*, 31–34.

Amos, A., Wiltshire, S., Bostock, Y., Haw, S. & McNeill, A. (2004). 'You can't go without a fag … you need it for your hash' – A qualitative exploration of smoking, cannabis and young people. *Addiction, 99*, 77–81.

Anderson, P. & Baumberg, B. (2006). *Alcohol in Europe: A public health perspective*. Brussels: European Commission. Retrieved 15 May 2007 from http://ec.europa.eu/health-eu/news_alcoholineurope_en.htm.

Barr, A. (1995). *Drink. An informal social history*. London: Bantam Press.

Bauman, Z. (2006). *Liquid fear*. Cambridge: Polity.

Bedi, G. & Redman, J. (2008). Ecstasy use and higher-level cognitive functions: Weak effects of ecstasy after control for potential confounds. *Psychological Medicine, 38*, 1319–1330.

Bean, P. (2004). *Drugs and crime* (2nd edn). Cullompton: Willan.

Beck, A.T., Wright, F.D., Newman, C.F. & Liese, B.S. (1993). *Cognitive therapy of substance abuse*. New York: Guilford Press.

Bertakis, K.D. & Azari, R. (2006). The influence of obesity, alcohol abuse and smoking on utilization of health care services. *Family Medicine, 38*, 427–434.

Coalition for Juvenile Justice (2006). *What are the implications of adolescent brain development for juvenile justice?* Washington, DC: Coalition for Juvenile Justice.

Coggans, N., Dalgarno, P., Johnson, L. & Shewan, D. (2004). Long-term heavy cannabis use: Implications for health education. *Drugs: Education, Prevention & Policy, 11*, 299–313.

Cohen, M., Solowij, N. & Carr, V. (2008). Cannabis, cannabinoids and schizophrenia: Integration of the evidence. *Australian and New Zealand Journal of Psychiatry, 42*, 357–368.

Collins, J.J., Hubbard, R.l., Rachal, J.V., Cavanaugh, E.R., Craddock, S.G. & Kristiansen, P.L. (1983). *Criminality in a drug treatment sample: Measurement issues and initial findings*. North Carolina: Research Triangle Institute.

Conner, M.T. & Norman, P. (Eds.) (2005). *Predicting health behaviour: Research and practice with social cognition models* (2nd edn). Milton Keynes: Open University Press.

Dalgarno, P. & Shewan, D. (2005). Reducing the risks of drug use: The case for Set and Setting. *Addiction Research and Theory, 13*, 259–265.

de Sola LLopis, S., Miguelez-Pan, M., Pena-Casanova, J., Poudevida, S., Farre, M., Pacifici, R. *et al.* (2008). Cognitive performance in recreational ecstasy polydrug users: A two-year follow-up study. *Journal of Psychopharmacology, 22*, 498–510.

Ditton, J. & Hammersley, R. (1996) *A very greedy drug: Cocaine in context*. Reading, MA: Harwood.

Drucker, E. & Clear, A. (1999). Harm reduction in the home of the war on drugs: Methadone and needle exchange in the USA. *Drug and Alcohol Review, 18*, 103–112.

Dunn, C., Deroo, L. & Rivara, F.P. (2001). The use of brief interventions adapted from motivational interviewing across behavioral domains: a systematic review. *Addiction, 96*, 1725–1742.

Durdle, H., Lundahl, L. H., Johanson, C. & Tancer, M. (2008). Major depression: The relative contribution of gender, MDMA, and cannabis use. *Depression and Anxiety, 25*, 241–247.

EMCDDA (2009). *State of the drugs problem in Europe*. European Monitoring Centre for Drugs and Drug Addiction. Retrieved 23 April 2009 from http://www.emcdda.europa.eu/themes/drug-situation#box29.

Ericson, R. (2006). *Crime in an insecure world*. Cambridge: Polity.

European Commission (2006). *Alcohol-related harm in Europe – Key data*. Brussels: Health & Consumer Protection Directorate General. Retrieved 23 April 2009 from http://ec.europa.eu/health/ph_determinants/life_style/alcohol/documents/alcohol_factsheet_en.pdf.

Farrell, M., Howes, S., Bebbington, P., Brugha, T., Jenkins, R., Lewis, G. *et al.* (2001). Nicotine, alcohol and drug dependence and psychiatric comorbidity. Results of a national household survey. *British Journal of Psychiatry, 179*, 432–437.

Fillmore, K.M., Golding, J.M., Leino, E.V., Motoyoshi, M., Ager, C.R., Ferrer, H.P. *et al.* (1994). Relationships of measures of alcohol consumption with alcohol-related problems in multiple studies – A research synthesis from the collaborative alcohol-related longitudinal project, *Addiction, 89*, 1143–1156.

Forsyth, A.J.M. (2007). *From illegal leisure to licensed disorder: Rave culture as marketing opportunity for the licensed trade (drinks) industry*. Glasgow: Glasgow Caledonian University.

Galloway, J., Forsyth, A.J.M. & Shewan, D. (2007). *Young people's street drinking behaviour: Investigating the influence of marketing & subculture*. London: Alcohol Education

Research Council. Retrieved 11 March 2009 from http://www.aerc.org.uk/documents/pdfs/finalReports/AERC_FinalReport_0030.pdf?zoom_highlight=galloway.

Godfrey, C., Weissing, L. & Hartnoll, R. (Eds.) (2001). *Modelling drug use: Methods to quantify and understand hidden processes.* EMCDDA Scientific Monograph Series. No. 6. Lisbon: European Monitoring Centre for Drugs and Drug Addiction.

Granfield, R. & Cloud, W. (1999). *Coming clean: Overcoming addiction without treatment.* New York: New York University Press.

Griffin, C., Measham, F., Moore, K., Morey, Y. & Riley, S. (Eds.) (2008). Special Issue: The social and cultural uses of ketamine. *Addiction Research and Theory, 16,* 205–303.

Guillot, C. & Greenway, D. (2006). Recreational ecstasy use and depression. *Journal of Psychopharmacology, 20,* 411–416.

Hammersley, R. (1994). A digest of memory phenomena for addiction research. *Addiction, 89,* 283–293.

Hammersley, R. (2008). *Drugs and crime: Theories and practices.* Cambridge: Polity.

Hammersley, R., Marsland, L. & Reid, M. (2003) *Substance use by young offenders: The impact of the normalization of drug use in the early years of the 21st century.* Home Office Research Study 261. London: Home Office Research and Statistics Directorate.

Hammersley, R. & Reid, M. (2009). Modelling transient mood changes after ingestion. *Neuroscience & Biobehavioral Reviews, 33,* 213–222.

Harthey, E., Orford, J.F., Dalton, S.I., Ferrins-Brown, M., Kerr, C.E.P. & Maslin, J. (2003). Untreated heavy drinkers: A qualitative and quantitative study of dependence and readiness to change. *Addiction Research and Theory, 11,* 317–337.

HM Government (2008). *Drugs: Protecting families and communities. The 2008 Drug Strategy.* London: HMSO.

Hoare, J. & Flatley, J. (2008) *Drug misuse declared: Findings from the 2007/08 British Crime Survey.* London: Home Office. Retrieved 11 March 2009 from http://www.homeoffice.gov.uk/rds/pdfs08/hosb1308.pdf.

Hogarth, L., Dickinson, A., Janowski, M., Nikitina, A. & Duka, T. (2008). The role of attentional bias in mediating human drug-seeking behaviour. *Psychopharmacology, 201,* 29–41.

Jones, B.T., Corbin, W. & Fromme, K. (2001). A review of expectancy theory and alcohol consumption. *Addiction, 96,* 55–70.

Kyrouz, E.M. & Humphreys, K. (1997). A review of research on the effectiveness of self-help/mutual aid groups. *International Journal of Psychosocial Rehabilitation, 1,* 12–17.

Liddle, H.A. & Dakof, G.A. (1995). Family-based treatment for adolescent drug use: State of the science. In E. Rahdert & D. Czechowicz (Eds.) *Adolescent drug abuse:*

Clinical assessment and therapeutic interventions (pp. 218–254). Rockville, MD: National Institute on Drug Abuse.

MacDonald, Z. & Pudney, S. (2000). Analysing drug abuse with British Crime Survey data: Modelling and questionnaire design issues. *Journal of the Royal Statistical Society Series C – Applied Statistics, 49,* 95–117.

Martinac, M. & Measham, F. (2008). *Swimming with crocodiles. The culture of extreme drinking.* London: Routledge.

Mathios, A., Avery, R., Bisogni, C. & Shanahan, J. (1998). Alcohol portrayal on prime-time television: Manifest and latent messages. *Journal of Studies on Alcohol, 59,* 305–310.

Miller, P. & Plant, M. (2002). Heavy cannabis use among UK teenagers: An exploration. *Drug and Alcohol Dependence, 65,* 235–242.

Miller, W.R. & Heather, N. (1998). *Treating addictive behaviors.* New York: Plenum.

Miller, W.R. & Rollnick, S. (1991). *Motivational interviewing: Preparing people to change addictive behavior.* New York: Guilford Press.

Monto, A., Currie, S. & Wright, T.L. (2008). Liver disease in injection drug users with hepatitis C, with and without HIV coinfection. *Journal of Addictive Diseases, 27,* 49–59.

Mukamal, K.J. (2004). Alcohol consumption and abnormalities of brain structure and vasculature. *American Journal of Geriatric Cardiology, 22*–28.

Murray-Lillibridge, K., Barry, J., Reagan, S., O'Flanagan, D., Sayers, G., Bergin, C. et al. (2006). Epidemiological findings and medical, legal, and public health challenges of an investigation of severe soft tissue infections and deaths among injecting drug users – Ireland, 2000. *Epidemiology and Infection, 134,* 894–901.

National Institute on Drug Abuse (2006). *What is addiction?* Retrieved 24 April 2007 from http://www.drugabuse.gov/tools/FAQ.html#Anchor-What-53617.

Nicholson, B. (2003). Responsible prescribing of opioids for the management of chronic pain. *Drugs, 63,* 17–32.

Norstrom, T. & Ramstedt, M. (2005). Mortality and population drinking: A review of the literature. *Drug and Alcohol Review, 24,* 537–547.

Nutt, D. (2009). Equasy: An overlooked addiction with implications for the current debate on drug harms. *Journal of Psychopharmacology, 23,* 3–5.

Orcutt, J.D. & Turner, J.B. (1993). Shocking numbers and graphic accounts: Quantified images of drug problems in the print media. *Social Problems, 40,* 190–206.

Orford, J. (2001). *Excessive appetites: A psychological view of the addictions* (2nd edn). Chichester: Wiley.

Perkins, H.W., Haines, M.P. & Rice, R. (2005). Misperceiving the college drinking norm and related problems: A nationwide study of exposure to prevention information, perceived norms and student alcohol misuse. *Journal of Studies on Alcohol, 66,* 470–478.

Rasitrick, D., Hodgson, R. & Ritson, B. (1999). *Tackling alcohol together: The basis for a UK alcohol policy.* London: Free Association Books.

Robins, L., Compton, W. & Horton, J. (2000). Is heroin the worst drug? Implications for drug policy. *Addiction Research, 8,* 527–548.

RSA (2007). *Drugs – facing facts: The report of the RSA Commission on Illegal Drugs, Communities and Public Policy.* London: Royal Society for the Encouragement of Arts, Manufactures and Commerce.

Schifano, F., Corkery, J., Deluca, P., Ovefeso, A. & Ghodse, A.H. (2006). Ecstasy (MDMA, MDA, MDEA, MBDB) consumption, seizures, retated offences, prices, dosage levels and deaths in the UK (1994–2003). *Journal of Psychopharmacology, 20,* 456–463.

Seivewright, N. (2000). *Community treatment of drug misuse: More than methadone.* Cambridge: Cambridge University Press.

Shewan, D. & Dalgarno, P. (2005). Evidence for controlled heroin use? Low levels of negative health and social outcomes among non-treatment heroin users in Glasgow (Scotland). *British Journal of Health Psychology, 10,* 33–48.

Stockwell, T., Donath, S., Cooper-Stanbury, M., Chikrizhs, T., Catalano, P. & Mateo, C. (2004). Under-reporting of alcohol consumption in household surveys: A comparison of quantity-frequency, graduated-frequency and recent recall. *Addiction, 99,* 1024–1033.

The Guardian (2009). Jacqui Smith slaps down drugs adviser for comparing ecstasy to horse riding. Retrieved 11 March 2009 from http://www.guardian.co.uk/politics/2009/feb/09/ecstasy-horse-riding.

Velleman, R.D.B. (2001). *Counselling for alcohol problems* (2nd edn). London: Free Association Books.

West, R. (2006). *Theory of addiction.* Oxford: Blackwell.

Young, J.E. (1999). *Cognitive therapy for personality disorders: A schema-focused approach.* Sarasota, FL: Professional Resource Press.

7

Sexual Health and Behaviour

Jeffrey T. Parsons and Brooke E. Wells

Chapter Outline

This chapter addresses sexual health and critical aspects of human sexual behaviour. First, we review definitions of sexual health and two theoretical models utilised to conceptualise and contextualise sexual health. Then, we summarise research focused on sexual dysfunction, disorders and dissatisfaction. Recognising that sexual health and behaviour is about more than such problems and issues, we turn our focus to the positive aspects of sexual health – pleasure and intimacy. We conclude by discussing four critical components of health promotion efforts which have proven efficacious. Important topics as sex therapy; pregnancy, childbirth, and contraception; or rates of HIV and STIs, are beyond the scope of this chapter.

Key Concepts

Cultural competency
Definitions of sexual health
Gender
Health benefits of sexual
    activity
Health promotion
    strategies
Pleasure and sexual health
Sexual dysfunction,
    disorders and
    dissatisfaction
Sexual health models
Sexual rights
Social determinants of
    sexual health

Introduction

Achieving and maintaining sexual health is a global public health challenge. A report by the World Health Organization (WHO) and the Joint United Nations Programme on HIV/AIDS (UNAIDS) estimates that, as of 2007, there were 33.2 million people in the world living with HIV, with prevalence rates at their highest in sub-Saharan Africa (UNAIDS & World Health Organization, 2007). Additionally, despite significant drops in teen pregnancy rates in most countries over the past 20–30 years, there are still an estimated 16 million teenage girls (15–19 years old) who become mothers every year, accounting for 11 per cent of births worldwide and adversely impacting maternal and infant health (World Health Organization, 2009). Prevalence rates for sexual dysfunction are difficult to estimate because of limited evidence-based literature for women and the fact that such dysfunction increases with age. A variety of recent epidemiological studies conducted worldwide suggest that about 35–45 per cent of women and 20–30 per cent of men have at least one apparent sexual dysfunction, such as erectile disorder (Lewis *et al.*, 2004; Nicolosi *et al.*, 2004; Nicolosi *et al.*, 2006). In light of the continued sexual health concerns facing researchers, policy makers and public health officials, a more complete understanding of sexual health and its components is warranted.

Definitions of Sexual Health

Definitions of sexual health inform models of sexual health, guide and reflect sexuality research agendas, and establish national and international public health agendas and health promotion efforts. Definitions of sexual health have evolved over time and vary across culture and setting, reflecting political and contextual influences (Giami, 2002). Reflecting newer definitions of sexual health published in the United States (Department of Health and Human Services, 2001) and in the United Kingdom (Department of Health, 2001), the World Health Organization (2002) has defined sexual health as:

> Sexual health is a state of physical, emotional, mental and social well-being related to sexuality; it is not merely the absence of disease, dysfunction or infirmity. Sexual health requires a positive and respectful approach to sexuality and sexual relationships, as well as the possibility of having pleasurable and safe sexual experiences, free of coercion, discrimination and violence. For sexual health to be attained and maintained, the sexual rights of all persons must be respected, protected and fulfilled.

This definition frames sexual health as a basic human right and focuses on the absence of disease and dysfunction and the importance of sexual pleasure. In its focus on the positive and pleasurable aspects of sexuality, this definition reflects a shift to sexual optimism and away from negative aspects of sexuality (Giami, 2002). Further, sexual health is situated as essential to sexual expression, now considered a basic human right (Giami, 2002). Finally, while defining sexual health does risk stigmatising behaviour which does not comply with these definitions, definitions of sexual health are critical in developing models of sexual health, establishing policy and research agendas, and in defining and upholding sexual rights around the globe.

Models of Sexual Health

In much sexual health research (which is primarily research on sexual risk behaviour), general health models have been adapted to address sexual health. Such health behaviour models include the health belief model (Hiltabiddle, 1996; Mahoney *et al.*, 1995), the information-motivation-behavior model (Fisher *et al.*, 2002; Kalichman *et al.*, 2001), theory of reasoned action (Munoz-Silva *et al.*, 2007; Terry *et al.*, 1993) and the transtheoretical model/stages of change model (Bowen & Trotter, 1995; Prochaska, 1994), to name a few. Increasingly, though, researchers are utilising current definitions of sexual health to conceptualise models that specifically apply to sexual health. This chapter identifies two broad models that attempt to identify the essential components of sexual health and the factors that impact sexual health. First, we review the sexual health model (Robinson *et al.*, 2002), wherein researchers have combined decades of experience and results to identify the essential components of sexual health. Second, we look at ecological models of sexual health, specifically describing a gendered model of adolescent sexual health inspired by the absence of gender in existing models of sexual health (Tolman *et al.*, 2003).

The sexual health model

Robinson *et al.* (2002) developed the sexual health model on the basis of years of experience in researching and treating sexual health issues. As central to their model, the creators identified the importance of open and honest communication, sexual pluralism, defined as an 'acceptance of the rights of others to differ from you in their choices and a belief that there is more than one way to achieve a moral life' (p. 46), and contextual factors. The authors intended the sexual health model to be a theoretical framework useful in developing HIV preventions and interventions.

The model first acknowledges the importance of background characteristics of the population, such as individual factors and sexual history. The authors then identify 10 key components they believe essential to sexual health and, thus, to the prevention of HIV. These 10 components, as outlined in Figure 7.1, hold equal importance in the model and can impact sexual behaviour directly or through their interaction with background characteristics. The first component, 'Talking about sex', recognises that effective sexual communication is essential to negotiate one's sexual health and to identify one's sexual values and beliefs. The second component, 'Culture and sexual identity', asserts that cultural factors, such as differential cultural meanings of sexual behaviour, should be considered when targeting sexual health messages to a specific population. Third, the authors identify the importance of a basic working knowledge of sexual anatomy and physiology, especially as they relate to sexual health behaviours such as condom use. In the fourth component, the authors identify basic health care behaviours, such as regular gynaecological and prostate examinations, and safer sex knowledge as essential to sexual health. The fifth component, 'Challenges', is conceptualised more broadly to identify the importance of overcoming any individual challenges to one's sexual health, such as a history of sexual abuse, sexual harassment or discrimination, and/or alcohol and drug abuse. Sixth, 'Body image' identifies the spe-

cific challenge of overcoming negative body image to establish an accepting view of one's body in relation to cultural standards of beauty. The seventh component of sexual health, 'Masturbation and fantasy', does not require these behaviours, but rather integrates demystifying these behaviours and establishing their importance in the context of abstinence and safer sex practices. The eighth component, 'Positive sexuality', reflects the increasing focus on positive sexuality and includes 'appropriate experimentation, affirming sensuality, attaining sexual competence through the ability to get and give sexual pleasure, and setting sexual boundaries based on what one prefers, as well as what one knows is safe and responsible'. The ninth component, 'Intimacy and relationships', situates sexuality within an interpersonal context and places the achievement of intimacy and respectful relationships as important in the prevention of HIV. Finally, the authors identify spirituality (encompassing both religion and other forms of spirituality) as important in so much as one's behaviour is congruent with one's moral, ethical and spiritual beliefs.

While the creators of this model recognise that all components of the model may not be necessary or even possible to include in any one intervention, they encourage tailored interventions that consider the interactions between the components and between background characteristics and the components of their model. In developing a model so broad, the authors also recognise the role of more general mental and physical health provision (such as substance abuse counselling) in improving sexual health. As such, they recommend partnerships between mental, community and sexual health experts. Finally, reflecting the overall tone of the model (and view of its creators), the researchers recommend that any implementation of an intervention based on the sexual health model 'should strive for a positive and empowering tone' (p. 53), which they consider essential to its success and relevant in the current sexual climate.

Gender matters

Ecological models of human behaviour have long been recognised as essential in understanding the interaction between individuals and their environment (Bronfenbrenner, 1977, 1979; Lewin, 1951/1972).

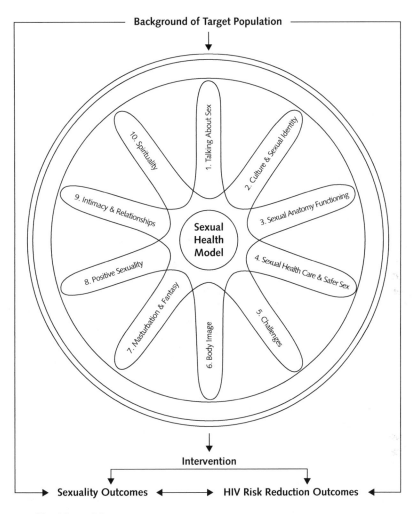

Figure 7.1 The sexual health model
Source: Robinson, B.B., Bockting, W.O., Rosser, B.R., Miner, M. & Coleman, E. (2002). The sexual health model: Application of a sexological approach to HIV prevention. *Health Education Research, 17*, 43–57.

Health psychologists have also recognised the importance of understanding health behaviour within an ecological framework that situates the individual in a particular interpersonal, sociocultural context (Ickovics *et al.*, 2001; Revenson, 1990). In this tradition of ecological models, Tolman and colleagues (Tolman *et al.*, 2003) developed a model of adolescent sexual health that places gender as an essential component of the individual and contextual components of sexual behaviour.

Tolman *et al.* (2003), in reviewing standard definitions of sexual health, recognised that gender was notably absent from these definitions. Taking a social constructionist perspective on gender, wherein socially constructed gendered understandings of sexual behaviour (and of individuals) serve to maintain a system of gender inequality, Tolman (Tolman, 1999; Tolman *et al.*, 2003) identified the ways in which gender constricts sexual health choices and relational power and dictates understandings of 'normal' sexuality that subsequently influence public health priorities. For example, scholars involved in the Women, Risk and AIDS Project (WRAP) demonstrated that cultural

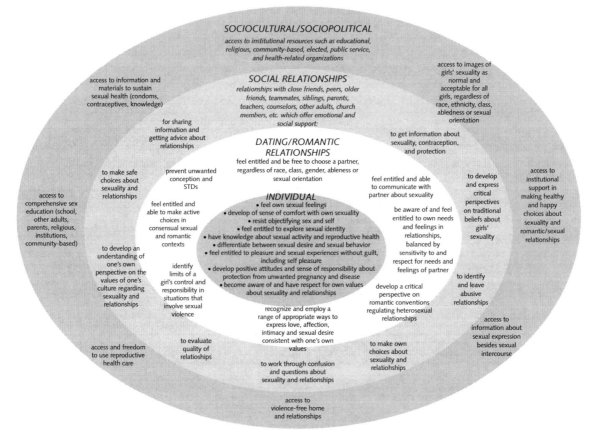

Figure 7.2   The model of adolescent sexual health
Source: Tolman, D.L. (1999). Femininity as a barrier to positive sexual health for adolescent girls. *Journal of the American Medical Women's Association, 54,* 133–38.

conceptions of women as passive and subordinate to male desire limited women's risk negotiation opportunities (Holland *et al.*, 1992). Amaro (1995) also articulated the importance of considering gendered realities in HIV prevention efforts. Tolman *et al.* (2003) argue that not including gendered factors that limit access to power and resources 'overlooks crucial barriers to … sexual health' (p. 7).

As such, Tolman and colleagues integrate several theoretical approaches to develop an ecological model of adolescent sexual health that centres around an understanding of gender within each level of the model. Their model strives to integrate various influences on sexual health and sexuality, moving beyond a focus on pregnancy or HIV/AIDS prevention and

intervention efforts. In their model, depicted in Figure 7.2, Tolman and colleagues (Tolman, 1999; Tolman *et al.*, 2003) identify the individual, interpersonal (dating/romantic relationships), social and sociocultural/sociopolitical contexts in which an individual is situated. Individual level factors include feelings about one's sexuality and sexual identity, knowledge about sexual and reproductive health, and awareness of one's own sexual values. At the interpersonal level (or, as they identify it, the dating/romantic relationships level), factors of influence include the ability to prevent unwanted conception and disease/infection transmission, feeling entitled to assert one's needs in a relationship, and being able to communicate effectively with one's partner about sexual matters. The social relationships context includes the social support provided by friends, family and peers, the ability to obtain information related to sexual health, and the ability to develop one's own perspective on sexual values and gender. Finally, the sociocultural/sociopolitical context includes access to institutional resources, social norms or images of gendered sexuality, access to safe relationships and living environments, and access to comprehensive sexuality education and the materials to ensure sexual health (condoms, contraception, health care, etc.).

While Tolman *et al.* (2003) developed this model to be specific to female adolescent sexual health, they also identify the ways in which a model for male adolescent sexual health would be very similar to the female version. Specifically, they define gender complementarity as the system under which gendered notions of sexuality are integrated and 'fit together to reproduce particular and limited forms of sexuality that are deemed to be "normal", all in the service of reproducing and sustaining compulsory heterosexuality' (p.10). In other words, the very systems that limit access to the pursuit of sexual health and expression for adolescent girls also limit such access for adolescent boys, though in varying (and complementary) ways. As such, they encourage researchers to develop models of sexual health that can be adapted to fit the needs of both men and women/boys and girls in ways that are useful to sexuality researchers and sexual health practitioners.

Moving forward

While these two models are both broad and ambitious in their attempts to model all of the factors that influence sexual health, there are two primary distinctions of importance. First, although both models take a positive approach to sexuality and sexual health, the impetus for each model is slightly different. In Robinson *et al.*'s (2002) sexual health model, the focus is on guiding HIV prevention and intervention efforts, thus responding directly to a sexual health crisis. In Tolman *et al.*'s (2003) model, on the other hand, they strive to develop a model of sexual health that will inform research efforts into sexual health and encourage researchers and sexual health practitioners to consider gender in their respective practices. Second,

these models are distinct in their placement and understanding of contextual factors. Tolman *et al.*'s model adapts an ecological approach to place all sexual factors in a specific context, reflecting the social constructionist framework informing their model. The sexual health model, on the other hand, situates background characteristics as potentially influencing each component of sexual health outlined in their model, but identifies each of these components, ultimately, as factors that can be modified at an individual level. These important distinctions between the two models are essential factors to consider in future attempts to conceptualise models of sexual health. Again, models of sexual health, while attempting the impossible in working to identify all of the factors influencing behaviour, should exert care to avoid normalising some behaviours and stigmatising others. Rather, these models should be developed as frameworks for research, policy, health practice and intervention and prevention efforts.

Sexual Dysfunction, Disorders and Dissatisfaction

The terminology used to differentiate 'normal' sexual functioning from problematic function is quite vague and varies significantly across researchers and clinicians. The *Diagnostic and Statistical Manual (DSM) of Mental Disorders*, 4th edition (text revision) of the American Psychiatric Association (2000) relies primarily on the term 'sexual disorders', while the International Classification of Diseases (ICD-10) system of the World Health Organization (WHO, 1992) uses the term 'sexual dysfunction'. The DSM categorises sexual disorders based on the four phases of sexual response according to Masters and Johnson (Masters & Johnson, 1966) and, unlike other disorders, does not require a specific duration for diagnosis (Balon *et al.*, 2007), although the disorder must be 'persistent or recurrent'. The ICD-10 system acknowledges that although some dysfunctions (e.g., orgasmic dysfunction) occur among both men and women, women tend to present with more subjective complaints regarding the quality of the sexual experience rather than the failure of some aspect of the sexual response cycle.

One of the central problems with defining sexual dysfunctions and disorders concerns the degree to which someone may experience symptomology but be fully satisfied with their sexual health. As such, some have turned to the term 'sexual dissatisfaction' to either factor in a person's own perceptions regarding the issues with their sexual health and/or as a requirement for classification as a 'sexual dysfunction' (that is, unless one is 'dissatisfied', one cannot have a problem despite having symptoms). The Working Group for a New View of Women's Sexual Problems (2001), a group of social scientists and clinicians, believe that medical classification systems (such as the DSM and ICD) are not appropriate for an understanding of female sexuality, and place dissatisfaction as a central tenet of their definition of sexual problems as: 'discontent or dissatisfaction with any emotional, physical, or relational aspect of sexual experience'. Certainly the term 'sexual dissatisfaction' better reflects some of the notions of sexual health described earlier in this chapter, however, the majority of research has emphasised the aspects of sexual dysfunction and disorders.

Reliable and valid information regarding the prevalence (the proportion of those with the disorder relative to the total population at risk at a particular point in time) and incidence (the number of new cases of a disorder that develop during a specified period of time) rates for sexual dysfunction are difficult to obtain. The vast majority of the heterogeneous studies in this area are observational or descriptive in nature, utilise a wide variety of methodological designs, and employ inconsistent definitions and time frames during which the sexual dysfunction may have occurred. This poses a challenge to pooling data for comparison purposes, particularly when many studies use imprecise measures. Some studies have focused on symptoms of sexual dysfunction (e.g., Do you have difficulty achieving an erection?), others have focused on problems as defined by distress (e.g., Are you distressed by the inability to achieve an erection?) and very few conduct a more formal assessment of a disorder (e.g., the assessment of erectile disorder using the DSM or ICD criteria). The research on sexual dysfunction is further complicated by the self-report nature of the behaviours and sexual responses under consideration, as well as the subjec-

tive nature of the perception of distress. Many sexual dysfunctions are associated with some degree of social stigma, and as such the extent of the problem may be under-reported (Boyle, 1999). Someone experiencing the lack of sexual desire may simply not perceive that it is a problem, or may minimise concerns, feeling that such problems do not compare to other health-related conditions. The presence or absence of regular sexual partners may also impact whether and to what degree a person experiences distress over even persistent sexual dysfunctions. In addition, it is critical to consider the influence of culture, religion and social norms and the ways in which these factors may influence the subjective experience of sexual dysfunctions as well as a person's willingness to discuss them.

One of the more recent attempts to examine the global extent of female and male sexual dysfunction was the Global Survey of Sexual Attitudes and Behaviors. Data from over 27,000 men and women (ages 40–80) in 29 countries were collected in 2001–2 (Nicolosi et al., 2004). Although numerous other efforts to examine the epidemiology of sexual dysfunction have been conducted (Derogatis & Burnett, 2008; Dunn et al., 2002; Hayes et al., 2006; Laumann et al., 1999; Rosen et al., 2004), this particular study was global in nature, utilised a standardised questionnaire, and was conducted after the advent of such medications to treat erection difficulties among men, such as Viagra (sildenafil), Levitra (vardenafil) and Cialis (tadalafil), which have helped to make discussion of male sexual dysfunctions more public (Slowinski, 2007). The specific research protocol used to collect the data varied by region, taking into consideration cultural differences. For example, random digit dialling methods and telephone interviews were used in such areas as North America, Europe and Australia, while door-to-door protocols were used in the Middle East and Africa. Sexual dysfunction was assessed by asking participants to indicate if they had ever experienced any of a list of sexual problems for at least two months during the previous year, and for those answering positively, whether the frequency was occasional, sometimes or frequent. Those reporting that a problem was occasional were excluded so that only those with a persistent sexual dysfunction were included.

Overall, the majority of these adult and elderly participants reported engagement in sexual intercourse in the past year (over 80 per cent of the men and 65 per cent of the women). The most commonly reported sexual dysfunctions were, among the men, early ejaculation (14 per cent) and erectile difficulties (10 per cent); among the women, lack of interest in sex (21 per cent), inability to achieve orgasm (16 per cent) and lubrication difficulties (16 per cent). Across countries, 28 per cent of men and 39 per cent of women reported at least one sexual problem. For both genders, reporting a sexual problem was significantly associated with a lower degree of satisfaction with sexual life. Although age was related to increased reporting of sexual problems, this was more so the case among men than among women. There were some between-country differences, with greater rates of early ejaculation and erectile difficulties reported among men from Asian countries, and greater rates of lack of interest in sex reported among women from South Asian and Middle Eastern areas of the world (Nicolosi *et al.*, 2004). When data from the five English-speaking countries (United States, Canada, United Kingdom, Australia and New Zealand) were examined, more regional differences were noted. For example, men and women in Canada (18 per cent and 28 per cent, respectively) were the least likely to report at least one sexual dysfunction whereas men and women in New Zealand (51 per cent and 57 per cent, respectively) were the most likely (Nicolosi *et al.*, 2006). Among those in these countries, 36 per cent of men and women reporting a sexual problem failed to seek any help or advice, and 32 per cent sought medical care (the remainder sought help from family, social support or information in the media). When asked why a physician had not been consulted for reported sexual problems, 72 per cent felt that the problem did not warrant such attention.

Defining sexual dysfunctions, disorders and dissatisfaction is a challenge to researchers and clinicians, and there is still a clear need for more studies to examine prevalence and incidence. Future studies, however, could benefit from the consideration of sexual health models, such that more precise definitions of dissatisfaction are provided. By incorporating a focus on pleasure and sexual intimacy as a component of dissatisfaction, we may arrive at a more nuanced understanding of what is healthy sexual functioning versus what is not.

Pleasure and Intimacy

Despite the risks inherent in sexual activity with others, sexuality still holds the potential for great pleasure and intimacy. In fact, a survey of the reasons people gave for engaging in sexual activity with another person showed that seeking pleasure and expressing love and affection were among the top 10 reasons for having sex (Meston & Buss, 2007). Additionally, research demonstrates the myriad physical and mental health benefits of sexual expression, pleasure and intimacy (Whipple *et al.*, 2003). Research in both arenas demonstrates the utility of including pleasure and intimacy components in definitions and models of sexual health.

Research demonstrates the role of sexual pleasure (and the potential disruption to pleasure) in determining acceptability and use of contraceptive and HIV and STI prevention techniques (Higgins & Hirsch, 2008; Higgins *et al.*, 2008; Montgomery *et al.*, 2008; Rahamefy *et al.*, 2008). Understanding the perceived and experienced impact of contraception and HIV/STI prevention techniques on sexual pleasure becomes increasingly important in testing new methods, such as microbicides. Intimacy, typically defined as the presence of love and affection, trust and self-disclosure, positively influences psychological health, physiological responses to stress and sexual communication (Hatfield & Rapson, 2007), all of which influence sexual health and, in fact, loosely correspond to the components outlined in the sexual health model (Robinson *et al.*, 2002).

Finally, though a discussion of the benefits of sexual activity has largely been absent in the wake of the AIDS epidemic, there is evidence that sexual activity is associated with a variety of mental and physical health benefits. A recent report of studies around the globe concludes that regular sexual activity is associated with longevity, a decreased likelihood of heart disease and breast cancer (possibly related to changes in hormone levels that occur during orgasm) and a strengthened immune system (Whipple *et al.*, 2003). Further, sexual activity positively impacts reproductive health through its protective effects against endometriosis, enhancing fertility, regulating the menstrual cycle and protecting against chronic nonbacterial prostatitis. Whipple *et al*.'s review (2003) also highlighted a variety of evidence that sexual satisfaction is a strong and consistent predictor of quality of life and is negatively associated with depression. Consistent with anecdotal evidence, sexual activity and orgasm can also reduce stress and induce relaxation. Finally, positive and satisfying sexual experiences can increase intimacy and bonding with one's partner, which, as noted above, can then positively influence communication and safer sex practices. In other words, satisfying sex may be associated with safer sexual practices.

Integrating Critical Components of Health Promotion Efforts

Because the specific content of health promotion efforts varies according to the goals of the intervention and prevention programmes (e.g. STI prevention, HIV testing, etc.), this chapter ends with a review of overarching components that have proven efficacious across health promotion content categories. We have identified four primary components proven effective in a variety of health promotion efforts: (i) cultural competency; (ii) a positive approach that incorporates the pleasurable aspects of sexuality; (iii) comprehensive information and educational components; and (iv) a clear theoretical framework.

Cultural competency

Cultural competency is '… a set of congruent behaviors, attitudes, and policies that come together in a system, agency, or among professionals and enable effective work in cross-cultural situations' (Anderson *et al*., 2003, p. 68). Research indicates that cultural appropriateness or sensitivity is an essential component of any sexual health intervention (DiClemente *et al*., 2008; Jemmott & Jemmott, 2000). For example, an HIV prevention intervention that emphasised values that were culturally relevant to African American women, including cultural pride, community concern and family responsibility (values were based on focus

groups with African American women and were directly linked to sexual health behaviours), resulted in an 18 per cent increase in HIV testing in the weeks post-intervention (Kalichman *et al*., 1993). Further, lack of cultural sensitivity or appropriateness has been reported as a barrier to accessing sexual health services (Beck *et al*., 2005).

Incorporating pleasure

In their exclusive focus on fear and danger, health promotion efforts position safe sex and pleasurable sex as mutually exclusive (Philpott *et al*., 2006), creating what some researchers titled the 'pleasure deficit' (Higgins & Hirsch, 2007). However, a review of interventions that focus on the positive or pleasurable aspects of sexuality (while also promoting sexually healthy behaviour) shows that incorporating the pleasurable aspects of condom use, such as the friction of the ring of the condom on the clitoris, the availability of studded condoms to enhance pleasure or the use of condoms to achieve delayed ejaculation/prolonged intercourse, is effective in increasing consistent condom use (Philpott *et al*., 2006). Again, Philpott recommends that these pleasure-promoting messages be tailored to the specific cultural context in which they are being delivered. Because of the lack of systematic research into the behavioural health effects of pleasure promotion, further research is warranted to better understand the specific effects and ramifications of incorporating a pleasure approach.

Comprehensive sexuality education and information

The debate surrounding sexuality education in the United States and elsewhere has fuelled a research agenda aimed at understanding health outcomes of comprehensive sexuality education, when compared to abstinence-only sexuality education. This research has definitively shown that comprehensive sexuality education is more efficacious in promoting sexually healthy behaviours, namely pregnancy and HIV/STI prevention behaviours (Fawole *et al*., 1999; Hoyt & Broom, 2002; Kohler *et al*., 2008). The effectiveness of comprehensive sexuality education is consistent with theoretical models that highlight the importance of information and education in health behaviour (e.g. the information-motivation-behavior model). A review of health education efforts concludes that educational efforts must aim to effect changes in psychological factors, such as self-efficacy, in addition to increasing knowledge (Schaalma et al., 2004). As noted above, though, the information provided and the manner in which sexuality is discussed should be culturally sensitive and relevant (Beck et al., 2005).

Theoretically grounded

Finally, research indicates that interventions grounded in a clear theoretical framework are associated with improved sexual risk outcomes and intervention efficacy (DiClemente et al., 2008; Schaalma et al., 2004). Health promotion efforts whose design and implementation are clearly guided by an underlying theory or theories are useful in that, when effective, they provide a clear outline of conceptual factors that are effective in changing the targeted behaviour. These conceptual factors can then be adapted to different populations in ways that preserve the theoretical and conceptual focus while allowing for culturally competent implementation of those concepts. Further, by testing clearly delineated concepts in a theoretical framework, researchers can pinpoint the specific elements that are effective in producing behaviour change. For example, research utilising the information-motivation-behavior model demonstrates the importance of motivation in changing behaviour and maintaining that behaviour change (Kalichman et al., 2008). Responding to this evidence, interventions are increasingly utilising motivational enhancement therapy and motivational interviewing to effect behaviour change, with highly promising results across behaviour goals and populations (Hettema et al., 2005).

An example

To illustrate the four critical components, we highlight one of the first behavioural interventions developed for HIV-positive persons and their HIV-negative partners (Parsons et al., 2000). This intervention was based on the transtheoretical model of stages of change (theoretically grounded), in which activities were developed to assist HIV-positive men with haemo-

philia across different stages of readiness to change, to prevent the transmission of HIV to their female partners. The intervention focused not only on condom use, but also on abstinence (comprehensive sexuality education and information). Several activities were specifically designed to help participants eroticise condom use as well as consider non-penetrative forms of sexual activity and pleasure (incorporating pleasure) which did not place their partners at risk of HIV. The intervention was developed based on considerable formative research (qualitative and quantitative) with members of the target population, taking into account unique cultural issues and opportunities for adaptation to ensure sensitivity to differences (cultural competency). The intervention was shown to be effective in reducing sexual risk behaviours and maintaining sexual safety, thus demonstrating the usefulness of integrating these four components into interventions to promote sexual health.

Conclusions

This chapter has focused on an examination of various definitions of sexual health, models of sexual health, sexual dysfunction and dissatisfaction, and pleasure and intimacy. In presenting sexual health as a relevant component of health psychology, we felt it more appropriate to address these areas, rather than focus on more of the negative aspects of sexuality such as HIV/STIs, unwanted pregnancy and sexual risk practices. Health promotion efforts need to recognise that humans are motivated to engage in sexual behaviours for a variety of reasons, and efforts should be culturally competent, emphasise the pleasurable aspects of sex and sexuality, provide comprehensive information and education, and be theoretically based whenever possible. We urge health psychologists to move beyond a disease-based (i.e., HIV/STIs) focus on sexual health, and to turn their attention to broader aspects of what makes a person sexually healthy – their ability to experience pleasure and intimacy and to be sexually satisfied. Certainly sexual risk behaviours which can compromise a person's overall health are important and must be examined as well, but this cannot come at the expense of research and clinical work around healthy sexuality.

Discussion Points

1 In what ways are the two sexual health models presented different and similar?
2 What are the inherent difficulties in defining and studying sexual dysfunctions and disorders?
3 What are the roles of pleasure and intimacy in a broader conceptualisation of sexual health?

4 What are the components with known efficacy for improving sexual health in health promotion efforts?
5 Why is it important for health promotion efforts to be theoretically grounded?

Further Reading

Robinson, B.B., Bockting, W.O., Rosser, B.R., Miner, M. & Coleman, E. (2002). The sexual health model: Application of a sexological approach to HIV prevention. *Health Education Research, 17*, 43–57.

Tepper, M.S. & Owens, A.F. (Eds) (2007). *Sexual health.* Westport, CT: Praeger.

Tolman, D.L., Striepe, M.I. & Harmon, T. (2003). Gender matters: Constructing a model of adolescent sexual health. *Journal of Sex Research, 40*, 4–12.

References

Amaro, H. (1995). Love, sex, and power: Considering women's realities in HIV prevention. *American Psychologist, 50*, 437–447.

Anderson, L.M., Scrimshaw, S.C., Fullilove, M.T., Fielding, J.E. & Normand, J. (2003). Culturally competent healthcare systems. A systematic review. *American Journal of Preventive Medicine, 24*, 68–79.

American Psychological Association (2000). *Diagnostic and statistical manual of mental disorders.* Washington, DC: American Psychological Association.

Balon, R., Segraves, R.T. & Clayton, A. (2007). Issues for DSM-V: Sexual dysfunction, disorder, or variation along normal distribution: Toward rethinking DSM criteria of sexual dysfunctions. *American Journal of Psychiatry, 164*, 198–200.

Beck, A., Majumdar, A., Estcourt, C. & Petrak, J. (2005). 'We don't really have cause to discuss these things, they don't affect us': A collaborative model for developing culturally appropriate sexual health services with the Bangladeshi community of Tower Hamlets. *Sexually Transmitted Infection, 81*, 158–162.

Bowen, A.M. & Trotter, R. II (1995). HIV risk in intravenous drug users and crack cocaine smokers: Predicting stage of change for condom use. *Journal of Consulting and Clinical Psychology, 63*, 238–248.

Boyle, P. (1999). Epidemiology of erectile dysfunction. In C. Carsons, R. Kirby & I. Goldstein (Ed.) *Textbook of erectile dysfunction* (pp.15–24). Oxford: Isis Medical Media.

Bronfenbrenner, U. (1977). Doing your own thing – our undoing. *Child Psychiatry & Human Development, 8*, 3–10.

Bronfenbrenner, U. (1979). *The ecology of human development: Experiments by nature and design.* Cambridge, MA: Harvard University Press.

Department of Health, UK (2001). *The National Strategy for Sexual Health and HIV.* Retrieved 12 February 2009 from www.dh.gov.uk/en/Publichealth/Healthimprovement/Sexualhealth/Sexualhealthgeneralinformation/DH_4002168.

Department of Health and Human Services, US (2001). *The Surgeon General's call to action to promote sexual health and responsible sexual behavior.* Rockville, MD: US Department of Health and Human Services.

Derogatis, L.R. & Burnett, A.L. (2008). The epidemiology of sexual dysfunctions. *Journal of Sexual Medicine, 5*, 289–300.

DiClemente, R.J., Crittenden, C.P., Rose, E., Sales, J.M., Wingood, G.M., Crosby, R.A. *et al.* (2008). Psychosocial predictors of HIV-associated sexual behaviors and the efficacy of prevention interventions in adolescents at-risk for HIV infection: What works and what doesn't work? *Psychosomatic Medicine, 70*, 598–605.

Dunn, K.M., Jordan, K., Croft, P.R. & Assendelft, W.J. (2002). Systematic review of sexual problems: Epidemiology and methodology. *Journal of Sex and Marital Therapy, 28*, 399–422.

Fawole, I.O., Asuzu, M.C., Oduntan, S.O. & Brieger, W.R. (1999). A school-based AIDS education programme for secondary school students in Nigeria: A review of effectiveness. *Health Education Research, 14*, 675–683.

Fisher, J.D., Fisher, W.A., Bryan, A.D. & Misovich, S.J. (2002). Information-motivation-behavioral skills model-based HIV risk behavior change intervention for inner-city high school youth. *Health Psychology, 21*, 177–186.

Giami, A. (2002). Sexual health: The emergence, development, and diversity of a concept. *Annual Review of Sex Research, 13*, 1–35.

Hatfield, E. & Rapson, R. L. (2007). Love and sexual health. In M.S. Tepper & A.F. Owens (Eds.) *Sexual health.* Westport, CT: Praeger.

Hayes, R.D., Bennett, C.M., Fairley, C.K. & Dennerstein, L. (2006). What can prevalence studies tell us about female sexual difficulty and dysfunction? *Journal of Sexual Medicine, 3*, 589–595.

Hettema, J., Steele, J. & Miller, W.R. (2005). Motivational interviewing. *Annual Review of Clinical Psychology, 1*, 91–111.

Higgins, J.A. & Hirsch, J.S. (2007). The pleasure deficit: Revisiting the 'sexuality connection' in reproductive health. *Perspectives in Sexual and Reproductive Health, 39*, 240–247.

Higgins, J.A. & Hirsch, J.S. (2008). Pleasure, power, and inequality: Incorporating sexuality into research on contraceptive use. *American Journal of Public Health, 98*, 1803–1813.

Higgins, J.A., Hirsch, J.S. & Trussell, J. (2008). Pleasure, prophylaxis and procreation: A qualitative analysis of intermittent contraceptive use and unintended pregnancy. *Perspectives in Sexual and Reproductive Health, 40*, 130–137.

Hiltabiddle, S.J. (1996). Adolescent condom use, the health belief model, and the prevention of sexually transmitted disease. *Journal of Obstetric, Gynecologic, & Neonatal Nursing, 25*, 61–66.

Holland, J., Ramazanoglu, C., Scott, S., Sharpe, S. & Thomson, R. (1992). Risk, power and the possibility of pleasure: Young women and safer sex. *AIDS Care, 4*, 273–283.

Hoyt, H.H. & Broom, B.L. (2002). School-based teen pregnancy prevention programs: A review of the literature. *Journal of School Nursing, 18*, 11–17.

Ickovics, J.R., Thayaparan, B. & Ethier, K.A. (2001). Women and AIDS: A contextual analysis. In A. Baum, T. A. Revenson & J. E. Singer (Eds.) *Handbook of health psychology* (pp. 817–839). Mahwah, NJ: Lawrence Erlbaum.

Jemmott, J.B., III & Jemmott, L.S. (2000). HIV risk reduction behavioral interventions with heterosexual adolescents. *AIDS, 14*, S40–S52.

Kalichman, S.C., Kelly, J.A., Hunter, T.L., Murphy, D.A. & Tyler, R. (1993). Culturally tailored HIV-AIDS risk-reduction messages targeted to African-American urban women: Impact on risk sensitization and risk reduction. *Journal of Consulting and Clinical Psychology, 61*, 291–295.

Kalichman, S.C., Picciano, J.F. & Roffman, R.A. (2008). Motivation to reduce HIV risk behaviors in the context of the Information, Motivation, and Behavioral Skills (IMB) model of HIV prevention. *Journal of Health Psychology, 13*, 680–689.

Kalichman, S.C., Rompa, D., DiFonzo, K., Simpson, D., Austin, J., Luke, W. *et al.* (2001). HIV treatment adherence in women living with HIV/AIDS: Research based on the Information-Motivation-Behavioral Skills model of health behavior. *Journal of the Association of Nurses in AIDS Care, 12*, 58–67.

Kohler, P.K., Manhart, L.E. & Lafferty, W.E. (2008). Abstinence-only and comprehensive sex education and the initiation of sexual activity and teen pregnancy. *Journal of Adolescent Health, 42*, 344–351.

Laumann, E.O., Paik, A. & Rosen, R.C. (1999). Sexual dysfunction in the United States: Prevalence and predictors. *Journal of the American Medical Association, 281*, 537–544.

Lewin, K. (1951/1972). *Field theory for the behavioral sciences.* Chicago: University of Chicago Press.

Lewis, R.W., Fugl-Meyer, K.S., Bosch, R., Fugl-Meyer, A.R., Laumann, E.O., Lizza, E. *et al.* (2004). Epidemiology/risk factors of sexual dysfunction. *Journal of Sexual Medicine, 1*, 35–39.

Mahoney, C.A., Thombs, D.L. & Ford, O.J. (1995). Health belief and self-efficacy models: Their utility in explaining college student condom use. *AIDS Education and Prevention, 7*, 32–49.

Masters, W.H. & Johnson, V. E. (1966). *Human sexual response.* Boston: Little Brown.

Meston, C.M. & Buss, D.M. (2007). Why humans have sex. *Archives of Sexual Behavior, 36*, 477–507.

Montgomery, C.M., Lees, S., Stadler, J., Morar, N.S., Ssali, A., Mwanza, B. *et al.* (2008). The role of partnership dynamics in determining the acceptability of condoms and microbicides. *AIDS Care, 20*, 733–740.

Munoz-Silva, A., Sanchez-Garcia, M., Nunes, C. & Martins, A. (2007). Gender differences in condom use prediction with Theory of Reasoned Action and Planned Behaviour: The role of self-efficacy and control. *AIDS Care, 19*, 1177–1181.

Nicolosi, A., Laumann, E.O., Glasser, D.B., Brock, G., King, R. & Gingell, C. (2006). Sexual activity, sexual disorders and associated help-seeking behavior among mature adults in five Anglophone countries from the Global

Survey of Sexual Attitudes and Behaviors (GSSAB). *Journal of Sex and Marital Therapy, 32*, 331–342.

Nicolosi, A., Laumann, E.O., Glasser, D.B., Moreira, E.D., Jr., Paik, A. & Gingell, C. (2004). Sexual behavior and sexual dysfunctions after age 40: The global study of sexual attitudes and behaviors. *Urology, 64*, 991–997.

Parsons, J.T., Huszti, H.C., Crudder, S.O., Rich, L. & Mendoza, J. (2000). Maintenance of safer sexual behaviours: Evaluation of a theory-based intervention for HIV seropositive men with haemophilia and their female partners. *Haemophilia, 6*(3), 181–190.

Philpott, A., Knerr, W. & Boydell, V. (2006). Pleasure and prevention: When good sex is safer sex. *Reproductive Health Matters, 14*, 23–31.

Prochaska, J.O. (1994). The transtheoretical model of change and HIV prevention: A review. *Health Education Quarterly, 21*, 471–486.

Rahamefy, O.H., Rivard, M., Ravaoarinoro, M., Ranaivoharisoa, L., Rasamindrakotroka, A.J. & Morisset, R. (2008). Sexual behaviour and condom use among university students in Madagascar. *Journal of Social Aspects of HIV/AIDS Research Alliance, 5*, 28–35.

Revenson, T.A. (1990). All other things are not equal: An ecological approach to personality and disease. In H.S. Friedman (Ed.) *Personality and disease* (pp. 65–94). New York: Wiley.

Robinson, B.B., Bockting, W.O., Rosser, B.R., Miner, M. & Coleman, E. (2002). The Sexual Health Model: Application of a sexological approach to HIV prevention. *Health Education Research, 17*, 43–57.

Rosen, R.C., Fisher, W.A., Eardley, I., Niederberger, C., Nadel, A. & Sand, M. (2004). The Multinational Men's Attitudes to Life Events and Sexuality (MALES) study: I. Prevalence of erectile dysfunction and related health concerns in the general population. *Current Medical Research and Opinion, 20*, 607–617.

Schaalma, H., Abraham, C., Gillmore, M.R. & Kok, G. (2004). Sex education as health promotion: What does it take? *Archives of Sexual Behavior, 33*, 259–269.

Slowinski, J. (2007). Sexual problems and dysfunctions in men. In M.S. Tepper & A.F. Owens (Eds.) *Sexual health* (Vol. 4, pp. 1–14). Westport, CT: Praeger.

Terry, D.H., Gallois, C. & McCamish, M. (1993). *The theory of reasoned action*. New York: Pergamon.

Tolman, D.L. (1999). Femininity as a barrier to positive sexual health for adolescent girls. *Journal of the American Medical Women's Association, 54*, 133–138.

Tolman, D.L., Striepe, M.I. & Harmon, T. (2003). Gender matters: Constructing a model of adolescent sexual health. *Journal of Sex Research, 40*, 4–12.

UNAIDS & World Health Organization (2007). *AIDS epidemic update*. Retrieved 14 February 2009 from www.unaids.org/en/KnowledgeCentre/HIVData/Epi Update/EpiUpdArchive/2007/default.asp.

Working Group for a New View of Women's Sexual Problems (2001). A new view of women's sexual problems. In E.T. Kaschak (Ed.) *A new view of women's sexual problems*. New York: Haworth Press.

Whipple, B., Knowles, J. & Davis, J. (2003). *The health benefits of sexual expression*. New York: Planned Parenthood Federation of America.

World Health Organization (1992). *Reproductive health: A key to a brighter future* (Bienniel Report). Geneva: World Health Organization.

World Health Organization (2002). *Gender and reproductive rights, glossary, sexual health*. Retrieved 13 February 2009 from www.who.int/reproductive-health/gender/glossary.html.

World Health Organization (2009). *Adolescent pregnancy: The facts*. Retrieved 14 February 2009 from www.who.int/making_pregnancy_safer/topics/adolescent_pregnancy/en/index.html.

Part II

Theoretical Approaches
to Health Behaviour Change

8

Interventions to Change Health-Related Behaviour Patterns

Charles Abraham

Chapter Outline

This chapter introduces a framework for intervention design and evaluation based on intervention mapping (Bartholomew *et al.*, 2006), the *information-motivation-behavioral skills* model (Fisher & Fisher, 1992), an integrative model of motivation (Fishbein *et al.*, 2001) and the RE-AIM criteria for external validity of intervention evaluations (Glasgow *et al.*, 2002). The chapter outlines key stages in the development of effective behaviour change interventions and highlights important considerations at each stage.

Key Concepts

Adoption and implementation of behavioural interventions
Behaviour change techniques
Behaviour patterns
Behavioural skills
Change objectives
Change processes
Evaluation of interventions
Information
Intervention design planning
Motivation
Multiple determinants

Targeting Health-Related Patterns of Behaviour

Patterns of individual behaviour contribute substantially to the major causes of premature death. In developed countries, these include cardiovascular disease (e.g. heart attacks and stroke), cancers (including lung cancer) and respiratory diseases. There is consistent evidence that behaviour patterns such as not smoking, engaging in regular physical activity, not overeating, eating vegetables and only consuming alcohol moderately are related to reduced morbidity and mortality (Belloc & Breslow, 1972; Khaw et al., 2008).

Health and longevity are also determined by many other factors including genetics, nutrition, family environment, work environments and stress (cf. Abraham et al., 2008). Social legislation, including the distribution of wealth within countries predicts longevity (Alder et al., 1994; Wilkinson, 1997). The risks associated with health-related behaviour patterns may be exacerbated by these other factors. For example, morbidity and mortality are more strongly associated with smoking and drinking for those with lower socioeconomic status (Hein et al., 1992; Hemmingsson et al., 1998). Consequently, effective health promotion policies need to consider changes at individual, organisational, community, national and international levels and to focus on people's control of their everyday lives, their access to resources as well as vested interests that work against adoption of health-promoting lifestyles. Within this context, there are strong arguments for targeting individual health-related behaviour patterns. For example, it has been estimated that alcohol consumption costs the UK economy £7 billion each year when indirect costs to families and employers are included. Overweight and obesity currently cost approximately the same but these costs are forecast to rise steeply. Indeed, the effectiveness and economic viability of health services in developed countries depends critically on public engagement in health care and maintenance (Wanless, 2002). Therefore, interventions which promote healthy lifestyles, enhance quality of life for those with long-term illness and reduce health service demand have the potential to make substantial differences to public health and to the viability of health services (Friedman et al., 1995).

An Intervention Mapping Approach to Intervention Planning

Careful planning is essential for the development and implementation of effective behaviour change interventions. One useful guide to this process entitled 'intervention mapping' (IM) has been provided by Bartholomew et al. (2006). IM is a sophisticated blueprint for intervention planning from initial design, through implementation to evaluation (see Kok et al., 2004 for a brief introduction and Tortolero et al., 2005 for an example of how this works in practice). IM highlights six key planning stages which can be briefly characterised as follows.

The first stage is *needs assessment*. This involves ascertaining whether, and how, a target group needs to change and specifying precisely the target behaviour/s that need to be changed. If this process is not completed then unneeded interventions or interventions that do not adequately or realistically target key behaviours may be wastefully developed and implemented. For example, consider the problems of unwanted teenage pregnancy and the spread of sexually transmitted infections (STIs) among teenagers. The key behaviour in these cases is unprotected teenage sexual intercourse. This does not, in itself, clarify what the needs of any particular teenage population are. Should health promoters discourage teenage sex or promote protected intercourse (Schaalma et al., 2004)? Is the problem linked to school or community-based norms? Are poverty and gender empowerment important elements? Is condom and emergency contraception accessibility relevant? Is the problem due to a failure to use already-existing services? Who needs to change? For example, is the target group all teenagers of a particular age, a small sub-group of teenagers, a small sub-group of parents and/or health-care practitioners and youth workers? Consideration of the societal and local context is critical to understanding the needs of a particular target group and, thereby, what kind of behaviour change intervention is likely to effectively improve the health and quality of life of that group. Careful needs assessment and specificity of targeting is critical to effective intervention (see Bartholomew et al., 2006, for details).

The second stage involves *setting change objectives*. This includes specifying precisely what behaviour changes the intervention is designed to induce and identifying potentially modifiable determinants of those behaviours such as key beliefs. For example, an intervention designed to promote condom use amongst sexually active teenagers may first focus on changing norms in relation to condom carrying at social events. In this case a key determinant of behaviour (perceived norms) and a crucial preparatory behaviour (condom carrying) have been identified.

The third stage involves *identifying change processes and effective change techniques*, that is, linking determinants and change mechanisms to a set of change techniques most likely to effectively change the target behaviour. This is a critical aspect of intervention design and it entails development of a good model of the processes which regulate behaviour and are involved in behaviour change. So, for example, if norms are targeted as a crucial determinant, providing information about teenagers' views and behaviours based on reliable research is one technique that can be used to change norms. Another approach would be to create role models and use opinion leaders to influence norms.

The fourth stage involves the translation of this theoretical model of determinants and change techniques into a *practical plan*. This will involve reviewing materials and methods (videos, leaflets, lesson plans, etc.) to implement the selected change techniques in the target setting with the target recipients. It is important to consult with potential recipients about materials (e.g. their appropriateness and attractiveness) and to pre-test materials, that is, to run small-scale experiments to see if exposure to the intervention materials has any effect on small groups of representative participants, prior to investing in the intervention as a whole. For example, Lemieux *et al.* (2008) designed, implemented and evaluated an innovated school-based intervention to reduce unprotected teenage sexual intercourse. They recruited musically talented opinion leaders to write, record and distribute music designed to prompt motivation, behavioural skills and action that would prevent the transmission of sexually transmitted infections (including HIV) in urban secondary schools. The intervention successfully promoted protective norms and behaviours.

Once the materials are selected and manuals have been written to describe in detail how the intervention should be delivered then the intervention is ready for the fifth stage, namely, *adoption and implementation*. This involves identifying those who will adopt and use the intervention (e.g. teachers in schools or worksite managers), negotiating its use with them and producing the intervention in a manner that facilitates accurate implementation (e.g. by providing training courses). It is crucial that those responsible for adoption of the intervention (head teachers, managers, mothers, teenagers, etc.) are persuaded at this stage. Consequently, it is prudent to involve respected opinion-leading representatives of this group in intervention development from stage 3 onwards. An opinion-leading 'champion', willing to persuade her peer group to adopt an intervention, can sometimes promote rolling adoption rather than rejection. Potentially effective interventions have no impact if they are not adopted!

The sixth and last stage is *evaluation*. This involves conducting research to discover whether the intervention worked, how well it worked and how it worked. This in turn may lead back to needs assessment to consider how the intervention can be developed or added to further meet the needs of the target group.

Identifying Behavioural Determinants: Information, Motivation and Behavioural Skills

In order to complete stages 2 and 3 of the intervention planning process described above, that is, *setting change objectives* and *identifying change processes and effective change techniques*, health promoters need to understand the determinants and causal processes which prompt and regulate the behaviours and behaviour change they hope to promote. A theoretical understanding of these regulatory processes provides insights into what type of intervention is most likely to be effective in changing behaviour.

The *information-motivation-behavioral skills* model (IMB; Fisher & Fisher, 1992; Fisher *et al.*, 2002, see Figure 8.1) provides a useful starting point for these phases of intervention design. For example the IMB provided the basis for the design of the music-based school intervention referred to above (Lemieux *et al.*, 2008). IMB proposes

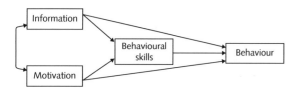

Figure 8.1　The information-motivation-behavioral skills model
Source: Fisher, J.D. & Fisher. W.A. (1992). Changing AIDS-risk behavior. *Psychological Bulletin, 111,* 455–471.

that, having identified key behaviours that they wish to promote among a specified target group, health promoters should initially ask themselves, 'What is missing in the target population that explains why these behaviours are not already being performed?' Do they lack key information? Is there a general lack of motivation? Alternatively, is the key problem a lack of behavioural skills required to translate informed motivation into action? In answering these questions it is critical to precisely define the target group – see the needs assessment stage outlined above. For example, having identified a low socioeconomic status group of teenagers as at risk of unwanted pregnancy and STIs – are they unaware of the risks they face, or are key drivers of motivation such as attitudes and norms absent or are forgetfulness and low goal priority key determinants of unprotected sex? Establishing whether the (precisely defined) target group lacks behaviour-relevant information, whether the key determinants of motivation are in place and whether the target group lacks any skills required to translate motivation into behaviour often necessitates preliminary research referred to as 'elicitation research'.

Information

If information provision is to influence action it must be relevant and readily accessible at the point of decision making. Information provision campaigns need to provide the information that the target group requires in a format that is attractive and accessible. They also need to provide relevant information that is accessible at key decision-making points. For example, even when packaged food includes comprehensive nutritional information, consumers may not know how much exercise they have to take to use the calories in a particular food choice. For example, how much exercise

would you have to do to burn off the calories in a cup of coffee? A woman weighing 11 stone walking somewhat faster than average (at 3.5 miles an hour) would need 45 minutes to burn off the 200 calories in a whole milk latte and 30 minutes to burn off the 120 calories in a skimmed milk latte (NHS Choices website). Imagine that all packaged foods and all restaurant meals were labelled with the number of minutes it would take the average adult to walk off the calories they include (e.g. 45 for a latte). Would this make a difference to food purchase and consumption decisions and so to eating patterns? If so, then a key factor in the so-called 'obesity epidemic' is a lack of readily accessible information about the calorie content of food at key decision-making points. Of course, while information about calorie content is critical to weight regulation, it is not the only information relevant to food choices and simple, readily accessible, health-related information symbols such as red (unhealthy), orange (neither healthy or unhealthy) or green (healthy) may influence consumer food purchases. The general point here is that making action-relevant information available at the point of decision making is a critical first step towards empowering people to make health-enhancing choices.

Motivation

Even when good information is readily available, people may not be motivated to change their behaviour. There are many theories modelling components of motivation (see Conner & Norman, 2005). A useful integration of many of these theories was undertaken by Fishbein *et al.* (2001) who reported on a workshop organised by the US National Institute of Mental Health in response to the need to promote HIV-preventive behaviours. The workshop sought to integrate insights from social cognitive theory (Bandura, 1999), the health belief model (Becker *et al.*, 1997), the theories of reasoned action and planned behaviour (Ajzen, 1991; Fishbein & Ajzen, 1975) and the theory of interpersonal behaviour (Triandis, 1977). Three prerequisites of action were identified:

1　a strong *intention*;
2　the necessary *skills* to perform the behaviour; and
3　an absence of *environmental constraints* that could prevent the behaviour.

These echo IMB in that they specify motivation (that is, intention) and behavioural skills. The model extends IMB by highlighting that, for some behaviours, it is not a lack of information, motivation or behavioural skills that prevents action but rather the way in which the environment impacts on motivation or the feasibility of action. What is relevant in the environment will vary according to the target behaviour. For example, the amount of money invested in advertising may be an important determinant of behaviour. Consequently, advertising bans (e.g. for tobacco) can be an effective behaviour change intervention. Alternatively, physical architecture may impede or facilitate health-related behaviours. For example, if people are to be encouraged to wash their hands then readily available, attractive hand-washing facilities and fast hand-drying options need to be available. Thus elicitation research must examine carefully various environmental prompts and barriers to the target behaviour prior to intervention design.

The Fishbein et al. (2001) model also provides a useful list of cognitions that are likely to enhance and sustain motivation (or intention). Motivation is likely to be strengthened when a person:

1 perceives the advantages (or benefits) of performing the behaviour to outweigh the perceived disadvantages (or costs);
2 perceives the social (normative) pressure (i.e. subjective and descriptive norms) to perform the behaviour to be greater than that not to perform the behaviour;
3 believes that the behaviour is consistent with his or her self-image;
4 anticipates the emotional reaction to performing the behaviour to be more positive than negative; and
5 has high levels of self-efficacy.

Further discussion of how these motivation components and the theories from which they are derived can be integrated to provide a framework for understanding behavioural motivation is provided by Abraham et al. (1998). However, each of these components could become the primary target of a behaviour change intervention if, first, a motivational deficit was identified among the target population through elici-

tation research and, second, this particular component was found to be the key deficit. For example, as we noted previously, teenage norms regarding condom carrying and use may be a critical determinant of teenage STI transmission (see point 2 above). Alternatively, if a campaign seeks to change the perceived benefits and costs of a behaviour (e.g. condom use) then intervention materials may use persuasive communication tailored to achieve this end (see point 1 above) – or to change the image of those seen to engage in this behaviour (see point 3 above). In each case the choice of behavioural change technique will depend on the motivational element found to be important and lacking in the target population.

A popular approach to enhancing motivation is to use fear appeals. However, perceived threat and fear responses often do not prompt behaviour change (e.g. Albarracín et al., 2005). For example, if people are not persuaded that the threat is personally relevant this may undermine intervention ('if the threat is not relevant to me why bother to take precautions?'). In addition, if people have low self-efficacy in relation to the recommended action they may protect themselves psychologically through defensive cognitive responses. When this happens, recipients of fear appeals may dismiss the message as untrustworthy – rejecting it altogether – or reject its relevance to them (Good & Abraham, 2008). Thus fear appeals should be used cautiously (Ruiter et al., 2001) and only when prior research demonstrates that low perceived susceptibility and susceptibility are important predictors of motivation amongst the target population. When employed, they should combine strong persuasive threat information with strong self-efficacy-enhancing messages (Witte & Allen, 2000).

Self efficacy (SE – see point 5 above), that is, the belief that one can successfully perform a given behaviour in a specified context, is a critical determinant of motivation and action. People rarely persist with goals they do not feel they can achieve. Those who believe they can succeed set themselves more challenging goals. They exert more effort, use more flexible problem-solving strategies and are more persistent *because* they believe they will eventually succeed. High SE also minimises stress which enhances skilled performance. Moreover, high SE facilitates concentration on the task rather than concerns about personal deficiencies or exaggeration of task demands. This minimises anxiety during performance and, thereby reduces the longer term effects of stress on cardiovascular and immune functioning (Bandura, 1997, 1999). Thus self-efficacy boosts motivation and behavioural skills and is often a critical prerequisite to effective behaviour change. SE can refer to distinct types of confidence. For example, Schwarzer (2008) distinguishes between *action* SE (believing one can succeed in completing a planned behaviour), *maintenance* SE (believing one can maintain the action over time) and *recovery* SE (believing one can adopt the behaviour again after a relapse).

Bandura (1997) identifies four main approaches to enhancing self-efficacy. First, *mastery experiences* (i.e. experience of successfully performing the behaviour) give people confidence that they can tackle new tasks because they know they have previously succeeded with similar challenges. This recommends that teachers and trainers guide learners towards success by identifying manageable tasks and only increasing difficulty as confidence and skill grow, that is by use of graded tasks. Second, *observation of others' success*, especially others like ourselves or those who we aspire to be like. Positive role models (that is, observation of successful others) can be SE-enhancing. Moreover, contrasts between current self and desired or ideal self can be motivating, that is, negative-self models combined with realistic goal-setting opportunities (Oettingen, 1996). Third, when direct experience and modelling are not available, SE can be enhanced through *verbal persuasion*. People can be persuaded by arguments demonstrating that others (like them) are successful in meeting challenges similar to their own (thereby changing descriptive norms) as well as persuasion highlighting the person's own skills, and past success. Finally, our own *physiological reactions* and our interpretations of these reactions affects SE. Stress and anxiety during performance can undermine SE so that interventions designed to reduce anxiety and encourage reinterpretation of arousal (as normal) may enhance SE and facilitate skilled performance.

Behavioural skills

Behaviour change may necessitate a variety of skills which people in the target group may or may not have already developed. It may be useful to think about three groups of prerequisite skills. Self-regulatory skills are cognitive skills which, for example, help people consider longer term consequences of current action, evaluate their current behaviour, set new goals, including graded tasks, prioritise goals in the face of other demands, plan action before and during goal-relevant experiences and prompt exertion of appropriate effort when opportunities present themselves. For example, implementation intention formation, refers to the formation of if-then plans in which the 'if' specifies a context or environmental prompt and the 'then' specifies the targeted behaviour (Sheeran et al., 2005). When helping people develop such skills, initial teaching may involve conscious rehearsal of the skill followed by practice over time with a view to longer term automatic initiation of self-regulatory processes. For example, Schinke and Gordon (1992) describe a culturally specific intervention including a self-completion book using comic strip characters and rap music verse to encourage effective safer sex regulation amongst black teenagers. The aim was to develop self-monitoring and planning skills as well as verbal resources which can be used to control and disrupt scripted interaction that could lead to unprotected sex.

Motor skills are also important to adoption of health-related behaviours. For example, correct condom use depends upon a basic understanding of infection control as well as the manual skills involved in opening and using a condom correctly. Certain medication regimes require patients to learn to use devices such as inhalers or needles and patients and medical staff may need instruction in apparently simple skills such as hand washing as part of infection control in hospitals (Pittet et al., 2000). Thus, sometimes, effective behaviour change intervention will focus on routinising apparently simple manual skills.

Another important group of skills is that required to seek others' support for change. For example, the skills to negotiate condom use with a reluctant partner or to insist on drinking non-alcoholic drinks in a bar or to refuse to eat traditional but unhealthy foods. The social skills required are likely to be determined by the target behaviour and the social resources available to individuals planning change. However, assertiveness training (that is, being able to express one's own wants and needs in an honest and non-aggressive manner) and negotiation skills are often prerequisite to managing interactions which arise when individuals begin to change their behaviour.

Selecting behaviour change techniques

Having modelled behavioural determinants that are prerequisite to the target behaviour and also missing in the targeted intervention recipients, intervention designers, working in stage 3, need to decide how to change or promote those determinants. In other words, they need to select behaviour change techniques (BCTs) that are likely to be most effective in promoting the target behaviour with the target recipients. Sometimes it is clear which techniques are the most likely candidates. For example, if recipients lack motor skills then behaviour-specific skill training programmes need to be developed. In each case behaviour change techniques such as information provision, instruction and demonstration may be necessary and these can be provided in face-to-face interaction or in carefully prepared leaflets (e.g. Kools *et al.*, 2006).

A wide range of BCTs are available and a crucial element of stage 3 planning is to review the relevant literature in relation to the target behaviour. A list of 26 distinct BCTs that have been reliably identified across a range of behaviour change interventions has been provided by Abraham and Michie (2008) and extended by Abraham *et al.* (2010). This list includes techniques designed to enhance information, change aspects of motivation, enhance self-regulatory skills including techniques derived from operant conditioning theory (Skinner, 1938) as well as sets of techniques frequently used together, for example, relapse prevention (Marlatt & Donovan, 2005), stress management, motivational interviewing (Rollnick & Miller, 1995) and time management. As an example, the BCT 'prompt self-monitoring of behaviour' was defined as: 'The person is asked to keep a record of specified behaviour/s. This could e.g., take the form of a diary or completing a questionnaire about their behaviour' (Abraham & Michie, 2008).

In a systematic review of interventions designed to promote physical activity and/or healthy eating, Michie *et al.* (2009) found that different intervention designers had selected different BCTs even when targeting very similar behaviours amongst very similar populations. Drawing upon the taxonomy of BCTs developed by Abraham and Michie (2008) and Carver and Scheier's (1981) control theory, Michie *et al.* (2009) examined whether BCT content made a difference to intervention effectiveness. It was hypothesised, on the basis of control theory, that interventions which targeted self-regulatory skills by including (i) prompting intention formation or goal setting; (ii) specifying goals in relation to particular contextualised actions; (iii) self-monitoring of behaviour; (iv) feedback on performance; and (v) reviewing previously set goals would be most effective. Controlling for other intervention characteristics using meta regression, the researchers found that interventions including self-monitoring and at least one of four other self-regulatory techniques were, on average, twice as effective as interventions not including these techniques in interventions designed to promote both physical activity and healthy eating. Thus choice of BCT can make a substantial difference to interventions' effectiveness and BCT selection should be based on identification of missing behavioural determinants.

To assess the impact of BCT inclusion on intervention effectiveness, Webb and Sheeran (2006) used meta-analysis to calculate the average effectiveness of interventions that included various BCTs. The interventions including information provision, persuasive communication, goal setting, modelling and skill training yielded small-to-medium effects on behaviour change (with *d*s around 0.3). Effects of this size are typical of behaviour change interventions and if achieved with populations, can produce worthwhile effects on public health (see Rose, 1992). The strongest effects were observed for interventions including the use of incentives and social support or pressure (with *d*s between 0.5 and 0.6). However, whether information provision about local group norms, or persuasive communication designed to change perceptions of the consequences of action (that is, change attitudes) or group-level instruction and demonstration (designed to enhance SE and behavioural skills) are most appropriate BCTs depends on the results of elicitation research and the outcomes of analyses completed in IM-based stages 1–3. It is important to note that the synergistic impact of combinations of BCTs in multi-technique interventions and other intervention characteristics could confound such analyses. Nonetheless the results are interesting. Future work is needed to discover which BCTs are effective for producing change in different behaviours with different populations.

Designing useful and sustainable interventions

Stage 5 of the intervention planning process outlined above refers to the adoption and implementation of behaviour change interventions. Interventions are adopted by intended users of the intervention when they are perceived to be useful, easy to implement, sustainable and affordable in the setting in which they have been tested. Glasgow *et al.* (2002) and Green and Glasgow (2006) discuss how we can assess these intervention features using the RE-AIM (reach, effectiveness, adoption, implementation and maintenance) framework.

Reach refers to how many of the target population were involved in an evaluation of an intervention and how representative they were. For example, if an intervention was evaluated using economically advantaged participants then questions would arise as to whether it would also be effective for economically less advantaged people. *Effectiveness* relates to the range of effects an intervention might have. For example, even if it changed behaviour, we would want to know whether it enhanced overall quality of life and whether it had any unintended consequences (e.g. did participants find it onerous or upsetting?) *Adoption* refers to whether the users (e.g. nurses or managers) are persuaded of the utility of the intervention. This is likely to depend on how easy it is implement, whether they or their clients like it and whether it is compatible with their other primary goals, including minimising cost. *Implementation* refers to the ease and feasibility of faithful delivery. If an intervention is complex, expensive or requires specialist training or teams of people to deliver it then it is less likely to be sustainable in real-world settings. *Maintenance* refers to the longer term sustainability of the intervention in real-world settings. For example, if a community does not have the resources to deliver an intervention then, no matter how efficacious, it will be dropped or changed over time. If the complexity of an intervention leads to it being changed or adapted then critical BCTs may be omitted so compromising effectiveness.

Unless these considerations are prioritised in stages 2, 3, and especially stage 4 (when practical intervention delivery procedures are developed) then potentially effective behaviour change interventions may never be widely implemented or may only be used for short periods, thereby, undermining their impact on health and quality of life. Although the RE-AIM criteria are particularly salient in stages 4 and 5 of the intervention development process, they need to be considered from the outset, that is from stage 2 (setting change objectives). For example, development of an intervention which is accurately based on identified information and motivational deficits in the target group and is found to be effective in changing these determinants may, nonetheless, have no health impact if it is not adopted because it requires resources that are unavailable in the local context. The RE-AIM criteria can be used to assess the degree to which an evaluation of a behaviour change intervention (i.e. IM stage 6) informs us about the likely utility and applicability of the intervention. These elements of intervention design and evaluation determine the external validity of an intervention study, that is, its relevance to behaviour change in practice.

Intervention Evaluation

As an important aspect of intervention adoption is confidence in the effectiveness of the intervention, rigorous, defensible evaluation is critical (IM stage 6). Evaluation involves comparison of outcomes between those who received the intervention and those who did not. This may involve a no-intervention control group or another intervention group (e.g. an active control group – as is the case when an intervention is compared to routine care) – or both. Typically post-intervention levels of outcome measures are compared, controlling for pre-intervention levels as we expect no difference between intervention and control groups at pre-intervention but a post-intervention improvement for the intervention group relative to the control group.

The internal validity of intervention evaluations, that is the extent to which they provide reliable estimates of the effectiveness of intervention, is dependent on a number of factors. The following are important.

First, the extent to which the design successfully controls for *confounding factors* (e.g., differences between control and intervention group participants or the variability of the effectiveness of routine care). Randomisation can control for potentially confounding variables but sometimes it is necessary to randomise at group level (e.g., school classes or doctors' surgeries), necessitating multilevel modelling to control for systematic biases that might exist between such groups. Second, the *statistical power* of the study. The number of participants in the intervention and control groups should be large enough to have a good chance to detect a pre-specified effect size. Third, use of *validated measures*, that is, measures of determinants and behaviour have been previously shown to be accurate and reliable. Fourth, intention to treat analysis may be important for interventions likely to suffer from high drop-out rates. For example, if 50 per cent of those in the intervention group drop out then, even if the intervention is very successful amongst the remaining 50 per cent (compared to no-intervention controls), the overall impact of this intervention may be limited. Intention-to-treat analysis involves retaining all randomised participants in the analyses and counting drop outs as showing no change.

It is important to be clear when designing evaluations what the main outcomes are. For example, in interventions designed to improve self-care among people with long-term illnesses one might want to examine outcomes such as quality of life, adherence to medication and use of health services. Alternatively, an intervention designed to decrease unprotected sexual intercourse among teenagers in schools could be powered so that the impact on area statistics relating to teenage pregnancy or STIs could be examined five years later. In addition, evaluations also need to assess psychological determinants assumed to be involved in the change process upon which the design is based. For example, if expected changes in such determinants occur in an effective intervention then the inclusion of these measures allows *mediation analyses* to be conducted, which test whether the hypothesised change mechanisms can account for the success of the intervention.

Interventions may be differentially successful for different groups (e.g. men versus women, older teenagers versus younger teenagers, patients with some conditions but not others etc.). Such *moderation analyses* can tell us for whom the intervention was effective. Anticipated moderation effects determine the number of participants required to achieve adequate power. For example, if men and women are to be compared as well as comparing intervention and control groups this may double the numbers needed in the evaluation study.

When an intervention is not effective, it is important to know why. Measures of targeted determinants of behaviour can be diagnostic in such cases. If the predicted impact on determinants (e.g. motivational measures) is not observed then the intervention did not work according to its design. Alternatively an intervention may fail even if it was capable of generating the predicted effects but was not delivered correctly (e.g. classes were not taught as described in the manual or participants did not attend to the intervention materials). To clarify this, a process evaluation is required. This involves examining whether delivery in practice matched delivery design. This may include interviewing those delivering and receiving the intervention, using surveys to assess their experience of the delivery and observing intervention groups to check for design fidelity in implementation.

Summary and Conclusions

Behaviour change interventions are an important component of effective health promotion. Intervention effectiveness depends on a clear understanding of the processes that regulate behaviour and behaviour change among the target population. Research-based insights must be applied within a structured planning process to develop and then evaluate, and finally disseminate and widely implement behaviour change interventions. Intervention mapping provides a helpful six- stage planning process which can be summarised as: (i) needs assessment; (ii) setting change objectives; (iii) identifying change processes and effective change techniques; (iv) developing a practical plan; (v) adoption and implementation; and, finally, (vi) evaluation. The information-motivation-behavioral skills model provides a useful basis for identifying what the key determinants of behaviour change are and many effective behaviour interventions have been based on this model (see http://www.chip.uconn. edu/int_res_int.htm for details).

Discussion Points

1   What are the dangers in focusing on behaviour change and ignoring the social, political and legal structures which shape health and quality of life?
2   How can behavioural scientists facilitate adoption of the IM planning process among health promoters faced with tight deadlines?
3   What skills do teams who design interventions to change behaviour need? See the UK National Institute for Health and Clinical Excellence guidance on behaviour change for one answer (www.nice.org.uk/guidance/PH6/Guidance/pdf/English).
4   What should behavioural scientists do when behavioural change agendas are dominated by political or religious values that run contrary to research evidence (see Schaalma *et al.*, 2004, for a discussion)?

Further Reading

Abraham, C., Conner, M., Jones, F. & O'Conner, D. (2008). *Health psychology*. London: Hodder (especially Chapters 8 and 9).

Abraham C., Kelly, M.P., West, R. & Michie, S. (2009). The UK National Institute for Health and Clinical Excellence (NICE) public health guidance on behaviour change: A brief introduction. *Psychology, Health & Medicine, 14*, 1–8.

Abraham, C. & Michie, S. (2008). A taxonomy of behavior change techniques used in interventions. *Health Psychology, 27*, 379–387.

Albarracín, D., Gillete, J.C., Earl, A.N., Glasman, L.R. & Durantini, M.R. (2005). A test of major assumptions about behavior change: A comprehensive look at the effects of passive and active HIV-prevention interventions since the beginning of the epidemic. *Psychological Bulletin, 131*, 856–897.

Bartholomew, L.K., Parcel, G.S., Kok, G. & Gottlieb, N.H. (2006). *Planning health promotion programs. An intervention mapping approach*. San Francisco: Jossey-Bass.

National Institute of Health and Clinical Excellence (2007) Behaviour change at population, community and individual levels (Public Health Guidance 6). London: NICE (www.nice.org.uk/guidance/PH6/Guidance/pdf/English).

References

Abraham, C., Conner, M., Jones, F. & O'Conner, D. (2008). *Health psychology*. London: Hodder.

Abraham C., Kelly, M.P., West, R. & Michie, S. (2009). The UK National Institute for Health and Clinical Excellence (NICE) public health guidance on behaviour change: A brief introduction. *Psychology, Health & Medicine, 14*, 1–8.

Abraham, C., Kok, G., Schaalma, H. & Luszczynska, A. (2010). Health promotion. In P.R. Martin *et al.* (Eds), *The International Association of Applied Psychology Handbook of Applied Psychology*. Oxford: Wiley-Blackwell.

Abraham, C. & Michie, S. (2008). A taxonomy of behavior change techniques used in interventions. *Health Psychology, 27*, 379–387.

Abraham, C., Sheeran, P. & Johnston, M. (1998). From health beliefs to self-regulation: Theoretical advances in the psychology of action control. *Psychology & Health, 13*, 569–591.

Albarracín, D., Gillete, J.C., Earl, A.N., Glasman, L.R. & Durantini, M.R. (2005). A test of major assumptions about behavior change: A comprehensive look at the effects of passive and active HIV-prevention interventions since the beginning of the epidemic. *Psychological Bulletin, 131*, 856–897.

Alder, N.E., Boyce, T., Chesney M.A., Cohen S., Folkman, S., Kahn, R.L. & Syme, S.L. (1994). Socio-economic status and health: The challenge of the gradient. *American Psychologist, 49*, 15–24.

Ajzen, I. (1991). The theory of planned behavior. *Organizational Behavior and Human Decision Processes, 50*, 179–211.

Bandura, A. (1997). *Self-efficacy: the exercise of control*. New York: Freeman.

Bandura, A. (1999). Health promotion from the perspective of social cognitive theory. *Psychology & Health, 13*, 623–650.

Bartholomew, L.K., Parcel, G.S., Kok, G. & Gottlieb, N.H. (2006). *Planning health promotion programs. An intervention mapping approach*. San Francisco: Jossey-Bass.

Becker, M.H., Haefner D.P., Kasl, S.V., Kirscht, J.P., Maiman, L.A. & Rosenstock, I.M. (1997). Selected psychosocial models and correlates of individual health-related behaviors. *Medical Care, 15*, 27–46.

Belloc, N.B. & Breslow, L. (1972). Relationship of physical health status and health practices. *Preventive Medicine, 9*, 469–421.

Carver, C.S. & Scheier, M.F. (1982). Control theory: A useful conceptual framework for personality-social, clinical and health psychology. *Psychological Bulletin, 92*, 111–135.

Conner, M.T. & Norman, P. (Eds.) (2005). *Predicting health behaviour: Research and practice with social cognition models* (2nd edn). Milton Keynes: Open University Press.

Fishbein, M. & Ajzen, I. (1975). *Belief, attitude, intention theory and research*. Reading, MA: Addison-Wesley.

Fishbein, M., Triandis, H.C., Kanfer, F.H., Becker, M., Middlestadt, S.E. & Eichler, A. (2001). Factors influencing behavior and behavior change. In A. Baum, T.A. Revenson & J.E. Singer (Eds.) *Handbook of health psychology* (pp. 3–17). Mahwah, NJ: Lawrence Erlbaum.

Fisher, J.D. & Fisher. W.A. (1992). Changing AIDS-risk behavior. *Psychological Bulletin, 111*, 455–471.

Fisher, J.D., Fisher, W.A., Bryan, A.D. & Misovich, S.J. (2002). Information-motivation-behavioral skills model-based HIV risk behavior change intervention for inner-city high school youth. *Health Psychology, 21*, 177–186.

Floyd, D. L., Prentice-Dunn, S. & Rogers, R., W (2000). A meta analysis of research on protection motivation theory. *Journal of Applied Social Psychology*, 30, 407–429.

Friedman, R., Sobel, D., Myers, P., Caudill, M. & Benson, H. (1995). Behavioral medicine, clinical health psychology and cost offset. *Health Psychology, 14*, 509–518.

Glasgow, R.E., Bull, S.S., Gillette, C., Klesges, L.M. & Dzewaltowski, D.M. (2002). Behavior change intervention research in healthcare settings: A review of recent reports with emphasis on external validity. *American Journal of Preventive Medicine, 23*, 62–69.

Good, A. & Abraham, C. (2008). Measuring defensive responses to threatening messages: A meta analysis of measures. *Health Psychology Review, 1*, 208–229.

Green, L.W. & Glasgow, R.E. (2006). Evaluating the relevance, generalization, and applicability of research: Issues in external validation and translation methodology. *Evaluation & the Health Professions, 29*, 126–153.

Hein, H.O., Suadicani, P. & Gyntelberg, F. (1992). Ischaemic heart disease incidence by social class and form of smoking: The Copenhagen Male Study – 17 years follow-up. *Journal of Internal Medicine, 231*, 477–483.

Hemmingsson, T., Lundber, I., Diderichsen, F. & Allebeck, P. (1998). Explanation of social class differences in alcoholism among young men. *Social Science & Medicine, 47*, 1395–1405.

Khaw, K.T., Wareham, N., Bingham, S., Welch, A., Luben, R. & Day, N. (2008). Combined impact of health behaviours and mortality in men and women: The EPIC-Norfolk prospective population study, *PLOS Medicine, 5*.

Kok, G., Schaalma, H., Ruiter, R.A.C., van Empelen, P. & Brug, J. (2004). Intervention mapping: A protocol for applying health psychology theory to prevention programmes. *Journal of Health Psychology, 9*, 85–98.

Kools, M., Van de Wiel, M.W.J., Ruiter, R.A.C. & Kok, G. (2006). Pictures and text in instructions for medical devices: Effects on recall and actual performance. *Patient Education & Counseling, 64*, 104–111.

Lemieux. A.F., Fisher, J.D. & Pratto, F. (2008). A music-based HIV prevention intervention for urban adolescents. *Health Psychology, 27*, 349–357.

Luszczynska, A., Sobczyk, A, & Abraham, C (2007). Planning to lose weight: RCT of an implementation intention prompt to enhance weight reduction among overweight and obese women. *Health Psychology, 26*, 507–512.

Marlatt, G.A. & Donovan, D.M. (Eds.) (2005). *Relapse prevention: Maintenance strategies in the treatment of addictive behaviors*. New York: Guilford Press.

Michie, S., Abraham, C., Whittington, C., McAteer, J. & Gupta, S. (2009). Identifying effective techniques in interventions: A meta-analysis and meta-regression. *Health Psychology, 28*, 690–701.

Mokdad, A.H., Marks, J.S., Stroup, D.F. & Gerberding, J.L. (2004). Actual causes of death in the United States, 2000. *Journal of the American Medical Association, 291*, 1238–1245.

Oettingen, G. (1996). Positive fantasy and motivation. In P.M. Gollwitzer & J.A. Bargh (Eds.) *The psychology of action: Linking cognition and motivation to behavior* (pp. 236–259). New York: Guilford Press.

Pittet, D.S., Hugonnet, S., Harbarth, P., Mourouga, V., Sauvan, S. & Perneger, T.V. (2000). Effectiveness of a hospital-wide programme to improve compliance with hand hygiene. *Lancet, 356*, 1307–1312.

Rose, G. (1992). *The strategy of preventive medicine*. Oxford: OUP.

Ruiter, R.A.C., Abraham, C. & Kok, G. (2001). Scary warnings and rational precautions: A review of the psychology of fear appeals. *Psychology & Health, 16*, 613–630.

Schaalma, H.P., Abraham, C., Gillmore, M.R. & Kok, G. (2004). Sex education as health promotion: What does it take? *Archives of Sexual Behavior, 33*, 259–269.

Schinke, S.P. & Gordon, A.N. (1992). Innovative approaches to interpersonal skills training for minority adolescents.

In R.J. DiClemente (Ed.) *Adolescents and AIDS: A generation in jeopardy*. Newbury Park, CA: Sage.

Schwarzer, R. (2008). Modeling health behavior change: How to predict and modify the adoption and maintenance of health behaviors. *Applied Psychology: An International Review, 57*, 1–29.

Sheeran, P., Milne, S., Webb, T.L. & Gollwitzer, P.M. (2005). Implementation intentions. In M. Conner & P. Norman (Eds.) *Predicting health behaviour: Research and practice with social cognition models* (2nd edn, pp. 276–323). Buckingham: Open University Press.

Skinner B.F. (1938). *The behavior of organisms*. New York: Appleton-Century-Crofts.

Tortolero, S.R., Markham, C.M., Parcel, G.S., Peters, R.J. Jr, Escobar-Chaves, S.L., Basen-Engquist, K. & Lewis, H.L. (2005). Using intervention mapping to adapt an effective HIV, sexually transmitted disease, and pregnancy prevention program for high-risk minority youth. *Health Promotion Practice, 6*, 286–298.

Rollnick, S., & Miller, W.R. (1995). What is motivational interviewing? *Behavioural and Cognitive Psychotherapy, 23*, 325–334

Triandis, H. (1977). *Interpersonal behavior*. Monterey, CA: Brooks-Cole.

Wanless, D. (2002). *Securing our future health: Taking a long-term view*. London: HMSO.

Webb, T.L. & Sheeran, P. (2006). Does changing behavioral intentions engender behavior change? A meta-analysis of the experimental evidence. *Psychological Bulletin, 132*, 249–268.

Wilkinson, R.G. (1997). Health inequalities: relative or absolute material standards? *British Medical Journal, 314*, 591–595.

Witte, K. & Allen, M. (2000). A meta-analysis of fear appeals: Implications for effective public health campaigns. *Health Education & Behavior, 27*, 591–615.

9

The Impact of Perceived Risk On Risk-Reducing Behaviours

Alison J. Wright

Chapter Outline

This chapter focuses on whether, and by what mechanisms, informing individuals about potential threats to their health is likely to be an effective strategy to change health behaviours. First, models of the psychosocial determinants of health behaviours that assign a key role to risk perceptions are examined. Subsequently, the manner in which information about health threats is processed, and how such cognitive processing may influence the adoption of protective behaviours, is considered.

Key Concepts

Boomerang interaction
Danger control
Defence-motivated
    processing
Efficacy appraisal
Extended parallel process
    model
Fear control
Heuristic-systematic model
Information processing
Protection motivation
    theory
Threat appraisal

Introduction

Risk perceptions can be simply defined as people's 'beliefs about a potential harm' (Brewer *et al.*, 2007). Risk perceptions interest health psychologists for several reasons. Firstly, informing individuals about potential threats to their health is a possible strategy for motivating risk-reducing behaviours. The likely effectiveness of this strategy is the focus of this chapter. However, psychologists may also undertake risk communication interventions to provide reassurance while avoiding false reassurance or to facilitate informed decision making (French & Marteau, 2007). For a discussion of risk communication strategies to increase risk comprehension, readers are referred to Lipkus's (2007) review. This chapter examines whether, and by what mechanisms, interventions targeting risk perceptions may be effective at changing health behaviours.

One such intervention is the use of graphic warning labels on cigarette packets. Making such warnings compulsory has become part of tobacco control policy in a number of countries. The debate about the likely effectiveness of these warnings illustrates some of the key controversies in this area. Based on a longitudinal survey of smokers in Canada, one of the first countries to adopt such warnings, Hammond *et al.* (2004, 2006) argued that providing graphic warnings provokes strong emotional reactions in smokers, which in turn increases quitting. In contrast, Ruiter and Kok (2005, 2006) argued that 'cigarette warning labels are useless'. In part, their objection stems from Hammond *et al.*'s study not being experimental, so limiting possible conclusions about the causal effects of tobacco warning labels. However, they also argued that such warnings increase fear arousal, which makes smokers defensive, resulting in less behaviour change than if such warning labels were not used.

To understand how such opposing viewpoints can arise, it is necessary to examine the models psychologists use to make predictions about the impact of risk perceptions on risk-reducing behaviour.

Models Relating Risk Perceptions to Protective Behaviour

Risk perceptions feature in a number of theoretical models describing the psychological determinants of health behaviours. This chapter focuses on models that assign an important role to risk perceptions. However, it should be noted that risk perceptions are also included in several other models of health behaviour (e.g. the health action process approach, Schwarzer, 2008). Here, two models specifically developed to explain the behavioural impact of health risk information, protection motivation theory and the extended parallel process model, are examined.

Protection motivation theory

According to protection motivation theory (PMT) (Rogers, 1983; Rogers & Prentice-Dunn, 1997), risk-reducing behaviour occurs when individuals have high *protection motivation*. Protection motivation is defined as a motive that arouses, sustains and directs activity (Floyd *et al.*, 2000) and is considered best measured by intentions for the relevant protective behaviour (Rogers & Prentice-Dunn, 1997). Protection motivation arises as the result of combining two cognitive appraisals: *threat appraisal* and *coping appraisal*.

The first of these, *threat appraisal*, considers the current risky behaviour (e.g. smoking). *Perceived vulnerability* is defined as the perceived likelihood of the adverse outcome occurring and is conditional upon continuing the risky behaviour. *Perceived severity* refers to the perceived extent of harm likely if the adverse outcome occurs. *Perceived rewards* of the risky behaviour increase the likelihood of its performance. In PMT, *fear* is viewed as only having only an indirect influence on protection motivation, with fear arousal influencing the appraisal of the threat's severity; threats that arouse more fear being viewed as more severe. The most recent formulation of PMT (Rogers & Prentice-Dunn, 1997) states that overall threat appraisal is the sum of perceived severity and vulnerability, minus the rewards of the maladaptive behaviour. For example, a smoker would have a high threat appraisal if she believed she was very likely to develop coronary heart disease (CHD) if she continued to smoke, that CHD is a life-threatening condition and that there were few benefits of continuing to smoke.

Coping appraisal considers the risk-reducing behaviour (e.g. quitting smoking). *Response efficacy* refers to the perceived effectiveness of the risk-reducing behaviour at reducing the threat. *Self-efficacy* concerns beliefs about one's ability to perform the risk-reducing behaviour. Beliefs about any physical or psychological costs (*response costs*) of the risk-reducing behaviour reduce its likelihood. Overall coping appraisal is the sum of response and self-efficacy, minus the perceived costs of the risk-reducing behaviour. For example, smokers might believe that quitting smoking would be an effective way to reduce their risk of CHD, feel somewhat confident that they have the ability to quit, but be concerned that quitting may cause weight gain.

According to PMT, threat and coping appraisals interact to influence motivation for risk-reducing behaviour. In other words, the impact of a person's threat appraisal on motivation is dependent on the level of his or her efficacy appraisal. The most recent formulation of PMT (Rogers & Prentice-Dunn, 1997) proposes that if people believe that they can cope with the threat (i.e. have high efficacy appraisals), then the greater the perceived threat, the greater their intentions for the risk-reducing behaviour. However, if people have low efficacy, then as perceived threat becomes greater, their intentions to perform the risk-reducing behaviour will decrease. Therefore, according to PMT, interventions that aim to increase perceived threat will be counterproductive in individuals who have low efficacy for the risk-reducing behaviour. Ruiter and Kok (2006) argued that most smokers would have low self-efficacy, due to having already made several unsuccessful quit attempts, and so their intentions to quit would decrease when faced with warning labels that increased their threat appraisals.

Rogers and Prentice-Dunn (1997) refer to the threat × efficacy interaction, leading to reduced motivation under conditions of high threat but low efficacy, as a 'boomerang effect'. They list six potential causal psychological processes for this interaction, but do not discuss which the evidence best supports. However, one of the most plausible explanations, which benefits from being subject to empirical investigation, is that provided by the extended parallel process model (EPPM).

The extended parallel process model

The EPPM (Witte, 1992, 1998) attempts to explain when increasing risk perceptions will or will not increase risk-reducing behaviour. In the EPPM, as in PMT, learning of a health threat initiates appraisals of threat and efficacy (Witte, 1998). Threat is appraised first. When people consider themselves to be at low likelihood of experiencing the health problem (low vulnerability) and/or believe that the threat is trivial (low severity), they do not experience fear arousal. As a result, they will not be motivated to appraise their efficacy for the protective behaviour. However, if perceived threat reaches a certain threshold, then fear is aroused. Experiencing fear arousal motivates individuals to make an efficacy appraisal, which is very similar to coping appraisal in PMT, with individuals examining their perceived self-efficacy and response efficacy for the risk-reducing behaviour. It should be noted that the EPPM assigns a greater role to fear arousal than does PMT, because, according to the model, individuals will only appraise their efficacy if they experience fear arousal.

Depending on the results of the efficacy appraisal, people will be motivated to engage in *danger control* or *fear control*. Danger control processes involve attempting to control the threat by being motivated to adopt the risk-reducing behaviour. Fear control processes are strategies that reduce the fear arousal associated with learning of the threat, rather than attempting to control the threat through behaviour. Fear control processes can include denial (e.g. stating one is not at risk of cancer), defensive avoidance (e.g. deliberately trying to avoid thinking about cancer) or reactance (e.g. stating that a health-related message is manipulative, and so ignoring it) (Witte & Allen, 2000).

Whether a person engages in danger control or fear control after learning of a threat is determined by perceived efficacy. When perceived efficacy is stronger than perceived threat, individuals will engage in danger control. However, if perceived threat overwhelms perceived efficacy, individuals will instead practise fear control, shifting their focus from managing the danger to managing their fear arousal. This shift of focus will decrease plans for, and actual, behavioural attempts to control the threat, leading to the 'boomerang effect'. The resulting lower level of motivation for risk-reducing behaviour will be associated with evidence of use of strategies to control fear arousal, such as avoidance, information derogation and threat minimisation. Therefore, according to the EPPM, interventions such as cigarette warning labels will be counterproductive for people who have low efficacy for the risk-reducing behaviour.

Table 9.1 Summary of results of meta-analyses of PMT and the EPPM

| | Witte & Allen (2000) | | Milne, Sheeran & Orbell (2000) | | |
	Intention	Behaviour	Intention	Concurrent behaviour	Subsequent behaviour
Threat appraisal					
Vulnerability	0.17	0.14	0.16	0.13	0.12
Severity	0.14	0.13	0.10	0.10	0.07, ns
Fear	0.13	0.16	0.20	0.26[a]	−0.04[a], ns
Efficacy appraisal					
Self-efficacy	0.17	0.13	0.33	0.36	0.22
Response efficacy	0.17	0.13	0.29	0.17	0.09, ns
Response costs	–	–	−0.34	−0.32	−0.25
Intention	–	–	–	0.82	0.40

Numbers are pooled average correlations.

ns – Average correlation not significantly different from zero. All other correlations significantly different from zero at $p < 0.05$ or less.

[a]Based on only one study.

Sources: Data from Witte, K. & Allen, M. (2000). A meta-analysis of fear appeals: Implications for effective public health campaigns. *Health Education & Behavior, 27*, 591–615 and Milne, S., Sheeran, P. & Orbell, S. (2000). Prediction and intervention in health-related behavior: A meta-analytic review of protection motivation theory. *Journal of Applied Social Psychology, 30*, 106–143.

Evidence for PMT and the EPPM

PMT and the EPPM have been applied to a wide variety of health threats and behaviours. Two meta-analyses examined the relationships between variables specified by the models and motivation for, and actual, risk-reducing behaviour (Milne *et al.*, 2000; Witte & Allen, 2000). A third meta-analysis (Floyd *et al.*, 2000) tested PMT's predictions, but did not differentiate between effects on intentions compared to effects on behaviour, and so is not as informative to discuss. The two meta-analyses reviewed here differ in terms of their aims and inclusion criteria, so both provide useful information regarding the validity of the models. The results are summarised in Table 9.1.

Milne and colleagues (2000) used the narrower inclusion criteria. Studies had to be an empirical application of PMT, assess both intention and concurrent or subsequent behaviour and concern a health-related behaviour. Therefore, they included both studies that manipulated PMT variables and those that assessed correlations between PMT variables and intentions and behaviour. In contrast, Witte and Allen (2000) only included experimental studies that manipulated fear or threat and measured attitudes, intentions or behaviour. They included studies testing PMT, the EPPM and a variety of other theories of how perceived threat influences a wide range of behaviours, both health related and not health related. Given these differences in inclusion criteria, it is unsurprising that Witte and Allen (2000) included 98 experimental studies, while Milne and colleagues (2000) identified 27 studies, of which 15 used correlational designs. Therefore, differences in the findings of the two meta-analyses may reflect differences in the research literature synthesised by each. In particular, only experimental designs permit conclusions regarding whether a change in a threat or efficacy appraisal variable causes a change in intentions or behaviour. Because Milne and colleagues (2000) include both experimental and correlational designs in their analysis, the resulting effect sizes provide less clear evidence of whether changes in threat and efficacy beliefs result in changes in intentions and behaviour.

Evidence for danger control processes Both meta-analyses found small effect sizes for the relationships between intentions and threat appraisal variables. Milne and colleagues (2000) found medium-sized effects for the relationships between self-efficacy, response efficacy and intentions, while Witte and Allen (2000) found small effect sizes for these relationships. Response costs had a medium strength negative association with intentions (Milne *et al.*, 2000).

Effect sizes for relationships between fear, vulnerability, severity or response efficacy and both concurrent behaviour (Milne *et al.*, 2000) and behaviour in general (Witte & Allen, 2000) were small. Self-efficacy had a medium strength effect on concurrent behaviour (Milne *et al.*, 2000), while Witte and Allen (2000) found it had a small effect on behaviour in general. Only Milne and colleagues (2000) examined the effects of PMT variables on subsequent behaviour, finding that vulnerability had a significant, yet small, effect size, self-efficacy and response costs had small to moderate effects, while the other beliefs' effects were not significant. Of all the constructs, intentions had the largest correlations with concurrent and subsequent behaviour, but were most strongly associated with concurrent behaviour.

Can interventions successfully alter threat and efficacy beliefs? The meta-analyses explored the effectiveness of attempts to manipulate threat and efficacy beliefs. Both found that fear was least successfully manipulated in experiments, $r = 0.30$ (Witte & Allen, 2000) and $r = 0.26$ (Milne *et al.*, 2000). Milne and colleagues (2000) found that severity ($r = 0.66$) and vulnerability ($r = 0.63$) were more successfully manipulated than response efficacy ($r = 0.42$) or self-efficacy ($r = 0.32$). Witte and Allen (2000) also found that severity was most successfully manipulated ($r = 0.44$), but effect sizes for manipulations of vulnerability, response efficacy and self-efficacy were all moderate, ranging from $r = 0.30$ to $r = 0.36$.

Evidence for the interaction between threat and efficacy appraisals Whether threat and efficacy appraisals interact to influence intentions is

important. If an interaction does exist, then interventions that increase threat perceptions without increasing perceived efficacy will backfire, reducing protective behaviour. In contrast, if the effects of threat and efficacy appraisals on intentions are additive, then increasing either type of belief will have a positive motivational effect. Milne *et al.* (2000) did not test for the existence of an interaction between threat and efficacy appraisals on intentions or behaviour, but Witte and Allen (2000) did. They found better support for an additive model, in which high levels of threat and higher levels of efficacy independently produced greater mean levels of danger control, than for the EPPM/PMT predictions of a threat × efficacy interaction. Therefore, these findings do not support the prediction that the impact of threat on risk-reducing behaviour depends on efficacy levels, nor that increasing threat perceptions in individuals with low efficacy will reduce risk-reducing behaviour.

Summary of meta-analytic evidence for danger control processes Together, the two meta-analyses suggest that variables specified by PMT and the EPPM have small to moderate relationships with intentions for, and actual, risk-reducing behaviour. Milne and colleagues (2000), focusing on health-related behaviours, found that PMT/EPPM constructs predicted intentions more strongly than behaviour, while Witte and Allen's (2000) review across a broader range of behaviours found similar strength of prediction for intentions and behaviour. Milne and colleagues (2000) found stronger relationships between self-efficacy and response efficacy and intentions/behaviour than between threat variables and intentions/behaviour, while the effect sizes reported by Witte and Allen (2000) for self-efficacy and response efficacy were small and very similar to those for the threat variables. Both groups of researchers found that the effect sizes for manipulations of response efficacy and self-efficacy manipulations were smaller than that for the severity manipulations. Therefore, the cognitions found to be most predictive of intentions and behaviour in the review focused on health-related behaviours (Milne *et al.*, 2000) were also those least effectively manipulated. This may reflect the choice of intervention techniques. Most experimental manipulations of PMT or EPPM variables have relied on written messages. This approach may be less suited for increasing self-efficacy than other PMT/EPPM constructs. According to Bandura (1997), verbal persuasion is a less strong influence on self-efficacy than enactive mastery experiences (e.g. successfully going a day without smoking) or vicarious mastery experiences (e.g., seeing someone similar to oneself successfully quit smoking).

Evidence regarding fear control processes   The EPPM predicts that individuals who perceive high threat but low efficacy should show the most evidence of fear control responses (Witte, 1998). Fewer studies have addressed this side of the model. Witte and Allen (2000) subjected this literature to meta-analysis, reporting that greater defensive responses were significantly associated with stronger fear appeals ($r = 0.20$), weaker efficacy messages ($r = -0.11$) and fewer danger control responses ($r = -0.18$). However, too few studies measured fear control processes to test for the predicted threat × efficacy interaction in the meta-analysis. Therefore, evaluation of this element of the EPPM requires examination of evidence from primary studies.

The prediction that fear control will be greatest when participants perceive high threat but low efficacy has received mixed support. In two studies that presented high-threat messages about either the human papillomavirus (Witte *et al.*, 1998) or breast cancer (Rippetoe & Rogers, 1987), women with lower efficacy beliefs scored higher on certain measures of fear control. However, other studies' results do not support the EPPM's predictions. For example, a study of the impact of learning of a genetic risk of heart disease assessed fear control in the form of threat minimisation and information derogation (Wright *et al.*, 2006). The authors found that threat and efficacy did not significantly predict information derogation, but did interact to significantly influence threat minimisation. However, this threat × efficacy interaction was not in the form predicted by the EPPM, because it was not high-risk individuals with low perceived efficacy who scored highest on threat minimisation. Similarly, a study of responses to breast cancer risk information found no evidence of a threat × efficacy interaction on three different measures of fear control (Ruiter *et al.*, 2003).

The relationship between danger control and fear control processes   Fear control processes, such as threat ministration or information derogation, are only problematic if they interfere with the performance of protective behaviour. The EPPM argues that if individuals are defensively avoiding the threat, they cannot be thinking about ways to protect themselves and so will not be motivated to perform the risk-reducing behaviour (Witte, 1992). In other words, there should be a strong negative correlation between the amount of fear control processes and the amount of danger control processes. Because of this theorised strong, negative correlation, it has been argued that any intervention that evokes fear control processes will be ineffective at changing behaviour (e.g. Ruiter & Kok, 2005). Although meta-analytic evidence demonstrated a negative correlation between fear and danger control, its magnitude was small (-0.18) (Witte & Allen, 2000). If only one type of process operated at one time, then this negative correlation would be much larger. Perhaps attempts to control the threat and to cope with emotional arousal operate at least somewhat in parallel, as suggested by other theorists (Leventhal, 1970). If this is the case, then interventions that evoke fear control may not be entirely ineffective at changing behaviour. Individuals may cope with the threat by changing their behaviour, while at the same time, cope with the emotional arousal associated with learning of the threat by using fear control processes.

Critical appraisal of studies testing PMT and the EPPM

The extent to which one can have confidence in the meta-analytic findings concerning the magnitude of relationships between threat and efficacy appraisals and intentions and behaviour depends upon the adequacy of the operationalisation of these constructs. Protection motivation and danger control are often operationalised as intentions for the risk-reducing behaviour. However, in many studies intentions are not measured with a time frame or are simply phrased in terms of performing the behaviour in the future, rather than in a specific time frame. This is problematic, as where subsequent behaviour is assessed, not assessing intentions in the corresponding time frame will reduce intention–behaviour relationships. Also, measuring intentions with a vague or no time frame may attenuate the observed magnitude of the relationship between intentions and threat and efficacy. For example, consider two smokers, one of whom has very high perceived vulnerability to CHD and one of whom has moderate perceived vulnerability to CHD. The first smoker is more likely than the second to strongly endorse the item 'I intend to quit smoking in the next month'. However, both of them might equally strongly endorse the item 'I intend to quit smoking in the future', the person with high perceived vulnerability because she plans to quit in the next month, but the person with moderate perceived vulnerability because she plans to quit in 20 years' time.

PMT or EPPM studies often do not assess behaviour as an outcome, instead focusing on intentions. Where behaviour is assessed, self-report rather than objective measures are generally used, with a few notable exceptions (e.g. Wurtele, 1988). Assessment of threat appraisals is also sometimes problematic. The reliability of perceived severity scales tends to be low, perhaps because perceived consequences of health threats are multidimensional, encompassing not only physical harm, but also potential social and psychological consequences (Milne et al., 2000). Despite the fact that PMT states that vulnerability perceptions are conditional upon continuing the risky behaviour, some studies do not use conditional vulnerability items. This is not ideal, as some respondents may report low vulnerability because they do not perceive the threat as probable, while others may report low vulnerability because they intend to begin protective behaviour, and figure their anticipated future behaviour into their reported vulnerability. Therefore, the true relationship between vulnerability and behaviour will be underestimated (van der Velde et al., 1996). An additional problem with assessing perceived vulnerability, though less easy to rectify, is that threat minimisation, a form of fear control, may result in individuals downgrading their reported vulnerability to a threat.

Another possible reason for the small relationships between risk perceptions and protective behaviour found in the meta-analyses is that risk perceptions may be more predictive of behaviours mainly intended to reduce specific health threats (e.g. being vaccinated) than of behaviours that have a variety of health,

social and economic consequences (e.g. diet) (Brewer et al., 2007). In support of this, the average correlation between perceived vulnerability and behaviour was stronger ($r = 0.26$) in a recent meta-analysis examining the ability of risk perceptions to predict vaccination (Brewer et al., 2007) than in either of the two PMT/EPPM meta-analyses discussed earlier, which included a wider range of behaviours.

Often, the choice of PMT and EPPM questionnaire items used in studies does not seem to have been based on developmental work to ensure that the most salient beliefs about the threat and the risk-reducing behaviour in the relevant population are captured in the questionnaire items. Another weakness in measurement is that studies rarely report the use of factor analysis to examine whether items load onto the factors specified by the theories (Norman et al., 2005).

As discussed earlier, predictions regarding fear control reactions have received mixed support. Such reactions can be assessed in a variety of ways. A recent meta-analysis (Good & Abraham, 2007) examined the ability of different measures of fear control processes to discriminate between groups expected to differ in terms of their defensiveness (e.g. those for whom a health threat was highly relevant versus those for whom the threat was less relevant). For many measures, there were too few experimental tests for the authors to draw clear conclusions. In contrast, avoidance was assessed in 25 per cent of the included studies, with meta-analytic results suggesting that avoidance measures had limited capacity to detect defensiveness. Therefore, the use of avoidance measures to assess fear control processes may have adversely affected researchers' ability to detect the operation of such processes.

One of the strengths of both PMT and the EPPM is that their predictions have been tested using experimental manipulations. However, these studies have been criticised for tending not to use mediation analyses to test whether the impact of the intervention on risk-reducing intentions or behaviour is due to changes in PMT/EPPM cognitions. Moreover, follow-up tends to be short term, so there is less evidence as to whether the impact of changes in PMT variables on intentions and behaviour is sustained over time (Norman et al., 2005).

Finally, both PMT and the EPPM focus on motivation for protective behaviours. However, positive intentions does not always translate into risk-reducing behaviour, as indicated by Milne *et al.*'s (2000) finding of an average correlation of 0.40 between intentions and subsequent behaviour. Adding interventions, such as implementation intention formation, that target volitional aspects of adopting a protective behaviour to a PMT-based intervention, has been found to help translate protection motivation into protective action (Milne *et al.*, 2002).

Cognitive Processing of Health Threat Information

Many PMT and EPPM intervention studies appear to assume that participants will process information about health threats in a carefully considered manner. However, dual process models of information processing, such as the heuristic-systematic model (HSM; Chen & Chaiken, 1999) argue that attitude change is the result of two types of information processing (see also the similar elaboration likelihood model; Petty & Wegener, 1999). *Systematic processing* involves an analytic and in-depth consideration of judgement-relevant information. *Heuristic processing* requires less cognitive effort, entailing the activation and application of heuristics: 'quick and easy' judgmental rules of thumb stored in memory.

According to the HSM, the *sufficiency principle* determines how information is processed. The principle states that individuals try to balance minimising cognitive effort with satisfying their current motivational concerns. The amount of cognitive effort they will expend depends on their desired confidence in a particular judgement. Individuals will only exert cognitive effort sufficient for their actual confidence in their judgement to be equal to their desired confidence. Systematic processing is more likely to occur when individuals desire greater confidence in their judgements, as heuristic processing alone is unlikely to result in their feeling sufficiently confident about their conclusions. Individuals are likely to want greater confidence about topics they view as personally relevant. For example, someone who drinks wine regularly is more likely to systematically process a newspaper article about a link between wine consumption

and cancer risk than someone who never drinks alcohol.

The HSM originally assumed that individuals would want to hold accurate attitudes and beliefs. However, the revised HSM (Chen & Chaiken, 1999) recognises that defence and impression motivation may coexist with or replace accuracy motivation. Impression and defence motivation serve different goals. Impression motivation reflects the desire to hold attitudes that satisfy current perceived social demands. Of greater interest to researchers examining the impact of health threat information is defence motivation, the desire to hold beliefs congruent with one's existing self-definitional beliefs. Self-definitional beliefs are those closely tied to the self, including those involved in one's values, social identities or personal attributes. These could include beliefs about one's susceptibility to health threats and about the adequacy of one's choices regarding risk-reducing behaviours. Receiving health threat information may well challenge such self-definitional beliefs and thus engender defence motivation. Although the HSM argues that the selective application of heuristics can serve defence motives, when defence motivation is high and cognitive resources are available, defence-motivated systematic processing is more probable. Defence-motivated processing involves effortful but biased scrutiny of information, with information supporting preferred conclusions being judged more favourably than information contradicting preferred conclusions. For example, faced with a newspaper report of research linking alcohol consumption to cancer, a person who drinks regularly will try hard to find flaws in the research. In contrast, she will devote less cognitive effort to considering a statement suggesting a need for further research to verify the link.

Implications of the HSM for the impact of health threat information interventions

Learning one is vulnerable to a health threat may increase desired confidence in one's conclusions about protective action and so engender systematic processing of information about the threat and possible protective actions. Experiencing fear in response to health threat information could also motivate systematic processing, as fear signals uncertainty and so a need for more effortful processing to reduce this uncertainty (Tiedens & Linton, 2001). Given that systematic processing results in attitudes that are more stable over time (Chen & Chaiken, 1999) and that more stable attitudes more strongly predict health behaviour (Cooke & Sheeran, 2004), providing health threat information could increase protective behaviour through increasing systematic processing. However, health threat information could also be processed in a defensive manner, which is a concern because negative attitudes to healthy behaviour formed as the result of defence-motivated systematic processing could be long-term deterrents to risk-reducing behaviour.

Researchers have investigated the effectiveness of various tactics to promote systematic yet accuracy-motivated processing in individuals for whom a health threat is most relevant. One possible strategy is self-affirmation, a procedure in which people reflect upon cherished values or attributes of the self, which has been shown to increase acceptance of health risk information (McQueen & Klein, 2006) and risk-reducing behaviour (Epton & Harris, 2008). However, before focusing solely on strategies to overcome defence-motivated processing, we should also note that defence-motivated processing is constrained by the bounds of rationality. Individuals are unlikely to be able to completely deny or derogate the existence of many health threats. Therefore, defensive processing will not always result in complete rejection of health threat information. In fact, given these constraints on defensive processing, de Hoog and colleagues (2007) argue that individuals are not only biased against accepting the threat information but also biased in favour of accepting risk-reducing behaviour recommendations, in order to feel protected from the health problem. In support of this, a recent meta-analysis found that manipulations that increased perceived severity and vulnerability resulted in both more defensive processing of threat information and more information-processing accepting action recommendations (de Hoog et al., 2007). However, these conclusions derive from only six studies, covering limited behaviours, some of which appear relatively easy to perform (e.g. attending repetitive strain injury prevention workshops). Further research needs to establish whether biased acceptance of action recommendations also occurs for behaviours to which there are greater barriers.

Conclusions

This chapter has explored the extent to which risk perceptions are associated with protective behaviour, and the psychological mechanisms underpinning this association. Evidence shows that perceived severity and perceived vulnerability have a small but significant relationship with motivation to protect oneself and to behaviour. This relationship may be stronger when the behaviour in question has mostly health-related consequences. Measurement and study design issues may also have served to cause the observed relationship between risk perceptions and behaviour to be an underestimate of the true relationship.

The EPPM and PMT suggest that the influence of risk perceptions on motivation for protective behaviour will depend on individuals' efficacy appraisals. However, the evidence is more consistent with there being main effects of threat and efficacy appraisals on motivation for protective behaviour. In fact, in a meta-analysis of PMT studies that focused only on health-related behaviours, self-efficacy and response efficacy were more predictive of behaviour than threat appraisal variables. Therefore, increasing these beliefs may be an optimal strategy to increase protective behaviours. However, self-efficacy in particular may be difficult to change through the provision of written health information. Predictions from EPPM and PMT that high perceived threat in individuals with low efficacy will be associated with defensive, fear control processes have also met with mixed support.

Learning one is at risk from a health threat will influence both how further information about the threat itself, and information about the recommended protective actions, is processed. Threatening health risk information may be processed systematically, but also in a defensive manner, resulting in negative attitudes towards the risk-reducing behaviour. However, recent work suggests that defence-motivated processing may encompass both threat minimisation and biased acceptance of, and therefore positive attitudes towards, recommended protective behaviours, a possibility that requires further investigation. Finally, all the models linking risk perceptions to protective behaviour reviewed in this chapter focus on motivational aspects of behavioural adoption. To maximise their impact on the adoption of risk-reducing behaviour, interventions targeting risk perceptions may benefit from also including components targeting volitional aspects of behaviour change.

Discussion Points

1   According to PMT/EPPM, what set of beliefs is most likely to result in risk-reducing behaviour?
2   How strongly does evidence show threat appraisal and efficacy appraisal variables are linked to intentions and behaviour?
3   Does evidence support the suggestion that increasing perceived risk only increases risk-reducing behaviour if people have high response efficacy and self-efficacy?
4   Does evidence to suggest that, for people with low response efficacy and self-efficacy, increasing severity and vulnerability perceptions will lead to fear control processes?
5   What will be the result of putting frightening pictures of the harms of smoking on cigarette packets?
6   What criticisms have been made of PMT and EPPM primary studies?
7   According to the heuristic-systematic model, how will information linking meat consumption to an increased risk of cancer be processed:
    – by a person who likes eating steak three times a week?
    – by a person who is a lifelong vegetarian?
8   To what extent is defence-motivated, systematic processing of health-related information a problematic response to someone planning an intervention to change behaviour?

Further Reading

de Hoog, N., Stroebe, W. & De Wit, J.B.F. (2007). The impact of vulnerability to and severity of a health risk on processing and acceptance of fear-arousing communications: A meta-analysis. *Review of General Psychology, 11,* 258–285.

Good, A. & Abraham, C. (2007). Measuring defensive responses to threatening messages: A meta-analysis of measures. *Health Psychology Review, 1,* 208–229.

Milne, S., Sheeran, P. & Orbell, S. (2000). Prediction and intervention in health-related behavior: A meta-analytic review of protection motivation theory. *Journal of Applied Social Psychology, 30,* 106–143.

Norman, P., Boer, H. & Seydel, E.R. (2005). Protection motivation theory. In M. Conner & P. Norman (Eds.) *Predicting health behaviour* (pp. 81–126). Maidenhead: Open University Press.

Witte, K. & Allen, M. (2000). A meta-analysis of fear appeals: Implications for effective public health campaigns. *Health Education & Behavior, 27,* 591–615.

References

Bandura, A. (1997). *Self-efficacy: The exercise of control.* New York: W.H. Freeman.

Brewer, N.T., Chapman, G.B., Gibbons, F.X., Gerrard, M. & McCaul, K.D. (2007). Meta-analysis of the relationship between risk perception and health behavior: The example of vaccination. *Health Psychology, 26,* 136–145.

Chen, S. & Chaiken, S. (1999). The heuristic-systematic model in its broader context. In S. Chaiken & Y. Trope (Eds.) *Dual process theories in social psychology* (pp. 73–96). New York: Guilford Press.

Cooke, R. & Sheeran, P. (2004). Moderation of cognition-intention and cognition-behaviour relations: A meta-analysis of properties of variables from the theory of planned behaviour. *British Journal of Social Psychology, 43,* 159–186.

de Hoog, N., Stroebe, W. & De Wit, J.B.F. (2007). The impact of vulnerability to and severity of a health risk on processing and acceptance of fear-arousing communications: A meta-analysis. *Review of General Psychology, 11,* 258–285.

Epton, T. & Harris, P.R. (2008). Self-affirmation promotes health behavior change. *Health Psychology, 27,* 746–752.

Floyd, D.L., Prentice-Dunn, S. & Rogers, R.W. (2000). A meta-analysis of research on protection motivation theory. *Journal of Applied Social Psychology, 30*, 407–429.

French, D.P. & Marteau, T.M. (2007). Communicating risk. In S. Ayers, A. Baum, C. McManus, S. Newman, K. Wallston, J. Weinman & R. West (Eds.) *Cambridge handbook of psychology, health and medicine* (2nd edn, pp. 431–435). Cambridge: Cambridge University Press.

Good, A. & Abraham, C. (2007). Measuring defensive responses to threatening messages: A meta-analysis of measures. *Health Psychology Review, 1*, 208–229.

Hammond, D., Fong, G.T., McDonald, P.W., Brown, S. & Cameron, R. (2004). Graphic Canadian cigarette warning labels and adverse outcomes: Evidence from Canadian smokers. *American Journal of Public Health, 94*, 1442–1445.

Hammond, D., Fong, G.T., Mcdonald, P.W., Brown, K.S. & Cameron, R. (2006). Showing leads to doing: Graphic cigarette warning labels are an effective public health policy. *European Journal of Public Health, 16*, 223–224.

Leventhal, H. (1970). Findings and theory in the study of fear communications. In L. Berkowitz (Ed.) *Advances in experimental social psychology* (pp. 119–186). New York: Academic Press.

Lipkus, I.M. (2007). Numeric, verbal and visual formats of conveying health risks: Suggested best practices and future recommendations. *Medical Decision Making, 27*, 696–713.

McQueen, A. & Klein, W.M. (2006). Experimental manipulations of self-affirmation: A systematic review. *Self and Identity, 5*, 289–354.

Milne, S., Orbell, S., & Sheeran, P. (2002). Combining motivational and volitional interventions to promote exercise participation: Protection motivation theory and implementation intentions. *British Journal of Health Psychology, 7*, 163–184.

Milne, S., Sheeran, P. & Orbell, S. (2000). Prediction and intervention in health-related behavior: A meta-analytic review of protection motivation theory. *Journal of Applied Social Psychology, 30*, 106–143.

Norman, P., Boer, H. & Seydel, E.R. (2005). Protection motivation theory. In M. Conner & P. Norman (Eds.) *Predicting health behaviour* (pp. 81–126). Maidenhead: Open University Press.

Petty, R.E. & Wegener, D.T. (1999). The elaboration likelihood model: Current status and controversies. In S. Chaiken & Y. Trope (Eds.) *Dual process theories in social psychology* (pp. 41–72). New York: Guilford Press.

Rippetoe, P.A. & Rogers, R.W. (1987). Effects of components of protection-motivation theory on adaptive and maladaptive coping with a health threat. *Journal of Personality and Social Psychology, 52*, 596–604.

Rogers, R.W. (1983). Cognitive and physiological processes in fear appeals and attitude change: a revised theory of protection motivation. In J.T. Cacioppo & R.E. Petty (Eds.) *Social psychophysiology: A source book* (pp. 153–176). New York: Guilford Press.

Rogers, R.W. & Prentice-Dunn, S. (1997). Protection motivation theory. In D.S. Gochman (Ed.) *Handbook of health behavior research 1: Personal and social determinants* (pp. 113–132). New York: Plenum.

Ruiter, R.A.C. & Kok, G. (2005). Saying is not (always) doing: Cigarette warning labels are useless. *European Journal of Public Health, 15*, 329.

Ruiter, R.A.C. & Kok, G. (2006). Response to Hammond *et al.* Showing leads to doing, but doing what? The need for experimental pilot-testing. *European Journal of Public Health, 16*, 225.

Ruiter, R.A.C., Verplanken, B., Kok, G. & Werrij, M.Q. (2003). The role of coping appraisal in reactions to fear appeals: Do we need threat information? *Journal of Health Psychology, 8*, 465–474.

Schwarzer, R. (2008). Modeling health behavior change: How to predict and modify the adoption and maintenance of health behaviors. *Applied Psychology – An International Review, 57*, 1–29.

Tiedens, L.Z. & Linton, S. (2001). Judgment under emotional certainty and uncertainty: The effects of specific emotions on information processing. *Journal of Personality and Social Psychology, 81*, 973–988.

van der Velde, F.W., Hooykaas, C. & van der Pligt, J. (1996). Conditional versus unconditional risk estimates in models of AIDS-related risk behaviour. *Psychology & Health, 12*, 87–100.

Witte, K. (1992). Putting the fear back into fear appeals – The extended parallel process model. *Communication Monographs, 59*, 329–349.

Witte, K. (1998). Fear as motivator, fear as inhibitor: Using the extended parallel process model to explain fear appeal successes and failures. In P.A. Andersen & L.K. Guerrero (Eds.) *Handbook of communication and emotion: Research, theory, applications and contexts* (pp. 423–449). New York: Academic Press.

Witte, K. & Allen, M. (2000). A meta-analysis of fear appeals: Implications for effective public health campaigns. *Health Education & Behavior, 27*, 591–615.

Witte, K., Berkowitz, J.M., Cameron, K.A. & Mckeon, J.K. (1998). Preventing the spread of genital warts: Using fear appeals to promote self-protective behaviors. *Health Education & Behavior, 25*, 571–585.

Wright, A.J., French, D.P., Weinman, J. & Marteau, T.M. (2006). Can genetic risk information enhance motivation for smoking cessation? An analogue study. *Health Psychology, 25*, 740–752.

Wurtele, S.K. (1988). Increasing women's calcium intake: The role of health beliefs, intentions, and health value. *Journal of Applied Social Psychology, 18*, 627–639.

10

Using Social Cognition Models to Develop Health Behaviour Interventions

The Theory of Planned Behaviour as an Example

Stephen Sutton

Chapter Outline

This chapter describes how to use social cognition models to develop health behaviour interventions, using the theory of planned behaviour (TPB) as an example. Following a description of the theory, the steps involved in developing an intervention to change salient beliefs are summarised. Then, a number of complexities are discussed, for example the consequences of using different scoring schemes for the belief components. Next, a detailed example of a TPB-based intervention is presented. The chapter concludes with recommendations for research and practice.

Key Concepts

Actual behavioural control
Attitude toward the
  behaviour
Elaboration likelihood
  model
Elicitation study
Intervention effect size
Modal salient beliefs
Perceived behavioural
  control
Subjective norm
Theory of planned
  behaviour
Unipolar and bipolar
  scaling

Introduction

The term 'social cognition models' is used to refer to theories that specify the proximal cognitive determinants of behaviour. These theories include, among others, social cognitive theory (Bandura, 1986, 1997), the theory of reasoned action (Ajzen & Fishbein, 1980), the theory of planned behaviour (TPB; Ajzen, 1991), the health belief model (Strecher & Rosenstock, 2002), protection motivation theory (Rogers, 1983), the 'continuum' version of the health action process approach (HAPA-C; Schwarzer, 2008; Sutton, 2008) and the information-motivation-behavioral skills model (Fisher & Fisher, 1992). Social cognition models are widely used in health psychology to predict and explain health behaviours such as condom use, physical activity, smoking cessation and medication adherence. Increasingly, they are being used to change health behaviours; in other words, as the basis for health behavioural interventions.

This chapter focuses on the use of theory to develop interventions to change behaviour. Theories are useful in intervention development because they specify determinants of behaviour that are potentially amenable to change. Thus, theories inform us which variables should be targeted in interventions – which variables we should try to change in order to produce the desired change in behaviour. These are also the variables that we should measure (along with the target behaviour) when evaluating the impact of an intervention. In particular, it is important to assess whether an intervention that is designed to target behavioural determinants such as self-efficacy or attitude actually produces changes in these variables. If it does not, this provides one plausible reason for a lack of an intervention effect on behaviour.

Conner and Norman (2005) provide a detailed exposition of the major theories of health behaviour. This chapter focuses on one theory, the TPB, and explains how to use it to develop interventions to modify health-related behaviours. The TPB has several advantages over alternative theories. First, by contrast to theories that are health specific (e.g. the health belief model) or behaviour or domain specific (e.g. the AIDS risk reduction model; Catania *et al.*, 1990), the TPB is a general theory. Stroebe argues that general models should be preferred for the sake of parsi-mony: 'it is not very economical to continue to entertain specific theories of health behaviour unless the predictive success of these models is greater than that of general models of behaviour' (2000, p. 27). Second, in the TPB, the constructs are clearly defined and the causal relationships between the constructs clearly specified. Third, there exist clear recommendations for how the constructs should be operationalised (Ajzen, 2006a). Fourth, the theory has been widely used to study health behaviours (Ogden, 2003). And finally, meta-analyses show that it accounts for a useful amount of variance in intentions and behaviour (but see Sutton, 2004, for a discussion of effective variance explained by social cognition models).

Although the chapter focuses on using the TPB to develop interventions, many of the comments are also applicable to other social cognition models.

The Theory of Planned Behaviour

The theory of planned behaviour (TPB; Ajzen, 1991, 2006b), an extension of the theory of reasoned action (Ajzen & Fishbein, 1980), is widely used to study the cognitive determinants of health behaviours (Conner & Sparks, 2005; Sutton, 2004).

According to the theory, behaviour is determined by the strength of the person's intention to perform that behaviour and the amount of actual control that the person has over performing the behaviour. According to Ajzen (2006b), intention is 'an indication of a person's readiness to perform a given behaviour, and … is considered to be the immediate antecedent of behavior', and actual behavioural control '… refers to the extent to which a person has the skills, resources, and other prerequisites needed to perform a given behavior.' Perceived behavioural control, similar to Bandura's (1986) construct of self-efficacy, refers to the person's perceptions of their ability to perform the behaviour and is assumed to reflect actual behavioural control more or less accurately. To the extent that perceived behavioural control is an accurate reflection of actual behavioural control, it can, together with intention, be used to predict behaviour (Figure 10.1).

The strength of a person's intention is determined by three factors: their attitude toward the behaviour, that is, their overall evaluation of performing the

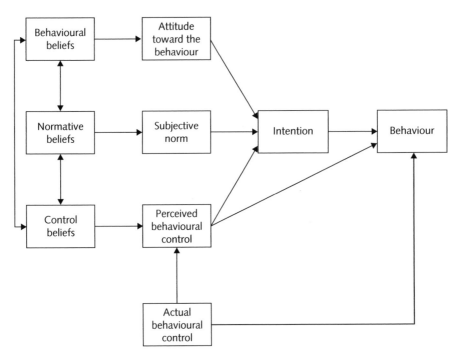

Figure 10.1   The theory of planned behaviour

behaviour; their subjective norm, that is, the extent to which they think that important others would want them to perform it; and their perceived behavioural control. Attitude toward the behaviour is determined by the total set of salient (readily accessible) behavioural beliefs about the personal outcomes of performing the behaviour. Specifically, attitude is determined by the belief strength for each salient outcome (the perceived likelihood that the outcome will occur if the behaviour is performed) multiplied by the evaluation of that outcome (its perceived desirability or undesirability), summed across outcomes. Similarly, subjective norm is determined by the total set of salient normative beliefs, that is, beliefs about the views of important others ('referents'). Specifically, subjective norm is determined by the belief strength for each salient referent (the perceived likelihood that the referent thinks the person should perform the behaviour) multiplied by his or her motivation to comply with that referent, summed across referents. Finally, perceived behavioural control is determined by the total set of salient control beliefs, that is, beliefs about

the presence of factors that may facilitate or impede performance of the behaviour. Specifically, perceived behavioural control is determined by the belief strength for each salient control factor (the perceived likelihood that a given control factor will be present) multiplied by the perceived power of the control factor (the extent to which the control factor will make it easier or more difficult to perform the behaviour), summed across control factors.

The direct path from perceived behavioural control to behaviour in Figure 10.1 is causally ambiguous (Sutton, 2004). It is not clear from descriptions of the theory whether perceived behavioural control is assumed to have a direct causal effect on behaviour or whether the arrow represents an association between perceived behavioural control and behaviour that is induced by actual control as the common cause. This has implications for intervention. If the second interpretation is correct, then changing perceived behavioural control would not lead to behaviour change directly (though it may lead to behaviour change indirectly via a change in intention). Under either interpretation, changing actual control (e.g. by increasing the individual's skills or opportunities to perform the behaviour) would influence behaviour both directly and indirectly (via perceived behavioural control and intention). Note that Figure 10.1 shows actual control influencing perceived control directly but it may be more accurate to show this effect as mediated by control beliefs.

The TPB has been used in numerous observational studies to predict and explain intentions and behaviour. Meta-analyses of these studies show that, on average, the TPB explains between 35 and 50 percent of the variance in intentions and between 26 and 35 percent of the variance in behaviour (Sutton, 2004). However, to date the theory has not been widely used to develop behaviour change interventions (Hardeman et al., 2002).

Applications of the TPB to developing behavioural interventions have focused on changing attitude, subjective norm and perceived behavioural control by changing the salient beliefs that are assumed to determine these constructs. There are three strategies for achieving this aim: change existing salient beliefs; make existing non-salient beliefs salient; or create new salient beliefs. The following section, which is based on Fishbein and Middlestadt (1989) and Sutton (2002b), summarises the steps involved in developing an intervention to change existing salient beliefs.

Of course, there is much more involved in developing and evaluating a behavioural intervention than can be covered here. The scope of this chapter is limited to those aspects of intervention development that are directly related to theory. For a broader picture, the reader is referred to the UK Medical Research Council (MRC) framework (Campbell et al., 2000) and the updated guidelines (Craig et al., 2008). In particular, the theory that is selected as the basis for the behavioural intervention can be embedded in a larger causal model that specifies the hypothesised causal relationships between the components of the proposed intervention (including the proposed behaviour change techniques), the determinants of the target behaviour, the behaviour itself and consequent clinical and health outcomes (Hardeman et al., 2005). Drawing a causal model is a useful early step in the process of planning and designing an intervention. Such a model also helps

in designing the evaluation of the intervention. In particular, it informs decisions about what should be measured; for example, measures of the theoretical determinants of the target behaviour should be included as intermediate outcomes. It also guides the analysis of the data; for example, if measures of the theoretical determinants are included, mediation analysis can be used to test hypotheses about causal pathways.

Steps in the Development of a TPB-based Intervention

1. Decide on the target behaviour and the target population

These are crucial decisions regardless of the theory that is being used to inform the intervention. However, in the TPB, the definition of the target behaviour assumes special importance because it also determines the definition of the constructs to be targeted in the intervention and the wording of the items used to assess these constructs, in accordance with the principle of correspondence or compatibility (Ajzen, 2005). Behaviours can be defined in terms of four components: action, target, time and context. The action component is a necessary part of the definition of any behaviour. The target component is usually necessary, though not always. Time and context are optional; they enable the definition of behaviour to be as specific as required. For example, consider the definition 'stop smoking cigarettes in the New Year when I am at work'. Here, 'stop smoking' is the action, 'cigarettes' is the target, 'in the New Year' is the time component and 'at work' is the context. Having defined the target behaviour in terms of these four components, the measures of the theory's constructs should incorporate this wording and the intervention should target beliefs about this particular behaviour.

2. Identify the modal salient beliefs

The second step is to conduct an elicitation study to identify those salient beliefs with respect to the target behaviour that are most common in a sample of people drawn from the target population. Those beliefs that

Table 10.1 Open-ended questions used in the elicitation study by Elliott, Armitage and Baughan (2005)

1. What do you believe are the *advantages* of keeping within the speed limit while driving in built-up areas?
2. What do you believe are the *disadvantages* of keeping within the speed limit while driving in built-up areas?
3. Is there anything else you think is good or bad about keeping within the speed limit while driving in built-up areas?
4. Which individuals or groups of people would *approve* of you keeping within the speed limit while driving in built-up areas?
5. Which individuals or groups of people would *disapprove* of you keeping within the speed limit while driving in built-up areas?
6. Are there any other individuals or groups who would approve or disapprove of you keeping within the speed limit while driving in built-up areas?
7. What factors or circumstances would make you *more* likely to keep within the speed limit while driving in built-up areas?
8. What factors or circumstances would make you *less* likely to keep within the speed limit while driving in built-up areas?
9. Are there any other factors you can think of that make keeping within the speed limit while driving in built-up areas easy or difficult?

Note: Questions 1 to 3 were designed to elicit salient behavioural beliefs, questions 4 to 6 salient normative beliefs and questions 7 to 9 salient control beliefs.
Source: Elliott, M.A., Armitage, C.J. & Baughan, C.J. (2005). Exploring the beliefs underpinning drivers' intentions to comply with speed limits. *Transportation Research Part F, 8*, 459–479. Elsevier.

are elicited first in response to open-ended questions such as those in Table 10.1 are assumed to be salient for the individual. Those elicited most frequently in the sample are designated the modal salient beliefs.

3. Decide which TPB components to target in the intervention

This decision can be informed by conducting a quantitative study in a second sample from the target population in which all the TPB variables, including the modal salient beliefs, are measured using a structured questionnaire. This second study is usually referred to as the main study. In the analysis, intention is regressed on attitude, subjective norm and perceived behavioural control; and behaviour is regressed on intention and perceived behavioural control. The findings are used to decide whether the intervention should target one, two or all three components. For example, suppose attitude is a relatively strong predictor of intention which is in turn a relatively strong predictor of behaviour, but subjective norm and perceived behavioural control have little independent predictive power. This pattern of findings could be used to justify focusing the intervention on the attitudinal component alone.

4. Decide which specific beliefs to target

The same dataset can be used to identify the beliefs that best discriminate between intenders and non-intenders (or between those who subsequently engage in the behaviour and those who do not). This is usually done by dividing the sample into two groups on the basis of intention or behaviour responses and examining differences in scores between groups on each of the belief measures in turn, for example by conducting a series of t-tests.

5. Develop and evaluate the intervention

The final step is to develop an intervention designed to change these key beliefs, and to evaluate the intervention using the TPB measures in another sample drawn from the target population. Table 10.2 lists the possible ways of changing existing behavioural, normative and control beliefs, using 'walking for more than 20 minutes a day' as the example target behaviour and assuming unipolar scoring (e.g. 1 to 7) for all six belief components.

Of course, variations on this procedure are possible. Relevant prior studies may already exist, which may obviate the need for collecting new data for steps 2 to 4.

Table 10.2   Ways of changing existing beliefs in the theory of planned behaviour, using 'walking for more than 20 minutes a day' as the example target behaviour

---

Behavioural beliefs

(a)   Increase belief strength
   (e.g. increase the perceived likelihood that walking for more than 20 minutes a day will improve fitness)

(b)   Increase outcome evaluation
   (e.g. increase the perceived desirability of the outcome 'will improve my physical fitness')

Normative beliefs

(c)   Increase belief strength
   (e.g. increase the recipient's perceived likelihood that his/her parents – or other significant referents – would approve if he/she walked for more than 20 minutes a day)

(d)   Increase motivation to comply
   (e.g. persuade the recipient that he/she wants to do what his/her parents want them to do)

Control beliefs

(e)   Increase belief strength
   (e.g. increase the recipient's perceived likelihood that they will have more time in the future)

(f)   Increase perceived power
   (e.g. persuade the recipient that having more time in the future will make it easier to walk for more than 20 minutes a day)

Note: These strategies assume the use, and validity, of a particular scoring scheme: unipolar scales for all six belief components, for example 1–7, where 1 means extremely unlikely (belief strength), extremely undesirable (outcome evaluation), extremely low (motivation to comply) and much more difficult (control belief power), and 7 means extremely likely (belief strength), extremely desirable (outcome evaluation), extremely high (motivation to comply) and much easier (control belief power).

In addition to changing existing salient beliefs, the intervention may aim to create new salient beliefs by presenting novel information. For example, an intervention to encourage smokers to quit may present evidence that smoking is a risk factor for osteoporosis.

As described, the procedure seems quite straightforward. However, there are several complexities of which researchers and practitioners need to be aware.

Complexities

Deciding which beliefs to include in the modal salient set

An important decision to be made is which of the beliefs from the elicitation study to include in the modal salient set for the questionnaire in the main study (step 3). This decision needs to be made for each of the three categories of beliefs (behavioural, normative, control). Ajzen and Fishbein (1980) suggest several possible decision rules: take the 10 or 12 most frequently mentioned beliefs; include all beliefs mentioned by at least 10 per cent or 20 per cent of the sample; select as many beliefs as necessary to account for a particular percentage (e.g. 75 per cent) of all beliefs elicited. Numerous variations on these rules could be devised. Application of these different rules may result in different sets of modal salient beliefs. Consider participants completing the TPB questionnaire in the main study. The ideal situation would be that each participant's personally salient beliefs are all included in the questionnaire (call this criterion 1) and no participant is presented with any belief items that are not personally salient to them (criterion 2). The second criterion is relevant because of the risk that, as a consequence of measuring them, non-salient beliefs may become salient, that is, that the questionnaire will be reactive (French & Sutton, in press). Increasing the number of beliefs in the questionnaire (i.e. the size of the modal set) will favour the first criterion at the expense of the second. The decision will therefore be a compromise. See Sutton *et al.* (2003) for a method of using the data from an elicitation study to optimise this trade-off.

Selecting the key beliefs

A commonly used procedure in step 4 is to divide the sample into 'intenders' and 'non-intenders' and to compare these two groups on each of the belief measures in turn using t-tests. For behavioural beliefs, such analyses may examine belief strength, outcome evaluation and/or the product term (belief strength multiplied by outcome evaluation). Those beliefs that best discriminate between the two groups (i.e. show the largest, or most statistically significant, difference in means) are selected for the intervention.

Apart from the loss of information incurred by artificially dichotomising the sample, the main limitation of this procedure is that, for a given belief score, the means for intenders and non-intenders will be partly based on participants for whom that belief is not salient. This proportion will generally be unknown but it may comprise the majority of participants (e.g. up to approximately 80 per cent if the decision rule is 'include all beliefs mentioned by at least 20 per cent of the sample'). A difference between intenders and non-intenders may be observed in the full sample even if there is no difference between intenders and non-intenders for whom the belief is salient. Conversely, if there is a difference in means between intenders and non-intenders for whom the belief is salient, this may not be reflected in an analysis that includes all intenders and non-intenders. Given the problems with this procedure, a pragmatic strategy is to drop step 4 and to target in the intervention a subset of the modal salient beliefs identified in step 2.

The notion that some salient beliefs are more important than others in influencing intention is actually inconsistent with a key assumption of the TPB (Sutton, 2002b). For example, for salient behavioural beliefs, the theory assumes that each belief strength × outcome evaluation product term has the same weight (equal to 1) in determining attitude (and therefore intention). In other words, all the product terms are equally important in determining attitude.

The problems outlined in this and the preceding section arise when the TPB is used to develop a generic intervention where information about individual recipients of the intervention is not available, for example a national campaign to increase condom use among young people. The theory can also be used to develop individually tailored interventions. In tailored interventions, open-ended questions can be used to elicit a participant's salient beliefs, and he or she is then asked to rate them with respect to belief strength, outcome evaluation and so on (e.g. Agnew, 1998; Rutter & Bunce, 1989). The intervention can then be individually targeted. Each individual receives a different version of the intervention, the exact content depending on their own idiosyncratic set of beliefs and belief scores.

The consequences of using different scoring schemes for the belief components

Table 10.2 assumes unipolar scoring (e.g. that responses to the belief questions are scored from 1 to 7) for all six belief components. This is just one of several scoring schemes that have been proposed. Different scoring schemes imply different strategies for changing beliefs. Suppose, for example, that a bipolar scoring scheme is used for behavioural belief strength and outcome evaluation (e.g., −3 to +3 with a midpoint of zero). If an individual believes that it is fairly unlikely (say, −2 on the belief strength scale) that a negative outcome such as 'getting swollen ankles' (say, −2 on the outcome evaluation scale) will occur if they walk for more than 20 minutes a day, then assuming that this 'double negative' belief is salient, it will contribute positively to his/her attitude toward engaging in this behaviour. Furthermore, the less likely the outcome is perceived to be and the more negatively it is evaluated, the greater the positive contribution to the person's attitude. This suggests an intervention strategy of persuading the individual that this outcome is even less likely and even worse than they thought it was, which is the direct opposite of the strategy implied by unipolar scoring.

The question of how belief components should be scored to most accurately reflect the underlying mechanism of how they combine is still unresolved (Ajzen & Fishbein, 2008; French & Hankins, 2003; O'Sullivan et al., 2008). Researchers and practitioners should carefully consider the implications of different scoring schemes for the strategies they select to change beliefs.

Changing beliefs

A limitation of the TPB and similar theories is that it does not specify how to change beliefs, only that belief change requires exposure to 'information', broadly conceived to include not just written information from leaflets and web pages, for example, and verbal information, such as advice from a health professional, but also direct experience with the target behaviour and observation of others performing the behaviour. The currently dominant dual-process theories of persuasion offer only general recommendations about changing beliefs. According to the elaboration likelihood model (ELM; Petty & Wegener, 1999), the kind of change in beliefs or attitudes that is usually regarded as desirable in the health behaviour field (i.e., enduring, resistant to counterpersuasion and predictive of behaviour) is most likely to be produced if a communication presents 'strong' arguments and if the recipients are able and motivated to think about and elaborate on these arguments. However, little research has been done on what makes a strong argument; empirical studies using the ELM have relied on pretesting to identify high-quality arguments. Furthermore, relatively few studies have used the theory in the context of health behaviour change; the typical ELM study investigates attitudes to issues or policies such as a proposed increase in tuition fees rather than beliefs or attitudes with respect to changing personal health behaviour.

Intervention developers therefore need to take an empirical approach to developing strategies to change beliefs. Pretesting of intervention materials and messages should be an important part of step 5 of the intervention development process.

Estimating the potential size of an intervention effect

In planning an intervention, it is useful to have an estimate of the potential size of the intervention effect. This can be used to calculate the sample size required for the evaluation study (Cohen, 1992). Such an estimate is also helpful in the pretesting stage to assess whether the intervention is producing sufficiently large increases in attitude, subjective norm and perceived behavioural control.

It is possible to calculate an estimate of the potential size of an intervention effect from observational data on the TPB (such as would be obtained from step 3 of the intervention development procedure). For example, in a study of medication adherence in a sample of 61 patients with psychiatric problems, TPB variables were assessed at baseline using 7-point scales, and self-reported behaviour was assessed at follow up, in terms of the percentage of time the participant had adhered to medication over the previous nine weeks (Conner et al., 1998). In the analysis, intention was regressed on attitude, subjective norm and perceived behavioural control and behaviour was regressed on intention and perceived behavioural control. Figure 10.2 shows the standardised and unstandardised partial regression coefficients. Results from observational studies of the TPB are often presented in this format or in a table displaying the same information.

Suppose the aim is to estimate the effect on behaviour of increasing attitude. The unstandardised coefficients can be used to derive this estimate in terms of the raw scores. Simply multiply the coefficient for the attitude–intention path by the coefficient for the intention–behaviour path. In this example, the estimate is 2.030 (= .504 × 4.027). This means that an intervention that increases attitude by one unit on the 7-point scale would be expected to produce an increase in medication adherence of about 2 percentage points. If an intervention increased attitude by one unit and subjective norm by 0.5 units, the estimate of the intervention effect would be 2.703 (= 2.030 + (0.5 × .334 × 4.027)). If the behaviour measure is a dichotomy (e.g. attended for a health check, yes/no, coded 1/0), the estimate can be interpreted as the increase in the probability of performing the behaviour or the increase in the proportion of participants who perform the behaviour.

The standardised coefficients can be used in the same way to yield an estimated intervention effect expressed in standard deviation units. For example, an intervention that increased attitude by 0.8 standard deviation units (a 'large' effect according to Cohen, 1992) would be estimated to increase behaviour by 0.8 × .423 × .400 = .135 standard deviation units – a 'small' effect.

This method of estimating potential intervention effect size is simpler and more direct than the simulation method used by Fife-Shaw et al. (2007).

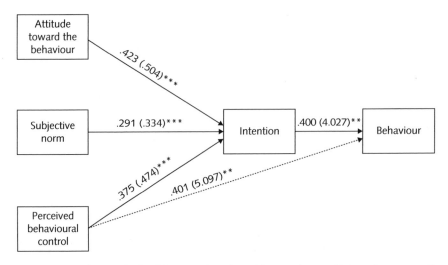

Figure 10.2 Standardised and unstandardised (in parentheses) partial regression coefficients from an application of the theory of planned behaviour to medication adherence in a psychiatric population. ★★ $p < .01$, ★★★ $p < .001$
Source: Conner, M., Black, K. & Stratton, P. (1998). Understanding drug compliance in a psychiatric population: An application of the theory of planned behaviour. *Psychology, Health & Medicine, 3*, 337–344. Taylor & Francis.

Such estimates are subject to a high degree of uncertainty. They will be imprecise, and the degree of imprecision will be greater in smaller samples. They may also be biased: drawing causal inferences from non-experimental data requires several strong assumptions (Sutton, 2002a). Nevertheless, in the absence of experimental data, it is necessary to rely on observational studies.

An Example of a TPB-based Intervention Study

Elliott and Armitage (2009) tested a generic TPB-based intervention to promote car drivers' compliance with speed limits. The target behaviour was compliance with 30 mph speed limits, which was selected because most accidents in Britain occur on 30 mph roads. Participants were sampled from a database of drivers residing in the south east of England.

Participants were randomly assigned to a control group ($N = 159$) who were sent a baseline questionnaire or to an experimental group ($N = 141$) who were also sent an eight-page intervention booklet to be read after completing the questionnaire. Both groups were followed up by postal questionnaire at

one month. The booklet included information about the risks of speeding in 30 mph areas and persuasive messages targeting behavioural, normative and control beliefs associated with complying with 30 mph speed limits. The beliefs to be targeted were those that predicted drivers' attitudes, subjective norms, perceived behavioural control and/or intentions to comply with speed limits in a previous study (Elliott *et al.*, 2005). The messages targeting behavioural beliefs focused on five positive outcomes (that complying with 30 mph speed limits would put pedestrians at less risk, reduce the chances of an accident, use less fuel, make it easier to detect hazards and make driving more relaxing) and one negative outcome (that complying with 30 mph speed limits would make it difficult to keep up with the traffic). Table 10.3 shows the message that was used to target the negative outcome. The normative message targeted three groups of referents (friends, spouses/partners, parents/children). Finally, messages targeting control beliefs consisted of strategies that drivers can use to help them to avoid speeding when late or in a rush, when other drivers are exceeding the speed limit, when the speed limit is not clearly signed and when driving on long straight roads.

The TPB measures used in this study were closely in line with Ajzen's recommendations (Ajzen, 2006a).

Table 10.3   Examples of messages used by Elliott and Armitage (2009) to target behavioural, normative and control beliefs with respect to complying with 30 mph speed limits

---

Behavioural beliefs

Keeping to 30 mph speed limits will not make it difficult to keep up with the traffic

Many drivers think that if they keep to the speed limit they will have difficulty keeping up with the traffic. However, this is a perception rather than a reality for the most part. Consider what driving in a 30 mph area is typically like. Even on larger 30 mph roads, there are roundabouts, traffic lights, pedestrian crossings, and other things that make it necessary for traffic to slow down or stop. If a vehicle in front starts to pull away from you, you will often find that by maintaining a speed of 30 mph you will catch up with that vehicle further up the road, because they have had to stop or slow down. They will have saved no significant amount of time and they will have gained little or no advantage.

Normative beliefs

Do the people important to you really want you or themselves to be involved in an accident?

Many drivers say that a reason why they sometimes drive faster than the speed limit is because they think other people would want them to do so. Drivers may think that people who are important to them, or people whose views they respect, would approve of them driving faster than the speed limit. However, is this really the case? It is a fact that increases in driving speed will increase the risk of a road traffic accident. It is also a fact that increases in driving speed will increase the severity of an accident, were it to occur. Ask yourself: *Do the people who are important to me really want me, or themselves, to be involved in a road accident? Do my friends really want this to happen? Does my girl/boyfriend, or my wife/husband want this to happen? Do my parents or my children want this to happen?*

Control beliefs

Driving in a hurry?

It's actually very easy to keep within the speed limit. Keeping to 30 mph speed limits is something everyone should, and can, do. Many drivers say that they speed because they are late or in a hurry. However, as mentioned above, driving faster than the speed limit does not actually save you that much time when driving in 30 mph areas. You are more likely to make your appointment on time and find it easier to keep to 30 mph speed limits if you plan ahead and make sure you leave plenty of time to reach your destination.

Source: Elliott, M.A. & Armitage, C.J. (2009). Promoting drivers' compliance with speed limits: Testing an intervention based on the theory of planned behaviour. *British Journal of Health Psychology, 100*, 111–132.

The measure of speeding behaviour was the mean of two items: 'How often have you kept within 30 mph speed limits when driving over the last month? (never–nearly all the time); and 'I have kept within 30 mph speed limits when driving over the last month' (strongly disagree–strongly agree).

The intervention had limited effects on cognitions. It influenced one of the control power items: compared with those in the control group, participants in the intervention group were significantly more likely to say that if they were to drive on long straight roads this would make it more likely that they would keep within the speed limit. Intervention participants also had higher perceived behavioural control at follow up. Finally, there was significant effect on the behaviour measure: intervention participants reported greater compliance with speed limits compared with controls. The effect size was small (0.19). Mediation analysis supported a model in which the effect of the intervention on behaviour was mediated by change in perceived behavioural control which was in turn mediated by change in control power for 'long straight roads'.

This study is a good example of a 'pure' TPB-based intervention. A number of observations can be made. The first concerns the target group. Ideally, the target population for such an intervention would be drivers who do not consistently comply with 30 mph speed limits. However, at baseline the study sample had on average strongly positive attitudes, subjective norms and perceived behavioural control with respect to the target behaviour and scored just over 5 on the 7-point self-report measure of compliance with the 30 mph speed limit. The authors comment that there was limited scope for changing many of the TPB variables. Second, the beliefs to be targeted in the intervention were originally identified in a small ($N = 16$) pilot elicitation study. All the beliefs were taken forward to a large quantitative study (Elliott *et al.*, 2005). Those beliefs that were significantly predictive of the TPB variables were selected as targets for the intervention. As noted in an earlier section, this procedure is of doubtful validity. Third, regarding the content of the intervention, note that the normative message (Table 10.3) included information that increases in driving speed increase the risk and severity of accidents, which is relevant to behavioural beliefs. This illustrates a potential difficulty in TPB-based interventions, namely that it is not always easy to design messages that target a single component of the theory.

Conclusions and Recommendations

The theory of planned behaviour offers a systematic approach to intervention development. It is recommended that a modified stepwise procedure is employed based on the steps outlined earlier but omitting step 4 and conducting a relatively large elicitation study in step 2.

More basic research is needed on salient beliefs. The left-hand side of the theory has been neglected

in research on the TPB to date. For example, there is little evidence on the stability of salient beliefs. In principle, different subsets of beliefs may be salient in different situations, which implies that a person's attitude, subjective norm, perceived behavioural control and intention may vary depending on the context. Research is needed that systematically tests the effect of behaviour change techniques (Abraham & Michie, 2008), including information provision, on behavioural, normative and control beliefs. For example, does self-monitoring increase the salience of behavioural beliefs about the affective outcomes of performing the target behaviour? Does offering rewards for behaviour change work by creating a new salient belief ('If I perform behaviour X, I will receive a reward') or does it have additional, less obvious, effects? More research is needed on the most appropriate way of scaling belief components to reflect the underlying mechanism. Ajzen and Fishbein (2008) suggest that this may depend on the behaviour under investigation, the nature of the outcome and the labels used in the questionnaire items. The potential reactivity of TPB questionnaires should also be investigated. Such issues can be studied as part of the process of developing and evaluating TPB-based interventions.

Discussion Points

1 What advantages and disadvantages does the TPB have compared with alternative social cognition models?
2 How can the TPB be used to develop individually tailored interventions?
3 How effective have TPB-based interventions been in changing behaviour?
4 What are the implications of using different decision rules for selecting modal salient beliefs?

5 What are the implications for intervention strategies of using different schemes for scoring belief components?
6 How useful are models of persuasion in informing how to change beliefs?
7 How can TPB-based interventions increase actual control over the target behaviour?
8 How can the reactivity of TPB questionnaires be tested?

Further Reading

Ajzen, I. & Fishbein, M. (1980). *Understanding attitudes and predicting social behavior.* Englewood Cliffs, NJ: Prentice-Hall.
Craig, P., Dieppe, P., Macintyre, S., Michie, S., Nazareth, I. & Petticrew, M. (2008). Developing and evaluating complex interventions: The new Medical Research Council guidelines. *British Medical Journal, 337,* a1655.
Hardeman, W., Sutton, S., Griffin, S., Johnston, M., White, A., Wareham, N.J. & Kinmonth, A.L. (2005). A causal modelling approach to the development of theory-based

behaviour change programmes for trial evaluation. *Health Education Research, 20,* 676–687.

Rutter, D. & Quine, L. (Eds.) (2002). *Changing health behaviour: Intervention and research with social cognition models.* Buckingham: Open University Press.

Sutton, S., French, D.P., Hennings, S.J., Mitchell, J., Wareham, N.J., Griffin, S., Hardeman, W. & Kinmonth, A.L. (2003). Eliciting salient beliefs in research on the theory of planned behaviour: The effect of question wording. *Current Psychology, 22,* 234–251.

References

Abraham, C. & Michie, S. (2008). A taxonomy of behavior change techniques used in interventions. *Health Psychology, 27,* 379–387.

Agnew, C.R. (1998). Modal versus individually-derived beliefs about condom use: Measuring the cognitive underpinnings of the theory of reasoned action. *Psychology & Health, 13,* 271–287.

Ajzen, I. (1991). The theory of planned behavior. *Organizational Behavior and Human Decision Processes, 50,* 179–211.

Ajzen, I. (2005). *Attitudes, personality and behavior* (2nd edn). Buckingham: Open University Press.

Ajzen, I. (2006a). Constructing a TpB questionnaire: Conceptual and methodological considerations. Retrieved 1 May 2009 from www.people.umass.edu/aizen/pdf/tpb.measurement.pdf.

Ajzen, I. (2006b). TpB Diagram. Retrieved 1 May 2009 from www.people.umass.edu/aizen/tpb.diag.html.

Ajzen, I. & Fishbein, M. (1980). *Understanding attitudes and predicting social behavior.* Englewood Cliffs, NJ: Prentice-Hall.

Ajzen, I. & Fishbein, M. (2008). Scaling and testing multiplicative combinations in the expectancy-value model of attitudes. *Journal of Applied Social Psychology, 38,* 2222–2247.

Bandura, A. (1986). *Social foundations of thought and action: A social cognitive theory.* Englewood Cliffs, NJ: Prentice-Hall.

Bandura, A. (1997). *Self-efficacy: The exercise of control.* New York: W.H. Freeman.

Campbell, M., Fitzpatrick, R., Haines, A., Kinmonth, A.L., Sandercock, P., Spiegelhalter, D. & Tyrer, P. (2000). Framework for the design and evaluation of complex interventions to improve health. *British Medical Journal, 321,* 694–696.

Catania, J.A., Kegeles, S.M. & Coates, T.J. (1990). Towards an understanding of risk behaviour: An AIDS risk reduction model (ARRM). *Health Education Quarterly, 17,* 53–72.

Cohen, J. (1992). A power primer. *Psychological Bulletin, 112,* 155–159.

Conner, M., Black, K. & Stratton, P. (1998). Understanding drug compliance in a psychiatric population: An application of the theory of planned behaviour. *Psychology, Health & Medicine, 3,* 337–344.

Conner, M. & Norman, P. (Eds.) (2005). *Predicting health behaviour: Research and practice with social cognition models* (2nd edn). Maidenhead: Open University Press.

Conner, M. & Sparks, P. (2005). Theory of planned behaviour and health behaviour. In M. Conner & P. Norman (Eds.) *Predicting health behaviour: Research and practice with social cognition models* (2nd edn, pp. 170–222). Maidenhead: Open University Press.

Craig, P., Dieppe, P., Macintyre, S., Michie, S., Nazareth, I. & Petticrew, M. (2008). Developing and evaluating complex interventions: The new Medical Research Council guidelines. *British Medical Journal, 337,* a1655.

Elliott, M.A. & Armitage, C.J. (2009). Promoting drivers' compliance with speed limits: Testing an intervention based on the theory of planned behaviour. *British Journal of Health Psychology, 100,* 111–132.

Elliott, M.A., Armitage, C.J. & Baughan, C.J. (2005). Exploring the beliefs underpinning drivers' intentions to comply with speed limits. *Transportation Research Part F, 8,* 459–479.

Fife-Shaw, C., Sheeran, P. & Norman, P. (2007). Simulating behaviour change interventions based on the theory of planned behaviour: Impacts on intention and action. *British Journal of Social Psychology, 46,* 43–68.

Fishbein, M. & Middlestadt, S. E. (1989). Using the theory of reasoned action as a framework for understanding and changing AIDS-related behaviors. In V.M. Mays, G.W. Albee & S.F. Schneider (Eds.) *Primary prevention of AIDS: Psychological approaches* (pp. 93–110). Newbury Park, CA: Sage.

Fisher, J.D. & Fisher, W.A. (1992). Changing AIDS risk behavior. *Psychological Bulletin, 111,* 455–474.

French, D.P. & Hankins, M. (2003). The expectancy-value muddle in the theory of planned behaviour – and some proposed solutions. *British Journal of Health Psychology, 8,* 37–55.

French, D.P. & Sutton, S. (in press). Reactivity of measurement in health psychology: How much of a problem is it? What can be done about it? *British Journal of Health Psychology.*

Hardeman, W., Johnston, M., Johnston, D.W., Bonetti, D., Wareham, N.J. & Kinmonth, A.L. (2002). Application of the theory of planned behaviour in behaviour change interventions: A systematic review. *Psychology & Health, 17,* 123–158.

Hardeman, W., Sutton, S., Griffin, S., Johnston, M., White, A., Wareham, N.J. & Kinmonth, A.L. (2005). A causal modelling approach to the development of theory-based behaviour change programmes for trial evaluation. *Health Education Research, 20,* 676–687.

Ogden, J. (2003). Some problems with social cognition models: A pragmatic and conceptual analysis. *Health Psychology, 22,* 424–428.

O'Sullivan, B., McGee, H. & Keegan, O. (2008). Comparing solutions to the 'expectancy-value muddle' in the theory of planned behaviour. *British Journal of Health Psychology, 13,* 789–802.

Petty, R.E. & Wegener, D.T. (1999). The elaboration likelihood model: Current status and controversies. In S. Chaiken & Y. Trope (Eds.) *Dual-process theories in social psychology* (pp. 41–72). New York: Guilford Press.

Rogers, R.W. (1983). Cognitive and physiological processes in fear appeals and attitude change: A revised theory of protection motivation. In J.T. Cacioppo, R.E. Petty & D. Shapiro (Eds.) *Social psychophysiology: A sourcebook* (pp. 153–176). New York: Guilford Press.

Rutter, D.R. & Bunce, D.J. (1989). The theory of reasoned action of Fishbein and Ajzen: A test of Towriss's amended procedure for measuring beliefs. *British Journal of Social Psychology, 28,* 39–46.

Schwarzer, R. (2008). Modeling health behavior change: How to predict and modify the adoption and maintenance of health behaviors. *Applied Psychology: An International Review, 57,* 1–29.

Strecher, V.J. & Rosenstock, I.M. (2002). The health belief model. In A. Baum, S. Newman, J. Weinman, R. West & C. McManus (Eds.) *Cambridge handbook of psychology, health and medicine* (pp. 113-117). Cambridge: Cambridge University Press.

Stroebe, W. (2000). *Social psychology and health* (2nd edn). Buckingham: Open University Press.

Sutton, S. (2002a). Testing attitude-behaviour theories using non-experimental data: An examination of some hidden assumptions. *European Review of Social Psychology, 13,* 293–323.

Sutton, S. (2002b). Using social cognition models to develop health behaviour interventions: Problems and assumptions. In D. Rutter & L. Quine (Eds.) *Changing health behaviour: Intervention and research with social cognition models* (pp. 193–208). Buckingham: Open University Press.

Sutton, S. (2004). Determinants of health-related behaviours: Theoretical and methodological issues. In S. Sutton, A. Baum & M. Johnston (Eds.) *The Sage handbook of health psychology* (pp. 94–126). London: Sage.

Sutton, S. (2008). How does the Health Action Process Approach (HAPA) bridge the intention-behavior gap? An examination of the model's causal structure. *Applied Psychology: An International Review, 57,* 66–74.

Sutton, S., French, D.P., Hennings, S.J., Mitchell, J., Wareham, N.J., Griffin, S., Hardeman, W. & Kinmonth, A.L. (2003). Eliciting salient beliefs in research on the theory of planned behaviour: The effect of question wording. *Current Psychology, 22,* 234–251.

11

Stage Models of Behaviour Change

Falko F. Sniehotta and Robert Aunger

Chapter Outline

This chapter introduces stage theories of behaviour change, a set of theoretical models describing the change process as a sequence of qualitatively different stages individuals pass through on their way to sustained behaviour change. Each of these stages is defined by specific barriers to stage progression and often by specific psychological states. Consequently, it is assumed that interventions matched to specific stages are more effective in supporting people to progress towards action.

The most important stage models for health psychology and standard tests of stage models are introduced, after which the evidence for these models is evaluated against these tests.

Key Concepts

Experimental matched-mismatched designs
Intention–behaviour gap
Mindsets
Precaution process model
Rubicon model of action phases
Stage matched interventions
Stage versus pseudo-stage models
Stages of change
Transtheoretical model

Introduction

Stage models of behaviour change assume that changing behaviour requires a sequence of qualitatively different changes in psychological factors and practices as individuals come gradually to adopt new behaviours. These changes can be conceptualised as distinct stages an individual passes through on the way to behaviour change. For example, in order to make an appointment to receive a vaccination, an individual must have first become aware of the potential illness and the availability of a vaccine, then deliberated if getting a vaccine would be a good idea and then called the GP practice to make the appointment. At each stage, different tasks and cognitions will be of relevance.

While the idea of stages may be intuitively compelling, most theoretical models of behaviour change suggest that people can adopt new patterns of behaviour with a single decision or change in belief. Traditional social cognition models specify a small set of psychological variables such as self-efficacy, outcome expectations and intentions, which are used to predict behaviour using a single equation. In stage models, several equations are needed to predict stage progression. This chapter discusses a selection of approaches that have been devoted to describing a process of behaviour adoption in terms of stages.

Stages can be defined as a set of categorically different, ordered states, which are similar internally in terms of cognitive, emotional and behavioural features, but psychologically different from each other. Stage models are characterised by four defining features (Weinstein, Rothman et al., 1998):

- **Stage definitions**: A diagnostic algorithm which assigns individuals to an exhaustive and distinctive set of stages in accordance with cognitive and/or emotional and/or behavioural qualities.
- **Sequence of stages**: The assumption that individuals sequentially pass through each stage on the way to adoption of new intentional behaviours and that regressions to previous stages are possible.
- **Common barriers within the same stage**: Barriers to progressing to the next stage are those things which need to be achieved to make progress

from the current to the next stage; often these barriers are associated with assumptions about common features such as stage-specific 'mindsets' or characteristic states resulting from successful transitions from previous stages and engagement with current barriers (Heckhausen, 1991).

- **Different barriers between different stages**: People at different stages face different barriers, need to master different tasks, or differ regarding their mindset, and thus benefit from different interventions toward behaviour change (i.e. the variables that differentiate between people in stages 1 and 2 are not the same ones that differentiate between people in stages 2 and 3).

According to stage models, people in different stages face particular challenges in progressing to the next stage of the change process, and differ in their thoughts and feelings about the behaviour the model is applied to in each stage. The important practical implication is that interventions 'tailored' to an individual's stage will be more effective than a 'one-size-fits-all' intervention. Individuals deciding whether or not to act would, for example, benefit more from provision of information about behavioural consequences, whereas those who have already decided to act would benefit more from information about opportunities to act.

The following sections introduce the most important stage models relevant to health psychology, standard types of tests for such stage models, and a summary of the evidence regarding these models for each of these kinds of tests (Weinstein, Lyon et al., 1998). A complete overview of all stage models is beyond the scope of this chapter and can be found elsewhere (Aunger & Curtis, in press).

Transtheoretical Model of Change (TTM)

Historically the first, and empirically the most frequently utilised, stage model is the 'transtheoretical' or 'stages of change' model of Prochaska and colleagues (Prochaska et al., 1993; Prochaska & Velicer, 1997) (http://www.uri.edu/research/cprc/transtheoretical. htm). The TTM integrates basic principles of behaviour

Table 11.1 Transtheoretical model: stages of change

Stage	Definition	Processes of change
Precontemplation	Not seriously thinking changing behaviour	**Consciousness raising:** Efforts by the individual to seek new information and to gain understanding and feedback about the problem behaviour **Dramatic relief:** Experiencing and expressing feelings about the problem behaviour and potential solutions **Environmental reevaluation:** Consideration and assessment of how the problem behaviour affects the physical and social environment
Contemplation	Seriously thinking about changing behaviour in the next 6 months + but not within the next 30 days + no attempt in the past year	**Self-reevaluation:** Emotional and cognitive reappraisal of values by the individual with respect to the problem behaviour
Preparation	Seriously thinking about changing behaviour in the next 30 days	**Self-liberation:** Choice and commitment to change the problem behaviour, including belief in the ability to change **Social liberation:** Awareness, availability and acceptance by the individual of alternative, problem-free lifestyles in society
Action	First 6 months of abstinence	**Stimulus control:** Control of situations and other causes which trigger the problem behaviour **Counter-conditioning:** Substitution of alternatives for the problem behaviour
Maintenance	Abstinence beyond 6 months	**Helping relationships:** Trusting, accepting and utilising the support of caring others during attempts to change the problem behaviour **Contingency management:** Rewarding oneself or being rewarded by others for making changes
(Termination)	Complete absence of temptation for previous behaviour	No more activities needed to maintain behaviour

Note: Definitions adapted from www.uri.edu/research/cprc/TTM/ProcessesOfChange.htm, retrieved 25 May 2009.

change from the major theories of intervention current at the time, based on clinical experience in the area of smoking cessation; hence the appellation 'transtheoretical'.

The TTM divides people into one of five, sometimes six different *stages of change* (see Table 11.1). Stage definitions differ slightly dependent on the target behaviour. For the example of smoking cessation, individuals in the 'precontemplation' stage are not thinking about stopping smoking within the next six months. Those in the 'contemplation' stage are seriously deliberating about stopping sometime in the medium-term future (usually defined as between one to six months). 'Preparation' is the stage in which individuals intend to quit in the near term (i.e. within

a month), and have taken steps to make themselves ready for quitting. 'Action' is the stage in which people have quit for less than six months. The individual enters the 'maintenance' stage once they have been continuously abstinent for more than six months. The first three stages are assumed to involve motivational processes, while the latter two are behavioural. People are assumed to move through each of these stages in the order listed, although the authors of the approach acknowledge that people might regress occasionally (i.e. move backward to an 'earlier' stage). In some applications, a sixth stage, 'termination' is added, where people have permanently adopted a new behaviour and no longer perceive any temptation to revert to their previous behaviour.

The TTM hypothesises that there are 10 independent experiential and behavioural 'processes of change' which facilitate stage progression, each of which is peculiar to one (or sometimes more) of these five stages (see Table 11.1). People in a particular stage use the associated processes to overcome the barriers of movement to the next stage. For example, those in the precontemplation stage are expected to seek out information (i.e. raise their consciousness) about the benefits of the target behaviour, or to reward themselves for making changes (reinforcement management). Thus, there are specific processes that differentiate one stage from the next, given the individual's readiness to change their behaviour. These processes are formulated in a way that allows linking behaviour change techniques to processes of change.

Furthermore, the TTM theorises that the decisional balance of pros and cons (positive and negative outcome expectations), self-efficacy (perceive ability to perform the target behaviour) and temptation function as intermediate or 'dependent' outcomes. These outcomes mediate the relationships between the processes of change and progress on the stages of change (Prochaska & Velicer, 1997).

Empirical evidence for the TTM

Cross-sectional tests Cross-sectional designs provide the weakest tests of stage model assumptions. They are, however, common because they are relatively simple to perform – one simply needs to compare people within a population at a single point in time.

Analytically, cross-sectional designs support stage models, to the extent that: (a) the variance within a stage of measures indicative of stage-specific mindsets is smaller than the variation between stages, indicating that people in the same stage are more similar to each other than those in different stages; (b) participants in different stages differ from those in other stages with regard to variables indicative of hypothesised mindsets; and (c) patterns of differences in key variables between the stages are in line with the assumptions above regarding stage models.

Remember, people in different stages should face different barriers for progress, require different strategies and have different mindsets. If stages vary on some dimensions continuously (say each successive stage shows significantly higher self-efficacy or reported strength of intention to perform the target behaviour), then even if those differences between stages are significantly different quantitatively, they could indicate a single continuous process of change (i.e. 'pseudo-stages'). Only a pattern of discontinuous change in relevant variables suggests that people are qualitatively different from each other, and thus likely to be in different stages (Sutton, 2000).

Cross-sectional evidence for the TTM Cross-sectional tests of the TTM show that patterns of differences in pros, cons, self-efficacy and temptation differ substantially over the stages of change for different health behaviours. However, in most cases, these measures show linear increases or decreases over stages, indicative of continuous differences rather than qualitative differences (Rosen, 2000). More recently, Armitage and Arden (2002) showed that the stages of change for adopting healthy food choices are a linear function of theory of planned behaviour measures. The current cross-sectional evidence, then, is consistent only with a 'pseudo-stage' mode of change.

Longitudinal tests A somewhat stronger test of stage assumptions can be conducted using prospective or longitudinal designs, following participants to determine if and how they have changed and which variables predict progress or regress from different stages. Longitudinal designs support stage models assumptions if:

1 progress follows the proposed sequence;
2 progression over time can be predicted from a different set of variables in each stage; and
3 stage allocation is predictive of future behaviour.

The rationale for prospective tests is that transitions from different stages would be predicted by different variables (matched to the barriers for progress defined in criteria 3 and 4). However, the predictive utility of measures is limited by their variability and stages usually limit the variability of key measures. For example, in stages defined by having an intention (e.g. preparation), motivational measures related to intentions (e.g. pros, cons or self-efficacy) will show reduced variance and are therefore less likely to be predictive of stage transitions than in stages with a wider range of intention levels. However, if one finds that the transition from having an intention to taking action is predicted by action planning and the transition from not thinking about changing to deliberating by knowledge, one would conclude that the finding is supportive of the idea that different factors promote stage transition at both of these hypothetical stages.

Longitudinal evidence for the TTM   The stages of change have some predictive value. For example, participants in the preparation stage for smoking cessation are more likely to subsequently quit than those in the precontemplation phase. However, when standard measures such as previous smoking behaviour and quitting history are controlled for, the stages lose their predictive utility. Likewise, long-term maintenance of cessation is better predicted by simple descriptive data about smoking patterns and quitting attempts than by the stages (Abrams *et al.*, 2000; Farkas, 1996). Similarly, de Vet and colleagues (2007a, 2007b) showed that the stages of change are less predictive of fruit intake than a continuous or dichotomous measure of intention.

Several studies have tested the utility of variables outside of the TTM for predicting stage progress in the stages of change and showed, for example, that theory of planned behaviour variables are predictive of stage progression. In a study of healthy food choice involving nearly 800 participants, it was found that sociodemographic variables and a stage-specific intervention predicted progression to particular stages, except for the most relevant movement from the preparation to the action stage, which was not correlated with any of the included variables (Armitage *et al.*, 2004). Likewise, it has been shown that the predictive power of other social cognitive measures is moderated by the stage allocation (Lippke & Plotnikof, 2009).

While there is a wealth of data showing different patterns of prediction for stage transitions and behaviour prediction, there is to date no clear evidence from longitudinal research that transitions from each of the stages of change are predicted by the stage-specific pattern of processes of change, pros, cons, self-efficacy and temptation that the theory suggests.

Experimental tests   Experiments provide the most rigorous tests of stage theories. They usually follow a 'matched–mismatched' design in which participants in at least two different stages are randomly assigned to at least two interventions, each of which is tailored to facilitate progress from one of the stages participants are in. Thus participants are either allocated to a condition matched or mismatched to their initial stage. If the theory has correctly defined the characteristics of stages, then the matched interventions should be more effective at promoting stage transition than the mismatched intervention. Consequently, the analysis for stage transition tests for an interaction between intervention and baseline. A theoretically weaker approach is based on experiments or randomised controlled trials in which interventions based on stage theories are compared against interventions based on other theories, or – even weaker – against passive control groups (Weinstein, Lyon *et al.*, 1998).

Experimental evidence for the TTM   An exemplary experimental test of the TTM was conducted by Blissmer and McAuley (2002) in a study on physical activity. The authors randomly allocated participants to one of four conditions: (i) receiving a stage matched TTM intervention; (ii) receiving one of the materials as used in condition 'i' but mismatched to participants' current state allocation; (iii) standard care, action-oriented leaflets developed by the American Heart Association; and (iv) a control condition. The authors found that the stage-matched interventions resulted in higher physical activity levels than stage-mismatched and control conditions. However, the action-related standard care intervention did as well as the stage-matched intervention and this intervention did not require the additional effort of stage diagnostics and tailoring.

Quinlan and McCaul (2000) tested the effects of a stage-matched (prompting participants to deliberate about quitting smoking) and a stage-mismatched (action-oriented intervention usually used for individuals in the preparation stage) intervention on quitting attempts amongst daily smokers in the precontemplation stage. Contrary to the assumptions in the TTM, participants receiving the *mismatched* intervention were more likely to make a quit attempt

(Quinlan & McCaul, 2000). This is in line with evidence showing that prompting deliberation and changing attitudes (indicative for the transition through the motivational stages of the TTM) is not effective in changing behaviour. Stage matching in accordance with the TTM can therefore involve denying more effective interventions to participants (West, 2005).

A recent systematic review identified 37 randomly controlled trials designed to facilitate change in seven different health-related behaviours (Bridle *et al.*, 2005). The authors found limited evidence that stage-based interventions facilitated progression through stages, regardless of the type of control treatment (e.g. alternative interventions, a care intervention, or no intervention). Only 6 of 18 comparisons showed greater forward movement through stages than controls, although overall, data quality was poor.

Overall evaluation of the TTM

As this brief review of empirical studies suggests, there is little evidence that people progress, as expected, from the first to last stage in order (Littell & Girvin, 2002), or that interventions designed for a given stage are more effective at moving people from that stage to the next than interventions which do not target stages (Adams & White, 2005; Aveyard *et al.*, 2009; Bridle *et al.*, 2003; Herzog *et al.*, 1999). Also, studies often use stage progress rather than actual behaviour change as dependent variables, which assumes the validity of the models rather than testing it. As a result of this poor empirical record, some have called for a moratorium on research using the TTM (West, 2005; Sutton, 2005).

The TTM has also been subjected to a number of theoretical criticisms (Sutton, 2001). First, some stages are defined by arbitrary criteria (e.g. a specific amount of time spent in the stage), which do not seem to map onto relevant psychological processes. For example, it is not compelling that people would progress to the maintenance phase just because they have been in the action phase for six months. Secondly, some authors have argued that behaviour change might be better described by specifying a smaller or larger number of stages with other specifications than those postulated by the TTM. Consequently, more recent stage models

use other means to define the criteria to categorise similar kinds of mindsets during the process of change, thus aiming for a stage model better supported by evidence.

Precaution Adoption Process Model

The precaution adoption process model (PAPM; Weinstein & Sandman, 1992) is a revision of the TTM, and overcomes many of the conceptual criticisms associated with it. Stage definitions are consistently based on psychological criteria rather than external factors (such as time). The PAPM aims at explaining the deliberative processes involved in making decisions about behaviour change and the translation of these decisions into action (e.g. taking a newly available vaccination). It does not aim to explain the gradual development of behaviour patterns such as diet or exercise or the adoption of risk behaviours (Weinstein *et al.*, 2008). Defining the range of intended applications is a crucial feature of scientific theories often neglected in psychology. The authors also acknowledge that the PAPM is unfinished, a model in development. A full model explicitly proposes the stages as well as the factors promoting transition from each stage.

PAPM has seven stages (Table 11.2). In the beginning, people are unaware of the health issue (stage 1). When they first learn something about the hazard, they can no longer be said to be unaware, and are starting to form opinions, but tend not to be engaged by it either (i.e. don't really think the issue applies to them, or are not susceptible to the health problem) (stage 2). People then reach the decision-making stage (stage 3), having become engaged by the issue, perhaps because they have had some personal experience with it. At this point, they begin to consider their response. This decision-making process can result in one of three outcomes. First, they may suspend judgement, remaining in stage 3 for the moment. Second, they may decide to take no action, at least for the time being (stage 4). These people have actively decided not to act respond differently to information, become more resistant to persuasion, and may engage in actions that protect their decision/position. Third, they may decide to adopt the target behaviour, and

Table 11.2   PAPM: Stages of precaution adoption

Stage	Psychological state	Progression/Step	Factors of change
1	Unaware	—	—
2	Unengaged	First learnings	Media messages about the hazard and precaution
3	Undecided	Suspend judgement	Communications from significant others
			Personal experience with hazard
4	Decided not to act	Take negative decision	Beliefs about hazard likelihood and severity
			Beliefs about personal susceptibility
5	Decided to act	Take positive decision	Beliefs about precaution effectiveness and difficulty
			Behaviours and recommendations of others
			Perceived social norms
			Fear and worry
6	Acting	Initiate behaviour	Time, effort and resources needed to act
			Detailed 'how-to' information
			Reminders and other cues to action
			Assistance in carrying out action
7	Maintenance	Engage in sustaining actions	

Source: Adapted from Weinstein, N.D. Sandman, P.M. & Blalock, S.J. (2008). The precaution adaption process model. In K. Glanz, B.K. Rimer & K. Viswanath (Eds.) *Health behavior and health education: Theory, research and practice* (4th edn, pp.123–149). San Francisco: Jossey-Bass.

thus move to stage 5. Those who decide to adopt should then begin to initiate the behaviour (stage 6). A seventh stage, if relevant, indicates that the behaviour has been maintained over time (stage 7).

Since stages 3, 4 and 5 are mutually exclusive, but all direct consequences of stage 2, there cannot be a strict progression through these three stages; instead, the individual is hypothesised to move from stage 2 into one of these, and if in stage 5, then straight on to stage 6; if stage 3, then potentially into stage 4 or 5 next; but if stage 4, then the individual moves no further. This is, in fact, the primary distinction between PAPM and TTM in terms of stages (although the definitions of these stages are also different).

As with TTM, PAPM suggests that there are specific factors associated with movement from one stage to the next (see Table 11.2) (Weinstein & Sandman, 1992). However, the authors of the theory argue these are not factors already proven to be associated with progress through stages, but rather reasonable candidates; users of the approach are invited to test these relationships and others they believe might hold true. To date, the PAPM does not specify in detail information the barriers at each stage and the critical factors

to overcome these barriers (Weinstein, Lyon *et al.*, 1998). The model is thus not strictly testable, but aims at inspiring research to explain the process of adopting precautious behaviours.

PAPM evidence

PAPM has been tested less than TTM. Cross-sectional stage comparisons find that the variables that distinguish one stage from another vary depending on which two stages are compared (Blalock *et al.*, 1996; Clemow *et al.*, 2000; Costanza *et al.*, 2005; Sniehotta *et al.*, 2005). These results give some support to the claim that the PAPM stages are qualitatively different, so the evidence for this model is more favourable than that for TTM (even though they are very similar!). For example, in a year-long prospective study of calcium supplement intake, isolated instances of adequate calcium intake were predicted by higher levels of knowledge and perceived benefits, whereas long-term maintenance was predicted by lower levels of perceived difficulty, providing some support that individuals in different stages had different characteristics (Blalock, 2007). De Vet and colleagues (2008) found that transitions from PAPM stages for fruit intake were predicted by different variables: attitude and social influences were predictive of stage transitions amongst those deciding whether to act or not, whereas self-efficacy was predictive of the transition from decided to act to taking action.

Recently, the TTM and the PAPM have been directly compared for their ability to predict transitions in fruit intake (De Vet *et al.*, 2007a, 2007b, 2008). Using a longitudinal design, a cohort of 700 adults completed questionnaires assessing fruit intake, stages of change and intention to increase fruit intake several times over a period of two months. The researchers found that PAPM better described the processes through which the individuals progressed than TTM, suggesting that a better definition of stages does produce better descriptions of the processes people actually go through.

Perhaps the strongest study to date (because it is an experimental, match–mismatch design) supports the fundamental distinction between the pre-intention versus post intention (Weinstein, Lyon *et al.*, 1998). This study concerns testing for the presence of radon in the home environment through a single do-it-yourself test. Radon is an invisible, odourless, radioactive gas produced by the decay of small amounts of naturally occurring uranium in soil. The home radon testing experiment focused on two stage transitions: from being undecided about testing one's home for radon (stage 3) to deciding to test (stage 5); and from deciding to test (stage 5) to ordering a test (stage 6). People in both stages 3 and 5 were subjected to theory-based interventions matched to their stage, or matched to the other stage in the experiment (or both interventions). Information about the local radon risk was chosen for stage 3, while the stage 5 interventions were designed to increase the ease of testing by providing information about do-it-yourself test kits and an actual test order form. Of the original sample 55 per cent progressed from stage 3 by the end of the experiment (versus 19 per cent in control group); from stage 5 36 per cent (versus 8 per cent in control group). Thus, the matched treatments worked significantly better, indicating that there are psychological differences between people who are uncommitted to change, and those who are (Weinstein, Lyon *et al.*, 1998).

Overall evaluation of the PAPM

Based on the present evidence, the PAPM might contribute to a better understanding of the process of adopting health behaviours. The model provides a particularly useful account of the early stages of behaviour adoption in response to new health threats (e.g. radon home testing, meat consumption during a livestock epidemic). However, the model's assumptions are less explicit than those in the TTM, so that empirical tests are less rigorous. The strongest experimental evidence from the PAPM research (Weinstein, Lyon *et al.*, 1998) supports the distinction between intenders and non-intenders. This distinction is also at the heart of the Rubicon model of action phases, discussed next.

Rubicon Model of Action Phases

The major contribution of the 'Rubicon' model of action phases (Heckhausen, 1991) is to provide clear criteria for defining boundaries between 'phases' (rather than stages), by hypothesising and testing features of phase-specific mindsets (see Table 11.3). The model describes behaviour change in four consecutive phases: (i) a preactional motivational phase, focussing on goal choice; (ii) a preactional volitional phase, focusing on planning; (iii) an actional volitional phase where action performance is managed; and (iv) a post-actional motivation phase in which the results of one's action are evaluated.

The model identifies three important boundaries or transitions between phases: from general motivation to a decision/intention; to the initiation of action; and then a transition back to motivational phase during which evaluation of the action takes place. In the pre-decisional, deliberative phase, the individual is assumed to consider the likely benefits from pursuing the goal, determining what the likely benefits are, and how much they value such benefits. They also consider the costs of changing, and whether they can achieve the goal through their own abilities (Heckhausen, 1991).

With the formation of an intention (i.e. the shift from goal setting to goal striving), the individual is postulated to move from a fluid state of contemplation

Table 11.3 Qualities of the mindsets associated with Rubicon model

Mindset	Content	Selectivity	Information processing
Motivational	Incentive focused anticipation of possible consequences of behaviour (value) Likelihood of different consequences to occur (realisation)	Low, open-minded reception of all available information about possible options	'Reality-oriented', unbiased by wishes and desires
Volitional	Focused on realisation of intentions and plans	High, cognitive shielding of the intention by ignoring incongruent information	'Realisation-oriented', accompanied by optimistic bias

(pre-decisional phase) to one of firm commitment (preactional volitional phase) – in analogy to the Roman emperor Julius Caesar crossing the Rubicon river, and thereby committing himself to a civil war. Ideally, people in this preactional phase should develop plans which specify exactly when, where and how goal-directed behaviour is to be performed – what Gollwitzer (1999) called 'implementation intentions' – which is assumed to facilitate the transition into the volitional action phase in which the goal is actively pursued. The postactional phase involves evaluating what has been achieved (using a motivational frame of mind so that the individual's values are available) compared to the initial goal. Indeed, the individual must determine whether action can cease because the goal has been reached, and whether the hoped-for benefits were forthcoming as a result of action.

As with the other stage models, specific tasks have to be solved in each stage. In this case, making a decision, planning the execution, initiating action and evaluating the outcome are considered to result in specific, characteristic mindsets (Gollwitzer, 1999). Cognitions in motivational and volitional mindsets are distinguished by their content (certain thoughts are more prevalent than in other mindsets), selectivity of information reception (certain information is more likely to be attended to and memorised) and information processing (information is processed with different aims in different phases).

This model has been tested in an experimental paradigm in which participants first get primed, for example by being asked to deliberate on an unsolved personal problem (deliberative mindset) or to plan the implementation of a recently set personal goal (implemental mindset). In a subsequent allegedly unrelated experiment, cognitive, self-evaluative and behavioural consequences of mindsets are assessed. There is good evidence that participants in deliberative mindsets think more about values of expected outcomes whereas participants in implemental mindsets think about when, where and how to act, and are more likely to attend to and recall stage-congruent information (Heckhausen, 1991). Moreover, there is a volitional bias after forming an intention. People in preintentional stages judge desirability and feasibility impartially whereas an implemental mindset is associated with strong optimistic biases (Heckhausen & Gollwitzer, 1987).

Overall evaluation of the Rubicon model

The Rubicon model of action phases has not yet been subjected to the typical stage model tests outlined above, nor directly applied to health psychology. However, the key ideas of this model have become extremely influential in health psychology. Forming an intention and adopting action are the most powerful moderators in the process of health behaviour change. Both events qualitatively change the psychological processes taking place with respect to a particular behaviour. All stage models incorporate these two transitions. In particular the health action process approach (HAPA; Schwarzer, 2008) has been influenced by this the Rubicon model. It distinguishes between an initial, motivation phase, during which people develop an intention to act, based on beliefs about risk, outcomes and self-efficacy, and the volition phase in which they plan the details of action, initiate action and deal with the difficulties of carrying out that action successfully. However, the HAPA is not formulated as a strict stage model and most studies use the model to investigate the mechanisms through which people translate their intentions into action (mediators), rather than as a stage model (Schwarzer et al., 2008).

'Intervention–Behaviour Gap' and Solutions

The strongest evidence for qualitative psychological changes in the process of adopting new behaviour supports the distinction of pre-intentional and post-intentional states (Gollwitzer, 1999; Schwarzer, 2008; Weinstein, Lyon et al., 1998). While intention formation is influenced by beliefs about the value of anticipated outcomes and perceived ability to perform the target behaviour (Fishbein & Ajzen, 1975), intentions are necessary, but not sufficient conditions for behaviour change. Amongst those who form an intention, however, more than half fail to put this intention into practice. This has been described as the intention–behaviour gap (Orbell & Sheeran, 1998).

Several approaches have been suggested to bridge this intention–behaviour gap by introducing post-intentional constructs focusing on how people pursue their goals after forming an intention. The most prominent examples are 'implementation intentions' or specific if-then plans, which have been shown to facilitate action adoption amongst intenders (Gollwitzer, 1999; Gollwitzer & Sheeran, 2006; Sniehotta, 2009) and specific self-efficacy beliefs about capabilities to cope with impediments ('coping self-efficacy') or to recover from lapses ('recovery self-efficacy') (Marlatt, 1996; Schwarzer, 2008). These approaches are not explicitly referred to as stage models but they do share the assumptions of sequence and qualitatively different psychological processes definitive of stage approaches.

Conclusion

To date, there is no conclusive evidence that the process of behaviour change can be reliably characterised as movement through a definite series of stages which can be differentiated on psychological grounds. This may be because stages have not as yet been properly characterised (except for the basic distinction between a pre- and post-intentional phase which is strongly supported by evidence). In particular, there is little evidence to support the key claim of these approaches that treatments are more successful when applied in a stage sequence than when applied in a random sequence.

It remains to be seen how many stages should be specified and whether a continuous change model better fits the data (although some have argued that the existing data from TTM and other stage models is more consistent with a continuous interpretation of change than discrete stages (De Vet et al., 2007a, 2007b; Sutton, 1996; Weinstein, Rothman et al., 1998).

The core principles of stage models are sequence and moderation (the importance of psychological variables and interventions depends on the progress made towards behaviour change). Some of the sequence is common-sense rather than the object of empirical tests: One cannot deliberate about using radon home tests before one has become aware of the radon risk and the possibility of testing. One cannot form an intention without some deliberation. Making a plan before one decides to act seems as unlikely as unintended adoption of new preventive behaviours. The key moderators in the stage models seem to be the formulation of an intention and the adoption of actual behaviour. Future research will need to show if combining these and other moderators in a unidimensional stage model is useful.

Health psychology is thus currently left in the unresolved situation of believing that behaviour change is probably a dynamic process, but without having a well-defined and empirically confirmed approach to understanding that process. The least well formulated model (TTM) is the most used and most tested, and appears not to be very efficacious. Better formulated models have been used less often, so it is not yet clear whether they work any better. Hopefully a theoretical breakthrough will occur in the near future, or one of the newer existing models will be shown to have substantial validity, thus remedying this situation.

Discussion Points

1 What are the differences between stage models and social cognition models of behaviour change?

2 How can stage model assumptions be tested? Which tests are the most rigorous?

3 How are mindsets defined in the Rubicon model of action phases?

4 What are the differences between the TTM and the PAPM?

5 Does evidence support the TTM? Discuss the evidence.

6 How would you develop a theory-based intervention to help people stop smoking based on any of the stage models described? How would that intervention differ from those developed based on a social cognition model?

7 What is the rationale for an experimental matched–mismatched test of a stage model?

Further Reading

Aunger, R. & Curtis. V. (in press). *Consolidating behaviour change theory*.

Sutton, S. (2001). Back to the drawing board? A review of applications of the transtheoretical model to substance use. *Addiction, 96*, 175–186.

Weinstein, N.D., Rothman A. & Sutton, S. (1998). Stage theories of health behavior. *Health Psychology, 17*, 290–299.

West, R. (2005). Time for a change: Putting the Transtheoretical (Stages of Change) Model to rest. *Addiction, 100*, 1036–1039.

References

Abrams, D.B., Herzog, T.A., Emmons, K.M. & Linnan, L. (2000). Stages of change versus addiction: A replication and extension. *Nicotine & Tobacco Research, 2*, 223–229.

Adams, J. & White, M. (2005). Why don't stage-based activity promotion interventions work? *Health Education Research, 20*, 237–243.

Armitage, C.J. & Arden, M.A. (2002). Exploring discontinuity pattern in the transtheoretical model: An application of the theory of planned behaviour. *British Journal of Health Psychology, 7*, 89–103.

Armitage, C.J., Sheeran, P., Conner, M. & Arden, M.A. (2004). Stages of change or changes of stage? Predicting changes in transtheoretical model stages in relation to healthy food choice. *Journal of Consulting and Clinical Psychology, 72*, 491–499.

Aunger, R. & Curtis, V. (in press). Consolidating behaviour change theory.

Aveyard, P., Massey, L., Parsons, A., Manaseki, S. & Griffin, C. (2009). The effect of transtheoretical model based interventions on smoking cessation. *Social Science & Medicine, 68*, 397–403.

Blalock, S.J. (2007). Predictors of calcium intake patterns: A longitudinal analysis. *Health Psychology, 26*, 251–258.

Blalock, S.J., DeVellis, R.F., Giorgino, K.B., DeVellis, B.M., Gold, D., Dooley, M.A., Anderson, J.B. & Smith, S.L. (1996). Osteoporosis prevention in premenopausal women: Using a stage model approach to examine the predictors of behaviour. *Health Psychology, 15*, 84–93.

Blissmer, B. & McAuley, E. (2002). Testing the requirements of stages of physical activity among adults: The comparative effectiveness of stage-matched, mismatched, standard care, and control interventions. *Annals of Behavioral Medicine, 24*, 181–189.

Bridle, C., Riemsma, R.P., Pattenden, J., Sowden, A.J., Mather, L., Watt, I.S. & Walker A. (2005). Systematic review of the effectiveness of health behavior interventions based on the transtheoretical model, *Psychology & Health, 20*, 283–301.

Clemow, L., Costanza, M.E., Haddad, W.P., Luckmann, R., White, M.J., Klaus D. & Stoddard, A.M. (2000). Underutilizers of mammography screening today: Characteristics of women planning, undecided about, and not planning a mammogram. *Annals of Behavioral Medicine, 22*, 80–88.

Costanza, M.E., Luckmann, R., Stoddard, A.M., White, M.J., Stark, J.R., Clemow, L. & Rosal, M.C. (2005). Applying a stage model of behavior change to colon cancer screening. *Preventive Medicine, 41*, 707–719.

De Vet, E., De Nooijer, J., De Vries, N.K. & Brug, J. (2007a). Comparing stage of change and behavioral intention to understand fruit intake. *Health Education Research, 22,* 599–608.

De Vet, E., De Nooijer, J., De Vries, N.K. & Brug, J. (2007b). Testing the transtheoretical model for fruit intake: Comparing web-based tailored stage-matched and stage-mismatched feedback. *Health Education Research, 23,* 218–227.

De Vet, E., De Nooijer, J., Oenema, A., De Vries, N.K. & Brug, J. (2008). Predictors of stage transitions in the Precaution Adoption Process Model for fruit intake. *American Journal of Health Promotion, 22,* 282–290.

Farkas, A.J., Pierce, J.P., Zhu, S.-H., Rosbrook, B., Gilpin, E.A., Berry, C. & Kaplan, R.M. (1996). Addiction versus stages of change models in predicting smoking cessation. *Addiction, 91,* 1271–1280.

Fishbein, M. & Ajzen, I. (1975). *Belief, attitude, intention, and behavior: An introduction to theory and research.* Reading, MA: Addison-Wesley.

Gollwitzer, P.M. (1999). Implementation intentions: Strong effects of simple plans. *American Psychologist, 54,* 493–503.

Gollwitzer, P.M. & Sheeran, P. (2006). Implementation intentions and goal achievement: A metaanalysis of effects and processes. *Advances in Experimental Social Psychology, 38,* 69–119.

Heckhausen, H. (1991). *Motivation and action.* New York: Springer.

Heckhausen, H. & Gollwitzer, P.M. (1987). Thought contents and cognitive functioning in motivational versus volitional states of mind. *Motivation and Emotion,* 11, 101–120.

Herzog, T.A., Abrams, D.B., Emmons, K.M., Linnan, L.A. & Shadel, W.G. (1999). Do processes of change predict smoking stage movements? A prospective analysis of the transtheoretical model. *Health Psychology,* 18, 369–375.

Lippke, S. & Plotnikoff, R.C. (2009). The protection motivation theory within the stages of the transtheoretical model – Stage-specific interplay of variables and prediction of stage transitions. *British Journal of Health Psychology,* 14, 211–229.

Littell, J.H. & Girvin, H. (2002) Stages of change. A critique. *Behavior Modification, 26,* 223–273.

Marlatt, G.A. (1996). Taxonomy of high-risk situations for alcohol relapse: Evolution and development of a cognitive-behavioral model. *Addiction, 91,* 37–50.

Orbell, S. & Sheeran, P. (1998). 'Inclined abstainers': A problem for predicting health-related behaviour. *British Journal of Social Psychology, 37,* 151–165.

Prochaska, J.O., Diclemente, C.C., Velicer, W.F. & Rossi, J.S. (1993). Standardized, individualized, interactive, and personalized self-help programs for smoking cessation. *Health Psychology, 12,* 399–405.

Prochaska, J.O. & Velicer, W.F. (1997). The Transtheoretical Model of health behavior change. *American Journal of Health Promotion, 12,* 38–48.

Quinlan, K.B. & McCaul, K.D. (2000) Matched and mismatched interventions with young adult smokers: Testing a stage theory. *Health Psychology, 19,* 165–171.

Rosen, C.S. (2000). Is the sequencing of change processes by stage consistent across health problems? A meta-analysis. *Health Psychology, 19,* 593–604.

Schwarzer, R. (2008). Modeling health behavior change: How to predict and modify the adoption and maintenance of health behaviors. *Applied Psychology, 57,* 1–29.

Schwarzer, R., Luszczynska, A., Ziegelmann, J.P., Scholz, U. & Lippke, S. (2008). Social-cognitive predictors of physical exercise adherence: Three longitudinal studies in rehabilitation. *Health Psychology, 27,* S54–S63.

Sniehotta, F.F. (2009). Towards a theory of intentional behaviour change: Plans, planning, and self-regulation. *British Journal of Health Psychology, 14,* 261–273.

Sniehotta, F.F., Luszczynska, A., Scholz, U. & Lippke, S. (2005). Discontinuity patterns in stages of the precaution adoption process model: Meat consumption during a livestock epidemic. *British Journal of Health Psychology, 10,* 221–235.

Sutton, S. (1996). Can 'stages of change' provide guidance in the treatment of addictions? A critical examination of Prochaska and DiClemente's model. In G. Edwards & C. Dare (Eds.) *Psychotherapy, psychological treatments and the addictions* (pp. 189–205). Cambridge: Cambridge University Press.

Sutton, S. (2000). Interpreting cross-sectional data on stages of change. *Psychology & Health, 15,* 163–171.

Sutton, S. (2001). Back to the drawing board? A review of applications of the transtheoretical model to substance use. *Addiction, 96,* 175–186.

Sutton, S. (2005). Another nail in the coffin of the transtheoretical model? A comment on West (2005). *Addiction, 100,* 1043–1046.

Weinstein, N.D., Lyon, J.E., Sandman, P.M. & Cuite, C.L. (1998). Experimental evidence for stages of precaution adoption. *Health Psychology, 17,* 445–453.

Weinstein, N.D., Rothman, A. & Sutton, S. (1998). Stage theories of health behavior. *Health Psychology, 17,* 290–299.

Weinstein, N.D. & Sandman, P.M. (1992). A model of the precaution adoption process: Evidence from home radon testing. *Health Psychology, 11,* 170–180.

Weinstein, N.D. Sandman, P.M. & Blalock, S.J. (2008). The precaution adaption process model. In K. Glanz, B.K. Rimer & K. Viswanath (Eds.) *Health behavior and health education: Theory, research and practice* (4th edn, pp. 123–149). San Francisco: Jossey-Bass.

West, R. (2005). Time for a change: putting the transtheoretical (stages of change) model to rest. *Addiction, 100,* 1036–1039.

Part III

Cognition, Emotion, Behaviour and Health Care

12

Illness-Related Cognition and Behaviour

Linda D. Cameron and Rona Moss-Morris

Chapter Outline

This chapter focuses on illness cognition within the context of the common-sense model of the self-regulation of illness behaviour. This model specifies that individuals hold mental representations of their illnesses that include beliefs about the identity, cause, timeline, consequences, cure/controllability and cause of their conditions. The purpose of the chapter is to show how these beliefs influence individuals' responses to their illness-related experiences. The responses include whether or not individuals seek help for symptoms, adhere to treatment recommendations, avoid dealing with the problem altogether or remain engaged in daily activities. Representations of illness and illness risk are shown to be important determinants of psychological adjustment to illness and motivators of health-protective behaviours such as cancer screening and regular medical check-ups. The final sections of the chapter address how concrete-experiential and emotional processes interact with cognitions to influence representations and behaviour and the influence of culture on the development of illness representations.

Key Concepts

Adherence
Appraisals
Attributions
Causal beliefs
Chronic illness
Common-sense model
Control beliefs
Coping
Cultural influences
Emotional adjustment
Emotional regulation
Emotional representations
Health behaviours
Illness cognitions
Illness consequences
Illness identity
Illness prototypes
Illness representations
Mood states
Psychological adjustment
Representational coherence
Risk representations
Self-regulation theory
Symptom perception
Timeline beliefs
Treatment representations

Introduction

Imagine waking up one morning with a splitting headache. The pounding pain flares as you lift your head off the pillow. You then notice that your eyes hurt when you move them and that your throat feels scratchy. You immediately try to figure out what is wrong: could it be a migraine headache, or the beginning of the flu? Or is it fatigue and overexertion from too much work? What you do next will depend on your beliefs about the nature of this episode. These beliefs will determine whether you spend the day in bed with the lights out, drink lots of fluids and take vitamin C tablets, or press on with your busy schedule after taking some aspirin and promising yourself an early bedtime that night.

As this scenario illustrates, illness-related beliefs critically shape our experiences and behaviours. Illness beliefs are assumed to be organised in memory into schemas or *representations* – that is, mental models for how a condition, event or object usually functions. An *illness representation*, therefore, is an organised set of beliefs regarding how the illness affects the body and its likely impact on life activities and experiences. Synonymous terms used in the literature include illness cognitions, illness perceptions, illness beliefs and illness schemata. We will use the term illness representations in discussing this large area of research.

People vary markedly in their representations of an illness. For example, one person may erroneously believe that HIV can be spread through mosquito bites and that it invariably leads to a rapid death. In contrast, another person may have more accurate beliefs that HIV is spread through the exchange of bodily fluids such as by sexual intercourse and the use of contaminated intravenous needles and that new treatments may prolong survival of HIV-infected individuals. Some may have an elaborate and detailed representation of an illness whereas others may know very little about it. Illness representations can also vary in terms of their *coherence*, or the extent to which they make sense to a person (Moss-Morris *et al.*, 2002). For example, one person may have beliefs about her diabetes that seem logical to her, whereas another person with diabetes may be perplexed as to how her obesity could have contributed to its development and how insulin relates to her body functioning.

Illness representations are critically important because they guide our reactions to symptoms, diagnoses and other types of illness-related information. Inaccurate representations can lead to problems such as delays in seeking medical care, non-adherence to medical prescriptions and undue distress.

A Self-Regulation Model of Illness Cognition and Behaviour

An overview

The self-regulation model of illness cognition and behaviour proposed by Leventhal and associates specifies how illness representations guide responses to illness-related experiences (see Figure 12.1; Leventhal *et al.*, 2003). It is a self-regulation model in that it focuses on how individuals select and monitor their behaviour over time in order to make progress towards their goals (e.g. being healthy, avoiding pain and suffering; Cameron & Leventhal, 2003). It is often called the *common-sense model* (CSM) because of its emphasis on personal, common-sense beliefs about illnesses. This model identifies five key components of illness representations.

- *Identity:* these beliefs concern the illness label or diagnosis (e.g. 'migraine headache') and associated symptoms (e.g. throbbing headache, nausea and visual disturbances).
- *Cause:* these beliefs concern the factors or conditions believed to have caused the illness (e.g. hereditary factors or stress).
- *Timeline:* these beliefs concern the expected duration of the illness. Beliefs about illness timelines can vary from acute or of limited duration (as with the flu); to cyclic, with episodes that come and go over time (as with migraines); and chronic or of long-term duration (as with diabetes).
- *Consequences*: these beliefs concern the expected effects of an illness on physical, social and psychological well-being (e.g. migraines interfere with performance at work or school and they limit one's ability to attend social gatherings).
- *Control/Cure*: these beliefs concern the extent to which the illness can be controlled or cured

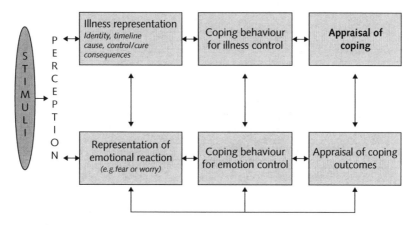

Figure 12.1   Leventhal's self-regulation model of illness cognition and behaviour
Source: Leventhal, H., Brissette, I. & Leventhal, E.A. (2003). The common-sense model of self-regulation of health and illness. In L.D. Cameron & H. Leventhal (Eds.) *The self-regulation of health and illness behaviour* (pp. 42–65). London: Routledge.

through treatment measures and behaviours (e.g. medication and stress reduction will control the migraines effectively).

Illness representations develop from exposure to a variety of social and cultural sources of information – media stories, education in schools, personal experiences of illness in oneself and others and other experiences. Representations include both abstract, conceptual information (represented by the linguistic phrases in memory, such as 'my migraines last about 24 hours') and concrete images (such as vivid memories of experiencing a migraine, staying in bed all day and waking up the next morning with no pain).

Figure 12.1 illustrates the role of illness representations in the self-regulation of health threats – that is, the process of selecting and monitoring behaviour aimed at controlling health threat conditions. Perceptions of stimuli (such as symptoms or disease-related information) activate illness representations stored in memory and a representation of the individual's present condition is formed through matching and integrating current symptoms and contextual information with these pre-existing beliefs. This representation guides the selection of coping behaviours (e.g. aspirin use or seeking medical care) and the outcomes of these actions are appraised in terms of their success in controlling the illness and its consequences. These outcome appraisals lead to refinements of the representation (e.g. its controllability, likely consequences, etc.) and the selection of new coping behaviours (e.g. maintaining the same action or switching to alternative strategies).

At the same time that symptoms or other cues trigger the activation and development of representations, they can also induce emotional responses (see the lower level of the model in Figure 12.1). For example, the discovery of a large, unusual lump may automatically induce a response of fear and the activation of an illness representation (e.g. cancer) can further fuel distress and worry. Awareness of these emotional responses (the emotional representation) prompts the selection and use of strategies for controlling these emotions, such as directing attention to either focus on or avoid the problem, expressing or suppressing one's feelings in communications with others or reappraising the problem in a positive manner. These emotion regulation efforts are then appraised for their success and these appraisals guide further efforts in emotional regulation. Illness representations therefore play an important role in generating emotional experiences and influencing behaviours aimed at controlling them.

Although illness representations are activated by symptoms, diagnoses and other cues that one is sick, they can also be evoked when a person is asymptomatic and illness-free. Beliefs regarding one's risk of illness can develop through matching beliefs about one's health status, health habits and family history with representational attributes (Cameron, 2008). These risk representations can motivate a variety of health-related behaviours. As noted in Chapter 9, this volume, risk-related beliefs predict prevention behaviours such as exercise and use of immunisations and screening behaviours such as mammograms (Brewer et al., 2007; Floyd et al., 2000). Risk appraisals are often discrepant with actual risk estimates (Wilcox & Stefanick, 1999), however, leading to inappropriate use of health-care procedures and protective behaviours.

In the following sections, we focus more closely on the each of the illness representation components. As will become clear, each component plays an important role in influencing behaviours, emotions and health outcomes.

Identity beliefs: label and symptoms

An illness label is closely linked with beliefs about associated symptoms; indeed, when asked to define an illness such as a cold, we almost invariably describe the physical experiences we associate with it. Moreover, when we experience atypical symptoms, we automatically try to determine whether they represent a specific illness by searching for possible matches with one of our illness representations. Evidence suggests that identity beliefs have a prototype structure (Bishop & Converse, 1986). A prototype is a mental model of the most representative case of a condition or entity and it is used as the standard with which to determine whether other cases are members of that category. If you experience six symptoms that closely match the prototypical symptoms of your representation of strep throat, then you may readily label your condition as strep throat. If, however, only two out of your six symptoms match your prototype for strep throat, then you may suspect that your condition is something else.

The process of matching symptoms with disease labels is often not an easy one. There may be considerable overlap among disease prototypes, making it difficult to discern which illness is more likely to be responsible for a particular symptom experience. Moreover, the same disease can cause markedly different types of symptoms in different people. For example,

symptoms associated with blood glucose levels vary considerably across diabetes patients (Gonder-Frederick et al., 1986). Moreover, symptoms can be caused by other factors besides illness – fatigue may produce headaches and lethargy and exercise may cause vague muscle or nerve pains.

Individuals recognise that stress can cause a variety of symptoms and they often attribute symptoms occurring during a stressful time to stress rather than to illness. Stress attributions are more likely to occur if the symptoms are unfamiliar or ambiguous rather than highly prototypical of a specific disease and if the stressor is highly salient (Baumann et al., 1989). In a study of community residents, individuals experiencing new and potentially serious symptoms were more likely to believe that their symptoms were due to stress rather than to illness if the symptoms were ambiguous in nature and they were less likely to seek care if they were facing recent, stressful events (Cameron et al., 1995).

Just as individuals experiencing atypical symptoms rely on identity beliefs to determine a 'diagnosis', individuals who receive a diagnosis (e.g. from a doctor) use identity beliefs to detect associated symptoms. When a woman is told she has heart disease, for example, she will think through her recent symptom experiences to identify symptoms that are likely to be caused by this condition. This process can lead to erroneous attributions of symptoms to a diagnosed illness. Consider, for example, the case of hypertension. Hypertension is an asymptomatic condition – there are no identifiable symptoms and people are not able to tell when their blood pressure is high or low (Baumann & Leventhal, 1985). Nevertheless, people diagnosed with hypertension can and do find symptoms to associate (erroneously) with this illness label. One study found that 80 per cent of hypertension patients agreed that people with hypertension cannot tell when their blood pressure is elevated. Yet 88 per cent of these same patients reported that *they* could tell when their blood pressure was elevated and they identified symptoms that they believed corresponded with their high blood pressure (Meyer et al., 1985).

Illness identity beliefs critically influence decisions to seek medical care. Evidence suggests that individuals are unlikely to seek medical attention for new symptoms unless they have a personal diagnosis or label for them (Cameron *et al.*, 1993). Moreover, the inaccurate labelling of symptoms can lead to dangerous delays in seeking care for symptoms, such as symptoms of a myocardial infarction (MI) or heart attack. People tend to have clear beliefs about MI symptoms as including breathlessness, crushing chest pain and sudden collapse. In fact, MI symptoms can vary markedly from this prototype. Common symptoms include nausea, coughing and flu-like symptoms; moreover, chest pain caused by MI can develop gradually or be relatively mild in nature. Individuals often fail to recognise these as MI symptoms and end up delaying seeking care for many hours (Dracup *et al.*, 1995). Among MI patients, discrepancies between their beliefs about symptoms associated with MI and their actual symptom experiences are associated with longer delays in getting to the hospital (Perry *et al.*, 2001). These delays may critically affect survival, as the risk of mortality is reduced by 40 per cent if treatment is started within one hour after symptom onset (Newby *et al.*, 1996).

Causal beliefs

Illnesses by their very nature are threatening and unwanted conditions and a natural response to a diagnosis is to ask, 'Why me? Why did I get this illness?' Attempts to identify the causes of an illness can be motivated by efforts to make sense of the experience and it may provide a sense of predictability and control, such as by enabling one to determine whether aspects of one's life can be changed to alter the course of the disease or to prevent recurrences. For certain illnesses, almost all patients develop causal beliefs. For example, Taylor and colleagues (Taylor *et al.*, 1984) found that over 95 per cent of women with breast cancer had developed strong beliefs about the likely causes, many of which were discrepant with medical science. For other illness experiences, there may be less motivation to formulate causal attributions. Sissons Joshi (1995) found that over 33 per cent of individuals with diabetes were disinclined to identify potential causes, apparently because they did not believe that it was important or helpful to do so.

What kinds of causes are identified by patients? People commonly attribute their illnesses to heredity, the actions of other people, the environment, fate or

chance and their own character and actions (Michela & Wood, 1986). Beliefs that God's will and sin play a causal role in the development of illnesses such as AIDS are also common, even among US university students (Klonoff & Landrine, 1994). Stress is implicated as a causal factor for a wide variety of illnesses. In fact, stress is one of the most commonly reported perceived causes among individuals with breast cancer (Taylor *et al.*, 1984), heart disease (French *et al.*, 2001), rheumatoid arthritis and multiple sclerosis (Moss-Morris *et al.*, 2002).

How do causal beliefs affect coping and emotional responses? Weiner's theory of causal attribution (Weiner, 1986) identifies three aspects of causal beliefs that are associated with coping and emotional adjustment: the locus of causality (whether the cause is an internal feature of the person or an external aspect of the environment); the stability (whether it changes over time); and the controllability (whether one can alter it). Beliefs that causes are stable and uncontrollable (such as intelligence or environmental pollution) are associated with the use of avoidance coping and poor psychological adjustment (Roesch & Weiner, 2001). In contrast, attributions to internal, unstable and controllable causes are associated with adaptive problem-focused and emotion-focused coping and with better adjustment (Roesch & Weiner, 2001).

Accumulating evidence suggests that causal beliefs may predict subsequent health behaviours and outcomes. For example, individuals who attribute their illness to stress and other psychological factors are more likely to use complementary and alternative treatments such as homeopathy and therapeutic massage (Bishop *et al.*, 2007). In a study of individuals surviving an MI (Martin *et al.*, 2005), attributions to diet and exercise were associated with healthy changes in these behaviours three months later. Of concern, however, was that women were less likely than men to attribute the heart condition to these behaviours even though they had comparably poor habits; moreover and possibly as a consequence of these causal attributions, women were less likely than men to improve their diet and exercise habits over time. Affleck and colleagues found that patients who attributed their MI to stress had greater disease progression eight years later compared to patients who did not make stress attributions. Moreover, those who blamed the initial

MI on other people were more likely than those who did not to suffer another MI (Affleck *et al.*, 1987).

Timeline

The timeline component constitutes the perceived time frame for the development and duration of the illness. As mentioned earlier in the chapter, patients tend to define illnesses in terms of three major timeline models: acute, cyclical and chronic. However, people often start out with a more acute model because childhood experiences of illness are typically with short-lived infectious diseases such as cold and flu (Leventhal *et al.*, 2003). These childhood experiences may lead people to develop a heuristic or implicit 'rule of thumb' that illnesses are acute and can be cured. When faced with a diagnosis of a more chronic condition, such as heart disease or diabetes, the adjustment to a chronic model can pose difficulties for many people. In some instances, it may take repeated symptom flare-ups and remissions or ongoing complications before patients realise the chronicity of their condition. A chronic illness often means accepting that the illness may not be amenable to cure and that the illness and the symptoms have to be managed over the long term.

It is therefore not surprising that the timeline component influences adherence to treatment. For example, patients who perceive their asthma to be a cyclical rather than chronic condition often fail to use their preventive medication as prescribed, apparently because they do not believe that the medication is necessary (Horne & Weinman, 2002). Similarly, believing diabetes is a cyclical illness is associated with poorer adherence to both medication and dietary recommendations (Barnes *et al.*, 2004).

In other instances, an acute rather than chronic model can be advantageous for patients. A study of illness perceptions in first-time MI patients demonstrated that those who believed that their illness would last a short time were more likely to return to work within six weeks of their MI (Petrie *et al.*, 1996). A study of predictors of chronic fatigue following glandular fever showed that people who believed their acute illness would last a long time were more likely to have ongoing fatigue and symptoms six months after the start of the infection (Candy *et al.*,

2003). Similarly, a prospective study of low back pain patients in primary care showed that patients who expected their back problem to last a long time and have serious consequences when they consulted their doctors were more likely to have a poor clinical outcome six months later (Foster *et al.*, 2008).

Consequences

Beliefs about the consequences of one's illness include physical, social and economic consequences and, in some cases, the prospect of imminent death. People's beliefs about the consequences of their illnesses are often related to their experience of symptoms. If the symptoms are seen to be severe or obtrusive, the common belief is that the illness is more serious. However, certain serious illnesses, such as heart disease, diabetes and cancer, have few symptoms in the early stages of the illness. If patients experience few symptoms it may be hard for them to see the serious nature of the condition. A classic example of this occurs in diabetes, an illness that is often regarded as a 'silent killer' by the medical profession. Poorly controlled diabetes can have severe consequences such as blindness, gangrenous limbs, renal failure and even death. However, patients with poorly controlled diabetes may not experience many symptoms (Gonder-Frederick & Cox, 1991). For these patients, the long-term consequences may be too abstract to motivate adherence behaviours, which require patients to carefully monitor their blood glucose levels, regulate their medication use and adhere to a strict dietary regimen.

Then there are other patients with medically unexplained illnesses such as chronic fatigue syndrome and fibromyalgia, which are not life-threatening and are generally regarded as less serious illnesses by the medical profession. Yet patients with these illnesses experience a wide range of symptoms which they believe signifies a serious disease with wide-ranging consequences (Fink, 1992).

Patients' perceptions of the consequences of their illness are important predictors of behavioural responses to the illness and adjustment to the condition. A meta-analysis of illness perception studies showed that MI patients who viewed their condition as having more symptoms and more severe consequences were more likely to attend cardiac rehabilitation (French *et al.*, 2006). In this context, beliefs in the negative consequence of the disease may have positive outcomes, as attendance at cardiac rehabilitation is associated with better outcome post MI.

For others, serious consequences beliefs may be less adaptive. Longitudinal studies of patients with rheumatoid arthritis have shown that even when controlling for medical indices of illness severity, beliefs in the adverse consequences of the illness are associated with more visits to the outpatient clinic, more tiredness and higher anxiety (Treharne *et al.*, 2008;). These studies suggest that patients' beliefs about the severity of the illness have a greater association with outcome than do clinical measures of illness severity. This pattern reinforces the idea that patients' beliefs may be just as important as the predictions of the medical profession in ultimately determining the prognosis for the patient.

Cure (Controllability)

The fifth illness representation component refers to beliefs about the controllability and/or curability of the illness and is closely related to inferences about the severity of the illness. A more severe illness is seen as less controllable and less curable than an illness that is perceived to be less severe (Lau & Hartman, 1983). Perceptions of control are also important indicators of coping behaviour. People with a strong sense of control over their illnesses may be more prepared to engage in treatment programmes to recover or to prevent further relapses. This is certainly true for patients who have experienced an MI. Patients with stronger beliefs at admission that their heart conditions can be controlled are more likely to attend cardiac rehabilitation programmes (French *et al.*, 2006).

On the other hand, patients who believe that the course of their illness is largely uncontrollable are more likely to use passive coping strategies to deal with their illness such as cognitive or behavioural avoidance (Moss-Morris *et al.*, 1996). Perceptions of low controllability are also related to higher hospital admissions in psoriasis patients (Scharloo *et al.*, 2000), which may reflect in part a greater reliance on hospital care than on self-care to manage the illness. Patients who lack confidence that self-care will be effective

may fail to make behavioural changes to manage their illness. They may end up going to hospital more frequently as a consequence because they are sicker and because they feel a greater need to be taken care of by hospital staff.

Although many researchers construe control as a single, broad dimension, it may be useful to separate control beliefs into two dimensions: personal control and treatment control (Moss-Morris *et al.*, 2002). Personal control includes beliefs that one's own actions will help to control the illness, whereas treatment control involves beliefs that one's prescribed treatments will be effective in controlling the condition. A study on multiple sclerosis suggests that these control dimensions may have differing effects on illness outcomes (Jopson & Moss-Morris, 2003). For instance, mental fatigue was associated with stronger beliefs in personal control, but lower beliefs in treatment control. It may be that maintaining a strong sense of personal control over an illness that can be unpredictable requires substantial mental effort, leading to mental fatigue. Having faith that treatment may control the illness may offer a more external source of control, which has positive benefits for mental fatigue. Although personal control appeared to tax mental stamina in these patients, it did have positive benefits for their psychological adaptation. Patients with a strong sense of personal control had higher self-esteem and were less distressed.

Patterns and Coherence in Representations of Illnesses and Health Actions

So far we have discussed the illness representation attributes separately. In many instances, however, the collection of beliefs, rather than the individual attributes, may be important in understanding outcomes. A study of chronic pain patients showed that those who appeared better adapted to their pain had more acute timeline beliefs, less pain-related consequences, stronger beliefs in personal and treatment control and a better understanding of their pain condition than did patients who were less well adapted (Hobro *et al.*, 2004). Patients seeking care for food poisoning showed that those who had stronger identity beliefs and who believed it was uncontrollable, would last a long time and have serious emotional consequences were more likely to develop irritable bowel syndrome six months later (Spence & Moss-Morris, 2007).

An important aspect of an illness representation is its coherence – that is, the extent to which the representational beliefs fit together so that the illness makes sense and the extent to which these beliefs have logical links with coping behaviours. Evidence suggests that individuals tend to develop coherent representations with attributes typically associated with each other in logical ways. For example, beliefs that an illness will last a long time and has numerous symptoms tend to be associated with more severe consequences and lower beliefs about disease control (Moss-Morris et al., 2002).

In order for the illness representation to motivate appropriate treatment or protection behaviour, it must link coherently with the representation of the behaviour: Not only do individuals need to know *what* action to take in order to control a health threat, they must understand *how* that action will do so. For example, consider women with abnormal Pap smears who smoke and who are advised to quit in order to reduce their risk of cervical cancer: Most women are unclear about the connection between smoking and cervical cancer. Researchers have shown that providing these women with clear information about the link can play an instrumental role in motivating them to quit (Bishop et al., 2005). They evaluated the efficacy of a pamphlet providing a concrete description of how cigarette chemicals enter the bloodstream and pass throughout the body to the cervix, where they harm the cells in ways that can result in cancer. Compared to women who did not receive this information, those receiving the pamphlet later reported that they had a more coherent understanding of the link between smoking and cervical cancer and higher intentions to stop smoking.

The links between representations of an illness and an associated treatment give rise to treatment perceptions involving needs and concerns (Horne, 2003). In research on understanding adherence to medications, *necessity* beliefs regarding the personal need for the treatment and *concerns* about negative effects such as unpleasant symptoms and long-term consequences have been found to predict uptake and adherence to medication regimens in a variety of patient groups, including those with HIV/AIDS, kidney disease and asthma (Horne, 2003; Horne & Weinman, 2002).

Concrete and Emotional Aspects of Illness Representations

Illness representations include not only conceptual, abstract information; they also incorporate vivid images and memories of experiences. These concrete-experiential cognitions can have particularly powerful effects on reactions and behaviour because they tend to be highly accessible to recall and closely linked with affect (Cameron & Chan, 2008).

A qualitative study of the mental images of cancer held by breast cancer survivors (Harrow et al., 2009) provides initial evidence of the nature and impact of imagery associated with illness identity. The women tended to differ in terms of whether they had a representation of cancer that was creature-like (e.g. like a black snake or jellyfish, with tentacles that spread or bodies that grew) or substance-like (e.g. as hard lumps or inert matter). Women with creature-like images appeared to be more distressed and have more intrusive thoughts relative to the ones who saw their cancer as hard lumps or inert matter.

In a study of skin cancer risk representations (Cameron, 2008), adults reported the images that came to mind when they thought about skin cancer. Content analyses revealed that most images fell neatly into the representational categories of identity, cause, consequences, timeline and control/cure. Moreover, 44 per cent reported a skin symptom image such as a large, black growth or an oozing sore. These symptom images proved to be important for motivating protective action, as intentions to engage in sun protection and skin self-examinations were high only for individuals who reported both skin symptom imagery and elevated worry about skin cancer.

Given the potential for mental images to influence behaviour, interventions that instil adaptive images may be particularly effective. Promising evidence is provided by a study evaluating an educational intervention for patients with end-stage renal disease, for whom controlling high phosphate levels is an important treatment goal (Karamanidou *et al.*, 2008). A transparent, stomach-shaped container was used to demonstrate how the phosphate-binding medication can effectively bind with phosphates (from foods such as nuts and chocolate) during the digestion process. Compared to a control group, this intervention group reported a better and more coherent understanding of the medication effects and its efficacy in disease control. Together, these studies provide promising support that mental images embedded in one's representation of a health threat may have a unique impact on adjustment and behaviour.

As illustrated in Figure 12.1, emotions play an important role in illness cognition. Illness beliefs can evoke powerful emotional experiences and these experiences can significantly influence coping responses and adjustment to illness. But cognitions and emotions are highly interactive: just as illness cognitions can activate emotions such as worry and distress, emotions can influence illness cognitions. For example, negative mood can influence the perception and interpretation of physical symptoms. In studies utilising mood induction techniques, people made to feel sad reported more physical symptoms and greater discomfort from them than did those made to feel happy (Salovey & Birnbaum, 1989). Similarly, happy moods have been found to reduce perceived risk for health problems, whereas sad moods increase these risk perceptions (Salovey & Birnbaum, 1989).

Mood states may influence these illness cognitions in several ways. First, people rely on their moods as indicators of how well they are doing. If they feel happy, they may perceive this mood as a sign that things are going well and there is little danger or need for worry (Slovic *et al.*, 2002). Positive mood may also enhance confidence that one is able to protect oneself from potential dangers. Moreover, negative mood enhances inward self-focus, which may increase awareness of bodily symptoms and stimulate worries about their implications for health and illness (Salovey, 1992). Finally, mood-congruent memory effects may be at work, such that negative moods may increase the accessibility of worrying, health-related thoughts and memories (Forgas, 2000).

Worry about a disease is an emotional factor that significantly influences illness cognition and behaviour (Cameron & Chan, 2008). Worry can promote rumination about the illness and motivate one to search for relevant information and so it can foster the development of more extensive and elaborate illness representations. Moreover, worry can heighten the accessibility of these cognitive representations in memory; one consequence of this may be that individuals remember to engage in protective behaviours, such as taking medications or scheduling medical appointments. Worry has been associated with a greater propensity to seek medical care and to use screening procedures such as mammograms (e.g. Hay *et al.*, 2006).

Illness Representations and Clinical Interventions

Substantial evidence suggests that identity, cause, timeline, consequences and cure/control beliefs all have unique contributions to illness outcomes. Of even greater clinical significance are findings that interventions can alter patients' illness representations and that these changes may affect health outcomes.

A study of chronic pain patients attending a four-week, cognitive-behavioural pain management programme showed that participants reduced their beliefs about the serious consequences of their pain and their emotional representations of their pain and increased their sense of coherence of their condition for up to six months post-treatment. Reductions in serious consequences beliefs were associated with improvements in physical functioning, while changes in coherence and emotional representations improved mental functioning (Moss-Morris *et al.*, 2007).

Researchers in Auckland used the common-sense model to design a brief, hospital-based intervention for recovery from MI (Petrie *et al.*, 2002). This intervention included eliciting patients' MI beliefs, explaining MI in the context of these beliefs with an emphasis on increasing control beliefs and decreasing consequences beliefs and developing action plans for recovery. This randomised controlled trial (RCT) showed that the intervention enhanced control/cure beliefs and reduced timeline and consequences beliefs. A three-month follow-up showed that intervention participants returned to work sooner and experienced less angina compared to participants receiving standard hospital care. These outcome results were replicated in an RCT which modified the intervention to include spouses (Broadbent *et al.*, 2009a). In this study, key changes occurred for causal and coherence beliefs rather than for consequences and timeline beliefs. These differences may reflect the fact that the two studies used different measures of illness representations. Spouses who attended an intervention session also showed changes in beliefs about MI and less anxiety about their partners' conditions, suggesting the utility of targeting support people (Broadbent *et al.*, 2009b). This is in line with a growing body of research demonstrating that partners' beliefs about illness affect outcomes for patients (Figueiras & Weinman, 2003; Kaptein *et al.*, 2007).

Researchers in the UK developed a six-hour self-management programme for people with type 2 diabetes, which was based in part on the common-sense model. The emphasis of this group-based programme was on eliciting personal beliefs about diabetes and then using these stories to educate people about managing diabetes and to develop self-management plans (Skinner *et al.*, 2006). An RCT showed that, one year later, programme participants reported higher serious consequences, timeline and personal responsibility beliefs relative to those receiving standard care (Davies *et al.*, 2009). In the context of diabetes, believing your illness has potentially serious consequences and is chronic is more accurate and therefore more likely to elicit the behaviour changes necessary to manage this disease. In support of this idea, the trial found that intervention participants showed greater improvements in smoking cessation and weight loss than did those receiving standard care. However, none of the trials conducted so far have tested mediation effects, i.e. whether changes in illness beliefs predict changes in behavioural outcomes. This is an important step in order to distinguish whether the changes in behaviour actually determine the changes in illness beliefs rather than the other way around.

Culture and Illness Representations

We have focused primarily on research concerning illness representations held by individuals in Western societies such as those in Europe, North America, New Zealand and Australia. These societies make up a small minority of the world's peoples, however, and research exploring illness beliefs in cultures around the globe reveals a diverse array of beliefs about health and illness. This is not surprising when you consider that illnesses are, in essence, culturally defined experiences (Adams & Salter, 2009; Landrine & Klonoff, 2001). Interestingly, the *structure* of representations as consisting of illness identity, cause, timeline, consequences and control/cure is highly consistent across cultures; however, the specific *contents* or beliefs vary considerably (Baumann, 2003). For example, individuals across cultures invariably develop causal beliefs about illnesses. In traditional cultures, though, attributions to supernatural causes (such as sorcery or mystical retribution for transgressions) and emotional causes (such as stress or fear) far outweigh attributions to natural causes such as infections, accidents or deterioration (Murdock, 1980). The common-sense model provides a sound theoretical framework with which to explore the rich variety of illness-related beliefs and behaviours across cultures.

Discussion Points

1 According to the common-sense model of illness self-regulation, how do illness representations influence health and illness behaviours?
2 How may the process of receiving a diagnostic label influence a patient's symptom reports?
3 What role do patients' beliefs about the causes of their illness play in their psychological adjustment to their condition?
4 How might childhood experiences with illness influence people's timeline and consequences beliefs of chronic illnesses such as heart disease and diabetes?
5 How might people's emotional reactions to their illness influence their cognitive illness representations?
6 In developing interventions aimed at promoting adjustment to illness, why is it important to consider the pictures and images used in the educational materials?

Further Reading

Cameron, L.D. & Leventhal, H. (Eds.) (2003). *The self-regulation of health and illness behaviour.* London: Routledge.

Hagger, M.S. & Orbell, S. (2003). A meta-analytic review of the common-sense model of illness representations. *Psychology & Health, 18,* 141–184.

Landrine, H. & Klonoff, E.A. (2001). Cultural diversity and health psychology. In A. Baum, T. Revenson & J. Singer (Eds.) *Handbook of health psychology* (pp. 851–892). New York: Erlbaum.

Moss-Morris, R., Weinman, J., Petrie, K.J., Horne, R., Cameron, L.D. & Buick, D. (2002). The Revised Illness Perception Questionnaire (IPQ-R). *Psychology & Health, 17,* 1–16.

Roesch, SC & Weiner, B. (2001). A meta-analytic review of coping with illness: Do causal attributions matter? *Journal of Psychosomatic Research, 50,* 205–219.

References

Adams, G. & Salter, P. S. (2009). Health psychology in African settings: A cultural-psychological analysis. *Journal of Health Psychology, 12,* 539–551.

Affleck, G., Tennen, H., Croog, S. & Levine, S. (1987). Causal attribution, benefits and morbidity after a heart attack: An 8-year study. *Journal of Consulting AND Clinical Psychology, 5,* 339–355.

Barnes, L., Moss-Morris, R. & Kaufusi, M. (2004). Illness beliefs and adherence in diabetes mellitus: A comparison between Tongan and European patients. *New Zealand Medical Journal, 117,* 1–9.

Baumann, L.C. (2003). Culture and illness representation. In L.D. Cameron & H. Leventhal (Eds.) *The self-regulation of health and illness behaviour* (pp. 242–253). London: Routledge.

Baumann, L.J., Cameron, L.D., Zimmerman, R.S. & Leventhal, H. (1989). Illness representations and matching labels with symptoms. *Health Psychology, 8,* 449–469.

Baumann, L.J. & Leventhal, H. (1985). I can tell when my blood pressure is up, can't I? *Health Psychology, 4, 203*–218.

Bishop, A.J., Marteau, T.M., Hall, S., Kitchener, H. & Hajek, P. (2005). Increasing women's intentions to stop smoking following an abnormal cervical smear test result. *Preventive Medicine, 41,* 179–185.

Bishop, F.L., Yardley, L. & Lewith, G.T. (2007). A systematic review of beliefs involved in the use of complementary and alternative medicine. *Journal of Health Psychology, 12,* 851–867.

Bishop, G.D. & Converse, S.A. (1986). Illness representations: A prototype approach. *Health Psychology, 5,* 95–114.

Brewer, N.T., Chapman, G.B., Gibbons, F.X., Gerrard, M., McCaul, K.D. & Weinstein, N.D. (2007). Meta-analysis of the relationship between risk perception and health behavior: The example of vaccination. *Health Psychology, 26,* 136–145.

Broadbent, E., Ellis, C.J., Thomas, J., Gamble, G. & Petrie K.J. (2009a). Further development of an illness perception intervention for myocardial infarction patients: A randomized controlled trial. *Journal of Psychosomatic Research, 67,* 11–15.

Broadbent, E., Ellis, C.J., Thomas, J., Gamble, G. & Petrie K.J. (2009b). Can an illness perception intervention reduce illness anxiety in spouses of myocardial infarction patients? A randomized controlled trial. *Journal of Psychosomatic Research, 67,* 17–23.

Cameron, L.D. (2008). Illness risk representations and motivations to engage in protective behavior: The case of skin cancer risk. *Psychology & Health, 23,* 91–112.

Cameron, L.D. & Chan, C.K.Y. (2008). Designing health communications: Harnessing the power of affect, imagery and self-regulation. *Personality & Social Psychology Compass, 2,* 262–282.

Cameron, L.D. & Leventhal, H. (Eds.) (2003). *The self-regulation of health and illness behaviour.* London: Routledge.

Cameron, L.D., Leventhal, E.A. & Leventhal, H. (1993). Symptom representations and affect as determinants of care seeking in a community-dwelling, adult sample population. *Health Psychology, 12,* 171–179.

Cameron, L.D., Leventhal, H. & Leventhal, E.A. (1995). Symptom ambiguity, life stress and decisions to seek medical care. *Psychosomatic Medicine, 57,* 37–47.

Candy, B., Chalder, T., Cleare, A.J., Peakman, A., Skowera, A., Wessely, S. *et al.* (2003). Predictors of fatigue following the onset of infectious mononucleosis. *Psychological Medicine, 33,* 847–855.

Davies, M.J., Heller, S., Skinner, T.C., Campbell, M.J., Carey, M.E. *et al.* (2009). Effectiveness of the diabetes education and self management for ongoing and newly diagnosed (DESMOND) programme for people with newly diagnosed type 2 diabetes: Cluster randomised controlled trial. *British Medical Journal, 336,* 491–495.

Dracup, K., Moser, D.K., Eisenberg, M., Meischke, H., Alonzo, A.A. & Braslow, A. (1995). Causes of delay in seeking treatment for heart attack symptoms. *Social Science & Medicine, 40,* 379–392.

Figueiras, M.J. & Weinman, J. (2003). Do similar patient and spouse perceptions of myocardial infarction predict recovery? *Psychology & Health, 18,* 201–216.

Fink, P. (1992). Physical complaints and symptoms of somatizing patients. *Journal of Psychosomatic Research, 36,* 125–136.

Floyd, D.L., Prentice-Dunn, S. & Rogers., R.W. (2000). A meta-analysis of research on protection motivation theory. *Journal of Applied Social Psychology, 30,* 407–429.

Forgas, J.P. (2000). Affect and information processing strategies: An interactive relationship. In J.P. Forgas (Ed.) *Feeling and thinking: The role of affect in social cognition* (pp. 253–280). Cambridge: Cambridge University Press.

Foster, N.E., Bishop, A., Thomas, E., Main, C., Horne, R., Weinman, J. & Hay, E. (2008). Illness perceptions of low back pain patients in primary care: What are they, do they change and are they associated with outcome? *Pain, 136,* 1–2.

French, D.P., Cooper, A. & Weinman, J. (2006). Illness perceptions predict attendance at cardiac rehabilitation following acute myocardial infarction: A systematic review with meta-analysis. *Journal of Psychosomatic Research, 61,* 757–767.

French, D.P., Senior, V., Weinman, J. & Marteau, T. (2001). Causal attributions for heart disease: A systematic review. *Psychology & Health, 16,* 77–98.

Gonder-Frederick, L.A. & Cox, D.J. (1991). Symptom perception, symptom beliefs and blood glucose discrimination in the self-treatment of insulin-dependent diabetes. In J.A. Skelton & R.T. Croyle (Eds.) *Mental representations in health and illness* (pp. 220–246). New York: Springer-Verlag.

Gonder-Frederick, L.A., Cox, D.J., Bobbitt, S.A. & Pennebaker, J. (1986). Blood glucose symptom beliefs in Type I diabetic adults. *Health Psychology, 3,* 327–341.

Hay, J.L., McCaul, K.D. & Magnan, R.E. (2006). Does worry about breast cancer predict screening behaviors? A meta-analysis of the prospective evidence. *Preventive Medicine, 42,* 401–408.

Hobro, N., Weinman, J. & Hankins, M. (2004). Using the self-regulatory model to cluster chronic pain patients: The first step towards identifying relevant treatments? *Pain, 108,* 276–283.

Horne, R. (2003). Treatment perceptions and self-regulation. In L.D. Cameron & H. Leventhal (Eds.) *The self-regulation of health and illness behaviour* (pp. 138–153). London: Routledge.

Horne, R. & Weinman, J. (2002). Self-regulation and self-management in asthma: Exploring the role of illness perceptions and treatment beliefs in explaining non-adherence to preventer medication. *Psychology & Health, 17,* 17–32.

Jopson, N. & Moss-Morris, R. (2003). The role of illness severity and illness representations in adjusting to multiple sclerosis. *Journal of Psychosomatic Research, 54,* 503–511.

Kaptein, A.A., Scharloo, M., Helder, D.I., Snoei, L., Van Kempen, G.M.J. *et al.* (2007). Quality of life in couples living with Huntington's disease: The role of patients' and partners' illness. *Quality of Life Research, 16,* 793–801.

Karamanidou, D., Weinman, J. & Horne, R. (2008). Improving haemodialysis patients' understanding of phosphate-binding medication: A pilot study of a psycho-educational intervention designed to change patients' perceptions of the problem and treatment. *British Journal of Health Psychology, 13,* 205–214.

Klonoff, E.A. & Landrine, H. (1994). Culture and gender diversity in commonsense beliefs about the causes of six illnesses. *Journal of Behavioral Medicine, 17,* 407–418.

Landrine, H. & Klonoff, E.A. (2001). Cultural diversity and health psychology. In A. Baum, T.A. Revenson & J.E. Singer (Eds.) *Handbook of health psychology* (pp. 851–892). Mahweh, NJ: Erlbaum.

Lau, R.R. & Hartman, K.A. (1983). Common sense representations of common illnesses. *Health Psychology, 2,* 167–185.

Leventhal, H., Brissette, I. & Leventhal, E.A. (2003). The common-sense model of self-regulation of health and illness. In L.D. Cameron & H. Leventhal (Eds.) *The self-regulation of health and illness behaviour* (pp. 42–65). London: Routledge.

Martin, R., Johnsen, E.L., Bunde, J., Bellman, B., Rothrock, N.E., Weinrib, A. & Lemos, K. (2005). Gender differences in patients' attributions for myocardial infarction: Implications for adaptive health behaviors. *International Journal of Behavioral Medicine, 12,* 39–45.

Meyer, D., Leventhal, H. & Gutmann, M. (1985). Common-sense models of illness: The example of hypertension. *Health Psychology, 4,* 115–135.

Michela, J.L. & Wood, J.V. (1986). Causal attribution in health and illness. In P.C. Kendall (Ed.) *Advances in cognitive-behavioral research and therapy* (pp. 179–235). New York: Academic Press.

Moss-Morris, R., Humphrey, K., Johnson, M.H. & Petrie, K.J. (2007). Patients' perceptions of their pain condition across a multidisciplinary pain management program: Do they change and if so does it matter? *Clinical Journal of Pain, 23,* 558–564.

Moss-Morris, R., Petrie, K.J. & Weinman, J. (1996). Functioning in chronic fatigue syndrome: Do illness perceptions play a regulatory role? *British Journal of Health Psychology, 1,* 15–25.

Moss-Morris, R., Weinman, J., Petrie, K.J., Horne, R., Cameron, L.D. & Buick, D. (2002). The Revised Illness Perception Questionnaire (IPQ-R). *Psychology & Health, 17,* 1–16.

Murdock, G.P. (1980). *Theories of illness: A world survey.* Pittsburgh: University of Pittsburgh Press.

Newby, L.K., Rutsch, W.R., Califf, R.M., Simons, M.L., Aylward, P.E., Armstrong, P.W. *et al.* (1996). Time from symptom onset to treatment and outcomes after thrombolytic therapy. *Journal of the American College of Cardiology, 27,* 1646–1655.

Perry, K., Petrie, K.J., Ellis, C.J., Horne, R. & Moss-Morris, R. (2001). Symptom expectations and delay in acute myocardial infarction patients. *Heart, 86,* 91–93.

Petrie, K.J., Cameron, L.D., Ellis, C., Buick, D. & Weinman, J. (2002). Changing illness perceptions following myocardial infarction: An early intervention randomized controlled trial. *Psychosomatic Medicine, 64,* 580–586.

Petrie, K.J., Weinman, J., Sharpe, N. & Buckley, J. (1996). Role of patients' view of their illness in predicting return to work and functioning after myocardial infarction: Longitudinal study. *British Medical Journal, 312,* 1191–1194.

Roesch, S.C. & Weiner, B. (2001). A meta-analytic review of coping with illness: Do causal attributions matter? *Journal of Psychosomatic Research, 50,* 205–219.

Salovey, P. (1992). Mood induced self-focused attention. *Journal of Personality and Social Psychology, 62,* 699–707.

Salovey, P. & Birnbaum, D. (1989). Influence of mood on health-relevant cognitions. *Journal of Personality and Social Psychology, 57,* 539–551.

Scharloo, M., Kaptein, A.A., Weinman, J., Bergman, W., Vermeer, B.J. & Rooijmans, H.G.M. (2000). Patients' illness perceptions and coping as predictors of functional status in psoriasis: A 1-year follow up. *British Journal of Dermatology, 142,* 899–907.

Sissons Joshi, M. (1995). Lay explanations of the causes of diabetes in India and the UK. In L. Markova & R.M. Farr (Eds.) *Representations of health, illness and handicap* (pp. 163–188). Reading: Harwood Academic.

Skinner, T.C., Carey, M.E., Cradock, S., Daly, H., Davies, M.J., Doherty, Y. *et al.* (2006). Diabetes education and self-management for ongoing and newly diagnosed (DESMOND): Process modelling of pilot study. *Patient Education and Counseling, 64,* 369–377.

Slovic, P., Finucane, M.L., Peters, E. & MacGregor, D.G. (2002). The affect heuristic. In T. Glovich, D. Griffin & D. Kahneman (Eds.) *Heuristics and biases: The psychology of human judgment* (pp. 397–420). New York: Cambridge University Press.

Spence, M. & R. Moss-Morris (2007). The cognitive behavioural model of irritable bowel syndrome. *Gut, 56,* 1066–1071.

Taylor, S.E., Lichtman, R.R. & Wood, J.V. (1984). Attributions, beliefs about control and adjustment to breast cancer. *Journal of Personality and Social Psychology, 46,* 489–502.

Treharne, G.J., Lyons, A.C., Hale, E.D., Goodchild, C.E., Booth, D.A. & Kitas, G.D. (2008). Predictors of fatigue over 1 year among people with rheumatoid arthritis. *Psychology, Health & Medicine, 13,* 494–504.

Weiner, B. (1986). *An attributional theory of motivation and emotion.* New York: Springer.

Wilcox, S. & Stefanick, M.L. (1999). Knowledge and perceived risk of major diseases in middle-aged and older women. *Health Psychology, 18,* 346–353.

13

Symptom Perception
and Help Seeking

Suzanne E. Scott

Chapter Outline

This chapter discusses research and theory on the awareness and interpretation of somatic information and its role in help-seeking behaviour. The first part of this chapter outlines how people become aware of bodily changes and how they appraise these changes. It will distinguish between biomedical and psychological models of symptom perception and highlight the relative inaccuracy of symptom perception and interpretation and the possible reasons for this. The second part of this chapter outlines the approaches used to understand help-seeking behaviour. This section also considers the implications of this work for interventions to encourage appropriate help seeking and concludes with a discussion of the methodological issues associated with this topic.

Key Concepts

Conceptually driven (top-down) perception
Data-driven (bottom-up) perception
Illness schema
Lay referral network
Patient delay
Somatic information
Symptom interpretation
Symptom perception

Introduction

Symptom perception and our decisions to seek help from health-care professionals are complex processes that have implications for our health, quality of life and treatment options; they also have implications for the cost of health-care services. For instance, if we do not notice, pay attention to or seek professional help for a change in our bowel habits, slurred speech or chest pain we may miss the signs of serious diseases such as colon cancer, stroke or myocardial infarction and in turn fail to receive a correct diagnosis and/or appropriate and prompt treatment. Conversely, if we access medical services for trivial complaints we may overload services and undergo unnecessary medical tests and procedures.

Symptom Perception

Perception of bodily changes is common. In fact, we notice signs and symptoms almost daily (Gijsbers van Wijk *et al.*, 1999). From a biomedical perspective, examples of 'signs' include a change in pulse or temperature, a fracture or an open wound. *Signs* are considered to be objective bodily events which can be measured and verified. *Symptoms* are considered to be a more subjective experience of physiological events. They are 'felt' by individuals and are therefore only apparent to the affected person unless communicated (Pennebaker & Brittingham, 1982). Examples of symptoms include nausea, pain, thirst and fatigue. Throughout this chapter a psychological perspective is adopted. The terms 'somatic information' and 'bodily changes' are used to refer to both signs and symptoms and the term 'symptom perception' to refer to awareness of this somatic information. Somatic information can arise from disease (e.g. a breast lump due to cancer), from emotions (e.g. increased heart rate due to anxiety) or from environmental conditions (e.g. change in hand temperature due to cold air) as well as from fluctuations in normal bodily processes (Kolk *et al.*, 2003). Somatic information includes both sensations and visible changes (e.g. rash, blushing, alteration of a mole).

Biomedical models of symptom perception imply a direct relationship between disease and symptom perception in that the presence of illness (i.e. pathology, injury) will directly cause bodily changes and these will be detected by the individual and perceived as indicators of illness. This model also purports that as the pathology or injury intensifies, the signs and symptoms will become more obvious and increasingly diagnostic. However, this biomedical model does not reflect the true nature of symptom perception (Kolk *et al.*, 2003). Using experimental tests of symptom perception, Pennebaker and Brittingham (1982) found that the correlation between physiological states (e.g. skin temperature) and symptoms (self-reported warm hands) is low. This finding is also evidenced outside the laboratory. For instance, people often miss the signs of cancer, or notice signs yet dismiss them, believing they are due to minor illness. In turn, the disease is only picked up during screening, or when additional signs and symptoms arise. Alternatively we have 'false alarms' whereby we notice and become preoccupied with bodily changes although no disease is present. This may impact our quality of life or lead us to use health services unnecessarily. In 25–50 per cent of all primary care visits, no somatic cause is found to explain the patient's presenting symptoms (Barsky & Borus, 1995; olde Hartman *et al.*, 2009).

Although we are well trained in noticing some bodily states (e.g. thirst, hunger, need to urinate) the 'false alarms' and 'misses' within symptom perception demonstrate the relative inaccuracy in our perceptual ability (Broadbent & Petrie, 2007). For those with chronic illnesses such as asthma and diabetes, self-monitoring and being aware of bodily changes is an integral part of disease management, because accurate and precise symptom perception is vital in ensuring appropriate use of medication. Even so, people with a chronic illness are often unable to accurately monitor the crucial signs of disease. For instance, many asthma patients are unable to detect changes in their lung function (Janssens *et al.*, 2009). Finally, people may report similar symptoms, yet have different pathology or have different pathology, yet report similar symptoms. Again, this challenges the biomedical model of symptom perception, indicating that we must look for alternative explanations of the perception of somatic information.

What influences symptom perception?

Psychological approaches to symptom perception (see Cioffi, 1991; Gijsbers van Wijk & Kolk, 1997) indicate that awareness of somatic information is the result of a combination of two processes: data-driven (bottom-up) perception and conceptually driven (top-down) perception. Data-driven perception relates to the quality and quantity of incoming information, whereas conceptually driven perception refers to the influence of cognitions.

Data-driven perception

Think of all the information you are currently receiving from your environment. For example, the words on this page, light, sounds, air temperature. Now think of internal information (i.e. somatic information). Are you hungry or thirsty? Are you sitting comfortably? Do you need to cough? Do you have any aches or pains? You will soon realise that in addition to the abundance of external information coming from the environment, our organs and body parts continually produce sensory information, which is forwarded to the brain (Rief & Broadbent, 2007). Given that we are limited in attentional and cognitive capacity and to prevent overstimulation of our brain with irrelevant information, we filter the incoming information. In turn, we are only consciously aware of a small proportion of the incoming data. 'Selective attention' is the term used to describe the regulation that determines the type and extent of information which we consciously process and thus are aware of. Selective attention to the body means we focus on the processing of somatic information, therefore increasing the likelihood of symptom detection (Rief & Broadbent, 2007).

Pennebaker (1982) argued that there is a 'competition of cues' between external and internal information. As external information increases, we have less cognitive capacity for somatic (internal) information and thus are less likely to process the multitude of physical changes occurring within our body. Conversely, when our environment is lacking in stimuli, we have more cognitive resources to focus on our body and less need to filter incoming internal information. Thus we attend to physical changes. This *competition of cues theory* is supported by data indicating

that those who live alone or have boring, undemanding jobs report more physical symptoms than those who co-habit or have demanding jobs (Gijsbers van Wijk & Kolk, 1997). The relationship between the ratio of internal and external information is not quite so simple however, as some external stimuli produce emotional reactions and physical sensations (e.g. stress due to work pressures). In such circumstances we appear to focus on internal information (and report more symptoms) even though the amount of external information is high. Furthermore, it should be noted that the competition of cues theory is difficult to test as it is almost impossible to know the quantity of an individual's somatic information, and it is difficult to control for the influence of cognitions.

Conceptually driven perception

Cognitions (e.g. expectations, beliefs) play an important role in the perception of somatic information. Anticipation of a symptom can influence subsequent symptom perception. For example, Lorenz et al. (2005) found that if low intensity pain stimuli are expected, experimentally induced pain is experienced as less intense, even though high intensity stimuli are given and vice versa. Similarly, Pennebaker and Skelton (1981) demonstrated the role of expectations in a study in which participants were told an ultrasonic noise (actually fictitious) will produce warm hands, cold hands or have no effect. Participants' subsequent symptom reports were consistent with the suggestions (although there was no observable difference in skin temperature). Another example of the influence of expectations on symptom detection is the placebo effect, whereby patients report a reduction in symptoms after taking medication even though the medication is inert. Conceptually driven perception is thought to arise because we use hypothesis-driven (or expectation-driven) selective attention which creates bias in our detection of somatic information. Thus we are more likely to detect somatic information that we are expecting, as opposed to that we did not anticipate (Cioffi, 1996; Janssens et al., 2009).

Conceptually driven perception is also thought to occur due to the influence of our beliefs about diseases and the somatic information we associate with different diseases. We are guided by a *symmetry rule*

(Leventhal & Diefenbach, 1991) between somatic information and the labels we apply to somatic information, whereby symptoms create labels and labels create symptoms. For instance, when we detect somatic information (e.g. increase in temperature, perspiration) we assign a label to it (e.g. fever). Conversely, if we have, or think we have a condition (e.g. fever), we will search for associated somatic information based on our beliefs about that condition. This phenomenon has been elegantly demonstrated by a series of studies concerning a (fabricated) saliva test for a (fictitious) enzyme deficiency. For example, participants who are told they have the fictitious illness are more likely to report symptoms consistent with their knowledge of that illness than individuals told they do not have that illness (Croyle & Sande, 1988). Such conceptually driven perception is also demonstrated by the occurrence of 'medical students' disease' whereby medical students believe they have contracted one of the illnesses they are learning about. The symptoms experienced are often modelled on those of a patient the students have seen (Sarafino, 2008).

Emotions also influence symptom perception. For instance, Costa and McCrae (1980) found individuals high in trait negative affectivity report 2–3 times as many symptoms as individuals low in negative affectivity. Experimental studies indicate that people made to feel sad report more physical symptoms than those made to feel happy (see Salovey et al., 2000). The mechanisms underlying this phenomenon are still under debate (see Mora et al., 2007). Negative affectivity may induce hyper-vigilance, which leads to an increase in scanning of the body. This in turn directs attention to the body and more somatic information is detected. Negative affectivity may also increase stress and therefore stress hormones, which in turn may lead to an increase in internal information to be detected (Golub, 1992).

The process of symptom interpretation

Just because we have detected somatic information, this does not mean the process of symptom perception is complete. After labelling the somatic information (e.g. decrease in temperature of hands can be labelled 'cold hands') we then attribute it to something (e.g. weather or bad circulation) (Cioffi, 1991,

1996). Our interpretation of the somatic information determines whether we believe it is due to disease, to a psychological state, or whether the sensations are fluctuations of normal bodily processes or responses to the environment, or a combination of these. This attribution is then used to form a hypothesis or 'working diagnosis'. But what influences our symptom interpretations and how do we make these attributions? With strong sensory signals (e.g. pain, bleeding) we are more likely to interpret this somatic information as illness as opposed to trivial or transient causes (Safer et al., 1979). However, many early symptoms of life-threatening illness have more ambiguous symptoms without pain or discomfort. The cognitive-perceptual process of symptom interpretation is subject to a multitude of psychological, social and contextual influences. Drawing on research from the fields of health psychology and social psychology, Cacioppo et al. (1986) developed the 'psychophysiological comparison theory' which identifies heuristics and biases that guide our symptom interpretations. One of the assumptions presented by psychophysiological comparison theory is that we are motivated to explain our physiological condition (i.e. we have a tendency to assign reasons to the presence of somatic information rather than leave it unexplained). The second assumption of psychophysiological comparison theory is that symptom interpretations are not necessarily accurate in terms of physiological aetiology. For example, just because I interpret chest pain as a heart attack, this does not mean it is a heart attack. Shaw et al. (2008) stressed this point when referring to the 'individual as a lay-diagnostician'. The basic tenet of psychophysiological comparison theory and the theories which underpin it (e.g. Self-Regulatory Model (Leventhal et al., 1980)) is that once we have detected a sign or symptom we compare this somatic information with salient situational events and known illness prototypes (see Chapter 12, this volume). The illness prototypes or schema hold facts and beliefs about normal physiological conditions and states (e.g. menopause, fatigue) and disease (e.g. heart attack) and can include beliefs about the associated symptoms, the causes, consequences, timeline and perceived controllability of the illness. Illness schemas can be informed by previous experience, observational learning (i.e. experience of a relative) or receipt of illness information (e.g. public health campaigns, the internet, reading newspaper articles). These schema are therefore idiosyncratic and do not necessarily reflect the 'medical reality'.

The influence of illness schemas is evidenced by the impact of perceptions about stereotypical sufferers of disease (Lalljee et al., 1993). For instance, there is a common stereotype that coronary heart disease is predominantly a male diagnosis and this is embedded in our illness schemas. Subsequently, when women experience cardiac-like symptoms, cardiac causes tend not to be considered (Martin et al., 2004). Other biases in symptom perception include the 'stress-illness rule' whereby we discount ambiguous symptoms during periods of stress (Cameron et al., 1995; Leventhal & Crouch, 1997). Age also influences symptom interpretation – as we grow older we increasingly attribute sensations to the ageing process rather than to illness, even though most illnesses occur in later life. In addition, we are guided by a 'recency rule'; those schema used recently are more likely to be triggered again (Fiske & Taylor, 2008). As we are more likely to experience a trivial illness this will most likely be the most recent, therefore will trigger a 'trivial' illness schema. This links to our optimistic tendency whereby innocuous explanations are generally more likely than serious illness attributions.

Of course we do not interpret our symptoms in isolation. Input from the lay referral network (Friedson, 1961; Moloczij et al., 2008), our social identity and the real or perceived illness schemas of others can assist and affect our symptom interpretations (Levine, 1999; St Claire, 2003). Furthermore, Robbins and Kirmayer (1991) suggested we have certain attributional styles whereby some people may have a tendency to make illness interpretations, whereas others may attribute symptoms to psychological states, while others tend to normalise symptoms. However, subsequent research has not shown full support for this concept as people can have more than one attribution (Lundh & Wangby, 2002).

Help Seeking

Perception of signs and symptoms is crucial in the decision to seek help from a health-care professional. However, although perception of signs and symptoms are often necessary for a visit to a health-care profes-

sional, they are by no means sufficient. Think about yourself in the last six months. How many times have you noticed somatic information? How many times have you thought you were ill? How many times have you visited a health-care professional? Presumably you will have noticed somatic information and/or felt ill more often than you have visited a health-care professional. In fact we notice signs and symptoms almost daily yet only seek help for a small proportion of these. This is because help seeking is only one of many possible reactions to symptom perception. Others include doing nothing, active or passive waiting (Patterson et al., 1992), resting, having time off work, self-medication and consulting others or resources (e.g. internet, medical encyclopaedia). Just as there seems to be no close correspondence between disease state and symptom perception, there is neither a strong relationship between symptom perception and seeking help from a health-care professional.

Definitions used in help-seeking research

The time from a patient's detection of a sign or symptom to the first consultation with a health-care professional regarding that sign or symptom has been termed 'patient delay' (Pack & Gallo, 1938). Patient delay is therefore distinct from 'professional delay', which refers to the time taken from the first consultation with a health-care professional to the receipt of a definitive diagnosis. For most conditions, when the duration of professional and patient delay are compared, patient delay is generally the longest (Allgar & Neal, 2005; Finn et al., 2007; Onizawa et al., 2003; Pattenden et al., 2002). The combined duration of patient and professional delay is called 'diagnostic' or 'total' delay. Dividing diagnostic delay into phases is advantageous as the factors which prolong patient delay may have different or no effects on professional delay and thus may be obscured if only diagnostic delay is considered (Safer et al., 1979). It should be noted that there is no consensus with regard to these definitions of delay. Some researchers use 'start of treatment' as the end point of the total delay period rather than receipt of a definitive diagnosis. Others (e.g. Finn et al., 2007) use totally different terms such as pre-hospital delay and hospital delay. This of course limits the ability to compare studies. Sisler (2003) suggested that 'presentation delay' and 'management delay' may be more appropriate than patient delay and professional delay as the latter terms assign undeserved blame. There have also been objections to the term 'delay' as some patients seek help almost immediately. Finally, although patient delay would be best treated as a continuous variable (i.e. number of days) most research has dichotomised duration of delay by specifying a particular duration (e.g. more than three months) to divide 'non-delayers' and 'delayers'. Although this can overcome the problems of skewed data, the selected duration for 'delayers' is often arbitrary with no documented clinical relevance.

Why do people delay seeking help?

A biomedical approach to help seeking purports that the quantity and severity of symptoms is negatively correlated with the time taken to seek help. Thus, those who have multiple or severe symptoms will seek help more promptly than those who have few or minimally invasive symptoms. It is true that some symptoms have higher correlations with (prompt) help seeking. For instance, those with sudden onset or which are particularly disabling. However, the majority of conditions are typified by much more ambiguous symptoms.

Furthermore, the quantity and severity of symptoms explain only a small amount of variance in the duration of patient delay, with persons with similar complaints behaving differently (Mechanic, 1978; Scott et al., 2008). The biomedical approach therefore appears to be too simplistic; other explanations are needed to aid our understanding of help-seeking decisions.

Dispositional approach

One approach to understanding help-seeking behaviour is the dispositional approach. This maintains that we have stable patterns of illness behaviour. Considering the extremes, some people may always rush to the doctor at the first sign of illness, whereas others rarely visit a health-care professional. Thus, the dispositional approach attempts to identify who delays and why. For example, gender differences have been found to exist in help-seeking behaviour. Women are more likely to report symptoms, to visit a doctor when they are ill and have higher rates of health-care utilisation for most

health-care services (Department of Health, 2000; OPCS, 1991). Young children and the elderly have more contact with the medical profession than adolescents and young adults (USDHHS, 1995). However, the dispositional approach has not gone beyond identifying the influence of sociodemographic factors or personality types. When sociodemographic factors have been identified, explanations are often suggested, yet these explanations are rarely compared or investigated empirically (Mechanic, 1982). Furthermore, for many conditions, sociodemographic factors do not appear to influence the duration of patient delay. The dispositional approach is also limited in that personality factors, by their very nature, are rarely amenable to change. A more fundamental criticism to this approach is that a person with similar symptoms at different time points often chooses to seek help on one occasion but not on another (Mechanic, 1978). Thus it appears that help-seeking decisions rely on more complex processes than the dispositional approach allows.

Health-care system approach

An alternative approach to understanding help-seeking behaviour is to study factors of the health-care system that influence help-seeking decisions. This mainly involves identification of problems with access to health-care services. Access, however, is not a single entity. Penchansky and Thomas (1981) identified five domains of access: 'availability' (e.g. the volume of existing services); 'accessibility' (e.g. the location of the services); 'affordability' (e.g. the cost of the services or getting to the services); 'accommodation' (e.g. opening hours of the services); and 'acceptability' (e.g. patients' attitudes about the health-care professional's personal and professional characteristics). These domains differ within and between health-care systems.

Access can also be limited by perceptions of when it is acceptable (or unacceptable) to use health-care services. For instance, we often feel that we should not bother the doctor with something that might not be serious (Rogers et al., 1999) or that we need to demonstrate the failure of self-medication to validate medical care seeking (Alonzo, 1986). Finally, other aspects of health-care systems that impact help-seeking decisions are the aspects of the physician–patient relationship. For instance, patients' previous interactions with health-care professionals impact subsequent help-seeking behaviour (Moore et al., 2004). Furthermore, patients' stereotypes and beliefs about physicians correlate with help seeking (Bogart et al., 2004). Thus, a good physician–patient relationship and clear, empathic communication are essential in encouraging prompt help seeking.

Focus on the health-care system is a useful approach to detect barriers to health-care utilisation and in turn identify targets for interventions. However, this approach assumes that patients perceive a need for care but are restricted in getting the help they desire. As we will see in the 'psychosocial approach' to help seeking, this is not always the case as patients frequently misinterpret symptoms. Furthermore, the health-care system approach tells us little about the processes involved in the decision to seek help.

Psychosocial approach

The psychosocial approach to help seeking focuses on symptom appraisal, the perceived need for health care and beliefs about accessing and using health-care services. Safer et al. (1979) proposed a three-stage model of the help-seeking process, with each stage governed by a distinct set of appraisal and decisional processes. In the first stage (appraisal delay) individuals are said to evaluate somatic information and decide if it is indicative of illness. They then move to the second stage (illness delay) and decide if the illness requires or will be ameliorated by professional care. Finally, during the third stage (utilisation delay), the decision is made as to whether seeking care is worth the costs associated with it. Andersen et al. (1995) subsequently expanded utilisation delay and suggested that after an individual has decided an illness requires medical attention, they plan whether or not to act on this decision (behavioural delay), actually attend an appointment (scheduling delay) and then begin treatment (treatment delay). Some researchers have suggested further adaptations of the model proposed by Andersen et al. (e.g. the addition of new stages or merging of existing stages) but at present there has not been a comprehensive adaptation or testing of any suggested adaptations (Bairati et al., 2005; Evans et al., 2007; Pitts et al., 2000; Salomaa et al., 2005). Although this model has been subject to criticism (e.g. it assumes people only seek help for treat-

ment of an illness whereas in reality people visit health-care professionals for a number of reasons including reassurance, social contact, symptomatic relief, to rule out serious disease or reduce uncertainty (St Claire, 2003)), it does offer a useful guide to understand the pathway leading to the decision to seek help.

When the stages of delay have been compared, appraisal delay appears to be the most important stage, constituting approximately 60 per cent of the overall delay time. Evidence of the importance of symptom interpretation and the deleterious effects of misinterpretation (appraisal delay) are found across a wide range of conditions. For instance, the belief that symptoms are those of a heart attack seems to be a strong predictor of early arrival in hospital (Clark et al., 1992; Horne et al., 2000; Reilly et al., 1994; Ruston et al., 1998). A qualitative synthesis of studies on patient delay for symptoms of cancer found failure to attribute symptoms to cancer was a major factor in patient delay (Smith et al., 2005). However, as the model of delay suggests, even though symptom interpretation plays the major role in a person's decision to seek help, it is not always sufficient for help seeking to occur. Taylor (2008) reported that the majority of those who have appraised themselves as ill do not seek professional help. This may simply be because we think the medical profession cannot help with our problem (Scambler & Scambler, 1985). Scanlon et al. (2006) found this to be the case in a group of Irish people living in England who reported they never heard of people recovering from cancer. In turn, they associated cancer with death, believing there was no chance of cure and thus little need to seek treatment promptly. If people do believe treatment is necessary, they may still not seek help because of their perceptions about the treatment, they may have other priorities (e.g. child care) or have difficulties accessing health care (Scott et al., 2006). In a fascinating study, Facione and Facione (2006) interviewed women who had noticed a change in their breast that they thought may be cancer, yet had decided not to seek help. The women chose not to seek help because they believed talking about breast cancer would be difficult, they had other things to do, they were uncertain as to whether it was cancer and feared ridicule from their doctor if it turned out to be benign.

The majority of research on help-seeking behaviour has focused on barriers to delay, whereas an important aspect is triggers to help seeking and the interaction between barriers and triggers. Key triggers include interference of symptoms with one's ability to work (Zola, 1973), persistence of symptoms (Scott *et al.*, 2009) and the switch from private symptoms to public symptoms (Hale *et al.*, 2007). This indicates that the decision to seek help is an interpersonal process. Indeed, Burgess *et al.* (1998) found that women with breast cancer who did not disclose the discovery of their symptoms to anyone were six times more likely to delay than those who did inform someone. Thus our significant others can encourage help-seeking behaviour and provide social permission to seek care or take on the 'sick role'. Thus people may seek help not because they think care is necessary, but because other people think it is. Of course, lay referral may not always result in recommendation to seek medical attention. Alternatives include recommending self-medication, suggesting who else to consult or offering no advice (Cornford & Cornford, 1999). This could worsen the condition or delay receipt of appropriate treatment.

A note on fear and denial

It is often assumed that people delay seeking help for signs and symptoms of serious illness because they are scared or in denial. However, the evidence for fear as a cause of delay is mixed. For instance, whereas some research (e.g. MacDonald *et al.*, 2006) has shown no relationship between fear and the duration of patient delay, others (e.g. Meechan *et al.*, 2003) found that *higher* levels of emotional response to the detection of symptoms to be related to *shorter* patient delay. Conversely, in their qualitative synthesis, Smith *et al.* (2005) found fear of cancer and fear of embarrassment to be common reasons for patient delay. The inconclusive results may be because fear is multifactorial (e.g. fear of diagnosis, fear of treatment, fear of ridicule, fear of disfigurement – see Facione, 1993) yet is often measured as a unitary construct. Furthermore, fear can motivate action as well as hinder (de Nooijer *et al.*, 2001).

There is also continuing debate as to the role of denial (Burgess & Ramirez, 2006; Stiefel, 2006). Denial is obviously a difficult concept to measure, yet when it has been investigated, many studies have found no correlation between denial and delay (Watson *et al.*, 1984; Wielgosz *et al.*, 1988). Furthermore, those who do delay often think a lot about their symptoms and their possible treatments (Leventhal, 1970; Safer *et al.*, 1979). It appears that although fear and denial may influence the decision to see help, their effects are not as great as those of other factors, such as symptom interpretation.

Interventions

Research into help-seeking behaviour has the potential to inform interventions to encourage appropriate help-seeking behaviour and reduce patient delay. However, we should not promote early detection just for the sake of it, as effective treatment is not always available (Canadian Health Services Research Foundation, 2007). General or mass media campaigns may just encourage those who would seek promptly anyway, to seek help even quicker (Dracup *et al.*, 2006; Waters *et al.*, 1983). As such, interventions should be targeted at those at high risk of the disease and those who are more likely to delay or present with advanced disease.

Despite an increasingly large literature on the reasons for patient delay, there have been few interventions to reduce patient delay. A recent review of early detection interventions (Burgess *et al.*, 2008) found most interventions were not methodologically rigorous nor theory based, demonstrated only short-lived effects or had no control group. Interventions that do exist often attempt to increase knowledge of the signs and symptoms of the disease in question. Knowledge about symptoms is a crucial factor in the symptom appraisal process as, for example, one cannot interpret a breast lump as a potential sign of breast cancer if we do not know that the two are linked. However, as has been discussed in this chapter, the relationship between knowledge, symptom interpretation and the decision to seek help is by no means definitive. Indeed, those interventions that have increased knowledge often fail to reduce actual or intended patient delay (Becker *et al.*, 2001; Finn *et al.*, 2007; Mandelzweig *et al.*, 2006). Interventions need to focus on encouraging accurate symptom interpretation, stress the importance of fast action (Zapka *et al.*, 2000) and adopt a positive 'gain framed' approach (Burgess *et al.*, 2008). De Nooijer *et al.* (2002) found tailored interventions to be more effective than non-tailored interventions, indicating that one-to-one delivery or personal mail outs may be a useful tool. More research is required to develop effective techniques for these interventions and to evaluate them thoroughly. Of course, all our efforts to assist more appropriate help-seeking decisions will be limited without an accessible health-care system.

Methodological Issues

Research into symptom perception and help seeking faces a number of methodological challenges. Due to the complex nature of the processes involved there are multiple factors to control. Research relies on an individual's ability to articulate their somatic experiences and decisional processes, which otherwise may not be voiced. There is potential for the research to impact the processes being studied. For instance, symptom lists in questionnaires may increase attention to the body, leading to increased detection and thus overestimation of somatic information (Kroenke, 2001). Similarly, asking a person if they have decided to seek help for a certain symptom may in fact prompt them to do so. The majority of help-seeking research has involved retrospective accounts of decisional

processes, but this adds potential error due to inaccurate recall of events or a biased sample (e.g. many studies do not include data from those who died or are too unwell to take part (Finn *et al.*, 2007)). Finally, symptom perception and help seeking are continuous processes rather than static events. For instance, people may reinterpret thier symptoms throughout the symptom episode (Scott *et al.*, 2007). Our study designs and data collection tools need to allow for this (St Claire, 2003).

Conclusion

This chapter has highlighted the complex processes involved in detecting and responding to bodily changes. Presence of disease may initiate somatic information, but this does not automatically result in perception of that somatic information. Even when somatic information is detected, it is open to interpretation, which in turn influences our responses. Furthermore, symptom perception and help seeking should not be regarded as an individual experience; they are the result of an interaction between psychological, bio-physiological, social, cultural and environmental factors.

Discussion Points

1   What are the limitations of the biomedical models of symptom perception and help seeking?
2   Sports players sometimes do not realise that they have a severe injury until after a match has finished. From your knowledge of symptom perception, how would you explain this phenomenon?

3   Why do some people decide not to visit a health-care professional after noticing a sign of illness?
4   Imagine you were asked to develop an intervention to encourage early presentation of cancer. What would be the content and format of the intervention? How would you evaluate the intervention? What difficulties might you encounter?

Further Reading

Andersen, B.L., Cacioppo, J.T. & Roberts, D.C. (1995). Delay in seeking a cancer diagnosis: delay stages and psychophysiological comparison processes. *British Journal of Social Psychology, 34,* 33–52.

Kolk, A.M., Hanewald, G.J.F.P., Schagen, S. & Gijsbers van Wijk, C.M.T. (2003). A symptom perception approach to common physical symptoms. *Social Science & Medicine, 57,* 2343–2354.

Pennebaker, J.W. (1982). *The psychology of physical symptoms.* New York: Springer.

St Claire, L. (2003). *Rival truths: Common sense and psychological explanations in health and illness.* Hove, East Sussex: Psychology Press.

References

Allgar, V.L. & Neal, R.D. (2005). Delays in the diagnosis of six cancers: Analysis of data from the National Survey of NHS Patients: Cancer. *British Journal of Cancer, 92,* 1959–1970.

Alonzo, A.A. (1986). The impact of the family and lay others on care seeking during life threatening episodes of suspected coronary artery disease. *Social Science & Medicine, 22,* 1297–1311.

Andersen, B.L., Cacioppo, J.T. & Roberts, D.C. (1995). Delay in seeking a cancer diagnosis: delay stages and psychophysiological comparison processes. *British Journal of Social Psychology, 34,* 33–52.

Bairati, I., Fillion, L., Meyer, F.A., Hery, C. & Larochelle, M. (2006). Women's perceptions of events impeding or facilitating the detection, investigation and treatment of breast cancer. *European Journal of Cancer Care, 15,* 183–193.

Barsky, A.J. & Borus, J.F. (1995). Somatization and medicalisation in the era of managed care. *Journal of the American Medical Association, 274,* 1931–1934.

Becker, K.J., Fruin, M.S., Gooding, T.D., Tirschwell, D.L., Love, P.J. & Manowski, T.M. (2001). Community-based education improves stroke knowledge. *Cerebrovascular Diseases, 11,* 34–43.

Bogart, L.M., Bird, S.T., Walt, L.C., Delahanty, D.L. & Figler, J.L. (2004). Association of stereotypes about physicians to health care satisfaction, help-seeking behavior and adherence to treatment. *Social Science & Medicine, 58,* 1049–1058.

Broadbent, E. & Petrie, K.J. (2007). Symptom perception. In S. Ayers, A. Baum, C. McManus, S. Newman, K. Wallston, J. Weinman & R. West (Eds.) *Cambridge handbook of psychology, health and medicine* (2nd edn, pp. 219–223). Cambridge: Cambridge University Press.

Burgess, C., Bish, A.M., Hunter, H.S., Salkovskis, P., Michell, M., Whelehan, P. & Ramirez, A.J. (2008). Promoting early presentation of breast cancer: development of a psychoeducational intervention. *Chronic Illness, 4,* 13–27.

Burgess, C. & Ramirez, A. (2006). Response to Letter to the Editor. *Journal of Psychosomatic Research, 60,* 311.

Burgess, C., Ramirez, A.J., Richards, M.A. & Love, S. B. (1998). Who and what influences delayed presentation in breast cancer? *British Journal of Cancer, 77,* 1343–1348.

Cacioppo, J.T. andersen, B.L., Turnquist, D.C. & Petty, R.E. (1986). Psychophysiological comparison processes: Interpreting cancer symptoms. In B.L. Andersen (Ed.) *Women with cancer: Psychological perspectives* (pp. 141–171). New York: Springer-Verlag.

Cameron, L., Leventhal, E.A. & Leventhal, H. (1995). Seeking medical care in response to symptom and life stress. *Psychosomatic Medicine, 57,* 37–47.

Canadian Health Services Research Foundation. (2007). Myth: early detection is good for everyone. *Journal of Health Services Research Policy, 12,* 125–126.

Cioffi, D. (1991). Beyond attentional strategies: A cognitive-perceptual model of somatic information. *Psychological Bulletin, 109,* 25–42.

Cioffi, D. (1996). Making public the private: Possible effects of expressing somatic experience. *Psychology & Health, 11,* 203–222.

Clark, L.T., Bellam, S.V., Shah, A H. & Feldman, J.G. (1992). Analysis of pre-hospital delay among inner-city patients with symptoms of myocardial infarction: implications for therapeutic intervention. *Journal of the National Medical Association, 84,* 931–937.

Cornford, C.S. & Cornford, H.M. (1999). 'I'm only here because of my family'. A study of lay referral networks. *British Journal of General Practice, 49,* 617–620.

Costa, P.T. & McCrae, R.R. (1980). Somatic complaints in males as a function of age and neuroticism: a longitudinal analysis. *Journal of Behavioral Medicine, 3,* 245–257.

Croyle, R.T. & Sande, G.N. (1988). Denial and confirmatory search: Paradoxical consequences of medical diagnosis. *Journal of Applied Social Psychology, 18,* 473–490.

de Nooijer, J., Lechner, L. & de Vries, H. (2001). A qualitative study on detecting cancer symptoms and seeking medical help; an application of Andersen's model of total patient delay. *Patient Education and Counselling, 42,* 145–157.

de Nooijer, J., Lechner, L. & de Vries, H. (2002). Tailored versus general information on early detection of cancer: a comparison of reactions of Dutch adults and the impact on attitudes and behaviours. *Health Education Research, 17,* 239–252.

Department of Health. (2000). *Press release: Reference 2000/0187.* London: Department of Health.

Dracup, K., McKinley, S., Riegel, B., Mieschke, H., Doering, L.V. & Moser, D.K. (2006). A nursing intervention to reduce prehospital delay in acute coronary syndrome: a randomized clinical trial. *Journal of Cardiovascular Nursing, 21,* 186–193.

Evans, J., Ziebland, S. & McPherson, A. (2007). Minimizing delays in ovarian cancer diagnosis: an expansion of Andersen's model of 'total patient delay'. *Family Practice, 24,* 48–55.

Facione, N.C. (1993). Delay versus help seeking for breast cancer symptoms: a critical review of the literature on patient and provider delay. *Social Science & Medicine, 36,* 1521–1534.

Facione, N.C. & Facione, P.A. (2006). The cognitive structuring of patient delay in breast cancer. *Social Science & Medicine, 63,* 3137–3149.

Finn, J.C., Bett, J.H.N., Shilton, T.R., Cunningham, C. & Thompson, P.L. (2007). Patient delay in responding to symptoms of possible heart attack: Can we reduce time to care? *Medical Journal of Australia, 187,* 293–298.

Fiske, S.T. & Taylor, S.E. (2008). *Social cognition: From brains to culture.* New York: McGraw-Hill.

Friedson, E. (1961). *Patients' view of medical practice.* New York: Russell Sage Foundation.

Gijsbers van Wijk, C.M.T., Huisman, H. & Kolk, A.M. (1999). Gender differences in physical symptoms and illness behavior. A health diary study. *Social Science & Medicine, 49,* 1061–1074.

Gijsbers van Wijk, C.M.T. & Kolk, A.M. (1997). Sex differences in physical symptoms: The contribution of symptom perception theory. *Social Science & Medicine, 45,* 231–246.

Golub, S. (1992). *Periods: From menarche to menopause.* New York: Sage.

Hale, S., Grogan, S. & Willott, S. (2007). Patterns of self-referral in men with symptoms of prostate disease. *British Journal of Health Psychology, 12,* 403–419.

Horne, R., James, D., Petrie, K., Weinman, J. & Vincent, R. (2000). Patients' interpretation of symptoms as a cause of delay in reaching hospital during acute myocardial infarction. *Heart, 83,* 388–393.

Janssens, T., Verleden, G., de Peuter, S., van Diest, I. & van den Bergh, O. (2009). Inaccurate perception of asthma symptoms: A cognitive–affective framework and implications for asthma treatment, *Clinical Psychology Review, 29,* 317–327.

Kolk, A.M., Hanewald, G.J.F.P., Schagen, S. & Gijsbers van Wijk, C.M.T. (2003). A symptom perception approach to common physical symptoms. *Social Science & Medicine, 57,* 2343–2354.

Kroenke, K. (2001). Studying symptoms: sampling and measurement issues. *Annals of Internal Medicine, 134,* 844–853.

Lalljee, M., Lamb, R. & Carnibella, G. (1993). Lay prototypes of illness: Their content and use. *Psychology & Health, 8,* 33–49.

Leventhal, H. (1970). Findings and theory in the study of fear communications. *Advances in Experimental Social Psychology, 5,* 119–186.

Leventhal, E.A. & Crouch, M. (1997). Are there differences in perceptions of illness across the lifespan? In K.J. Petrie & J.A. Weinman (Eds.) *Perceptions of health and illness* (pp. 77–102). Amsterdam: Harwood Academic.

Leventhal, H. & Diefenbach, M. (1991). The active side of illness cognition. In J.A. Skelton & R.T. Croyle (Eds.) *Mental representations in health and illness* (pp. 247–272). New York: Springer-Verlag.

Leventhal. H., Meyer, D. & Nerenz, D.R. (1980). The common-sense model of illness danger. In S. Rachman (Ed.), *Medical Psychology* (Vol. II, pp. 7–30). New York: Pergamon Press.

Levine, R.M. (1999). Identity and illness: The effects of identity salience and frame of reference on evaluation of illness and injury. *British Journal of Health Psychology, 4,* 63–80.

Lorenz, J., Hauck, M., Paur, R.C., Nakamura, Y., Zimmermann, R., Bromm, B. & Engel, A. K. (2005). Cortical correlates of false expectations during pain intensity judgements – a possible manifestation of placebo/nocebo cognitions. *Brain, Behavior, and Immunity, 19,* 283–295.

Lundh, M.P. & Wangby, M. (2002). Causal thinking about somatic symptoms – How is it related to the experience of symptoms and negative affect? *Cognitive Therapy and Research, 26,* 701–717.

MacDonald, S., Macleod, U., Campbell, N.C., Weller, D. & Mitchell, E. (2006). Systematic review of factors influencing patient and practitioner delay in diagnosis of upper gastrointestinal cancer. *British Journal of Cancer,* 94, 1272–1280.

Mandelzweig, L., Goldbourt, U., Boyko, V. & Tanne, D. (2006). Perceptual, social and behavioural factors associated with delays in seeking medical care in patients with symptoms of acute stroke. *Stroke, 37,* 1248–1253.

Martin, R., Lemos, C., Rothrock, N., Bellman, S.B., Russell, D., Tripp-Reimer, T. *et al.* (2004). Gender disparities in common sense models of illness among myocardial infarction victims. *Health Psychology, 23,* 345–353.

Mechanic, D. (1978). *Medical sociology* (2nd edn). New York: Free Press.

Mechanic, D. (1982). The epidemiology of illness behaviour and its relationship to physical and psychological distress. In D. Mechanic (Ed.) *Symptoms, illness behaviour and help-seeking* (pp. 1–24). New York: Prodist Press.

Meechan, G., Collins, J. & Petrie, K.J. (2003). The relationship of symptoms and psychological factors to delay in seeking medical care for breast symptoms. *Preventative Medicine, 36,* 374–378.

Moloczij, N., McPherson, K.M., Smith, J.F. & Kayes, N.M. (2008). Help-seeking at the time of stroke: stroke survivors' perspectives on their decisions. *Health & Social Care in the Community, 16,* 501–510.

Moore, P.J., Sickel, A.E., Malat, J., Williams, D. & Alder, N.E. (2004). Psychosocial factors in medical and psychological treatment avoidance: the role of the doctor–patient relationship. *Journal of Health Psychology, 9,* 421–433.

Mora, P.A., Halm, E., Leventhal, H. & Ceric, F. (2007). Elucidating the relationship between negative affectivity and symptoms: the role of illness-specific affective responses. *Annals of Behavioral Medicine, 34,* 77–86.

olde Hartman, T.C., Borghuis, M.S., Lucassen, P.L., van de Laar, F.A., Speckens, A.E. & van Weel, C. (2009). Medically unexplained symptoms, somatisation disorder and hypochondriasis: Course and prognosis. A systematic review. *Journal of Psychosomatic Research, 66,* 363–377.

Onizawa, K., Nishihara, K., Yamagata, K., Yusa, H., Yanagawa, T. & Yoshida, H. (2003). Factors associated with diagnostic delay of oral squamous cell carcinoma. *Oral Oncology, 39,* 781–788.

OPCS (Office of Population Censuses and Surveys) (1991). *General Household Survey.* London: HMSO.

Pack, G.T. & Gallo, J.S. (1938). The culpability for delay in the treatment of cancer. *American Journal of Cancer, 33,* 443–462.

Pattenden, J., Watt, I., Lewin, R.J. & Stanford, N. (2002). Decision-making processes in people with symptoms of acute myocardial infarction: Qualitative study. *British Medical Journal, 324,* 1006–1009.

Patterson, E.T., Douglas, A.B., Patterson, P.M. & Bradle, J.B. (1992). Symptoms of preterm labor and self-diagnostic confusion. *Nursing Research, 41,* 367–372.

Penchansky, R. & Thomas, J.W. (1981). The concept of access: definition and relationship to consumer satisfaction. *Medical Care, 19,* 127–140.

Pennebaker, J.W. (1982). *The psychology of physical symptoms.* New York: Springer.

Pennebaker, J.W. & Brittingham, G.L. (1982). Environmental and sensory cues affecting the perception of physical symptoms. In A. Baum, S.E. Taylor & J.E. Singer (Eds.) *Advances in environmental psychology IV* (pp. 115–136). Hillsdale, NJ: Erlbaum.

Pennebaker, J.W. & Skelton, J.A. (1981). Selective monitoring of physical sensations. *Journal of Personality and Social Psychology, 41,* 213–223.

Pitts, M.K., Woolliscroft, J., Cannon, S., Johnson, I. & Singh, G. (2000). Factors influencing delay in treatment seeking by first-time attenders at a genitourinary clinic. *International Journal of STD & AIDS, 11,* 375–378.

Reilly, A., Dracup, K. & Dattolo, J. (1994). Factors influencing pre-hospital delay in patients experiencing chest pain. *American Journal of Critical Care, 13,* 350–356.

Rief, W. & Broadbent, E. (2007). Explaining medically unexplained symptoms – models and mechanisms. *Clinical Psychology Review, 27,* 821–841.

Robbins, J.M. & Kirmayer, L.J. (1991). Attributions of common somatic symptoms. *Psychological Medicine, 21,* 1029–1045.

Rogers, A., Chapple, A. & Sergison, M. (1999). 'If a patient is too costly they tend to get rid of you': the impact of people's perceptions of rationing on the use of primary care. *Health Care Analysis, 7,* 225–237.

Ruston, A., Clayton, J. & Calnan, M. (1998). Patients' action during their cardiac event: qualitative study exploring differences and modifiable factors. *British Medical Journal, 316,* 1060–1065.

Safer, M.A., Tharps, Q.J., Jackson, T.C. & Leventhal, H. (1979). Determinants of three stages of delay in seeking care at a medical clinic. *Medical Care, 17,* 11–29.

Salomaa, E.R., Sallinen, S., Hiekkanen, H. & Liippo, K. (2005). Delays in the diagnosis and treatment of lung cancer. *Chest, 128,* 2282–2288.

Salovey, P., Rothman, A.J., Detweiler, J.B. & Steward, W.T. (2000). Emotional states and physical health. *American Psychologist, 55,* 110–121.

Sarafino, E.P. (2008). *Health psychology: Biopsychosocial interactions* (6th edn, pp. 247–251). New York: Wiley.

Scambler, A. & Scambler, G. (1985). Menstrual symptoms, attitudes and consulting behaviour. *Social Science & Medicine, 20,* 1065–1068.

Scanlon, K., Harding, S., Hunt, K., Petticrew, M., Rosato, M. & Williams, R. (2006). Potential barriers to prevention of cancers and to early cancer detection among Irish people living in Britain: a qualitative study. *Ethnicity & Health, 11,* 325–341.

Scott, S.E., Grunfeld, E.A., Auyeung, V. & McGurk, M. (2009). Barriers and triggers to seeking help for potentially malignant oral symptoms: Implications for interventions. *Journal of Public Health Dentistry, 61,* 34–40.

Scott, S.E., Grunfeld, E.A., Main, J. & McGurk, M. (2006). Patient delay in oral cancer: A qualitative study of patients' experiences. *Psycho-Oncology, 15,* 474–485.

Scott, S.E., McGurk, M. & Grunfeld, E.A. (2007). The process of symptom appraisal: cognitive and emotional responses to detecting potentially malignant oral symptoms. *Journal of Psychosomatic Research, 62,* 621–630.

Scott, S.E., McGurk, M. & Grunfeld, E.A. (2008). Patient delay for potentially malignant oral symptoms. *European Journal of Oral Sciences, 116,* 141–147.

Shaw, C., Brittain, K., Tansey, R. & Williams, K. (2008). How people decide to seek healthcare: A qualitative study. *International Journal of Nursing Studies, 45,* 1516–1524.

Sisler, J.J. (2003). Delays in diagnosing cancer. Threat to the patient–physician relationship. *Canadian Family Physician, 49,* 857–863.

Smith, L.K. Pope, C. & Botha, J.L. (2005). Patients' help-seeking experiences and delay in cancer presentation: a qualitative synthesis. *Lancet, 366,* 825–831.

St Claire, L. (2003). *Rival truths: Common sense and psychological explanations in health and illness.* Hove: Psychology Press.

Stiefel, F. (2006). Letter to editor. *Journal of Psychosomatic Research, 60,* 309–310.

Taylor, S.E. (2008). *Health Psychology* (7th edn). New York: McGraw-Hill.

USDHHS (United States Department of Health & Human Services) (1995). *Health United States: 1994 (Publication*

No. PHS 95-1232). Washington, DC: US Government Printing Office.

Waters, W.E., Wheeller, M.J., Fraser, J.D. & Hayes, A.J. (1983). Evaluation of a health education campaign to reduce the delay in women presenting with breast symptoms. *Community Medicine, 5,* 104–108.

Watson, M., Greer, S., Blake, S. & Shrapnell, K. (1984). Reaction to a diagnosis of breast cancer. Relationship between denial, delay and rates of psychological morbidity. *Cancer, 53,* 2008–2012.

Wielgosz, A.T.J., Nolan, R.P., Earp, J.A., Biro, E. & Wielgosz, M. B. (1988). Reasons for patients' delay in response to symptoms of acute myocardial infarction. *Canadian Medical Association Journal, 139,* 853–857.

Zapka, J.G., Oakes, J.M., Simons-Morton, D.G., Mann, N.C., Goldberg, R., Sellers, D.E. *et al.* (2000). Missed opportunities to impact fast response to AMI symptoms. *Patient Education and Counseling, 40,* 67–82.

Zola, I.K. (1973). Pathways to the doctor – from person to patient. *Social Science & Medicine, 7,* 677–689.

14

Adherence to Advice and Treatment

Rob Horne and Jane Clatworthy

Chapter Outline

This chapter begins by describing the extent and importance of adherence to advice and treatment in health care. Difficulties in defining and measuring adherence are discussed. It presents the perceptions and practicalities approach, an explanatory model for understanding adherence and why previous interventions have had limited effects. It will summarise research into people's perceptions of treatment and show how a better understanding of the psychology of adherence can inform the development of more effective adherence support.

Key Concepts

Evidence-based adherence
    interventions
Necessity concerns
    framework
Operationalising adherence
Perceptions and
    practicalities approach

Introduction

Defining adherence

Adherence is the extent to which a patient's behaviour matches agreed recommendations from their health professional (Horne *et al.*, 2006; NICE, 2009a). In developed economies, the most common health intervention is the prescription of medication. It is unsurprising that most adherence research is concerned with the extent to which medication is taken as prescribed, and this will be the primary focus of this chapter. There is, however, growing awareness of the vital role of lifestyle factors in managing chronic illness, and we will also explore adherence to non-pharmaceutical treatments and advice such as recommendations regarding physical activity and diet modification.

Rates of non-adherence

It has been suggested that approximately a third to half of all medication prescribed for long-term conditions is not taken as directed (World Health Organization, 2003) with rates varying widely between 5–100 per cent (DiMatteo, 2004). There are numerous reasons for this including varying behavioural demands across treatments (Haynes *et al.*, 2002) and differences in methods of assessment.

There is no universally accepted way of operationalising non-adherence (i.e. measuring it or defining cut-offs that distinguish between 'adherers' and 'non-adherers'), yet the method adopted impacts on the rates obtained. For example, in a review of the extent of non-adherence to phosphate-binding medication in renal disease, serum phosphorus levels deemed to be indicative of non-adherence ranged across studies from 4.5 mg/dl to 7.5 mg/dl. This difference in opinion over what represented acceptable levels of phosphorus control was reflected in the reported rates of non-adherence, with the study adopting the highest cut-off reporting the lowest rates of non-adherence (22 per cent) and the study adopting the lowest cut-off reporting one of the highest rates of non-adherence (68 per cent) (Karamanidou *et al.*, 2008).

Impact of adherence

The implicit assumption behind adherence research is that adherence improves patient outcomes. This premise was not, however, thoroughly tested until DiMatteo and colleagues (2002) reviewed 63 studies investigating the relationship between adherence to medical advice (including prescribed medication, diet modification, physical activity and eye patching) and outcomes (including survival, reported pain, blood pressure control, visual acuity, cholesterol levels and organ rejection) (DiMatteo *et al.*, 2002). Overall, the odds of having a good treatment outcome were three times higher among high adherers than low adherers.

Focusing specifically on medication adherence and using an objective outcome measure, a review of 21 studies found the odds of dying among those with high adherence to medication were almost half those of the group with low adherence (Simpson *et al.*, 2006). Interestingly, while those who adhered to medication were significantly less likely to die than those who adhered to placebo, there was also an 'adherence effect' in the placebo group, with the odds of dying among high adherers to placebo being approximately half those of low adherers to placebo. The explanation for the observed 'healthy adherer' effect is not clear. It may be due to the fact that patients who are highly adherent to medication are more likely to engage in other health behaviours. It may also reflect the fact that high adherence is a behavioural marker of the placebo effect.

The impact of adherence varies across conditions, ranging from minor effects on outcomes in some conditions, to making the difference between life and death in others. A key priority for adherence research and the development of adherence interventions is therefore to focus on the conditions where adherence matters most (i.e. in conditions where there is strong evidence supporting the benefits of medication and where high levels of adherence to treatment are essential to ensure efficacy or prevent problems such as treatment resistance, for example in HIV, transplantation, moderate-severe asthma (Horne *et al.*, 2006)).

Cost of non-adherence

If we assume the recommended treatment was appropriate, non-adherence can have numerous costs in addition to the missed opportunity for health gain for the patient. Non-adherence to medication places a substantial financial burden on health-care providers. A recent report published by the UK National Institute for Health and Clinical Excellence (NICE, 2009b) estimates that hospital admissions resulting from medication non-adherence cost the UK National Health Service (NHS) up to £196 million annually. In addition, the report suggests that up to £4 billion per year is wasted on prescribed medication that is not taken as directed. Lack of therapeutic benefit due to undisclosed non-adherence could also lead to escalating treatment costs (increased dose/switch to more expensive regimen) or further costly diagnostic tests (Hughes *et al.*, 2001). The wider economic costs of non-adherence have not been fully evaluated and further health economics modelling studies are needed to improve our understanding of the effects of non-adherence on health utilities.

Operationalising Adherence

Defining and measuring adherence for clinical and research purposes is notoriously difficult. There are numerous ways in which patients' behaviour can differ from recommendations, with varying implications for clinical outcomes. For example, a patient could take all the required doses of a medication but not at the correct time, miss occasional doses, take 'drug holidays' (i.e. miss three or more days' doses), take lower or fewer doses than prescribed, never take the medication or take larger or more frequent doses than prescribed. Despite the huge diversity in non-adherent behaviours, most studies reduce the measurement of adherence to a simple dichotomous variable, with patients being labelled as 'adherent' or 'non-adherent'.

Ideally, where adherence is dichotomised, the cut-offs should be based on values that are clinically meaningful (Vitolins *et al.*, 2000), for example, defining non-adherence as taking less medication than found necessary for clinical efficacy (Horne *et al.*, 2007).

Unfortunately it is often not clear what the precise clinically relevant 'cut-offs' should be. Consequently most adherence cut-offs are approximate or arbitrary. The precise definition of adherence in a given study depends to a large extent on the way in which it is measured, as different measurement approaches will be sensitive to different types of non-adherence. There is no 'gold standard' method, with each having its advantages and disadvantages. Table 14.1 illustrates the issues using medication adherence as an example. At first sight it may appear that 'direct' measures such as biological assays would be the best methods of assessing adherence, but the amount of a drug or drug metabolite in a biological fluid is determined not only by the amount taken but also by individual variation in pharmacokinetic processes (e.g. the absorption, distribution, metabolism and elimination of the medicine). These measures can therefore indicate whether someone has taken *any* of the medicine but are unlikely to be sensitive to dose or timing variations (i.e. they are qualitative but not quantitative measures of adherence).

Indirect, behavioural measures of adherence such as electronic monitoring of medication containers or wearing pedometers to assess physical activity may offer objective measures of adherence but are subject to the Hawthorne effect (i.e. people may change their behaviour because they know they are being monitored). In this way they may in themselves act as adherence interventions rather than giving an accurate estimation of adherence levels. While self-report measures of adherence are often criticised for being subjective and prone to response bias (e.g. people overestimate their adherence), they are the only methods that allow us to find out *why* the person was non-adherent (e.g. was it intentional or unintentional?). For example, a self-report measure of adherence revealed that after 10 days of taking a new medication prescribed for a chronic illness, 30 per cent of patients were non-adherent, 55 per cent of whom reported that their non-adherence was unintentional and 45 per cent intentional (Barber *et al.*, 2004). The accuracy of self-report may be improved by taking steps to reduce self-presentational bias by 'normalising' non-adherence and by limiting questions to behaviours rather than reasons for behaviours (see the Medication Adherence Report Scale (MARS; Horne & Weinman, 2002) as an example).

Table 14.1 Methods of measuring medication adherence

Method	Example	Advantages	Disadvantages
Direct			
Observation	Adherence assessment is made by directly observing patients taking their medication. Widely used in the treatment of tuberculosis but as an intervention to improve adherence rather than a means of measuring adherence	Accurate	Costly Inconvenient for patient and assessor
Biological assays	Usually blood or urine samples are taken and analysed to detect levels of the drug/drug metabolites	Objective	Not available for all drugs Only assesses adherence in the time immediately preceding the assessment Hard to establish cut-offs as there are individual differences in the way drugs are metabolised Expensive May be inconvenient for patients Subject to 'white coat adherence' whereby patients take medication immediately before assessment
Indirect			
Pill count	Patients are asked to bring all their medication containers to their appointment. The remaining tablets are counted and the percentage of prescribed doses taken is calculated	Objective	Time consuming Dependent on patients bringing all their medication containers to appointments Pills may be thrown away to indicate adherence
Self-report	Patients are asked to describe their adherence either in an interview or through completion of a questionnaire or diary	Inexpensive Simple Enables identification of nonadherent cohort (unlikely to be lying)	Dependent on patients accurately recalling medication use Response bias (social desirability, recency effects)
Repeat prescription/ pharmacy refill records	Records of when the patients collect or fill prescriptions are monitored. Actual collect/fill date compared with date medication would have been needed if all doses had been taken as prescribed	Inexpensive Prospective or retrospective assessment	Assumes a prescription is filled/filled prescription is taken Dependent on patients collecting/filling their prescription at the same place Crude indicator – patients are unlikely to collect/ fill prescriptions precisely when they need them
Electronic monitor	Caps of medication bottles contain a computer chip and record each time the container is opened. Caps are scanned and the data downloaded onto a computer	Objective Enables detailed assessment of patterns of adherence, including exact timing of doses	Assumes medication is taken each time the container is opened Does not allow for patients decanting medication into other containers Expensive May require health professionals to decant medication into the containers Requires patients to bring containers with them to appointments for data to be downloaded May act as an intervention if people know they are being monitored

Unfortunately, as the different methods of assessing non-adherence are often sensitive to different types of non-adherence (e.g. a self-report method of adherence could give subjective information on adherence over the last month, urine analysis could give objective information on whether any drug has been taken in the last three days), correlations between rates of adherence indicated by the different methods are often very small, even in the same sample (Velligan et al., 2007). This can lead to a confusing picture and more attention needs to be paid to finding meaningful ways of combining adherence measures (Vitolins et al., 2000). One example in the field of medication adherence would be the use of urine analysis as a 'check' for response bias in self-report adherence measures (i.e. anyone who reports high adherence but who has no detectable drug metabolites in their urine could be reclassified as a low adherer).

The Limited Effects of Interventions to Improve Adherence

Despite the potentially high costs of non-adherence to individuals and society, effective interventions are elusive. The positive finding that adherence behaviours can be changed is moderated by the disappointing result that even effective interventions have relatively small and short-lived effects. For example, a review of 95 randomised controlled trials (RCTs) of adherence interventions reported that the overall increase in adherence resulting from the interventions was a modest 4–11 per cent (Peterson et al., 2003). A major Cochrane review of RCTs assessing medication adherence interventions' impact on both adherence and outcomes revealed that less than half of the 81 interventions examined were associated with improvements in adherence and less than a third had any impact on clinical outcomes (Haynes et al., 2008). These findings are not restricted to interventions to enhance medication adherence. A review of interventions to improve adherence to fluid restrictions in kidney disease reported similarly disappointing results (Sharp et al., 2005).

Changing health-related behaviours, such as adherence, is difficult and we are unlikely to produce large and sustained improvements in adherence rates unless we identify and address the limitations of previous interventions. A review, commissioned by the UK National Institute for Health Research (Horne & Kellar, 2005), identified the reasons for the lack of sustained improvement in adherence to medication, which may also be relevant to other health-related behaviours. It also provided a framework for the development of more cost-effective approaches informed by recent advances in our understanding of the causes of adherence. Previous interventions have had limited effects because of poor design and inadequate development:

- *Limitations in design:* the interventions were not specific enough. Few interventions addressed proven determinants of adherence. Most adopted a 'one-size-fits-all' approach and were not tailored to the specific barriers to adherence for each individual.
- *Limitations in development:* the content of interventions was often not specified in enough detail to identify the active ingredient(s). For example an intervention might be described as 'adherence support' without specifying the particular components targeting specific causes of non-adherence (e.g. reminders to address forgetting, educational interventions to improve understanding). The pharmacological equivalent of this approach would be to propose that 'we treat hypertension with a red pill', without providing details of the specific pharmacological agent within the red pill! Adherence interventions are often tested using a 'black-box' approach, usually in expensive randomised trials. Typically, studies measure *outcome* variables such as adherence but do not assess *process* variables (i.e. the specific causes of adherence that are being addressed by the intervention). The result is that we know whether or not the intervention has worked but do not know *why*. We cannot tell why some interventions work and other, similar interventions do not. We cannot build an accumulative knowledge base to inform future interventions but have to 'start from scratch' each time.

The problem of describing interventions may be addressed by a new taxonomy of theory-based behaviour change techniques (Abraham & Michie, 2008;

Michie *et al.*, 2008). This enables a more thorough evaluation of which techniques are useful in effecting behaviour change and which are not successful. For example, when this taxonomy was applied in a review of interventions to increase healthy eating and exercise, those interventions using the specific technique 'self-monitoring' had a larger effect on health behaviour than those that did not (Michie, 2008).

We can distinguish two ways in which applying theory might help to develop more effective interventions to support adherence:

• Theories of adherence behaviour to identify potentially modifiable causes of non-adherence.
• Theories of behaviour change to identify the best techniques for addressing the modifiable causes of non-adherence.

The first point can inform the second. The selection of approaches to change a particular behaviour will depend on the likely antecedents of the behaviour. Over the last decade or so, research into medication adherence has identified potentially modifiable causes of non-adherence and contributed to the development of theory (see Horne, 2006 for an overview). These explanatory studies have proceeded in parallel to many of the randomised controlled trials included in the Cochrane systematic reviews of adherence interventions and their findings can now be used to inform the development of theory-based pragmatic interventions to improve the efficacy of adherence support.

Understanding Non-adherence: Towards Theory-Based Interventions

Non-adherence cannot be explained by the type or severity of disease with rates of between 25–30 per cent noted across 17 disease conditions (DiMatteo, 2004). Regimen complexity may be a barrier to adherence but reducing the frequency of dosage administrations does not always solve the problem (Claxton *et al.*, 2001; Ingersoll & Cohen, 2008). Furthermore, providing clear information, although essential, is not enough to guarantee adherence and information-based interventions do not tend to

improve adherence to long-term treatments (Kripalani *et al.*, 2007). Knowing *how* is not enough.

There is little evidence that adherence behaviours can be explained in terms of trait personality characteristics. Similarly there are no clear and consistent links between adherence and sociodemographic variables such as gender and age in adults (DiMatteo, 2004; Horne, 1998). This is not to say that sociodemographic or dispositional characteristics are irrelevant, but rather that trait characteristics and sociodemographic factors influence the adherence behaviour of some patients more than others. The notion of the 'non-adherent patient' is a myth: most of us are non-adherent some of the time. Non-adherence is a variable behaviour and not a trait characteristic. Moreover, sociodemographic variables and trait characteristic are fixed variables. They can help identify groups 'at risk' for non-adherence but can do little to inform the type or content of these interventions. For this, we need to identify potentially modifiable causes of non-adherence.

Identifying potentially modifiable causes of non-adherence: the perceptions and practicalities approach

As with most other behaviours relating to health and illness, the many causes of non-adherence can be grouped as intentional and unintentional. The recognition that human behaviour can often be understood as a combination of volitional and non-volitional factors is fundamental to modern psychology. The classification of non-adherent behaviours into intentional and unintentional is the basis of the perceptions and practicalities approach (PPA) (Horne, 2001 see Figure 14.1) for understanding non-adherence and developing interventions to support optimal adherence.

Unintentional non-adherence occurs when the patient's intentions to adhere to treatment are thwarted by barriers such as poor recall or comprehension of instructions, difficulties in administering the treatment, financial costs of the treatment, or simply forgetting to take it. Intentional non-adherence occurs when the patient decides not to follow the treatment recommendations. Intentional non-adherence can be understood in terms of the beliefs and preferences influencing the person's motivation to start and

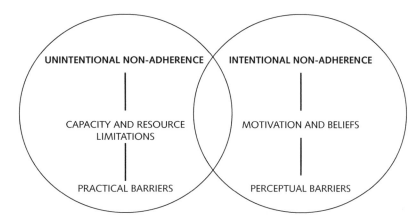

Figure 14.1 The perceptions and practicalities approach
Source: Horne, R. (2001). Compliance, adherence and concordance. In K. Taylor & G. Harding (Eds.) *Pharmacy practice* (pp. 165–184). London: Taylor & Francis.

continue with treatment. Clearly there is a degree of overlap between intentional and unintentional non-adherence: motivation may overcome resource barriers and resource barriers may reduce motivation. The PPA is not meant to be a comprehensive 'boxes and arrows' model of adherence but rather provides a simple framework for developing the content of interventions. The key principles of the approach are:

- To understand non-adherence and facilitate adherence, we need to consider two issues: motivation and resources.
- People's motivation to start and continue with treatment will be influenced by treatment-related cognitions and emotions and these can form *perceptual* barriers leading to intentional non-adherence.
- Limitations in resources (including abilities) constitute practical barriers leading to unintentional non-adherence.

Perceptual and practical barriers need to be addressed by different types of interventions. For example, perceptual barriers might be addressed by cognitive behavioural techniques or motivational interviewing whereas practical barriers might be overcome by interventions that increase capacity or improve ability (e.g. reminder systems to reduce forgetting).

Each individual will have a unique mix of perceptual and practical barriers to adherence and interventions should be tailored to meet the needs of individuals by first assessing the specific barriers and then selecting appropriate techniques to address each barrier.

The perceptual and practical barriers for each individual will be affected by sociodemographic, cultural and economic factors and trait characteristics. However, the effect of these variables will vary among individuals. For this reason the assessment of the specific perceptual and practical barriers for each individual should be the starting point for adherence interventions. One size does not fit all.

In order to apply the PPA in the development of effective interventions for helping people to get the best from treatments, we need methods for operationalising the salient perceptual and practical factors influencing adherence that can be used in routine practice.

Perceptions

Health psychologists have developed a range of structured models integrating various beliefs thought to influence health behaviours. A detailed description of these models is beyond the scope of this chapter but see Ogden (2007) for an overview. There is increasing interest in understanding how people make value judgements about treatments and how perceptions of treatment and illness influence behaviours (Cameron & Leventhal, 2003). Work identifying the salient beliefs influencing adherence to medication offers an example.

Treatment beliefs and the necessity concerns framework (NCF) Research into perceptions of medicines identified two categories of medication beliefs: general beliefs about medicines as a class of treatment and specific beliefs about a particular prescribed medication (Horne et al., 1999). Specific beliefs were the more salient in relation to adherence (Horne & Weinman, 1999) but these were influenced by general beliefs which provide the context for the evaluation of specific medicines prescribed for the patient (Horne, 1997). Principal components analysis of items derived from interview-based studies showed that the salient beliefs about prescribed medicines could be grouped as *necessity* beliefs and *concerns* (Horne et al., 1999).

Necessity beliefs. To arrive at a necessity belief we ask the question 'How much do I need this treatment?'. Perceived necessity is not a form of efficacy belief. Although views about efficacy are likely to contribute to perceived necessity, the constructs are not synonymous. We might believe that a treatment will be effective but not that we need it. Conversely, we might perceive a strong need for a treatment that we believe to be only moderately effective, because we know that it is the only treatment that is available. Necessity beliefs are influenced by perceptions of the condition being treated (Horne & Weinman, 2002) as well as by symptom expectations and experiences (Cooper, 2004).

Concerns. The concerns construct represents the personal impact of potential costs and has an emotional as well as a cognitive component (e.g. 'I worry about side effects'). There is a striking similarity in the type of concerns that patients report about prescription medicines. One obvious source of concern is the experience of symptoms as medication 'side effects' and the disruptive effects of medication on daily living; but this is not the whole picture. Many patients receiving regular medication who have not experienced adverse effects are still worried about possible problems in the future. These often arise from the

belief that regular use can lead to dependence or that the medication will accumulate within the body and lead to long-term effects, and these are related to the social representations of medicines as intrinsically harmful substances that are over prescribed (Horne & Weinman, 1999). Other concerns are specific to the particular class of medicine. For example, worries that corticosteroid inhalers prescribed for asthma will result in weight gain (Horne & Weinman, 2002) or that regular use of analgesic medication now will make it less effective in the future (Gill & Williams, 2001).

Medication cost as a concern and adherence barrier. Out-of-pocket prescription expenses are a serious concern for many patients and have been identified as a significant practical barrier to medication access and adherence in the USA (Piette et al., 2004a, 2004b). This work has also resulted in a theoretical model integrating aspects of cost and perceived value with the necessity concerns framework (Piette et al., 2006). The way in which patients respond to cost pressures and how that impinges on treatment choices is strongly influenced by the *value* they place on specific components of the treatment.

Studies involving patients from a wide range of illness groups including asthma (Horne & Weinman, 2002; Menckeberg et al., 2007), renal transplantation (Butler et al., 2004), diabetes, cancer and coronary heart disease (Horne & Weinman, 1999), bipolar disorder (Clatworthy et al., 2009), depression (Aikens et al., 2005; Hunot et al., 2007), HIV/AIDS (Gonzalez et al., 2007; Horne et al., 2007), rheumatoid arthritis (Neame & Hammond, 2005) and haemophilia (Llewellyn et al., 2003) have found that low rates of adherence are related to doubts about personal need for medication and concerns about potential adverse effects.

A meta-analysis of over 30 peer-reviewed studies confirms the utility of the NCF in operationalising the salient medication beliefs influencing adherence across a range of therapeutic categories, cultures, sociodemographic groups and countries (Horne et al., manuscript in preparation).

Necessity-concerns dilemma. The motivation to start and persist with treatment is influenced by the way in which the individual judges their personal need for the treatment *relative* to their concerns about potential adverse effects. Many patients are faced with a necessity-concerns dilemma. They believe that they need the treatment to maintain or improve health but also harbour concerns about potential adverse effects. Non-adherence is often a 'common-sense' response to this dilemma: they take some but not all. Although, this might not make sense from a medical perspective, as it might compromise efficacy, it is a logical response based on the patient's perceived value of the treatment. The effect on adherence may be implicit as well as explicit (Horne, 2003). For example, in some situations, non-adherence could be the result of a deliberate strategy to minimise harm by taking less medication. Alternatively, it might simply be a reflection of the fact that patients who do not perceive their medication to be important are more likely to forget to take it. The impact of perceptions of treatment on adherence will also be influenced by beliefs about adherence, such as the importance of strict adherence to achieve the desired outcome (Siegel *et al.*, 2000).

Recent research suggests that the NCF may also be applied to other treatment-related behaviours such as attendance at cardiac rehabilitation classes (Cooper *et al.*, 2005). Doubts about necessity and concerns about potential adverse effects of treatment are potentially modifiable determinants of adherence. However, in order to challenge doubts about personal need for medication and allay concerns we need to understand their origins. The following section presents ideas and research improving our understanding of how individuals evaluate the necessity of treatment and develop concerns. It will also illustrate how common-sense representations of illness and treatment might explain illness-related behaviours within the context of Leventhal's common-sense model (see Horne 2003 for a more detailed description of an extended common-sense model).

The common-sense origins of necessity beliefs and concerns

Prior to treatment, necessity beliefs and concerns may be thought of as higher order outcome expectancies that are influenced by beliefs about the illness (e.g. identity, cause, consequences, timeline and capacity for control/cure) as well as by more general 'social representations' of and preferences for classes of treatments. Once treatment has

commenced appraisal processes are also influential as the person checks how well the 'treatment is working'.

Medication necessity beliefs. In order to be convinced of a personal need for ongoing medication we must first perceive a good fit between the *problem* (the illness or condition) and the *solution* (the medication). Patients' common-sense perceptions of illness influence their beliefs about the necessity of medication (see Horne, 2003 for a review). Symptoms perceptions relative to expectations are key. Until we experience a chronic condition most of our experience of illness is symptomatic and acute. We know we are ill because we experience symptoms. We know when we are better because the symptoms go away. We carry these expectations of symptoms and illness with us when we encounter long-term conditions. For many long-term conditions the medical rationale for maintenance treatment is based on a prophylaxis model. The benefits of treatment are often silent and long term. This may be in stark contrast to our intuitive common-sense model of 'no symptoms no problem'. Moreover missing doses may not lead to an immediate deterioration in symptoms, so reinforcing the (erroneous) perception that high adherence to the medication may not be necessary. Related to this is the fact that people often stop taking treatment when they judge that the condition has improved. These judgements are often based on potentially erroneous symptoms perceptions rather than on objective clinical indicators of disease severity.

Medication concerns are related to prototypic 'background beliefs' about the nature of pharmaceuticals as a class of treatments (Horne *et al.*, 1999). Many people are suspicious of pharmaceuticals and the pharmaceutical industry. They tend to view all medicines as having common properties. The benefits of medicines are often taken for granted with a focus on the potential negative effects. In this view medicines are often seen as intrinsically harmful addictive substances that are overused by doctors and the health-care system. These 'social representations' of medicines are linked to wider concerns about scientific medicine, lack of trust in doctors and an increasing interest in alternative or complementary health care (Calnan *et al.*, 2005).

General medication beliefs influence the way in which people evaluate *specific* medication prescribed for a particular medical condition. They frame initial expectations of the outcome of taking the prescribed medication (Cooper *et al.*, 2004), as well as how subsequent events are interpreted – for example whether symptoms are attributed to the illness or the treatment (Siegel *et al.*, 1999). General beliefs about medicines may also contribute to perception of medication necessity and could even influence outcome directly through the placebo effect although this has yet to be empirically tested.

Practicalities

Forgetting is the most commonly reported reason for treatment non-adherence (Bulloch *et al.*, 2006; Franks *et al.*, 2005), although this may in part be due to a reporting bias, as it may be more socially acceptable to disclose unintentional than intentional non-adherence. There are two separate memory processes linked to adherence – remembering the treatment instructions (retrospective memory) and remembering to take/engage in the treatment at the right time (prospective memory – see Ellis, 1998). Memory performance has been associated with adherence to medication across a range of chronic conditions, including HIV (Woods *et al.*, 2009), diabetes (Vedhara *et al.*, 2004) and chronic obstructive pulmonary disease (Incalzi *et al.*, 1997). Interventions using reminder systems to combat forgetting can be effective but the effects are typically modest (Vincent *et al.*, 1995; Wise & Operario, 2008), perhaps because they fail to address perceptual barriers.

Other interventions designed to reduce forgetting focus on the development of plans known as 'implementation intentions' (Gollwitzer, 1993). Implementation intentions tie a specific adherence behaviour to an environmental cue by planning how and when the behaviour can be carried out. Turning an intention (e.g. 'I will take my medicine') into a more specific implementation intention (e.g. 'I will take my medicine every morning immediately after I clean my teeth') increases the likelihood of the behaviour being performed (Gollwitzer & Brandstattter, 1997). The formation of implementation intentions has been found to increase adherence to a range of health recommendations such as diet modification, preventive screening and increased exercise, at least in the short term (Gollwitzer & Sheeran, 2006; Schweiger Gallo & Gollwitzer, 2007). Further research is required to investigate the effect of developing implementation intentions on adherence to medication.

Other factors and challenges

Emotion and affect are likely to influence both perceptual and practical barriers to adherence as well as individual responses to efforts to overcome them. A meta-analysis of 25 studies found that the relationship between depression and non-adherence to medication prescribed for chronic illnesses (other than depression) was substantial. Anxiety had little effect (DiMatteo *et al.*, 2000). A further area for future research is the effect of social support. Social support appears to have broadly positive effects on adherence but we know little about the mechanism or the type of support that works best in what situations.

Summary and Future Directions

Low rates of adherence to treatment are a major problem, both in terms of lost opportunity for health gain for patients and also cost to health-care providers. The development of effective, equitable and efficient interventions to facilitate informed adherence where adherence matters most is the key challenge. The goal of intervention is to support informed choice and support optimal adherence. A patient can be considered to have made an informed choice if they can demonstrate knowledge of relevant information about the treatment and then act according to their beliefs (Michie *et al.*, 2003). This concept of informed choice has been extended to address *informed adherence* to treatment recommendations (Horne & Weinman, 2004). To enable informed adherence, evidence-based medicine should be used to guide initial recommendations for treatment. The recommendations should then be presented to patients in a way that takes account of their individual beliefs and preferences and attempts to help them resolve any incompatibilities between their personal beliefs and the prevailing evidence.

This chapter has outlined the reasons why previous adherence interventions have met with only limited success and presented a perceptions and practicalities approach as a possible framework to develop comprehensive adherence interventions. This approach conceptualises non-adherence as unintentional and intentional behaviours with internal and external determinants. The 'internal' factors influencing motivation and capacity may be moderated by 'external' variables, such as the quality of communication between the patient and health-care provider and by the wider societal contexts such as access to resources and societal policy and practice. Future interventions may be more effective if they address both the perceptual factors influencing motivation to initiate and persist with the recommended behaviour, as well as facilitating the implementation of intentions to adhere, for example by addressing the capacity and resource limitations that act as barriers. All patients will have their own unique mix of practical and perceptual barriers to adherence which need to be elicited and addressed in order to facilitate adherence. If using a medicine does not make 'common sense' to the patients (e.g. taking regular inhaled steroid in the absence of symptomatic benefit), they are unlikely to take it, even if the regimen is convenient and easy to use.

The perceptions and practicalities approach has been adopted in new NICE adherence guidelines (NICE, 2009a), developed to help health professionals support patients in making informed choices about and adhering to prescribed medication.

Interventions can be developed at several levels:

- The individual patient level such as cognitive behavioural approaches. The available evidence suggests that these are likely to be more effective if they address both motivational factors and capacity limitations (the perceptions and practicalities approach).
- Interventions focusing on others, for example, changing the behaviour of health-care practitioners (e.g. providing adherence support training for clinicians), facilitating support from non-professional helpers (e.g. the Expert Patient programme; www.expertpatients.nhs.uk/), or targeting the household unit.
- Organisational or service modification such as introducing an additional 'medicines-management' consultation with a pharmacist as part of programme of care for elderly patients.
- Population-level interventions such as media-delivered information or behaviour change campaigns often known as social marketing.

We need to develop interventions of varying complexity from simple minimal interventions targeted to all patients through to more comprehensive interventions targeted to patients most at risk of non-adherence. We need to apply 'technologies' for behaviour change and adherence support, combining cognitive behavioural approaches with innovative applications of existing and new technologies (e.g. reminders to address forgetting). Such interventions should be developed in a systematic manner. The Medical Research Council has recently published updated guidelines to improve the design and evaluation of complex interventions (Craig et al., 2008) and these approaches can be applied to develop interventions to support adherence (Horne & Kellar, 2005).

Discussion Points

1 How can adherence best be measured?
2 Why does non-adherence occur?
3 Why are the interventions designed to improve adherence often unsuccessful?

4 How can we improve the quality of adherence support?

Further Reading

Craig, P., Dieppe, P., Macintyre, S., Michie, S., Nazareth, I. & Petticrew, M. (2008). Developing and evaluating complex interventions: The new Medical Research Council guidance. *British Medical Journal, 337*, a1655.

DiMatteo, M.R. (2004). Variations in patients' adherence to medical recommendations: A quantitative review of 50 years of research. *Medical Care, 42*, 200–209.

Horne, R., Weinman, J., Barber, N., Elliott, R.A. & Morgan, M. (2005). *Concordance, adherence and compliance in medicine taking: A conceptual map and research priorities.* London:

National Coordinating Centre for NHS Service Delivery and Organisation (NCCSDO).

Horne, R. (2003). Treatment perceptions and self-regulation. In L.D. Cameron & H. Leventhal (Eds.) *The self-regulation of health and illness behaviour* (pp. 139–153). London: Routledge.

NICE. (2009). *Clinical Guideline 76: Medicines adherence – involving patients in decisions about prescribed medicines and supporting adherence.* London: National Institute for Health and Clinical Excellence.

References

Abraham, C. & Michie, S. (2008). A taxonomy of behavior change techniques used in interventions. *Health Psychology, 27*, 379–387.

Aikens, J.E., Nease, D.E. *et al.* (2005). Adherence to maintenance-phase antidepressant medication as a function of patient beliefs about medication. *Annals of Family Medicine, 3*, 23–30.

Barber, N., Parsons, J. *et al.* (2004). Patients' problems with new medication for chronic conditions. *Quality and Safety in Health Care, 13*, 172–175.

Bulloch, A.G., Adair, C.E. *et al.* (2006). Forgetfulness: A role in noncompliance with antidepressant treatment. *Canadian Journal of Psychiatry, 51*, 719–722.

Butler, J.A., Peveler, R.C. *et al.* (2004). Modifiable risk factors for non-adherence to immunosuppressants in renal transplant recipients: A cross-sectional study. *Nephrology Dialysis Transplantation, 19*, 3144–3149.

Calnan, M., Montaner, D. *et al.* (2005). How acceptable are innovative health-care technologies? A survey of public beliefs and attitudes in England and Wales. *Social Science & Medicine, 60*, 1937–1948.

Cameron, L.D. & Leventhal, H. (2003). *The self-regulation of health and illness behaviour.* London: Routledge.

Clatworthy, J., Bowskill, R. *et al.* (2009). Understanding medication non-adherence in bipolar disorders using a Necessity-Concerns Framework. *Journal of Affective Disorders, 116*, 51–55.

Claxton, A.J., Cramer, J. *et al.* (2001). A systematic review of the associations between dose regimens and medication compliance. *Clinical Therapeutics, 23*, 1296–1310.

Cooper, A.F., Jackson, G. *et al.* (2005). A qualitative study investigating patients' beliefs about cardiac rehabilitation. *Journal of Clinical Rehabilitation, 19*(1), 87–96.

Cooper, V. (2004). *Explaining adherence to Highly Active Anti-Retroviral Therapy (HAART): The utility of an extended self-regulatory model.* PhD thesis, University of Brighton, UK.

Cooper, V., Gellaitry, G. *et al.* (2004). Treatment perceptions and self-regulation in adherence to HAART. *International Journal of Behavioral Medicine, 11*, 81.

Craig, P., Dieppe, P. *et al.* (2008). Developing and evaluating complex interventions: The new Medical Research Council guidance. *British Medical Journal, 337*, a1655.

DiMatteo, M.R. (2004). Variations in patients' adherence to medical recommendations: a quantitative review of 50 years of research. *Medical Care, 42*: 200–209.

DiMatteo, M.R., Giordani, P.J. *et al.* (2002). Patient adherence and medical treatment outcomes: A meta-analysis. *Medical Care, 40*: 794–811.

DiMatteo, M.R., Lepper, H.S. *et al.* (2000). Depression is a risk factor for noncompliance with medical treatment: Meta-analysis of the effects of anxiety and depression on patient adherence. *Archives of Internal Medicine, 160*, 2101–2107.

Ellis, J. (1998). Prospective memory and medicine taking. In L.B. Myers & K. Midence (Eds.) *Adherence to treatment in medical conditions.* Amsterdam: Harwood Academic.

Franks, T.J., Burton, D.L. *et al.* (2005). Patient medication knowledge and adherence to asthma pharmacotherapy: a pilot study in rural Australia. *Therapeutics and Clinical Risk Management, 1*, 33–38.

Gill, A. & Williams, A.C. (2001). Preliminary study of chronic pain patients' concerns about cannabinoids as analgesics. *Clinical Journal of Pain, 17*, 245–248.

Gollwitzer, P.M. (1993). Goal achievement: The role of intentions. *European Review of Social Psychology, 4*, 141–185.

Gollwitzer, P.M. & Brandstattter, V. (1997). Implementation intentions and effective goal pursuit. *Journal of Personality and Social Psychology, 73*, 186–189.

Gollwitzer, P.M. & Sheeran, P. (2006). Implementation intentions and goal achievement: A metaanalysis of effects and processes. *Advances in Experimental Social Psychology, 38*, 70–110.

Gonzalez, J., Penedo, F. et al. (2007). Physical symptoms, beliefs about medications, negative mood, and long-term HIV medication adherence. *Annals of Behavioural Medicine, 34*, 46–55.

Haynes, R.B., Ackloo, E. et al. (2008). Interventions for enhancing medication adherence. *Cochrane Database of Systematic Reviews* (2): CD000011.

Haynes, R.B., McDonald, H.P. et al. (2002). Helping patients follow prescribed treatment: Clinical applications. *Journal of the American Medical Association, 288*(22), 2880–2883.

Horne, R. (1997). Representations of medication and treatment: Advances in theory and measurement. In K.J. Petrie & J.A. Weinman (Eds.) *Perceptions of health and illness: Current research and applications* (pp. 155–188). London: Harwood Academic Press.

Horne, R. (1998). Adherence to medication: A review of existing research. In L. Myers & K. Midence (Eds.), *Adherence to treatment in medical conditions* (pp. 285–310). London: Harwood Academic.

Horne, R. (2000). Nonadherence to medication: causes and implications for care. In P. Gard (Ed.) *A behavioural approach to pharmacy practice.* Oxford: Blackwell Science.

Horne, R. (2001). Compliance, adherence and concordance. In K. Taylor & G. Harding (Eds.) *Pharmacy Practice* (pp. 165–184). London: Taylor & Francis.

Horne, R. (2003). Treatment perceptions and self regulation. In L.D. Cameron & H. Leventhal (Eds.), *The self-regulation of health and illness behaviour* (pp. 138–153). London: Routledge.

Horne, R. (2006). Beliefs and adherence to treatment: The challenge for research and clinical practice. In P.W. Halligan & M. Aylward (Eds.) *The power of belief: Psychosocial influence on illness, disability and medicine* (pp. 115–136). Oxford: Oxford University Press.

Horne, R., Cooper, V. et al. (2007). Patients' perceptions of highly active antiretroviral therapy in relation to treatment uptake and adherence: the utility of the Necessity-Concerns Framework. *Journal of Acquired Immune Deficiency Syndrome, 45*, 334–341.

Horne, R. & Kellar I. (2005). Interventions to facilitate adherence. In R. Horne, J. Weinman, N. Barber, R.A. Elliott & M. Morgan (Eds.) *Concordance, adherence and compliance in medicine taking.* London: National Institute for Health Research (NIHR) Service Delivery and Organisation (SDO).

Horne, R. & Weinman J. (1999). Patients' beliefs about prescribed medicines and their role in adherence to treatment in chronic physical illness. *Journal of Psychosomatic Research, 47*, 555–567.

Horne, R. & Weinman J. (2002). Self-regulation and self-management in asthma: Exploring the role of illness perceptions and treatment beliefs in explaining non-adherence to preventer medication. *Psychology & Health, 17*, 17–32.

Horne, R. & Weinman J. (2004). The theoretical basis of concordance and issues for research. In C. Bond (Ed.) *Concordance* (pp. 119–146). London: Pharmaceutical Press.

Horne, R., Weinman, J. et al. (2006). *Concordance, adherence and compliance in medicine taking: A conceptual map and research priorities.* London: National Coordinating Centre for NHS Service Delivery and Organisation (NCCSDO).

Horne, R., Weinman, J. et al. (1999). The Beliefs about Medicines Questionnaire: the development and evaluation of a new method for assessing the cognitive representation of medication. *Psychology & Health, 14*, 1–24.

Hughes, D.A., Bagust, A. et al. (2001). The impact of non-compliance on the cost-effectiveness of pharmaceuticals: a review of the literature. *Health Economics, 10*, 601–615.

Hunot, V., Horne, R. et al. (2007). A cohort study of adherence to antidepressants in primary care: The influence of antidepressant concerns and treatment preferences. *The Primary Care Companion to the Journal of Clinical Psychiatry, 9*, 91–99.

Incalzi, R.A., Gemma, A. et al. (1997). Verbal memory impairment in COPD: Its mechanisms and clinical relevance. *Chest, 112*, 1506–1513.

Ingersoll, K.S. & Cohen J. (2008). The impact of medication regimen factors on adherence to chronic treatment: a review of literature. *Journal of Behavioral Medicine, 31*, 213–224.

Karamanidou, C., Clatworthy, J. et al. (2008). A systematic review of the prevalence and determinants of nonadherence to phosphate binding medication in patients with end-stage renal disease. *BMC Nephrology, 9*, 2.

Kripalani, S., Yao, X. et al. (2007). Interventions to enhance medication adherence in chronic medical conditions: A systematic review. *Archives of Internal Medicine, 167*, 540–550.

Llewellyn, C., Miners, A. et al. (2003). The illness perceptions and treatment beliefs of individuals with severe haemophilia and their role in adherence to home treatment. *Health Psychology, 18*, 185–200.

Menckeberg, T.T., Bouvy, M.L. et al. (2007). Beliefs about medicines predict refill adherence to inhaled corticosteroids. *Journal of Psychosomatic Research, 64*, 47–54.

Michie, S. (2008). Designing and implementing behaviour change interventions to improve population health. *Journal of Health Services & Research Policy, 13*, 64–69.

Michie, S., Dormandy, E. *et al.* (2003). Informed choice: Understanding knowledge in the context of screening uptake. *Patient Education and Counseling, 50,* 247–253.

Michie, S., Johnston, M. *et al.* (2008). From theory to intervention: Mapping theoretically derived behavioural determinants to behaviour change techniques. *Applied Psychology: An International Review, 57,* 660–680.

Neame, R. & Hammond, A. (2005). Beliefs about medications: A questionnaire survey of people with rheumatoid arthritis. *Rheumatology, 44,* 762–767.

NICE (2009a). *Clinical Guideline 76: Medicines adherence: Involving patients in decisions about prescribed medicines and supporting adherence.* London: National Institute for Health and Clinical Excellence.

NICE (2009b). *Costing Statement: Medicines adherence: Involving patients in decisions about prescribed medicines and supporting adherence.* London: National Institute for Health and Clinical Excellence.

Ogden, J. (2007). *Health psychology: A textbook.* Buckingham: Open University Press.

Peterson, A.M., Takiya, L. *et al.* (2003). Meta-analysis of trials of interventions to improve medication adherence. *American Journal of Health-System Pharmacy, 60,* 657–665.

Piette, J.D., Heisler, M. *et al.* (2004a). Cost-related medication under-use among chronically ill adults: What treatments do people forego? How often? Who is at risk? *American Journal of Public Health, 94.*

Piette, J.D., Heisler, M. *et al.* (2004b). Cost-related medication underuse: Do patients with chronic illnesses tell their doctors? *Archives of Internal Medicine, 164,* 1749–1755.

Piette, J.D., Heisler, M. *et al.* (2006). A conceptually based approach to understanding chronically ill patients' responses to medication cost pressures. *Social Science & Medicine, 62,* 846–857.

Schweiger Gallo, I. & Gollwitzer, P.M. (2007). Implementation intentions: A look back at fifteen years of progress. *Psicothema, 19,* 37–42.

Sharp, J., Wild, M.R. *et al.* (2005). A systematic review of psychological interventions for the treatment of non-adherence to fluid-intake restrictions in people receiving hemodialysis. *American Journal of Kidney Diseases, 45,* 15–27.

Siegel, K., Dean, L. *et al.* (1999). Symptom ambiguity among late middle aged and older adults with HIV. *Research on Aging, 21,* 595–618.

Siegel, K., Schrimshaw, E.W. *et al.* (2000). Accounts for non-adherence to antiviral combination therapies among older HIV-infected adults. *Psychology, Health & Medicine, 5,* 29–42.

Simpson, S.H., Eurich, D.T. *et al.* (2006). A meta-analysis of the association between adherence to drug therapy and mortality. *British Medical Journal, 333,* 15.

Vedhara, K., Wadsworth, E. *et al.* (2004). Habitual prospective memory in elderly patients with Type 2 diabetes: Implications for medication adherence. *Psychology, Health & Medicine, 9,* 17–28.

Velligan, D.I., Wang, M. *et al.* (2007). Relationships among subjective and objective measures of adherence to oral antipsychotic medications. *Psychiatric Services, 58,* 1187–1192.

Vincent, E.C., Hardin, P.A. *et al.* (1995). The effects of a computer-assisted reminder system on patient compliance with recommended health maintenance procedures. *Proceedings of the Annual Symposium on Computer Application in Medical Care,* 656–60.

Vitolins, M.Z., Rand, C.S. *et al.* (2000). Measuring adherence to behavioral and medical interventions. *Controlled Clinical Trials, 21,* 188S–194S.

Wise, J. & Operario, D. (2008). Use of electronic reminder devices to improve adherence to antiretroviral therapy: A systematic review. *AIDS Patient Care STDS, 22,* 495–504.

Woods, S.P., Dawson, M.S. *et al.* (2009). Timing is everything: Antiretroviral nonadherence is associated with impairment in time-based prospective memory. *Journal of the International Neuropsychological Society, 15,* 42–52.

World Health Organization (2003). *Adherence to long-term therapies: Evidence for action.* Geneva: World Health Organization.

15

Health-Care Professional Behaviour

Enhancing Evidence-Based Health Care

Jill Francis and Marie Johnston

Chapter Outline

For many years psychologists have focused on doctors' consulting behaviours (e.g. communication; Byrne & Long, 1976) and their effect on patient outcomes such as satisfaction (Frostholm *et al.*, 2005), coping styles (Ong *et al.*, 1999) and adherence to medication (Ley, 1982). This chapter will focus more on the clinical behaviours of a range of health-care professionals (HCPs), that is, their clinical decisions and actions rather than their communication style. The outcomes of disease are influenced to a large extent by such clinical behaviours. For example, if people experiencing symptoms are not accurately diagnosed, if appropriate evidence-based treatments are not prescribed or if chronic illnesses are not adequately monitored, people are more likely to experience health problems. Furthermore, HCPs are expected to change their behaviours in line with constantly evolving biomedical evidence. There is a growing field of research about the effectiveness of attempts to assist HCPs to change their clinical behaviours. Some of this research is based on theories, methods and behaviour change techniques from health psychology but much is based on the intuitive ideas of clinical researchers. In this chapter we:

- trace the trends in research about behaviours that constitute evidence-based health care;
- identify the role of theories of behaviour and behaviour change;
- describe research about health professional behaviour change that is based on theories, methods and interventions from health psychology;
- discuss issues that require special attention;
- propose directions for further research.

Key Concepts

Behaviour change interventions
Behaviour change techniques
Evidence-based practice
Evidence-practice gap
Implementation of clinical guidelines
Professional behaviour
Theories of behaviour

Trends in Research about HCP Behaviours

Since the 1970s, research in evidence-based health care can be described in terms of the following phases:

1970s: Randomised controlled trials to determine best practice. Randomised controlled trials (RCTs) were conducted to build an evidence base about treatments that were effective. RCTs are experiments used to evaluate the effects of health-care interventions (such as a drug, surgical procedure or therapy). They involve the random allocation of participants to at least one treatment group and a comparable control group. Where possible, participants are 'blinded' (i.e. they do not know which group they have been allocated to, for example, by the use of a placebo treatment) and researchers who measure the outcome variable are also unaware of the participants' treatment allocation (to avoid bias associated with assessors' expectations).

In the databases PsycINFO and Medline, the first time that 'randomised controlled trial' appeared in the title of a publication was in 1969 (Kennedy & Connell, 1969), with a further 47 papers in this category published in the 1970s.[1] One notable RCT was the first of several to evaluate the effects of aspirin in the prevention of early mortality following myocardial infarction (Elwood & Williams, 1979). Another RCT tested the effects of vitamin C in treatment of the common cold (Elwood *et al.*, 1976). Behaviour change interventions were also trialled. For example, an intervention involving recall of middle-aged smokers for an interview with a physician about smoking cessation was tested in an early RCT (Rose & Hamilton, 1978). An intervention involving yoga and bio-feedback compared with placebo therapy (general relaxation) was evaluated for the management of hypertension (Patel & North, 1975). Treatments for phobic patients were tested using a randomised factorial design to compare flooding, desensitisation and a specially constructed non-specific control treatment (Gelder *et al.*, 1973). The effectiveness of electroconvulsive therapy (ECT) compared with simulated ECT was evaluated as a treatment for depression (Freeman *et al.*, 1978). Testing of these interventions identified some clinical behaviours that were likely to result in improved health outcomes and some that were unlikely to be effective.

Following Archie Cochrane's (1972) now-famous distinction between effectiveness and efficiency in health care, the economic basis of health care was also examined using RCTs. One early trial (Gerson & Berry, 1976) compared 'early transfer of hospital inpatients to home care' with controls. The group of patients discharged earlier performed at least as well as controls on outcome variables such as return to work, leisure and household roles, indicating that the measured health outcomes were not diminished following the less expensive intervention.

1980s: Synthesis of trial evidence. In addition to further RCT research, there was a focus in the 1980s on integrating the evidence. The methodology for synthesising the evidence from RCTs included the use of systematic search criteria, quality criteria to assess existing evidence and systematic methods of evidence synthesis, such as meta-analysis. This procedure for quantitative synthesis was first proposed by Glass in 1976 and applied to 375 studies of the effects of psychotherapy by Smith and Glass (1977). Systematic reviews increased certainty about the evidence base and it became clearer that it was possible to base health care on robust scientific evidence. In 1992, the *Journal of the American Medical Association* (*JAMA*) published a ground-breaking article entitled 'Evidence-based medicine: A new approach to teaching the practice of medicine' (Evidence-Based Medicine Working Group, 1992).

1990s: Identification of evidence-practice gaps and trials testing 'implementation' interventions to change HCPs' behaviour. Medical research continues to build the evidence base using RCTs and systematic reviews, but with the idea of evidence-based medicine came a concern with identifying discrepancies between the evidence base and HCPs' behaviour. It became increasingly clear that the publication of systematic reviews (and clinical guidelines or protocols based on available evidence) was often not, in itself, sufficient to ensure either the implementation of effective health-care practices or the discontinuation of ineffective practices. For example, a large systematic review of clinical behaviours in primary care identified that 'in almost all studies, the processes of care did not attain the standards set out in national guidelines' (Seddon et al., 2001, p. 132). (There are direct parallels between this evidence-practice gap among HCPs and the widespread evidence of non-adherence to recommended treatment in patients (see Chapter 14, this volume) and other health-protective behaviours.) Additional 'strategies', or interventions, were needed. Hence, interventions were developed and evaluated to identify what might work to increase the evidence-based clinical behaviours of HCPs. Examples are presented in Table 15.1.

Table 15.1 shows that:

- trials attempted to change a large range of clinical behaviours in many clinical contexts;
- intervention labels had variable levels of generality (e.g. 'multifaceted' versus 'performance feedback');
- interventions were sometimes defined by the behaviour change goal ('strategies to improve asthma management') rather than by the content of the intervention;
- from the intervention descriptions, there is little to suggest that these interventions were based on theories of behaviour and behaviour change.

Furthermore, many interventions in this list did not appear to change clinical behaviour. However, a more systematic approach to identifying such trials and synthesising the evidence they produced would be needed before drawing a firm conclusion. Indeed, as early as 1992 (Davis et al., 1992), researchers were pioneering the use of systematic reviews to synthesise evidence about HCP behaviour change interventions and the Cochrane group,[2] Effective Practice and Organisation of Care (EPOC), was also formed in the 1990s. The review by Davis et al. (1992) was limited to continuing medical education (CME) interventions. Although CME was defined broadly as any method by which physician learning and

clinical practice might be altered by educational or persuasive means, it is clear that the authors had two implicit models of behaviour change (see Table 15.2). Another early systematic review of 'trials of educational interventions in the health care professions' (Oxman et al., 1995, p. 1423) sought to update the 1992 review and to define specific 'types of interventions' (p. 1424). This early, systematic work inspired a much larger body of systematic review activity in the 2000s.

2000s: Systematic reviews of trials to change HCPs' behaviour. The common-sense typology proposed by Oxman et al. (1995) consisted of 10 intervention categories that were also reported by Grimshaw et al. (2004) in their large review of RCTs targeting HCPs' behaviours (synthesising evidence from 235 studies reporting 309 comparisons). These intervention labels and descriptions are presented in Table 15.2.

Table 15.2 also includes a column (that we have added) describing the implicit processes of change that can be inferred from each intervention description. It shows that, although there had been some theoretical development since Davis et al. (1992) proposed two models of change, researchers had nevertheless used a fairly restricted range of implied models of change (relative to the wealth of theories available in psychology). The taxonomy of interventions was an important attempt to use an explicit basis for grouping interventions but was dependent on adequate reporting of interventions in published reports of RCTs. Concurrent work was developing guidance for researchers about the standards for reporting interventions. First, the evidence-based guideline, CONSORT (Consolidated Standards of Reporting Trials) was extended to non-pharmacological trials (Moher et al., 2001), including the recommendation that more precise details of interventions be reported. More importantly for this chapter, Davidson et al. (2003) proposed a detailed list of what should be included in intervention descriptions (Box 15.1). These recommendations are not 'merely' about reporting; they are profoundly about developing the science of behaviour change, as they can radically influence the way

Table 15.1 Examples of RCTs to evaluate interventions designed to change HCP behaviour

Clinical context; Unit of randomisation (sample size)	Evidence-based target behaviours	Study design	Intervention labels	Descriptions of (1) Control treatment and (2) Intervention treatment(s)	Major findings	Authors, year of publication
Acute myocardial infarction; community hospitals (37)	Increased use of (specified) lifesaving drugs; decreased use of a (specified) potentially harmful therapy	Before-and-after 2-arm cluster randomised controlled trial	Clinical education by local opinion leaders and performance feedback	(1) Mailed performance feedback (2) Small and large group discussion and informal consultation with opinion leader, focusing on evidence, comparative performance, barriers to change	Increase in use of target drugs significantly higher in intervention hospitals. No differences in decrease (of 50%) in use of harmful therapy	Soumerai et al., 1998
Lumbar spine pain and knee pain; general practices (244)	Decrease in number of radiograph requests (measured as requests per 1000 patients per year)	Before-and-after cluster randomised controlled trial with 2×2 factorial design	(a) Audit and feedback; (b) Educational reminder messages	(1) No intervention (2) 6-monthly feedback of audit data; attachment of educational reminder messages to radiographs	No significant group differences following audit and feedback. Following reminder messages, relative reduction of 20% in requests for lumbar spine and knee radiographs	Eccles et al., 2001
Asthma and angina; general practices (81)	Adherence to 10 recommendations about asthma management and 14 recommendations about angina management	Before-and-after cluster randomised controlled trial with incomplete block design	Guidelines, prioritised review criteria and feedback	(1) Full guidelines (2) Reduced guidelines in the form of prioritised review criteria; review criteria supplemented by feedback	No group differences in GPs' behaviour	Baker et al., 2003
Care of acute low back pain; primary care physician groups (14; 120 individuals)	Guideline-consistent behaviour (not specified in abstract)	Cluster randomised controlled trial with 2×2 factorial design	Multifaceted guideline implementation intervention: education and feedback	(1) No intervention (2) Clinician intervention: education/ audit/ feedback model with local peer opinion leaders. Patient education intervention: written and videotaped materials on the care of low back pain	Clinician intervention: significant increase in guideline-consistent behaviour. Patient intervention: no effect	Schechtman et al., 2003

Setting	Outcome	Study design	Intervention	Intervention details	Results	Reference
Induced abortion care; hospital gynaecology units (26)	Compliance with five key guideline recommendations	Two-arm cluster randomised controlled trial	Tailored multifaceted strategy	(1) Printed guideline summaries (2) Audit and feedback, educational meetings, dissemination of structured case records, promotion of a patient information booklet	No effect for any key recommendation	Foy et al., 2004
Lower third molar management; dental practices	Referral of patients for removal of asymptomatic impacted third molars	Two-arm cluster randomised controlled trial with pre-and post-assessments	Multifaceted intervention	(1) No intervention (2) Feedback, reminders and interactive meeting.	Dentists' knowledge significantly improved in intervention group. No group differences in guideline-consistent patient referral rates	Van der Sanden et al., 2005
Management of diabetes in primary care; general practices (58)	Various management behaviours	Two-arm cluster randomised controlled trial	Diabetes recall and management system	(1) Computerised diabetes register (2) Extended, computerised diabetes register incorporating a full structured recall and management system, including patient management prompts	Patients in intervention practices were more likely to have the following recorded: at least one diabetes appointment, foot check, receiving dietary advice, blood pressure reading	Eccles et al., 2007
Management of childhood asthma in general practice; GPs	Management of childhood asthma (unspecified)	Three-arm randomised controlled trial	Strategies to improve childhood asthma management	(1) Dissemination of a guideline (2) Dissemination of a guideline plus an educational session; dissemination of a guideline plus an educational session plus individualised treatment advice	No difference in primary outcome: severity of airway hyper-responsiveness after 1 year (in 362 children)	Hagmolen et al., 2008

Note: As these trials take several years to complete and there is then some delay before publication, it is likely that the studies in this table were designed and commenced in the 1990s.

Table 15.2 Classification of Cochrane Effective Practice and Organisation of Care (EPOC) interventions directed towards HCPs, intervention descriptions (adapted from Grimshaw et al., 2004, Box 2) and the processes of behaviour change they imply for increasing evidence-based (EB) clinical behaviour

Intervention label	Intervention description	Implicit process of change
1. Distribution of educational materials	Distribution of published or printed recommendations for clinical care including practice guidelines; audiovisual materials; electronic publications. The materials may be delivered personally or through mass mailings	Correction of knowledge deficits → EB behaviour
2. Educational meetings: small group (active participation) or large group (passive participation)	Participation of HCPs in conferences, lectures, workshops or training sessions outside their own practice settings	Correction of knowledge deficits and social persuasion → EB behaviour
3. Local consensus processes	Inclusion of participating providers in discussion to ensure that they agree that the chosen clinical problem is important and the approach to managing the problem is appropriate	Correction of knowledge deficits and social persuasion → EB behaviour
4. Educational outreach visits	Use of a trained person who meets with providers in their practice settings to provide information with the intent of changing the provider's practice. The information given may include feedback on providers' performance	Correction of knowledge deficits and social persuasion → EB behaviour
5. Local opinion leaders	Use of providers nominated by their colleagues as 'educationally influential'	Correction of knowledge deficits and social persuasion → EB behaviour
6. Patient-mediated interventions	Any intervention aimed at changing the performance of healthcare providers where information was sought from or given directly to patients by others e.g. direct mailings; counselling; materials given to patients or placed in waiting rooms	Social persuasion (patients' expectations) → EB behaviour
7. Audit and feedback: (i) Internal audit (performed by providers) (ii) External (others – not patients – provide performance data)	Any information or summary of clinical performance of health care over a specified period of time. Written or oral format; may include recommendations for clinical action. Performance information may be from medical records; computerised data bases; observation; or from patients	Correction of knowledge deficits and feedback about own behaviour → EB behaviour
8. Reminders	Manual or computerised information that prompts the health-care provider to perform or avoid a clinical action. Includes computerised decision support; drugs dosage; concurrent reports; inter-visit reminders; enhanced lab report; administrative support; implicit reminders	Correction of forgetting → EB behaviour
9. Marketing	Use of personal interviewing, group discussion ('focus groups'), or a survey of targeted providers to identify barriers to change and subsequent design of an intervention that addresses identified barriers	Barrier identification and plans for overcoming barriers → EB behaviour
10. Mass media	(1) Varied use of communication that reaches great numbers of people including television, radio, newspapers, posters, leaflets and booklets; (2) targeted at the population level	Correction of knowledge deficits and social persuasion (patients' expectations) → EB behaviour

Note: The EPOC taxonomy includes a first-line classification of interventions into professional, organisational, financial and regulatory. Only the 'professional' sub-categories are presented here, although readers will be aware that financial rewards for health professional behaviours are firmly supported by learning theory and that there may be both intended and unintended consequences of reward systems.

Box 15.1 Details to include when describing and reporting behaviour change interventions

1. Content (including elements or components) of the intervention
2. Mode of delivery (e.g. face to face, printed material)
3. Intensity (e.g. contact time)
4. Duration (e.g. number of sessions over a given period)
5. Characteristics of the setting
6. Characteristics of people who will deliver the intervention
7. Adherence to intervention protocol
8. Characteristics of the recipients

(Adapted from Davidson, K. W., Goldstein, M., Kaplan, R.M., Kaufmann, P.G., Knatterund, G.L., Orleans, C.T. *et al.* (2003). Evidence-based behavioral medicine: what is it and how do we achieve it? *Annals of Behavioral Medicine*, 26, 161–171.)

in which researchers think about the design and delivery of interventions.

Comparison of the intervention descriptions in Table 15.2 with the guidelines for describing interventions in Box 15.1 shows some interesting differences. For example, Table 15.2 (Column 2) more often described modes of delivery (e.g. printed materials, lectures, interactive group sessions, opinion leaders) than the content of the interventions. The content of interventions, the 'active ingredients', would be more effectively represented in terms of evidence-based behaviour change techniques, such as those listed and defined by Abraham and Michie (2008; now available at www.interventiondesign; see also Chapter 8, this volume).

The point here is that systematic reviews of interventions described by mode of delivery (e.g. local opinion leader) *may* be synthesising evidence from comparable interventions – or they may not. Without clear specification of the content of the interventions (e.g. the behaviour change techniques delivered by an opinion leader), it is impossible to be sure that an

intervention has been replicated in a trial using the same label. Therefore, processes of evidence synthesis (across different studies that have delivered 'the intervention') are likely to be flawed.

In Column 3 of Table 15.2 we suggest the implicit processes of change that might underlie each intervention as described. As mentioned above, there is a predominance of interventions that assume that non-evidence-based clinical behaviours are the result of knowledge deficits and therefore require information, education or persuasion. At best, some of these interventions might be delivered in groups or through social interaction, which may reflect the need for efficiency but could also be an acknowledgement of the role of social influences in changing behaviour. Nevertheless, even without an explicit theoretical basis, trials of implementation strategies have demonstrated consistent but variable and modest effects (Grimshaw *et al.*, 2004), suggesting that changing clinical behaviour is a realistic goal.

Thus, there is this considerable scope for theories and behaviour change techniques from health psychology to improve the effectiveness and efficiency of interventions to change HCPs' behaviour. But there is also an important role for theory in the evidence synthesis that is the goal of systematic reviews. Indeed, Grol *et al.* (2005; Chapter 2) reported that the application of theories of behaviour change to systematic reviews of HCP behaviour change interventions gives a greater understanding of intervention effects.

In summary, the Grimshaw *et al.* (2004) review of RCTs to evaluate behaviour change interventions targeting HCPs reported that most interventions resulted in modest improvements in care. However, there was considerable variation in effects both within and across interventions and the authors recommended the development of a theoretical framework of HCP behaviour change. In other words, most of the research activity had been based on intuitive or common-sense models, which were found to be lacking. Consequently, there was a failure to build a cumulative science of HCP behaviour change based on scientific theories tested using replicable methods. It is an irony worthy of note that rigorous, carefully specified (and therefore replicable), scientific methods based on physiologically plausible (theoretical) models were used to amass evidence about what works clinically. However, when it came to implementing this evidence in the form of HCP behaviour change, poorly specified (and therefore non-replicable) interventions were tested and there was rarely an attempt to base these interventions on psychologically plausible (theoretical) models, when amassing evidence about what works behaviourally. Recent developments in collaborative work between health psychologists and clinical researchers are addressing this situation.

The Role of Behaviour and Behavioural Theory

This apparent failure of implementation researchers to acknowledge the importance of behaviour reflects the problem described by Johnston and Dixon (2008): researchers had neglected the label 'behaviour', thereby missing a large body of literature from psychology and health psychology that could inform (and be informed by) and shape the research agenda. Research that investigates and seeks to change the clinical behaviours of HCPs goes under many labels, e.g. implementation research, knowledge transfer research, quality improvement research, quality of care research. All these labels refer to efforts to increase the clinical behaviours that fit the evidence about what works and to decrease the clinical behaviours that fit the evidence about what does not work or may be harmful. Clinical behaviours that might be the object of this kind of research are often labelled in their specific form (e.g. prescribing, referral, management, guideline adherence) without using the term, 'behaviour'. However, if these actions are labelled 'behaviour', it immediately becomes clear that models of behaviour and behaviour change are relevant and that there is a large literature reporting theoretical development, behaviour change techniques and empirical evidence that can inform this field. Using the body of knowledge from health psychology avoids the use of: (i) implicit models

that, by definition, cannot be operationalised or tested (Johnston, 1995); (ii) isolated or undefined constructs (e.g. 'barriers' and 'enablers') that can have many meanings and thus give rise to untestable hypotheses; and (iii) naive hypotheses that have poor empirical support (e.g. the 'knowledge–attitude–behaviour–health' model; Johnston, 1995).

Marteau and Johnston (1990) identified that the behaviour of HCPs is a source of variation in health outcomes. This variation was not well explained by differences in HCPs' knowledge and they identified cognitive and behavioural theories that show more promise than the educational model in both predicting and changing the clinical behaviours of HCPs. However, clinical researchers have expressed scepticism about the role of theories of behaviour in changing clinical behaviours (e.g. Oxman et al., 2005). Why might this be so?

Knowledge and skill. A dominant but often implicit belief is that knowledge and skill account for most of the variation in clinical behaviour (Marteau & Johnston 1990). In the health-care context, the challenges of self-regulation (e.g. failure to translate intentions into action) are not self-evident. Hence, information provision and education are assumed to be the most effective interventions.

Professional role and identity. HCPs are trained to play the role of expert within health-care consultations and may be reluctant to reflect on how they might improve their self-regulation skills (as opposed to their clinical skills).

Time pressures in health-care contexts. Health care is often delivered in time-pressured contexts and HCPs tend to develop habits, routines and scripts in order to act and react quickly. For some, this feels inconsistent with the more considered and rational approaches that are the apparent bases of social cognition models, but may be explicable in terms of learning theories as habits, or 'conditioned responses', acquired with reinforcers experienced in the context of time pressures.

Confidentiality. To protect patients' privacy clinical consultations are held 'in secret'. Hence, there is a reluctance to subject the consultation to the sort of observation and critique that could lead to improvements. By contrast, some health care (e.g. surgery) can be delivered in relatively public contexts and, although the behaviours might be observable by others, it may be ethically problematic to report individual events.

Use of proxy outcomes. Research to test the effectiveness of interventions to change HCPs' behaviour often fails to measure behaviour *per se* but measures factors further down the causal chain (e.g. Hagmolen *et al.*, 2008; Hardeman *et al.*, 2005). For example, physiological indicators (such as patients' blood pressure or blood sugar levels to measure prescribing behaviour) are often used as proxy measures of clinical behaviour. Attrition along the causal chain (e.g. the imperfect relationships between HCPs' behaviour and patient adherence) makes these very blunt measures of clinical behaviour. Even if adherence is high, we tend to rely on epidemiological and clinical evidence that such behaviours reliably affect physiological indicators. This is unlikely to be true for every patient.

Involvement of teams. Increasingly, especially in the context of the management of chronic disease, health care is delivered by clinical teams rather than individual HCPs. Some have argued that, therefore, theories of individual behaviour are not relevant. There is potential to take up this challenge by adapting models of group behaviour (e.g. bystander apathy, Darley & Latané, 1968; role theory, Biddle, 1986) and extending existing models of individual behaviours to team-level behaviours. This is a feasible goal (e.g. Eccles *et al.*, 2009) but provides interesting challenges as the research becomes more complex.

Contextual factors may distinguish clinical behaviours from health-related behaviours more generally. Behaviours of HCPs are performed within a particular kind of relationship that may be construed as unequal in terms of power, or in terms of imposing a level of responsibility on HCPs arising from professional norms (e.g. the responsibilities associated with the Hippocratic oath) and legal accountabilities (e.g. the potential for litigation if something goes wrong). Consequently, clinicians tend to see 'consequences of the behaviour' (e.g. behavioural beliefs within a theory of planned behaviour framework) as encompassing consequences for the *patient*. Data from interview studies (e.g. Kolehmainen *et al.*, 2006) show that clinicians often do not see the point of questions about consequences for the professional (i.e. the 'actor'). The stance of health psychology is that our models of behaviour are applicable to HCPs and can be operationalised across different contexts, but this is not necessarily accepted by our clinical collaborators. Nevertheless, systematic review evidence (e.g. Eccles *et al.*, 2006; Godin *et al.*, 2008) demonstrates that the patterns and strength of prediction across social cognition models are very similar for clinical behaviours and health behaviours. Empirical evidence is thus consistent with the view that the models of behaviour that apply to people in general also apply to HCPs.

Research about HCP Behaviour Change

In this field the focus of investigation is on specific clinical behaviours rather than commencing with a commitment to specific theories. So, a question arises, which theory or theories are relevant and applicable to a particular behaviour in a given clinical context? Similarly, this field is not characterised by a commitment to one type of intervention or behaviour change technique. Rather, researchers address the question, what are the best ways to develop and deliver interventions that are most likely to be operationalisable (i.e. acceptable to HCPs, feasible to deliver) and effective in changing a specific clinical behaviour? A common approach thus focuses on multiple theories and a range of behaviour change techniques. In this section we describe empirical studies that have been conducted to: (i) predict and explain the behaviour of HCPs and (ii) change the behaviour of HCPs in order to increase the uptake of evidence-based clinical guidelines.

Selecting theories

Marteau and Johnston (1990) suggested that cognitive and behavioural theories such as attribution theory (Weiner, 1986) and subjective expected utility models (Edwards, 1961) might be used in investigating HCP behaviour. Attribution theory notes that systematic attributional biases influence behaviour. According to subjective expected utility models, behaviour is influenced by the individual's beliefs about the consequences (of a clinical action or treatment) weighted by beliefs about the importance of each consequence. Marteau and Johnston argued that these kinds of processes help to explain the variation in HCP behaviour. It is now generally (although not universally) recognised that research about clinical behaviours is more robust when based on theory. Typically in this field, a rationale is given for the selection of specific theories as the basis for a piece of research. For example, the PRIME study (Walker *et al.*, 2003) used multiple theories to predict five evidence-based clinical behaviours of physicians and dentists. The criteria for selecting theories were:

1. Rigorous evaluation in other settings.
2. Explanation of *behaviour* in terms of factors that are amenable to change (e.g. beliefs, attitudes, self-efficacy and actual or perceived external constraints) rather than unchangeable features (e.g. personality or intelligence).
3. Inclusion of non-volitional components, i.e. the assumption that individuals do not always have complete control over their actions.
4. Inclusion of motivational theories (e.g. emphasis on predicting intention) and action theories (e.g. emphasis on direct predictors of behaviour).

Other studies have started with the extensive range of theoretical domains relevant to HCP behaviours (identified in a consensus process by Michie *et al.*, 2005) and then used interview methods to select relevant theoretical constructs. The IMPLEMENT trial (concerning managing acute low back pain in general practice; McKenzie *et al.*, 2008) identified two key behaviours, from the clinical guideline, for which adherence was low: giving advice to stay active and managing the patient without referring for plain x-ray. It used the theoretical construct domains as the basis for semi-structured interviews (the 'theoretical domains interview', or TDI) with 42 GPs in 11 focus groups. The interview data were used to identify the relevant theoretical domains: beliefs about consequences; beliefs

about capabilities; skills; knowledge; social influences; and environmental context and resources. These domains were mapped on to behaviour change techniques (using the matrix report in Michie *et al.*, 2008) to select the techniques most likely to be effective for changing the target behaviours. The techniques were operationalised in a complex intervention (McKenzie *et al.*, 2008).

This approach streamlined the process of exploration from the initial exploratory study through to intervention development. However, it involved the use of constructs isolated from their theoretical context. Furthermore, asking HCPs what they think is important in changing their behaviour, although important, provides evidence at the level of attribution (Weiner, 1986) rather than at the level of prediction. A later study of transfusion practice in intensive care units (Francis *et al.*, in press), used the TDI to gather attribution-level evidence of the likely important domains by interviewing 18 intensive care consultants across the UK. The interview data were used to identify specific constructs within those domains that were likely to be relevant to transfusion behaviour. The specific constructs were then used to select whole theories on which to base a predictive study and a subsequent intervention design.

Predictive studies

Several studies have used theories of behaviour to predict 'actual' (objectively recorded) behaviour of HCPs. The largest study of this kind, the PRIME study (Walker *et al.*, 2003), tested the predictive power of theoretical constructs drawn from a range of theories. Further details about this study are published elsewhere (Bonetti *et al.*, 2006; Eccles *et al.*, 2007; Francis *et al.*, 2007) but here we report data relating to two motivational theories (social cognitive theory (Bandura, 1977) and the theory of planned behaviour (Ajzen, 1991)) and two action theories (operant learning theory (Skinner, 1953) and implementation intentions (Gollwitzer, 1993)). Most of these theories and constructs assessed in PRIME have been described in Part II of this book.

In the PRIME study, operant learning theory (OLT) was assessed by two constructs. The theory

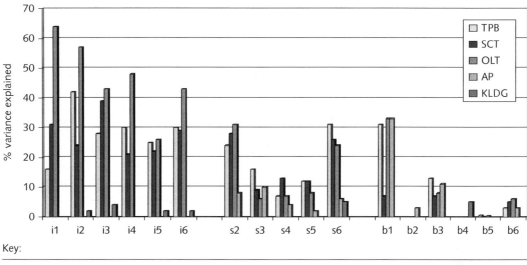

Key:

Theories	Behaviours	Dependent variables
TPB: Theory of planned behaviour	1 Applying sealants – ERUPT Study (dental)	i: Intention
SCT: Social cognitive theory	2 Applying sealants – PRIME Study (dental)	s: Simulated behaviour
OLT: Operant learning theory	3 Taking intra-oral radiographs (dental)	b: Routinely recorded
AP: Action planning (or implementation	4 Restoring carious teeth (dental)	behaviour
intention)	5 Referring for lumbar spine x-ray (medical)	
KLDG: Knowledge	6 Prescribing antibiotic for URTI (medical)	

Figure 15.1 Predicting intention, behavioural simulation and clinical behaviour: how do models of behaviour perform?

proposes that behaviours that have positive consequences for the individual are likely to be repeated, whereas those that have unpleasant consequences will become less frequent. These consequences can take a variety of forms, from material (e.g. financial rewards), to social (e.g. maintaining a positive relationship) and personal (e.g. achieving a desired goal). As rewarded behaviours are repeated and may become 'habitual', the frequency of past behaviour can be a powerful predictor of future behaviour. So the PRIME study included two theoretical constructs derived from OLT: perceived consequences of the clinical behaviour and the habitual nature of the behaviour in the past.

Behaviour was assessed using routinely recorded data. However, there are validity issues associated with such measures. Briefly, it is very difficult to be sure of achieving correspondence between routine records and the behaviour as specified in a questionnaire (e.g.

for a particular GP, managing a patient with uncomplicated sore throat without prescribing antibiotics). Hence, simulated behaviour was also measured. This was achieved by presenting a series of simulations of clinical situations (written descriptions of patient scenarios) and asking the clinician to make a series of decisions about the clinical management.

Figure 15.1 presents the results of a number of predictive studies based on multiple theories (i.e. the constructs of at least four theories were measured within each sample of HCPs). These studies investigated specific evidence-based behaviours of general medical practitioners (GPs) and general dental practitioners (GDPs). The behaviours were:

- Applying sealants to children's teeth (by 133 GDPs). (ERUPT study; Bonetti *et al.*, in press).
- Applying sealants to children's teeth (by 106 GDPs). (PRIME study; Walker *et al.*, 2003).

- Taking intra-oral radiographs (by 214 GDPs). (PRIME study; Bonetti *et al.*, 2006).
- Restoring carious teeth in children (by 116 GDPs). (PRIME study; Walker *et al.*, 2003).
- Referring patients with low back pain for lumbar spine x-ray (by 280 GPs). (PRIME study; Walker *et al.*, 2003).
- Prescribing antibiotics for upper respiratory tract infections (URTI) (by 228 GPs). (PRIME study; Eccles *et al.*, 2007).

In each study, the behaviour was measured using data that are routinely recorded, either as the basis of payment (e.g. for GDP behaviours) or through existing computer systems (e.g. for GP prescribing). Each study also measured intention and most measured simulated behaviour. For the purposes of contrasting theory-based approaches with the 'knowledge deficit' assumption (see Table 15.2), we also included a measure of knowledge in each study.

Figure 15.1 presents the percentages of variance in intention (i), simulated behaviour (s) and routinely recorded behaviour (b) that were significantly predicted by each theoretical model (and knowledge). One of the clearest findings across the six studies reported is that knowledge was, overall, a poor predictor compared with the theoretical models and a very poor predictor of intention. It did, however, predict small amounts of variance in simulated behaviour for prescribing antibiotics for upper respiratory tract infections and routinely recorded behaviour for restoring carious teeth in children.

A further clear finding is that the theoretical models did much better in predicting intention than in predicting either simulated behaviour or routinely recorded behaviour (see Armitage & Conner, 2001, for other behaviours). The models generally predicted simulated behaviour better than routinely recorded behaviour, but as mentioned, it is not necessarily the case that the latter was a more accurate measure.

Figure 15.1 also shows that OLT was at least as effective as the other theories in predicting intention, simulated behaviour and recorded behaviour. Although there are clearly some methodological issues to be addressed in the context of this theory (in

particular, the notion of creating self-report measures), it appears that this theory offers possibilities for future research, especially as it includes behaviour change techniques with a highly elaborated and strong evidence base.

Clearly, the benefit of predictive studies is that they may inform the development of behaviour change interventions. If constructs from specific theories fail to predict a target behaviour then we would be less likely to invoke those theories as the basis of interventions. However, predictive studies do not test the causal hypothesis that is the basis of intervention, and experimental evidence is required (Collins *et al.*, 2005). Therefore, in the next section we describe one example of an intervention that used a predictive study to design a theory-based intervention, which was then evaluated in an 'intervention modelling experiment'.

Experimental studies

Overprescribing of antibiotics is an important problem in primary care. Figure 15.1 shows that managing patients with upper respiratory tract infection (URTI) without prescribing antibiotics was predicted by a range of models and this finding is consistent with an earlier study of the same behaviour (Walker *et al.*, 1991). Thus, there was robust evidence on which to design a behaviour change intervention. As RCTs of HCP behaviour typically cost millions of pounds and take around five years to complete, it has been argued (Bonetti *et al.*, 2005) that it is efficient to 'model' the intervention using an experimental design to establish the underlying mechanisms of change.

In the TRACII project (pronounced 'Tracy': 'Translating clinicians' beliefs into implementation interventions'; Hrisos *et al.*, 2008a, 2008b), predictive studies identified 'anticipated consequences' and 'self-efficacy' as predictors of antibiotic use in the context of managing URTI. These constructs were summarised as the theoretical domains: 'beliefs about consequences' and 'beliefs about capabilities' (Michie *et al.*, 2005) and mapped on to behaviour change techniques using the matrix reported in Michie *et al.* (2008). 'Persuasive communication' and 'graded task' were selected as the two techniques to be tested in a

2×2 randomised factorial design using a paper-based mode of delivery. The results showed that the graded task intervention increased self-efficacy scores but did not increase intention or simulated behaviour. The persuasive communication intervention (operationalised in the form presented in Figure 15.2) was effective in changing both the proximal outcome (attitude) and the distal outcomes (intention and simulated behaviour).

A different theory-based intervention was evaluated in a full-scale RCT in the ERUPT trial (Clarkson *et al.*, 2008), which used a 2×2 factorial design to test an intervention based on OLT and an educational intervention based on the intuitive 'knowledge deficit' model. The participants were general dental practitioners (GDPs) in Scotland and the evidence-based target behaviour was placing preventive fissure sealant[3] on children's teeth. After adjustment for baseline differences, the OLT-based intervention (contingent reinforcement in the form of a financial reward) resulted in a 9.8% increase (measured 12 months post-intervention) in the target behaviour. There was no significant increase following the educational intervention.[4]

In summary, experimental studies to test interventions designed to change HCP behaviour have demonstrated that theory-based interventions can be both feasible and effective. This kind of research thus demonstrates both the utility and effectiveness of theory-based approaches to intervention design.

Issues that Require Special Attention

Although we have argued that HCP behaviour is influenced by the same theoretical principles as health behaviour generally, there are some practical and scientific issues specific to this field that require careful consideration.

Validity issues in the measurement of clinical behaviour

Objective measurement is regarded as a 'gold standard' in the measurement of behaviour but there are ethical and practical issues that make such objectivity challenging. Many clinical actions take place in the context of a confidential consultation; some are routinely recorded (e.g. prescription of a particular drug, specific surgical procedures, if they are paid for) but there are several potential sources of bias. It may be difficult to link the recorded clinical behaviour to a particular clinician, patient condition or time period.

HCP behaviour change research is concerned with whether a particular clinical action is appropriate, i.e. evidence-based, given the target (a patient with specific clinical characteristics), the context (e.g. during a consultation) and the time (e.g. 12 months since the action was last taken). Routine records are regarded as 'objective' measures of behaviour and, at first glance, may seem to be the 'gold standard' measure, as they are unlikely to be contaminated by social desirability bias or recall bias. However, routinely recorded data can contain inaccuracies. In particular, they can usually identify how many times a clinician performs the action (e.g. number of prescriptions of Drug A) but often not how many opportunities occurred (*Was Drug A the appropriate drug for this patient at this time?* And *would Drug A have been appropriate for other patients?*). In addition, in certain sections of the health system, the HCP performing the action may not be identified (i.e., Drug A was prescribed to patient N but it may not be clear which physician wrote the prescription). By contrast, self-report measures of behaviour can include social desirability bias and recall bias – but at least they do record estimates of both the behaviour and of the opportunities and it is clear who (supposedly) performed the behaviour.

A potential solution – although still not perfect – is to measure 'simulated behaviour'. A simulation of a real clinical situation may take the form of a verbal description, a patient chart representing a set of test results, a computer screen representing the patient's clinical history or a video clip of the patient in a consultation. The HCP is then asked to report the clinical decision based on the information provided in the simulated situation. While this type of measure can include social desirability bias, it does not include recall bias, the clinical decision is recorded and the scenario description specifies conditions for judging whether the action was appropriate. Thus,

A Week in the life of two GPs......

Dr A manages patients with URTI by prescribing antibiotics

Penicillin 3 times daily

"I'm worried about our Colin, he's got a dreadful cough and a sore throat."

"You should take him to Dr A for some antibiotics."

"More sore throats – does Dr A have any appointments left for this week?"

"I'm sorry I gave you my cold, here, have some of the antibiotics Dr A gave me."

"Not another four extras with sore throats wanting antibiotics!"

Dr B manages patients with URTI symptomatically

Paracetamol, fluids, bed rest

"I'm worried about our Colin, he's got a dreadful cough and a sore throat."

"Our Martin had that last week. A couple of days of Calpol and he was fine."

"That's another 'flu vac clinic booked up."

"I'm sorry I gave you my cold, here, let me get you some paracetamol."

"No extras today – I'll enjoy this cup of tea before I start my visits!"

Whose patients have more expectation of getting antibiotics?

Whose practice is more likely to have opportunities for prevention?

Whose patients are more likely to share antibiotics?

On balance, who has the easier life?

who are you most like ?

Figure 15.2 Intervention materials for TRACII study, which used this persuasive communication intervention to address anticipated consequences of managing URTIs by prescribing antibiotics (Dr A) or without prescribing antibiotics (Dr B)

measures of simulated behaviour may be at least as informative as measures of behaviour based on routinely recorded data. They have the added advantage that they provide opportunities for manipulating specific clinical or contextual features of the situation to test the effects of such factors on the clinical decision.

Typology of behaviours

It is clear (e.g. from Figure 15.1) that there is a lot of variation in the effects found in studies using the same theoretical model across different behaviours and contexts. Hopefully this is not only the result of random error, or variations in the skill of researchers, but tells us something about the behaviours themselves. A typology of behaviours would assist in identifying when certain theories or techniques are most likely to be appropriate. For example, we know from learning theory that different techniques are used to increase the frequency of a behaviour (e.g. positive consequence) and to decrease the frequency (e.g. negative consequence). Are there other dimensions along which behaviour vary, that would assist in developing a generalisable body of knowledge? For example, developing habits requires a different approach than introducing a new action into the behavioural repertoire. As a discipline we need to discern these and other fundamental differences between behaviours that will clarify the range of applicability of theories and techniques.

Standardised nomenclature for behaviour change techniques

The evidence base relating to behaviour change techniques is growing but can be synthesised into a coherent evidence base only if the discipline agrees to use a standardised form of words for labelling techniques. This applies of course to HCP behaviour change and to health-related behaviour change in general. It is vital that the nomenclature be reliable and consistent to aid reporting and replicability of interventions (see WIDER network; http://interventiondesign.co.uk).

Use of a theoretical basis for evidence synthesis

We have progressed beyond the time when intuitive models were acceptable. For further progress to be made in the science of behaviour change, it is important that we use the current evidence base, in the form of robust and generalisable theory, to make sense of existing evidence.

Directions for Further Research

Further research on the behaviour of HCPs in delivering evidence-based clinical practice will have much of the same requirements as research seeking to understand and change any health-related behaviour. We suggest that key issues are the use of research designs that assess causal links as a basis for intervention, the use of theories that incorporate behaviour change techniques, good reporting of behaviour change interventions and more emphasis on investigating the effects on patients' behaviour of changing HCPs' behaviour.

An important aspect of testing behaviour change techniques is the use of experimental rather than correlational designs (Collins et al., 2005; Weinstein, 2007). Because full-scale randomised controlled trials to change the behaviour of HCPs are very expensive and time consuming, we have proposed the use of intervention modelling experiments to filter out the interventions least likely to be effective and to take only the 'best bets' forward into full-scale RCTs.

As a discipline, perhaps we should place more emphasis on developing those theories that incorporate behaviour change techniques. At the very least we need to develop clearer links between theory and behaviour change techniques. That is, we need theories of behaviour change rather than of behaviour prediction.

Good reporting of behaviour change interventions requires the use of a shared terminology, estimates of the fidelity of delivery of the intervention and making intervention protocols available. The publication of study protocols prior to analysis of the study has become a marker of best practice in clinical and implementation research. Clearly, this facilitates accountability of researchers and ensures a clear distinction between results that confirm *a priori* predictions and results that are the result of data dredging. However, intervention protocols for behaviour change interventions continue to be unsatisfactory both for replication and for evidence synthesis. To this end, the development and refinement of a nomenclature for behaviour change techniques is vital. It is not just an exercise in semantics; it is fundamentally a research activity and will shape the future research agenda identifying replicable, evidence-based behaviour change techniques. With good descriptions of behaviour change techniques, it is possible to assess and report the fidelity of interventions as delivered, an issue central to research about their effectiveness (e.g. Hardeman *et al.*, 2008).

A lot of health care is based on the assumption of a 'behaviour change cascade', e.g. the GP's behaviour changes to giving more behaviour change advice with resulting behaviour change in patients. This is inher-ently an attenuation model that should be examined carefully but it may be the best or most feasible way to proceed in attempts to increase health outcomes gen-erally. This raises the importance of using multi-level models in this field (both in theory development and data analysis).

Conclusion

In summary, in this chapter we have identified trends in research about the evidence-based clinical behav-iours of health care professionals over four decades. We have discussed the role of theories and techniques of behaviour change. Our description of research about health professional behaviour change that is based on theories, methods and interventions from health psychology has raised issues that require special attention. Finally, we have proposed directions for fur-ther research. There is a large agenda for theory-based research to change HCP behaviour to increase evi-dence-based practice and improve health outcomes.

Discussion Points

1   Professional behaviour could be referred to as 'clinical practice', 'patient care', 'management of [a clinical condition]', 'delivery of clinical proce-dures' and so on. What might be some advan-tages for clinical researchers in calling it 'behaviour'?
2   What would be an appropriate list of criteria for deciding to undertake a study to change the behaviour of health-care professionals?
3   From Figure 15.1, what conclusions can be drawn about:
   –   the predictive utility of the different theoreti-cal models?
   –   the extent to which an understanding of *actual* behaviour is informed by measuring and predicting routinely recorded behav-iour, simulated behaviour and behavioural intention?
   –   how the results might inform the develop-ment of interventions to change the clinical behaviours investigated?
4   Comment on the advantages and disadvantages of conducting 'intervention modelling experiments' (IMEs).
5   How would you explain each of the following theories to a clinical collaborator who was unfa-miliar with them?
   –   theory of planned behaviour
   –   operant learning theory
   –   social cognitive theory

Notes

1. This is not to say that these 47 were the only RCTs published, as it only gradually became common practice to use 'randomised controlled trial' in the title.

2. The Cochrane collaboration (www.cochrane.org) is a global network that aims to improve health-care deci-sion making through systematic reviews of health-care

interventions. These reviews are published in the Cochrane library.

3. A fissure sealant is a plastic coating that is applied to teeth to prevent dental caries.

4. It is not possible to comment on whether this behaviour was sustained for longer than 12 months post-

intervention, as this study influenced a change in policy with a fee-for-service for preventive sealant application that was introduced in Scotland in November 2005.

Further Reading

Clarkson, J.E., Turner, J., Grimshaw, J.M., Ramsay, C.R., Johnston, M., Scott, A. *et al.* (2008). Changing clinicians' behavior: a randomized controlled trial of fees and education. *Journal of Dental Research, 87,* 640–644.

Hrisos, S., Eccles, M., Johnston, M., Francis, J.J., Kaner, E.F.S., Steen, N. & Grimshaw, J. (2008). Developing the content of two behavioural interventions. Using theory-based interventions to promote GP management of upper respiratory tract infection without prescribing antibiotics #1. *BMC Health Services Research, 8,* 11.

Marteau, T.M. & Johnston, M. (1990). Health professionals: a source of variation in health outcomes. *Psychology & Health, 5,* 47–58.

Walker, A.E., Grimshaw, J., Johnston, M., Pitts, N., Steen, N., Eccles, M. (2003). PRIME – Process modeling in ImpleMEntation research: selecting a theoretical basis for interventions to change clinical practice. *BMC Health Services Research, 3,* 1–22.

References

Abraham, C. & Michie, S. (2008). A taxonomy of behavior change techniques used in interventions. *Health Psychology, 27,* 379–387.

Ajzen, I. (1991). The theory of planned behaviour. *Organizational Behaviour & Human Decision Processes, 50,* 179–211.

Armitage C.J. & Conner, M. (2001). Efficacy of the theory of planned behaviour: a meta-analytic review. *British Journal of Social Psychology, 40,* 471–499.

Baker, R., Fraser, R.C., Stone, M., Lambert, P., Stevenson, K. & Shiels, C. (2003). Randomized controlled trial of the impact of guidelines, prioritized review criteria and feedback on implementation of recommendations for angina and asthma. *British Journal of General Practice, 53,* 284–291.

Bandura, A. (1977). Self-efficacy: towards a unifying theory of behaviour change. *Psychological Review, 84,* 191–215.

Biddle, B.J. (1986). Recent developments in role theory. *Annual Review of Sociology, 12,* 67–92.

Bonetti, D., Eccles, M., Johnston, M., Steen, N., Grimshaw, J., Baker, R. *et al.* (2005). Guiding the design and selection of interventions to influence the implementation of evidence-based practice: an experimental simulation of a complex intervention trial. *Social Science & Medicine, 60,* 2135–2147.

Bonetti, D., Johnston, M., Clarkson, J. & Turner, S. (in press). Applying multiple models to predict clinicians' behav-

ioural intention and objective behaviour when managing children's teeth. *Psychology & Health.*

Bonetti, D., Pitts N.B., Eccles, M., Grimshaw, J., Johnston, M., Steen, N. *et al.* (2006). Applying psychological theory to evidence-based clinical practice: identifying factors predictive of taking intra-oral radiographs. *Social Science & Medicine, 63,* 1889–1899.

Byrne, P.P. & Long, B.E.L. (1976). *Doctors talking to patients: A study of the verbal behavior of general practitioners consulting in their surgeries.* London: HSMO/RCGP.

Clarkson, J.E., Turner, J., Grimshaw, J.M., Ramsay, C.R., Johnston, M., Scott, A. *et al.* (2008). Changing clinicians' behavior: a randomized controlled trial of fees and education. *Journal of Dental Research, 87,* 640–644.

Cochrane A.L. (1972). *Effectiveness and efficiency. Random reflections on health services.* London: Nuffield Provincial Hospitals Trust.

Collins, L.M., Murphy, S.A., Nair, V.N. & Strecher, V.J. (2005). A strategy for optimising and evaluating behavioral interventions. *Annals of Behavioral Medicine, 30,* 65–73.

Darley, J.M. & Latané, B. (1968). Bystander intervention in emergencies: diffusion of responsibility. *Journal of Personality and Social Psychology, 8,* 377–383.

Davidson, K.W., Goldstein, M., Kaplan, R.M., Kaufmann, P.G., Knatterund, G.L., Orleans, C.T. *et al.* (2003). Evidence-based behavioral medicine: what is it and how do we achieve it? *Annals of Behavioral Medicine, 26,* 161–171.

Davis, D.A., Thomson, M.A., Oxman, A.D. (1992). Evidence for the effectiveness of CME: a review of 50 randomized controlled trials. *Journal of the American Medical Association, 268,* 1111–1117.

Eccles, M.P., Grimshaw, J.M., Johnston, M., Steen, N., Pitts, N.B., Thomas, R. *et al.* (2007). Applying psychological theories to evidence-based clinical practice: identifying factors predictive of managing upper respiratory tract infections without antibiotics. *Implementation Science, 2,* 26.

Eccles, M.P., Hrisos, S., Francis, J., Kaner, E.F.S., Dickinson, H.O., Beyer, F. & Johnston, M. (2006). Do self-reported intentions predict clinicians' behaviour: a systematic review. *Implementation Science, 1,* 1–10.

Eccles, M.P., Hrisos, S., Francis, J., Steen, N. & Johnston, M. (2009). Can the collective intentions of individual professionals within healthcare teams predict the team's performance: developing methods and theory. *Implementation Science, 4,* 24.

Eccles, M.P., Steen, N., Grimshaw, J., Thomas, L., McNamee, P., Soutter, J. *et al.* (2001). Effect of audit and feedback and reminder & on primary-care radiology referrals: a randomised trial. *Lancet, 357,* 1406–1409.

Eccles, M.P., Whitty, P.M., Speed, C., Steen, I.N., Vanoli, A., Hawthorne, G.C. *et al.* (2007). A pragmatic cluster randomised controlled trial of a Diabetes REcall And Management system: the DREAM trial. *Implementation Science, 2,* 6.

Edwards, W. (1961). Behavioral decision theory. *Annual Review of Psychology, 12,* 472–498.

Elwood, P.C., Lee, H.P., St Leger, A.S., Baird, I.M. & Howard, A.N. (1976). A randomized controlled trial of vitamin C in the prevention and amelioration of the common cold. *British Journal of Preventive & Social Medicine, 30,* 193–196.

Elwood, P.C. & Williams, W.O. (1979). A randomized controlled trial of aspirin in the prevention of early mortality in myocardial infarction. *Journal of the Royal College of General Practitioners, 29,* 413–416.

Evidence-Based Medicine Working Group. (1992). Evidence-based medicine. A new approach to teaching the practice of medicine. *Journal of the American Medical Association, 268,* 2420–2425.

Foy, R., Penney, G.C., Grimshaw, J.M., Ramsay, C.R., Walker, A.E., MacLennan, G. *et al.* (2004). A randomized controlled trial of a tailored multi-faceted strategy to promote implementation of a clinical guideline on induced abortion care. *International Journal of Obstetrics & Gynaecology, 111,* 726–733.

Francis, J., Stockton, C., Eccles, M.P., Johnston, M., Cuthbertson, B.H., Grimshaw, J.M. *et al.* (2009). Evidence-based selection of theories for designing behaviour change interventions: using methods based on theoretical construct domains to understand clinicians' blood transfusion behaviour. *British Journal of Health Psychology, 14,* 625–646.

Francis, J., Johnston, M., Bonetti, D., Glidewell, L., MacLennan, G., Eccles, M., Grimshaw, J., on behalf of the PRIME project group. (2007). Health psychology research advances theory by addressing problems: illustrations from theory-based studies of health professional behaviour. *European Health Psychologist, 9,* 20–25.

Freeman, C.P.L., Basson, J.V. & Crighton, A. (1978). Double-blind controlled trial of electroconvulsive therapy (ECT) in depressive illness. *Lancet,* 8 April, 738–740.

Frostholm, L., Toft, T., Kaj, S., Christenson, K.S., Oernboel, F., Fink, P. *et al.* (2005). The uncertain consultation and patient satisfaction: the impact of patients' illness perceptions and training communication skills. *Psychosomatic Medicine, 67,* 897–905.

Gelder, M.G., Bancroft, J., Gath, D., Johnston, D.W., Mathews, A. & Shaw, P. (1973). Specific and non-specific factors in behaviour therapy. *British Journal of Psychiatry, 23,* 450–462.

Gerson, L. & Berry, A.F. (1976). Psychosocial effects of home care: results of a randomized trial. *International Journal of Epidemiology, 5,* 59–165.

Glass, G.V. (1976). Primary, secondary and meta-analysis of research. *The Educational Researcher, 10,* 3–8.

Godin, G., Belanger-Gravel, A., Eccles, M.P. & Grimshaw, J. (2008). Healthcare professionals' intention and behaviours: a systematic review of studies based on the social cognitive theories. *Implementation Science, 3,* 36.

Gollwitzer, P.M. (1993). Goal achievement: the role of intentions. In W. Stroebe & M. Hewstone (Eds.) *European review of social psychology, volume 4* (pp. 141–185). Chichester: Wiley.

Grimshaw, J.M., Thomas, R.E., MacLennan, G., Fraser, C., Ramsay, C.R., Vale, L. *et al.* (2004). Effectiveness and efficiency of guideline dissemination and implementation strategies. *Health Technology Assessment, 8,* 1–72.

Grol, R., Wensing, M., Hulscher, M. & Eccles, M. (2004). Theories on implementation of change in healthcare. In R. Grol, M. Wensing & M. Eccles (Eds.) *Improving patient care. The implementation of change in clinical practice* (pp. 15–40). Oxford: Elsevier.

Hagmolen, H.W., van den Berg, N.J., van der Palen, J., van Aaldern, W.M. & Bindels, P.J. (2008). Implementation of an asthma guideline for the management of childhood asthma in general practice: a randomized controlled trial. *Primary Care Respiratory Journal, 17,* 90–96.

Hardeman, W., Michie, S., Fanshawe, T., Prevost, A.T., McLoughlin, K. & Kinmonth, A.L. (2008). Fidelity of delivery of a physical activity intervention: predictors and consequences. *Psychology & Health, 23*, 11–24.

Hardeman, W., Sutton, S., Griffin, S., Johnston, M., White, A., Wareham, N.J. & Kinmonth, A.L. (2005). A causal modelling approach to the development of theory-based behaviour change programmes for trial evaluation. *Health Education Research, 20*, 676–687.

Hrisos, S., Eccles, M., Johnston, M., Francis, J.J., Kaner, E.F.S., Steen, N. & Grimshaw, J. (2008a). Developing the content of two behavioural interventions. Using theory-based interventions to promote GP management of upper respiratory tract infection without prescribing antibiotics #1. *BMC Health Services Research, 8*, 11.

Hrisos, S., Eccles, M., Johnston, M., Francis, J.J., Kaner, E.F.S., Steen, N. & Grimshaw, J. (2008b). An intervention modelling experiment to change GPs' intentions to implement evidence-based practice: using theory-based interventions to promote GP management of upper respiratory tract infection without prescribing antibiotics #2. *BMC Health Services Research, 8*, 10.

Johnston, M. (1995). Health related behaviour change. In F. Sharp for the National Heart Forum (Ed.) *Preventing coronary heart disease in primary care* (pp. 37–47). London: HMSO.

Johnston, M. & Dixon D. (2008). Current issues and new directions in psychology and health: what happened to behaviour in the decade of behaviour? *Psychology & Health, 23*, 509–513.

Kennedy, T. & Connell, A.M. (1969). Selective or truncal vagotomy? A double-blind randomised controlled trial. *Lancet, 1*, 899–901.

Kolehmainen, N., Francis, J. & McKee, L. (2006). *Investigating treatment provision behaviour in occupational therapy: a mixed methods approach.* Oral presentation at UK Society for Behavioural Medicine Annual Scientific Meeting, Cambridge, December.

Ley, P. (1982). Satisfaction, compliance and communication. *British Journal of Clinical Psychology, 21*, 241–254.

Marteau T.M. & Johnston M. (1990). Health professionals: a source of variation in health outcomes. *Psychology & Health, 5*, 47–58.

McKenzie, J.E., French, S.D., O'Connor, D.A., Grimshaw, J.M., Mortimer, D., Michie, S. et al. (2008). IMPLEmenting a clinical practice guideline for acute low back pain evidence-based manageMENT in general practice (IMPLEMENT): cluster randomised controlled trial study protocol. *Implementation Science, 3*, 11.

Michie, S., Johnston, M., Abraham, C., Lawton, R., Parker, D., Walker, A. et al. (2005). Making psychological theory useful for implementing evidence based practice: a con-

sensus approach. *Quality and Safety in Health Care, 14*, 26–33.

Michie, S., Johnston, M., Francis, J.J., Hardeman, W. & Eccles, M.P. (2008). From theory to intervention: mapping theoretically derived behavioural determinants to behaviour change techniques. *Applied Psychology: An International Review, 57*, 660–680.

Moher, D., Schultz, K.F., Altman, D.G. & CONSORT Group (2001). The CONSORT statement: revised recommendations for improving the quality of reports of parallel-group randomized trials. *Lancet, 357*, 1191–1194.

Ong, L.M.L., Visser, M.R.M., van Zuuren, F., Rietbroek, R.C., Lammes, F.B. & de Haes, J.C.J.M. (1999). Cancer patients' coping styles and doctor–patient communication. *Psycho-Oncology, 8*, 155–166.

Oxman, A., Fretheim, A. & Flottorp, S. (2005). The OFF theory of research utilization. *Journal of Clinical Epidemiology, 58*, 113–116.

Oxman, A.D., Thomas, M.A., Davis, D.A. & Haynes, B.H. (1995). No magic bullets: a systematic review of interventions to improve professional practice. *Canadian Medical Association Journal, 153*, 1423–1431.

Patel, C. & North, W.R. (1975). Randomized controlled trial of yoga and bio-feedback in management of hypertension. *Lancet, 2*, 93–95.

Rose, G. & Hamilton, P.J. (1978). A randomised controlled trial of the effect on middle-aged men of advice to stop smoking. *Journal of Epidemiology & Community Health, 32*, 275–281.

Schechtman, J.M., Schroth, W.S., Verme, D. & Voss, J.D. (2003). Randomized controlled trial of education and feedback for implemenetation of guidelines for acute low back pain. *Journal of General Internal Medicine, 18*, 773–780.

Seddon, M.E., Marshall, M.N., Campbell, S.M. & Roland, M.O. (2001). Systematic review of studies of quality of clinical care in general practice in the UK, Australia and New Zealand. *Quality in Health Care, 10*, 152–158.

Skinner, B.F. (1953). *Science and human behavior.* New York: Macmillan.

Smith M.L. & Glass G.V. (1977). Meta-analysis of psychotherapy outcome studies. *American Psychologist, 32*, 752–760.

Soumerai, S.B., McLaughlin, B., Gurwitz, J.H., Guadagnoli, E., Hauptman, P.J., Borbas, C. et al. (1998). Effect of local opinion leaders on quality of care for acute myocardial infarction: A randomized controlled trial. *Journal of the American Medical Association, 279*, 1358–1363.

Van der Sanden, W.J., Mettes, D.G., Plasschaert, A.J., Grol, R.P., Mulder, J. & Verdonschot, E.H. (2005). Effectiveness of clinical practice guideline implementation on lower third molar management in improving clinical decision-making: a randomized controlled trial. *European Journal of Oral Sciences, 113,* 349–354.

Walker, A.E., Grimshaw, J., Johnston, M., Pitts, N., Steen, N. & Eccles, M. (2003). PRIME – Process modeling in ImpleMEntation research: selecting a theoretical basis for interventions to change clinical practice. *BMC Health Services Research, 3,* 1–22.

Walker, A.E., Grimshaw, J.M. & Armstrong, E.M. (2001). Salient beliefs and intentions to prescribe antibiotics for patients with a sore throat. *British Journal of Health Psychology, 6,* 347–360.

Weiner, B. (1986). An *attributional theory of motivation and emotion.* New York: Springer-Verlag.

Weinstein, N.D. (2007). Misleading tests of health behavior theories. *Annals of Behavioral Medicine, 33,* 1–10.

16

Psychological Interventions in Chronic Illness

Alison J. Wearden and Chris Bundy

Chapter Outline

Health psychology interventions for long-term conditions have three broad aims: to help patients to achieve optimum health; to reduce symptoms and improve functioning; and to facilitate good adjustment to illness. A variety of techniques informed by psychological theory are used. In this chapter, a brief introduction to several different types of intervention is provided, illustrated with reference to some common long-term conditions such as heart disease, diabetes and cancer. Interventions discussed include information and education programmes, motivational interventions, formulation-based cognitive behavioural approaches, coping skills training and written emotional disclosure. The role and needs of significant others of chronically ill patients are considered. The chapter briefly outlines the use of new technology to deliver psychological interventions in novel ways. Finally the chapter identifies the particular challenges that health psychologists face when researching, designing and delivering interventions and communicating the results of studies across discipline boundaries.

Key Concepts

Cognitive behavioural
   interventions
Condition management
Coping skills
Illness perception
   interventions
Intervention mapping
Novel intervention delivery
   methods
Patient education
Psychological adjustment
   to illness/anxiety and
   depression
Significant others
Written emotional
   disclosure

Introduction

Chronic illnesses, or 'long-term conditions', are health conditions which persist over an extended period of time and for which a realistic aim is ongoing management rather than cure. With a decline in early death from infectious illness, and an increase in life expectancy, more people are living with long-term conditions and living for longer. In the 2001 General Household Survey of 13,000 British households, 63 per cent of those aged 75 or over, and 32 per cent of all respondents, reported a longstanding condition. The average number of conditions reported by those with a longstanding illness was 1.5, and 19 per cent reported a condition which limited them in some way (Walker *et al.*, 2002). The commonest conditions in Britain were musculoskeletal conditions such as arthritis and back problems (146/1000), heart and circulatory system conditions (106/1000), asthma and other respiratory conditions (62/1000), and endocrine or metabolic conditions, principally diabetes (44/1000) (Walker *et al.*, 2002). Health professionals face the challenge of helping those affected by these conditions to achieve a good quality of life in spite of their chronic ill health (Wilson *et al.*, 2005).

While long-term conditions have some common features and people living with them face some common challenges, it is clear that illnesses differ along a number of dimensions. A condition may be relatively symptom free, symptoms may fluctuate, or there may be a gradual or episodic deterioration. Some conditions have greater general health implications than others – the potential complications of diabetes, such as microvascular disease, are wide ranging and can produce problems in most bodily systems. The degree to which long-term conditions can be controlled by medication or lifestyle management varies significantly. The range of impacts of chronic illness is large, including potential impact on the ability to work, or on the ability to undertake social and leisure activities. Long-term conditions may affect the lives of family members, and conversely, family members may play an important role in helping or hindering patients in the management of their condition.

Health psychology interventions for long-term conditions target a range of outcomes, use a variety of techniques (Abraham & Michie, 2008), and may be aimed at patients, significant others or both (Martire *et al.*, 2004). Some interventions are clearly underpinned by theoretical understandings of what motivates, regulates and maintains health behaviours while in other cases, interventions are more technique driven and the theoretical underpinning is less clear (Hardeman *et al.*, 2002; Michie, Hardeman *et al.*, 2008; Michie, Johnston *et al.*, 2008). Health psychologists aim to understand what is mediating the change when successful interventions work and to examine whether evidence for the effect of mediating variables is consistent with theoretical predictions. Additionally, health psychologists are interested in the factors moderating the effect of an intervention, whether individual, interpersonal or environmental.

Furthermore, health psychologists may be involved in interventions for long-term conditions in a variety of roles. They may be engaged in pre-intervention research, developing and testing theory, or carrying out acceptability and feasibility studies; they may provide advice and expertise to other health professionals; they may deliver interventions themselves or, more commonly, train and supervise others to carry out this role. Modern technology, such as the internet or mobile phones, may be used for delivering interventions. Increasingly, health psychologists are involved in intervention research, contributing towards guidelines for good practice, and conducting trials of treatments (Craig *et al.*, 2008).

Nicassio and colleagues (Nicassio *et al.*, 2004) categorised health psychology interventions into: (i) those which help patients to manage their condition with a view to improving or maintaining physical health or slowing down the progress of the condition; (ii) those which aim to treat what they called 'psychophysiological disorders' (p. 132) such as chronic pain, often aimed at alleviating symptoms and improving functioning; and (iii) those which address psychological adjustment to illness, including co-morbidities such as depression and anxiety. This broad framework is used here to illustrate the varied role which health psychologists have played in developing, delivering and testing interventions. Examples will be provided of each of the three types of intervention, highlighting the theoretical underpinnings and the techniques which have been used. There will be a brief discussion of interventions which include or are aimed at significant others. The use of modern technology to deliver interventions for people with long-term conditions will be outlined. Finally future developments in psychological interventions for long-term conditions will be considered.

Interventions to Help Patients to Manage their Illness

Educational or information-based interventions

In order for people to be able to manage a long-term condition effectively, they need to know what it is, and what actions are recommended. People with diabetes need to understand how diet, activity and medication interact to maintain blood glucose levels. They need to know how to test for blood glucose levels and how to modify them. However, merely knowing about a condition may not be enough to promote effective management strategies (Newman et al., 2004). One study of young people showed that knowledge of diabetes was unrelated to the level of glycaemic control achieved (Coates & Boore, 1996), while a review of asthma education studies showed that providing information about asthma reduces the level of symptoms reported but does not impact on self-management skills or hospitalisation rates (Gibson et al., 2003).

In the recently reported Diabetes Education and Self-Management for Ongoing and Newly Diagnosed (DESMOND) trial, participants who received a six-hour structured group education programme, delivered by diabetes educators over 1–2 sessions showed greater weight loss and were less likely to smoke than those in a control condition, but there was no significant effect on glycaemic control (Davies et al., 2008). On the other hand, a somewhat longer, community-based, group-structured education programme for adults with type 2 diabetes – the X-PERT programme – (Deakin et al., 2006) was effective both in increasing diabetes knowledge and improving a range of outcomes, including glycaemic control. At 14-month follow-up, patients who had been randomised to six 2-hour group sessions had lower cholesterol, reduced weight, higher physical activity levels and better diet

than patients in a standard individual care control condition. It could, however, be argued that the X-PERT programme was more than education, as it attempted to empower patients, by increasing confidence and mastery and included problem-solving and goal-setting components.

Interventions targeting motivation and the control of behaviour

If equipping patients with knowledge and information is necessary but not sufficient, what else can be done to help patients to manage a long-term condition better? Health psychology interventions to improve self-management draw on a number of different psychological theories and models in order to address two factors: motivation and control of action. Motivational interventions may attempt to bring about change in beliefs and attitudes which generate the intention to perform desired illness-related behaviours. Such techniques are increasingly used in health-care settings to help patients to consider different possible courses of action and determine priorities (Knight et al., 2006; Rollnick et al., 2008). In order to help patients to translate intentions into appropriate actions, a range of behavioural techniques are used, such as teaching problem solving (Welschen et al., 2007), behavioural experimentation with feedback to increase self-efficacy (Lorig et al., 2001) and the collaborative development of 'implementation intentions' (Gollwitzer, 1999) or if–then action plans (Leventhal et al., 2008) to guide behaviour and overcome barriers.

Leventhal's common-sense model (CSM) (Leventhal et al., 1980) provides a useful framework for self-management interventions (Petrie et al., 2003; Wearden & Peters, 2008). According to this model, when people encounter a health threat, such as chronic illness, they develop a coherent personal model, or set of representations of that threat, which then generate congruent behavioural responses. Cognitive representations (or illness perceptions) generate behaviours to regulate the threat, while emotional representations generate emotion regulation strategies. Although these processes operate in parallel they also interact in a dynamic way. Appraisals of threat regulatory and emotion regulatory behaviours operate to modify both the representations and future regulatory behaviours, in a dynamic feedback loop. The model provides a rationale for improving patients' management of a long-term condition by helping them to develop more adaptive perceptions of their illness with consequent effects on behaviours. Petrie and colleagues (Petrie *et al.*, 2002), showed that a brief, three-session, nurse-delivered, intervention to modify illness perceptions of patients who had just had a heart attack led to patients feeling better prepared for leaving hospital, returning to work more quickly and experiencing fewer angina symptoms.

The techniques used in interventions based on the CSM incorporate techniques from cognitive behaviour therapy (CBT) (McAndrew *et al.*, 2008). They include eliciting patients' own illness models, examining where these models lead to non-optimal management behaviours, and encouraging patients to consider alternative understandings of their condition by providing information and engaging in discussion. The patient's newly formulated illness models are then used to develop action plans which include anticipation of potential barriers to change and specifications as to how they may be overcome. The illness perception intervention for post-heart attack patients described above has recently been replicated (Broadbent *et al.*, in press), and the general model has been employed in the design of interventions for the management of diabetes and asthma (French *et al.*, 2008; Keogh *et al.*, 2007; McAndrew *et al.*, 2008). This is an area where health psychologists have a role in training physicians and other health-care professionals in the skills needed to elicit and work with patients' illness models (Theunissen *et al.*, 2003).

Developing interventions for the management of long-term conditions

The protocol for an intervention to improve adherence to medication in patients with type 2 diabetes (Farmer *et al.*, 2008) provides a good example of the ways in which health psychologists can be involved in developing and evaluating treatments for long-term conditions. As recommended by the UK Medical Research Council's Complex Intervention Guidelines (Craig *et al.*, 2008) Farmer and colleagues' intervention was developed from an initial exploratory study of the beliefs of patients with type 2 diabetes about their hypoglycaemic medication. The components of

the intervention were then developed, and include belief elicitation, reinforcement of positive beliefs using tailored information, problem solving and the use of implementation intentions. The next role for the health psychologist is in training practice nurses to deliver the intervention; the training is specified in a manual and sets the therapeutic techniques in their theoretical context. Assessment measures operationalise theoretical constructs and are designed to allow the researchers to examine processes of change, and thereby to relate any observed change to theoretical predictions.

Interventions to Treat Symptoms

Interventions for the management of symptoms in conditions such as chronic pain, multiple sclerosis, cancer and rheumatoid arthritis differ from other health psychology interventions in being driven by a model of the condition or symptoms to be managed rather than by overarching theories of health behaviours. Such interventions are often based on cognitive behavioural type formulations similar in format (although not necessarily in content) to those developed by clinical psychologists for conditions such as depression and anxiety. In this section, a cognitive behavioural formulation of fatigue is presented which has formed the basis for treatments of chronic fatigue syndrome (CFS), a condition in which severe, disabling fatigue is the principal symptom and also for the fatigue experienced in other conditions such as multiple sclerosis.

Current models of CFS distinguish between predisposing, precipitating and maintaining factors (Surawy *et al.*, 1995). Precipitating factors may include infection, chronic stress or trauma. A slower than expected recovery with long periods of reduced activity can lead to cardiovascular and muscular deconditioning, and disturbance of sleep–wake rhythms (Convertino *et al.*, 1997). Thereafter, attempts to increase activity and get back to normal may be accompanied by symptoms related to deconditioning, such as delayed muscle soreness after activity. Continued symptoms may be interpreted as a relapse of the illness and thus feed back into the emotional and behavioural responses of demoralisation and activity restriction

(Deale *et al.*, 1998; Silver *et al.*, 2002). Limiting activity leads to further deconditioning, and a vicious cycle is set up. Thus the model attempts to relate cognitive factors (such as expectations about the time course of the illness and evaluations of symptoms), to emotional responses (such as demoralisation), to behavioural attempts at management (such as activity restriction), and to physiological changes (such as deconditioning). Interactions with others who may have different understandings of the meaning of symptoms and who may provide helpful or unhelpful support attempts are also incorporated into the model (Schmaling *et al.*, 2000).

A similar model of fatigue has been at the basis of a number of psychological interventions. Several studies have shown the value of CBT which attempts to help patients to break out of the vicious cycle of fear avoidance, inactivity, deconditioning and perpetuation of symptoms (Price *et al.*, 2008). Similar models have been developed for a number of other illnesses where fatigue is a prominent symptom, such as multiple sclerosis, rheumatoid arthritis and cancer (e.g. Armes *et al.*, 2007). A cognitive behavioural intervention for the treatment of fatigue in multiple sclerosis included behavioural techniques such as activity scheduling and regularisation of sleep patterns, techniques to encourage more adaptive beliefs about MS, such as discussion of symptom attribution, and management of stress and negative emotions (van Kessel *et al.*, 2008). The intervention was delivered by a psychologist, and significantly reduced fatigue when compared with a relaxation therapy control group.

Interventions to Address Psychological Adjustment to Illness

Psychological adjustment to a long-term condition is complex, encompassing adaptation to limitations imposed by the condition, achieving good quality of life in various domains (e.g. work, social and leisure), the maintenance of satisfying relationships and the absence of negative emotions or psychological disorders such as depression and anxiety (de Ridder *et al.*, 2008). Health psychology interventions to help patients to adjust to chronic illness include the use of CBT and

coping skills training to reduce and manage stress, and interventions which focus specifically on the regulation of emotions by encouraging healthy or effective emotional expression. Each of these is considered briefly below.

Stress management techniques have been studied particularly in the context of living with HIV infection and cancer. A particular set of techniques, known as cognitive behavioural stress management (CBSM), has been developed and subjected to considerable testing, much of it by health psychologists based at the University of Miami. The intervention contains a number of components aimed at reducing anxiety through techniques such as relaxation and meditation, encouraging more positive appraisals of stressors by cognitive reframing, and enhancing social support by interpersonal skills training. There is also an emphasis on engendering a greater sense of control, and the prioritising of coping resources to those aspects of living with long-term conditions that are controllable and amenable to change (Antoni *et al.*, 2000). There is now considerable evidence that CBSM can improve quality of life, reduce depression, enhance benefit finding and reduce social disruption (Antoni *et al.*, 2006; Compas *et al.*, 1998). Increased benefit finding in turn has been shown to be associated with reduced cortisol levels in women being treated for breast cancer (Cruess *et al.*, 2000), illustrating the interdependence of cognitive, emotional and physiological variables. There is also emerging evidence that the reduction in negative emotion in HIV-positive men may impact directly on immune functioning (Antoni *et al.*, 2005).

Coping skills training has been used extensively with patients with a number of conditions including chronic pain from osteo- and rheumatoid arthritis, with the aim of improving patients' confidence and belief in their ability to deal with pain. In many cases the intervention has been extended to involve spouses or significant others as well as the patient. Coping skills training involves systematic instruction and practice, with feedback, of pain-coping skills and has been shown to be effective in increasing self-efficacy (Compas *et al.*, 1998) and reducing disability. Patients may also be taught how to maintain their treatment gains by early identification of potential relapse, practising skills to deal with symptom exacerbations and training in self-control skills (Carson *et al.*, 2006). In addition to its application in arthritic pain conditions, coping skills training has been used with young people with sickle cell disease (Gil *et al.*, 2001) and adolescents with diabetes (Grey *et al.*, 2000).

Given the demands that living with a long-term condition can place upon a person it is unsurprising that many experience a range of negative emotions, with a significant proportion fulfilling diagnostic criteria for depression or anxiety disorders. For example, it has been estimated that 20 per cent of patients with coronary heart disease suffer from major depression at some point during their illness (Lustman *et al.*, 2000), while adults with type 2 diabetes are more than twice as likely to suffer from generalised anxiety disorder than adults in the general community (Fisher *et al.*, 2008). Many patients suffer from more than one chronic condition, and this places them at even greater risk of emotional disorder (Egede, 2005). Negative emotional states or co-morbid psychological disorders may exacerbate the impact or expression of the condition itself (Katon *et al.*, 2007)). For example, anxiety and depression are both associated with a higher risk of cardiac events in patients with stable cardiac disease (Frasure-Smith & Lesperance, 2008). In addition, negative emotional states may interfere with patients' attempts to manage their condition – for example, via loss of motivation or loss of cognitive control over self-management behaviours (Cluley & Cochrane, 2001). Finally, negative emotional states contribute an additional burden and impair quality of life. Health psychologists therefore attach considerable importance to helping people to cope with the emotions engendered by long-term conditions (Detweiler-Bedell *et al.*, 2008).

In Western cultures, avoiding dealing with emotions or inhibiting the expression of emotions is often associated with poorer outcomes while venting emotions *per se* is not always adaptive (de Ridder *et al.*, 2008). What does seem to be helpful is the expression of emotion in a context which allows for a degree of reappraisal of the threat. Empirical observations that people who had had the opportunity to process a severe trauma tended to have fewer health problems later in life, led to the development of an intervention technique, which induces patients to express emotions via the medium of structured writing. An early application of the intervention was carried out with women completing treatment for breast cancer, who were allocated one of three conditions in which they wrote on four occasions about either: their deepest thoughts and feelings; positive thoughts and feelings; or facts about breast cancer. Women who wrote about emotions had fewer symptoms and fewer medical consultations at follow-up. Additionally, the authors demonstrated a moderating effect of pre-intervention coping styles. Women who habitually used avoidant emotion-coping strategies had better outcomes in the positive thoughts and feelings group, while non-avoidant women did better in the emotion-focused group (Stanton *et al.*, 2002). The written emotional expression intervention has now been tested in a number of different illness conditions, as diverse as fibromyalgia (Broderick *et al.*, 2005), asthma (Harris *et al.*, 2005), HIV infection (Petrie *et al.*, 2004) and psoriasis (Vedhara *et al.*, 2007), targeting a variety of outcomes including disease status, quality of life and well-being. The findings of these studies have been mixed, some studies showing positive benefits of writing and others showing none (Frisina *et al.*, 2004). The paradigm has generated a large amount of research on the possible mechanisms of action. For example, it has been suggested that the intervention works when it encourages cognitive restructuring (Warner *et al.*, 2006), and there is also some evidence for the mediating role of habituation to negative emotion (Low, *et al.*, 2006).

In recent years, the potential role of family members (or significant others) in both the management of and adjustment to a long-term condition has been increasingly recognised. Family members may support (or hinder) patients' attempts at self-management in a number of ways. They may provide practical assistance, or help to create a family environment which supports the patient's needs. Obvious examples would be making adjustments to family diet in the case of diabetes, or taking exercise with a patient (Lagreca *et al.*, 1995). Family members may provide emotional support, or conversely, may undermine a patient's attempts at self-management through criticism (Wearden *et al.*, 2000). A recent review and meta-analysis of interventions for chronic illness which involved family members revealed that family interventions had a small impact on patient depression over a range of different conditions. However, there was stronger evidence of benefits for family members themselves, with reductions in depression, anxiety and burden (Martire *et al.*, 2004).

The Use of New Technology – Internet, Telephone and Mobile Phone Interventions

Over the past 10 or so years, there has been an explosion of interest in using new technologies, particularly the internet, to deliver health interventions to patients, and several new journals are dedicated to this topic. While many of the internet interventions are targeted at prevention and health promotion in general, there is a clear case for using this medium to reach people with long-term conditions. A recent review (Griffiths *et al.*, 2006) noted a number of advantages to delivery of interventions over the internet, including low cost for both users and providers, potential to reach patients who could not access services, convenience for patients and reduction in stigma. Other advantages of internet interventions include the presentation of information in a variety of formats, the relative ease of tailoring advice to patient's personal profiles, and the provision of automated encouragement, feedback and reminders. In the UK, the Economic and Social Research Council (ESRC) and the National Centre for e-Social Science are supporting the development of a web-based 'Behavioural Intervention Grid' (LifeGuide, www.lifeguideonline.org). LifeGuide will allow researchers and clinicians to quickly set up and test psychological interventions using components available in the grid, and will also provide a forum for discussion and dissemination of intervention research.

Testing Interventions

The UK Medical Research Council (MRC) recently updated its guidelines for the conduct of trials of complex interventions, and for the first time, health psychologists were integral to the consultation and development of the guidelines (Craig *et al.*, 2008). The guidelines emphasise the need for careful development work, including testing of theory and work to determine the acceptability and feasibility of interventions. This is in line with the current move towards 'intervention mapping' in health psychology, a set of techniques for producing and evaluating theory- and evidence-based interventions (Kok *et al.*, 2004). It is recommended that initial tests of new interventions enable the examination of processes of change, using both quantitative measures of mediating variables, and post-intervention qualitative work to explore patients' views and experiences. The process of developing and testing interventions is iterative, with each new advance feeding back into further development work.

Conclusions and Future Directions

This chapter provided a brief overview of some of the interventions that health psychologists have developed in the context of long-term conditions, and has illustrated the many and varied roles and tasks that health psychologists undertake, and the many settings in which they work. Health psychologists aim to design interventions which are theory based and advance psychological knowledge, which are acceptable to patients, manageable for the rest of the multidisciplinary team and feasible in the social, economic and environmental circumstances (Schaalma & Kok, 2009). Health psychologists should consider the issue of where to publish their interventions research, taking into account the dual aims of advancing psychological theory and of influencing practice more generally.

Discussion Points

1 What are the challenges faced by health psychologists working with patients with long-term physical conditions?

2 To what extent are health psychology interventions theory based?

3 Are atheoretical interventions acceptable?

4 What are the most important aspects of the design of a new psychological intervention for a long-term condition?

5 Is it possible or desirable to design 'pure' psychological interventions for patients with long-term conditions?

6 What are the advantages and disadvantages of using new technology to deliver interventions in health psychology?

Further Reading

Abraham, C. & Michie, S. (2008). A taxonomy of behavior change techniques used in interventions. *Health Psychology, 27*(3), 379–387.

Craig, P., Dieppe, P., Macintyre, S., Mitchie, S., Nazareth, I. & Petticrew, M. (2008). Developing and evaluating complex interventions: the new Medical Research Council guidance. *British Medical Journal, 337*(7676).

Detweiler-Bedell, J.B., Friedman, M.A., Leventhal, H., Miller, I.W. & Leventhal, E. A. (2008). Integrating co-morbid depression and chronic physical disease management: identifying and resolving failures in self-regulation. *Clinical Psychology Review, 28*(8), 1426–1446.

Frisina, P.G., Borod, J.C. & Lepore, S.J. (2004). A meta-analysis of the effects of written emotional disclosure on the health outcomes of clinical populations. *Journal of Nervous and Mental Disease, 192*(9), 629–634.

Hardeman, W., Johnston, M., Johnston, D.W., Bonetti, D., Wareham, N.J. & Kinmonth, A.L. (2002). Application of the theory of planned behaviour in behaviour change interventions: a systematic review. *Psychology & Health, 17*(2), 123–158.

Kok, G., Schaalma, H., Ruiter, R. .C., Van Empelen, P. & Brug, J. (2004). Intervention mapping: a protocol for applying health psychology theory to prevention programmes. *Journal of Health Psychology, 9*(1), 85–98.

Leventhal, H., Weinman, J., Leventhal, E.A. & Phillips, L. A. (2008). Health psychology: the search for pathways between behavior and health. *Annual Review of Psychology, 59*, 477–505.

Low, C.A., Stanton, A.L. & Danoff-Burg, S. (2006). Expressive disclosure and benefit finding among breast cancer patients: mechanisms for positive health effects. *Health Psychology, 25*(2), 181–189.

Nicassio, P.M., Meyerowitz, B.E. & Kerns, R.D. (2004). The future of health psychology interventions. *Health Psychology, 23*(2), 132–137.

Schaalma, H. & Kok, G. (2009). Decoding health education interventions: the times are a-changin'. *Psychology & Health, 24*(1), 5–9.

Wearden, A. & Peters, S. (2008). Therapeutic techniques for interventions based on Leventhal's common sense model. *British Journal of Health Psychology, 13*, 189–193.

References

Abraham, C. & Michie, S. (2008). A taxonomy of behavior change techniques used in interventions. *Health Psychology, 27*, 379–387.

Antoni, M.H., Carrico, A.W., Duran, R.E., Spitzer, S., Penedo, F., Ironson, G. *et al.* (2006). Randomized clinical trial of cognitive behavioral stress management on human immunodeficiency virus viral load in gay men treated with highly active antiretroviral therapy. *Psychosomatic Medicine, 68*, 143–151.

Antoni, M.H., Cruess, D.G., Cruess, S., Lutgendorf, S., Kumar, M., Ironson, G. *et al.* (2000). Cognitive-behavioral stress management intervention effects on anxiety, 24-hr urinary norepinephrine output, and T-cytotoxic/suppressor cells over time among symptomatic HIV-infected gay men. *Journal of Consulting and Clinical Psychology, 68*, 31–45.

Antoni, M.H., Cruess, D.G., Klimas, N., Carrico, A.W., Maher, K., Cruess, S. *et al.* (2005). Increases in a marker of immune system reconstitution are predated by decreases in 24-h urinary cortisol output and depressed mood during a 10-week stress management intervention in symptomatic HIV-infected men. *Journal of Psychosomatic Research, 58*, 3–13.

Armes, J., Chalder, T., Addington-Hall, J., Richardson, A. & Hotopf, M. (2007). A randomized controlled trial to evaluate the effectiveness of a brief, behaviorally oriented intervention for cancer-related fatigue. *Cancer, 110*, 1385–1395.

Broadbent, E., Ellis, C. J., Thomas, J., Gamble, G. & Petrie, K.J. (2009). Further development of an illness perception intervention for myocardial infarction patients: a randomised controlled trial. *Journal of Psychosomatic Research, 67*, 17–23.

Broderick, J.E., Junghaenel, D.U. & Schwartz, J.E. (2005). Written emotional expression produces health benefits in fibromyalgia patients. *Psychosomatic Medicine, 67*, 326–334.

Carson, J.W., Keefe, F.J., Affleck, G., Rumble, M.E., Caldwell, D.S., Beaupre, P.M. *et al.* (2006). A comparison of conventional pain coping skills training and pain coping skills training with a maintenance training component: a daily diary analysis of short- and long-term treatment effects. *Journal of Pain, 7*, 615–625.

Cluley, S. & Cochrane, G.M. (2001). Psychological disorder in asthma is associated with poor control and poor adherence to inhaled MED steroids. *Respiratory Medicine, 95*, 37–39.

Coates, V.E. & Boore, J.R.P. (1996). Knowledge and diabetes self-management. *Patient Education and Counseling, 29*, 99–108.

Compas, B.E., Haaga, D.A.F., Keefe, F.J., Leitenberg, H. & Williams, D.A. (1998). Sampling of empirically supported psychological treatments from health psychology: smoking, chronic pain, cancer, and bulimia nervosa. *Journal of Consulting and Clinical Psychology, 66*, 89–112.

Convertino, V.A., Bloomfield, S.A. & Greenleaf, J.E. (1997). An overview of the issues: Physiological effects of bed rest and restricted physical activity. *Medicine & Science in Sports & Exercise, 29*, 187–190.

Craig, P., Dieppe, P., Macintyre, S., Mitchie, S., Nazareth, I. & Petticrew, M. (2008). Developing and evaluating complex interventions: the new Medical Research Council guidance. *British Medical Journal, 337*.

Cruess, D.G., Antoni, M.H., McGregor, B.A., Kilbourn, K.M., Boyers, A.E., Alferi, S.M. *et al.* (2000). Cognitive-behavioral stress management reduces serum cortisol by enhancing benefit finding among women being treated for early stage breast cancer. *Psychosomatic Medicine, 62*, 304–308.

Davies, M.J., Heller, S., Skinner, T.C., Campbell, M.J., Carey, M.E., Cradock, S. *et al.* (2008). Effectiveness of the diabetes education and self management for ongoing and newly diagnosed (DESMOND) programme for people with newly diagnosed type 2 diabetes: cluster randomised controlled trial. *British Medical Journal, 336*, 491–495.

de Ridder, D., Geenen, R., Kuijer, R. & van Middendorp, H. (2008). Psychological adjustment to chronic disease. *Lancet, 372*, 246–255.

Deakin, T.A., Cade, J.E., Williams, R. & Greenwood, D.C. (2006). Structured patient education: the Diabetes X-PERT Programme makes a difference. *Diabetic Medicine, 23*, 944–954.

Deale, A., Chalder, T. & Wessely, S. (1998). Illness beliefs and treatment outcome in chronic fatigue syndrome. *Journal of Psychosomatic Research, 45*, 77–83.

Detweiler-Bedell, J.B., Friedman, M.A., Leventhal, H., Miller, I.W. & Leventhal, E.A. (2008). Integrating comorbid depression and chronic physical disease management: Identifying and resolving failures in self-regulation. *Clinical Psychology Review, 28*, 1426–1446.

Egede, L.E. (2005). Effect of comorbid chronic diseases on prevalence and odds of depression in adults with diabetes. *Psychosomatic Medicine, 67*, 46–51.

Farmer, A.J., Prevost, A.T., Hardeman, W., Craven, A., Sutton, S., Griffin, S.J. *et al.* (2008). Protocol for SAMS (Support and Advice for Medication Study): a randomised controlled trial of an intervention to support patients with type 2 diabetes with adherence to medication. *BMC Family Practice, 9*.

Fisher, L., Skaff, M.M., Mullan, J.T., Arean, P., Glasgow, R. & Masharani, U. (2008). A longitudinal study of affective and anxiety disorders, depressive affect and diabetes distress in adults with Type 2 diabetes. *Diabetic Medicine, 25*, 1096–1101.

Frasure-Smith, N. & Lesperance, F. (2008). Depression and anxiety as predictors of 2-year cardiac events in patients with stable coronary artery disease. *Archives of General Psychiatry, 65*, 62–71.

French, D.P., Wade, A.N., Yudkin, P., Neil, H.A.W., Kinmonth, A.L. & Farmer, A.J. (2008). Self-monitoring of blood glucose changed non-insulin treated type 2 diabetes patients' beliefs about diabetes and self-monitoring in a randomised trial. *Diabetic Medicine 25*, 1218–1228.

Frisina, P.G., Borod, J.C. & Lepore, S.J. (2004). A meta-analysis of the effects of written emotional disclosure on the health outcomes of clinical populations. *Journal of Nervous and Mental Disease, 192*, 629–634.

Gibson, P.G., Ram, F.S.F. & Powell, H. (2003). Asthma education. *Respiratory Medicine, 97*, 1036–1044.

Gil, K.M., Anthony, K.K., Carson, J.W., Redding-Lallinger, R., Daeschner, C.W. & Ware, R.E. (2001). Daily coping practice predicts treatment effects in children with sickle cell disease. *Journal of Pediatric Psychology, 26*, 163–173.

Gollwitzer, P.M. (1999). Implementation intentions – Strong effects of simple plans. *American Psychologist, 54*, 493–503.

Grey, M., Boland, E.A., Davidson, M., Li, J. & Tamborlane, W.V. (2000). Coping skills training for youth with diabetes mellitus has long-lasting effects on metabolic control and quality of life. *Journal of Pediatrics, 137*, 107–113.

Griffiths, F., Lindenmeyer, A., Powell, J., Lowe, P. & Thorogood, M. (2006). Why are health care interventions delivered over the Internet? A systematic review of the published literature. *Journal of Medical Internet Research, 8*(2).

Hardeman, W., Johnston, M., Johnston, D.W., Bonetti, D., Wareham, N.J. & Kinmonth, A.L. (2002). Application of the theory of planned behaviour in behaviour change interventions: a systematic review. *Psychology & Health, 17*, 123–158.

Harris, A.H.S., Thoresen, C.E., Humphreys, K. & Faul, J. (2005). Does writing affect asthma? A randomized trial. *Psychosomatic Medicine, 67*, 130–136.

Katon, W., Lin, E.H.B. & Kroenke, K. (2007). The association of depression and anxiety with medical symptom burden in patients with chronic medical illness. *General Hospital Psychiatry, 29*, 147–155.

Keogh, K.M., White, P., Smith, S.M., McGilloway, S., O'Dowd, T. & Gibney, J. (2007). Changing illness perceptions in patients with poorly controlled type 2 diabetes, a randomised controlled trial of a family-based intervention: protocol and pilot study. *BMC Family Practice, 8*.

Knight, K.M., McGowan, L., Dickens, C. & Bundy, C. (2006). A systematic review of motivational interviewing in physical health care settings. *British Journal of Health Psychology, 11*, 319–332.

Kok, G., Schaalma, H., Ruiter, R.A.C., Van Empelen, P. & Brug, J. (2004). Intervention mapping: A protocol for applying health psychology theory to prevention programmes. *Journal of Health Psychology, 9*, 85–98.

Lagreca, A.M., Auslander, W.F., Greco, P., Spetter, D., Fisher, E.B. & Santiago, J.V. (1995). I get by with a little help from my family and friends – adolescent support for diabetes care. *Journal of Pediatric Psychology, 20*, 449–476.

Leventhal, H., Weinman, J., Leventhal, E.A. & Phillips, L.A. (2008). Health psychology: the search for pathways between behavior and health. *Annual Review of Psychology, 59*, 477–505.

Leventhal, H.J., Meyer, D. & Nerenz, D. (1980). The common sense representation of illness danger. In S. Rachman (Ed.) *Contributions to medical psychology* (Vol. 2, pp. 17–30). New York: Pergamon Press.

Lorig, K.R., Ritter, P., Stewart, A.L., Sobel, D.S., Brown, B.W., Bandura, A. *et al.* (2001). Chronic disease self-management program – 2-year health status and health care utilization outcomes. *Medical Care, 39*, 1217–1223.

Low, C.A., Stanton, A.L. & Danoff-Burg, S. (2006). Expressive disclosure and benefit finding among breast cancer patients: Mechanisms for positive health effects. *Health Psychology, 25*, 181–189.

Lustman, P.J., Anderson, R.J., Freedland, K.E., de Groot, M., Carney, R.M. & Clouse, R.E. (2000). Depression and poor glycemic control – a meta-analytic review of the literature. *Diabetes Care, 23*, 934–942.

Martire, L.M., Lustig, A.P., Schulz, R., Miller, G.E. & Helgeson, V.S. (2004). Is it beneficial to involve a family member? A meta-analysis of psychosocial interventions for chronic illness. *Health Psychology, 23*, 599–611.

McAndrew, L.M., Musumeci-Szabo, T.J., Mora, P.A., Vileikyte, L., Burns, E., Halm, E.A. *et al.* (2008). Using the common sense model to design interventions for the prevention and management of chronic illness threats: From description to process. *British Journal of Health Psychology, 13*, 195–204.

Michie, S., Hardeman, W., Fanshawe, T., Prevost, A.T., Taylor, L. & Kinmonth, A.L. (2008). Investigating theoretical explanations for behaviour change: The case study of ProActive. *Psychology & Health, 23*, 25–39.

Michie, S., Johnston, M., Francis, J., Hardeman, W. & Eccles, M. (2008). From theory to intervention: mapping theoretically derived behavioural determinants to behaviour change techniques. *Applied Psychology – An International Review – Psychologie Appliquee-Revue Internationale, 57*, 660–680.

Newman, S., Steed, L. & Mulligan, K. (2004). Self-management interventions for chronic illness. *Lancet, 364*, 1523–1537.

Nicassio, P.M., Meyerowitz, B.E. & Kerns, R.D. (2004). The future of health psychology interventions. *Health Psychology, 23*, 132–137.

Petrie, K.J., Broadbent, E. & Meechan, G. (2003). Self-regulatory interventions for improving the management of chronic illness. In L.D. Cameron & H. Leventhal (Eds.) *The self-regulation of health and illness behaviour* (pp. 257–277). London: Routledge.

Petrie, K.J., Cameron, L.D., Ellis, C.J., Buick, D. & Weinman, J. (2002). Changing illness perceptions after myocardial infarction: An early intervention randomized controlled trial. *Psychosomatic Medicine, 64*, 580–586.

Petrie, K.J., Fontanilla, I., Thomas, M.G., Booth, R.J. & Pennebaker, J.W. (2004). Effect of written emotional expression on immune function in patients with human immunodeficiency virus infection: a randomized trial. *Psychosomatic Medicine, 66*, 272–275.

Price, J.R., Mitchell, E., Tidy, E. & Hunot, V. (2008). Cognitive behaviour therapy for chronic fatigue syndrome in adults. *Cochrane Database of Systematic Reviews* (3).

Rollnick, S., Miller, W.R. & Butler, C.C. (2008). *Motivational interviewing in health care*. New York: Guilford Press.

Schaalma, H. & Kok, G. (2009). Decoding health education interventions: the times are a-changin'. *Psychology & Health, 24*, 5–9.

Schmaling, K.B., Smith, W.R. & Buchwald, D.S. (2000). Significant other responses are associated with fatigue and functional status among patients with chronic fatigue syndrome. *Psychosomatic Medicine, 62*, 444–450.

Silver, A., Haeney, M., Vijayadurai, P., Wilks, D., Pattrick, M. & Main, C.J. (2002). The role of fear of physical movement and activity in chronic fatigue syndrome. *Journal of Psychosomatic Research, 52,* 485–493.

Stanton, A.L., Danoff–Burg, S., Sworowski, L.A., Collins, C.A., Branstetter, A.D., Rodriguez-Hanley, A. *et al.* (2002). Randomized, controlled trial of written emotional expression and benefit finding in breast cancer patients. *Journal of Clinical Oncology, 20,* 4160–4168.

Surawy, C., Hackmann, A., Hawton, K. & Sharpe, M. (1995). Chronic fatigue syndrome – a cognitive approach. *Behaviour Research and Therapy, 33,* 535–544.

Theunissen, N.C.M., de Ridder, D.T.D., Bensing, J.M. & Rutten, G. (2003). Manipulation of patient–provider interaction: discussing illness representations or action plans concerning adherence. *Patient Education and Counseling, 51,* 247–258.

van Kessel, K., Moss-Morris, R., Willoughby, E., Chalder, T., Johnson, M.H. & Robinson, E. (2008). A randomized controlled trial of cognitive behavior therapy for multiple sclerosis fatigue. *Psychosomatic Medicine, 70,* 205–213.

Vedhara, K., Morris, R.M., Booth, R., Horgan, M., Lawrence, M. & Birchall, N. (2007). Changes in mood predict disease activity and quality of life in patients with psoriasis following emotional disclosure. *Journal of Psychosomatic Research, 62,* 611–619.

Walker, A., O'Brien, M., Traynor, J., Fox, K., Goddard, E. & Foster, K. (2002). *Living in Britain. Results from the 2001 General Household Survey.* London: Office for National Statistics.

Warner, L.J., Lumley, M.A., Casey, R.J., Pierantoni, W., Salazar, R., Zoratti, E.M. *et al.* (2006). Health effects of written emotional disclosure in adolescents with asthma: a randomized, controlled trial. *Journal of Pediatric Psychology, 31,* 557–568.

Wearden, A. & Peters, S. (2008). Therapeutic techniques for interventions based on Leventhal's common sense model. *British Journal of Health Psychology, 13,* 189–193.

Wearden, A.J., Tarrier, N. & Davies, R. (2000). Partners' expressed emotion and the control and management of Type 1 diabetes in adults. *Journal of Psychosomatic Research, 49,* 125–130.

Welschen, L.M.C., van Oppen, P., Dekker, J.M., Bouter, L.M., Stalman, W.A.B. & Nijpels, G. (2007). The effectiveness of adding cognitive behavioural therapy aimed at changing lifestyle to managed diabetes care for patients with type 2 diabetes: design of a randomised controlled trial. *BMC Public Health, 7.*

Wilson, T., Buck, D. & Ham, C. (2005). Rising to the challenge: will the NHS support people with long term conditions? *British Medical Journal, 330,* 657–661.

17

Screening and Prevention

Kate Brain

Chapter Outline

This chapter examines the psychological impact of screening and prevention. Definitions of terms are provided, along with a brief historical background and outline of criteria for the introduction of screening. (For a comprehensive review of the history of screening, see Holland & Stewart, 2005.) An important distinction is made between screening in the general population and family history-based screening, both of which may involve an analysis of the individual's genetic inheritance. The emotional consequences, both positive and negative, of the screening process are explored, with examples drawn from population and family history screening studies. Cognitive and behavioural consequences of screening are also considered. Factors which moderate the impact of screening are examined, highlighting particular subgroups of people who may be more prone to adverse experiences of screening. Finally, some reflections are made on the implications of the growing availability of commercial genetic screening tests.

Key Concepts

Commercial genetic
  screening
False-positive results
Family history screening
Population screening
Psychological
  consequences
Screening criteria

Definition of Terms

Screening to detect medical symptoms at an early asymptomatic stage is available for a wide array of conditions throughout the life cycle. Holland and Stewart (2005, p. 6) define screening as the process of 'actively seeking to identify a disease or pre-disease condition in people who are presumed and who presume themselves to be healthy'. The UK National Screening Committee website (www.nsc.nhs.uk) gives a more comprehensive definition of screening as 'a public health service in which members of a defined population, who do not necessarily perceive they are at risk of, or are already affected by a disease or its complications, are asked a question or offered a test, to identify those individuals who are more likely to be helped than harmed by further tests or treatment to reduce the risk of a disease or its complications'. Further definitions of some terms associated with screening are:

- *Sensitivity*: the extent to which the screening test is able to give a positive (i.e. abnormal) result when the individual being screened has the condition in question. A positive result usually leads to further diagnostic tests to confirm the presence of disease.
- *Specificity*: the extent to which the screening test is able to give a negative (i.e. normal or clear) result when the individual being screened does not have the condition.
- *False-positive result*: when an individual screens positive but does not have the condition. This initial abnormal result may lead to further diagnostic tests or investigations before the situation is resolved.
- *False-negative result*: when an individual screens negative but does in fact have the condition.
- *Inconclusive results*: screening tests may sometimes give an inadequate or unsatisfactory result, for example in cervical screening there may not be enough epithelial cells in the smear sample to allow an accurate assessment.

Prevention refers to any intervention which is aimed at halting disease before it develops and operates on three levels. *Primary prevention* involves modifying risk factors in an effort to stop disease occurring in the first place, for example lowering cholesterol to reduce the risk of coronary heart disease or stopping smoking to reduce the risk of lung cancer. *Secondary prevention* involves tests or interventions to detect illness at an early stage before symptoms progress, such as cervical screening. *Tertiary prevention* focuses on ameliorating symptoms in people who have developed disease, through treatment and rehabilitation. The focus of this chapter will be on screening as a form of secondary prevention. Other forms of secondary prevention include self-screening practices such as breast and testicular self-examination and home-testing kits for diabetes and cholesterol. However, these will not be covered in depth because they do not conform to the accepted principles of screening, which are considered in the next section.

Historical Background

The second half of the 20th century saw a gradual shift in medicine away from diagnosis and treatment towards a 'predict and prevent' approach to disease. One of the first examples of this sea-change was mass screening for tuberculosis in the 1950s and 1960s, the effectiveness of which led to widespread acceptance of screening by health-care professionals and the public. However, with the rapid expansion of population screening services in the 1960s came an increasing awareness of the need to regulate screening by judging the evidence in favour of its effectiveness in detecting disease or abnormality and establishing criteria that would have to be fulfilled before a screening programme could be introduced into health-care services. Although no screening test is foolproof and some errors will inevitably occur, the basic criteria that should be satisfied were first set out by Wilson and Jungner in 1968 and are summarised in Table 17.1.

According to the principles established by Wilson and Jungner, screening should occur at a whole-population level. In practice, however, the term screening tends to be more loosely applied to testing on an individual basis. For example, the prostate-specific antigen (PSA) test for prostate cancer is

Table 17.1 Summary of criteria for screening

Category	Criteria
Condition	The condition sought should be an important health problem whose natural history, including development from latent to declared disease, is adequately understood. The condition should have a recognisable latent or early symptomatic stage
Diagnosis	There should be a suitable diagnostic test that is available, safe and acceptable to the population concerned. There should be an agreed policy, based on respectable test findings and national standards, as to whom to regard as patients and the whole process should be a continuing one
Treatment	There should be an accepted and established treatment or intervention for individuals identified as having the disease or pre-disease condition and facilities for treatment should be available
Cost	The cost of case finding (including diagnosis and treatment) should be economically balanced in relation to possible expenditure on medical care as a whole

Source: Reproduced by kind permission of the authors and copyright holder. Holland, W.W. & Stewart, S. (2005). *Screening in Disease Prevention: What Works?* Oxford: Radcliffe Publishing.

controversial because there is a high level of public demand without evidence of benefit. It has a low level of accuracy and a high rate of false-positive results and the efficacy of prostate cancer treatments is uncertain. Consequently, PSA testing is not offered on a routine population basis, but is available for individuals who actively seek it through the Prostate Cancer Risk Management Programme in primary care. Screening can therefore be seen as a continuum, with highly organised screening programmes at one end and individual testing at the other end. Some examples of organised screening programmes include smear tests aimed at detecting cervical cancer at a pre-cancerous stage and sight-threatening diabetic retinopathy screening for people with diabetes. The UK national breast screening programme was introduced after the Forrest Report in 1987 and offers three-yearly mammograms to women aged between 50 and 70 years on population registers. A colorectal cancer screening programme is also available, involving annual faecal occult blood (FOB) testing and possible flexible sigmoidoscopy to detect pre-cancerous polyps. Screening programmes such as these are conducted within a framework of rigorous evaluation to ensure that they adhere to the Wilson and Jungner principles. The UK National Screening Committee recently added a further principle to those set out in Table 17.1, which was that that the benefits of screening must outweigh any physical and psychological harm caused by the process of screening. This reflects a growing recognition in recent years of the potential for psychological side effects of screening.

Population Screening vs. Family History Screening

It is important to distinguish *population* screening programmes aimed at detecting problems in the general population from screening targeted at individuals with a *family history* of a particular disease. For example, women who are identified as being at increased risk due to a strong family history of breast or ovarian cancer are able to have breast/ovarian screening at an earlier age than women in the general population, as part of highly organised research studies to evaluate the clinical effectiveness of these forms of surveillance. Due to their own personal experiences of disease in the family, these individuals are likely to perceive themselves as 'at risk' of the disease in question and to actively pursue screening because of these concerns (Brain *et al.*, 2000). In contrast, individuals in the general population are typically invited by health professionals to undergo screening for a condition of which they may have little prior experience or awareness. The different psychological issues in these groups have implications for their experiences of screening and this will be explored later on in the chapter.

Developments in molecular genetics technology have enabled many individuals with a family history of conditions such as Huntington's disease and hereditary cancers to become involved in organised programmes of genetic assessment and testing. However, the terms 'genetic testing' and 'genetic screening' are often used interchangeably. A further distinction needs to be made between *genetic screening of large population groups* (e.g. prenatal genetic screening, newborn screening and screening to identify unaffected carriers of genetic diseases such as cystic fibrosis and Duchenne muscular dystrophy) and *genetic testing of individuals with a family history* to detect mutations in specific susceptibility genes (see Harper & Clarke, 1997, pp. 7–8). Again, the psychological issues in genetic population screening are different to those in family history-based genetic counselling and testing. As Clarke (in Harper & Clarke, 1997 p. 75) points out, the latter 'entails responding to concerns that are already there in a family; [population-based genetic screening] involves raising concerns that may not otherwise exist'. This chapter will use a range of examples drawn from both population screening studies and family history screening and testing studies in order to highlight the contrasting impact of screening in these different contexts.

Psychological Consequences of Screening

Negative emotional consequences

The screening process involves a number of stages which have the potential to cause distress, anxiety or worry. In the very early stages of routine (i.e. general population) screening, receiving an invitation letter may generate anticipatory anxiety. The screening encounter itself may cause pain and discomfort, for example women may report pain during routine mammography screening and invasive procedures such as cervical smears and colonoscopies may be found uncomfortable or embarrassing. Potential outcomes of screening include true/false-positive results, true/false-negative results and inconclusive results.

The psychological costs associated with unfavourable screening outcomes have been highlighted in studies of different types of population screening. For example, many studies have reported adverse emotional consequences in women from the general population who receive false-positive mammogram results

(e.g. Brett *et al.*, 1998; Meystre-Agustoni *et al.*, 2001; Olsson *et al.*, 1999). Compared to women who receive clear mammogram results straight away, those who have to undergo further tests are likely to experience significant anxiety which may still be evident three years on at their next routine mammogram (Brett & Austoker, 2001; Brett *et al.*, 2005). Similarly, studies have found evidence of heightened worry about ovarian cancer in community samples up to two years after a false-positive ovarian screening result (Anderson *et al.*, 2007; Wardle *et al.*, 1994) and of long-term generalised distress in women who had undergone false-positive oophorectomy following an abnormal result (i.e. ovaries were removed but subsequently found to be disease-free) (Wardle *et al.*, 1994). Marteau *et al.* (1992) also found evidence for persistent anxiety in pregnant women who received false-positive results of routine screening for Down syndrome. Women with positive or mildly abnormal results of routine cervical screening report increased anxiety and cancer-specific concerns compared to women with normal results (Lerman *et al.*, 1991; Wardle *et al.*, 1995) and inadequate smear test results may generate levels of anxiety and worry equivalent to those in women with abnormal results (French *et al.*, 2004). A further example of the potential for adverse effects of population screening is that of human papillomavirus (HPV) testing during routine cervical screening, in which testing positive for HPV has been associated with anxiety, distress and concern (Maissi *et al.*, 2004; McCaffery *et al.*, 2004). Not surprisingly, receiving an unexpected diagnosis of cancer, i.e. detected through routine screening rather than symptomatically, may be met with alarm and distress (Miles *et al.*, 2003). Emotional benefits of unfavourable screening outcomes have been observed in general population studies, for example Wardle *et al.* (2003) found positive effects in those who had polyps detected during flexible sigmoidoscopy screening for colorectal cancer. However, this was a highly organised research trial with an emphasis on quality of care which may be less evident in other population screening contexts.

Although negative screening results are generally associated with reduced anxiety (e.g. Brett *et al.*, 2005; Sutton *et al.*, 1995; Wardle *et al.*, 2003), this may not be the case for those who come to screening with high-risk expectations. Michie *et al.* (2003) investigated responses to negative genetic test results in individuals at high risk due to a family history of familial adenomatous polyposis (FAP, an inherited form of bowel cancer). A lack of reassurance in these individuals was associated with their cognitive representations of genetic testing, i.e. doubts about the accuracy of the test. Those not reassured by negative test results were sceptical about whether an apparently simple blood test could predict the development of cancer located in the bowel. Similarly, women with a family history of breast cancer who are given a 'low' risk result of genetic assessment may fail to be reassured by this ostensibly favourable information (Bish *et al.*, 2002). The lack of reassurance in these individuals stems from a mismatch between their expectations of being at increased personal risk and the actual low-risk outcome, which may lead them to mistrust the results (Michie *et al.*, 2002). While much research has focused on increased or unaltered anxiety as a negative consequence of screening, another potential pitfall of screening is the phenomenon of false reassurance, whereby individuals are less motivated to engage in ongoing screening and prevention despite continuing risk. Psychological costs of screening, such as those outlined, may be offset by the provision of adequate information and support.

Positive emotional consequences

Traditionally there has been an emphasis on negative emotional sequelae of screening. However, there is growing evidence for positive consequences in individuals who undergo family history-based genetic counselling and testing. Studies of the psychological impact of genetic counselling for familial breast/ovarian cancer indicate that, overall, this process does not cause adverse psychological outcomes and often leads to reduced distress and worry in individuals with a family history (e.g. Braithwaite *et al.*, 2004; Watson *et al.*, 1999). Similarly, disclosure of BRCA1/2 gene test results does not appear to cause increased distress (e.g. Schwartz *et al.*, 2002). Broadstock *et al.* (2000) carried out a systematic review of the psychological impact of genetic testing for a range of adult-onset inherited conditions, including hereditary breast/ovarian cancer and Huntington's disease and found no evidence of adverse long-term conse-

quences in gene carriers or non-carriers. Any transient increases in anxiety and worry in individuals who undergo genetic counselling and testing tend to disappear by 12 months follow-up. The provision of careful information and support in part explains the positive psychological outcomes seen in these individuals.

Adverse emotional outcomes appear to be more prevalent in the context of general population screening than in cancer screening for individuals with a family history. Rijnsburger *et al.* (2004) reported no adverse effects of breast screening on health-related quality of life in women with a familial risk, with levels significantly better than those of women in the general population. Despite a higher rate of false-positive results in women with a family history of breast/ovarian cancer, such results do not appear to generate negative effects. In a comparative study, Gilbert *et al.* (1998) found no evidence for sustained anxiety in women with a family history who had false-positive mammograms and concluded that breast screening may be less stressful for these women than for those without a family history. Regular mammographic screening appears to be psychologically beneficial for women with a family history regardless of screening outcome and in fact women with false-positive results reported more benefits of screening than women who had an initial clear result (Tyndel *et al.*, 2007). Studies of the impact of familial ovarian cancer screening are less clear-cut, for example Wardle *et al.* (1993) reported transient increases in anxiety associated with false-positive results, whereas Kauff *et al.* (2005) reported longer term effects. There is some evidence, however, that even false-positive oophorectomy – a radical outcome of ovarian screening – may confer psychological benefits in women with a family history. In contrast with the long-term distress seen in a community sample of women who had undergone the same procedure (Wardle *et al.*, 1994), the women in the Pernet *et al.* (1992) study reported feeling reassured that the removal of healthy ovaries had removed their risk of ovarian cancer.

The positive psychological consequences of family history screening and testing are partly due to psychological preparedness in those at increased risk. Individuals with a family history are likely to be better prepared than those in the general population for a possible transition from health to illness because of their experiences of living at increased risk, in some cases for many years. During this time, most individuals will have done 'the work of worry' and developed strategies for coping with the threat associated with a family history (McAllister, 2002). According to stress and coping theory, a moderate amount of worry and concern encourages the mobilisation of coping resources for adaptation to a stressful event such as an abnormal screening result (Lazarus & Folkman, 1984). Individuals who are at increased risk due to a family history often actively seek out referrals for information and screening, whereas individuals in the general population who are offered screening by health professionals may have little awareness or experience of the condition in question with which to prepare themselves for the potential impact of unfavourable results. Therefore most individuals come to routine population screening with the expectation that 'all will be well'. An unfavourable screening result or a diagnosis of cancer may be less shocking or devastating for individuals with a family history than for those without, because their high-risk expectations have been confirmed (Clements et al., 2008).

Being part of an organised screening/testing programme is also stress buffering for individuals at increased risk due to a family history. For these individuals, screening represents an active, problem-focused strategy for coping with increased genetic risk which minimises or averts any negative effects of the screening process and from which a great deal of reassurance may be derived. Although psychologically beneficial, however, the clinical effectiveness of regular cancer screening for individuals with a familial cancer risk is unproven. Familial cancer screening programmes are in the process of being evaluated both in medical outcomes (effectiveness in early detection of cancer) and psychological outcomes (impact of screening on anxiety and predictors of impact). This raises an important question: how will policy decisions about implementing screening be made if there are conflicting findings of medical and psychological evaluation studies, for example if screening is ineffective yet people are reassured by it? Primary prevention, involving active efforts to reduce the risk of developing cancer through lifestyle changes,

may become especially pertinent in high-risk groups if screening is not proven to be of medical benefit.

Cognitive and behavioural consequences

The focus of much screening evaluation research has been on emotional consequences, with less research on cognitive and behavioural outcomes of screening. However, recent studies have investigated the impact of genetic testing on individuals' cognitive representations of illness and subsequent behaviour, using the self-regulation model (Leventhal et al., 1997) as a theoretical framework. Marteau and colleagues have carried out a programme of research on genetic testing for familial hypercholesterolaemia (FH) in individuals at increased risk of coronary heart disease due to a family history, exploring how they make sense of their risk and the impact of causal beliefs on motivation to engage in risk-reducing behaviours. Of particular concern is the possibility that genetic causal attributions may lead to a sense of fatalism, which then reduces motivation to change behaviour (Senior et al., 2002). However, in a randomised controlled trial of family history-based genetic testing for FH, Marteau et al. (2004) found that positive gene test results did not reduce people's overall perception of control but did alter their perceptions of how control could be best achieved, i.e. through biological (cholesterol-lowering medication) rather than behavioural (adopting a low-fat diet) strategies. Subsequent studies lend further support to the idea that genetic testing for preventable diseases reinforces genetic causal models of coronary heart disease and the perceived effectiveness of biological vs. behavioural methods (Senior et al., 2004). This is of concern if behavioural methods are at least as effective as biological methods. On the whole, individuals at increased risk are already likely to be engaging in behavioural strategies for coping with an increased risk, having had time to regulate their emotional and cognitive representations of the threat associated with having a family history (Senior & Marteau, 2007). However, population-based genetic testing may engender fatalism and reduce motivation to change behaviours in people without a family history who have previously been unaware of their risk. This effect has been observed in community-based studies of smokers given information about their genetic susceptibility to lung cancer (Audrain et al., 1997; Lerman et al., 1997).

Other studies have examined inaccuracies in the understanding of screening results and the impact on subsequent behaviours. In a three-year study of population-based cystic fibrosis carrier screening, Axworthy *et al.* (1996) found poor long-term recall of the test result and its significance. Women given a 'low' risk result of genetic assessment for breast/ovarian cancer have also been found to have an inaccurate understanding of their risk, which may partly explain their failure to be reassured by this information (Fry *et al.*, 2003). Such misunderstanding may lead to continued desire for unnecessary tests or surveillance as a means of seeking reassurance. For example, Michie *et al.* (1996) found that individuals given a low-risk result of gene testing for familial adenomatous polyposis still wanted regular bowel screening, even though this favourable result negated the need for regular screening. Unrealistic expectations of continued access to screening were predicted by doubts about the accuracy of the test as well as high levels of worry about developing bowel cancer (Michie *et al.*, 2002). In general population screening, high anxiety or worry seems to have the opposite effect in discouraging people from re-attending future screening appointments. For example, Brett and Austoker (2001) found that the anxiety generated by a false-positive mammogram result decreased attendance at subsequent appointments in routine breast screening, perhaps reflecting avoidance of screening due to fear of finding breast cancer. Similarly in cervical screening, heightened anxiety in response to an inadequate smear test may lead women to avoid attending for a repeat smear within the recommended three months (French *et al.*, 2004). Such studies highlight the negative behavioural consequences of screening. It remains to be seen whether any positive emotional consequences of screening translate into the adoption of healthy lifestyle behaviours such as smoking cessation, alcohol reduction and dietary improvement.

Factors Moderating the Impact of Screening

While most people cope well with the screening process, there are subgroups of people who may be more susceptible to adverse effects of screening.

A range of factors has been shown to moderate the psychological impact of both general population screening and family history screening/testing, including the screening encounter itself and characteristics of the individual being screened.

In a longitudinal study of women recalled for further investigations in routine breast screening, Brett and Austoker (2001) found that aspects of the screening process predicted negative emotional outcomes, including dissatisfaction with the information given, longer waiting time between the recall letter and recall appointment and having had a false-positive result in the past. Experiencing pain and fear during previous routine mammogram appointments (Drossaert *et al.*, 2002) and longer delays in receiving unfavourable cervical screening results (Wardle *et al.*, 1995) have also been associated with greater distress. The communication skills of health-care professionals can be an important factor influencing people's emotional responses to screening: for example, inadequate information and counselling during routine antenatal screening has been linked to distress and anxiety in pregnant women (Smith *et al.*, 1994). In women who received an inconclusive smear test result, residual concern at three months follow-up was strongly predicted by dissatisfaction with information, in spite of a subsequent normal result (French *et al.*, 2006). Maissi *et al.*'s (2004) study of women who received borderline results of HPV smear testing found that high levels of anxiety were associated with lower understanding of the meaning of test results. This underlines the importance of providing accurate, clear information conveyed in a sensitive manner at all stages of the screening process.

Demographic and psychological characteristics of the individual also moderate the impact of screening. Younger age has been shown to predict negative responses to both breast screening in the general population (Lindfors *et al.*, 2001) and cancer genetic risk assessment and testing in those with a family history (Brain *et al.*, 2000; Lodder *et al.*, 1999). Individuals with less formal education (Loken *et al.*, 1998; Meystre-Agustoni *et al.*, 2001) and from a lower socioeconomic background (Olsson *et al.*, 1999) also tend to be more prone to negative reactions to routine breast screening and to genetic testing for colorectal cancer (Vernon *et al.*, 1997). However, the psychological attributes that people bring with them to the screening encounter are the most powerful influence in shaping their responses to screening. Both general population and family history studies indicate that pre-existing anxiety and worry is the strongest predictor of anxiety following screening, regardless of the actual screening result (e.g. Brain *et al.*, 2008; Broadstock *et al.*, 2000; Meystre-Agustoni *et al.*, 2001). Individual differences in personality have also been shown to predict adaptation to screening. For example, O'Neill *et al.* (2006) found that women with low tolerance for uncertainty reported increased distress in response to uninformative results of testing for the BRCA1/2 gene mutation. A monitoring coping style has been shown to predict increased distress in response to abnormal ovarian screening results, both in women with and without a family history of ovarian cancer (Wardle *et al.*, 1993; Wardle *et al.*, 1994). Low dispositional optimism is a risk factor for adverse reactions to breast cancer risk information (Norman & Brain, 2007) and abnormal ovarian screening results (Andrykowski *et al.*, 2004), as well as distress during the period of waiting for genetic test results (Lodder *et al.*, 1999). On the other hand, Tibben *et al.* (1993) found that people with overly optimistic situation-specific expectations of the outcome of genetic testing for Huntington's disease were more likely to be distressed after an unfavourable result of testing. As explored earlier in the chapter, adverse emotional reactions to screening can be predicted by a mismatch between people's expectations or perceptions of their risk and the actual screening outcome. People's prior cognitive representations also predict the behavioural impact of genetic risk information, with genetic information having a greater impact on individuals whose pre-existing causal beliefs are primarily genetic rather than behavioural or environmental (Marteau & Weinman, 2006). In Michie *et al.*'s (2003) study of FAP genetic testing, negative test results were perceived as more accurate in those whose illness representations included genes as the single cause, whereas individuals whose representations were multi-causal received the result with less certainty and less reassurance.

Commercial Genetic Screening

The mapping of the human genome presents a challenge to accepted definitions and principles of screening (Andermann *et al.*, 2008). In recent years there has been a proliferation of commercial genetic tests to identify those in the general population who may be 'genetically at risk' for common multifactorial diseases such as cancer, diabetes and coronary heart disease, offered by companies such as 23andMe (i.e. 23 chromosomes). These 'direct-to-consumer' genetic tests contravene the basic principles of screening outlined earlier in the chapter, one of which is that screening should only take place within a context of regulation and an awareness of its limitations. According to Lenzer and Brownlee (2008), such tests are unlikely to provide clinically useful or definitive information, yielding a high rate of false-positive results and an array of further tests and investigations that do more harm than good. The gold standard for genetic testing is that it takes place within a formal and well-evaluated counselling protocol designed to facilitate informed choices, interpret test results and minimise adverse psychological consequences (Harper & Clarke, 1997). Indeed, the good psychological outcomes of genetic testing are partly explained by the provision of in-depth counselling protocols which aim to prepare people for possible psychological consequences of their decision (Broadstock *et al.*, 2000). Adverse consequences are more likely if individuals are not given balanced information about the possible benefits and harms of their screening choice, including the likelihood of receiving false-positive results. As we have seen in research on the emotional, cognitive and behavioural consequences of screening, mass genetic screening may lead to increased worry, reduced perceptions of control and reduced motivation to engage in health behaviours such as healthy lifestyle and ongoing surveillance in people who are unprepared for and unaware of their risk. If molecular genetics technology is applied to the general population through commercial genetic susceptibility screening, adequate preparation regarding the possible consequences of testing will be even more necessary given their lack of personal experience and awareness of risk, combined with unrealistic expectations about what such tests can achieve. Adequate information and support should be a prerequisite to such testing, particularly for vulnerable individuals who may be most susceptible to any ill-effects.

Marteau and Weinman (2006) highlight the importance of trying to achieve goodness-of-fit between individuals' pre-existing cognitive representations of illness and the information given, though it is not clear how complex risk information based on interactions between multiple genetic and environmental factors would be communicated in a commercial screening context. The Prostate Cancer Risk Management Programme for individuals who seek PSA testing is an example of an unproven screening test only being available in the context of balanced information and follow-up care.

Summary

In recent years, widespread enthusiasm for screening has been replaced by a more measured appraisal of its potential for psychological harm. Studies of screening in the general population highlight in particular the negative impact of false-positive, abnormal and inconclusive test results. This underlines the importance of offering and carrying out screening tests within a framework of careful preparation and support to minimise negative psychological consequences. There is growing evidence for psychological benefits of screening and genetic testing in high-risk groups such as individuals with a strong family history of cancer. This reflects the higher level of psychological preparation and awareness in individuals at increased risk, partly due to their experiences of living 'at risk' and partly due to the safety net of supportive care that they receive through being part of a family history screening and testing programme. In both general population and

family history contexts, however, people's prior expectations, beliefs and personality have a powerful moderating effect on their psychological responses to screening. Vulnerable individuals, such as those with high pre-existing anxiety, unrealistic expectations and a need for certainty, may require extra support and preparation.

The 21st century is witnessing a further paradigm shift away from a traditional biomedical model of detecting illness at an asymptomatic stage (secondary prevention), towards a psychological model of preventing illness through behaviour change strategies such as stopping smoking, healthy diet and exercise (primary prevention). There has also been an increase in health-related information available through the media and internet and access by the general public to screening in the form of over-the-counter home-testing kits. In the future, commercial screening tests may be used to identify those in the general population who are 'genetically at risk' and target them for lifestyle modifications. However, care must be taken that this latest paradigm shift towards individual responsibility is not a step too far. Information for its own sake may do more harm than good if there are no safeguards in place to help people prepare for the potential negative consequences of screening, particularly for vulnerable individuals. The highly patient-centred care that is available through family history-based screening programmes will not be available to the public on a large commercial scale. The challenge for health psychology will be to help ameliorate the psychological consequences of commercial genetic susceptibility screening by developing interventions that help people to make informed and empowered lifestyle choices.

Discussion Points

1   Should screening (secondary prevention) be abandoned in favour of efforts to change health behaviours (primary prevention)? To what extent would this empower individuals to take responsibility for their own health or stigmatise those who do not adopt a healthy lifestyle?
2   If people are highly reassured by being part of an organised screening programme, should it be imple-

mented without evidence of clinical effectiveness? What might be the psychological consequences of discontinuing screening in this situation?
3   What type of information and support could be available to help people who are considering commercial genetic screening, particularly for common multifactorial conditions such as heart disease and cancer?

Further Reading

An interesting overview of the issues surrounding commercial genetic screening is given by Lenzer, J. & Brownlee, S. (2008). Knowing me, knowing you. *British Medical Journal, 336*, 858–860.

For a challenging and critical perspective on screening, read Kaplan, R.M. (2000). Two pathways to prevention. *American Psychologist, 55*(4), 382–396.

References

Andermann, A., Blancquaert, I., Beauchamp, S. & Déry, V. (2008). Revisiting Wilson and Jungner in the genomic age: A review of screening criteria over the past 40 years. *Bulletin of the World Health Organization, 86*, 241–320.

Anderson, M.R., Drescher, C.W., Zheng, Y.Y., Bowen, D.J. & Wilson, S. (2007). Changes in cancer worry associated with participation in ovarian cancer screening. *Psycho-Oncology, 16*, 814–820.

Andrykowski, M.A., Boerner, L.M., Salsman, J.M. & Pavlik, E. (2004). Psychological response to test results in an ovarian cancer screening program: A prospective, longitudinal study. *Journal of Health Psychology, 23*, 622–630.

Audrain, J., Boyd, N.R., Roth, J., Main, D., Caporaso, N.E. & Lerman, C. (1997). Genetic susceptibility testing in smoking-cessation treatment: One-year outcomes of a randomized trial. *Addictive Behaviours, 22*, 741–751.

Axworthy, D., Brock, D.J.H., Bobrow, M. & Marteau, T.M. (1996). Psychological impact of population-based carrier testing for cystic fibrosis: 3-year follow-up. *Lancet, 347*, 1443–1446.

Bish, A., Sutton, S., Jacobs, C., Levene, S., Ramirez, A. & Hodgson, S. (2002). Changes in psychological distress after cancer genetic counselling: A comparison of affected and unaffected women. *British Journal of Cancer, 86*, 43–50.

Brain, K., Gray, J., Norman, P., Parsons, E., Clarke, A., Rogers, C. et al. (2000). Why do women attend familial breast cancer clinics? *Journal of Medical Genetics, 37*, 197–202.

Brain, K., Henderson, B., Tyndel, S., Bankhead, C., Watson, E., Clements, A. & Austoker, J. (2008). Predictors of breast cancer related distress following mammographic screening in younger women on a family history breast screening programme. *Psycho-Oncology, 17*, 1180–1188.

Braithwaite, D., Emery, J., Walter, F., Prevost, A.T. & Sutton, S. (2004). Psychological impact of genetic counselling for familial cancer: a systematic review and meta-analysis. *Journal of the National Cancer Institute, 96*, 122–133.

Brett, J. & Austoker, J. (2001). Women who are recalled for further investigation for breast screening: psychological consequences 3 years after recall and factors influencing re-attendance. *Journal of Public Health Medicine, 23*, 292–300.

Brett, J., Austoker, J., Ong, G. (1998). Do women who undergo further investigation for breast screening suffer adverse psychological consequences? A multi-centre follow-up study comparing different breast screening result groups five months after their last breast screening appointment. *Journal of Public Health Medicine, 204*, 396–403.

Brett, J., Bankhead, C., Henderson, B., Watson, E. & Austoker, J. (2005). The psychological impact of mammographic screening. A systematic review. *Psycho-Oncology, 14*, 917–938.

Broadstock, M., Michie, S. & Marteau, M. (2000). Psychological consequences of predictive genetic testing: A systematic review. *European Journal of Human Genetics, 8*, 731–738.

Clements, A., Henderson, B.J., Tyndel, S., Evans, G., Brain, K, Austoker, J. & Watson, E. (2008). Diagnosed with breast cancer while on a family history screening programme: An exploratory qualitative study. *European Journal of Cancer Care, 17*, 245–252.

Drossaert, C.H., Boer, H., Seydel, E.R. (2002). Monitoring women's experiences during three rounds of breast cancer screening: Results from a longitudinal study. *Journal of Medical Screening, 9*, 168–175.

Forrest Report. (1987). *Breast Cancer Screening*. Report to the Health Ministers of England, Wales, Scotland and Northern Ireland by a Working Group chaired by Sir Patrick Forrest. London: HMSO.

French, D.P., Maissi, E. & Marteau, T.M. (2004). Psychological costs of inadequate cervical smear test results. *British Journal of Cancer, 91*, 1887–1892.

French, D.P., Maissi, E. & Marteau, T.M. (2006). The psychological costs of inadequate cervical smear test results: Three-month follow-up. *Psycho-Oncology, 15*, 498–508.

Fry, A., Cull, A., Appleton, S., Rush, R., Holloway, J. & Gorman, D. (2003). A randomised controlled trial of breast cancer genetics services in South East Scotland: psychological impact. *British Journal of Cancer, 89*, 653–659.

Gilbert, F.J., Cordiner, C.M., Affleck, I.R., Hood, D.B., Mathieson, D. & Walker, L.G. (1998). Breast screening:

The psychological sequelae of false-positive recall in women with and without a family history of breast cancer. *European Journal of Cancer, 34*, 2010–2014.

Harper, P.S & Clarke, A.J. (1997). *Genetics, society and clinical practice.* Oxford: BIOS Scientific.

Holland, W.W. & Stewart, S. (2005). *Screening in disease prevention: What Works?* Oxford: Radcliffe.

Kauff, N.D., Hurley, K.E., Hensley, M.L., Robson, M.E., Lev, G., Goldfrank, D. *et al.* (2005). Ovarian carcinoma screening in women at intermediate risk. *Cancer, 104*, 314–320.

Lazarus, R.S. & Folkman, S. (1984). *Stress, appraisal and coping.* New York: Springer.

Lenzer, J. & Brownlee, S. (2008). Knowing me, knowing you. *British Medical Journal, 336*, 858–860.

Lerman, C., Miller, S.M., Scarborough, R., Hankani, P., Nolte, S. & Smith, D. (1991). Adverse psychologic consequences of positive cytologic cervical screening. *American Journal of Obstetrics & Gynecology, 165*, 658–662.

Lerman, C., Gold, K., Audrain, J., Lin T.H., Boyd, N.R., Orleans, C.T. *et al.* (1997). Incorporating biomarkers of exposure and genetic susceptibility into smoking cessation treatment: Effects on smoking-related cognitions, emotions and behavior change. *Journal of Health Psychology, 16*, 87–99.

Leventhal, H., Benyamini, Y., Brownlee, S., Diefenbach, M.A., Leventhal, E.A., Patrick-Miller, L. *et al.* (1997). Illness representations: theoretical foundations. In K.J. Petrie & J.A. Weinman (Eds.) *Perception of health and illness* (pp. 19–46). Amsterdam: Harwood Academic.

Lindfors, K.K., O'Connor, J. & Parker, R.A. (2002). False-positive screening mammograms: Effect of immediate versus later work-up on patient stress. *Radiology, 218*, 247–253.

Lodder, L.N., Frets, P., Trijsburg, R., Meijers-Heijboer, E., Klijn, J. & Duivenvoorden, H. (1999). Presymptomatic testing for BRCA1 and BRCA2: How distressing are the pre-test weeks? *Journal of Medical Genetics, 36*, 906–913.

Loken, K., Steine, S. & Laerum, E. (1998). Mammography: influence of departmental practice and women's characteristics on patient satisfaction. Comparison of six departments in Norway. *Quality in Health Care, 7*, 136–141.

Maissi, E., Marteau, T.M., Hankins, M., Moss, S., Legood, R. & Gray, A. (2004). Psychological effect of human papillomavirus testing in women with borderline or mildly dyskaryotic cervical smear test results: Cross-sectional questionnaire study. *British Medical Journal, 328,* 1293.

Marteau, T.M., Cook, R. & Kidd, J. (1992). The psychological effects of false-positive results in prenatal screening for fetal abnormality: a prospective study. *Prenatal Diagnosis, 12*, 205–214.

Marteau, T., Senior, V., Humphries, S.E., Bobrow, M., Cranston, T. & Crook, M.A. (2004). Psychological impact of genetic testing for familial hypercholesterolemia within a previously aware population: A randomized controlled trial. *American Journal of Medical Genetics, 128A*, 285–293.

Marteau, T.M. & Weinman, J. (2006). Self-regulation and the behavioural response to DNA risk information: A theoretical analysis and framework for future research. *Social Sciences & Medicine, 62*, 1360–1368.

McAllister, M. (2002). Predictive genetic testing and beyond: A theory of engagement. *Journal of Health Psychology, 7*, 491–508.

McCaffery, K., Waller, J., Forrest, S., Cadman, L., Szarewski, A. & Wardle, J. (2004). Testing positive for human papillomavirus in routine cervical screening: Examination of psychosocial impact. *British Journal of Obstetrics & Gynaecology, 111*, 1437–1443.

Meystre-Agustoni, G., Paccaud, F., Jeannin, A. & Dubois-Arber, F. (2001). Anxiety in a cohort of Swiss women participating in a mammographic screening programme. *Journal of Medical Screening, 8*, 213–219.

Michie, S., McDonald, V. & Marteau, T. (1996). Understanding responses to predictive genetic testing: A grounded theory approach. *Psychology & Health, 11*, 455–470.

Michie, S., Smith, J., Senior, V. & Marteau, T.M. (2003). Predictive genetic testing: Understanding why negative test results sometimes fail to reassure. *American Journal of Medical Genetics, 119A*, 340–347.

Michie, S., Weinman, J., Miller, J., Collins, V., Halliday, J. & Marteau, T.M. (2002). Predictive genetic testing: High risk expectations in the face of low risk information. *Journal of Behavioral Medicine, 25*, 33–50.

Miles, A., Wardle, J. & Atkin, W. (2003). Receiving a screen-detected diagnosis of cancer: The experience of participants in the UK flexible sigmoidoscopy trial. *Psycho-Oncology, 12*, 784–802.

NHS Cancer Screening Programmes. (2002). Prostate Cancer Risk Management Programme: An information pack for primary care. NHS Cancer Screening Programmes, Sheffield: www.nelc.org.uk.

Norman, P. & Brain, K. (2007). Optimism, perceived risk and breast cancer worries among women attending risk assessment clinics. *Journal of Psychosomatic Research, 63*, 247–254.

O'Neill, S.C., Demarco, T., Peshkin, B.N., Rogers, S., Rispoli, J., Brown, K. *et al.* (2006). Tolerance for uncertainty and perceived risk among women receiving uninformative BRCA 1/2 test results. *American Journal of Medical Genetics, 142C*, 251–259.

Olsson, P., Armelius, K., Nordahl, G., Lenner, P. & Westman, G. (1999). Women with false positive screening mammograms: How do they cope? *Journal of Medical Screening, 6,* 89–93.

Pernet, A.L., Wardle, J., Bourne, T.H., Whitehead, M.I., Campbell, S. & Collins, W.P. (1992). A qualitative evaluation of the experience of surgery after false positive results in screening for familial ovarian cancer. *Psycho-Oncology, 1,* 217–233.

Rijnsburger, A.J., Essink-Bot, M.L., van Dooren, S., Borsboom, G.J.J.M., Seynaeve, C., Bartels, C.C.M. *et al.* (2004). Impact of screening for breast cancer in high-risk women on health-related quality of life. *British Journal of Cancer, 91,* 69–76.

Schwartz, M.D., Peshkin, B.N., Hughes, C., Main, D., Isaacs, C. & Lerman, C. (2002). Impact of BRCA1/BRCA2 mutation testing on psychologic distress in a clinic-based sample. *Journal of Clinical Oncology, 15,* 514–520.

Senior, V., Smith, J.A., Michie, S. & Marteau, T.M. (2002). Making sense of risk: an interpretive phenomenological analysis of vulnerability to heart disease. *Journal of Health Psychology, 7,* 157–168.

Senior, V., Marteau, T.M., Weinman, J. On behalf of the Genetic Risk Assessment for FH Trial (GRAFT) Study Group. (2004). Self-reported adherence to cholesterol-lowering medication in patients with familial hypercholesterolaemia: The role of illness perceptions. *Cardiovascular Drugs and Therapy, 18,* 475–481.

Senior, V. & Marteau, T.M. (2007). Causal attributions for raised cholesterol and perceptions of effective risk-reduction: Self-regulation strategies for an increased risk of coronary heart disease. *Psychology & Health, 22,* 699–717.

Smith, D.K., Shaw, R.W. & Marteau, T.M. (1994). Informed consent to undergo serum screening for Down's syndrome: The gap between policy and practice. *British Medical Journal, 309,* 776.

Sutton, S., Saidi, G., Bickler, G. & Hunter, J. (1995). Does routine screening for breast cancer raise anxiety? Results from a three wave prospective study in England. *Journal of Epidemiology & Community Health, 49,* 413–418.

Tibben, A., Frets, P.G., van de Kamp, J.J., Niermeijer, M.F., Vegter-van der Vlis, M., Roos, R.A. *et al.* (1993). Presymptomatic DNA-testing for Huntington's disease: Pretest attitudes and expectations of applicants and their partners in the Dutch program. *American Journal of Medical Genetics, 48,* 10–16.

Tyndel. S., Henderson, B., Austoker, J., Brain, K., Bankhead, C., Clements, A. & Watson, E. (2007). What is the psychological impact of mammographic screening on younger women with a family history of breast cancer? Findings from a prospective cohort study by the PIMMS management group. *Journal of Clinical Oncology, 25,* 3823–3830.

Vernon, S.W., Perz, C.A., Gritz, E.R., Peterson, S.K., Amos, C.I., Baile, W.F. & Lynch, P.M. (1997). Correlates of psychologic distress in colorectal cancer patients undergoing genetic testing for hereditary colon cancer. *Journal of Health Psychology, 16,* 73–86.

Wardle, J., Collins, W., Pernet, A., Whitehead, M.I., Bourne, T.H. & Campbell, S. (1993). Psychological impact of screening for familial ovarian cancer. *Journal of National Cancer Institute, 85,* 653–657.

Wardle, J., Pernet, A., Collins, W. & Bourne, T. (1994). False positive results in ovarian cancer screening: One year follow-up of psychological status. *Psychology & Health, 10,* 33–40.

Wardle, J., Pernet, A. & Stephens, D. (1995). Psychological consequences of positive results in cervical cancer screening. *Psychology & Health, 10,* 185–194.

Wardle, J., Williamson, S., Sutton, S., Biran, A., McCaffery, K., Cuzick, J. & Atkin, W. (2003). Psychological impact of colorectal cancer screening. *Health Psychology, 22,* 54–59.

Watson, M., Lloyd, S., Davidson, J., Meyer, L., Eeles, R., Ebbs, S. & Murday, V. (1999). The impact of genetic counselling on risk perception and mental health in women with a family history of breast cancer. *British Journal of Cancer, 79,* 868–874.

Wilson, J.M.G. & Jungner, G. (1968). *Principles and practice of screening for disease.* Geneva: Word Health Organization.

18

Hospitalisation and Stressful Medical Procedures

Kim G. Smolderen and Ad Vingerhoets

Chapter Outline

Hospitalisation and undergoing medical procedures have the potential to induce strong ambivalent feelings in patients. On the one hand, relief from their physical discomfort and an increase of their quality of life in the long run may be expected, while, on the other hand, the more immediate prospect is less pleasurable. Being hospitalised or being subjected to medical interventions can elicit feelings of distress and is often associated with separation from significant others, loss of control, anxiety and pain. What exactly makes hospitalisation and medical procedures aversive? And what can be done to make patients feel more comfortable and to help them to cope better with such interventions? Finally, are there psychological interventions which are cost-effective and have beneficial effects on both subjective well-being and more objective clinical outcomes? This chapter provides an overview of the literature describing the impact of hospitalisation and medical procedures on adults and children. In addition, recent developments in the preparation of patients for stressful medical procedures and interventions that can alleviate patients' distress levels during their hospital stay will be discussed.

Key Concepts

Adult care
Anxiety
Hospitalisation
Medical procedures
Paediatric care
Stress
Stress reduction
Surgical preparation

Hospitalisation

Although hospitalisation in itself can greatly disrupt patients' lives and daily activities, its impact has not frequently been examined from a patient's perspective. Most studies evaluating the effects of adult hospitalisation heretofore focused on painful medical procedures and critical illness, whereas in paediatric care there has also been more interest in the experience of being hospitalised as a stressful event on its own. Frequently reported hospital stressors, across patient populations, include aspects of the physical hospital environment (e.g. having to sleep in a strange bed, having machines around) (Ahmadi, 1985; Koenig *et al.*, 1995; White & Ritchie, 1984), being separated from one's familiar environment or worries about one's family (van Servellen *et al.*, 1990; White & Ritchie, 1984) and lack of control as well as loss of autonomy (Koenig *et al.*, 1995). Finally, communication difficulties in the staff–patient interaction are often indicated as another major source of distress (Koenig *et al.*, 1995; White & Ritchie, 1984). Patients additionally often report a lack of clear, understandable information about procedures, diagnosis, and prognosis, leaving them with many uncertainties about their stay, the treatments they have to undergo and the implications for their further life (Koenig *et al.*, 1995).

Most hospital stressors identified in adult patient care also apply to paediatric clinical care, but studies in this specific area also have identified some additional features that require special attention. Hospitalisation of children increases both children's and caregivers' levels of anxiety and these increased levels of distress may, in different ways, extend well into the post-discharge period (Leidy *et al.*, 2005). For example, preoperative anxiety in particular can act as a possible barrier for postoperative recovery; high levels of anxiety before surgery, for example, are associated with negative behavioural changes (McCann & Kain, 2001). In addition, research among adults has shown that high presurgical levels of anxiety stimulate the release of stress hormones, such as cortisol and adrenalin, which may prevent quick postoperative recovery (Kiecolt-Glaser *et al.*, 1998).

Repeated and long-lasting hospitalisations, in particular in the case of serious disease, may be experienced as a traumatic experience and can interfere considerably with normal cognitive and socioemotional development. Adequate care for these children requires interventions at different levels of the hospital organisation, with involvement of the child, the parents, the family and hospital staff. Making health-care providers more aware of the possible damaging effects of hospitalisation and chronic illness on the child's development is a first and necessary step in this process. Last but not least, adequate attention should be given to palliative care in children, as well as separation anxiety and homesickness, which are significant sources of distress for both the hospitalised child and its caregivers (Thurber & Walton, 2007).

Challenges that come into play when patients are confronted with an illness, injury, hospitalisation or a burdensome medical procedure can be summarised by the 'crisis theory' of physical illness formulated by Moos and Schaefer (1984). These challenges may represent a turning point in an individual's life and may be associated with changes in identity, in environment, in role, in social support, and in prospects for the future. In addition, the crisis nature of illness may be exacerbated by factors that are often specific to illness such as lack of information on the precise nature of the illness and uncertainty about its course. How individuals cope with these various aspects is determined by the cognitive appraisal of the situation. The patient evaluates the seriousness, significance and consequences of the condition. Factors like social support, prior knowledge or experience and illness representations may influence this appraisal process. Patients will need to handle various disease-specific tasks, such as: (i) dealing with pain, incapacitation and other symptoms; (ii) dealing with the hospital environment and special treatment procedures; and (iii) developing and maintaining adequate relationships with health-care staff, as well as general tasks, including preserving a reasonable emotional balance, preserving a satisfactory self-image and maintaining a sense of competence and mastery, sustaining relationships with family and friends and preparing for an uncertain future (Figure 18.1). How patients deal with these challenges will affect a broad range of outcomes: psychological outcomes (e.g. depressive symptoms, anxiety, post-traumatic stress symptoms), health status and quality of life, illness-specific outcomes (e.g. recovery, rehabilitation process

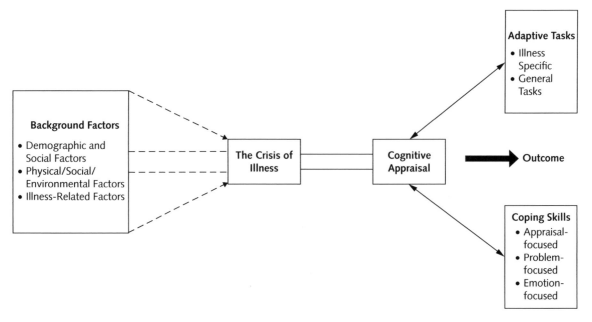

Figure 18.1 Crisis theory of physical illness
Source: Adapted from Ogden, J. (2000). *Health psychology: A textbook* (2nd edn, p.58). Buckingham: Open University Press.

and utilisation of health resources and costs (e.g. longer hospital length of stay, complications).

Stressful Medical Procedures

Apart from the experience of being hospitalised, patients have to cope with uncomfortable, sometimes painful medical procedures. We briefly discuss a selection of potentially stressful medical procedures and highlight patient groups that have to deal with them on a regular basis. This overview is not exhaustive, but provides merely examples of treatment, which are frequently addressed in literature. Some medical interventions (e.g. vaccinations, venipuncture, (minor) surgery or catheter insertion) concern large groups of patients, because of the very nature of the procedure, but the interventions may also be limited to specific patient groups (e.g. bone marrow aspirations or chemotherapy for oncology patients). Occasionally, a medical procedure may be very distressing for special groups such as children, or patients suffering from a specific phobia (e.g. claustrophobia, blood phobia or needle phobia).

Below we provide some examples of frequently applied medical procedures and interventions, which may cause distress and pain.

Diagnostic procedures

A well-known example of a diagnostic medical examination that may induce anxiety in patients is upper gastrointestinal endoscopy. This procedure implies the insertion of a tube or a scope through one's mouth in order to examine the oesophagus, stomach and duodenum to detect gastrointestinal and digestive disorders and pathology. There is substantial variation among clinicians whether or not patients are being sedated intravenously and it is not a standard procedure to administer local anaesthetics in the throat. Therefore, an adequate preparation procedure addressing all possible patient concerns will be indispensable in order to undergo this procedure with minimal pain and discomfort. Frequently reported concerns related to this procedure are: (i) sensory discomfort like pain, gagging that is invoked by inserting the scope and fear of needles; (ii) fear of discovering a malignancy; (iii) anxiety that is evoked by perceived incompetence or inconvenience (e.g. not enough sedation or insufficient knowledge of the procedure); and (iv) general concerns (e.g. fear of doctors, concerns about others watching the procedure) (Drossman et al., 1996).

Another frequently applied stressful diagnostic procedure that often evokes anxiety is magnetic resonance imaging (MRI). MRI is a non-invasive scanning method that provides detailed anatomical imaging information and can be used across a broad range of disorders (e.g. neurology, orthopaedics, internal medicine) (Bolejko et al., 2008). This procedure can be very demanding for some patients, who must lie down and stay immobile in a narrow tunnel during 20 to 90 minutes. Although the procedure in itself is painless, the noise and limited space are experienced as burdensome by a substantial number of patients. In fact, severe feelings of anxiety and claustrophobia are experienced by approximately one-third of patients and occasionally the procedure needs to be stopped prematurely or patients will not show up for the examination because of anticipatory anxiety (Bolejko et al., 2008; Katz et al., 1994; McIsaac et al., 1998; Melendez & McCrank, 1993).

Oncology

Among the most stressful treatments for cancer is chemotherapy, an intense and cyclic treatment with many dramatic side effects (e.g. hair loss, nausea, vomiting, diarrhoea, neuropathies). The long periods of treatment, repeated hospitalisations and serious side effects may cause a lot of distress. Sometimes, one-trial conditioning takes place, implying that side effects such as nausea and emesis occur even at the mere sight of the hospital or health-care provider ('anticipatory nausea') (Pandey et al., 2006). Although a lot of efforts are undertaken to minimise the burden associated with chemotherapy treatment, recent evidence shows that medical staff often fails to pay adequate attention to the concerns and worries of patients undergoing chemotherapy (Farrell et al., 2005; Mulders et al., 2008). The nature of these concerns may be related to specific aspects of their illness and treatment (e.g. hair loss) (Mols et al., 2009), future perspectives, inability to perform work or household activities, hobbies and family. Furthermore, environmental and organisational influences, like waiting

times and being confronted with the suffering of fellow patients, determine patients' experiences.

Patients undergoing chemotherapy in a day hospital labelled maintaining a sense of normality and absence of the sick role as positive aspects of being treated in day care, whereas negative associations concerned the dehumanising, factory-like system (McIlfatrick et al., 2007). Addressing these concerns in an integrated care setting, both directed at biomedical and psychosocial factors will be mandatory, because failure to do so may result in later development of psychological morbidity, such as anxiety and depression.

Another therapeutic modality that is offered frequently to both adult and young oncology patients is bone marrow transplantation (BMT). BMT is a relatively new medical procedure to treat several life-threatening conditions like leukaemia, aplastic anaemia, lymphomas, multiple myeloma, immune deficiency disorders and some cases of solid tumours. Although most studies have focused on long-term adjustment after BMT, stressors related to hospitalisation (i.e. lack of information provided by medical staff, family-related stress, side effects) are considered as most serious by patients even several years following treatment (Heinonen et al., 2005). In fact, a recent longitudinal study on the adaptation to the stress of BMT underscored the impact of the initial hospitalisation period as being the most stressful for the transplant patient (Fife et al., 2000). This period is characterised by intensive therapy, isolation, relative inactivity, and uncertainty regarding the outcome.

Gynaecology

Women who undergo in vitro fertilisation (IVF) treatment also deserve special attention; IVF is a taxing procedure requiring women to follow a strict regimen of hormone treatments and to schedule their sexual intercourse as a function of the treatment. Repeated failure of IVF treatment is especially burdensome and may cause feelings of distress that increase along with the number of treatment cycles. Type of IVF treatment strategy may be particularly important for psychological outcomes following treatment failure in women. Although standard IVF treatment, including double embryo transfer, increases the chance of being pregnant, failure of treatment following less aggressive strategies like mild ovarian stimulation and single embryo transfer seems to result in fewer short-term symptoms of depression as compared with failure after a standard treatment strategy (de Klerk et al., 2007).

In some cases, it is even not a strict medical procedure that arouses distress. A minority of women may suffer from extreme fear of childbirth, which can be so intense that it prevents them from becoming pregnant, despite desperately wanting a baby (Bewley & Cockburn, 2002). But also, once pregnant, these women can suffer from a wide variety of fears, like the fear that they will die during delivery or that they will do harm to their child (Fava et al., 1990). Additionally, some women will actively seek out an obstetrician who will perform an elective caesarean section before deciding to become pregnant for the first time (Bewley & Cockburn, 2002; Hofberg & Ward, 2003). In addition, the extreme fear of childbirth may increase the risk of experiencing the delivery as traumatic, resulting in the development of post-natal post-traumatic stress disorder (PTSD). PTSD as a consequence of childbirth, in its turn, may have many possible wide-ranging effects on the well-being of the women and the bonds with their babies (Ayers et al., 2006; Nicholls & Ayers, 2007).

Critical care unit

A group of patients who require special consideration are those admitted to an intensive care unit (ICU). Referral to an ICU generally implies critical or life-threatening conditions and as such, the mere admission to an ICU, can be considered as a stressful life event (van de Leur et al., 2004). Apart from patients' condition, the ICU stay itself can be taxing. Patients' unpleasant recollections are all related to feelings of discomfort during the ICU hospitalisation: anxiety, pain, thirst, sleeplessness, disorientation, shortness of breath, inability to move, painful medical interventions and the presence of an endotracheal tube are examples of factors that may contribute to the high levels of discomfort of these patients (Granja et al., 2005; van de Leur et al., 2004). Patients who do not have factual recollections of their ICU stay, but report amnesia for the early period of critical illness, may be particularly at risk of developing PTSD symptoms

post-ICU stay (Granja et al., 2008). In fact, a recent review (Davydow et al., 2008) points out that one out of five ICU survivors develops a PTSD. Consistent predictors of post-ICU PTSD include pre-ICU psychopathology, greater ICU benzodiazepine administration and frightening and/or psychotic experiences. Other predictors include female sex and younger age, whereas severity of critical illness does not consistently predict PTSD incidence. Needless to say, that the development of PTSD, will impact ICU survivors' subsequent quality of life.

Reducing Stress in Hospitalised Patients

Adult care

A wide variety of psychological interventions are available to help patients coping with stressful medical procedures (see Table 18.1). Several of them have been shown to be effective across a range of health outcomes, ranging from patient satisfaction, levels of anxiety and distress, to pain reduction, decreased use of medication, and reduced hospital stay (Devine & Cook, 1986; Hathaway, 1986; Johnston & Vögele, 1993). Unfortunately, the relative effect of the different strategies is difficult to determine, because of the fact that very often treatment 'packages' are offered in which different strategies are combined. Such an approach does not allow an evaluation of the effectiveness of each of the specific components. In addition, there is a wide variation in outcome measures. Therefore, evidence is often fragmentary and findings are not always replicated, which may be due to the small sample sizes and variations in the applied methods, settings, and research methodology. Below, we will address some of the most frequently applied interventions. These interventions can be categorised on the basis of the coping skills that are addressed when dealing with the challenges of a physical illness and its treatment as identified by the 'crisis theory' (Figure 18.1).

Appraisal-focused coping refers to attempts to understand the illness and searching for meaning. Examples of this type of coping include logical analysis or mental preparation. *Problem-focused coping* involves dealing with

Table 18.1 Frequently applied psychological interventions to help patients coping with the stress and pain associated with undergoing medical procedures

Cognitive interventions	
Cognitive distraction	Cognitive techniques to shift attention away from procedure (e.g. counting, non-procedural talk)
Imagery	Techniques to encourage the patient to cope with the pain/distress of the procedure by having them imagine a pleasant object or experience (e.g. sunny beach, enchanted forest)
Hypnosis	Dissociation from painful experience and distress via hypnotic induction, suggestions and imagined fantasy; similar to but more involved than imagery
Preparation/information	Explaining the steps of the procedures and/or providing sensory information associated with the procedure (e.g. providing instructions about what the procedure will involve)
Thought-stopping	The patient repeats 'stop' or a similar statement during times of distress/pain, to block out negative thoughts
Coping self-statements	The patient repeats a set of positive thoughts (e.g. 'I can do this'; 'This will be over soon')
Suggestion	Providing verbal or non-verbal cues to the patient suggesting that the administered intervention will or can reduce pain and/or distress
Memory change	Helping the patient to reframe negative memories of the procedure into positive ones
Parent training (specific for the paediatric setting)	Training the parent (not the patient) to engage in one of the above cognitive strategies. The goal is to decrease the parent's distress that in turn may decrease the patient's distress or pain, or both
Behavioural interventions	
Behavioural distraction	Behavioural techniques to shift attention away from procedure (e.g. videotapes, games, virtual reality)
Muscle relaxation	Tensing and relaxing various muscle groups of the body
Breathing exercises	Deep breathing or breathing from the diaphragm rather than the chest (e.g. using party blowers, blowing bubbles, pretending to inflate or deflate a tire through inhaling/exhaling)
Modelling	Demonstration of positive coping behaviours during a mock procedure by another patient
Rehearsal	Practice using positive coping behaviours demonstrated during modelling
Desensitisation	Gradual systematic exposure to the feared stimuli, generally involving a hierarchy of feared stimuli
Positive reinforcement	Providing positive statements and/or tangible rewards (e.g. toys) to the patient following the procedure
Parent training (specific for the paediatric setting)	Training the parent (not the patient) to engage in one of the above behavioural strategies
Combined cognitive behavioural therapy (CBT) definition	
Combined CBT	Any intervention using at least one of the above cognitive interventions in combination with at least one of the above behavioural interventions

Source: Adapted from Uman, L.S., Chambers, C.T., McGrath, P.J. & Kisely, S. (2008). A systematic review of randomized controlled trials examining psychological interventions for needle-related procedural pain and distress in children and adolescents: an abbreviated Cochrane review. *Journal of Pediatric Psychology, 33*(8), 842–854.

the problem and redefining or reconstructing it as manageable (e.g. learning specific procedures and behaviours during a diagnostic procedure). Finally, *emotion-focused coping* involves managing emotions and maintaining emotional equilibrium. Different types of emotion-focused coping can be discerned: affective coping refers to maintaining hope when dealing with a stressor; emotional discharge involves venting of feelings; and resigned acceptance refers to coming to terms with inevitable outcomes of an illness. (Figure 18.1)

Information, social support and skills training

Providing information, social support, skills training (behavioural, cognitive, relaxation techniques) are the most frequently applied and best-evaluated techniques. Procedural information includes objective information about the sequence of events, which procedures are carried out and why, the equipment used and the timing of experiences, while sensory information refers to the sensations that patients may experience before, during and following the procedure. Preparatory information and patient education specifically have the capacity to decrease anxiety levels in patients undergoing surgery (McDonald *et al.*, 2004) or diagnostic procedures (Galaal *et al.*, 2007).

Another information strategy, often used in paediatric care, is modelling. This implies the provision of information by patient models. Typically, a preparatory videotape is shown, depicting a specific patient (the model) undergoing the medical procedure. Modelling interventions, either alone or in combination with other preparatory strategies, may in particular have benefits for patients undergoing invasive medical procedures, during which patients are required to stay awake and focused (O'Halloran & Altmaier, 1995).

Evaluation studies among surgical patients reveal that most psychological interventions (giving procedural or sensational information, cognitive or behavioural coping strategies, relaxation, psychological support) have some benefit, but prior research was not always able to demonstrate consistent positive effects for all these different kinds of interventions on all outcome variables (O'Halloran & Altmaier, 1995). Nevertheless, it can be concluded that psychological adjuncts to increase patients' comfort levels may have promising potential. For example, an elegantly designed study among patients undergoing percuta-neous vascular and renal procedures, comparing intra-operatively standard care, structured attention, or self-hypnotic relaxation, demonstrated not only greater decreases in anxiety in the intervention groups compared with standard care, but also lower use of medication and significantly shorter procedure times (Lang *et al.*, 2000). In another randomised trial among coronary artery bypass graft surgery patients, a combination of an educational and supportive intervention was provided presurgery and outcomes were compared with patients receiving standard care (Arthur *et al.*, 2000). The presurgery intervention had beneficial effects on quality of life, but also on postoperative length of stay.

A final example concerns women with extreme fear of childbirth, whose intervention consisted of extensive psycho-education, combined with cognitive therapy. Moreover, an appointment with the midwife and visits to the obstetric ward were recommended to obtain more practical information about pain relief and possible interventions during labour and delivery. Written information was given at the first session regarding the pros and cons of vaginal delivery versus a caesarean delivery, as well as information about alternative modes of pain relief available in the hospital. The care as usual group received standard information and routine obstetric check-ups, as well as written information about the pros and cons of vaginal versus caesarean delivery and the pain relief that is offered routinely in the hospital. After intervention, in both groups 62 per cent of all of those originally requesting a caesarean delivery chose to deliver vaginally. In women delivering vaginally, however, labour lasted on average 1.7 hours shorter in the intensive intervention group than in the conventional group (Saisto *et al.*, 2001).

Patient control and optimising patients' comfort

Providing patients more control, while undergoing medical procedures, may have a positive effect on their well-being and distress. 'Patient-controlled analgesia' (PCA) is a relatively new technique currently routinely used as an analgesic strategy postsurgery. Patients can self-administer opioids intravenously by means of a specially designed programmable pump. Although patients receiving PCA tend to use somewhat higher doses of medication, occasionally resulting in a higher occurrence of side effects like itching, this procedure generally provides better pain control and increased patient satisfaction compared with conventional methods (Hudcova *et al.*, 2006).

In addition to the more established psychological interventions that can be applied with patients to help them to cope with the stress of hospitalisation and undergoing painful medical procedures, there are also attempts to alleviate distress and pain with alternative methods, such as music or virtual reality applications. In a recent systematic overview (Evans, 2002) the effectiveness of music as an intervention for hospital patients was examined. The author concluded that little or no effects on physiological outcome measures had been demonstrated, whereas anxiety, specifically during normal care delivery, not when undergoing procedures like bronchoscopy or sigmoidoscopy, was positively influenced. Likewise, virtual reality techniques have been proposed as a promising adjunct analgesic technique during medical procedures; offering visual, auditory and/or kinaesthetic distraction can tax patients' limited attention capacity, resulting in distraction and subsequent pain reduction (Wismeijer & Vingerhoets, 2005). The number of studies which have adequately evaluated the effectiveness of these alternative strategies is very limited, but given their relatively low costs and the lack of negative side effects, these strategies deserve further investigation as they may have great potential to be used as an adjunct to normal care practices.

Individual differences An issue that requires further attention is whether the effects of psychological interventions to help patients coping with stressful medical procedures may differ as a function of individual patient characteristics. Often evaluated is the distinction between 'monitors' and 'blunters'. Central concepts in this context are attention and avoidance. Patients who focus on the threatening situation or who seek information as a way of preparing for a threatening procedure are called monitors. In contrast, blunters tend to apply a coping style of avoidance and they are more open for distraction. It has been suggested that both groups cope better if the preparatory strategy is in accordance with their coping style, but the evidence is not consistent (van Vliet *et al.*, 2004). Preparatory strategies

have also been investigated as a function of gender, locus of control or patients' anxiety levels, but findings often could not be replicated (Schultheis *et al.*, 1987). Large studies using standardised measures and well-described interventions are a prerequisite to obtain more insight into this issue.

Paediatric care

Children are a special vulnerable group in the hospital setting, because their developmental stage and maturing cognitive skills may prevent them from understanding the necessity and objectives of hospitalisation and medical procedures. In addition, there is the threat of being separated from the parents. Not surprisingly, pain and anxiety are the major issues, which deserve the attention of researchers and clinicians. Since pain and anxiety are often interwoven, interventions specially designed for children address both aspects. Below, we will briefly discuss specific interventions that are most frequently being applied in current clinical care settings. Collectively, these strategies will require efforts both on: (i) an institutional level by organising quality-of-care initiatives creating an 'ouchless' environment for children (e.g. education programmes for hospital staff) and (ii) an individual level by stimulating close collaboration and optimising communication between physicians, staff and family (e.g. ask patient and family about perceptions of prognosis) (Pao *et al.*, 2007).

Information As with adult care, the provision of information about procedures to children can be offered as a tailor-made intervention, which can alleviate distress in unfamiliar situations because it increases the predictability and feelings of control. Also, in the case of children, it is important to make a clear distinction between procedural information, focusing on the details of the procedures to be applied and sensory information, addressing the experiences associated with the procedures. Providing this latter information is primarily aimed at reassuring the child that particular (painful) sensations are a normal part of the procedure and do not signal that there is something wrong. Also helpful are suggestions how to deal best with such negative experiences and discomfort: information about swallowing techniques, which position to take or how to breathe are examples of coping instructions that may be offered in the context of unpleasant medical procedures.

For younger children (2–7 years), it is recommended to combine verbal information with the use of pictures, cartoons or videos. For this group, emphasis should be in particular on the sensory information since this better fits their cognitive abilities. Trying to explain rather complex procedural issues may promote feelings of lack of control resulting in an increase rather than a decrease in distress (van Broeck, 1993).

Medical play may also be an alternative or adjunct to the provision of information to paediatric patients (Bolig et al., 1991). It is based on the notion that children's (mis)conceptions and unfamiliarity with the medical setting may be an important source of distress. Given the heterogeneity in approaches and intervention strategies (e.g. Is it a single episode or integrated with other activities?; Is the child forced to participate?), outcome studies evaluating the effects of medical play in children are needed to obtain adequate insight into which specific elements must be considered crucial to the intervention.

Modelling can be considered a more advanced way to provide information and to educate children about hospitalisation and painful medical procedures. There is some evidence that matching age and sex of the model with that of the patient is important; identification with the model is further facilitated when s/he expresses what and how s/he feels and thinks. It is also important to make clear that it is effortful for the model to deal with the threat. Alternatively, children may profit from social learning, such as when the child has the possibility to observe a fellow patient or live model undergoing the same procedure. In particular if the model is a child who has broad experience with the procedure and demonstrates that s/he can adequately deal with it, this may be very effective.

Skills training: behavioural strategies and regulation of emotions Being exposed to an aversive (pain) stimulus in a specific environment (hospital room) by a specific person (nurse or doctor in the white coats) may result in stimulus generalisation, which implies that the conditioned fear is extended to people in white coats and/or hospitals or hospital rooms in general. This generalisation can be prevented by pre-exposure, based on the learning principle of latent inhibition. In practice, this means that the child is exposed to the treatment room and the involved doctors and nurses under neutral conditions. Such neutral interaction and exposure is effective in decreasing the risk of the development of fast generalisation of fear responses.

In particular children who respond with increased distress and arousal to a wide variety of stimuli after a pain experience may profit from exposure to the same stimuli in a neutral or positive emotional context. This process can be stimulated by creating a play situation, in which the child fulfils the role of the physician, examining and treating their dolls or pets (Van Broeck, 1993). The interventions and medical procedures applied to their 'patients' are those the child is familiar with and, if possible, real medical materials are used, such as thermometers, empty medicine bottles, syringes (without needle) and bandages. In particular for children in the age range from four to nine, this kind of play contributes to a kind of 'natural' desensitisation. In systematic desensitisation, the child is exposed in a safe and controlled way to the object or situation of his fear. The most commonly used exposure therapy involves gradual encounters with the fear-producing object, first in the imagination and then in reality.

Play therapy can also be helpful for the child to come to terms with its painful experiences and it may stimulate the expression of the emotions, which might have been inhibited in the real situation. Not exceptionally, this kind of play is characterised by aggression and revenge, but also sadness, powerlessness, frustration, pity and tenderness. These feelings are a normal response and for the most part should be allowed and supported. It has been suggested that children who spontaneously start with this kind of play are better equipped to cope with stressful situations. Facilitating this behaviour by providing the necessary ingredients is therefore recommended. This therapeutic play can also be used in combination with modelling interventions. Although play therapy is currently widely used in hospitals, there is hardly any systematic research which has evaluated its effects.

In accordance with findings in adults, the application of hypnosis has also been reported as a successful strategy for children to reduce their distress during painful or frightening medical procedures. For example, children with urinary tract problems having to undergo a painful radiological procedure were randomly allocated to either a hypnosis condition or routine care (Butler *et al.*, 2005). Compared with usual care, more positive results of hypnosis were observed on four dimensions: (i) the parents of the children in the hypnosis condition indicated that the procedure was now less traumatic for their children than the previous procedures; (ii) observational data yielded less signs of distress in the hypnosis group; (iii) the medical staff reported fewer problems with the procedure in the hypnosis condition; and (iv) the total procedure time of the hypnosis group was significantly shorter. This study – performed in a naturalistic setting – thus demonstrated considerable positive effects of a non-invasive procedure with minimal risk, on both subjective and objective outcomes, having consequences both for quality of care and procedural costs. These favourable effects of hypnosis have recently been supported by a systematic review on psychological interventions for needle-related procedural pain; hypnosis was one of the strategies yielding the largest effect sizes for reducing pain and distress (Uman *et al.*, 2006).

Recent reviews further demonstrate that distraction is among the most promising techniques to reduce pain and distress. This may vary from simple counting aloud, blowing a party blower, playing with toys, to the use of multimedia including virtual reality, which is very promising even in the case of very painful wound-care procedures in burn patients (Blount *et al.*, 2006; Powers, 1999; Uman *et al.*, 2006, 2008; Wismeijer & Vingerhoets, 2005). Unless the parents are too emotional, which in turn may cause serious distress in the children, it is generally recommended to involve parents and to provide them with an active role as a model, or by stimulating them to provide information, or emotional support. Using parents as coaches to promote coping or to distract their children has been rather successful (Walker *et al.*, 2006).

Patient control and optimising comfort Since unpredictability and uncontrollability increase feelings of distress, one possibility to reduce distress is to increase control. This can be done by offering the child the opportunity to start and stop the procedure and to allow pauses. This procedure may be particularly useful for children older than eight with chronic diseases, who repeatedly have to undergo the same procedures (van Broeck, 1993).

In the case of babies, very young children or children with mental retardation, the possibilities for the use of verbal interventions or films and models are limited or non-existent. Close physical contact in these cases is prescribed. Rhythmic rocking, caressing and tenderly petting appear to have a calming effect and reduce distress. Holding hands is an act that even in adults may have a pain-reducing effect. In addition, it has been suggested to administer sucrose to babies in case of short-live procedural pain, like vaccinations.

Conclusion

The last few decades have shown a considerable increase in attention for how the patient – and in particular children – experience hospitalisation and medical procedures. A wide variety of psychological interventions has been developed to help patients to cope better with painful medical procedures. Very often, behavioural therapeutic principles form the basis of these interventions. Modelling, social learning, systematic desensitisation and distraction are, together with the provision of information, the most frequently applied interventions. Less frequently applied, but with promising results, is the application of hypnosis (Butler *et al.*, 2005; Lang *et al.*, 2000; Uman *et al.*, 2006).

As revealed by recent overviews (Blount *et al.*, 2006; Powers, 1999; Uman *et al.*, 2006, 2008), well-designed evaluation studies focusing on the effects of interventions on different outcome measures are very limited in number. In addition, very often 'treatment packages' are offered, which prove to be rather effective, but also prevent the disentanglement of the effects of its individual components. Occasionally, psychological and medical interventions (e.g. pharmacological) are combined.

Outcome variables may vary considerably among studies, ranging from self-reported pain to the use of medication and duration of the medical procedure. An important question is whether the adequate use of psychological interventions may not only contribute significantly to the well-being of hospitalised patients, but also may have positive clinically and/or economically relevant effects. Especially in times when cost-effectiveness issues are critical, expensive and time-consuming treatment packages should – if possible – be replaced by simpler methods if they render similar results. It is the challenge for medical psychologists to further examine and develop ways to prevent unnecessary pain and discomfort in hospitalised adults and children and in all those who have to undergo demanding medical procedures.

Discussion Points

1 How would you design a randomised controlled trial to demonstrate the effectiveness of hypnosis as an adjunct strategy for pain management for women in labour? How many treatment arms would you foresee in your protocol? Which outcome measures would you use to evaluate the intervention?
2 How can optimal preparation of patients undergoing surgery or other stressful medical procedures contribute to the reduction of health-care costs?
3 Parental stress during their child's hospitalisation may negatively affect the child's well-being. What strategies would you apply to prevent the increase of distress in the paediatric patient and how would you engage the parents in supporting the young patient?

Further Reading

Galaal, K.A., Deane, K., Sangal, S. & Lopes, A.D. (2007). Interventions for reducing anxiety in women undergoing colposcopy. *Cochrane Database of Systematic Reviews* (3), CD006013.

Smith, C.A., Collins, C.T., Cyna, A.M. & Crowther, C.A. (2006). Complementary and alternative therapies for pain management in labour. *Cochrane Database of Systematic Reviews* (4), CD003521.

Uman, L.S., Chambers, C.T., McGrath, P.J. & Kisely, S. (2008). A systematic review of randomized controlled trials examining psychological interventions for needle-related procedural pain and distress in children and adolescents: An abbreviated Cochrane review. *Journal of Pediatric Psychology, 33*(8), 842–854.

References

Ahmadi, K.S. (1985). The experience of being hospitalized: Stress, social support and satisfaction. *International Journal of Nursing Studies, 22*(2), 137–148.

Arthur, H.M., Daniels, C., McKelvie, R., Hirsh, J. & Rush, B. (2000). Effect of a preoperative intervention on preoperative and postoperative outcomes in low-risk patients awaiting elective coronary artery bypass graft surgery. A randomized, controlled trial. *Annals of Internal Medicine, 133*(4), 253–262.

Ayers, S., Eagle, A. & Waring, H. (2006). The effects of childbirth-related post-traumatic stress disorder on women and their relationships: A qualitative study. *Psychology, Health & Medicine, 11*(4), 389–398.

Bewley, S. & Cockburn, J. (2002). Responding to fear of childbirth. *Lancet, 359*(9324), 2128–2129.

Blount, R.L., Piira, T., Cohen, L.L. & Cheng, P. S. (2006). Pediatric procedural pain. *Behavior Modification, 30*(1), 24–49.

Bolejko, A., Sarvik, C., Hagell, P. & Brinck, A. (2008). Meeting patient information needs before magnetic resonance imaging: Development and evaluation of an information booklet. *Journal of Radiology Nursing, 27*(3), 96–102.

Bolig, R., Yolton, K.A. & Nissen, H.L. (1991). Medical play and preparation: Questions and issues. *Children's Health Care, 20*(4), 225–229.

Butler, L.D., Symons, B.K., Henderson, S.L., Shortliffe, L.D. & Spiegel, D. (2005). Hypnosis reduces distress and duration of an invasive medical procedure for children. *Pediatrics, 115*(1), e77–85.

Davydow, D.S., Gifford, J.M., Desai, S.V., Needham, D.M. & Bienvenu, O.J. (2008). Posttraumatic stress disorder in general intensive care unit survivors: A systematic review. *General Hospital Psychiatry, 30*(5), 421–434.

de Klerk, C., Macklon, N.S., Heijnen, E.M., Eijkemans, M.J., Fauser, B.C., Passchier, J. *et al.* (2007). The psychological impact of IVF failure after two or more cycles of IVF with a mild versus standard treatment strategy. *Human Reproduction, 22*(9), 2554–2558.

Devine, E.C. & Cook, T.D. (1986). Clinical and cost-saving effects of psychoeducational interventions with surgical patients: A meta-analysis. *Research in Nursing & Health, 9*(2), 89–105.

Drossman, D.A., Brandt, L.J., Sears, C., Li, Z., Nat, J. & Bozymski, E.M. (1996). A preliminary study of patients' concerns related to GI endoscopy. *American Journal of Gastroenterology, 91*(2), 287–291.

Evans, D. (2002). The effectiveness of music as an intervention for hospital patients: A systematic review. *Journal of Advanced Nursing, 37*(1), 8–18.

Farrell, C., Heaven, C., Beaver, K. & Maguire, P. (2005). Identifying the concerns of women undergoing chemotherapy. *Patient Education and Counseling, 56*(1), 72–77.

Fava, G.A., Grandi, S., Michelacci, L., Saviotti, F., Conti, S., Bovicelli, L. et al. (1990). Hypochondriacal fears and beliefs in pregnancy. *Acta Psychiatrica Scandinavica, 82*(1), 70–72.

Fife, B.L., Huster, G.A., Cornetta, K.G., Kennedy, V.N., Akard, L.P. & Broun, E.R. (2000). Longitudinal study of adaptation to the stress of bone marrow transplantation. *Journal of Clinical Oncology, 18*(7), 1539–1549.

Galaal, K.A., Deane, K., Sangal, S. & Lopes, A.D. (2007). Interventions for reducing anxiety in women undergoing colopscopy. *Cochrane Database of Systematic Reviews* (3), CD006013.

Granja, C., Gomes, E., Amaro, A., Ribeiro, O., Jones, C., Carneiro, A. et al. (2008). Understanding posttraumatic stress disorder-related symptoms after critical care: The early illness amnesia hypothesis. *Critical Care Medicine, 36*(10), 2801–2809.

Granja, C., Lopes, A., Moreira, S., Dias, C., Costa-Pereira, A. & Carneiro, A. (2005). Patients' recollections of experiences in the intensive care unit may affect their quality of life. *Critical Care, 9*(2), R96–109.

Hathaway, D. (1986). Effect of preoperative instruction on postoperative outcomes: A meta-analysis. *Nursing Research, 35*(5), 269–275.

Heinonen, H., Volin, L., Zevon, M.A., Uutela, A., Barrick, C. & Ruutu, T. (2005). Stress among allogeneic bone marrow transplantation patients. *Patient Education and Counseling, 56*(1), 62–71.

Hofberg, K. & Ward, M.R. (2003). Fear of pregnancy and childbirth. *Postgraduate Medical Journal, 79*(935), 505–510, quiz 508–510.

Hudcova, J., McNicol, E., Quah, C., Lau, J. & Carr, D.B. (2006). Patient controlled opioid analgesia versus conventional opioid analgesia for postoperative pain. *Cochrane Database of Systematic Reviews* (4), CD003348.

Johnston, M. & Vögele, C. (1993). Benefits of psychological preparation for surgery: A meta-analysis. *Annals of Behavioral Medicine, 15*(4), 245–256.

Katz, R.C., Wilson, L. & Frazer, N. (1994). Anxiety and its determinants in patients undergoing magnetic resonance imaging. *Journal of Behavior Therapy and Experimental Psychiatry, 25*(2), 131–134.

Kiecolt-Glaser, J.K., Page, G.G., Marucha, P.T., MacCallum, R.C. & Glaser, R. (1998). Psychological influences on surgical recovery. Perspectives from psychoneuroimmunology. *The American Psychologist, 53*(11), 1209–1218.

Koenig, H.G., George, L.K., Stangl, D. & Tweed, D.L. (1995). Hospital stressors experienced by elderly medical inpatients: Developing a hospital stress index. *International Journal of Psychiatry in Medicine, 25*(1), 103–122.

Lang, E.V., Benotsch, E.G. Fick, L.J., Lutgendorf, S., Berbaum, M.L., Berbaum, K.S. et al. (2000). Adjunctive non-pharmacological analgesia for invasive medical procedures: a randomised trial. *Lancet, 355*(9214), 1486–1490.

Leidy, N.K., Margolis, M.K., Marcin, J.P., Flynn, J.A., Frankel, L.R., Johnson, S. et al. (2005). The impact of severe respiratory syncytial virus on the child, caregiver and family during hospitalization and recovery. *Pediatrics, 115*(6), 1536–1546.

McCann, M.E. & Kain, Z.N. (2001). The management of preoperative anxiety in children: An update. *Anesthia and Analgesia, 93*(1), 98–105.

McDonald, S., Hetrick, S. & Green, S. (2004). Pre-operative education for hip or knee replacement. *Cochrane Database of Systematic Reviews* (1), CD003526.

McIlfatrick, S., Sullivan, K., McKenna, H. & Parahoo, K. (2007). Patients' experiences of having chemotherapy in a day hospital setting. *Journal of Advanced Nursing, 59*(3), 264–273.

McIsaac, H.K., Thordarson, D.S., Shafran, R., Rachman, S. & Poole, G. (1998). Claustrophobia and the magnetic resonance imaging procedure. *Journal of Behavioral Medicine, 21*(3), 255–268.

Melendez, J.C. & McCrank, E. (1993). Anxiety-related reactions associated with magnetic resonance imaging examinations. *Journal of the American Medical Association, 270*(6), 745–747.

Mols, F., van den Hurk, C.J., Vingerhoets, A.J. & Breed, W.P. (2009). Scalp cooling to prevent chemotherapy-induced hair loss: Practical and clinical considerations. *Supportive Care in Cancer, 17*(2), 181–189.

Moos, R.H. & Shaefer, J.A. (1984). The crisis of physical illness: An overview and conceptual approach. In R.H. Moos (Ed.) *Coping with physical illness: New perspectives* (Vol. 2, pp. 3–25). New York: Plenum.

Mulders, M., Vingerhoets, A. & Breed, W. (2008). The impact of cancer and chemotherapy: Perceptual similarities and differences between cancer patients, nurses and physicians. *European Journal of Oncology Nursing, 12*(2), 97–102.

Nicholls, K. & Ayers, S. (2007). Childbirth-related post-traumatic stress disorder in couples: A qualitative study. *British Journal of Health Psychology, 12*(4), 491–509.

O'Halloran, C.M. & Altmaier, E.M. (1995). The efficacy of preparation for surgery and invasive medical procedures. *Patient Education and Counseling, 25*(1), 9–16.

Pandey, M., Sarita, G.P., Devi, N., Thomas, B.C., Hussain, B.M. & Krishnan, R. (2006). Distress, anxiety and depression in cancer patients undergoing chemotherapy. *World Journal of Surgical Oncology, 4*, 68.

Pao, M., Ballard, E.D. & Rosenstein, D.L. (2007). Growing up in the hospital. *Journal of the American Medical Association, 297*(24), 2752–2755.

Powers, S.W. (1999). Empirically supported treatments in pediatric psychology: Procedure-related pain. *Journal of Pediatric Psychology, 24*(2), 131–145.

Saisto, T., Salmela-Aro, K., Nurmi, J.E., Kononen, T. & Halmesmaki, E. (2001). A randomized controlled trial of intervention in fear of childbirth. *Obstetrics & Gynecology, 98*(5 Pt 1), 820–826.

Schultheis, K., Peterson, L. & Selby, V. (1987). Preparation for stressful medical procedures and person × treatment interactions. *Clinical Psychology Review, 7*(3), 329–352.

Thurber, C.A. & Walton, E. (2007). Preventing and treating homesickness. *Pediatrics, 119*(1), 192–201.

Uman, L.S., Chambers, C.T., McGrath, P.J. & Kisely, S. (2006). Psychological interventions for needle-related procedural pain and distress in children and adolescents. *Cochrane Database of Systematic Reviews* (4), CD005179.

Uman, L.S., Chambers, C.T., McGrath, P.J. & Kisely, S. (2008). A systematic review of randomized controlled trials examining psychological interventions for needle-related procedural pain and distress in children and adolescents: An abbreviated Cochrane review. *Journal of Pediatric Psychology, 33*(8), 842–854.

Van Broeck, N. (1993). Medical play. In *Behandeling van zieke kinderen (Treatment of ill children)*. Houten, Netherlands: Bohn Stafleu Van Loghum.

van de Leur, J.P., van der Schans, C.P., Loef, B.G., Deelman, B.G., Geertzen, J.H. & Zwaveling, J.H. (2004). Discomfort and factual recollection in intensive care unit patients. *Critical Care, 8*(6), R 467–473.

van Servellen, G., Lewis, C.E. & Leake, B. (1990). The stresses of hospitalization among AIDS patients on integrated and special care units. *International Journal of Nursing Studies, 27*(3), 235–247.

van Vliet, M.J., Grypdonck, M., van Zuuren, F.J., Winnubst, J. & Kruitwagen, C. (2004). Preparing patients for gastrointestinal endoscopy: The influence of information in medical situations. *Patient Education and Counseling, 52*(1), 23–30.

Walker, L.S., Williams, S.E., Smith, C.A., Garber, J., Van Slyke, D.A. & Lipani, T.A. (2006). Parent attention versus distraction: Impact on symptom complaints by children with and without chronic functional abdominal pain. *Pain, 122*(1–2), 43–52.

White, M. & Ritchie, J. (1984). Psychological stressors in antepartum hospitalization: Reports from pregnant women. *Maternal–Child Nursing Journal, 13*(1), 47–56.

Wismeijer, A.A. & Vingerhoets, A.J. (2005). The use of virtual reality and audiovisual eyeglass systems as adjunct analgesic techniques: A review of the literature. *Annals of Behavioral Medicine, 30*(3), 268–278.

Part IV

Psychological Aspects
of Health and Illness

19

Stress, Health and Illness

The Effects of Prolonged Physiological Activity and Perseverative Cognition

Julian F. Thayer and Jos F. Brosschot

Chapter Outline

In this chapter we will discuss how stress can affect health and illness. We first present two models of the effect of stress on health and illness – the reactivity model and the prolonged activation model. We then discuss the cognitive mechanism of prolonged physiological activation namely perseverative cognition. We show that perseverative cognition is associated with health complaints and with physiological arousal. Importantly we try to show the brain processes involved in the physiological effects of perseverative cognition. We end by providing a 'glimpse into the future' by discussing anticipatory stress and unconscious perseverative cognition.

Key Concepts

Autonomic nervous system
Health
Heart rate variability
Illness
Perseverative cognition
Prolonged physiological
   activity
Stress

Introduction

Psychological stress is a widespread problem and a substantial cause or co-determinant of organic disease presenting an ever-growing humanitarian and economic burden (Krantz & McCeney, 2002; Schwartz et al., 2003). However, it is not clear how stress 'gets under the skin' to cause or influence physiological processes and ultimately health and disease. For decades, this health risk has been explained by theorising that stressful events are accompanied by increased physiological responses, which, if frequent and intense, may cause bodily harm. This idea has been termed 'the reactivity hypothesis' (see Figure 19.1). However, the often reported lack of relationship between reactivity in the laboratory and real-life stress responses as well as the tenuous association between laboratory reactivity and disease markers or end-points has led many to question the reactivity hypothesis as an explanation for the stress–disease relationship.

Why Stress has Physiological Effects

Psychological stress responses are largely similar to negative emotions. Emotions, according to leading emotion theorists, involve tendencies to certain actions. These actions involve vigorous physiological activity, especially in the case of negative emotions such as anger and fear. Psychological stressors by definition do not themselves involve direct physical damage, but are composed of threats to the physical or psychological integrity of the individual. It is the *cognitive representation* of these threats that causes a 'fight-or-flight' action tendency (Frijda, 1988), followed by a cascade of biological events, starting in the brain inducing peripheral stress responses such as increases in heart rate, blood pressure and stress hormones including cortisol (Lovallo, 2004).

From Reactivity to Prolonged Activity

The domain of stress and health is currently facing a change of scope, from reactivity (during stressors) to prolonged activity (before and after stressors)

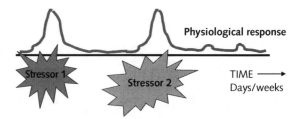

Figure 19.1   The reactivity model

(Brosschot et al., 2005; Brosschot et al., 2006; Brosschot & Thayer, 1998; Linden et al., 1997; Pieper & Brosschot, 2005; Ursin & Eriksen, 2004; Ursin & Murison, 1983). The reactivity hypothesis described above has received only weak and inconsistent support and has recently been argued to be insufficient, because it does not account for prolonged increased physiological activity (Brosschot & Thayer, 1998; Linden et al., 1997; Gerin, in press; Schwartz et al., 2003). Prolonged physiological activity, instead of occasional increases, is believed to lead to the bodily wear and tear that can finally cause or codetermine disease (Brosschot et al., 2005). Physiological activity during stressful events (i.e. stress reactivity) will only become a critical health threat when it is sustained long after these events, or when physiological activity is already present in *anticipation* of these events, sometimes even far before them (see Figure 19.2). Importantly, a large amount of our stress responses may occur in anticipation of events that in fact never happen! Stressful events include severe life events such as the death of a loved one as well as common daily stressors and stressful work situations after which it is often difficult to 'unwind'. What counts is the stress response's total load on the organism, not only what happens during their occurrence. Although this notion of prolonged stress-related physiological activity has been explicit in early stress theories, it has remained implicit and under-investigated since then (Selye, 1950; Ursin, 1978). One of the early modern stress theorists was Hans Selye. He proposed the 'general adaptation syndrome' in which an organism's response to a threat, if prolonged, would eventually lead to the complete exhaustion of the organism's coping resources and ultimately its death. Only recently have researchers

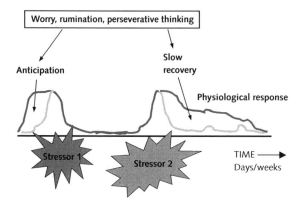

Figure 19.2 The prolonged activation model

returned to a more thorough examination of the role of time or prolonged activation in the stress–disease relationship.

Evidence for Prolonged Activity

Consequently, there is only limited evidence, mainly for cardiovascular disease, that prolonged physiological activity predicts pathogenic states and organic disease. This research has recently been reviewed and the researchers concluded that, whereas the evidence for psychological stress producing prolonged physiological activity exists, the link to disease is less clear (Pieper & Brosschot, 2005).

Moreover as a result of focusing on reactivity alone, remarkably few studies have measured and shown prolonged stress-related physiological activity, most of them being laboratory studies (Brosschot et al., 2005; Dorr et al., 2007; Linden et al., 1997; Pieper & Brosschot, 2005). Recently, however, researchers have started to provide evidence for prolonged stress-related physiological activity in ambulatory studies in which individuals are monitored during their daily life (Brosschot et al., 2002; Brosschot et al., 2007; Brosschot & Thayer, 2003; Pieper et al., 2007). There is now evidence that stressors have prolonged physiological effects, at least cardiovascular effects (Pieper & Brosschot, 2005). The big question now is, what causes this prolonged physiological activity?

The Role of Continuing Stressful Thoughts: 'Perseverative Cognition'

To date, apart from a few researchers, this fundamental question has rarely been addressed. Of course, this is again related to the continued focus on reactivity in stress research. To explain prolonged activity, we formulated the *perseverative cognition hypothesis*, which is based on two core arguments (Brosschot et al., 2005; Brosschot et al., 2006).

Recovery after physical and after psychological stressors

The first argument is that slow recovery after stressors or long anticipatory responses before stressors cannot be due to biological mechanisms alone. The physiological response to an average daily stressor is comparable to that of mild physical exercise, for example a brisk bike ride of 10 minutes, or walking stairs to the fifth floor (Lovallo, 2004). Recovery of the autonomic nervous system after such a physical stressor is much faster (a matter of minutes) than from most psychological stressors (Linden et al., 1997). In addition, there is often an anticipatory response. The exact cause of these extended responses is not yet adequately clarified. A promising candidate is the fact that psychological stressors can make people 'linger on' mentally. This brings us to the second argument.

Human brains look backwards and forwards

A special feature of the human brain is that it can look back and learn from the past and look ahead planning for the future. Unfortunately, this often leads to ruminating about the past and worrying about the future, especially in the case of the more important stressors, such as problems in relationships, income and health. Thus, in humans these stressful representations can manifest themselves virtually at any time before or after stressors, together with their potentially harmful physiological effects. Thus, chronic stress responses are likely to be a rather recent invention of mankind, with no analogue in other species. This makes stress research in animals far less relevant – that is, for understanding the *psychological* mechanisms – than what its dominance in half a century of stress literature suggests.

The second argument, therefore, is that humans make mental representations of stressors, long before and long after these events occur or are believed to occur. This continued cognitive representation of stressful events, before or after their occurrence and even regardless of their actual occurrence, we called perseverative cognition (PC) (Brosschot *et al.*, 2006; Watkins, 2008). By extending and repeating the mental representation of stressors, PC prolongs their physiological effects too. It is likely that by far the most stress-related physiological activity in daily life is not due to stressful events themselves, but to frequent and often spontaneous thinking about them. This is true whether it concerns occasional brief quarrels as well as the chronic stress of low socioeconomic status, racial discrimination or caring for an Alzheimer's patient at home (Baumgarten *et al.*, 1992; Clark *et al.*, 1999; Mackenbach *et al.*, 2008). Stressors without continuous worrying or other mechanisms that prolong the mental representation of stress (or, perhaps more precisely, 'threat') are not likely to influence one's health.

The Nature of Perseverative Cognition

Perseverative cognition, common to a number of negative affective states and dispositions, including depression, anxiety disorders, post-traumatic stress disorder and perhaps many medically unexplained syndromes, is repetitive, abstract and involuntary and represents a failure of inhibitory neural processes (Thayer & Lane, 2000). Later in the chapter we will discuss this inhibitory nature in more detail. This cognitive mode is thought to serve several different functions. The most straightforward function attributed to worry and perseverative cognition is an attempt, albeit thwarted, at constructive mental problem solving (Davey, 1994). In support of this role, Davey (1994) and co-workers found positive correlations between worry and problem-focused coping, but only after partialling out the effect of trait anxiety. Thus, worry appeared to be associated with a habitual tendency for active problem solving combined with low confidence in succeeding in it. Tallis and Eysenck (1994)

proposed a tripartite function of worry. First, worry serves an alarm function, acting to interrupt ongoing behaviour and directing awareness towards an issue demanding immediate solution. Second, worry has a prompt function, continuously representing unresolved threatening situations to awareness. Third, worry is proposed to have a preparation function, anticipating threat and readying the organism for a situation in which intense motor activation is needed. Obviously, such a situation is rare relative to typical levels of worry and perseverative cognition. Thus, perseverative cognition theoretically engenders a protracted state of psychophysiological 'action preparation' without resolution.

Perseverative cognition reflects a disinhibition of a potentially adaptive frontal lobe mechanism in higher organisms. The frontal lobes have reciprocal neural connections with more evolutionarily primitive subcortical structures that are partially responsible for basic approach and avoidance behaviour. When these structures are disinhibited, a number of processes associated with threat responses are unleashed, including hypervigilance and fear, as well as increased heart rate and blood pressure. These processes could be viewed as sensitisation-like as well as disinhibitory and their behavioural 'hallmarks' of hypervigilance and fear might pertain to any threat, including work stress, low socioeconomic status, or discrimination and racism.

The classical finding of a large orienting response followed by a lack of habituation is an example of sensitisation (Ursin, 1998). Similarly, the phenomenon of long-term potentiation, so important for memory, can be viewed as a type of sensitisation (Thayer & Friedman, 2002). The tuning of the organism to novel stimuli followed by habituation to innocuous stimuli is characteristic of healthy and adaptive functioning. In contrast, failure to habituate to innocuous stimuli leads to vigilance and defensiveness that is the hallmark of pathologies such as anxiety disorders. This maladaptive mode exemplifies perseverative behaviour that can be seen as a positive feedback loop. Interruption of this ongoing state is associated with inhibition and negative feedback.

These mechanisms could operate outside of conscious awareness at a precognitive or preconscious level. These findings are consistent with classic work on perceptual defence (see Mackinnon & Dukes,

1962, for review) and the psychophysiology of attention (e.g. Graham & Clifton, 1966; Sokolov, 1963), as well as more contemporary notions of preattentive discrimination and selective processing of threat in anxiety (Mathews, 1990).

Several recent studies further highlight the fact that perseverative cognition can have effects outside of conscious awareness. In one study, healthy individuals were brought into a sleep laboratory and randomly divided into two groups (Hall et al., 2004). One group was told that in the morning they would be asked to give a speech that would be evaluated (stress group). The other participants were told that they would be allowed to read popular magazines upon awakening (control group). The results indicated that relative to the control group, the stress group had decreased heart rate variability during both rapid eye movement (REM) and non-REM sleep. They also had poorer sleep maintenance and lower automated delta counts, indicative of high cortical arousal, assessed via electroencephalography. Another recent study found that daytime worry and daily hassles were associated with decreased heart rate variability and increased heart rate on the succeeding night (Brosschot et al., 2007). Taken together, these studies suggest that the effects of perseverative cognition are not restricted to periods when such activity is consciously perceived, but can have effects that extend to periods in which perseverative cognition is not accessible to conscious awareness.

Perseverative Cognition and Perceived Control

Perseverative cognition is a central feature of many psychological disorders that have also been associated with poor physical health outcomes. For example, chronic and transient episodes of anxiety, depression and anger all have been associated with cardiovascular disease (Kubzansky, 2007). A core characteristic of these perseverative states is the perception that control over a stressor is threatened. Only when a threat to control is perceived is the stressor's full potential for activating the organism manifested, because there is no apparent way to cope with the stressor. Perceived uncontrollability of stress (or related concepts like

hopelessness) has been documented as a chief characteristic of both stressors and individuals that accounts for potentially pathogenic physiological states and health problems (Brosschot et al., 1998; Everson et al., 1996).

Thus, perseverative cognition might be viewed as the cognitive manifestation and source of nourishment of the deeper underlying experience of perceived uncontrollability. The concept of perseverative cognition may, therefore, help to explain the health effects of perceived uncontrollability by accounting for the prolongation of its physiological effects. Specifically, perseverative cognition sustains the physiological response to a stressor by prolonging uncertainty over stressor control in the coping process. A theoretical implication of this concept is an emphasis on the time dimension in stress research. Associations between perseverative cognition on the one hand and physiological and health consequences on the other are implicit in view of the crucial role of uncertainty and uncontrollability in the stress–disease link.

Perseverative Cognition and Health

Preliminary evidence for a positive association between dispositional worry and general health exists. In an exploratory study of 171 students (Brosschot & van der Doef, 2006), the disposition to worry (Borkovec, 1985) was found to be correlated with subjective health complaints ($r = .41$, $p < .001$). The association was lower when the effect of trait anxiety was controlled (partial $r = .23$, $p < .001$), which suggests that the association was at least partly due to 'pure' worry tendencies and not entirely to the disposition to express negative affect. In addition, further evidence accrued for a causal role for worry. These same students were instructed to keep a log of their worries during one week. Compared to three days prior to initiating this procedure, the students that worried more and longer had more health complaints during the last three days of the intervention week. In addition, half of these students were asked to limit worry every day to a 30-minute designated 'worry period' late in the day, for one week. This worry 'postponement' group had fewer health complaints during the last three days of the intervention week. The range of complaints (e.g. coughing and flu-like symptoms, neck pain, breathing difficulties and stomach pains) covered several bodily systems and were not restricted to the typical 'psychosomatic' complaints such as headache. These results collectively imply that time spent worrying and health complaints are positively related.

Perseverative Cognition and Heart Rate Variability

Another way in which perseverative cognition may be causally related to prolonged physiological activation and disease is by decreased vagally mediated heart rate variability (HRV). Diminished tonic HRV and the associated reduction of vagally mediated cardiovascular control has been associated with a variety of pathological states and dispositions, including diabetes, myocardial infarction, congestive heart failure and hypertension (for a review see Thayer & Lane, 2007). As an index of vagally mediated cardiovascular activity, HRV reflects a negative feedback mechanism that is crucial for the self-regulation of behaviour. Vagal activity has beneficial effects on cardiovascular function by restraining cardiac rate and electrical conduction speed, which is vital to attain cardiac stability, responsiveness and flexibility (Thayer *et al.*, 2008).

In an early landmark study, chronic worry was shown to be related to increased risk of coronary heart disease (Kubzansky *et al.*, 1997). In a recent study of the stress associated with the 9/11 attacks in the United States, worry about terrorism post-9/11 was associated with an increased risk of physician–diagnosed heart problems 2–3 years after the attack (Holman *et al.*, 2008). Thus, the perseverative cognition, characteristic of worry, not only can lead to increased anxiety, but is also associated with an increased cardiovascular disease risk. Transitory worry has been associated with decreased vagal activity (Thayer *et al.*, 1996). Thus, one mechanism that might link worry to elevated disease risk is low vagal activity. Similar models of decreased vagal activity have been proposed to describe the relationship between other psychological factors and physiological health. For example, Brosschot and Thayer (1998) relate diminished vagal activity to hostility and cardiovascular disease risk and low vagal activity has been suggested as

the link between psychological factors and myocardial ischaemia (Kop *et al.*, 2001).

Perseverative Cognition and the Brain

A possible key role in this process is played by decreased medial prefrontal cortex activity. The frontal cortex may tonically inhibit limbic (amygdala) activity (Thayer & Lane, 2009) and this limbic activity has been associated with autonomically mediated defensive behaviour, including increased heart rate and blood pressure. Direct and indirect pathways by which the frontal cortex modulates limbic activity, especially via parasympathetic activity, have been identified (Ter Horst, 1999; Thayer & Lane, 2009). Ter Horst relates these connections to increased risk of re-infarction and death in post-myocardial infarction depression. The thrust of this proposal is that when faced with threat, tonic inhibitory limbic control can be rapidly decreased, leading to sympathoexcitatory fight-or-flight survival responses. Disruption of this inhibitory control allows a rigid, defensive behavioural pattern to emerge with associated hypervigilance and perseverative behaviour, manifested in cognitive, affective and autonomic inflexibility.

Perseverative cognition and low HRV may, in fact, reflect the breakdown of a common reciprocal inhibitory cortical–subcortical neural circuit. This network of reciprocally interconnected structures allows the prefrontal cortex to inhibit subcortical activity associated with defensive behaviour and thus foster flexible control of behaviour in response to changing environmental demands. As noted earlier, disruption of this network might lead to disinhibition of defensive perseverative behaviours, including hypervigilance.

The Physiological Profile of Perseverative Cognition

We have written extensively about perseverative cognition and its physiological concomitants (for a review see Brosschot *et al.*, 2006). There is now evidence that experimentally manipulated worry has physiological effects (i.e. enhanced autonomic activity) (Davis *et al.*, 2002; Lyonfields *et al.*, 1995; Thayer *et al.*, 1996; Verkuil *et al.*, 2009). Importantly, these effects can persist into restorative periods such as recovery from stressors and sleep. The combined autonomic effects of stressful events and worry that we found were of the same magnitude as for smoking (Brosschot *et al.*, 2002, 2007; Pieper *et al.*, 2007). Evidence has begun to appear that perseverative cognition in addition to having direct physiological effects, mediates prolonged effects of stressors – confirming the perseverative cognition hypothesis, namely prolonged autonomic activity in real life during waking as well as sleeping (indisputably our most important restorative period), slow blood pressure recovery after anger provocation and other emotional stress and slow cortisol recovery after a speech stressor (Brosschot *et al.*, 2007; Key *et al.*, 2008; Zoccola *et al.*, 2008). Notably, these real-life and laboratory effects of worry were independent of negative mood (the effect of which was negligible), lifestyle factors such as smoking, coffee and alcohol intake and physical activity and thus seemed exclusively due to perseverative cognition.

Thus the physiological concomitants of perseverative cognition include autonomic imbalance as indexed by decreased HRV, decreased prefrontal cortex activity, increased amygdala activity, excess and prolonged cortisol responsivity, altered immune function, increased blood pressure and peripheral resistance responses in anticipatory coping, increased blood pressure and peripheral resistance during recovery from stress, sustained and prolonged pupil dilation and poor tolerance to and delayed recovery from stress in general. All of these physiological responses are associated with poor health outcomes.

Perseverative Cognition as a Balance between Inhibition and Excitation

In a normal, relaxed and safe environment, the prefrontal cortex tonically inhibits limbic activity while it is responsively monitoring internal and external stimuli and guiding goal-directed behaviour. The prefrontal cortex is receptive to a broad range of information, but is not specifically directed to potential concerns (e.g. fears such as work stress or racism and discrimination) of the organism. Such is the case in situations in which the organism does not expect

threat or immediate danger. However, when the situation becomes ambiguous or threat becomes more imminent, or is ever present, prefrontal inhibition of the limbic brain is partially released, potentially generating hypervigilance and perseverative cognition. This partial disinhibition is associated with a hyper-alert state of action readiness. In this situation, the organism is obviously not switched completely into a defensive, fight–flight excitatory state. Instead, under limbic influence, the nature of prefrontal function is converted from flexible and open to experience into a state of anticipatory rehearsal of feared scenarios and vigilant scanning of available information. Under immediate threat, however, the prefrontal cortex is disengaged nearly completely, albeit temporarily, in normal or healthy subjects, resulting in the full and sometimes explosive manifestation of the emotion (anger attack, actual flight, shouting, panicking).

Thus, perseverative cognition can be viewed as a demonstration of the reciprocal nature of prefrontal-amygdala communication. The amygdala sends signals of threat warning to the prefrontal cortex, leading to hypervigilance and rehearsal of feared scenarios, but it is able to do this because of prefrontal disinhibition itself. The disinhibition is in turn due to the rapid and rough perception of immediate threat, which emerges from the integration of ongoing environmental perception with memory associations (conditioned responses), the storage and activation of which is, again, largely under amygdala influence (LeDoux, 2000). In other words, in a bottom-up manner, lower brain centres, in cooperation with memory, demand the prefrontal cortex to occupy itself with rehearsing feared scenarios and stimulate vigilant and biased scanning of internal and external information. At the same time, in a top-down mode, the prefrontal inhibition of lower brain centres is maintained. Perseverative cognition may in fact lead to solutions to the threat, resulting in diminished activation and restoration of the relaxed state dominated by prefrontal inhibition of subcortical sympathoexcitatory circuits.

Finally, it is clear from these findings and theoretical considerations that hypervigilance and perseveration have physiological consequences, that is, signs of stress and limbic-induced autonomic imbalance such as low HRV, elevated heart rate and cortisol and particularly elevated blood pressure and peripheral resistance (the so-called 'vigilance reaction'; see Winters *et al.*, 2000). Due to partially maintained limbic inhibition by the prefrontal cortex, this activation is often moderate and may appear blunted (cf. Young *et al.*, 1998). But prolonged vagal withdrawal renders the autonomic nervous system (ANS) inflexible and unresponsive to changing environmental demands. Therefore autonomic activation is still high enough (and – more importantly – *sustained*) to cause damage (e.g. hypertension and cardiovascular disease) (Brosschot & Thayer, 1998), but also low enough, for example, for anxious subjects to learn to worry to prevent the full manifestation of fear responses (Borkovec & Hu, 1990). Thus, the autonomic imbalance associated with anticipatory coping and delayed physiological recovery from discrete stressors may be associated with hypervigilance and perseveration due to partial release of prefrontal inhibition of the amygdala. That these anticipatory and recovery responses have been associated with increased blood pressure and peripheral resistance (Gregg *et al.*, 1999) has special importance because this pattern has been linked to increased hypertension and related morbidity and mortality particularly for example in African Americans.

The Psychological Profile of Perseverative Cognition

A psychological profile associated with perseverative cognition has also emerged. This profile is marked by hypervigilance to threat and failure to habituate to innocuous stimuli, impaired cognitive function on tasks demanding delayed responding and executive functions, a lack of inhibitory behaviour, denial and an avoidant coping style, increased neuroticism, decreased conscientiousness and impulse control, thought intrusions, lack of perceived control and greater levels of depression, anxiety and hostility. Again, all of these psychological responses are linked to poor health outcomes. It is important to note that these responses can occur in

anticipation of the stress event or even when no actual stress event occurs.

Anticipated Stress

One important implication of this view is that, as we mentioned earlier, obviously a large part of our daily stress experience consists of worries about future events. People fear far more events than those that actually turn out to happen, but their bodies have responded to them all the same, repeatedly and often continuously. Unfortunately, for decades stress research almost exclusively assessed past or ongoing stressors, such as life events, daily hassles or work stressors. Thus, conventional stress theories, by being guided by the reactivity hypothesis, led to missing a potentially large source of stress responses. In contrast, perseverative cognition theory, by proposing cognitive representations of stress and thus 'what is in the mind', aggregates many more stress sources, including stressors that never actually occur, but that are nonetheless anticipated long before. Moreover, the stressors that people perseverate about in this way are likely to be the most personally relevant, yielding the strongest and longest physiological effects. In summary, this chapter states that perseverative cognition is a form of maladaptive coping with stressors and is the main cause of prolonged activity.

Other Psychological Mediators of Prolonged Stress-Related Activity

Still, even after adding worry as an additional factor, our studies explained only about half of the variance in prolonged activity, which made clear that there is still potentially much more unexplained stress-related prolonged activity (Brosschot *et al.*, 2002, 2007; Pieper *et al.*, 2007). There must be another, unmeasured stress source responsible for this still unexplained part. It should be noted that worry and rumination are not the only possible mediators of prolonged activity. There are several other potential candidates, of which the most promising seem to be 'prolonged problem solving' and 'unconscious perseverative cognition'.

Prolonged problem solving

In a recent experiment, we found that experimental worry as well as problem solving increased heart rate and decreased heart rate variability in comparison with relaxation (Verkuil *et al.*, 2009). However, worry and problem solving did not differ from each other in their cardiac effects. We speculated that in real life, much (or most?) of the autonomic effects of worry are in fact due to the mental effort involved and not (so much) to the negative affective part. This is in line with our failure to find any independent effects for negative affect in ambulatory studies. Before the reader asks sceptically 'So, since when is problem solving unhealthy', it should be realised that normal problem solving is typically of short duration, because either a solution is found or the problem is (temporarily at least) abandoned. If not, problem solving turns into worry, with its above-described prolonged physiological effects. Still – and this is the point we want to make – there are many cases in which problem solving might be continued without being experienced as worry. Think of the school director working late at night, or the surgeon or therapist carrying problems with her/him at home, or the executive working literally day and night. In all these cases, problem solving is continuous, often without being experienced as and therefore not measurable as worry, but it nevertheless involved the prolonged representation of a stressor (problem). We speculate that these situations may cause a considerable part of prolonged activity. Thus, these people may be characterised as 'chronic problem solvers' (personal communication, D. Strunk) and may run serious health risks because of their special type of perseverative cognition. There are several studies showing prolonged physiological activity related to overwork (Sluiter *et al.*, 2001) that support these ideas in a certain sense, but in these studies, problem solving and worry or rumination have not been measured, let alone that their physiological effects have been disentangled.

Unconscious perseverative cognition

In the past 20 years it has become clear that *conscious* cognition may be very limited and that moment-to-moment psychological self-regulation is for the larger part controlled by unconscious processes (Aarts, 2007; Bargh & Chartrand, 1999; Bargh & Morsella, 2008). There is also evidence that this is true for unconscious emotional cognition too (LeDoux, 2000). Thus the challenge for the next generation of stress researchers is to try to find the factors, some of which may be outside of conscious awareness, that may account for the prolonged physiological activation that accompanies much of our daily life but eludes our attempts to measure them.

Summary and Conclusions

We all 'know' that stress is bad for us. However, we are still at the beginning of understanding exactly how stress 'gets under the skin' to influence physiology and possibly disease. In this chapter we have tried to provide some ideas about how stress can affect physiology and disease. We have proposed that prolonged physiological activation must accompany stress if it is to lead to a chronic pathogenic state and ultimately disease. But we also noted that most of us are 'stressed' by events that may occur in the future as well as by those events that in fact never occur. How is this possible? What we have tried to show is that the mental representation of a stressor can have physiological consequences when the mental representation is activated. That this mental representation can be repeatedly and continuously activated we have called perseverative cognition. We showed that perseverative cognition is repetitive, abstract and involuntary and represents a failure of inhibitory neural processes. Moreover evidence is accumulating that perseverative cognition is associated with significant physiological activation which, if prolonged, may be the source of the chronic pathogenic state necessary for disease to take hold. Importantly, much of perseverative cognition may occur outside of conscious awareness. This provides a challenge for researchers as we try to understand the relationship between stress, prolonged physiological activation and perseverative cognition.

Discussion Points

1 How does stress 'get under the skin'?
2 What is the evidence for the 'reactivity hypothesis'?
3 What is the evidence for the 'prolonged activation hypothesis'?
4 How does the perception of control influence our reactions to threatening situations?

5 What is the role of the brain in stress, illness and health?
6 What are the implications of unconscious perseverative cognition?

Further Reading

Brosschot, J.F, Gerin, W. & Thayer, J.F. (2006). Worry and health: The perseverative cognition hypothesis. *Journal of Psychosomatic Research, 60*, 113–124.

Brosschot, J.F., Pieper, S. & Thayer, J.F. (2005). Expanding stress theory: Polonged activation and perseverative cognition. *Psychoneuroendocrinology, 30*(10), 1043–1049.

Kubzansky, L.D. (2007). Sick at heart: The pathophysiology of negative emotions. *Cleveland Clinic Journal of Medicine, 74*, S67–S72.

LeDoux, J.E. (2000). Emotion circuits in the brain. *Annual Reviews in Neuroscience, 23*, 155–184.

Linden, W., Earle, T.L, Gerin, W. & Christenfeld, N. (1997). Physiological stress reactivity and recovery: Conceptual siblings separated at birth? *Journal of Psychosomatic Research, 42*, 117–135.

Rosengren, A., Hawken, S., Ounpuu, S., Sliwa, K., Zubaid, M., Almahmeed, W.A. *et al.* & INTERHEART investigators (2004). Association of psychosocial risk factors with risk of acute myocardial infarction in 11,119 cases and 13,648 controls from 52 countries (the INTERHEART study): Case-control study. *Lancet, 364*(9438), 953–962.

Schwartz, A.R., Gerin, W., Davidson, K.W., Pickering, T.G., Brosschot, J.F. *et al.* (2003). Toward a causal model of cardiovascular responses to stress and the development of cardiovascular disease. *Psychosomatic Medicine, 65*, 22–35.

Thayer, J.F. & Lane, R.D. (2009). Claude Bernard and the heart-brain connection: Further elaboration of a model of neurovisceral integration. *Neuroscience & Biobehavioral Reviews, 33*, 81–88.

References

Aarts, H. (2007). On the emergence of human goal pursuit: The nonconscious regulation and motivation of goals. *Social & Personality Psychology Compass, 1*, 183–201.

Bargh, J.A. & Chartrand, T.L. (1999). The unbearable automaticity of being. *American Psychologist, 54*, 462–479.

Bargh, J.A. & Morsella, E. (2008). The unconscious mind. *Perspectives on Psychological Science, 3*, 73–79.

Baumgarten, M., Battista, R.N., Infante-Rivard, C., Hanley, A., Becker, R. & Gauthier, S. (1992). The psychological and physical health of family members caring for an elderly person with dementia. *Journal of Clinical Epidemiology, 45*, 61–70.

Borkovec, T.D. (1985). Worry: A potentially valuable concept. *Behaviour Research and Therapy, 23*(4), 481–482.

Borkovec, T.D. & Hu, S. (1999). The effect of worry on cardiovascular response to phobic imagery. *Behaviour Research and Therapy, 28*(1), 69–73.

Brosschot, J.F, Gerin, W. & Thayer, J.F. (2006). Worry and health: The preservative cognition hypothesis. *Journal of Psychosomatic Research, 60*, 113–124.

Brosschot, J.F., Godaert, G.L.R., Benschop, R.J., Olff, M., Ballieux, R.E. & Heijnen, C.J. (1998). Experimental stress and immunological reactivity: A closer look at perceived uncontrollability. *Psychosomatic Medicine, 60*(3), 359–361.

Brosschot, J.F., Pieper, S. & Thayer, J.F. (2005). Expanding stress theory: Prolonged activation and perseverative cognition. *Psychoneuroendocrinology, 30*(10), 1043–1049.

Brosschot, J.F. & Thayer, J.F. (1998). Anger inhibition, cardiovascular recovery and vagal function: A model of the link between hostility and cardiovascular disease. *Annals of Behavioral Medicine, 20*, 1–8.

Brosschot, J.F. & Thayer, J.F. (2003). Heart rate response is longer after negative emotions than after positive emotions. *International Journal of Psychophysiology, 50*, 181–187.

Brosschot, J.F., Van Dijk, E. & Thayer, J.F. (2002). Prolonged autonomic activation, perseverative negative cognition and daily stressors. *International Congress Series, 1241C*, 329–336.

Brosschot, J.F., van Dijk E. & Thayer, J.F. (2007). Daily worry is related to low heart rate variability during waking and the subsequent nocturnal sleep period. *International Journal of Psychophysiology, 63*, 39–47.

Brosschot, J.F. & Van der Doef, M. (2006). Daily worrying increases somatic complaints: A simple worry reduction intervention helps. *Psychology & Health, 21*, 19–31.

Clark, R. Anderson, N.B., Clark, V.R. & Williams, D.R. (1999). Racism as a stressor for African Americans: A biopsychosocial model. *American Psychologist, 54*, 805–816.

Davey, G.C.L. (1994). Pathological worrying as exacerbated problem solving. In G.C.L. Davey & F. Tallis (Eds.) *Worrying: Perspectives on theory, assessment and treatment* (pp. 35–60). New York: Wiley.

Davis, M., Montgomery, I. & Wilson, G. (2002). Worry and heart rate variables: Autonomic rigidity under challenge. *Journal of Anxiety Disorders, 16*, 639–659.

Dorr, D., Brosschot, J.F., Sollers III, J.J. & Thayer J.F. (2007). Damned if you do, damned if you don't: The differential effect of expression and inhibition of anger on cardiovascular recovery in black and white males. *International Journal of Psychophysiology, 66*, 125–134.

Everson, S.A., Goldberg, D.E., Kaplan, G.A., Cohen, R.D. *et al.* (1996). Hopelessness and risk of mortality and incidence of myocardial infarction and cancer. *Psychosomatic Medicine, 58*(2), 113–121.

Frijda, N.H. (1988). The laws of emotion. *American Psychologist, 43*, 349–358.

Gerin, W. (in press) Cardiovascular reactivity. In S.R. Waldstein, W.J. Kop, L.I. Katzel (Eds.) *Handbook of cardiovascular behavioral medicine.* New York: Springer.

Graham, F.K. & Clifton, R.K. (1966). Heart-rate change as a component of the orienting response. *Psychological Bulletin, 65*, 305–320.

Gregg, M.E., Matyas, T.A. & James, J.E. (2002). A new model of individual differences in hemodynamic profile and blood pressure reactivity. *Psychophysiology, 39*, 64–72.

Hall, M., Vasko, R., Buysse, R., Thayer, J.F., Ombao, H., Chen, Q. *et al.* (2004). Acute stress affects autonomic tone during sleep. *Psychosomatic Medicine, 66*, 56–62.

Holman, E.A., Silver, R.C., Poulin, M., Andersen, J., Gil-Rivas, V. & McIntosh, D.N. (2008). Terrorism, acute stress, and cardiovascular health. *Archives of General Psychiatry, 65*, 73–80.

Key, B.L., Campbell, T.S., Bacon, S.L. & Gerin, W. (2008). The influence of trait and state rumination on cardiovascular recovery from a negative emotional stressor. *Journal of Behavioral Medicine, 31*(3), 237–248.

Kop, W.J., Verdino, R.J., Gottdiener, J.S., O'Leary, S.T., Merz, C.N.B. & Krantz, D.S. (2001). Changes in heart rate and heart rate variability before ambulatory ischemic events. *Journal of the American College of Cardiology, 38*, 742–749.

Krantz, D. S. & McCeney, M. K. (2002). Effects of psychological and social factors on organic disease: Aa critical assessment of coronary heart disease. *Annual Review of Psychology, 53*, 341–369.

Kubzansky, L.D. (2007). Sick at heart: the pathophysiology of negative emotions. *Cleveland Clinic Journal of Medicine, 74*, S67–S72.

Kubzansky, L.D., Kawachi, I., Spiro, A., III, Weiss, S.T., Vokonas, P.S. & Sparrow, D. (1997). Is worrying bad for your heart? A prospective study of worry and coronary heart disease in the Normative Aging Study. *Circulation, 95*(4), 818–824.

LeDoux, J.E. (2000). Emotion circuits in the brain. *Annual Reviews in Neuroscience, 23*, 155–184.

Linden, W., Earle, T.L, Gerin, W. & Christenfeld, N. (1997). Physiological stress reactivity and recovery: conceptual siblings separated at birth? *Journal of Psychosomatic Research, 42*, 117–135.

Lovallo, W.R. (2004). *Stress and Health: Biological and psychological interactions* (2nd edn). Thousand Oaks, CA: Sage.

Lyonfields, J.D., Borkovec, T.D. & Thayer, J.F. (1995). Vagal tone in generalized anxiety disorder and the effects of aversive imagery and worrisome thinking. *Behavior Therapy, 26*, 457–466.

Mackenbach, J.P., Stirbu, I., Roskam, A.J., Schaap, M.M., Menvielle, G., Leinsalu, M. & Kunst, A.E. (2008). European Union Working Group on Socioeconomic Inequalities in Health. Socioeconomic inequalities in health in 22 European countries. *New England Journal of Medicine, 358*(23), 2468–2481.

Mackinnon, D.W. & Dukes, W. (1962). Repression. In L. Postman (Ed.) *Psychology in the Making: Histories of selected research problems* (pp. 662–744). New York: Alfred A. Knopf.

Mathews, A. (1990). Why worry? The cognitive function of anxiety. *Behaviour Research and Therapy, 28*, 455–468.

Pieper, S. & Brosschot, J.F. (2005). Prolonged stress-related cardiovascular activation: Is there any? *Annals of Behavioral Medicine, 30*(2), 91–103.

Pieper, S., Brosschot, J.F., van der Leeden, R. & Thayer, J.F. (2007). Cardiac effects of momentary assessed worry episodes and stressful events. *Psychosomatic Medicine, 69*, 901–909.

Schwartz, A.R., Gerin, W., Davidson, K.W., Pickering, T.G., Brosschot, J.F. *et al.* (2003). Toward a causal model of cardiovascular responses to stress and the development of cardiovascular disease. *Psychosomatic Medicine, 65*, 22–35.

Selye H. (1950). *Stress.* Montreal: Acta.

Sluiter, J.K., Frings-Dresen, M.H.W., van der Beek, A.J. *et al.* (2001). The relation between work-induced neuroendocrine reactivity and recovery, subjective need for recovery, and health status. *Journal of Psychosomatic Research, 50*, 29–37.

Sokolov, E.N. (1963). *Perception and the orienting response.* New York: Macmillan.

Tallis, F. & Eysenck, M.W. (1994). Worry: Mechanisms and modulating influences. *Behavioural and Cognitive Psychotherapy, 22*(1), 37–56.

Ter Horst, G.J. (1999). Central autonomic control of the heart, angina and pathogenic mechanisms of post-myocardial infarction depression. *European Journal of Morphology, 37*, 257–266.

Thayer, J.F. & Friedman, B.H. (2002). Stop that! Inhibition, sensitization and their neurovisceral concomitants. *Scandinavian Journal of Psychology, 43*, 123–130.

Thayer, J.F., Friedman, B.H. & Borkovec, T.D. (1996). Autonomic characteristics of generalized anxiety disorder and worry. *Biological Psychiatry, 39*, 255–266.

Thayer, J.F., Hansen, A.L. & Johnsen, B.H. (2008). Non-invasive assessment of autonomic influences on the heart: impedance cardiography and heart rate variability. In L.J. Luecken & L.C. Gallo (Eds.) *Handbook of physiological research methods in health psychology* (pp. 183–209). Newbury Park, CA: Sage.

Thayer, J.F. & Lane, R.D. (2000). A model of neurovisceral integration in emotion regulation and dysregulation. *Journal of Affective Disorders, 61*, 201–216.

Thayer, J.F. & Lane, R.D. (2007). The role of vagal function in the risk for cardiovascular disease and mortality. *Biological Psychology, 74*, 224–242.

Thayer, J.F. & Lane, R.D. (2009). Claude Bernard and the heart-brain connection: Further elaboration of a model of neurovisceral integration. *Neuroscience & Biobehavioral Reviews, 33*, 81–88.

Ursin, H. (1978). Activation, coping and psychosomatics. In H. Ursin, E. Baade & S. Levine (Eds.) *Psychobiology of Stress: A study of coping men* (pp. 201–228). New York: Academic Press.

Ursin, H. (1998). The psychology in psychoneuroendocrinology. *Psychoneuroendocrinology, 23*, 555–570.

Ursin, H. & Eriksen, H.R. (2004). The cognitive activation theory of stress. *Psychoneuroendocrinology, 29*, 567–592.

Ursin, H. & Murison, R. (1983). *Biological and psychological basis of psychosomatic disease.* (Advances in the Biosciences, vol. 42. pp. 269–277). Oxford: Pergamon.

Verkuil, B., Brosschot, J.F., Borkovec, T. & Thayer, J.F. (2009). Acute autonomic effects of experimental worry and cognitive problem solving: why worry about worry? *International Journal of Clinical and Health Psychology, 9*, 439–453.

Watkins, E.R. (2008). Constructive and unconstructive repetitive though. *Psychological Bulletin, 134*(2), 163–206.

Winters, R.W., McCabe, P.M., Green, E.J. & Schneiderman, N. (2000). Stress responses, coping and cardiovascular neurobiolojgy: Central nervous system circuitry underlying learned and unlearned affective responses to stressful stimuli. In P.M. McCabe, N. Schneiderman, T. Field & A.R. Wellens (Eds.) *Stress, coping and cardiovascular disease.* Mahwah, NJ: Lawrence Erlbaum.

Young, E.A., Neese, R.M., Weder, A. & Julius, S. (1998). Anxiety and cardiovascular reactivity in the Tecumseh population. *Journal of Hypertension, 16*(12), 1727–1733.

Zoccola, P.M., Dickerson, S.D. & Zaldivar, F.P. (2008). Rumination and cortisol responses to laboratory stressors. *Psychosomatic Medicine, 70*(6), 661–667.

20

Psychoneuroimmunology

Elizabeth Broadbent and Patricia Loft

Chapter Outline

This chapter introduces psychoneuroimmunology (PNI), an inter-disciplinary field that combines psychology with immunology and the neurosciences. The immune system was once thought to be an autonomous defence system, independent of the nervous and endocrine systems. Yet research has built over many years to demonstrate clear links between these systems (Ader, 1995). Two key figures in developing the field have been Aaron Rasmussen, who demonstrated that stress could increase susceptibility to herpes simplex virus in mice as early as 1957 (Rasmussen *et al.*, 1957) and George Solomon (Solomon & Moos, 1964). These and many other researchers have helped to gather an evidence base for the effects of stress on immune changes in humans. The first section of this chapter explains what PNI is, describing the pathways and systems involved. The next section examines how PNI is relevant to health outcomes and the last section summarises how PNI principles can be applied to improve health. The field contains some fascinating work and we hope that this introductory chapter broadens your understanding and ignites your interest.

Key Concepts

Acute and chronic stress
Catecholamines
Cognitive behavioural
   interventions
Cortisol
Emotional disclosure
Endocrine system
Hypothalamic-pituitary-
   adrenal axis (HPA)
Immune system
Inflammation
Natural immunity
Specific immunity
Sympathetic adrenal
   medullary system (SAM)

What is Psychoneuroimmunology?

As human beings we have evolved to respond quickly to threatening events thus increasing our potential for survival. Immediately upon cognition of a threat or challenge to well-being (whether it be escaping from a wild animal or avoiding a swerving vehicle), a cascade of physiological events unfold that instantly prepares our bodies for survival. At this time, a complex network of signalling is triggered between the central nervous system (CNS), the endocrine system and the immune system, with the bi-directional communication between these systems leading to physical changes that boost the chance of surviving the challenge.

Two interrelated endocrine systems become activated when the brain perceives a threat: the sympathetic adrenal medullary system (SAM) and the hypothalamic-pituitary-adrenal axis (HPA). Activation of these systems culminates in increased secretion of stress hormones. The SAM system is activated by the autonomic nervous system (ANS) and is characterised by the 'fight-or-flight' response of the sympathetic nervous system (SNS). SNS activation results in secretion of catecholamines, with norepinephrine released from sympathetic nerve terminals of the heart, lungs and other major organs and epinephrine released into general circulation from the adrenal medulla. The release of catecholamines increases sensory and motor activity, marked by increased vigilance, elevated heart rate and blood pressure, increased blood flow to essential organs and mobilisation of immune function. At the same time non-essential physiological activity such as reproduction and digestion are inhibited (Kaye & Lightman, 2005).

SAM activation enables an instant physiological response to a threatening event. Several minutes later the HPA axis becomes activated and provides additional energy resources. The HPA axis is initiated in the hypothalamus, a region of the brain that regulates functions such as growth, reproduction and appetite and when activated corticotrophin-releasing hormone (CRH) is released from the paraventricular nucleus of the hypothalamus. This stimulates the release of adrenocorticotropin hormone (ACTH) from the anterior pituitary gland culminating in the release of glucocorticoids (cortisol in humans) from the zona fasciculata region of the adrenal cortex (Miller *et al.*, 2007). Daily secretion of cortisol is vital for the effective function and regulation of many physiological systems including metabolism, glucose storage and use and is essential to learning, memory and emotion. Within the immune system cortisol secretion stimulates lymphocyte maturation and regulates inflammatory responses. Cortisol release is subject to daily fluctuations and patterns of the circadian rhythm and secretion may vary widely over a 24-hour period with morning peaks and evening troughs (John & Buckingham, 2003). During stress exposure, cortisol secretion enhances the cardiovascular activity promoted by catecholamine release and importantly, regulates the intensity and duration of the stress response by suppressing the SAM and immune systems.

The secretion of stress hormones offers significant physiological benefits when life is in danger, enabling immediate energy release, yet a problem can occur when the same biological response systems are activated when survival is not threatened, such as when anticipating public speaking or worrying about academic examinations. During these relatively benign events, increased concentrations of cortisol and catecholamines cause alterations in the distribution and activity of immune cells that can lead to poorer immune function (Rabin, 2005).

The immune system includes a variety of cells that identify and eliminate foreign matter in our bodies (antigens) (Rabin, 2005). The immune system can be divided into natural (innate) and specific (acquired) immune responses. Natural immunity consists of all-purpose cells that attack many different pathogens (disease-causing antigens) within minutes or hours; some of these include phagocytic cells (e.g. neutrophils, monocytes, macrophages) and natural killer (NK) cells. Specific immunity consists of immune cells that only respond to specific antigens and can take up to several days to respond. It involves three types of lymphocytes: B-lymphocytes (produce antibodies); T-helper cells (produce cytokines – soluble proteins that regulate immune responses); and T-cytotoxic cells (destroy cells). The response to an antigen or tissue damage causes inflammation (with heat, pain, swelling, redness); acute inflammation involves the rapid movement of neutrophils and monocytes to the site. Failure of the acute inflammatory response to remove the agent quickly, can lead to activation of the specific response and chronic inflammation.

A comprehensive meta-analytic review of almost 300 studies that have investigated stress-related changes in immune parameters, found that the nature and duration of the stressor influences immune activity (Segerstrom & Miller, 2004). Acute stress, such as laboratory stress tests, was found to upregulate parameters of natural immunity, with rises in the number of neutrophils and NK cells in peripheral blood suggesting redistribution of immune cells in preparation for infection or injury. There was some evidence for acute stress to downregulate specific immunity. Chronic stress, such as the long-term stress experienced by informal caregivers, was associated with the most immunosuppression, with decreases observed in both natural and specific immunity. Overall this review suggests that short-term stressful events elicit potentially beneficial immune changes, whereas chronic stress elicits immune changes that are potentially detrimental.

It is predominantly through neuorendocrine pathways that stresses and worries can lead to adverse health consequences, such as increased susceptibility to colds and influenza and inflammatory or autoimmune conditions such as arthritis and lupus. We examine such consequences in the following section.

How Clinically Relevant is PNI to Health Outcomes?

This section addresses the question of whether the effects of psychological factors on immune parameters are large enough to alter health outcomes in a meaningful way. Many of the changes in immune functioning caused by stress still remain in the normal range and in these cases the consequences for health are unclear (Bachen et al., 2007). Nevertheless, a number of studies support the hypothesis that psychological stress can impair health outcomes and that the effects are mediated by changes in immune functioning. Here, we focus on four areas of health in which PNI research has been performed; wound healing; colds; infections/vaccinations; and heart disease.

Wound healing

Wound healing presents a good model for studying how psychological parameters can affect immune function as well as tissue healing. The immune system is heavily involved in wound repair. In the initial stages of healing, pro-inflammatory cytokines, such as interleukin-1 (IL-1), attract phagocytes to the wound, which remove infectious agents and prepare the site for the growth of new tissue.

Evidence for the effects of stress on healing comes from both animal and human studies. Mice placed under restraint stress have shown higher glucocorticoid secretion, less inflammation, impaired bacterial clearance and slower healing compared to other mice (Padget et al., 1998; Rojas et al., 2002). Most human studies have been laboratory based and used 3.5 mm punch biopsy or induced blister wounds, where a variety of stressors have been shown to affect healing. In a classic study of chronic stress, punch biopsy wounds were made to the arms of 13 women caring for relatives with dementia and to 13 age-matched controls. Healing was on average nine days slower in the carers, who also had lower IL-1 responses to antigen stimulation in peripheral blood (Kiecolt-Glaser et al., 1995). Brief naturalistic stress has also been associated with slower healing. Eleven dental students were given 3.5 mm biopsy wounds to the hard palate in their mouths during vacation time and again (on the other side of the mouth) three days before examinations. The wounds took on average three days longer to heal during examinations than during vacation time (Marucha et al., 1998). Forty-two married couples were given blister wounds to the arm on two occasions: one occasion was followed by a supportive interaction and one occasion was followed by a marital disagreement. Healing was one day slower after the marital disagreement (Kiecolt-Glaser et al., 2005). The effects of stress on wound healing in laboratory settings are moderate to large (Kiecolt-Glaser et al., 1998).

Research has also shown that anger and depression can influence healing. An inability to control anger was associated with both higher cortisol and slower healing in a community sample of 98 participants who received biopsy wounds to the arm (Gouin et al., 2008). Participants with more depressive symptoms were likely to demonstrate slower healing in a sample of 193 students given 3.5 mm wounds to the hard palate (Bosch *et al.*, 2007).

A few studies have extended these laboratory findings to clinical populations. Higher pre-operative stress and worry about surgery in participants undergoing hernia repair have been associated with lower levels of IL-1 and matrix metalloproteinase-9 (involved in tissue remodelling) in wound drain fluid over 24 hours, as well as higher pain and a slower recovery (Broadbent *et al.*, 2003). Among patients with chronic leg ulcers, those with higher depression and anxiety were found to be more likely to have delayed healing (Cole-King & Harding, 2001). Later work has corroborated this finding, showing slower healing and higher recurrence of foot ulcers in diabetic patients who are higher in depressive symptoms (Monami *et al.*, 2008).

Cold studies

Stress-related changes in enumerative (counts of cell types) and functional (responses to a challenge) immune parameters are often reported in PNI research, such as decreases in lymphocyte number and function. Investigating relationships between psychosocial stress and immune response to viral infections occurring *in vivo* (within an organism), such as human immunodeficiency virus (HIV) infection and progression (Cole *et al.*, 1996), reactivation of latent herpes viruses (Glaser & Kiecolt-Glaser, 1997) and susceptibility to the common cold (Cohen *et al.*, 1998), provides realistic and clinically relevant information on stress-related immune function and health.

Throughout the year we are continually exposed to infectious agents such as common cold viruses, yet only a proportion of individuals go on to develop an infectious illness. A key study in this field was able to demonstrate a positive association between self-reported stress and incidence of upper respiratory infection when 394 healthy participants were intentionally inoculated with nasal drops containing one of five respiratory viruses and quarantined in an apartment for one week (Cohen *et al.*, 1991). At the study outset participants reported on the number of major stressful life events experienced during the previous 12 months and how unpredictable, uncon-

trollable and overwhelming they considered their lives to be. Findings revealed that the number of respiratory infections and clinical colds experienced by participants increased in a dose-response manner with the level of reported psychological stress, that is, the more life stress experienced, the more likely the person was to become infected with the virus or suffer a clinical cold.

Other common cold studies add further complexity to the relationship between stress and susceptibility to infectious disease. A study similarly investigating stress and resistance to the common cold following nasal inoculation with a cold virus and weekly quarantine, observed a higher risk of developing a common cold in participants reporting severe chronic stress over a period of more than one month compared with participants reporting severe acute stress for less than one month (Cohen *et al.*, 1998). Research exploring naturally occurring illness incidence found that individuals reporting higher numbers of life events and weekly stress plus exhibiting a higher cortisol response to a stressful speech task also experienced an increased natural incidence of upper respiratory illness (Cohen *et al.*, 2002). Other research has found that personality factors, such as a positive emotional style, predicted greater resistance to rhinovirus infection after nasal inoculation followed by a quarantine period, whereas negative emotional style was not associated with disease resistance (Cohen *et al.*, 2003). In addition to this, pro-inflammatory cytokine production was found to mediate the relationship between emotional style and incidence of upper respiratory illness, with higher positive emotional style associated with fewer signs and symptoms of infection and lower interleukin-6 (IL-6) levels (Doyle *et al.*, 2006).

Infections and vaccinations

Vaccinations are commonly administered to prevent diseases such as influenza and hepatitis A and B, with widespread use of vaccinations for health protection offering a useful immune paradigm for PNI research. A healthy immune response to vaccination is indicated by a measurable rise in antibody levels (titers) during the post-vaccination period, which signifies that the person has seroconverted (produced antibodies in response to the vaccine). Some vaccines require a specified rise in antibody titers to be considered clinically adequate, such as a fourfold rise in antibody titers following influenza vaccination required for sufficient protection from the virus. As with the common cold studies, investigating immune responses to vaccination allows the researcher to gain clinically relevant evidence of immune competence and potential vulnerability to infectious disease. An overview of vaccination research predominantly indicates immunological impairment in response to natural stressors, such as the stress experienced by spousal caregivers and in students undergoing academic examinations.

Influenza vaccination provides important health protection to the elderly prior to the yearly influenza season, yet several studies indicate poorer responses to influenza vaccination in elderly informal caregivers of dementia sufferers compared with non-caregivers (Kiecolt-Glaser et al., 1996; Vedhara et al., 1999). A study of 117 elderly individuals identified that the 50 spousal caregivers produced impaired antibody responses to a trivalent (containing three viral strains) influenza vaccination compared with a well-matched group of non-caregivers, with fewer caregivers producing a fourfold increase in antibody titers to one viral strain in the 28 days following vaccination (Vedhara et al., 1999). Importantly, other research has identified that former spousal caregivers have shown the same impaired influenza immunity as current caregivers, suggesting that these elderly individuals remain at risk of infectious disease even following the death of the ailing spouse (Glaser et al., 1998). As the elderly undergo a natural age-related decline in immune function these studies highlight the potential for health-related issues in chronically stressed elderly individuals.

Research also indicates diminished antibody responses to vaccination in young healthy individuals when exposed to academic examinations or reporting higher distress. Higher levels of self-reported stress significantly impaired antibody responses to a three-dose hepatitis B vaccination series in a group of 48 healthy medical students who received each vaccine dose on the final day of an examination period (Glaser et al., 1992). Students reporting lower perceived stress and anxiety during examinations seroconverted one month after the first vaccine dose, whereas following

the third and final vaccine dose, those reporting higher social support and lower anxiety exhibited a more robust immune response to the vaccine. Other studies have found that students reporting higher stress and higher numbers of stressful life events exhibited poorer antibody responses five months following influenza vaccination (Burns et al., 2003) and students reporting higher numbers of life events produced lower antibody responses to meningococcal C vaccination (Phillips, Burns et al., 2005).

A wide range of psychosocial variables, such as perceptions of adequate social support and loneliness, have been found to influence vaccination responses. Elevated feelings of loneliness and smaller social network size were associated with lower antibody responses to influenza vaccination (Pressman et al., 2005) and higher levels of stress, insomnia and social dysfunction were found in those producing lower antibody responses to meningococcal C vaccination (Burns et al., 2002). Students reporting lower social support produced poorer antibody responses to pneumococcal vaccination, whereas students reporting greater numbers of stressful life events produced poorer responses to hepatitis A vaccination (Gallagher et al., 2008). Research also indicates that individual differences predict vaccination outcomes, with higher positive affect in individuals with more robust antibody responses to hepatitis B vaccination (Marsland et al., 2006) and higher neuroticism scores in those producing lower antibody responses to influenza vaccination (Phillips, Carroll et al., 2005).

Heart disease

There is growing evidence for the influence of psychological factors on the development and progression of heart disease. Several longitudinal studies have shown that higher stress leads to a higher incidence of cardiac disease. A 14-year Whitehall study found that workers who reported chronic stress were more than twice as likely to develop metabolic syndrome (a cluster of risk factors for cardiovascular disease) than those without stress (Chandola et al., 2006). A study of 6395 men followed over a mean of 11.8 years showed those with higher stress at baseline were more likely to have developed coronary artery disease (Rosengren et al., 1991). Occupations involving high psychological workload and low decision latitude (job strain) have been associated with past myocardial infarction in representative US samples when controlling for other risk factors (Karasek *et al.*, 1988). A review of 17 empirical studies concluded that there is strong consistent evidence for an association between job strain and cardiovascular disease (Belkic *et al.*, 2004). Other work has compared 11,119 cases of heart attack with 13,648 matched controls and demonstrated that higher stress (work, family or financial) is associated with increased risk of myocardial infarction across regions, ethnicities and gender (Rosengren *et al.*, 2004). Depression was also more frequent in those who had heart attacks than controls.

The immunological pathways through which psychological factors influence heart disease are not fully known. Evidence suggests that chronic, episodic and acute psychological factors may influence different stages of heart disease (Kop, 2003). Chronic psychological factors, such as chronic stress or a hostile personality type, encourage atherosclerosis (the build up of plaque in the arteries) through increased lipid deposition and inflammatory processes. Episodic psychological factors, such as depression, may act to destabilise atherosclerotic plaques through activation of the ACTH pathway. Acute stressors, such as anger outbursts, are known to cause cardiac ischaemia (lack of blood supply) and trigger acute coronary syndromes by promoting the rupture of plaques. Steptoe and Brydon (2005) describe the pathways that link stress to biological responses, which promote inflammation and thrombosis (formation of a blood clot), leading to acute coronary syndromes and atherosclerosis. Genetic vulnerability and health behaviours are likely moderators of the influence of stress on heart disease.

Recent studies continue to define these pathways. Inflammatory stress responses have been linked to structural changes in artery walls. Higher prolonged fibrinogen (involved in blood clotting) and higher levels of the cytokine TNFα in response to an acute laboratory-based stress test were associated with arterial stiffness in healthy volunteers at a three-year follow-up (Ellins *et al.*, 2008). Disruption of the HPA axis has been linked with a type-D personality (characterised by high negative affectivity and social inhibition) in survivors of acute cardiac events (Molloy *et al.*, 2008).

How can PNI be used to Improve Health Outcomes?

The previous sections have described how psychological factors can influence immune parameters and contribute to poorer health, using examples in the areas of wound healing, susceptibility to colds, responses to vaccinations and coronary artery disease. An important question now is 'can psychological interventions impact immune system responses sufficiently to improve health?'

The way psychological interventions, such as stress management, relaxation training, emotional disclosure and hypnosis, could operate is by decreasing negative mood states with associated decreases in sympathetic nervous system and hormonal activation, in turn regulating immune processes (Miller & Cohen, 2001). A number of trials have found evidence supporting the benefits of such interventions, although meta-analyses combining the evidence across all trials have been less convincing, depending on the type of intervention, outcome measured and study population. Here we discuss some of the main interventions and findings.

Emotional disclosure

Emotional disclosure is a central tenet of psychotherapy. It refers to acknowledging and discussing deeply personal issues with attention to labelling the problem and discussing its causes and consequences (Pennebaker, 1997). Over the past 20 years, research led by Jamie Pennebaker has revealed a rather remarkable phenomenon. Writing about important emotional issues and exploring one's own deepest thoughts and feelings for three to five consecutive days for 15–30 minutes each day, can impact physician visits, immune function and autonomic activity, as well as improvements in mood (Pennebaker, 1997). A therapist does not need to be present for the benefits of emotional disclosure to occur. It is thought that emotional disclosure may help reduce stress by reappraisal and cognitive processing of the event.

Emotional writing can cause increases in distress during the writing process and immediate effects on immune responses, but it is likely that the longer term effects have more impact on health outcomes (Booth,

2005). A notable trial in this area showed that healthy medical students who wrote continuously for 20 minutes about traumatic or upsetting life events over four consecutive days resulted in enhanced antibody response to hepatitis B vaccination four and six months post-vaccination compared with a control group who wrote about unemotional daily events (Petrie *et al.*, 1998). Other work has shown that asthma patients experienced improvements in lung function and arthritis patients experienced reductions in disease activity four months following the writing intervention compared to a control group (Smyth *et al.*, 1999). Furthermore, a trial of 36 healthy people randomised to either expressive writing or time management writing and given a punch biopsy wound two weeks later, showed that wounds were smaller at 14 and 21 days after wounding in the emotional disclosure group (Weinman *et al.*, 2008). It is useful to compare these studies to a trial in which African Americans were asked to write about their experiences with racial discrimination; they exhibited poorer antibody responses to influenza vaccination compared to those writing about neutral topics (Stetler *et al.*, 2006). Those participants who were unable to make clear causal attributions for the upsetting events had the poorest responses, which underlines the importance of appraisal in emotional disclosure interventions.

A meta-analysis on written emotional expression, which reported a moderate overall effect size d of .47, supported the ability of this type of intervention to improve reported physical health, psychological well-being, physiological and general functioning, but not health behaviours (Smyth, 1998). A larger meta-analysis of 146 studies using a random effects approach concluded that emotional disclosure was effective with an effect size, r = .075 (Frattaroli, 2006). This is interpreted as worthwhile, especially considering its low-cost, non-invasive nature. Having at least three writing sessions of at least 15-minute duration, disclosure of more recent trauma, instructions that no one will read the writing, writing about previously undisclosed topics, disclosure in a private setting and follow-up of less than one month, led to greater effect sizes. Stronger effects were seen in populations with physical health problems, a history of trauma, males and non-students. This suggests that emotional disclosure might work best under these conditions.

Cognitive behaviour therapy and psychotherapy

Cognitive behavioural interventions have been applied to clinical groups to alleviate the distress of medical treatments, to prevent disease progression and to enhance physical and emotional well-being (Antoni, 2005). A study of 73 HIV-infected men identified that the group who attended a 10-week cognitive behavioural stress management (CBSM) intervention reported decreased anxiety, anger and stress and exhibited lower urinary epinephrine and higher numbers of T lymphocytes compared with the waitlist control group (Antoni *et al.*, 2000). Similarly, a 10-week CBSM intervention provided positive immune benefits to HIV-infected males who exhibited reduced herpes simples virus (HSV-2) antibody titers following the intervention (Cruess *et al.*, 2000).

A study investigating 43 elderly spousal carers of dementia patients, a group known to suffer high levels of chronic stress, showed that those who attended an eight-week CBSM intervention that included weekly one-hour counselling that focused on the caregiver role, relaxation training and cognitive restructuring, exhibited enhanced antibody responses to a trivalent influenza vaccination following the intervention compared with the non-intervention groups (Vedhara *et al.*, 2003).

There has been mixed evidence for the effects of psychological interventions on cancer survival. A well-known study found that of 86 women with metastatic breast cancer, those who participated in weekly sessions of expressive supportive group therapy for one year survived 18 months longer over a 10-year period compared with a control group (Spiegel *et al.*, 1989). However, a recent replication of this trial found no overall statistically significant effect on survival time (Spiegel *et al.*, 2007). Other research supporting a link between psychological therapy, the immune system and cancer survival includes a trial with melanoma patients who underwent a six-week intervention of education, coping and stress management techniques. Patients exhibited increased immune activity and survived longer than the control group, with melanoma recurrence in almost twice as many control group participants (Fawzy *et al.*, 1993). Two meta-analyses concluded that there was no effect of psychotherapy on survival time (Chow *et al.*, 2004; Edwards *et al.*, 2004), although one found support for individual but not group interventions (Smedslund & Ringdal, 2004). More recently Coyne *et al.* (2007) examined each trial in detail, finding methodological weaknesses and concluding that trials to date have been underpowered and the available evidence for effects on survival does not justify a larger trial. Cancer patients who are distressed may be the most likely to benefit from psychological interventions because significant reductions in their distress may be achievable. To help establish the utility of psychological interventions, future trials need to target this group.

Relaxation and exercise

Exercise and relaxation interventions have generated positive immune benefits in non-patient populations. Many of these trials have aimed to improve immune responses in older persons, as old age tends to make us more susceptible to infections. Elderly individuals who participated in progressive muscle relaxation training for one month exhibited increased NK cell activity and decreased antibody titers to herpes simplex virus (Kiecolt-Glaser *et al.*, 1985). Participation in a 15-week tai chi programme resulted in improved health functioning and immune benefits in community-dwelling elderly who exhibited heightened immunity to varicella-zoster virus following the intervention (Irwin *et al.*, 2003).

The effects of acute mental stress and exercise on vaccination response have been studied in a younger population. Sixty young healthy college students were assigned to one of three experimental conditions immediately prior to receiving influenza and meningococcal A and C vaccination: a stressful mental arithmetic task; 45-minute dynamic exercise condition (cycling); or control condition. Females assigned to the mental stress and exercise conditions, although not males, produced an elevated antibody response to the A/Panama influenza viral strain 4 and 20 weeks post-vaccination (Edwards *et al.*, 2006). In contrast, males (but not females) exposed to the exercise and mental stress conditions exhibited enhanced meningococcal A antibody responses 4 and 20 weeks post-vaccination (Edwards *et al.*, 2008). For each gender, stress-induced immunoenhancement was only manifest when the same gender in the control group produced a poor immune response. This suggests that acute stressors may enhance vaccine responses in individuals whose immune responses are less robust.

Meditation is a form of mental relaxation that has been found to afford positive consequences to physical and psychological health, such as reduced anxiety and depression (Kabat-Zinn *et al.*, 1992; Teasedale *et al.*, 2000). A study of 48 healthy individuals found that those who attended an eight-week meditation training programme that included 2–3 hour weekly classes in the workplace with some home practice, produced increased antibody responses to influenza vaccination and showed increased brain electrical activity (measured by EEG) that is normally associated with positive effect (Davidson *et al.*, 2003). Students exposed to self-hypnosis training over a three-week period prior to examinations exhibited improved mood and increased NK and CD8 cell numbers (Gruzelier *et al.*, 2001).

Although there is considerable observational evidence that stress is associated with impaired wound healing, few experimental studies have tested the hypothesis that interventions to reduce stress can improve wound repair. A surgical trial showed that relaxation training and guided imagery improved anxiety, urinary cortisol and wound erythema (redness) compared to a control group (Holden-Lund, 1988). However, a study of blister wound healing found that relaxation training made no difference to healing (Gouin *et al.*, 2008).

Conclusion

The SAM and HPA are two bi-directional endocrine pathways that connect psychological states such as stress to functioning of the immune system. While responses to short-term stressors may be adaptive, chronic stress leads to immune changes that are potentially detrimental. Research has shown that stress can have effects on our health, including impaired wound healing, increased susceptibility to infections, altered immune responses to immunisations and increased heart disease. Interventions designed to increase health and well-being vary widely in nature and duration. Research nonetheless illustrates that interventions in both clinical and healthy groups can enhance immune functioning and impact health outcomes. To further determine the effectiveness of interventions, future trials need to employ careful methodology, target the right populations to the intervention type, ensure adequate statistical power and choose appropriate outcome measures which permit an examination of clinical relevance as well as mechanisms (Miller & Cohen, 2001).

It is not easy to do research in psychoneuroimmunology. Choosing which parameters to measure, when and in whom can be difficult, but guides to immune measures can assist (e.g. Wetherell & Vedhara, 2005). There are complex interrelationships between immune parameters and findings can be difficult to interpret. However, the rewards of carefully planned and performed research are substantial. Research in PNI helps us to understand how we as human beings function and how our cognitions, emotions and behaviour can contribute to our health and well-being.

Discussion Points

1 Why is the duration of a stressor important in determining its influence on health?
2 Should doctors administer a stress test before giving vaccinations?
3 Why are the areas of wound healing, susceptibility to infections, responses to vaccinations and the development of heart disease good for studying mechanisms and effects in psychoneuroimmunology?

4 What other illness populations would be suitable to investigate the effects of psychological factors on immune function and health and why?
5 What kinds of interventions would be most helpful for people living with long-term stressors, such as caring for a relative with dementia?
6 How do you think stress reduction interventions might be tailored to people with chronic health conditions?

Further Reading

Ader, R. (Ed.) (2007). *Psychoneuroimmunology* (4th edn). Amsterdam: Academic Press.
Segerstrom S.C. & Miller, G.E. (2004). Psychological stress and the human immune system: A meta-analytic study of 30 years of inquiry. *Psychological Bulletin, 130,* 601–630.
Vedhara, K. & Irwin, M.R. (Eds.) (2005). *Human psychoneuroimmunology.* Oxford: Oxford University Press.

References

Ader, R. (1995). Historical perspectives on psychoneuroimmunology. In H. Friedman, T.W. Klein & A.L. Friedman (Eds.) *Psychoneuroimmunology, stress and infection.* Florida: CRC Press.
Antoni, M. (2005). Behavioural interventions and psychoneuroimmunology. In K. Vedhara & M.R. Irwin (Eds.) *Human psychoneuroimmunology* (pp. 285–318). Oxford: Oxford University Press.
Antoni, M., Cruess, D.G., Cruess, S., Lutgendorf, S., Kumar, M., Ironson, G. *et al.* (2000). Cognitive-behavioral stress management intervention affects on anxiety, 24-hr urinary norepinephrine output and T-cytotoxic/suppressor cells over time among symptomatic HIV-infected gay men. *Journal of Consulting and Clinical Psychology, 68,* 31–45.
Bachen, E., Cohen, S. & Marsland, A. (2007). Psychoneuroimmunology. In S. Ayers, A. Baum, C. McManus, S. Newman, K. Wallston, J. Weinman & R. West (Eds.) *Cambridge handbook of psychology, health and medicine* (2nd edn, pp. 167–172). Cambridge: Cambridge University Press.
Belkic, K.L., Landsbergis, P.A., Schnall, P.L. & Baker, D. (2004). Is job strain a major source of cardiovascular disease risk? A critical review of the empirical evidence, with a clinical perspective. *Scandinavian Journal of Work Environment & Health, 30,* 85–128.
Bosch, J.A., Engeland, C.G., Cacioppo, J.T. & Marucha, P.T. (2007). Depressive symptoms predict mucosal wound healing. *Psychosomatic Medicine, 69,* 597–605.

Booth, R. (2005). Emotional disclosure and psychoneuroimmunology. In K. Vedhara & M.R. Irwin (Eds.) *Human psychoneuroimmunology* (pp. 319–341). Oxford: Oxford University Press.

Broadbent, E., Petrie, K.J., Alley, P.G. & Booth, R.J. (2003). Psychological stress impairs early wound repair following surgery. *Psychosomatic Medicine, 65*, 865–869.

Burns, V.E., Carroll, D., Drayson, M., Whitham, M. & Ring, C. (2003). Life events, perceived stress and antibody response to influenza vaccination in young, healthy adults. *Journal of Psychosomatic Research, 55*, 569–572.

Burns, V.E., Drayson, M., Ring, C., & Carroll, D. (2002). Perceived stress and psychological well-being are associated with antibody status after meningitis C conjugate vaccination. *Psychosomatic Medicine, 64*, 963–970.

Chandola, T., Brunner, E. & Marmot, M. (2006). Chronic stress at work and the metabolic syndrome: Prospective study. *British Medical Journal, 332*, 521–525.

Chow, E., Tsao, M.N. & Harth, T. (2004). Does psychosocial intervention improve survival in cancer? A meta-analysis. *Palliative Medicine, 18*, 25–31.

Cohen, S., Doyle, W.J., Turner, R.B., Alper, C.M. & Skoner, D.P. (2003). Emotional style and susceptibility to the common cold. *Psychosomatic Medicine, 65*, 652–657.

Cohen, S., Frank, E., Doyle, W.J., Skoner, D.P., Rabin, B.S. & Gwaltney, J.M. (1998). Types of stressors that increase susceptibility to the common cold in healthy adults. *Health Psychology, 17*(3), 214–223.

Cohen, S., Hamrick, N., Rodriguez, M.S., Feldman, P.J., Rabin, B.S. & Manuck, S.B. (2002). Reactivity and vulnerability to stress-associated risk for upper respiratory illness. *Psychosomatic Medicine, 64*, 302–310.

Cohen, S., Tyrrell, D.A.J. & Smith, A.P. (1991). Psychological stress and susceptibility to the common cold. *New England Journal of Medicine, 325*, 606–612.

Cole, S., Kemeny, M.E., Taylor, S.E., Visscher, B.R. & Fahey, J.L. (1996). Accelerated course of human immunodeficiency virus infection in gay men who conceal their homosexual identity. *Psychosomatic Medicine, 58*, 219–231.

Cole-King, A. & Harding, K.G. (2001). Psychological factors and delayed healing in chronic wounds. *Psychosomatic Medicine, 63*, 216–220.

Coyne, J.C., Stefanek, M. & Palmer, S.C. (2007). Psychotherapy and survival in cancer: The conflict between hope and evidence. *Psychological Bulletin, 133*, 367–394.

Cruess, S., Antoni, M., Cruess, D., Fletcher, M.A., Ironson, G., Kumar, M. *et al.* (2000). Reductions in herpes simplex virus type 2 antibody titers after cognitive behavioral stress management and relationships with neuroendocrine function, relaxation skills and social support in HIV-positive men. *Psychosomatic Medicine, 62*, 828–837.

Davidson, R.J., Kabat-Zinn, J., Schumacher, J., Rosenkranz, M., Muller, D. Santorelli, S.F. *et al.* (2003). Alterations in brain and immune function produced by mindfulness meditation. *Psychosomatic Medicine, 65*, 564–570.

Doyle, W.J., Gentile, D.A. & Cohen, S. (2006). Emotional style, nasal cytokines and illness expression after experimental rhinovirus exposure. *Brain, Behavior, and Immunity, 20*, 175–181.

Edwards, A.G., Hailey, S. & Maxwell, M. (2004). Psychological interventions for women with metastatic breast cancer. *Cochrane Database Systems Review, CD004253.*

Edwards, K.M., Burns, V.E., Adkins, A.E., Carroll, D., Drayson, M. & Ring, C. (2008). Meningococcal A vaccination response is enhanced by acute stress in men. *Psychosomatic Medicine, 70*, 147–151.

Edwards, K.M., Burns, V.E., Reynolds, T., Carroll, D., Drayson, M. & Ring, C. (2006). Acute stress exposure prior to influenza vaccination enhances antibody response in women. *Brain, Behavior, and Immunity, 20*, 159–168.

Ellins, E., Halcox, J., Donald, A., Field, B., Brydon, L., Deanfield, J. & Steptoe, A. (2008). Arterial stiffness and inflammatory response to psychophysiological stress. *Brain, Behavior, and Immunity, 22*, 941–948.

Fawzy, F.I., Fawzy, N.W., Hyun, C.S., Elashoff, R., Guthrie, D., Fahey, J.L. et al. (1993). Malignant melanoma: Effects of an early structured psychiatric intervention, coping, and affective state on recurrence and survival 6 years later. *Archives of General Psychiatry, 50*, 681–689.

Frattaroli, J. (2006). Experimental disclosure and its moderators: A meta-analysis. *Psychological Bulletin, 132*, 823–865.

Gallagher, S., Phillips, A.C., Ferraro, A.J., Drayson, M.T. & Carroll, D. (2008). Psychosocial factors are associated with the antibody response to both thymus-dependent and thymus-independent vaccines. *Brain, Behavior, and Immunity, 22*, 456–460.

Glaser, R. & Kiecolt-Glaser, J. (1997). Chronic stress modulates the virus-specific immune response to latent herpes simplex virus type-1. *Annals of Behavioral Medicine, 19*, 78–82.

Glaser, R., Kiecolt-Glaser, J.K., Bonneau, R.H., Malarkey, W., Kennedy, S. & Hughes, J. (1992). Stress-induced modulation of the immune response to recombinant hepatitis B vaccine. *Psychosomatic Medicine, 54*, 22–29.

Glaser, R., Kiecolt-Glaser, J.K., Malarkey, W.B. & Sheridan, J. F. (1998). The influence of psychological stress on the immune response to vaccines. *Annals of the New York Academy of Sciences, 840*, 649–655.

Gouin, J.P., Kiecolt-Glaser, J.K., Malarkey, W.B. & Glaser, R. (2008). The influence of anger expression on wound healing. *Brain, Behavior, and Immunity, 22*, 699–708.

Gruzelier, J., Smith, F., Nagy, A. & Henderson, D. (2001). Cellular and humoral immunity, mood and exam stress: The influences of self-hypnosis and personality predictors. *International Journal of Psychophysiology, 42*, 55–71.

Holden-Lund, C. (1988) Effects of relaxation with guided imagery on surgical stress and wound healing. *Research in Nursing & Health, 11*, 235–244.

Irwin, M.R., Pike, J.L., Cole, J.C. & Oxman, M.N. (2003). Effects of a behavioral intervention, tai chi chih, on varicella-zoster virus specific immunity and health functioning in older adults. *Psychosomatic Medicine, 65*, 824–830.

John, C.D. & Buckingham, J.C. (2003). Cytokines: Regulation of the hypothalamic-pituitary-adrenal axis. *Current Opinion in Pharmacology, 3*, 78–84.

Kabat-Zinn, J., Massion, A.O., Kristeller, J., Peterson, L.G., Fletcher, K.E., Pbert, L. *et al.* (1992). Effectiveness of a meditation-based stress reduction program in the treatment of anxiety disorders. *American Journal of Psychiatry, 149*, 936–943.

Karasek, R.A., Theorell, T., Schwartz, J.E., Schnall, P.L., Pieper, C.F. & Michela, J.L. (1988). Job characteristics in relation to the prevalence of myocardial infarction in the US Health Examination Survey (HES) and the Health and Nutrition Examination Survey (HANES). *American Journal of Public Health, 78*, 910–918.

Kaye, J. & Lightman, S. (2005). Psychological stress and endocrine axes. In K. Vedhara & M.R. Irwin (Eds.) *Human psychoneuroimmunology* (pp. 25–52). Oxford: Oxford University Press.

Kiecolt-Glaser, J.K., Glaser, R., Gravenstein, S., Malarkey, W.B. & Sheridan, J. (1996). Chronic stress alters the immune response to influenza virus vaccine in older adults. *Proceedings of the National Academy of Sciences, 93*, 3043–3047.

Kiecolt-Glaser, J.K., Glaser, R., Williger, D., Stout, J., Messick, G., Sheppard, S. *et al.* (1985). Psychosocial enhancement of immunocompetence in a geriatric population. *Health Psychology, 4*, 25–41.

Kiecolt-Glaser, J.K., Loving, T.J., Stowell, J.R., Malarley, W.B., Lemeshow, S., Dickenson, S.L. & Glaser, R. (2005). Hostile martial interactions, proinflammatory cytokine production and wound healing. *Archives of General Psychiatry, 62*, 1377–1384.

Kiecolt-Glaser, J.K., Marucha, P.T., Malarkey, W.B., Mercado, A.M. & Glaser, R. (1995). Slowing of wound healing by psychological stress. *Lancet, 346*, 1194–1196.

Kiecolt-Glaser, J.K, Page, G.G., Marucha, P.T., MacCallum, R.C. & Glaser, R. (1998). Psychological influences on surgical recovery: Perspectives from psychoneuroimmunology. *American Psychologist, 53*, 1209–1218.

Kop, W.J. (2003). The integration of cardiovascular behavioural medicine and psychoneuroimmunology: New developments based on converging research fields. *Brain, Behavior, and Immunity, 17*, 233–237.

Marsland, A.L., Cohen, S., Rabin, B.S. & Manuck, S.B. (2006). Trait positive affect and antibody response to hepatitis B vaccination. *Brain, Behavior, and Immunity, 20*, 261–269.

Marucha, P.T., Kiecolt-Glaser, J.K. & Favagehi, M. (1998). Mucosal wound healing is impaired by examination stress. *Psychosomatic Medicine, 60*, 362–365.

Miller, G.E. & Cohen, S. (2001). Psychological interventions and the immune system: A meta-analytic review and critique. *Health Psychology, 20*, 47–63.

Miller, G.E., Chen, E. & Zhou, E.S. (2007). If it goes up, must it come down? Chronic stress and the hypothalamic-pituitary-adrenocortical axis in humans. *Psychological Bulletin, 133*, 25–45.

Molloy, G., Perkins-Porras, L., Strike, P. & Steptoe, A. (2008). Type-D personality and cortisol in survivors of acute coronary syndrome. *Psychosomatic Medicine, 70*, 863–868.

Monami, M., Longo, R., Desideri, C.M., Masotti, G., Marchionni, N. & Mannucci, E. (2008). The diabetic person beyond a foot ulcer: Healing, recurrence and depressive symptoms. *Journal of the American Podiatric Medical Association, 98*, 130–136.

Pennebaker, J.W. (1997). Writing about emotional experiences as a therapeutic process. *Psychological Science, 8*, 162–166.

Petrie, K.J., Booth, R.J., Pennebaker, J.W., Davison, K.P. & Thomas, M.G. (1995). Disclosure of trauma and immune response to a hepatitis B vaccination program. *Journal of Consulting and Clinical Psychology, 63*, 787–792.

Phillips, A.C., Burns, V.E., Carroll, D., Ring, C. & Drayson, M. (2005). The association between life events, social support and antibody status following thymus-dependent and thymus-independent vaccinations in healthy young adults. *Brain, Behavior, and Immunity, 19*, 325–333.

Phillips, A.C., Carroll, D., Burns, V.E. & Drayson, M. (2005). Neuroticism, cortisol reactivity and antibody response to vaccination. *Psychophysiology, 42*, 232–238.

Pressman, S.D., Cohen, S., Miller, G.E., Barkin, A., Rabin, B.S. & Treanor, J.J. (2005). Loneliness, social network size and immune response to influenza vaccination in college freshmen. *Health Psychology, 24*, 297–306.

Rabin, B.S. (2005). Introduction to immunology and immune-endocrine interactions. In K. Vedhara & M.R. Irwin (Eds.) *Human psychoneuroimmunology* (pp. 1–24). Oxford: Oxford University Press.

Rasmussen, A.F. Jr, Marsh, J.T. & Brill, N.Q. (1957). Increased susceptibility to herpes simplex in mice subjected to avoidance-learning stress or restraint. *Proceedings of the Society for Experimental Biology and Medicine, 96*, 183–189.

Rojas, I.G., Padgett, D.A., Sheridan, J.F. & Marucha, P. T. (2002) Stress-induced susceptibility to bacterial infection during cutaneous wound healing. *Brain Behavior, and Immunity, 16*, 74–84.

Rosengren, A., Tibblin, G. & Wilhelmsen, L. (1991). Self-perceived psychological stress and incidence of coronary artery disease in middle-aged men. *American Journal of Cardiology, 68*, 1171–1175.

Rosengren, A., Hawken, S., Ounpuu, S., Sliwa, K., Zubaid, M., Almahmeed *et al.* for the INTERHEART investigators (2004). Association of psychosocial risk factors with risk of acute myocardial infarction in 11,119 cases and 13,648 controls from 52 countries (the INTERHEART study): case-control study. *Lancet, 364*, 953–962.

Segerstrom S.C. & Miller, G.E. (2004). Psychological stress and the human immune system: A meta-analytic study of 30 years of inquiry. *Psychological Bulletin, 130*, 601–630.

Smedslund, G. & Ringdal, G.I. (2004). Meta-analysis of the effects of psychosocial interventions on survival time in cancer patients. *Journal of Psychosomatic Research, 57*, 123–131.

Smyth, J. (1998). Written emotional expression: effect sizes, outcome types and moderating variables. *Journal of Clinical and Consulting Psychology, 66*, 174–184.

Smyth, J.M., Stone, A.A., Hurewitz, A. & Kaell, A. (1999). Effects of writing about stressful experiences on symptom reduction in patients with asthma or rheumatoid arthritis: A randomized trial. *Journal of American Medical Association, 281*, 1304–1309.

Solomon, G.F. & Moos, R.H. (1964). Emotions, immunity and disease: A speculative theoretical integration. *Archives of General Psychiatry, 11*, 657–674.

Spiegel, D., Bloom, J.R., Kraemer, H.C. & Gottheil, E. (1989). Effect of psychosocial treatment on survival of patients with metastatic breast cancer. *Lancet, 2*, 888–891.

Spiegel, D., Butler, L.D., Giese-Davis, J., Koopman, C., Miller, E., DiMiceli, S. *et al.* (2007). Supportive-expressive group therapy and survival in patients with metastatic breast cancer: A randomized clinical intervention trial. *Cancer, 110*, 1130–1138.

Steptoe, A. & Brydon, L. (2005). Psychoneuroimmunology and heart disease. In K. Vedhara & M.R. Irwin (Eds.) *Human psychoneuroimmunology* (pp. 107–136). Oxford: Oxford University Press.

Stetler, C., Chen, E. & Miller, G. E. (2006). Written disclosure of experiences with racial discrimination and antibody response to an influenza vaccine. *International Journal of Behavioral Medicine, 13*, 60–68.

Teasedale, J.D., Segal, Z.V., Williams, J.M., Ridgeway, V.A., Soulsby, J.M. & Lau, M.A. (2000). Prevention of relapse/recurrence in major depression by mindfulness-based cognitive therapy. *Journal of Consulting and Clinical Psychology, 68*, 615–623.

Vedhara, K., Bennett, P.D., Clark, S., Lightman, S.L., Shaw, S., Perks, P. *et al.* (2003). Enhancement of antibody responses to influenza vaccination in the elderly following a cognitive-behavioural stress management intervention. *Psychotherapy and Psychosomatics, 72*, 245–252.

Vedhara, K., Cox, N.K.M., Wilcock, G.K., Perks, P., Hunt, M. anderson, S. *et al.* (1999). Chronic stress in elderly carers of dementia patients and antibody response to influenza vaccination. *Lancet, 353*, 627–631.

Weinman, J., Ebrecht, M., Scott, S., Walburn, J. & Dyson, M. (2008). Enhanced wound healing after emotional disclosure intervention. *British Journal of Health Psychology, 13*, 95–102.

Wetherell, M. & Vedhara, K. (2005). The measurement of physiological outcomes in health and clinical psychology. In J. Miles & P. Gilbert (Eds.) *Handbook of research methods for clinical and health psychology* (pp. 47–63). New York: Oxford University Press.

21

Coping with Stress

Joshua M. Smyth and Kelly B. Filipkowski

Chapter Outline

This chapter presents the concept of stress and its relation to health or illness. How one interprets, or appraises, a potentially stressful encounter will determine how one deals with the event. In this chapter many factors associated with how individuals cope with stressful events will be reviewed. An overview of coping is provided initially – discussing what coping is and why it is important to psychological and physical well-being. This is followed by a review of the wide range of styles of coping that individuals use, specifically noting the importance of matching the coping style to the requirements of the situation and the importance of understanding coping goals. Further, the concept of stress moderators, or factors that may influence how well one copes with a stressor, are introduced. Finally, this chapter concludes with a brief review of strategies that can be used to manage stress.

Key Concepts

Active coping style
Avoidant coping style
Blunting
Coping
Coping flexibility
Emotional approach coping
Emotional disclosure
Emotion-focused coping
External locus of control
Internal locus of control
Monitoring
Optimism
Pessimistic explanatory
 style
Primary appraisal
Proactive coping
Problem-focused coping
Secondary appraisal
Self-efficacy

Coping with Stress

It is clear that stress can negatively impact health and well-being – particularly when stress is intense and prolonged. Many theorists use a 'transactional' model to study stress and coping; this approach explicitly acknowledges the ongoing interactions between a person and his/her environment. In other words, stressful experiences are construed as person–environment transactions created initially by an individual's appraisal of the stressor and subsequently influenced by ongoing appraisals of available coping resources, effectiveness of coping behaviours and so forth. When faced with a stressor – something in the environment that may hold potential for threat or harm – a person evaluates the potential threat. This *primary appraisal* is a person's judgement about the significance of a stressor as being a threat (producing stress) or benign/irrelevant (not stressful). If a stressor is judged as threatening, *secondary appraisal* follows, which is an assessment of one's coping resources (Lazarus & Folkman, 1984). Secondary appraisals address what one believes – both about the nature of the stressor as well as what one can do to manage the circumstance (see Figure 21.1).

Actual *coping efforts* will unfold subsequent to these appraisal processes and, in turn, shape the outcome of the coping process.

If events occur that are appraised as stressful, they may pose health risks. There are multiple pathways through which stress can impact health; broadly defined, one can think about these as 'direct' and 'indirect' pathways. Direct pathways are the effects stress *directly* produces on biological systems such as the activation of the sympathetic nervous system or endocrine system (e.g. 'stress' hormones), or compromised immune functioning. Such physiological changes, especially when they are extreme or persistent, can influence health, posing a risk for the onset of new disease or the exacerbation of existing illnesses/conditions. Indirect pathways refer to alterations in behaviour. For instance, when under stress a person may sleep more poorly, drink alcohol to excess or be less adherent to a self-care regimen (e.g. taking medication). These behavioural changes in response to stress may *indirectly* pose health risks – again either by the onset of new conditions or exacerbation of health conditions that are already present. The degree to which stress is a risk for poorer health is strongly influenced by efforts to manage stress. The

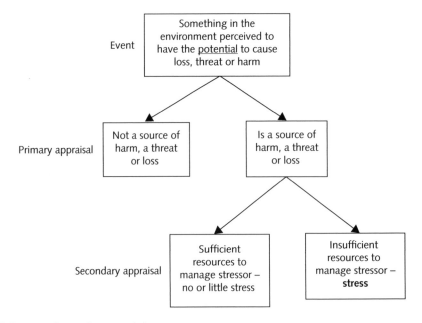

Figure 21.1 Primary and secondary appraisal

degree of success or failure in managing stress and accompanying emotional responses will help shape the short- and long-term adaptation to life's many challenges.

What is Coping?

Coping with a stressor is the process of dealing with both internal and environmental demands that are perceived to be overwhelming and exceeding the personal resources of the individual (Lazarus & Folkman, 1984). Coping consists of the wide range of efforts made to respond to, tolerate and attempt to resolve stressful events. In a broad sense, any behaviour could be considered coping – the key is that an individual engages in that behaviour in some attempt to manage stress and its consequences. It is also important to recognise that coping is a dynamic process in which the demands of the environment, available resources and characteristics of the event/stressor are constantly evolving and influencing each other. Thus, coping is not a one-time response to dealing with a stressor, but a balance of situational and personal factors that unfold over time.

Why is Coping Important?

Stressful experiences can disrupt one's normal functions and routines. This poses a risk for maladaptive outcomes, particularly when the stress is prolonged or extreme. To the degree people cope successfully, they promote a return to physiological, emotional and behavioural normalcy (or homeostasis). Coping can therefore strongly influence the degree to which people are negatively impacted by stress and help determine the balance between adaptive and maladaptive outcomes when faced with stressors. Early work on coping (e.g. Cohen & Lazarus, 1979) outlined five coping goals thought to be central to coping efforts:

- To reduce harmful environmental conditions and enhance the prospects of recovery.
- To tolerate or adjust to negative events or realities.
- To maintain a positive self-image.

- To maintain emotional equilibrium.
- To continue satisfying relationships with others.

Cohen and Lazarus (1979) further provided some general guidelines for evaluating if coping is successful. In particular, it is helpful to consider if the individual maintained (or returned to) healthy and normal psychological functioning. Similarly, effective coping should allow a person to resume, as much as possible, their usual activities and routines. It is worth recalling that stress is connected to the balance between health and illness through direct and indirect pathways. Effective coping can positively influence health and well-being through both of these pathways. For example, a coping response such as relaxation can blunt *direct* stress-related changes in physiological function (e.g. the release of 'stress' hormones, such as cortisol; e.g. Smyth *et al.*, 2001). Coping can also have an *indirect* effect on health-related behaviours or even consist of health behaviours. That is, engaging in effective coping strategies may result in a decreased likelihood of negative stress-related changes in behaviour (e.g. poor sleep or diet). Additionally, coping efforts may constitute specific behaviours that have health relevance; some with typically positive health impacts, such as exercise, others with typically negative health impact, such as smoking or binge drinking.

It is important to note that the impact of specific coping efforts may be mixed (i.e. both good and bad), depending on the outcome in question. Staying up all night to write a paper may result in a positive academic outcome (if not as positive as doing the paper in advance!), but the resultant fatigue and irritability may have negative impacts on health or interpersonal relationships. These types of mixed results are common and they start to provide a sense of why people choose strategies that can appear maladaptive. Behaviours such as excessive drinking may be serving, quite successfully, a very specific coping goal to an individual (e.g. escaping from an immediate negative mood state). Thus, efforts made to understand coping need to understand what goal(s) an individual is trying to meet. Often, successful attempts to change coping behaviours need to focus on changing coping *goals* in addition to changing coping *strategies*.

Coping Styles

Given the range of stressors a person may face, both in terms of severity and content, it is not surprising that there is a wide array of coping responses. Early work found some evidence that different individuals may be more or less likely to report engaging in specific coping strategies (see Carver *et al.*, 1989). Although it is tempting to assume that individuals have a limited coping repertoire that they apply to all circumstances, this is likely not to be the case. Often people appear unaware of their coping efforts if they are asked to report them after the fact. For instance, one study asked moderately stressed individuals to keep daily logs on palmtop computers of the moment-to-moment stressors and coping efforts they faced over a two-day period (Stone *et al.*, 1998). After these two days of self-monitoring their coping efforts, participants were interviewed about stressors they had coped with over the prior two days. People were surprisingly inaccurate about the strategies they endorsed only a day or two previous. In general, they were more likely to under-report using cognitive methods (e.g. 'concentrate on the next step') and over-report having used behavioural tactics (e.g. 'did something to relax'). This work suggests that − even when people report that they engage in certain coping behaviours consistently over time − actual coping behaviours may be quite dissimilar from those reported by the individual.

Actual coping efforts and behaviours are often determined by the specific circumstances an individual finds him/herself in at that time. Depending on the stressor and the context, someone may choose to avoid the problem altogether, others may tackle the problem and face it head on, while others may need to seek emotional support from a loved one. *Coping style* is used to refer to the general manner in which someone attempts to manage a stressful event and it is a simple way of categorising these coping behaviours. Although there is not perfect agreement on the ideal number or nature of distinctions to best describe coping styles, several of the major distinctions commonly made are described below.

Avoidant vs. active strategies

Sometimes people may choose to ignore a stressful event, distract themselves from the problem, or otherwise avoid any exposure to the stressor. In general,

these kinds of coping efforts are classified as an *avoidant coping style*. In contrast, an *active coping style* typically involves taking direct action to influence or manage a problem. Although much 'folk wisdom' suggests that avoidance and denial are 'bad', and active problem solving is 'good', the reality is a bit more complicated. In particular, it is critical that the coping efforts 'match' the demands of the circumstance (an idea explored in detail a bit later). More generally, each approach seems to have both advantages and disadvantages dependent upon the context (particularly the type of stressful event that is occurring).

Avoidant styles seem to be more effective with short-term threats (Suls & Fletcher, 1985), but may interfere with utilising cognitive resources to effectively manage more long-term concerns (Taylor & Clark, 1986). Attempts to wilfully suppress one's thoughts can actually backfire and create a rebound effect where one actually thinks *even more* about the forbidden thought (Wegner *et al.*, 1987)! Even when people engaging in an avoidant coping style report less stress, they can exhibit larger physiological responses than those using active coping strategies (Nyklícek *et al.*, 1998). This suggests that − even if avoidant coping might lead to an immediate cognitive and emotional distance from a stressor − more physiological pathways are not demonstrating the same benefit. There are, similarly, limitations in the capacity of active coping to manage stress. Active attempts to solve a problem may result in greater anxiety and distress in the short run (Smith *et al.*, 2000), even when it is related to better long-term adjustment. In addition, attempts to 'fix' a problem that has no solution can result in considerably more distress than efforts to avoid such problems.

Problem-focused vs. emotion-focused coping

Another distinction commonly made is between the two broad styles of coping referred to as problem-focused and emotion-focused coping. Someone who has just failed an exam and chooses to meet regularly with the professor and hires a tutor is thought to be engaging in *problem-focused coping*. That is, they are doing something constructive about the source of the problem and taking actions to resolve the stressor (this would be active and emotional coping – the categories are not exclusive!). On the other hand, *emotion-focused coping* are those efforts made to regulate the emotions associated with the stressor. Someone who is nervous about examination results may find comfort in talking to friends about the examination while they are waiting. Attempting to classify an approach as solely problem- or emotion-focused may be difficult. For instance, talking to a friend about a problem may be considered emotion-focused coping if the primary reason for doing so is to disclose feelings to a supportive listener. If, on the other hand, the goal of talking to a friend is to solicit their specific advice to develop a plan of action, then that strategy may also be thought of as problem-focused. Thus, it is important to consider the intent and motive for using a strategy in determining what type of approach it constitutes.

There exists a large range of specific coping efforts that fall within the broad definition of an emotion-focused approach. One important distinction that has been made regarding emotion-focused coping is between rumination and more active cognitive processing. Ruminating about a stressor, typically defined as the recurrence of intrusive negative thoughts, tends to increase negative mood states (e.g. depression; Morrow & Nolen-Hoeksema, 1990) and has been related to compromised immune functioning (Thomsen *et al.*, 2004). A more recent conceptualisation argues that earlier work has often unintentionally combined the assessment of emotion-focused coping with measures of emotional distress. An alternate approach is to carefully assess the acknowledgement, understanding and expression of emotions – a constellation of processes referred to as *emotional approach coping* (Austenfeld & Stanton, 2004). Efforts to clarify, reflect about and work through emotions are more likely to lead to positive adjustment regarding daily concerns, cancer, various chronic conditions, pain and issues surrounding fertility, among others (see Austenfeld & Stanton, 2004).

Responsive vs. proactive coping

Many of the coping styles illustrated are generally discussed in terms of responsive coping. That is, a stressful situation presents itself and the individual reacts to cope with the consequences. People sometimes, however, anticipate a potentially stressful situation before it happens and take measures to avoid it or alleviate it in advance, a process called *proactive coping* (Aspinwall & Taylor, 1997). This is typically a beneficial approach as being prepared for the stressful event may help one cope more effectively and, in fact, merely the act of preparing for a stressor can make it seem less overwhelming. Although useful, proactive coping may result in expending effort for an event that – when it occurs – may not be stressful, or the anticipated event may not occur at all.

Matching Coping Styles with Coping Demands

Most people use multiple types of coping, both within and across situations (Folkman & Lazarus, 1980). What is most critical to effective coping is that individual goals and coping style should match or fit the environmental demands, as some situations will be optimally addressed by utilising one approach over the other (or some combination of both). For instance, problem-focused coping may be most beneficial when the individual has control over the situation (e.g. work stressors) and can successfully execute some course of action. When control over the source and/or solution of the problem is not possible (e.g. bereavement) emotion-focused (or even avoidant) coping may be more beneficial (e.g. Stroebe *et al.*, 2005). In general, individuals who are able to alter their coping strategies in response to the situation demonstrate *coping flexibility* (Cheng, 2001). They generally fare better with stressors than those less flexible in their approach to coping; a more varied coping approach may allow for better matching between the coping strategy and the needs of a particular situation.

Personality and the Coping Response

In addition to the coping styles an individual utilises to manage stressful circumstances, personality characteristics can influence coping efforts. A few key areas where personality influences perceptions of stress, coping and health outcomes are reviewed.

Information-seeking styles

The manner in which people use or ignore information can lead to different coping styles. Information-seeking style is typically assessed by asking someone to imagine a stress-provoking scenario (e.g. 'Imagine you are afraid of flying and have to go somewhere by plane') and then report how they would use information to cope with the stressor. Miller and Mangan (1983) demonstrated that some people are *monitors*, or information seekers (e.g. 'I would read and reread the safety instruction booklet') and some are *blunters*, or information avoiders (e.g. 'I would watch the in-flight film even if I had seen it before'). They found that both monitors and blunters were least stressed when they were provided with the amount of information consistent with their coping strategy.

Repression

Some individuals tend to suppress, or divert, aversive thoughts from their conscious minds. These individuals are called repressors and they tend to score low on self-reported trait anxiety measures, but high on scores of defensiveness (Weinberger et al., 1979). When involved in a stressful circumstance, repressors are likely to avoid unpleasant thoughts and report low levels of distress; in contrast, however, they exhibit high physiological reactivity, such as long-term sensitivity to pain (Elfant et al., 2008) as well as increased heart rate and blood pressure (see Myers et al., 2008 for a review).

Negative affect and pessimism

Negative affect is described as a pervasive negative mood marked by anxiety, depression, hostility and general maladjustment across a wide range of situations (Watson & Clark, 1984). This general negative disposition has been described as a 'disease-prone' personality, as negative affect has been associated with poor health such as asthma, arthritis, ulcers, headaches and coronary artery disease (see Friedman & Booth-Kewley, 1987). Individuals with more negative affect are also more likely to experience illness vulnerability and use health-care services (Cohen & Williamson, 1991), perhaps due to their tendency to be hypervigi-lant about bodily sensations and interpret them as poor health (Pennebaker & Watson, 1991). Thus, even though there may be nothing objectively wrong with the individual, those with more negative affect are more likely to think they have a health problem, report symptoms and utilise health services.

Researchers have also suggested the existence of a general *pessimistic explanatory style* in which negative events are described in terms of internal, stable and global causes. Explanations that are internal refer to something residing within the individual, as in his or her personal characteristics; stable explanations refer to the perception of causes as being relatively permanent and do not change with the situation. Global explanations are those that are considered to be pervasive across all domains of life. Using this combination of explanations, someone with a pessimistic explanatory style will perceive negative events as being caused by something wrong with him/herself that is consistent across multiple domains and situations. This is, unsurprisingly, problematic as it can lead to feelings of helplessness and has been associated with poorer health more generally (Maruta et al., 2002).

Optimism

Optimism refers to a general expectancy that good things will happen or that desired outcomes will occur (e.g. Carver & Scheier, 1981). An optimistic disposition may lead one to perceive stress less often (Chang, 1998). Even when stress is encountered, someone higher in optimism may perceive a stressor to be lower in severity, is less likely to become depressed when faced with stress (Brissette et al., 2002) and tends to be more active and persistent with coping efforts (Segerstrom et al., 2003). Having a more optimistic outlook appears to enhance one's health; it has been associated with lower blood pressure (Räikkönen et al., 1999), protective effects on heart disease (Kubzansky et al., 2001) and better recovery after surgery (Scheier et al., 1989).

Control and self-efficacy

How much control one believes s/he has over the current situation has also been shown to affect coping efforts. Early work by Rotter (1966) distinguished between internal and external factors associated with perceptions of control. *Internal locus of control* refers to the perception that an individual has control over his/her life and the events that occur. Individuals exhibiting an *external locus of control*, on the other hand, perceive life events as being determined by luck, fate and the acts of others. More recent work often discusses personal control – the general belief of being able to direct one's own behaviour, impact one's own environment and have an effect on one's desired outcomes (additionally, Bandura (1977) discusses *self-efficacy*, a more narrow belief of self-control regarding a *specific* event or behaviour). Having a sense of personal control has been related to a variety of psychological and physical health benefits.

A landmark study examined this by providing nursing home residents with greater control over decisions in their daily lives, such as what leisure activities to engage in, taking care of oneself and one's room and caring for a plant. Compared to residents who had decisions made for them, residents provided greater perceived control over these small domains in their lives were happier and more active (Langer & Rodin, 1976). Furthermore, residents provided with an enhanced sense of control were more likely to still be living 18 months later than were the other residents (Rodin & Langer, 1977). More recently, a longitudinal study demonstrated that individuals with higher internal locus of control at age 10 had a significantly lower risk of hypertension, psychological distress, lower self-rated health and being overweight or obese as adults (Gale *et al.*, 2008). Looking at physiological consequences, perceptions of control have been shown to relate to improved immune responses (Chen *et al.*, 2003).

Similarly, some early research suggested that there is a personality characteristic that influences the amount of personal control one assumes. The hardy personality model proposes that psychological health is reflected in one's ability to take active control of the stress experience (Kobasa, 1979). This personality trait was described as a commitment to the self and a meaningful life, an internal locus of control and being cognitively flexible to perceive stress as a challenge rather than a threat and was related to better general health (Kobasa, 1979). This model, however, has also been criticised. Specifically, critics assert that the three

components do not constitute hardiness (Benishek, 1996) and that neuroticism or general maladjustment may largely account for the relationship between hardiness and health (Funk, 1992).

Self-esteem

Levels of general self-esteem have also been implicated in stress, coping and health-related outcomes. High self-esteem has been shown to ameliorate physical health problems during law and medical students' first year (Pritchard *et al.*, 2007) and appears to buffer the impact of negative feedback on cardiovascular reactivity (Hughes, 2007). Likewise, self esteem may influence risky health-related behaviours. Women with lower self-esteem are more likely to report initiating sex at an earlier age, having more risky partners and engaging in more unprotected sex than females with higher self-esteem levels (Ethier *et al.*, 2006). Recently, a person's self-esteem has been shown to predict symptom reports of chronic illness patients during daily life. Using palmtop computers, asthma and arthritis patients answered survey questions several times a day, for one week. Those individuals with higher self-esteem reported less stress and less severe symptoms of their disease (Juth *et al.*, 2008). Thus, higher self-esteem appears to act as a coping resource, protecting us from the negative effects of stressful events, while also facilitating the enactment and maintenance of positive health behaviours.

Intervening to Help People Cope with Stress

There are many strategies and approaches aimed at helping people cope with a stressful event and return to normal activities. In general, most approaches to helping people effectively manage stress consist of three main phases. First is the education phase, where stress is defined and individuals are shown how to identify potential stressors in their own lives. During the next phase, the acquisition of skills, participants acquire and practise coping skills. Lastly, in the application phase, individuals apply coping skills to target situations and monitor their usefulness, noting where they were successful and working to adapt those coping strategies that were not effective (Cameron & Meichenbaum, 1980). Therapeutic interventions have also long advocated reinforcing positive and avoiding negative self-talk (e.g. 'I can't do it'; see Meichenbaum, 1975), as persistent negative self-talk can perpetuate stress and impede effective coping.

Relaxation training

Whereas some strategies focus on cognitive insight into the stress and coping experience, others are aimed at reducing physiological reactivity. Relaxation training is a well-supported coping technique meant to reduce the physiological arousal associated with the stress response. Although a full review of relaxation training is beyond the scope of this chapter, a few of the major strategies are briefly described. *Guided imagery* takes the approach that a person cannot be both relaxed and stressed simultaneously and trains an individual to maintain focus on a soothing image to promote calm and 'displace' stress. In *meditation* the general goal is to maintain a comfortable physical position and emotionally passive attitude. Some approaches advocate keeping focus on a repetitive word or sound to eliminate distracting thoughts; other meditative perspectives do not try to ignore thoughts, but rather to maintain an awareness and acknowledge their presence to gain insight. *Progressive muscle relaxation* begins with getting in a comfortable position and becoming relaxed by focusing on one's breathing. Then, in a systematic manner, the individual picks a muscle group to contract and 'squeeze' for about 10 seconds, at which point the muscle(s) are released. This facilitates awareness of what it feels like when the muscles are relaxed and leads to greater relaxation over time. Lastly, in *biofeedback* biological responses are recorded on an electronic instrument in order to provide the person with a visual representation of his/her stress response. Through skill acquisition, the person eventually learns how to control the various psychological responses.

Social support

One of the most important resources in shaping stress and coping responses is social support. Social support is often defined as the belief that one is valued and cared for by others and a perception of being connected to larger social groups or networks. In general, feeling that one is valued and connected appears to reduce stress and promote better coping. Additionally, having an extended social network may serve to help provide more tangible support for coping efforts (e.g. getting a ride, borrowing money, having someone to talk to). Chapter 22, this volume, discusses social support in more detail.

Emotional disclosure

Emotional disclosure refers to the expression of thoughts and feelings by talking or writing about events that precipitated those emotions. Cross-cultural studies indicate that people from most cultures are inclined to share their emotions with others (Rimé, 1995), supporting the view that social sharing is a common coping strategy. Evidence suggests that emotional disclosure to a supportive and safe listener is often associated with positive adjustment (see Smyth & Nazarian, 2004). Recent work has become interested in ways that might promote positive emotional disclosure under circumstances where someone is less willing or able to disclose to another person (e.g. lacking a supportive listener, shame or social stigma about the problem to be disclosed, etc.). One such approach is to have people disclose their deepest thoughts and feelings through writing (Pennebaker & Beall, 1986), a process often referred to as expressive writing. Across many studies, individuals asked to complete expressive writing exercises have shown improvements in a wide array of health and well-being measures compared to people writing about mundane topics (Frattaroli, 2006). For example, studies have demonstrated that expressive writing facilitates faster wound healing (Weinman et al., 2008), better adjustment to AIDS (Petrie et al., 2004), cancer (Stanton et al., 2002) and post-traumatic stress disorder (Smyth et al., 2008), as well as improvements in objective indicators of disease function (Smyth et al., 1999). The role of emotional disclosure in coping – whether through speaking, writing, or emerging techniques of email, internet 'blogs' or SMS – is certainly an exciting and ongoing avenue of exploration.

In Summary

In earlier chapters it was shown how stress can exert a large impact on both the psychological and physiological well-being of the individual. The goal of this chapter was to introduce the concept of coping – efforts made to manage or 'deal with' stress – and how such efforts can influence the degree of stress experienced. Effective coping can be protective against stress-related disease and dysfunction, but ineffective coping may not help (or can even make things worse!). Many different types of coping were discussed – from the more passive to the more active, those tailored to fixing a problem and those focused on emotional responses – accompanied by a reminder of the need to consider the individual's unique context and coping goals. In particular, it is important to remember that coping is most effective when the coping behaviours utilised fit the demands of the situation. The ability to be flexible and shift from one coping style to another, rather than using a 'one-size-fits-all' approach, may be very important in dealing effectively with stress. In addition, there are various personality factors that may serve to help or hinder one's coping efforts. Finally, a brief review of some of the more formalised techniques that are aimed to improve efforts to cope with stress was provided.

Discussion Points

1 Stress can affect one's health via direct and indirect pathways. Discuss examples of each of these pathways and how they may relate to one another.

2 What makes events stressful? Include in your discussion Lazarus and Folkman's model of psychological appraisal in the experience of stress.

3 Coping is the method of responding to, managing and resolving demands that are considered to tax the resources of an individual. Why is coping considered a dynamic process?

4 How can we distinguish 'good' coping from 'bad' coping and how might this vary according to the perspective one takes?

5 Individuals use a wide variety of strategies for managing stressful events, often referred to as a coping style. Discuss the importance of coping styles and approaches (e.g. avoidant, active, emotion-focused, problem-focused, proactive and responsive strategies).

6 Individual coping styles may prove either effective or maladaptive, depending on the stressor. Of most importance is the 'match' between coping style and the demands of the situation. Discuss evidence that individuals employing a range of various coping styles in response to a stressor demonstrate coping flexibility and typically fare much better overall.

7 Individual differences (e.g. personality) will affect one's coping behaviours and responses. Discuss examples of how such influences, such as information-seeking styles, general mood dispositions, beliefs in control and self-esteem levels may influence coping behaviours and outcomes.

8 Given the importance of coping, discuss strategies to promote better coping. Which factors may help? What skills or interventions may promote better coping and health?

Further Reading

Aspinwall, L.G. & Taylor, S.E. (1997). A stitch in time: Self-regulation and proactive coping. *Psychological Bulletin, 121,* 417–436.

Austenfeld, J.L. & Stanton, A.L. (2004). Coping through emotional approach: A new look at emotion, coping and health-related outcomes. *Journal of Personality, 72,* 1335–1364.

Carver, C.S., Scheier, M.F. & Weintraub, J.K. (1989). Assessing coping strategies: A theoretically based approach. *Journal of Personality and Social Psychology, 56,* 267–283.

Cheng, C. (2001). Assessing coping flexibility in real-life and laboratory settings: A multimethod approach. *Journal of Personality and Social Psychology, 80,* 814–833.

Gale, C.R., Batty, G.D. & Deary, I.J. (2008). Locus of control at age 10 years and health outcomes and behaviors at age 30 years: The 1970 British Cohort Study. *Psychosomatic Medicine, 70,* 397–403.

Scheier, M.F., Matthews, K.A., Owens, J.F., Magovern, G.J., Lefebvre, R.C., Abbott, R.A. & Carver, C.S. (1989). Dispositional optimism and recovery from coronary artery bypass surgery: The beneficial effects on physical and psychological well-being. *Journal of Personality and Social Psychology, 57,* 1024–1040.

Stone, A.A., Schwartz, J.E., Neale, J.M., Shiffman, S., Marco, C.A., Hickcox, M. *et al.* (1998). A comparison of coping assessed by ecological momentary assessment and retrospective recall. *Journal of Personality and Social Psychology, 74,* 1670–1680.

Suls, J. & Fletcher, B. (1985). The relative efficacy of avoidant and nonavoidant coping strategies: A meta-analysis. *Health Psychology, 4,* 249–288.

References

Aspinwall, L.G. & Taylor, S.E. (1997). A stitch in time: Self-regulation and proactive coping. *Psychological Bulletin, 121,* 417–436.

Austenfeld, J.L. & Stanton, A.L. (2004). Coping through emotional approach: A new look at emotion, coping and health-related outcomes. *Journal of Personality, 72,* 1335–1363.

Bandura, A. (1977). Self-efficacy: Toward a unifying theory of behavioral change. *Psychological Review, 84,* 191–215.

Benishek, L.A. (1996). Evaluation of the factor structure underlying two measures of hardiness. *Assessment, 3,* 423–435.

Brissette, I., Scheier, M.F. & Carver, C.S. (2002). The role of optimism in social network development, coping and psychological adjustment during a life transition. *Journal of Personality and Social Psychology, 82,* 102–111.

Cameron, R. & Meichenbaum, D. (1980). Cognition and behaviour change. *Australian and New Zealand Journal of Psychiatry, 14,* 121–125.

Carver, C.S. & Scheier, M.F. (1981). *Attention and self-regulation: A control-theory approach to human behavior.* New York: Springer.

Carver, C.S., Scheier, M.F. & Weintraub, J.K. (1989). Assessing coping strategies: A theoretically based approach. *Journal of Personality and Social Psychology, 56,* 267–283.

Chang, E.C. (1998). Dispositional optimism and primary and secondary appraisal of a stressor: Controlling for confounding influences and relations to coping and psychological and physical adjustment. *Journal of Personality and Social Psychology, 74,* 1109–1120.

Chen, E., Fisher, E.B., Bacharier, L.B. & Strunk, R.C. (2003). Socioeconomic status, stress and immune markers in adolescents with asthma. *Psychosomatic Medicine, 65,* 984–992.

Cheng, C. (2001). Assessing coping flexibility in real-life and laboratory settings: A multimethod approach. *Journal of Personality and Social Psychology, 80,* 814–833.

Cohen, F. & Lazarus, R. (1979). Coping with the stresses of illness. In G.C. Stone, F. Cohen & N.E. Adler (Eds.) *Health psychology: A handbook* (pp. 217–254). San Francisco: Jossey-Bass.

Cohen, S. & Williamson, G.M. (1991). Stress and infectious disease in humans. *Psychological Bulletin, 109,* 5–24.

Elfant, E., Burns, J.W. & Zeichner, A. (2008). Repressive coping style and suppression of pain-related thoughts: Effects on responses to acute pain induction. *Cognition & Emotion, 22,* 671–696.

Ethier, K.A., Kershaw, T.S., Lewis, J.B., Milan, S., Niccolai, L.M. & Ickovics, J.R. (2006). Self-esteem, emotional distress and sexual behavior among adolescent females: Interrelationships and temporal effects. *Journal of Adolescent Health, 38,* 268–274.

Folkman, S. & Lazarus, R.S. (1980). An analysis of coping in a middle-aged community sample. *Journal of Health and Social Behavior, 21,* 219–239.

Frattaroli, J. (2006). Experimental disclosure and its moderators: A meta-analysis. *Psychological Bulletin, 132,* 823–865.

Friedman, H.S. & Booth-Kewley, S. (1987). The 'disease-prone personality': A meta-analytic view of the construct. *American Psychologist, 42,* 539–555.

Funk, S.C. (1992). Hardiness: A review of theory and research. *Health Psychology, 11,* 335–345.

Gale, C.R., Batty, G.D. & Deary, I.J. (2008). Locus of control at age 10 years and health outcomes and behaviors at age 30 years: The 1970 British Cohort Study. *Psychosomatic Medicine, 70,* 397–403.

Hughes, B.M. (2007). Self-esteem, performance feedback and cardiovascular stress reactivity. *Anxiety, Stress & Coping: An International Journal, 20,* 239–252.

Juth, V., Smyth, J.M. & Santuzzi, A. (2008). How do you feel? Self-esteem predicts affect, stress, social interaction and symptom severity during daily life in patients with chronic illness. *Journal of Health Psychology, 13,* 884–894.

Kobasa, S.C. (1979). Stressful life events, personality and health: An inquiry into hardiness. *Journal of Personality and Social Psychology, 37,* 1–11.

Kubzansky, L.D., Sparrow, D., Vokonas, P. & Kawachi, I. (2001). Is the glass half empty or half full? A prospective study of optimism and coronary heart disease in the normative aging study. *Psychosomatic Medicine, 63*, 910–916.

Langer, E.J. & Rodin, J. (1976). The effects of choice and enhanced personal responsibility for the aged: A field experiment in an institutional setting. *Journal of Personality and Social Psychology, 34*, 191–198.

Lazarus, R.S. & Folkman, S. (1984). *Stress, appraisal and coping.* New York: Springer.

Maruta, T., Colligan, R.C., Malinchoc, M. & Offord, K.P. (2002). Optimism-pessimism assessed in the 1960s and self-reported health status 30 years later. *Mayo Clinic Proceedings, 77*, 748–753.

Miller, S.M. & Mangan, C.E. (1983). Interacting effects of information and coping style in adapting to gynecologic stress: Should the doctor tell all? *Journal of Personality and Social Psychology, 45*, 223–236.

Meichenbaum, D.H. (1975). A self-instructional approach to stress management: A proposal for stress inoculation training. In C.D. Spielberger & I.G. Sarason (Eds.) *Stress and anxiety* (Vol. 2, pp. 237–264). New York: Wiley.

Morrow, J. & Nolen-Hoeksema, S. (1990). Effects of responses to depression on the remediation of depressive affect. *Journal of Personality and Social Psychology, 58*, 519–527.

Myers, L.B., Burns, J.W., Derakshan, N., Elfant, E., Eysenck, M.W. & Phipps, S. (2008). Current issues in repressive coping and health. In A. Vingerhoets, I. Nyklíček & J. Denollet (Eds.) *Emotion regulation: Conceptual and clinical issues.* New York: Springer.

Nyklíček, I., Vingerhoets, A.J.J.M., Van Heck, G.L. & Van Limpt, M.C.A.M. (1998). Defensive coping in relation to casual blood pressure and self-reported daily hassles and life events. *Journal of Behavioral Medicine, 21*, 145–161.

Pennebaker, J.W. & Beall, S.K. (1986). Confronting a traumatic event: Toward an understanding of inhibition and disease. *Journal of Abnormal Psychology, 95*, 274–281.

Pennebaker, J.W. & Watson, D. (1991). The psychology of somatic symptoms. In L.J. Kirmayer & J.M. Robbins (Eds.) *Current concepts of somatization: Research and clinical perspectives* (pp. 21–35). Washington, DC: American Psychiatric Association.

Petrie, K.J., Fontanilla, I., Thomas, M.G., Booth, R.J. & Pennebaker, J.W. (2004). Effect of written emotional expression on immune function in patients with human immunodeficiency virus infection: A randomized trial. *Psychosomatic Medicine, 66*, 272–275.

Pritchard, M.E., Wilson, G.S. & Yamnitz, B. (2007). What predicts adjustment among college students? A longitudinal panel study. *Journal of American College Health, 56*, 15–21.

Räikkönen, K., Matthews, K.A., Flory, J.D., Owens, J.F. & Gump, B.B. (1999). Effects of optimism, pessimism and trait anxiety on ambulatory blood pressure and mood during everyday life. *Journal of Personality and Social Psychology, 76*, 104–113.

Rimé, B. (1995). Mental rumination, social sharing and the recovery from emotional exposure. In J.W. Pennebaker (Ed.) *Emotion, disclosure and health* (pp. 271–291). Washington, DC: American Psychological Association.

Rodin, J. & Langer, E.J. (1977). Long-term effects of a control-relevant intervention with the institutionalized aged. *Journal of Personality and Social Psychology, 35*, 897–902.

Rotter, J.B. (1966). Generalized expectancies for internal versus external control of reinforcement. *Psychological Monographs: General & Applied, 80*, 1–28.

Scheier, M.F., Matthews, K.A., Owens, J.F., Magovern, G.J., Lefebvre, R.C., Abbott, R.A. & Carver, C.S. (1989). Dispositional optimism and recovery from coronary artery bypass surgery: The beneficial effects on physical and psychological well-being. *Journal of Personality and Social Psychology, 57*, 1024–1040.

Segerstrom, S.C., Castañeda, J.O. & Spencer, T.E. (2003). Optimism effects on cellular immunity: Testing the affective and persistence models. *Personality and Individual Differences, 35*, 1615–1624.

Smith, T.W., Ruiz, J.M. & Uchino, B.N. (2000). Vigilance, active coping and cardiovascular reactivity during social interaction in young men. *Health Psychology, 19*, 382–392.

Smyth, J.M., Hockemeyer, J.R. & Tulloch, H. (2008). Expressive writing and post-traumatic stress disorder: Effects on trauma symptoms, mood states and cortisol reactivity. *British Journal of Health Psychology, 13*, 85–93.

Smyth, J.M., Litcher, L., Hurewitz, A. & Stone, A. (2001). Relaxation training and cortisol secretion in adult asthmatics. *Journal of Health Psychology, 6*, 217–227.

Smyth, J.M. & Nazarian, D. (2004). Disclosure and health. In A.J. Christensen, R. Martin & J.M. Smyth (Eds.) *Encyclopedia of health psychology* (pp. 86–89). New York: Kluwer Academic Press.

Smyth, J.M., Stone, A.A., Hurewitz, A. & Kaell, A. (1999). Effects of writing about stressful experiences on symptom reduction in patients with asthma or rheumatoid arthritis: A randomized trial. *Journal of the American Medical Association, 281*, 1304–1309.

Stanton, A.L., Danoff-Burg, S., Sworowski, L.A., Collins, C.A., Branstetter, A.D., Rodriguez-Hanley, A. *et al.* (2002). Randomized, controlled trial of written emotional expression and benefit finding in breast cancer patients. *Journal of Clinical Oncology, 20*, 4160–4168.

Stone, A.A., Schwartz, J.E., Neale, J.M., Shiffman, S., Marco, C.A., Hickcox, M. *et al.* (1998). A comparison of coping assessed by ecological momentary assessment and retrospective recall. *Journal of Personality and Social Psychology, 74,* 1670–1680.

Stroebe, M., Schut, H. & Stroebe, W. (2005). Attachment in coping with bereavement: A theoretical integration. *Review of General Psychology, 9,* 48–66.

Suls, J. & Fletcher, B. (1985). The relative efficacy of avoidant and nonavoidant coping strategies: A meta-analysis. *Health Psychology, 4,* 249–288.

Taylor, S.E. & Clark, L.F. (1986). Does information improve adjustment to noxious medical procedures? In M.J. Saks & L. Saxe (Eds.) *Advances in applied social psychology* (Vol. 3, pp. 1–28). Hillsdale, NJ: Lawrence Erlbaum.

Thomsen, D.K., Mehlsen, M.Y., Hokland, M., Viidik, A., Olesen, F., Avlund, K. *et al.* (2004). Negative thoughts and health: Associations among rumination, immunity

and health care utilization in a young and elderly sample. *Psychosomatic Medicine, 66,* 363–371.

Watson, D. & Clark, L.A. (1984). Negative affectivity: The disposition to experience aversive emotional states. *Psychological Bulletin, 96,* 465–490.

Wegner, D.M., Schneider, D.J., Carter, S.R. & White, T.L. (1987). Paradoxical effects of thought suppression. *Journal of Personality and Social Psychology, 53,* 5–13.

Weinberger, D.A., Schwartz, G.E. & Davidson, R J. (1979). Low-anxious, high-anxious and repressive coping styles: Psychometric patterns and behavioral and physiological responses to stress. *Journal of Abnormal Psychology, 88,* 369–380.

Weinman, J., Ebrecht, M., Scott, S., Walburn, J. & Dyson, M. (2008). Enhanced wound healing after emotional disclosure intervention. *British Journal of Health Psychology, 13,* 95–102.

22

Social Support

Ralf Schwarzer and Nina Knoll

Chapter Outline

The chapter deals with social factors and how they might exert an influence on health and longevity. First, a distinction is made between the concepts of social integration and social support. Following this, a more fine-grained differentiation of various social support phenomena is offered and different approaches to their measurement are described. Individual differences in support mobilisation, provision and receipt are addressed. Evidence is provided for the association of social integration and social support with stress, life expectancy, medical conditions and bereavement. The role of social factors in the onset and course of severe health conditions, such as myocardial infarction and cancer, is examined. Moreover, the functional relationships of social support with other constructs such as stress, coping and perceived self-efficacy are discussed as well as the physiological correlates of support.

Key Concepts

Bereavement and loss
Gender differences
Instrumental, informational and emotional support
Longevity and survival
Onset and course of chronic illness
Oxytocin
Perceived versus received social support
Social integration, social networks and social ties
Social support
Support and coping

What is Social Support?

More than a century ago, the French sociologist Durkheim (1897) observed that suicide occurred more frequently among individuals who had no ties or only weak connections to other people. Today, it is common knowledge that poor mental health is more prevalent among people with low social integration. Physical health and longevity appear to depend in part on social factors. What exactly these social factors are and how they operate, continue to be difficult questions. Bowlby's (1969) attachment theory was a theoretical advancement. According to this theory, emotional attachment in early life promotes a sense of security and self-esteem that ultimately provides the basis on which individuals develop lasting, secure and loving relationships in adult life. Subsequent research has established a pattern of psychosocial variables that are connected to diverse health outcomes. People can be predisposed to illness by long-term social isolation, neglect, loneliness and social stress (Cacioppo & Patrick, 2008).

This chapter presents an introduction to social support and its relationship to stress, coping and health. Before discussing mechanisms that operate between social factors (as predictors) and health, illness and death (as outcomes), the conceptual background of the former needs to be clarified. Conceptually, it is important to distinguish between social integration and social support.

Social integration: structure and quantity of social relationships

The term 'social support' is often used in a broad sense, including social integration. However, *social integration* refers to the structure and quantity of social relationships, such as the size and density of networks and the frequency of interaction, but also sometimes to the subjective perception of embeddedness. *Social support*, in contrast, refers to the function and quality of social relationships, such as perceived availability of help or support actually received. It occurs through an interactive process and can be related to altruism, a sense of obligation and the perception of reciprocity (Schwarzer & Leppin, 1991).

Epidemiological studies have linked mortality rates to social networks, indicating that social factors have a beneficial effect on longevity (e.g. House *et al.*, 1988; Sbarra & Nietert, 2009). Social integration can be assessed in a sophisticated manner, but researchers usually choose a straightforward approach: the most common demographic indicator being marital status. It makes a difference whether individuals are single, married, divorced, etc. Based on this information only, one can conclude that, on average, married couples live longer than individuals in the other groups. A more comprehensive way to assess these constructs is a social network index that also includes the number of roles one assumes in the family and in organisations, such as church, as well as the frequency of contact to other members of such groups. Duration of contacts and degree of reciprocity are also important. A social network represents a web of relationships that encircles an individual together with network characteristics, such as range or size (number of members), density (degree of interconnection), boundedness (extent of closeness such as kin, workplace, neighbourhood) and homogeneity (similarity of members; Berkman *et al.*, 2000). There are various ways to assess these aspects (for an overview, see Cohen *et al.*, 2000). Advanced network analyses have been used to document the dynamic spread of happiness and the clustering of happiness at the community level over two decades (Fowler & Christakis, 2008).

Social support: function and quality of social relationships

Social support in the narrow sense has been defined in various ways. For example, it may be regarded as resources provided by others, as coping assistance or as an exchange of resources. Several types of social support have been investigated, such as instrumental (e.g. assist with a problem, donate goods), informational (e.g. give advice) and emotional (e.g. give reassurance). Health and well-being are not merely the result of actual support provision, but are also a consequence of participation in a meaningful social context. The most common distinction made is the one between *perceived* available support and actually *received* support. The former may pertain to anticipating help in time of need and the latter to help provided within a given time period. The former is often prospective, the latter always retrospective. This is an essential distinction because these two constructs need not necessarily have much in common. They can be closely related in some studies, but in others they may be unrelated, depending on wording and context. Expecting support in the future may be rather like a personality disposition (Sarason *et al.*, 1990) being intertwined with optimism, whereas support provided or received in the past is rather based on actual circumstances. Moreover, comparing the effects of perceived support and received support on self-reported well-being outcomes, the former is a more consistent predictor of better well-being than the latter (Sarason *et al.*, 1990). To which degree this distinction emerges empirically also depends on the amount of specificity in the item wordings. The more diffuse and general the questions are, the more the responses may be influenced by the respondents' personality characteristics. To illustrate the distinction between perceived support and received support, we use items from the Berlin Social Support Scales (BSSS; Schwarzer & Schulz, 2000).

Perceived available support. This is measured with items such as, 'There is always someone there for me when I need comforting' (emotional), or 'There are people who offer me help when I need it' (instrumental). One can generate more situation-specific items such as running errands, lending money, taking the dog out for a walk, etc. However, such specificity often prevents the use of sum scores because items are not closely related to each other.

Received support. The main feature of support that has been received lies in its retrospective nature. A time window can be provided such as 'last week', followed by items such as 'This person has comforted me when I was feeling bad' (emotional) or 'This person took care of many things for me' (instrumental).

Sources of support. Some measures of received support also consider the particular source that has provided help in a specific situation such as spouse, friend or colleague. In a study on the multidimensional nature of received social support in gay men (Schwarzer *et al.*, 1994), the UCLA Social Support Inventory was used to examine to what degree partners, friends, family and organisations provided assistance, gave advice, were reassuring or listened empathically. The four sources were nested within each kind of support.

There are a multitude of other psychometric tools available to assess support (for an overview, see Cohen *et al.*, 2000).

Spouse Support: Role and Gender Differences

Gender differences in social networks and social support have been discussed by various authors (cf. Glynn *et al.*, 1999). Throughout the life cycle, women generally have more close friends than men do, and women provide more emotional support to both men and women and they get more help in return (Klauer & Winkeler, 2002). Explanations for such discrepancies typically focus on gender differences in emotionality and emotional expressiveness (e.g. Maltz & Borker, 1982). This higher social integration and support in women may buffer stress even if they receive less support from their husbands in return. Thus, although men and women both benefit from social support in times of crisis, they may do so to a different degree and their sources may be different. When women receive less support from their spouses than men do from theirs, this is called the 'support gap hypothesis' (Cutrona, 1996). The support gap hypothesis has been confirmed, for example, in a study on tumour surgery patients. Men reported receiving more emotional support than women did. This remained stable across the entire stress episode of more than six months post surgery. In contrast, women reported not only less received support, but also a decline; support reached its lowest level at the last measurement point in time, six months after surgery. Being a female tumour patient and having a male caregiver was associated with less support receipt than was being a male tumour patient with a female caregiver (Luszczynska, Boehmer *et al.*, 2007).

Another study examined types and sources of received support among Costa Rican employees (Schwarzer & Gutiérrez-Doña, 2005). Gender and age differences were considered. Four types of support (advice giving, assistance, reassurance and empathic listening) were measured as received from four sources, namely friends, family, spouses and groups/organisations. It turned out that support types were not very distinct, but sources were discriminant. This means that it may be more important to consider sources than types.

For spousal support, a significant gender effect was found and an interaction between gender and age. Young men and women reported equal levels of spousal support, but, with increasing age, women reported continuously less support received from their partners. This interaction reflects a widening gap between men and women in terms of what they get from each other.

Women might be more sensitive to many kinds of social interaction than men are. Moreover, women seem to be particularly sensitive to relationship quality as a prerequisite of received support (Uchino, 2006). Thus it would appear that, to benefit from support, the partner must also be a positive source of social interaction.

Social Integration, Social Support and Longevity: Who Dies Prematurely?

Community-based prospective epidemiological studies have documented a link between lack of social integration on the one hand and morbidity/mortality on the other. Socially isolated people are at risk for a variety of diseases and fatal health outcomes. Social integration, or the lack of it, can influence the onset, progression and recovery from illness.

A distinction can be made between large-scale epidemiological studies and life-event studies. Life-event research on social support and mortality comes primarily from two sources: after severe medical occurrences or procedures and after conjugal loss. In epidemiological studies in which indicators of social integration (e.g. marital status) were correlated with longevity, it was found that the relative risk of dying within a given time period is higher for socially isolated than for socially integrated individuals. In the classic Alameda County Study, for example, the mortality risk of people with weak social integration is about twice as high than of those who are socially well integrated (Berkman & Syme, 1979).

Hemingway and Marmot (1999) distinguish between two kinds of epidemiological studies: prospective aetiological investigations in healthy samples and prognostic studies in patient samples. In a review, they found that five out of eight prospective studies documented an effect of social integration on coronary heart disease. Moreover, they found that nine out of ten prognostic studies confirmed evidence for a link between social integration and coronary heart disease.

In the Terman Life-Cycle Study (Tucker et al., 1999) the relationship between social ties and mortality was examined in 697 men and 544 women at four assessment points over a period of 51 years (1940–1991). They found that men who were always married had a significantly lower mortality risk compared to those who were separated, divorced or widowed, or who had remarried. For women, no such effect of marital status emerged. Instead, their mortality risk was lower when they had a greater number of children and belonged to more organisations. Embeddedness in social networks and social participation means something different for older men compared to older women.

Social Support and Health

To better understand the association between social integration, health and longevity, researchers have looked for qualitative aspects of social embeddedness, such as social support. Effects of network parameters on health may be explained by a higher availability of social support that aids individuals in recovery from illness, engaging in healthier lifestyles and experiencing less distress (Berkman et al., 2000). This proposal will now be considered.

Recovery from disease or surgery

Studies among cardiac patients have found social support to be beneficial for recovery from surgery. Some researchers have focused on the mere existence of social networks, whereas others have examined perceived or actually received social support. Kulik and Mahler (1989), for example, studied men who underwent coronary artery bypass graft surgery. Those whose spouses visited them often in the hospital were, on average, released earlier than those who received few visits. In a longitudinal study, the same authors also found that emotional support from spouses had positive effects on patients after surgery (Kulik & Mahler, 1993). King *et al.* (1993) found that perceived availability of support was associated with emotional and functional outcomes up to a year following coronary artery surgery. In particular, esteem support (that one is respected and valued by others) appeared to be related to improved health outcomes over the follow-up period. Thus, some types of social support are better than others when matched to the situation at hand. Emotional and esteem support, more so if extended from women to men, may be beneficial because it instils optimistic self-beliefs and equips the patient with more hardiness to cope with barriers and setbacks.

Close network members of patients make a difference in how patients adjust to their disease, depending on their interaction with each other (Coyne & Smith, 1991). Helgeson (1993) found that patients' perceived availability of information support was a good predictor of recovery. Negative marital interaction predicted poor adjustment and spousal disclosure predicted patients' life satisfaction.

Change of health- and illness-related behaviour: couple- and family-oriented approaches

Interaction with others has an impact on health-relevant behaviour. Network partners may be role models for health-enhancing as well as for health-compromising behaviours, they may exert control over a target, they may support behaviour change by offering instrumental help or by reducing distress when changing one's lifestyle.

Martire and Schulz (2007) reported findings from two reviews on the efficacy of interventions that included family members to help chronically ill patients in changing illness-related behaviours. Interventions were targeted at different patient populations and included psycho-education for patients

and family members, social support training for network members (couples being counselled in dealing with breast cancer) and partner programmes for changing lifestyle aspects or helping the patient acquire new behaviours and techniques to cope with their illness (e.g. spouses of patients suffering from chronic pain were taught to conduct relaxation interventions).

The first review included findings from 70 intervention studies for patients and family members comparing integrated interventions with standard care. Samples included patients suffering from dementia, coronary heart disease, cancer, chronic pain, stroke, rheumatoid arthritis or traumatic brain injury, and their family members. Interventions including groups of family members (e.g. spouses and adult children) did not yield overall positive effects when compared with standard care. However, patients with coronary heart disease who received family-group interventions using strategies based on cognitive behavioural therapy were found to have a slightly lower mortality risk. Generally, family members also benefited from the interventions, their indicators of well-being increased following the interventions and levels of caregiver burden decreased slightly (Martire & Schulz, 2007).

In a second review, the authors reported about 12 studies that compared family-oriented interventions with interventions targeted at patients only. Samples included patients with chronic back pain, arthritis, cancer or coronary heart disease. In about half of the studies positive effects of family interventions were reported, some of these effects were even larger than those observed in patient-only interventions. For example, individuals with chronic back pain who attended exercise sessions and received couple-oriented behavioural therapy showed greater lessening of pain and pain behaviour and greater diminishment of the impact of pain on their lives, than did individuals who received only an exercise intervention. The remainder of the studies showed either negative effects of family-oriented interventions or patient characteristics (e.g. patient gender) further moderated intervention effects on outcomes. An example for differential effects of family-oriented interventions comes from a study with cancer patients and their spouses by Wing *et al.* (1991). A couple-oriented behavioural programme for obese individuals with type 2 diabetes yielded more weight loss for female patients only. However, male patients lost more weight in the (individual) patient-oriented programme. Regardless of their gender, partners who participated in the couple-oriented programme lost more weight than spouses of individuals in the patient-oriented programme. Martire and Schulz (2007) conclude that the generally small effects of family-centred interventions may be explained by a less than optimal focus of interventions on two aims: (i) the reduction of familial interactions that compromise healthy behaviour in the patient (e.g. by making the patient dependent on support) and increase distress in the patient; (ii) the strengthening of interactions that increase healthy behaviour and emotional well-being (Knoll et al., 2007).

Social support and physiological stress reactions

Social support's potential stress-reducing function is discussed to constitute another pathway linking social network with longevity. Changes in perceived distress, but also in stress-related physiological responses as a consequence of the receipt or perception of available support have been examined by means of correlational and experimental studies for over 50 years. Studies investigated both ego-relevant (e.g. exam situations) as well as physically relevant (e.g. illnesses, injuries, painful medical procedures) stress episodes.

Laboratory studies examining physiological stress reactions usually have discovered positive buffering effects of experimentally varied social support interactions on parameters such as cardiovascular, neuroendocrine and immune responses (e.g. Uchino, 2006). Experimental paradigms use standardised stress induction procedures and manipulate the nature of received or available support, e.g. evaluative vs. non-evaluative support (Allen et al., 2002), verbal vs. non-verbal support (Ditzen et al., 2007), or support by familiar persons vs. strangers (e.g. Edens et al., 1992). Field studies on naturalistic social support interactions and physiological stress reactions generally yield weaker and less consistent results.

A meta-theory on the psychophysiology of social support was introduced by Taylor (2006) who describes the female stress reaction as generally characterised by tending (nurturant activities, protecting self and offspring) and befriending (creation and maintenance of social networks that help reduce distress). Taylor proposes oxytocin to be a central mediator of this reaction.

Oxytocin is a neuropeptide that has been linked with different facets of social interaction. In humans, Kosfeld et al. (2005) showed that transnasal oxytocin led to higher interpersonal trust. Also, oxytocin may benefit certain prerequisites of social support interactions. Domes et al. (2007) showed that a higher availability of oxytocin was associated with higher accuracy in reading others' emotional facial expressions.

One fascinating implication of the oxytocin–social support link might be its capacity to explain in part the gender differences in support interactions. Men also produce oxytocin, but in smaller quantities than women. However, men also benefit from increases in available oxytocin.

In an experimental study Heinrichs et al. (2003) gave men transnasal oxytocin or a placebo before a stress induction. Additionally, half of the men received support from a friend while the other half did not. Received support combined with oxytocin yielded the smallest stress response when compared to the other groups. This was true for men's cortisol response as well as their self-reported affect. Oxytocin may enhance a stress-reducing effect of received support. Based on their results and findings from animal studies, authors suggest that oxytocin might play a key role in explaining the stress-reducing effects of social support.

Mechanisms: Social Support in the Stress and Coping Context

According to transactional stress theory (e.g. Lazarus & Folkman, 1984), social support represents one resource factor, among others, that influences the cognitive appraisal of stressful encounters. Coping is then a result of this cognitive appraisal. Consequently, the theory suggests that greater support is associated with better coping, i.e. social support represents a coping resource which not only influences coping, but also outcomes

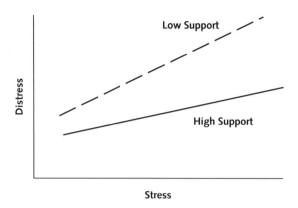

Figure 22.1 Social support as a buffer of stress

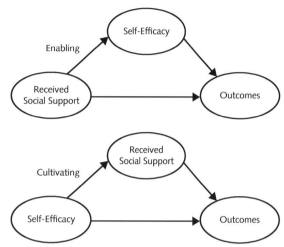

Figure 22.2 The enabling and cultivating effects

related to coping. In this way, coping and support are intimately connected, with the ability to utilise one's support being a marker of 'better coping'.

In a study (Luszczynska *et al.*, 2005), support and self-efficacy were found to act as resources of coping among cancer surgery patients, resulting in higher levels of post-traumatic growth. Boehmer *et al.* (2007) found that support and self-efficacy predicted active coping, which led to a higher quality of life in tumour patients.

In terms of its functional value, social support can have a *main effect* on various outcomes, or it can interact with the experience of stress. It has been postulated that social support might reveal its beneficial effect on health and emotions only in times of distress, as it buffers the negative impact of stressful events. This moderating impact is known as the *stress-buffering effect* (Cohen & Wills, 1985). Figure 22.1 illustrates how the association between experiencing a stressful episode (e.g. a critical life event) and the resulting distress (or strain) is moderated by levels of social support. Receiving support alleviates distress to some degree.

Moreover, there are a number of mediator effects that characterise the mechanisms through which social support operates in the stress and coping process, or by which social support is established and maintained (Schwarzer & Knoll, 2007). As an example of such mediator effects we choose the relation between social support and self-efficacy in terms of coping outcomes. Specifically, we compare the enabling hypothesis with the cultivation hypothesis.

The enabling hypothesis: social support enables self-efficacy

Social support constitutes a potential protective cushion against environmental demands. Moreover, support providers may facilitate an individual's self-regulation by enabling one's adaptive capabilities to face challenges and to overcome adversity (see Figure 22.2). In that, social support may provide an opportunity to engage in vicarious experiences in dealing with a stressor at hand. This should be especially true when support is granted by persons who have to deal with the same stressor and demonstrate competency in doing so. On the other hand, social support may represent a symbolic experience in which members of the network provide verbal assurances of the support recipient's competency to deal with the problem. A third possible pathway connecting social support with increases in self-efficacy may place the reduction of negative affect in a mediator position. Negative affect and stress-related arousal may be used as a source of information concerning one's own competency to cope with a situation at hand. Social support may reduce stress-related arousal and thus provide another source of increased self-efficacy. This last pathway then combines the enabling hypothesis with the stress-reducing function of social support.

Evidence for the enabling hypothesis of perceived social support comes from a number of studies on recovery from traumatic stress. Benight and Bandura (2004) have demonstrated that perceived social support generates favourable outcomes only to the extent that it is associated with higher perceived self-efficacy to overcome challenging demands.

Moreover, received support has also been shown to be associated with higher levels of self efficacy. For example, Luszczynska, Sarkar *et al.* (2007) have examined predictors of adherence to highly active antiretroviral therapy in AIDS patients. Outcomes such as physical functioning, benefit finding and adherence to therapy were related to received social support. However, these effects of received support were mediated by levels of perceived self-efficacy.

In a longitudinal study on 193 cardiac patients in the week after surgery, Schröder *et al.* (1998) found that received support delivered its beneficial effect on physical symptom experience through perceived self-efficacy. Amount of self-reported physical symptoms (e.g. discomfort, pain) one week post surgery was chosen as the indicator of recovery. It was found that social support was only an indirect predictor of recovery, while levels of self-efficacy operated as a full mediator of its effect. Thus, even recovery from surgery might in part be based on personal enablement.

The cultivation hypothesis: self-efficacy maintains and cultivates social support

The enabling function of support represents only one possible mechanism within the stress and adaptation process. The reverse pathway is also possible (see Figure 22.2 for a comparison of the two models). Self-efficacy may operate as an establisher of support. This is accomplished by self-regulatory social activities. People take initiative, they go out and make social contacts, they take action to maintain valuable social relationships and they invest effort to improve, extend and cultivate their networks. The better their self-efficacy, the better their supportive resources become. Various empirical findings can be reinterpreted with this perspective in mind.

One example is the research on work stress experienced by factory employees in Costa Rica (Schwarzer & Gutiérrez-Doña, 2005). Self-efficacy was assessed at the beginning of the study and received support and depressive mood half a year later. At the second

measurement point in time, six months later, depressive mood was negatively associated with initial self-efficacy. However, this relationship was accounted for in part by received support. Thus, received support partially mediated the effect of self-efficacy on emotional state, pointing to the possibility that active establishment or improvement of supportive relationships was instrumental for alleviating depressive mood.

In sum, evidence points to associations of social support with agency beliefs, with the latter likely explaining a considerable part of the former's potential positive outcomes (enabling hypothesis of support). Moreover, findings from other studies suggest that the relationship among self efficacy and social support may go both ways in that self-efficacy may also enhance social resources (cultivation hypothesis).

Conclusion

Engaging in social interaction, be it on the providing or receiving end, emerges as a very complex concept that researchers only recently have started to disentangle. A promising first step seems to be the differentiation between social network and social support as well as different subcategories of the latter. The mechanisms by which support concepts seem to act on health and ultimately longevity are also manifold. This chapter reviewed work showing that social relationships may aid persons in recovery from illness and encourage a healthy lifestyle. Social support was furthermore related to lower subjective and physiological stress levels and thus to the mastery of taxing situations. Perceived support is a more consistent predictor of better well-being than received support (Sarason *et al.*, 1990). Receipt of support may also be associated with negative outcomes, particularly with increases in self-report indicators of distress (e.g. negative affect; Bolger *et al.*, 2000; Coyne *et al.*, 1988; Kienle *et al.*, 2009; Revenson *et al.*, 1991). The assumptions about the functional roles of received social support as enabling, facilitating coping or constituting a transfer of resources cannot account for evidence, indicating that being provided with and receiving support may at times harm recipients' well-being instead of being supportive. Future model expansions and research thus need to focus on moderators that further qualify the relationships between support transactions and both positive and negative outcomes thereof.

The puzzle on how social interactions may help to improve our health or even prolong our life expectancy is thus likely to remain complex. Various types of support (e.g. emotional, instrumental) may exert their impact on health and lifetime prolonging factors via a number of behavioural and cognitive mediators that are closely linked to immune functions and cardiovascular reactivity.

A close examination of these mediating mechanisms will advance our understanding of desirable and undesirable aspects of support and help explain individual differences in the ability to benefit from it in terms of physical health. The rapid development of research in this field already promises the unearthing of several crucial pieces of this puzzle in the near future.

Discussion Points

1   What is the difference between 'social integration' and 'social support'?
2   Who receives more support, women or men? How is this gender difference in network size, support provision and receipt explained?
3   Which aspect of social embeddedness seems to be associated with:
    – surviving a life-threatening illness?
    – longevity following bereavement (especially for men)?
    How can these associations be explained?

4   What are the differences between the direct-effect hypothesis and the buffering hypothesis of social support? What might be ideal study designs to test these hypotheses?
5   Is the differentiation between several aspects of social interaction/support useful? Which are the costs and benefits of a differentiated approach to measuring social interaction/support?
6   Is being single a health risk? Does this change as people grow older?

Further Reading

Cacioppo, J.T. & Patrick, B. (2008). *Loneliness: Human nature and the need for social connection.* New York: W.W. Norton.

Cohen, S., Underwood, S. & Gottlieb, B. (2000). *Social support measures and intervention.* New York: Oxford University Press.

Revenson, T.A., Kayser, K. & Bodenmann, G. (Eds.) (2005). *Couples coping with stress: Emerging perspectives on dyadic coping.* Washington, DC: American Psychological Association.

Schwarzer, R. & Knoll, N. (2007). Functional roles of social support within the stress and coping process: a theoretical and empirical overview. *International Journal of Psychology, 42*(4), 243–252.

Taylor, S. E. (2006). Tend and befriend: biobehavioral bases of affiliation under stress. *Current Directions in Psychological Science, 15,* 273–277.

References

Allen, K., Blascovich, J. & Mendes, W.B. (2002). Cardiovascular reactivity and the presence of pets, friends and spouses: the truth about cats and dogs. *Psychosomatic Medicine, 64,* 727–739.

Benight, C. & Bandura, A. (2004). Social cognitive theory of posttraumatic recovery: the role of perceived self-efficacy. *Behaviour Research and Therapy, 42,* 1129–1148.

Berkman, L.F., Glass, T., Brissette, I. & Seeman, T.E. (2000). From social integration to health: Durkheim in the new millennium. *Social Science & Medicine, 51,* 843–857.

Berkman, L.F. & Syme, S.L. (1979). Social networks, host resistance and mortality: a nine-year follow-up study of Alameda county residents. *American Journal of Epidemiology, 109,* 186–204.

Boehmer, S., Luszczynska, A. & Schwarzer, R. (2007). Coping and quality of life after tumor surgery: personal and social resources promote different domains of quality of life. *Anxiety, Stress, and Coping, 20,* 61–75.

Bolger, N., Zuckerman, A. & Kessler, R.C. (2000). Invisible support and adjustment to stress. *Journal of Personality and Social Psychology, 79,* 953–961.

Bowlby, J. (1969). *Attachment and loss*. New York: Basic Books.

Cacioppo, J.T. & Patrick, B. (2008). *Loneliness: Human nature and the need for social connection*. New York: W.W. Norton.

Cohen, S. & Wills, T.A. (1985). Stress, social support and the buffering hypothesis. *Psychological Bulletin, 98*, 310–357.

Cohen, S., Underwood, S. & Gottlieb, B. (2000). *Social support measures and intervention*. New York: Oxford University Press.

Coyne, J.C., Wortman, C.B. & Lehman, D.R. (1988). The other side of social support: emotional overinvolvement and miscarried help. In B.G. Gottlieb (Ed.) *Marshaling social support: Formats, processes and effects* (pp. 305–330). Newbury Park, CA: Sage.

Coyne, J.C. & Smith, D.A.K. (1991). Couples coping with a myocardial infarction: a contextual perspective on wives' distress. *Journal of Personality and Social Psychology, 61*, 404–412.

Cutrona, C.E. (1996). *Social support in couples*. Thousand Oaks, CA: Sage.

Ditzen, B., Neumann, I.D., Bodenmann, G., Dawans, B., von Turner, R., Ehlert, U. & Heinrichs, M. (2007). Effects of different kinds of marital interaction on cortisol and heart rate responses to stress in women. *Psychoneuroendocrinology, 32*, 565–574.

Domes, G., Heinrichs, M., Michel, A., Berger, C. & Herpertz, S. (2007). Oxytocin improves 'mind-reading' in humans. *Biological Psychiatry, 61*, 731–733.

Durkheim, E. (1897/1952). *Le Suicide: Suicide, a study in sociology*. Glencoe, IL: Free Press.

Edens, J.L., Larkin, K.T. & Abel, J.L. (1992). The effect of social support and physical touch on cardiovascular reactions to mental stress. *Journal of Psychosomatic Research, 36*, 371–381.

Fowler, J.H. & Christakis, N.A. (2008). Dynamic spread of happiness in a large social network: longitudinal analysis over 20 years in the Framingham Heart Study. *British Medical Journal,* Online First.

Glynn, L.M., Christenfeld, N. & Gerin, W. (1999). Gender, social support and cardiovascular responses to stress. *Psychosomatic Medicine, 61*, 234–242.

Heinrichs, M., Baumgartner, T., Kirschbaum, C. & Ehlert, U. (2003). Social support and oxytocin interact to suppress cortisol and subjective responses to psychological stress. *Biological Psychiatry, 54*, 1389–1398.

Helgeson, V.S. (1993). The onset of chronic illness: its effect on the patient–spouse relationship. *Journal of Social and Clinical Psychology, 12*, 406–428.

Hemingway, H. & Marmot, M. (1999). Psychosocial factors in the aetiology and prognosis of coronary heart disease: systematic review of prospective cohort studies. *British Medical Journal, 318*, 1460–1467.

House, J.S., Landis, K.R. & Umberson, D. (1988). Social relationships and health. *Science, 241*, 540–545.

Kienle, R., Luszczynska, A., Pfüller, B. & Knoll, N. (2009). Appraisal detection bias and well-being in close relationships: Couples experiencing assisted reproduction treatment. *Applied Psychology: Health and Well-Being, 1*, 165–187.

King, K.B., Reis, H.T., Porter, L.A. & Norsen, L.H. (1993). Social support and long-term recovery from coronary artery surgery: effects on patients and spouses. *Health Psychology, 12*, 56–63.

Klauer, T. & Winkeler, M. (2002). Gender, mental health status and social support during a stressful event. In G. Weidner, M. Kopp & M. Kristenson (Eds.) *Heart disease: Environment, stress and gender. NATO Science Series, Series I: Life and Behavioural Sciences, Vol. 327* (pp. 223–236). Amsterdam: IOS Press.

Knoll, N., Kienle, R., Bauer, K., Pfüller, B. & Luszczynska, A. (2007). Affect and enacted support in couples undergoing in-vitro fertilization: when providing is better than receiving. *Social Science & Medicine, 64*, 1789–1801.

Kosfeld, M., Heinrichs, M., Zak, P.J., Fischbacher, U. & Fehr, E. (2005). Oxytocin increases trust in humans. *Nature, 435*, 673–676.

Kulik, J.A. & Mahler, H.I.M. (1989). Social support and recovery from surgery. *Health Psychology, 8*, 221–238.

Kulik, J.A. & Mahler, H.I.M. (1993). Emotional support as a moderator of adjustment and compliance after coronary bypass surgery: q longitudinal study. *Journal of Behavioral Medicine, 16*, 45–63.

Lazarus, R.S. & Folkman, S. (1984). *Stress, Appraisal and Coping*. New York: Springer.

Luszczynska, A., Boehmer, S., Knoll, N., Schulz, U. & Schwarzer, R. (2007). Emotional support for men and women with cancer: do patients receive what their partners provide? *International Journal of Behavioral Medicine, 14*, 156–163.

Luszczynska, A., Mohamed, N.E. & Schwarzer, R. (2005). Self-efficacy and social support predict benefit finding 12 months after cancer surgery: the mediating role of coping strategies. *Psychology, Health & Medicine, 10*, 365–375.

Luszczynska, A., Sarkar, Y. & Knoll, N. (2007). Received social support, self-efficacy and finding benefits in being HIV-infected as predictors of adherence to antiretroviral therapy. *Patient Education and Counseling, 66*, 37–42.

Maltz, D.N. & Borker, R.A. (1982). A cultural approach to male–female discommunication. In J.J. Gumperz (Ed.) *Language and social identity* (pp. 196–216). Cambridge: Cambridge University Press.

Martire, L. & Schulz, R. (2007). Involving family in psychosocial interventions for chronic illness. *Current Directions in Psychological Science, 16*(2), 90–94.

Revenson, T.A., Schiaffino, K.M., Majerovitz, S.D. & Gibofsky, A. (1991). Social support as a double-edged sword: the relation of positive and problematic support to depression among rheumatoid arthritis patients. *Social Science & Medicine, 33*, 807–813.

Sarason, B.R., Pierce, G.R. & Sarason, I.G. (1990). Social support: the sense of acceptance and the role of relationships. In B.R. Sarason, G. Sarason & G.R. Pierce (Eds.) *Social support: An interactional view* (pp. 97–128). Chichester: Wiley.

Sbarra, D.A. & Nietert, P.J. (2009). Divorce and death. Forty years of the Charleston Heart Study. *Psychological Science, 20*, 107–113.

Schröder, K.E.E., Schwarzer, R. & Konertz, W. (1998). Coping as a mediator in recovery from heart surgery: a longitudinal study. *Psychology & Health, 13*, 83–97.

Schwarzer, R. & Gutiérrez-Doña, B. (2005). More spousal support for men than for women: a comparison of sources and types of support. *Sex Roles: A Journal of Research, 52*, 523–532.

Schwarzer, R. & Knoll, N. (2007). Functional roles of social support within the stress and coping process: a theoretical and empirical overview. *International Journal of Psychology, 42*(4), 243–252.

Schwarzer, R. & Leppin, A. (1991). Social support and health: a theoretical and empirical overview. *Journal of Social and Personal Relationships, 8*, 99–127.

Schwarzer, R. & Schulz, U. (2000). *Berlin Social Support Scales (BSSS)*. Available from www.coping.de.

Schwarzer, R., Dunkel-Schetter, C. & Kemeny, M. (1994). The multidimensional nature of received social support in gay men at risk of HIV infection and AIDS. *American Journal of Community Psychology, 22*, 319–339.

Taylor, S.E. (2006). Tend and befriend: biobehavioral bases of affiliation under stress. *Current Directions in Psychological Science, 15*, 273–277.

Tucker, J.S., Schwartz, J.E., Clark, K.M. & Friedman, H.S. (1999). Age-related changes in the associations of social network ties with mortality risk. *Psychology and Aging, 14*, 564–571.

Uchino, B. (2006). Social support and health: a review of physiological processes potentially underlying links to disease outcomes. *Journal of Behavioral Medicine, 29*(4), 377–387.

Wing, R.R., Marcus, M.D., Epstein, L.H. & Jawad, A. (1991). A 'family-based' approach to the treatment of obese type II diabetic patients. *Journal of Consulting and Clinical Psychology, 59*, 156–162.

23

Personality, Health and Illness

Deborah J. Wiebe, Linda M. Drew and Andrea Croom

Chapter Outline

People have long been fascinated by the possibility that enduring characteristics of individuals – their dispositional thoughts, emotions and behaviours – can determine whether they stay healthy, get sick or die. This notion has come of age with the burgeoning of the field of health psychology. Why should health psychologists study personality? Although progress has been made in understanding biomedical contributions to illness, large amounts of variance remain unexplained raising the possibility that psychosocial factors are important. The primary causes of mortality in industrialised countries are chronic illnesses, which are heavily influenced by behavioural risks over long periods of time. Personality may create the fairly stable influences necessary to move people towards health-enhancing or health-damaging trajectories across the lifespan. Indeed, personality measured in childhood predicts longevity at magnitudes comparable to elevated serum cholesterol and resting systolic blood pressure measured in adulthood (Friedman *et al.*, 1993). By understanding personality–health associations and their underlying mechanisms, researchers and clinicians gain a more thorough picture of health as a biopsychosocial process which can guide more efficient and effective interventions. In the present chapter, we briefly discuss how personality has been defined and measured in health psychology. We then describe theoretical models that may explain personality–health associations and review some well-developed literatures linking personality to physical health. We conclude by discussing the research and clinical implications of this exciting area of enquiry.

Key Concepts

Conscientiousness
Coping behaviours
Five-factor model of
  personality
Health behaviour
  model
Health damaging
  behaviours
Health enhancing
  behaviours
Hostility
Illness behaviour model
Illness behaviours
Neuroticism
Optimism
Personality traits
Personality–health
  relationships
Risk and reliance
  factors
Stress appraisals
Transactional stress-
  moderation model
Type A behaviour

How is Personality Defined and Measured?

Much of personality–health research has focused on personality as a collection of traits that were either observed or theoretically expected to co-occur with illness. Early work was hampered by a lack of convergence in concepts and measures, resulting in often idiosyncratically defined traits that were not validly measured. The development of the five-factor model (Costa & McCrae, 1992) has brought structure and empirically validated measures to the field. This model emerged out of demonstrations that the extreme diversity of human traits is captured by five broad dimensions (neuroticism, extraversion, openness to experience, agreeableness and conscientiousness), each composed of more specific facets. With this taxonomy, we can evaluate old and new personality constructs using a common lens and can examine personality at multiple levels (e.g. specific facets, single broad dimensions or combinations of dimensions). The most recent wave of personality–health research has begun to benefit from this perspective.

Health psychology's focus on static trait–health relationships remains limited, however, because it ignores the dynamic influences of personality in our day-to-day lives that are central to current personality psychology (e.g. Cantor, 1990). From this perspective, personality, behavioural and physiological processes influence each other in ongoing transactions that become reflected in health-relevant trajectories across development (Friedman, 2000). For example, the interpersonal beliefs and behaviours of hostile individuals may generate interpersonal stress and minimise social support (Smith, 2003). These processes may not only contribute to the hostile person's poor health, but reverberate back to confirm his or her antagonistic behaviours toward others. Such short and long cycles of personality influences on health remain understudied.

How Might Personality Affect Physical Health?

Transactional stress-moderation model

The most common explanation of how personality influences health is by moderating the health–damaging effects of stress. Stress activates the sympathetic

and neuroendocrine systems and deregulates the immune system, resulting in a cascade of physiological responses that contribute to illness. Stress-moderation models posit that personality influences health by changing the intensity, frequency or duration of stress-induced physiological arousal. Personality may do so by altering both one's appraisal of and coping responses to potential stressors. This basic stress-moderation model is limited by its static view of personality, where personality is believed to create stable *responses* to ongoing life experiences, but not to shape the nature of those experiences. The more complex *transactional stress-moderation model* considers personality as actively creating different types of life experiences in addition to influencing our responses once such events occur.

Health behaviour model

Personality may also affect illness by altering one's likelihood of engaging in health-enhancing or health-damaging behaviours. Health behaviours are well-established predictors of illness and longitudinal studies demonstrate that personality predicts health behaviours over decades (e.g. Friedman *et al.*, 1995). Personality may contribute to health behaviours by shaping health beliefs (e.g. risk perceptions, self-efficacy beliefs) and motivational propensities. For example, Cooper *et al.* (2000) demonstrated neuroticism and extraversion promote risky behaviours (i.e., alcohol and sexual practices) through different affect regulation needs, where neurotic individuals engaged in risky behaviours to cope with negative mood while extraverted individuals did so to enhance positive moods.

Illness behaviour model

Illness behaviours represent actions people take when they *believe* they are sick (e.g. attend to and report symptoms, visit a physician, take medication). Such behaviours increase in the face of disease and are crucial to the ongoing management of health and illness (Cameron & Leventhal, 2003). However, illness behaviour is also related to dispositional aspects of symptom perception and illness cognition and may occur independent of underlying pathology (Watson & Pennebaker, 1989). This model is particularly important to consider if the measure of health outcomes plausibly reflects illness behaviour rather than objective pathology (e.g. symptom reports, health-care utilisation). In these cases, personality may *appear* associated with health in the absence of actual disease, highlighting the need to obtain unambiguous 'hard' measures of health when studying personality–health relationships (e.g. mortality, immune function, neuroendocrine arousal).

Specific Examples of Personality–Health Associations

A comprehensive review of personality–health associations is beyond our scope (see Vollrath, 2006, for review). Instead, we focus on traits that have compelling evidence for prospectively predicting unambiguous signs of illness. For each variable, we review the strongest evidence of associations with health and discuss the mechanisms examined to explain these associations.

Hostility, Type A behaviour and anger

Type A individuals are hard-driving, work-oriented individuals who frequently become impatient, irritable and annoyed. Hostility is the toxic component of this multi-faceted construct and is among the most well-studied health-relevant personality variables. Hostility is a personality trait with attitudinal (cynicism and mistrust), emotional (anger) and behavioural (overt and repressed aggression) components (Smith, 2003). In five-factor model terminology, hostility reflects both high neuroticism and low agreeableness.

Hostility and related constructs have been explicitly linked to coronary heart disease (CHD) at various stages of disease progression. Non-symptomatic individuals high in trait anger have a 50–75 per cent increased risk of developing CHD (Williams *et al.*, 2000), and hostility is associated with coronary artery calcification (Iribarren *et al.*, 2000), higher incidence of coronary events (Kawachi *et al.*, 1998) and early indications of atherosclerosis (Bleil *et al.*, 2004). Following a cardiovascular event, hostility predicts a higher likelihood of recurrent myocardial infarction (Chaput *et al.*, 2002). Hostility also predicts both CHD mortality and all-cause mortality in multiple prospective studies (e.g. Boyle *et al.*, 2004; Matthews, Gump *et al.*, 2004).

In support of the transactional stress-moderation model, hostile individuals create more interpersonal conflict in their lives and respond to conflict with more frequent and prolonged physiological reactivity. Hostile individuals experience chronic stress, displaying overactive physiological reactivity (Hughes *et al.*, 2003). In addition, hostile individuals report lower social support (O'Neil & Emery, 2002) and more interpersonal conflict (Siegler *et al.*, 2003) than individuals low in hostility. Therefore, hostility appears to influence both the situations individuals encounter and their physiological reactions to these situations, creating a unique constellation of psychosocial vulnerability (Smith, 2003).

Processes described in the health behaviour model are also important. Cross-sectional and longitudinal studies indicate hostility is associated with poor health behaviours (e.g. smoking and alcohol use, poorer exercise and diet) (Bunde & Suls, 2006; Siegler *et al.*, 2003). Everson *et al.* (1997) found that poor health behaviours mediate the relationship between hostility and subsequent CHD.

The influence of hostility on illness behaviour has received little empirical attention, although the mistrust of hostile individuals may impair their adherence to physicians' advice (Christensen *et al.*, 1997). Type A individuals are less likely to detect symptoms of myocardial infarction, particularly when work is highly demanding (Matthews *et al.*, 1983), and may be more likely to reject the sick role and return to work before recovering from illness (Alemagno *et al.*, 1991). These associations appear to reflect the competitive and hard-driving facets of type A, rather than hostility.

Neuroticism and negative affect

Neuroticism is a broad dimension of personality in the five-factor model that represents the disposition to experience negative emotions (e.g. anxiety, depression). The hypothesis that neuroticism is damaging to one's health has a controversial history due to concerns that associations reflected illness behaviour rather than objective health (Watson & Pennebaker, 1989). Although inconsistent findings continue, comprehensive reviews conclude that negative emotions such as anxiety and depression prospectively predict 'hard' health endpoints (e.g. Suls & Bunde, 2005).

Neuroticism is also associated with subsequent illness progression in patients with HIV (Ickovics et al., 2001) and renal failure (Christensen et al., 2002).

Neuroticism has been linked to stress and coping, making stress moderation likely. Neuroticism prospectively predicts higher stress and interpersonal conflict, suggesting neurotic individuals create stressful lives for themselves (e.g. Bolger & Zuckerman, 1995; Kendler et al., 2003). Neurotic individuals appraise experienced stressors as more threatening and less manageable (Schneider, 2004) and display greater emotional reactivity when psychological stress is encountered (Bolger & Zuckerman, 1995; Schneider, 2004). Neurotic individuals also report less adaptive coping strategies such as avoidance and denial (Watson & Hubbard, 1996).

Neuroticism has also been associated with risky health behaviours such as increased smoking (Terracciano & Costa, 2004), although inconsistent findings occur. Inconsistencies may occur because other variables moderate associations between neuroticism and health behaviours. For example, neuroticism may be damaging primarily when combined with low conscientiousness (Vollrath, 2006), or when risky behaviours are used to cope with high stress (Cooper et al., 2000).

Neuroticism clearly influences illness behaviour, which may explain some inconsistent findings. Neuroticism is associated with greater symptom complaints after exposure to a virus, even when objective disease is statistically controlled (Cohen et al., 1995). Although neurotic individuals appear accurate at detecting objectively determined illness-related symptoms, they do over-interpret the meaning of somatic sensations (i.e., misattribute benign sensations to illness or treatment) (Cameron & Leventhal, 2003; Wiebe et al., 1994) and perceive heightened threat in the face of illness symptoms (Skinner et al., 2002). Such processes may have health benefits by promoting early illness detection (Cameron & Leventhal, 2003), reducing delay in seeking help (Ristvedt & Trinkhaus, 2005) and promoting adherence (Skinner et al., 2002). These same processes, however, may impair health in other contexts by misguiding patients' and physicians' treatment decision making. For example, Wiebe and colleagues (1994) found trait anxious adolescents with diabetes who reported using symptoms to guide treatment decisions (e.g. when to take insulin) had poorer metabolic control; presumably, their symptom misattributions provided poor guides to effective illness management. In an analogue study, Ellington and Wiebe (1999) found neuroticism was associated with an elaborate style of describing symptoms in a medical context (e.g. exaggerating symptoms and inserting information about negative emotions and stress), which made it difficult for physicians to discern illness severity and recommend appropriate treatment.

Conscientiousness

Conscientiousness is another broad dimension in the five-factor model which captures tendencies to follow socially prescribed norms, be goal-directed, persistent and dependable and have strong impulse control and delay of gratification (Costa & McCrae, 1992). Although a relative newcomer to the personality–health literature, conscientiousness has impressively consistent relationships to positive health outcomes. A prospective lifespan study revealed characteristics of conscientiousness measured in childhood predict longevity and all-cause mortality over a seven-decade period (Friedman et al., 1993, 1995). In a recent meta-analysis, Kern and Friedman (2008) reported conscientiousness-related traits predicted increased longevity across 20 independent samples. Such associations are found when conscientiousness is measured in childhood and middle-age and among those with chronic illnesses such as HIV and chronic renal insufficiency (e.g. Christensen et al., 2002; Ironson & Hayward, 2008).

People high on conscientiousness tend to engage in active coping under stressful conditions, suggesting stress moderation is a potential mechanism. In particular, conscientiousness is associated with lower perceived stress, more positive appraisal and problem-focused coping (Grant & Langan-Fox, 2006; Kern & Friedman, 2008). Korotkov (2008) specifically reported that conscientiousness buffers negative emotional responses to stress. Consistent with a transactional perspective, conscientious individuals report fewer daily hassles over a four-week daily diary (O'Connor et al., 2009) and less stressful marriage and work environments across decades (Roberts & Bogg, 2004).

Health behaviours appear to mediate the link between conscientiousness and health (Friedman *et al.*, 1995). Conscientiousness is associated with lower behavioural risks such as tobacco use, risky sex, less physical activity and unhealthy eating, all of which contribute to health problems (Bogg & Roberts, 2004). Martin and Friedman (2007) found the relationship between conscientiousness and subsequent mortality was statistically mediated by reduced smoking and alcohol use.

Conscientiousness may also promote more adaptive illness behaviours. Conscientiousness is associated with better adherence (Wiebe & Christensen, 1996), potentially due to different illness perceptions. For example, conscientious adolescents with type 1 diabetes display better adherence partially because they have higher beliefs in treatment effectiveness (Skinner *et al.*, 2002).

Optimism

Optimism is defined as a generalised and stable expectation that good things will happen (Scheier & Carver, 1985). Individuals with high optimism show lower risk of nonfatal myocardial infarction (Kubzansky *et al.*, 2001), slower progression of coronary artery disease (Matthews, Raikkonen *et al.*, 2004) and fewer rehospitalisations and a faster return to normal life following coronary artery bypass surgery (Scheier *et al.*, 2003). Prospective population-based studies indicate optimism predicts lower cardiovascular and all-cause mortality (Brummett *et al.*, 2006; Kubzansky *et al.*, 2001). Furthermore, among patients with cancer or HIV, optimism predicts slower disease progression and lower mortality (Allison *et al.*, 2003; Ickovics *et al.*, 2006).

Some research suggests that there might be an optimal level of optimism, such that extreme optimism or optimism in the face of uncontrollable situations might actually be maladaptive (Milam *et al.*, 2004; Tomakowsky *et al.*, 2001). Careful attention to stress-moderation processes may clarify this relationship. Segerstrom (2005) suggested that inconsistent associations between optimism and immune functioning may reflect unmeasured interactions with the stress context. If optimism promotes active engagement and coping when a stressor is uncontrollable, the optimistic individual may experience short-term physiological costs, while still having longer term benefits (Nes

et al., 2005). Although such data suggest optimism could be detrimental in the context of uncontrollable stress, optimists appear to flexibly modify their coping beliefs and behaviours to match the situation at hand (Aspinwall *et al.*, 2001).

In regards to the health behaviour model, there has been concern that optimism may function like denial, reducing perceptions of health risk and motivation to engage in health-promoting behaviours (Davidson & Prkachin, 1997), as well as leaving optimists more vulnerable to negative reactions to unexpected health events and disappointment to poor recovery (Tennen & Affleck, 1987). However, Aspinwall and Brunhart (1996) found optimism actually predicts greater attention to risk information and multiple studies support a relationship between optimism and positive health practices (Mulkana & Hailey, 2001). For example optimists are more likely to use positive coping strategies (e.g. exercising) during times of stress rather than turning to health risks, such as alcohol or smoking. In addition, individuals with optimistic tendencies reported fewer daily hassles, lower negative mood and more positive social interactions (Baker, 2007; Steptoe *et al.*, 2008).

Optimism also appears to play a role in illness behaviours. Optimists are more likely to engage in problem-focused coping, including seeking information from physicians, are less likely to dwell on the negatives of recovery or deny physical symptoms (Scheier *et al.*, 2003) and have a greater likelihood of achieving adherence to their medication regimen (Milam *et al.*, 2004). The impact of optimism is highly related to the extent to which the specific illness can be controlled through self-care. Optimism is particularly helpful when self-care is limited, but optimism is not harmful when the disease is controllable (i.e. optimism does not interfere with people performing necessary illness behaviours; Fournier *et al.*, 2002). Taken together, optimism associations with health are likely to reflect a variety of complex processes that may work differently across the range of optimism scores and stress contexts.

Implications and Conclusions

This steady accumulation of knowledge suggests that personality has the potential to affect health and illness. Across experimental, cross-sectional, daily diary and lifespan longitudinal studies, personality predicts health in ways that cannot be readily explained by reverse causation (e.g. personality changes in response to disease), weak measures of health that reflect illness behaviour or shared associations with a third variable (e.g. genetic factors simultaneously predict personality and longevity). The five-factor model has brought structure to the field and identified conscientiousness, neuroticism and potentially low agreeableness (hostility) as active health-relevant traits. The full influence of personality is beginning to be recognised as the additive and interactive effects of these broad personality dimensions are examined. Finally, the mechanisms underlying these associations are beginning to be understood, although much work is needed to have a comprehensive understanding of these relationships (Vollrath, 2006; Wiebe & Fortenberry, 2006).

Personality–health research holds important implications for clinical health psychologists. Given the consistent press personality makes towards health-enhancing or health-damaging trajectories across the lifespan, personality may identify those at risk from early ages. Psychologists can use this risk information to target and tailor interventions towards health promotion and ill-

ness prevention more effectively. Personality provides much information about an individual's profile of cognitive, behavioural and emotional propensities and this information may inform the best approaches for helping patients manage illness and promote health. In this context, personality may also moderate the effectiveness of accepted interventions. Neurotic patients, for example, did not respond well to a health education intervention for myocardial infarction patients, presumably because the problem-focused intervention interfered with the neurotic individual's emotion-regulation needs (Cameron et al., 2005). Finally, there is some evidence that health-relevant personality traits are mutable and can be directly changed to promote health and well-being (Vollrath, 2006). For example, a cognitive behavioural hostility reduction intervention simultaneously lowered hostility, blood pressure and subsequent hospital days among hostile myocardial infarction patients (Gidron et al., 1999). Clinical research that rigorously tests interventions to alter personality traits or their health-relevant processes is important to move the field past simply describing personality–health associations, towards explaining and altering such associations and enhancing health and well-being.

Discussion Points

1   What are the benefits and limitations of the five-factor model for promoting personality–health research?
2   How do your personality traits contribute to or hinder your overall health? Discuss these influences based on the three models of personality–health associations.
3   Assume the role of a sceptic and develop an argument for the statement 'It is time to acknowledge

that the notion that personality can affect disease is largely folklore'. Then develop an argument against this statement. What additional scientific evidence would strengthen each of your arguments?
4   Do you believe that interventions to alter personality traits can be successful? Why or why not? Find an example in the literature to support your claim.

Further Reading

Cantor, N. (1990). From thought to behavior: 'Having' and 'doing' in the study of personality and cognition. *American Psychologist, 45,* 735–750.

Friedman, H.S. (2000). Long-term relations of personality and health: Dynamisms, mechanisms, tropisms. *Journal of Personality, 68,* 1089–1107.

Friedman, H.S., Tucker, J.S., Schwartz, J.E., Martin, L.R., Tomlinson-Keasey, C., Wingard, D.L. & Criqui, M.H.

(1995). Childhood conscientiousness and longevity: Health behaviors and cause of death. *Journal of Personality and Social Psychology, 68,* 696–703.

Scheier, M.F., Matthews, K.A., Owens, J.F., Schulz, R., Bridges, M.W., Magovern, G.J. & Carver, C.S. (1999). Optimism and rehospitalization after coronary artery bypass graft surgery. *Archives of Internal Medicine, 159,* 829–835.

Smith, T.W. (1992) Hostility and health: Current status of a psychosomatic hypothesis. *Health Psychology, 11,* 139–150.

Suls, J. & Bunde, J. (2005). Anger, anxiety and depression as risk factors for cardiovascular disease: The problems and implications of overlapping affective dispositions. *Psychological Bulletin, 131,* 260–300.

Vollrath, M.E. (Ed.) (2006). *Handbook of personality and health.* Chichester: Wiley.

References

Allison, P.J., Guichard,, C., Fung, K. & Gilain, L. (2003). Dispositional optimism predicts survival status 1 year after diagnosis in head and neck cancer patients. *Journal of Clinical Oncology, 21*(3), 543–548.

Alemagno, S.A., Zyzanski, S.J., Stange, K.C., Kercher, K., Medalie, J.H. & Kahana, E. (1991). Health and illness behavior of Type A persons. *Journal of Occupational Medicine, 33,* 891–895.

Aspinwall, L.G. & Brunhart, S.M. (1996). Distinguishing optimism from denial: Optimistic beliefs predict attention to health threats. *Personality and Social Psychology Bulletin, 22,* 993–1003.

Aspinwall, L.G., Richter, L. & Hoffman, R.R. (2001). Understanding how optimism works: An examination of optimists' adaptive moderation of belief and behavior. In E.C. Edwards (Ed.) *Optimism and pessimism: Implications for theory, research and practice* (pp. 217–238). Washington, DC: American Psychological Association.

Baker, S.R. (2007). Dispositional optimism and health status, symptoms and behaviours: Assessing idiothetic relationships using a prospective daily dairy approach. *Psychology & Health, 22*(4), 431–455.

Bleil, M.E., McCaffery, J.M., Muldoon, M.F., Sutton-Tyrell, K. & Manuck, S.B. (2004). Anger-related personality traits and carotid artery aterosclerosis in untreated hypertensive men. *Psychosomatic Medicine, 66,* 633–639.

Bogg, T. & Roberts, B.W. (2004). Conscientiousness and health-related behaviors: A meta-analysis of the leading behavioral contributors to mortality. *Psychological Bulletin, 130,* 887–919.

Bolger, N. & Zuckerman, A. (1995). A framework for studying personality in the stress process. *Journal of Personality and Social Psychology, 69*(5), 890–902.

Boyle, S.H., Williams, R.B. & Mark, D.B. (2004). Hostility as a predictor of survival in patients with coronary artery disease. *Psychosomatic Medicine, 66,* 629–632.

Brummett, B.H., Helms, M.J., Dahlstrom, W.G. & Siegler, I.C. (2006). Prediction of all-cause mortality by the Minnesota Multiphasic Personality Inventory Optimism-Pessimism scale scores: Study of a college sample during a 40-year follow-up period. *Mayo Clinic Proceedings, 81*(12), 1541–1544.

Bunde, J. & Suls, J. (2006). A quantitative analysis of the relationship between the Cook-Medley Hostility Scale and traditional coronary artery disease risk factors. *Health Psychology, 25*(4), 493–500.

Cameron, L.D. & Leventhal, H. (Eds.) (2003). *The self-regulation of health and illness behaviour.* London: Routledge.

Cameron, L.D., Petrie, K.J., Ellis, C.J., Buick, D. & Weinman, J.A. (2005). Trait negative affectivity and responses to health education intervention for myocardial infarction patients. *Psychology & Health, 20,* 1–18.

Cantor, N. (1990). From thought to behavior: 'Having' and 'doing' in the study of personality and cognition. *American Psychologist, 45,* 735–750.

Chaput, L.A., Adams, S.H., Simon, J.A., Blumenthal, R.S., Vittinghoff, E. & Lin, F. (2002). Hostility predicts recurrent events among postmenopausal women with coronary heart disease. *American Journal of Epidemiology, 156,* 1092–1099.

Christensen, A.J., Ehlers, S.L., Wiebe, J.S., Moran, P.J., Raichle, K, Ferneybough, K. *et al.* (2002). Patient personality and mortality: A 4-year prospective examination of chronic renal insufficiency. *Health Psychology, 21,* 315–320.

Christensen, A.J., Wiebe, J.S. & Lawton, W.J. (1997). Cynical hostility, powerful other control expectancies and patient adherence in hemodialysis. *Psychosomatic Medicine, 59,* 307–312.

Cohen, S., Doyle, W.J., Skoner, D.P., Fireman, P., Gwaltney, J.M. Jr. & Newsom, J.T. (1995). State and trait negative affect as predictors of objective and subjective symptoms of respiratory viral infections. *Journal of Personality and Social Psychology, 68,* 159–169.

Cooper, M.L., Agocha, V.S. & Sheldon, M.S. (2000). A motivational perspective on risky behaviors: The role of personality and affect regulatory processes. *Journal of Personality, 68,* 1059–1088.

Costa, P.T. Jr & McCrae, R.R. (1992). *Manual for the Revised NEO Personality Inventory (NEO PI-R) and NEO Five-Factor Inventory (NEO-FFI).* Odessa, FL: Psychological Assessment Resources.

Davidson, K. & Prkachin, K. (1997). Optimism and unrealistic optimism have an interacting impact on health-promoting behavior and knowledge changes. *Personality and Social Psychology Bulletin, 23*(6), 617–625.

Ellington, L & Wiebe, D.J. (1999). Neuroticism, symptom presentation and medical decision making. *Health Psychology, 18,* 634–643.

Everson, S.A., Kauhanen, J., Kaplan, G., Goldberg, D., Julkunen, J., Tuomilehto, J., Salonen, J.T. (1997). Hostility and increased risk of mortality and myocardial infarction: The mediating role of behavioral risk factors. *American Journal of Epidemiology, 146,* 142–152.

Fournier, M., de Ridder, D. & Bensing, J. (2002). How optimism contributes to the adaptation of chronic illness: A prospective study into the enduring effects of optimism on adaptation moderated by the controllability of chronic illness. *Personality and Individual Differences, 33,* 1163–1183.

Friedman, H.S. (2000). Long-term relations of personality and health: Dynamisms, mechanisms, tropisms. *Journal of Personality, 68,* 1089–1107.

Friedman, H.S., Tucker, J.S., Schwartz, J.E., Martin, L.R., Tomlinson-Keasey, C., Wingard, D.L. & Criqui, M.H. (1995). Childhood conscientiousness and longevity: Health behaviors and cause of death. *Journal of Personality and Social Psychology, 68,* 696–703.

Friedman, H.S., Tucker, J.S., Tomlinson-Keasey, C., Schwartz, J.E., Wingard, D.L. & Criqui, M.H. (1993). Does childhood personality predict longevity? *Journal of Personality and Social Psychology, 65,* 176–185.

Gidron, Y., Davidson, K. & Bata, I. (1999). The short-term effects of a hostility-reduction intervention in CHD patients. *Health Psychology, 18,* 416–420.

Grant, S. & Langan-Fox, J. (2006). Occupational stress, coping and strain: The combined/interactive effect of the Big Five traits. *Personality and Individual Differences, 41,* 719–732.

Hughes, J.W., Sherwood, A., Blumenthal, J.A., Suarez, E.C. & Hinderliter, A.L. (2003). Hostility, social support and adrenergic receptor responsiveness among African-American and White men and women. *Psychosomatic Medicine, 65,* 582–587.

Ickovics, J.R., Haven, C.T., Hamburger, M.E., Vlahov, D., Schoenbaum, E.E., Schuman, P. *et al.* (2001). Mortality, CD4 cell count decline and depressive symptoms among HIV-seropositive women: Longitudinal analysis from the HIV epidemiology research study. *Journal of the American Medical Association, 285,* 1466–1474.

Ickovics, J.R., Milan, S., Boland, R., Schoenbaum, E., Schuman, P. & Vlahov, D. (2006). Psychological resources protect health: 5-year survival and immune function among HIV-infected women from four US cities. *AIDS, 20*(14), 1851–1860.

Iribarren, C., Sidney, S., Bild, D.E., Liu, K., Markovitz, J.H., Roseman, J.M. & Matthews, K. (2000). Association of hostility with coronary artery risk development in young adults: The CARDIA study. *Journal of the American Medical Association, 283,* 2546–2551.

Ironson, G.H. & Hayward, H. (2008). Do positive psychosocial factors predict disease progression in HIV-1? A review of the evidence. *Psychosomatic Medicine. 70,* 546–554.

Kawachi, I., Sparrow, D., Kubzansky, L.D., Spiro, A., Vokonas, P.S. & Weiss, S.T. (1998). Prospective study of a self-report type: a scale and risk of coronary heart disease: test of the MMPI-2 type A scale. *Circulation, 98*(5), 405–412.

Kendler, K.S., Gardner, C.O. & Prescott, C.A. (2003). Personality and the experience of environmental adversity. *Psychological Medicine, 33,* 1193–1202.

Kern, M.L. & Friedman, H.S. (2008). Do conscientious individuals live longer? A quantitative review. *Health Psychology, 27,* 505–512.

Korotkov, D. (2008). Does personality moderate the relationship between stress and health behavior? Expanding the nomological network of the five factor model. *Journal of Research in Personality, 42,* 1418–1426.

Kubzansky, L.D., Sparrow, D. & Vokonas, P. (2001). Is the glass half empty or half full? A prospective study of optimism and coronary heart disease in the normative aging study. *Psychosomatic Medicine, 63,* 910–916.

Martin, L.R. & Friedman, H.S. (2007). Personality and mortality risk across the life span: The importance of conscientiousness as a biopsychosocial attribute. *Health Psychology, 26,* 428–436.

Matthews, K.A., Gump, B.B., Harris, K.F., Haney, T.L. & Barefoot, J.C. (2004). Hostile behaviors predict cardiovascular mortality among men enrolled in the Multiple Risk Factor Intervention Trial. *Circulation, 109,* 66–70.

Matthews, K.A., Raikkonen, K., Sutton-Tyrrell, K. & Kuller, L.H. (2004). Optimistic attitudes protect against progression of carotid atherosclerosis in healthy middle-aged women. *Psychosomatic Medicine, 66,* 640–644.

Matthews, K.A., Siegel, J.M., Kuller, L.H., Thompson, M. & Varat, M. (1983). Determinants of decisions to seek medical treatment by patients with acute myocardial infarction symptoms. *Journal of Personality and Social Psychology, 44,* 1144–1156.

Milam, J.E., Richardson, J.L. & Marks, G. (2004). The roles of dispositional optimism and pessimism in HIV disease progression. *Psychology & Health, 19,* 167–181.

Mulkana, S.S. & Hailey, B.J. (2001). The role of optimism in health-enhancing behavior. *American Journal of Health Behavior, 25,* 388–395.

Nes, L.S., Segerstrom, S.C. & Sephton, S.E. (2005). Engagement and arousal: Optimism's effects during a brief stressor. *Personality and Social Psychology Bulletin, 31,* 111–120.

O'Connor, D.B., Conner, M., Jones, F., & Ferguson, E. (2009). Exploring the benefits of conscientiousness: An investigation of the role of daily stressors and health behaviors. *Annals of Behavioral Medicine*. Annals of Behavioral Medicine, 37, 184–196.

O'Neil, J.N. & Emery, C.F. (2002). Psychosocial vulnerability, hostility and family history of coronary heart disease among male and female college students. *International Journal of Behavioral Medicine, 9,* 17–36.

Ristvedt, S.L. & Trainkhaus, K.M. (2005). Psychological factors related to delay in consultation for cancer symptoms. *Psycho-Oncology, 14,* 339–350.

Roberts, B.W. & Bogg, T. (2004). A longitudinal study of the relationships between conscientiousness and the social-environmental factors and substance-use behaviors that influence health. *Journal of Personality, 72,* 325–353.

Scheier, M.F. & Carver, C.S. (1985). Optimism, coping and health: assessment and implications of generalized outcome expectancies. *Health Psychology, 4,* 219–247.

Scheier, M.F., Matthews, K.A., Owens, J.F., Magovern, G.J., Lefebvre, R.C., Abbott, R.A. & Carver, C.S. (2003). Dispositional optimism and recovery from coronary artery bypass surgery: The beneficial effects of physical and psychological well-being. In P. Salovey & A.J. Rothman (Eds.) *Social psychology of health* (pp. 342–361), New York: Psychology Press.

Schneider, T.R. (2004). The role of neuroticism on psychological and physiological stress responses. *Journal of Experimental Social Psychology, 40,* 795–804.

Segerstrom, S.C. (2005). Optimism and immunity: Do positive thoughts always lead to positive effects? *Brain, Behavior, and Immunity, 19,* 195–200.

Siegler, I.C., Costa. P.T. & Brummett, B.H. (2003). Patterns of change in hostility from college to midlife in the UNC Alumni Heart Study predict high-risk status. *Psychosomatic Medicine, 65,* 738–745.

Skinner, T.C., Hampson, S.E. & Fife-Schaw, C. (2002). Personality, personal model beliefs and self-care in adolescents and young adults with Type 1 diabetes. *Health Psychology, 21,* 61–70.

Smith, T.W. (2003). Hostility and health: Current status of a psychosomatic hypothesis. In P. Salovey & A.J. Rothman (Eds.) *Social psychology of health: Key readings* (pp. 325–341). New York: Psychology Press.

Steptoe, A., O'Donnell, K., Marmot, M. & Wardle, J. (2008). Positive affect and psychosocial processes related to health. *British Journal of Psychology, 99*(2), 211–227.

Suls, J. & Bunde, J. (2005). Anger, anxiety and depression as risk factors for cardiovascular disease: The problems and implications of overlapping affective dispositions. *Psychological Bulletin, 131,* 260–300.

Tennen, H. & Affleck, G. (1987). The costs and benefits of optimistic explanations and optimism. *Journal of Personality, 55,* 376–393.

Terracciano, A & Costa, P.T. Jr. (2004). Smoking and the five-factor model of personality, *Addiction, 99,* 472–481.

Tomakowsky, J., Lumley, M.A., Markowitz, N. & Frank, C. (2001). Optimism explanatory style and dispositional optimism in HIV-infected men. *Journal of Psychosomatic Research, 51*(4), 577–587.

Vollrath, M. (2006). *Handbook of personality and health.* Chichester: Wiley.

Watson, D. & Hubbard, B. (1996). Adaptational style and dispositional structure: Coping in the context of the five-factor model. *Journal of Personality, 64,* 737–774.

Watson, D. & Pennebaker, J. (1989). Health complaints, stress and distress: Exploring the central role of negative affectivity. *Psychological Review, 96,* 234–254.

Wiebe, D.J., Alderfer, M.A., Palmer, S.C., Lindsay, R. & Jarrett, L. (1994). Behavioral self-regulation in adolescents with type 1 diabetes: Negative affectivity and blood glucose symptom perception. *Journal of Consulting and Clinical Psychology, 62,* 1204–1212.

Wiebe, D.J. & Fortenberry, K. (2006). Mechanisms linking personality and health. In M. Vollrath (Ed.), *Handbook of personality and health* (pp. 137–156). Chichester: Wiley.

Wiebe, J.S. & Christensen, A.J. (1996). Patient adherence in chronic illness: Personality and coping in context. *Journal of Personality, 64,* 815–835.

Williams, J.E., Paton, C.C., Siegler, I.C., Eigenbrodt, M.L., Nieto, F.J. & Tyroler, H.A. (2000). Anger proneness predicts coronary heart disease risk: Prospective analysis from the Atherocsclerosis Risk in Communities (ARIC) study. *Circulation, 101,* 2034–2039.

24

Pain

H. Clare Daniel and Amanda C. de C. Williams

Chapter Outline

Pain is represented in health care mainly as a physical health problem, with a focus on identifying the aetiology and treating the problem. But many people obtain little lasting benefit from treatment and often have no clear understanding of the reason for their continuing pain. Persistent pain is prevalent, with estimates from 10 per cent to 20 per cent (Breivik *et al.*, 2006; Elliott *et al.*, 1999); 7.8 million people in the United Kingdom according to a recent UK government report (Donaldson, 2009); reports for the international prevalence vary from 10.1 per cent to 55.2 per cent (Harstall & Ospina, 2003). It is because of this high prevalence and the persistence of disabling and distressing pain that psychologically based interventions for this condition have been developed. However, encounters with mental health services, for many people with chronic pain, become a dispute over the reality of the pain. Our dualistic heritage of notions of psychological problems presenting as, or overflowing into, persistent pain informs lay and professional discourses of 'psychological pain', despite their lack of scientific support and their rejection by people with pain. What we present in this chapter is a description of persistent pain in terms of an integrated model developed in scientific studies of pain, of the profound impact it has on many of those who experience it and on how psychology can contribute to assessment and treatment. Finally, possibilities for further research are addressed.

Key Concepts

Assessment
Behavioural
Cognitive
Management
Pain

Pain and Pain Mechanisms

Pain is defined as 'an unpleasant sensory and emotional experience associated with actual or potential tissue damage, or described in terms of such damage' (International Association for the Study of Pain, 1979). This definition emphasises the inherently aversive nature of pain and shifts the focus away from understanding pain as exclusively a physical experience, or one that can only be confirmed by anatomical or physiological findings, to an experience which is possible in the absence of tissue damage, but it neglects behaviour characteristics of pain (Sullivan, 2008). Chronic or persistent pain is defined by time scale; pain lasting three or more months, or beyond the usual time for healing or resolution of pathology which could be responsible for pain onset. Chronic or persistent pain tends to refer to pain that is not attributable to a life-shortening or progressive disease, although longer survival with cancer and pain as an adverse effect of cancer treatments, are blurring the distinctions. Pain can develop spontaneously, or may follow acute injury, including surgery.

People with persistent pain generally suffer more than the pain itself. Its physical and psychological impact varies enormously across individuals, but it is frequently pervasive and detrimental. Losses include employment, relationships, friendships, social roles, enjoyment, a sense of achievement; distress can take the form of depression, anxiety, fear, frustration; everyday life is difficult with self-care, domestic routines and social and leisure activities compromised by limited mobility and physical capacity (Turk & Monarch, 2002). This pervasive impact can influence others around the person with pain. Communication suffers, roles alter and dependence on others develops. It is these secondary effects of persistent pain, rather than pain relief, which are the focus of pain management.

Integrated pain processing was first clearly described in the gate control model (Melzack & Wall, 1965). It is now understood that pain processing occurs by fine dynamic balance of excitation and inhibition of pain transmission at synapses from the periphery or organ to the brain and within the brain, driven both by bottom-up and top-down processes. Cognitive content transmitted via the descending pathways represents the individual's state of alertness and arousal; fears, hopes and expectations; memories and previous learning about painful events.

An essential survival mechanism, pain helps us to recognise and respond rapidly to harmful and life-threatening situations; subsequently, it prioritises whatever behaviour promotes healing and avoids further damage (Wall, 1999). As with any alarm system, the cost of efficiency in detecting threat is a high rate of false positives which interrupt and demand action when none is needed. This is underpinned by mechanisms which produce central sensitisation, spontaneous pain signals, amplification of background 'noise' to the level of a consistent pain message, excessive firing to non-noxious stimuli or firing at a lower threshold and recruitment of other modalities such as touch and temperature to the pain system. Changes also occur in cortical representation (Flor et al., 1997; Wall, 1999). Despite uncertainties in interpretation and a predominance of experimental over clinical subjects, understanding is advancing through functional imaging of the brain (Gracely et al., 2004; Petrovic & Ingvar, 2002; Price, 1999).

Psychological Models of Pain

The description of mechanisms makes clear why pain can occur and persist in the absence of change detectable on imaging or other investigations (Breslau & Seidenwurm, 2000). Unfortunately, where understanding of pain is poor and clinical pain is not 'explained' by the conventional mechanisms of lesion or pathology, spurious, highly abstract and theoretically weak psychological mechanisms are often invoked as a cause, such as 'pain of psychosomatic origin' or 'excessive pain' (Crombez et al., 2009; Sharpe & Mayou, 2004; Sharpe & Williams, 2002). The implication is that pain is 'all in the mind', which is distressing for those who experience genuine, constant pain and its consequences. Pejorative labels, such as somatisation, do not help the majority of patients understand their pain and therefore are of little help in their subsequent treatment (Daykin & Richardson, 2004).

The application of psychological models to pain management began with the behavioural model

(Fordyce, 1976). This placed considerable emphasis on pain behaviours, which are responses to pain which also communicate suffering to others who may in turn respond contingently, so that the behaviours become operantly controlled. These behaviours – from guarding or sparing a painful part to seeking analgesia or other help – are influenced by psychological and social factors such as culture and context and if under operant control as described, they are subject to the effects of learning and reinforcement. Thus behavioural management sought to extinguish pain behaviours and reinforce adaptive behaviours. However, this approach oversimplified influences on behaviour and ignored social and cultural norms and the extent to which adaptiveness of behaviour was contextually determined. The next major development in the application of psychological theory to pain management was the incorporation of the cognitive behavioural model. Although this continues to address behaviour, cognitive behavioural pain management searches for its meaning in cognitive content and process (Rudy et al., 2003; Watson, 1999), especially in unhelpful appraisals of and decisions about pain. A third phase of pain management is on the horizon. It focuses on the development of strategies that encourage mindfulness in relation to pain (Baer, 2003; Burch, 2008) and acceptance of pain (McCracken et al., 2004).

Assessment

Any assessment tool is a compromise between the richness of patients' own descriptions and the need for economical and standardised measurement. Choice of tools depends on the purpose of assessment: diagnosis, decision about treatment, evaluation of treatment effects or predicting response to treatment (Turk & Okifuji, 2003), as well as the usual qualities of measures (Fitzpatrick et al., 1998). Unsystematic use and scant overlap between measures selected for studies of physical and psychologically based treatments means it is hard to devise a list of appropriate measures, although Turk and colleagues (2003) have attempted to do this. Assessment of persistent pain should consider pain experience, psychological content and process, mood, function and use of health-care

resources (McDowell & Newell, 1996; Turk & Melzack, 2001; Williams 2007a).

Pain experience

Pain dimensions are commonly described as sensory/intensity, emotional/motivational and cognitive aspects and interference with everyday life (Holroyd et al., 1999; Price, 1999). Dimensions of pain co-vary somewhat loosely and predict different aspects of patients' function and psychological state (Clark & Yang, 2001; Jensen & Karoly, 2001). Since there is no external referent for pain, there can be no validation; reliability of different forms vary, but rating is itself recursive (Williams et al., 2000).

Location of pain is often oversimplified, but more sites of pain tend to mean greater disability (Blyth et al., 2003) and different sites of pain can produce different limitations. Pain can be rated over different time scales (now; average over the last week; etc.). Temporal variation is also frequently oversimplified and while duration is consistently reported, beyond the first year or two it is associated with surprisingly few other aspects of function.

Pain scales   The visual analogue scale remains one of the most popular measures, despite the slightly superior reliability and practicality of numerical rating scales (Jensen & Karoly, 2001; Jensen et al., 1999; Turk & Okifuji, 2003; Williams et al., 2000). Surprisingly, there is virtually no research on the effect of verbal anchors (e.g. 'worst pain', 'most intense pain imaginable') for the highest level of pain on these scales. Pain relief is usually measured as a percentage: 50 per cent pain relief is a common, if arbitrary, criterion for success of treatment. Ideally, pain relief would be titrated against a primary outcome.

Entirely verbal scales, easy to administer and high in face validity, can present problems for scaling and scoring (Jensen & Karoly, 2001); standardised expressive faces may be substituted for use by children and people with cognitive impairment (Hadjistavropoulos et al., 2001). Another widely used verbal measure, the McGill Pain Questionnaire (MPQ: Melzack, 1975; short form Melzack, 1987), provides sensory, affective and evaluative factors (Melzack & Katz, 1999), although a single total is often used. There is surprisingly little use of patients' own descriptions of pain quantity or quality, such as 'good/bad days'.

Where possible, averaged frequent recordings are preferable to single retrospective ratings of pain (Bolton, 1999; Jensen & Karoly, 2001; Stone *et al.*, 2003); reactivity does not seem to be a significant problem (Stone *et al.*, 2003). Adherence is better with electronic media than pen and paper (Jamison *et al.*, 2001; Stone *et al.*, 2002), as well as allowing random sampling and automatic data downloads (Peters *et al.*, 2000; Stone *et al.*, 2003).

Behavioural expression of pain Pain is reliably expressed in the face, although culture and context modify expressiveness (Craig *et al.*, 2001; Williams, 2002). However, facial expression requires more detailed assessment than is usually practicable (Craig *et al.*, 2001), but may be the only unique indicator of pain in people with compromised or underdeveloped communication capacities (Hadjistavropoulos *et al.*, 2001). Other motor behaviours, particularly guarding, are of interest and can be assessed by observation (Keefe *et al.*, 2001), preferable to self-reporting of those behaviours.

Psychological content and process

Psychosocial variables measured soon after onset of pain, or even before, account for a substantial amount of variance in predicting who will develop persistent, disabling pain (Linton, 2002). Psychological questionnaires are often used in pain assessment without consideration of the population on which they were developed, or the inclusion of items that have a different meaning for those with pain than for those (on whom it was standardised) with no significant pain problem.

Coping The term coping is often used by patients and health-care providers and is one of the most discussed psychological variables in the pain literature (Van Damme, 2008). Although it has considerable face validity, measures rely on an oversimplification of behaviour, without reference to the context in which a coping strategy is used and the outcome of its use which render it adaptive or not. There may also be inconsistency between short- and long-term effects and personal and social outcomes. For example, using a walking stick may help a person achieve immediate goals, but elicit unhelpful responses from others and reduce opportunities to improve independent weight bearing. A recent review (Van Damme *et al.*, 2008) has sought to describe a motivational model of coping, which focuses on the function of behaviour in context and offers a more dynamic understanding of this construct than the common *a priori* classification into active or passive.

Content of beliefs A widely used measure of beliefs about illness, the Illness Perception Questionnaire (Weinman *et al.*, 1996; revised IPQ-R, Moss-Morris *et al.*, 2002; www.uib.no/ipq/), is increasingly used in pain studies. Other pain belief questionnaires sample the threat inherent in pain (Vlaeyen & Linton, 2000), each with a different focus (Williams, 2007a). Although fear of pain is important in predicting short- and long-term behaviour, it is not universal among those struggling with persistent pain. Formulations based on locus of control have been overtaken by the more predictive self-efficacy (Asghari & Nicholas, 2001; Lorig *et al.*, 1989).

Cognitive processes Catastrophising currently appears to be the most robust construct in predicting distress, depression and disability in persistent pain (Rosenstiel & Keefe, 1983; Sullivan *et al.*, 2001; Sullivan *et al.*, 1995). In relation to pain, it is described as a tendency to attend to pain stimuli, overestimate their threat value and underestimate the capacity to manage that threat (Sullivan *et al.*, 2001). Catastrophising is associated with fears and anxiety about pain, depressed mood and depressive thought content. Other measures that focus on cognitive processing are in development and include the acceptance of persistent pain (McCracken *et al.*, 1999). For a wider range of measures, see Turk and Melzack (2001) and Williams (2007a).

Mood Many measures of mood, in particular of depression and anxiety, have been imported from the mental health/psychiatric field into the pain field without adequate concern for their applicability. Most contain somatic items which are part of the persistent pain experience and on which alone scores of clinical concern may be achieved, without any cognitive or affective content (Pincus & Williams, 1999). Studies in persistent pain suggest differences in content and reference of mood difficulties between them and the standardisation samples. Measures are rarely re-standardised in populations with illness or pain.

Commonly used measures include the Beck Depression Inventory (Beck *et al.*, 1996) and the Center for Epidemiologic Studies Depression Scale (CES-D: Radloff, 1977), both of which are subject to inflation of total score by somatic content. The Hospital Anxiety and Depression Scale (HADS: Zigmond & Snaith, 1983) avoids the problems of the somatic items, but unnecessarily sacrifices cognitive content. Measures of depression and anxiety that exclude somatic content are the Depression Anxiety Stress Scales (Lovibond & Lovibond, 1995; see also www.psy.unsw.edu.au/Groups/Dass/) and, developed specifically for the pain population, the Depression, Anxiety and Positive Outlook Scale (Pincus *et al.*, 2004, www.dapos.org).

Measures of function

Function can incorporate many concepts and thus can be addressed by many instruments, although argu-ably not fully addressed by one. There is little theory informing measurement in this area, although some useful constructs are developing (Sullivan, 2008), as is recognition that psychological factors influence all behaviour measured (Rudy *et al.*, 2003). The concepts at this level include:

- measures of physical performance;
- impact or interference of pain;
- quality-of-life measures;
- work (or equivalent) status;
- health-care use.

Physical performance Measurement of activity is important but physical performance on a test may be unrelated to performance in daily activities and is subject to cognitive and affective influences (Rudy *et al.*, 2003; Verbunt *et al.*, 2005). Automated assessment using a pedometer or actimeter (attached to the wrist it measures any movement) provide cumulative measures which are promising.

Disability and quality of life Using disability questionnaires to ascertain physical performance can be problematic. Pain problems are often more specific than the supposedly representative items of inventories; the comparison point is unclear and relies on memory; domains of coverage represent researchers' and health-care staff concerns, not patients'. Two brief and fairly widely used questionnaires sampling impact of pain across diverse activities are the Brief Pain Inventory (BPI: Daut *et al.*, 1983; see also Tan *et al.*, 2004) and the Pain Disability Index (PDI: Tait *et al.*, 1987; Tait *et al.*, 1990).

Quality of life, its domains and the content within the domains, can mean different things for different people. There is little research on this concept (Bowling, 1995; Fitzpatrick *et al.*, 1998; Gagliese, 2001; Gladis *et al.*, 1999), which makes it hard to validate these measures and ascertain their responsiveness to change (Terwee *et al.*, 2003). The most widely used quality-of-life measure for people with pain is the SF-36 (Ware & Sherbourne, 1992; Ware *et al.*, 1993), although it may lack sensitivity to change (Bowling, 1997). (See also Chapter 26, this volume.)

Due to the economic impact, return to work as an outcome of pain management is of wide interest, but difficulties are presented by varied definitions of work (some do not include full-time home-making or car-ing); by the non-interchangeability of work status with other measures of function (Dionne *et al.*, 1999); and the frequent need for additional specific interven-tions to achieve return to work (Patel *et al.*, 2004; Watson *et al.*, 2004). The benefits of work for psycho-logical health may depend on the job, its demands and on pay and conditions. Additionally, a patient's con-cerns about work demands and losing entitlement to hard-won welfare benefits may be more immediate than the anticipated satisfactions of work (Marhold & Linton, 2002) and multiple extraneous factors affect return to work rates (Okifuji & Turk, 2001).

Health-care use Health-care use is often quoted as an important reason for pain management but is less often measured. £584 million a year is spent on prescriptions for pain in the United Kingdom (Donaldson, 2009), some unnecessary or detrimental, but patients are often keen to reduce their dose given adequate support. Visits to the general practitioner and outpatient visits are more commonly used measures, consistent with the goal of self-management.

Treatment

Evidence for the efficacy of psychological models for pain management other than the cognitive behavioural model is currently lacking (Raine *et al.*, 2002). Cognitive behavioural pain management is described in detail by Main *et al.* (2008) and Nicholas *et al.* (2003); and for patients by Berry (2001) and Lee *et al.* (2009). Cognitive behavioural therapy (CBT) for pain management is provided by a multidisciplinary team, most often in group format, either on an inpatient or outpatient basis. Groups are cheaper than individual interventions and provide group members with the opportunity to learn from one another (Keefe *et al.*, 2002). Patients often welcome the group support and the normalising effects of meeting others with pain and similar problems.

The team consists of clinical psychologists, physiotherapists and doctors (often consultants in pain management, sometimes rheumatologists or GPs); it may include nurses and occupational therapists. All involved staff must have a shared model of pain and receive ongoing training and supervision (British Pain Society, 2007).

The overall aim of pain management is not primarily to reduce pain intensity but to help people understand their pain better, to develop skills to reduce distress and disability and to move forward with their life goals despite continuing pain. At a more abstract level, it aims to improve the patient's pain experience by changing the pain's meaning and implications. The programme content is delivered as an integrated multicomponent package. Although there are core elements to the package, it differs in many ways across services, unfortunately too rarely evaluated to offer any guidance to others.

Knowledge and information

A lack of understanding about the body's repair mechanisms often results in people believing that pain must imply damage. This belief reinforces rest, avoidance of activity and looking to the medical profession to find, diagnose and resolve the problem. This search, often continuing for years, can increase distress and disability. Many people receive conflicting diagnoses or no diagnosis at all, or hear that scan results are 'normal' or show signs of degeneration, wear and tear or arthritis (usually normal age-related changes which do not necessarily cause pain); repeated failures of intervention confuse the picture further.

Despite appreciating the complexity of pain, well-meaning health-care providers may continue to investigate and treat, unwittingly reinforcing the conviction that the problem must be medically resolvable. Of course, some treatment is effective and some effective but at a cost in adverse effects which undermine long-term adherence (Bandolier, 2003). Pain clinics often overlook people's psychosocial needs, possibly because of the erroneous belief that a reduction in pain will necessarily be followed by a reduction or cessation of psychological and functional difficulties (Sullivan & Ferrell, 2005).

Enabling people to develop an alternative model and understanding of their pain helps to reduce these problems. Understanding persistent pain helps people recognise why, in the absence of ongoing damage, a focus on healing is futile and rehabilitation is the issue. This helps people to develop a new narrative for their pain and medical history; to place their experiences within a persistent pain model; and to contemplate strategies of self-management.

Behavioural reactivation

Over time, many people with persistent pain notice an overall decrease in their level of activity. Factors underlying this include:

- beliefs about damage and the need for rest (as used for acute pains);
- fears of increased pain or damage on movement;
- increasing activity during a period of 'better' pain but resting during times of increased pain (see Nicholas *et al.*, 2003, for more detail).

Despite the logic of the model of reduced activity being followed by muscle weakness and imbalance and joint stiffness, which in turn contribute to ongoing pain, evidence is inconsistent (Verbunt *et al.*, 2005).

Whatever the cause, increased pain with movement or effort reinforces beliefs about the advisability of rest and caution. What follows is withdrawal from activities that once provided a sense of achievement and/or enjoyment and a detrimental impact on mood, self-efficacy and confidence.

A first step to break this cycle is to increase activity level towards goals that are enjoyable and/or provide a sense of mastery. All too often people are instructed to work on specific exercises without an explicit link with functional goals. Exercise-only programmes tend to make rather small changes (Hayden *et al.*, 2005); and may not be well generalised to goal-directed activity. Once set, goals are analysed into components addressed with exercise and gradual increases on baseline, known as pacing (Birkholtz *et al.*, 2004; Main *et al.*, 2008). The increments are often time, but could be distance, speed or demand such as gradient. There is an important element of exposure to this technique (Vlaeyen *et al.*, 2002) and it can be difficult to distinguish practical adaptations of posture or position from avoiding ones which are best tackled; safety behaviours are an under-recognised problem (Thwaites & Freeston, 2005). Although pacing has not been rigorously evaluated and there are variations in practice (Gill & Brown, 2009), it is commonly mentioned by patients as a crucial principle for remaining active and is included in all professional and patient literature (Lee *et al.*, 2009; Main *et al.*, 2008; Nicholas *et al.*, 2003).

As with the majority of the components of pain management, behavioural reactivation is more successful if carried out alongside all the other components of pain management. The reason for this is conveyed in the central tenet of the cognitive behavioural model: that thoughts, behaviour and emotions are inextricably associated. So, for example, fears about movement or strain may be the major determinant of a low activity level. These are targeted in cognitive work alongside behavioural reactivation.

Cognitive intervention

The cognitive behavioural model proposes that cognitions strongly influence behaviour and emotion. Developing a formulation with the patient in the context of her/his beliefs about pain and their emotional, interpersonal and social lives, helps to develop a shared understanding of the unhelpful cognitive, emotional and behavioural responses to the pain that affect the ability to live a fulfilling life. Many if not all of the patient's behaviours and emotions are understandable in this light and it helps to prevent clinicians (and patients) taking a blaming stance or applying negative labels. Unhelpful cognitions and cognitive biases are then the focus for reflection and change, aiming for helpful alternatives. This process of re-evaluating erroneous beliefs and of reinforcing new, more helpful behaviours is supported by using behavioural experiments (Bennett-Levy *et al.*, 2004). (See also Chapter 12, this volume.)

Two important areas for cognitive intervention are fearful and depressive thinking. Fearful thinking is often associated with avoidance (Asmundson *et al.*, 2004; Vlaeyen & Linton, 2000) and catastrophising (Sullivan *et al.*, 2001). Addressing fear within a cognitive framework must be carried out alongside increasing the patient's knowledge about pain. Gathering new information about pain mechanisms and the role of investigations and treatments helps patients to re-evaluate unhelpful beliefs and fears about the pain's aetiology, the meaning of increases in pain and the issues of diagnosis and pain relief. These new understandings help support the patient in attempting new, often feared behaviours. Unless worry is addressed, it will undermine this new learning. Worry is a cognitive process that aims to problem solve a situation that has an uncertain outcome, one or more of these outcomes being negative (Borkovec *et al.*, 1983). Applied to pain, problem solving focuses on the search for pain reduction, but for the vast majority of people experiencing persistent pain, this focus is futile and they become trapped in attempts to solve the unsolvable (Eccleston & Crombez, 2007). Intervention shifts the focus away from pain reduction and towards living a fulfilling life despite pain.

Many patients describe depression or low mood, commonly assumed by health-care providers to be primary rather than secondary to pain. This can be reinforced by the prescription of antidepressants, which have some analgesic properties but where these are not explained to the recipient of the prescription, poor adherence and loss of trust in the therapeutic relationship can result. More usefully, discussion and acknowledgement of the losses of roles, activities and social contacts and of uncertainties about the future, can reveal cognitive biases which contribute to and maintain depressed mood.

'Third-wave therapies' are attracting increasing attention in pain management. The foundations for these are found in the concept of acceptance (Hayes *et al.*, 2004; McCracken *et al.*, 2004) and in mindfulness principles (Burch, 2008; Kabat-Zinn *et al.*, 1985; Segal *et al.*, 2002). Mindfulness refers to 'paying attention in a particular way; on purpose, in the present moment and non-judgmentally' (Kabat-Zinn, 1994). Chronic pain was one of the first problems addressed using mindfulness-based stress reduction (MBSR) (Kabat-Zinn *et al.*, 1985). More recently, MBSR in combination with some principles of cognitive therapy has been evaluated as an intervention called mindfulness-based cognitive therapy (MBCT). One of the main aims of MBCT is to help people observe unhelpful thoughts and physical experiences but without engaging in them on an emotional level. Evaluation in depressed populations (Ma & Teasdale, 2002; Segal *et al.*, 2002; Teasdale *et al.*, 2000) is promising and although there is to date little evaluation on MBCT for chronic pain, its use is spreading rapidly in clinical environments. This enthusiasm should be tempered with caution until further evaluation is available. Acceptance principles are drawn from acceptance and commitment therapy (Hayes *et al.*, 2003) and suggest that attempts to control pain are futile. In the chronic pain field, acceptance interventions aim to help people to cease trying to change their pain but instead have a 'willingness' to have pain without struggling to control or eliminate it and to pursue their goals despite pain. Studies suggest that acceptance is associated with reduced emotional distress and disability (McCracken *et al.*, 2004; McCracken & Vowles, 2006), a higher quality of life in a low back pain population (Mason *et al.*, 2008) and an increase in engagement in meaningful activities (McCracken & Yang, 2006).

Relaxation

Muscle tension underlying persistent pain is often cited to be the reason behind learning relaxation techniques. However, this model of tension and pain is dated and muscle tension appears to involve timing and coordination not normally under voluntary control in particular movements (Watson *et al.*, 1997). Tension often arises in response to emotional stresses

(Flor *et al.*, 1992); and a sense of control over musculature may be more important than the actual level of relaxation achieved. Relaxation as an intervention for persistent pain is not supported by randomised controlled studies (Knost *et al.*, 1999; www.jr2.ox.ac.uk/bandolier/booth/painpag/Chronrev/Other/CP080.html).

Use of aids and reliance on health care

People with pain may find themselves relying on aids, drugs and consultations with health-care providers, but the short-term benefits tend to be outweighed by long-term problems. Aids such as walking sticks and crutches can put strain on the arms and neck, distort posture and increase the likelihood of falls. Adapted furniture may help in the home or work environment but can reduce confidence to cope elsewhere. Although medication can be useful it usually has costs in adverse effects and some people feel undermined by having to take long-term medication. Health-care consultations may provide short-term reassurance, but can also be distressing and confusing and can perpetuate the cycle of investigations and treatments.

An open discussion about the advantages and disadvantages of these supports and of alternatives promotes long-term self-management.

Outcome

Several systematic reviews and meta-analyses support the efficacy of CBT for persistent pain, over no treatment or standard treatments, across a range of outcomes (Eccleston *et al.*, 2009; Guzmán *et al.*, 2001; Morley *et al.*, 1999; Raine *et al.*, 2002). Individual studies have shown reduced health-care use (e.g. Williams *et al.*, 1996; Williams *et al.*, 1999) and costs compared to other treatments (Goossens & Evers, 1997; Okifuji *et al.*, 1999). Reviews of interventions for back pain have placed cognitive interventions in the highest category of evidence of effectiveness (Burton *et al.*, 2004; Koes *et al.*, 2006). One review (Koes *et al.*, 2006) ranked cognitive interventions above analgesics, antidepressants, spinal manipulation, back school and exercise. Given the persistent nature of pain and associated problems, concern is often expressed about maintenance of treatment gains.

The difficulty and expense of repeated follow-up assessment and the lack of theory about maintenance, make this an area urgently requiring development.

Although trial methodology is improving, treatments remain very heterogeneous, content guided by unspecified hypotheses and many recent larger trials are of very brief treatments, arguably too brief to achieve adequate psychological and behavioural change (see Eccleston *et al.*, 2009; Guzmán *et al.*, 2001; Williams *et al.*, 1999). The costs of effective programmes and the accessibility only to a minority of patients, has led to the development of more widely available community-based psychoeducation and support programmes, such as the Expert Patient Programmes in the UK, but these drew little on available research and have failed to show any of the promised benefits (Greenhalgh, 2009; Griffiths *et al.*, 2007; Williams, 2007b). The answer may lie in better integration into primary care of evidence-based care for pain, rather than in dilution of effective but intensive secondary care.

The Future

To date, it seems that cognitive behavioural pain management is the most effective intervention to improve psychological and physical function in the presence of persistent pain. Its proponents recognise that further research is needed to continue to improve this already effective intervention, particularly on process variables such as staff skills, integration of programme components and therapeutic alliance between staff and patients (Morley & Williams, 2002; Yates *et al.*, 2005).

Since psychological variables are major predictors of the development of disabling persistent pain (Linton, 2000; Pincus *et al.*, 2002), there is increasing interest in early intervention with the aim of preventing persist-

ent pain. In particular, avoiding work loss is preferable to intervening some time after someone has lost his or her job. However, early rehabilitation attempts, with psychological intervention delivered by minimally trained GPs or physiotherapists (Jellema *et al.*, 2005; UK BEAM, 2004), have been disappointing (Main, 2005). The American stepped care model (Von Korff & Moore, 2001) is being adapted in UK health care, with early triage to direct patients to the appropriate treatment pathway at the appropriate intensity.

There is a risk that this system fits patients to existing services, as if their needs are uniform (Turk, 2005; Turk & Okifuji, 2001). However, it is hard to know how best to match interventions to patients for maximum effectiveness; evaluated trials are still scarce (Daniel & van der Merwe, 2006; Daniel *et al.*, 2008). Patients are most often grouped by pain site, but could be grouped by mechanisms of pain (for example, neuropathic), or by psychological problems, or by primary goals (for example, return to work). Reducing the variability within each group could enable more tailored interventions within a group programme, perhaps with a modular design. Useful discussion of advantages and disadvantages of different approaches can be found in Eccleston *et al.* (2003), Turk (2005) and Turk and Okifuji (2001).

The iatrogenic contribution to persistence of pain and the disability and distress which is so often associated with it, is probably still underestimated. Psychologists have an important role to play in ensuring that an integrated model of pain, not just a physical one, is disseminated and applied throughout the health service, from primary to highly specialist care. Given the good evidence for cognitive and behavioural interventions, psychologists also have a central role in mitigating the effects of persistent pain on patients' well-being, whether the pain is of recent onset or of many years.

Discussion Points

1 Rather than taking a dualistic stance and focusing on physical or psychological causes for reported pain, it is essential that one uses an integrated approach as highlighted in the current models of pain processing.

2 It is normal for there to be a lack of correlation between reported pain intensity and the results of medical investigations.

3 Despite classifications in the literature, chronic pain is no longer a medically unexplained symptom.

4 Pain can have wide-ranging effects and this must be reflected when assessing those with pain. Assessment must address the physical, psychological and social impact of pain and understand how these might further increase people's difficulties.

5 To date, the outcome literature for pain management supports the use of cognitive behavioural approaches.

Further Reading

Crombez, G., Beirens, K., Van Damme, S., Eccleston, C. & Fontaine, J. (2009). The unbearable lightness of somatisation: A systematic review of the concept of somatisation in empirical studies of pain. *Pain, 145,* 31–35.

Eccleston, C., Williams, A.C.deC. & Morley, S. (2009). Psychological therapies for the management of chronic pain (excluding headache) in adults. *Cochrane Database of Systematic Reviews,* CD003968.

Turk, D.C., Dworkin, R.H., Allen, R.R., Bellamy, N., Brandenburg, N., Carr, D.B. *et al.* (2003). Core outcome domains for chronic pain clinical trials: IMMPACT recommendations, *Pain, 106,* 337–345.

Wall, P.D. (1999). *Pain: The science of suffering.* London: Weidenfeld & Nicolson.

Van Damme, S., Crombez, G. & Eccleston, C. (2008). Coping with pain: A motivational perspective. *Pain, 139,* 1–4.

References

Asghari, A. & Nicholas, M.K. (2001). Pain self-efficacy beliefs and pain behaviour: A prospective study. *Pain, 94,* 85–100.

Asmundson, G.J.G., Vlaeyen, J.W.S. & Crombez, G. (Eds.) (2004). *Understanding and treating fear of pain.* Oxford: Oxford University Press.

Bandolier (2003). *Bandolier's little book of pain.* Oxford: Oxford University Press.

Baer, R.A. (2003). Mindfulness training as a clinical intervention: A conceptual and empirical review. *Clinical Psychology: Science & Practice, 10*(2), 125–143.

Beck A.T., Steer, R.A. & Brown, G.K. (1996). *Manual for the Beck Depression Inventory-II.* San Antonio, TX: Psychological Corporation.

Bennett-Levy, J., Butler, G., Fennell, M. & Mueller, M. (2004). *Oxford guide to behavioural experiments in cognitive therapy.* Oxford: Oxford University Press.

Berry, N. (2001). *Living with chronic pain.* At www.chronicpain.org.uk.

Birkholtz, M., Aylwin, L. & Harman, R.M. (2004). Activity pacing in chronic pain management: One aim, but which method? Part one: introduction and literature review. *British Journal of Occupational Therapy, 67,* 447–452.

Blyth, F.M., March, L.M., Nicholas, M.K. & Cousins, M.J. (2003). Chronic pain, work performance and litigation, *Pain, 103,* 41–47.

Bolton, J.E. (1999). Accuracy of recall of usual pain intensity in back pain patients. *Pain, 83,* 533–539.

Bowling, A. (1995). The concept of quality of life in relation to health. *Medicina nei secoli, 7,* 633–645.

Borkovec, T.D., Robinson, E., Pruzinsky, T. & Dupree, J.A. (1983). Preliminary exploration of worry: Some characteristics and processes. *Behavior Research and Therapy, 21,* 9–16.

Breivik, H., Collett, B., Ventafridda, V., Cohen, R. & Gallacher, D. (2006). Survey of chronic pain in Europe: Prevalence, impact on daily life and treatment. *European Journal of Pain, 10,* 287–333.

Breslau, J. & Seidenwurm, D. (2000). Socioeconomic aspects of spinal imaging: impact of radiological diagnosis on lumbar spine-related disability. *Topics in Magnetic Resonance Imaging, 11,* 218–223.

British Pain Society (2007). *Recommended guidelines for pain management programmes for adults.* London: The British Pain Society.

Burch, V. (2008). *Living well with pain and illness.* London: Wisdom Books.

Burton, A.K., Balagué, F., Cardon, G., Eriksen, H.R., Henrotin, Y., Lahad, A. *et al.* COST B13 Working Group on Guidelines for Prevention in Low Back Pain. (2006). European guidelines for prevention in low back pain. *European Spine Journal, 15,* S136–S168.

Clark, W.C. & Yang, J.C. (2001). What do simple unidimensional pain scales really measure? *Journal of Pain, 2,* 6.

Craig, K.D., Prkachin, K.M. & Grunau, R.E. (2001). The facial expression of pain. In D.C. Turk & R. Melzack (Eds.) *Handbook of pain assessment* (2nd edn, pp. 153–169). New York: Guilford Press.

Crombez, G., Beirens, K., Van Damme, S., Eccleston, C. & Fontaine, J. (2009). The unbearable lightness of somatisation: A systematic review of the concept of somatisation in empirical studies of pain. *Pain, 145,* 31–35.

Daniel, H.C. & Van Der Merwe, J. (2006). Cognitive behavioural approaches and neuropathic pain. In F. Cervero & T.S. Jensen (Eds.) *Handbook of clinical neurology* (pp. 885–868). Edinburgh: Elsevier.

Daniel, H.C., Narewska, J., Serpell, M., Johnson, R., Hoggart, B. & Rice, A. (2008). Comparison of psychological and physical function in neuropathic pain and nociceptive pain: Implications for cognitive behavioural pain management programs. *European Journal of Pain, 12,* 731–741.

Daut, R.L., Cleeland, C.S. & Flaner, R.C. (1983). Development of the Wisconsin Brief Pain Questionnaire to assess pain in cancer and other diseases. *Pain, 17,* 197–210.

Daykin, A.R. & Richardson, B. (2004). Physiotherapists' pain beliefs and their influence on the management of patients with chronic low back pain. *Spine, 29,* 783–795.

Dionne, C.E., Von Korff, M. & Koepsell, T.D. (1999). A comparison of pain, functional limitations and work status indices as outcome measures in back pain research. *Spine, 24,* 2339–2345.

Donaldson, L. (2009). *150 years of the annual report of the chief medical officer: On the state of public health 2008* (pp. 32–39). London: Department of Health.

Eccleston, C. & Crombez, G. (2007). Worry and chronic pain: A misdirected problem solving model. *Pain, 132,* 233–236.

Eccleston, C., Williams, A. & Morley, S. (2003). Cognitive behavioural therapy for chronic pain in adults. In T.S. Jensen, P.R. Wilson & A.S.C.R. Rice (Eds.) *Clinical pain management: Chronic pain* (pp. 325–333). London: Arnold.

Eccleston, C., Williams, A.C. deC. & Morley, S. (2009). Psychological therapies for the management of chronic pain (excluding headache) in adults. *Cochrane Database of Systematic Reviews*, Issue 2, CD003968.

Elliott, A.M., Smith, B.H., Penny, K.I., Smith, W.C. & Chambers, W.A. (1999). The epidemiology of chronic pain in the community, *Lancet, 354,* 1248–1252.

Fitzpatrick, R., Davey, C., Buxton, M.J. & Jones, D.R. (1998). Evaluating patient-based outcome measures for use in clinical trials. *Health Technology Assessment, 2,* 1–74.

Flor, H., Birbaumer, N., Schugens, M.M. & Lutzenberger, W. (1992). Symptom-specific psychophysiological responses in chronic pain patients. *Psychophysiology, 29,* 452–460.

Flor, H., Braun, C., Elbert, T. & Birbaumer, N. (1997). Extensive reorganization of primary somatosensory cortex in chronic back pain patients. *Neuroscience Letters, 224,* 5–8.

Fordyce, W.E. (1976). *Behavioral methods for chronic pain and illness.* St Louis: Mosby.

Gagliese, L. (2001). Assessment of pain in elderly people. In D.C. Turk & R. Melzack (Eds.) *Handbook of pain assessment* (2nd edn, pp. 119–133). New York: Guilford Press.

Gill, J.R. & Brown, C.A. (2009). A structured review of the evidence for pacing as a chronic pain intervention. *European Journal of Pain, 13,* 214–216.

Goossens, M.E.J.B. & Evers, S.M.A.A. (1997). Economic evaluation of back pan interventions. *Journal of Occupational Rehabilitation, 7,* 15–32.

Gladis, M.M., Gosch, E.A., Dishuk, N.M. & Crits-Cristoph, P. (1999). Quality of life: Expanding the scope of clinical significance. *Journal of Consulting and Clinical Psychology, 67,* 320–331.

Gracely, R.H., Geisser, M.E., Giesecke, T., Grant, M.A.B., Petzke, F., Williams, D.A. & Clauw, D.J. (2004). Pain catastrophizing and neural responses to pain among persons with fibromyalgia. *Brain, 127,* 835–843.

Greenhalgh, T. (2009). Patient and public involvement in chronic illness: Beyond the expert patient. *British Medical Journal, 338,* b49.

Griffiths, C., Foster, G., Ramsay, J., Eldridge, S. & Taylor, S (2007). How effective are expert patient (lay led) education programmes for chronic disease? *British Medical Journal, 334,* 1254–1256.

Guzmán, J., Esmail, R., Karjalainen, K., Irvin, E. & Bombadier, C. (2001). Multidisciplinary rehabilitation for chronic low back pain: Systematic review. *British Medical Journal, 322,* 511–516.

Hadjistavropoulos, T., von Baeyer, C. & Craig, K.D. (2001). Pain assessment in persons with limited ability to communicate. In D.C. Turk & R. Melzack (Eds.) *Handbook of pain assessment* (2nd edn, pp. 134–149). New York: Guilford Press.

Hayden, J.A., van Tulder, M.W., Malmivaara, A.V. & Koes, B.W. (2005). Meta-analysis: Exercise therapy for nonspecific low back pain. *Annals of Internal Medicine, 142,* 765–775.

Hayes, S.C., Strosahl, K.D. & Wilson, K.G. (2003). *Acceptance and commitment therapy: An experiential approach to behaviour change.* New York: Guilford Press.

Harstall, C. & Ospina, M. (2003). How prevalent is chronic pain? *Pain: Clinical Updates, XI,* 1–4.

Holroyd, K.A., Malinoski, P., Davis, M.K. & Lipchik, G. L. (1999). The three dimensions of headache impact: Pain, disability and affective distress. *Pain, 83,* 571–578.

International Association for the Study of Pain (1979). Pain terms: A list with definitions and notes on usage. *Pain, 6,* 249–252.

Jamison, R.N., Raymond, S.A., Levine, J.G., Slawsby, E.A., Nedeljkovic, S.S. & Katz, N.P. (2001). Electronic diaries for monitoring chronic pain: 1-year validation study, *Pain, 91,* 277–285.

Jellema P., van der Windt D.A.W.M., van der Horst, H.E., Twisk, J.W.R., Stalman W.A.B. & Bouter, L.M. (2005). Should treatment of (sub)acute low back pain be aimed at psychosocial prognostic factors? Cluster randomised clinical trial in general practice. *British Medical Journal, 331(7508),* 84.

Jensen, M.P. & Karoly, P. (2001). Self-report scales and procedures for assessing pain in adults. In D.C. Turk & R. Melzack (Eds.) *Handbook of pain assessment* (2nd edn, pp. 15–34). New York: Guilford Press.

Jensen, M.P., Turner, J.A., Romano, J.M. & Fisher, L.D. (1999). Comparative reliability and validity of chronic pain intensity measures. *Pain, 83,* 157–162.

Kabat-Zinn, J. (1994). *Wherever you go, there you are: Mindfulness meditation in everyday life.* New York: Hyperion.

Kabat-Zinn, J., Lipworth, L. & Burney, R. (1985). The clinical use of mindfulness meditation for the self regulation of chronic pain. *Journal of Behavioral Medicine, 8,* 163–190.

Keefe, F.J., Beaupré, P.M., Gil, K.M., Rumble, M.E. & Aspnes, A.K. (2002). Group therapy with patients with chronic pain. In D.C. Turk & R.J. Gatchel (Eds.) *Psychological approaches to pain management: A practitioner's handbook* (2nd edn, pp. 234–255). New York: Guilford Press.

Keefe, F.J., Williams, D.A. & Smith, S.J. (2001). Assessment of pain behaviors. In D.C. Turk & R. Melzack (Eds.) *Handbook of pain assessment* (2nd edn, pp. 170–187). New York: Guilford Press.

Knost, B., Flor, H., Birbaumer, N. & Schugens, M.M. (1999). Learned maintenance of pain: Muscle tension reduces central nervous system processing of painful stimulation in chronic and subchronic pain patients. *Psychophysiology, 36,* 755–764.

Koes, B.W., van Tulder, M.W. & Thomas, S. (2006). Diagnosis and treatment of low back pain. *British Medical Journal, 332,* 1430–1434.

Lee, J., Brook, S. & Daniel, H.C. (2009). *Back pain: The facts.* Oxford: Oxford University Press.

Linton, S.J. (2000). A review of psychological risk factors in back and neck pain. *Spine, 25,* 1148–1156.

Linton, S.J. (Ed.) (2002). *New avenues for the prevention of chronic musculoskeletal pain and disability.* Amsterdam: Elsevier.

Lorig, K., Chastain, R.L., Ung, E., Shoor, S. & Holman, H.R. (1989). Development and evaluation of a scale to measure perceived self-efficacy in people with arthritis. *Arthritis & Rheumatism, 32,* 37–44.

Lovibond, P.F. & Lovibond, S.H. (1995). The structure of negative emotional states: Comparison of the depression anxiety stress scales (DASS) with the Beck Depression and Anxiety Inventories. *Behaviour Research and Therapy, 33,* 335–343.

McCracken, L.M., Carson, J.W., Eccleston, C. & Keefe, F.J. (2004). Acceptance and change in the context of chronic pain. *Pain 109,* 4–7.

McCracken, L.M., Spertus, I.L., Janeck, A.S., Sinclair, D. & Wetzel, F.T. (1999). Behavioral dimensions of adjustment in persons with chronic pain: pain-related anxiety and acceptance. *Pain, 80,* 283–289.

McCracken, L.M. & Vowles, K.E. (2006). Acceptance of chronic pain. *Current Pain Headache Reports, 10,* 90–94.

McCracken, L.M. & Yang, S.Y. (2006). The role of values in a contextual cognitive-behavioral approach to chronic pain. *Pain, 123,* 137–145.

McDowell, I. & Newell, C. (1996) *Measuring health: A guide to rating scales and questionnaires* (2nd edn). New York: Oxford University Press.

Ma, S.H. & Teasdale, J.D. (2004). Mindfulness-based cognitive therapy for depression: Replication and exploration of differential relapse prevention effects. *Journal of Consulting and Clinical Psychology, 72,* 31–40.

Main, C.J. (2005). Commentary: Early psychosocial interventions for low back pain in primary care. *British Medical Journal, 331(7508),* 88.

Main, C.J., Sullivan M.J.L. & Watson, P.J. (2008). *Pain management* (2nd edn). Edinburgh: Churchill Livingstone.

Marhold, C. & Linton, S.J. (2002). Identification of obstacles for chronic pain patients to return to work: evaluation of a questionnaire. *Journal of Occupational Rehabilitation, 12,* 2–65.

Mason, V.L., Mathias, B. & Skevington, S.M. (2008). Accepting low back pain: Is it related to a good quality of life? *Clinical Journal of Pain, 24,* 22–29.

Melzack, R. (1975). The McGill Pain Questionnaire: Major properties and scoring methods. *Pain, 1,* 277–299.

Melzack, R. (1987). The short-form McGill pain questionnaire. *Pain, 30,* 191–197.

Melzack, R. & Katz, J. (1999). Pain measurement in persons in pain. In R. Melzack & P.D. Wall (Eds.) *Textbook of pain* (4th edn, pp. 409–426). Edinburgh: Churchill Livingstone.

Melzack, R. & Wall, P. (1965). Pain mechanisms: A new theory. *Science 150,* 971–979.

Morley, S., Eccleston, C. & Williams, A. (1999). Systematic review and meta-analysis of randomized controlled trials of cognitive behaviour therapy and behaviour therapy for chronic pain in adults, excluding headache. *Pain, 80,* 1–13.

Morley, S. & Williams, A.C.de C. (2002). Conducting and evaluating treatment outcome studies. In R.J. Gatchel & D.C. Turk (Eds.) *Psychosocial factors in pain* (2nd edn, pp. 52–68). New York: Guilford Press.

Moss-Morris, R., Weinman, J., Petrie, K.J., Horne, R., Cameron, L.D. & Buick, D. (2002). The Revised Illness Perception Questionnaire (IPQ–R). *Psychology & Health, 17,* 1–16.

Nicholas, M., Molloy, A., Tonkin, L. & Beeston, L. (2003). *Manage your pain: Practical and positive ways of adapting to persistent pain* (2nd edn). London: Souvenir Press.

Okifuji, A. & Turk, D.C. (2001). Assessment of treatment outcomes in clinical practice: A survival guide. In D.C.

Turk & R. Melzack (Eds.) *Handbook of pain assessment* (2nd edn, pp. 639–658). New York: Guilford Press.

Okifuji, A., Turk, D.C. & Kalauokalani, D. (1999). Clinical outcome and economic evaluation of multidisciplinary pain centers. In A.R. Block, E.F. Kremer & E. Fernandez (Eds.) *Handbook of pain syndromes* (pp. 77–97). New Jersey: Lawrence Erlbaum.

Patel, S., Greasley, K. & Watson, P.J. (2007). Barriers to rehabilitation and return to work for unemployed chronic pain patients: a qualitative study. *European Journal of Pain, 11,* 831–840.

Peters, M.L., Sorbi, M.J., Kruise, D.A., Kerssens, J.J., Verhaak, P.F.M. & Bensing, J.M. (2000). Electronic diary assessment of pain, disability and psychological adaptation in patients differing in duration of pain. *Pain, 84,* 181–192.

Petrovic, P. & Ingvar, M. (2002). Imaging cognitive modulation of pain processing. *Pain, 95,* 1–5.

Pincus, T., Burton, A.K., Vogel, S. & Field, A.P. (2002). A systematic review of psychological factors as predictors of chronicity/disability in prospective cohorts of low back pain. *Spine, 27,* 109–120.

Pincus, T. & Williams, A. (1999). Models and measurements of depression in chronic pain. *Journal of Psychosomatic Research, 47,* 211–219.

Pincus, T., Williams, A.C.deC., Vogel, S. & Field, A. (2004). The development and testing of the depression, anxiety and positive outlook scale (DAPOS). *Pain, 109,* 181–188.

Price, D.D. (1999). *Psychological mechanisms of pain and analgesia.* Seattle, WA: IASP Press.

Radloff, L.S. (1977). The CES-D scale: a self-report depression scale for research in the general population. *Applied Psychological Measurement, 1,* 385–401.

Raine, R., Haines, A., Sensky, T., Hutchings, A., Larkin, K. & Black, N. (2002). Systematic review of mental health interventions for patients with common somatic symptoms: Can research evidence from secondary care by extrapolated to primary care? *British Medical Journal, 325,* 1082–1093.

Rosenstiel, A.K. & Keefe, F.J. (1983). The use of coping strategies in chronic low back pain patients: Relationship to patient characteristics and current adjustment. *Pain, 17,* 33–44.

Rudy, T.E., Lieber, S.J., Boston, J.R., Gourley, L.M. & Baysal, E. (2003). Psychosocial predictors of physical performance in disabled individuals with chronic pain. *Clinical Journal of Pain, 19,* 18–30.

Segal, Z.V., Williams, J.M.G. & Teasdale, J.D. (2002). *Mindfulness-based cognitive therapy for depression.* New York: Guilford Press.

Sharpe, M. & Mayou, R. (2004). Editorial. Somatoform disorders: A help or hindrance to good patient care? *British Journal of Psychiatry, 184,* 465–467.

Sharpe, M. & Williams, A.C.deC. (2002). Treating patients with somatoform pain disorder and hypochondriasis. In D.C. Turk & R. Gatchel (Eds.) *Psychological approaches to pain management: A practitioner's handbook* (2nd edn, pp. 515–533). New York: Guilford Press.

Stone, A.A., Broderick, J.E., Schwartz, J.E., Shiffman, S., Litcher-Kelly, L. & Calvanese, P. (2003). Intensive momentary reporting of pain with an electronic diary: Reactivity, compliance and patient satisfaction. *Pain, 104,* 343–351.

Stone, A.A., Shiffman, S., Schwartz, J.E., Broderick, J.E. & Hufford, M.R. (2002). Patient non-compliance with paper diaries. *British Medical Journal, 324,* 1193–1194.

Sullivan, M.J.L. (2008). Toward a biopsychomotor conceptualization of pain. *Clinical Journal of Pain, 24,* 281–290.

Sullivan, M.J.L., Bishop, S.R. & Pivik, J. (1995). The Pain Catastrophizing Scale: Development and validation. *Psychological Assessment, 7,* 524–532.

Sullivan, M.J.L. & Ferrell, B. (2005). Ethical challenges in the management of chronic nonmalignant pain: Negotiating through the cloud of doubt. *Journal of Pain, 6,* 1–9.

Sullivan, M.J.L., Thorn, B., Haythornthwaite, J.A., Keefe, F., Martin, M., Bradley, L.A. & Lefevre, J.C. (2001). Theoretical perspectives on the relation between catastrophising and pain. *Clinical Journal of Pain, 17,* 53–61.

Tait, R.C., Pollard, C.A., Margolis, R.B., Duckro, P.N. & Krause, S.J. (1987). The Pain Disability Index: Psychometric and validity data. *Archives of Physical Medicine and Rehabilitation, 68,* 438–441.

Tait, R.C., Chibnall, J.T. & Krause, S. (1990). The Pain Disability Index: Psychometric properties. *Pain, 40,* 171–182.

Tan, G., Jensen, M.P., Thornby, J.I. & Shanti, B.F. (2004). Validation of the Brief Pain Inventory for chronic nonmalignant pain. *Journal of Pain, 5,* 133–137.

Teasdale, J.D., Segal, Z.V., Williams, J.M.G., Ridgeway, V.A., Soulsby, J.M. & Lau, M.A. (2000). Prevention of relapse/recurrence in major depression by mindfulness-based cognitive therapy. *Journal of Consulting and Clinical Psychology, 68,* 615–623.

Terwee, C.B., Dekker, F.W.S., Wiersinga, W.M., Prummel, M.F. & Bossuyt, P.M.M. (2003). On assessing responsiveness of health-related quality of life instruments: Guidelines for instrument evaluation. *Quality of Life Research, 12,* 349–362.

Thwaites, R. & Freeston, M. (2005). Safety-seeking behaviours: fact or fiction? How can we clinically differentiate between safety behaviours and adaptive coping strategies across anxiety disorders? *Behavioural and Cognitive Psychotherapy, 33,* 177–188.

Turk, D.C. (2005). The potential of treatment matching for subgroups of chronic pain patients: Lumping vs. splitting. *Clinical Journal of Pain, 21,* 44–55.

Turk, D.C., Dworkin, R.H., Allen, R.R., Bellamy, N., Brandenburg, N., Carr, D.B., Cleeland, C. *et al.* (2003). Core outcome domains for chronic pain clinical trials: IMMPACT recommendations. *Pain, 106,* 337–345.

Turk, D.C. & Melzack, R. (2001). The measurement of pain and the assessment of people experiencing pain. In D.C. Turk & R. Melzack (Eds.) *Handbook of pain assessment* (2nd edn, pp. 3–10). New York: Guilford Press.

Turk, D.C. & Monarch, E.S. (2002). Biopsychosocial perspective on chronic pain. In D.C. Turk & R.J. Gatchel. (Eds.) *Psychological approaches to pain management: A practitioner's handbook* (pp. 3–29). New York: Guilford Press.

Turk D.C. & Okifuji, A. (2001). Matching treatment to assessment of patients with chronic pain. In D.C. Turk & R. Melzack (Eds., *Handbook of pain assessment* (2nd edn, pp. 400–413). New York: Guilford Press.

Turk, D.C. & Okifuji, A. (2003). Clinical assessment of the person with chronic pain. In T.S. Jensen, P.R. Wilson & A. Rice (Eds.) *Clinical pain management: Chronic pain* (pp. 89–100). London: Arnold.

UK BEAM Trial Team (2004). United Kingdom back pain exercise and manipulation (UK BEAM) randomised trial: Effectiveness of physical treatments for back pain in primary care. *British Medical Journal, 329,* 1381.

Verbunt, J.A., Seelen, H.A., Vlaeyen, J.W., Bousema, E.J., van der Heijden, G.J., Heuts, P.H. & Knottnerus, J.A. (2005). Pain-related factors contributing to muscle inhibition in patients with chronic low back pain: An experimental investigation based on superimposed electrical stimulation. *Clinical Journal of Pain, 21,* 232–240.

Vlaeyen, J.W., de Jong, J., Geilen, M., Heuts, P.H. & van Breukelen, G. (2002). The treatment of fear of movement/(re)injury in chronic low back pain: Further evidence on the effectiveness of exposure in vivo. *Clinical Journal of Pain, 18,* 251–261.

Vlaeyen, J.W. & Linton, S.J. (2000). Fear-avoidance and its consequences in chronic musculoskeletal pain: a state of the art. *Pain, 85,* 317–332.

Van Damme, S., Crombez, G. & Eccleston, C. (2008). Coping with pain: A motivational perspective. *Pain, 139,* 1–4.

Von Korff, M. & Moore, J. (2001). Stepped care for back pain: Activating approaches for primary care. *Annals of Internal Medicine, 134,* 911–917.

Wall, P.D. (1999). *Pain: The science of suffering.* London: Weidenfeld & Nicolson.

Ware, J.E. & Sherbourne, C.D. (1992). The MOS 36-item short-form health survey (SF-36): I. Conceptual framework and item selection. *Medical Care, 30,* 473–483.

Ware, J.E., Snow, K.K., Kosinski, M. & Gandek, B. (1993). *SF-36 Health Survey: manual and interpretation guide.* Health Institute, New England Medical Center, Boston.

Watson, P.J. (1999.) Non-physiological determinants of physical performance in musculoskeletal pain. In M. Max (Ed.) *Pain 1999 – An updated review* (pp. 153–157). Seattle: IASP Press.

Watson, P.J., Booker, C.K., Main, C.J. & Chen, A.C. (1997). Surface electromyography in the identification of chronic low back pain patients: the development of the flexion relaxation ratio. *Clinical Biomechanics, 11,* 165–171.

Watson, P.J., Booker, C.K., Moores, L. & Main, C.J. (2004). Returning the chronically unemployed with low back pain to employment. *European Journal of Pain, 8,* 359–369.

Weinman, J., Petrie, K.J., Moss-Morris, R. & Horne, R. (1996). The Illness Perception Questionnaire: a new method for assessing the cognitive representations of illness. *Psychology & Health, 11,* 431–446.

Williams, A.C.deC. (2002). Facial expression of pain: an evolutionary account. *Behavioural and Brain ScienceS, 25,* 439–488.

Williams A.C.deC. (2007a). Chronic pain: investigation. In S. Lindsay & G. Powell (Eds.) *The handbook of clinical adult psychology* (3rd edn, pp. 689–707). Hove: Routledge.

Williams, A.C.deC. (2007b). Expert Patient Programmes: disappointing for patients and clinicians, *British Medical Journal,* www.bmj.com/cgi/eletters/334/7606/1254.

Williams, A.C.deC., Davies, H.T.O. & Chadury, Y. (2000). Simple pain rating scales hide complex idiosyncratic meanings. *Pain, 85,* 457–463.

Williams, A.C.deC., Nicholas, M.K., Richardson, P.H., Pither, C.E. & Fernandes, J. (1999). Generalizing from a controlled trial: the effects of patient preference versus randomization on the outcome of inpatient versus outpatient chronic pain management. *Pain, 83,* 57–65.

Williams, A.C.deC., Richardson, P.H., Nicholas, M.K., Pither, C.E., Harding, V.R., Ridout, K.L. *et al.* (1996). Inpatient vs. outpatient pain management: results of a randomised controlled trial. *Pain, 66,* 13–22.

Yates, S., Morley, S., Eccleston, C. & Williams, A.C.deC. (2005). A scale for rating the quality of psychological trials for pain. *Pain, 117,* 314–325.

Zigmond, A.S. & Snaith, R.P. (1983). The Hospital Anxiety and Depression Scale. *Acta Psychiatrica Scandinavica, 67,* 361–370.

25

Disability

Diane Dixon and Marie Johnston

Chapter Outline

This chapter describes three distinct conceptual approaches to disability: biomedical, social and behavioural. The utility of an integrated model of disability, able to account for the factors of interest to each approach, is discussed. An integrated model based on the World Health Organization's taxonomy of health outcomes and behavioural models is available. We describe the development of measures of disability consistent with the integrated model; these measures enable the model to be tested. The implications of the integrated model for the conceptualisation of disability and its management are discussed.

Key Concepts

Behaviour
Disability
ICF
Measurement
Social cognition models
Theory

Introduction

As a population we are living longer and advances in public health and biomedicine mean more people who experience a health crisis, such as a cerebrovascular accident or cancer, survive. While this increase in life expectancy is to be welcomed it is accompanied by increased risk of chronic illness and disability. Epidemiological evidence indicates that the prevalence of disability rises with age. For example, the prevalence of locomotor disability in adults aged over 65 has been reported at 30 per cent and 33 per cent in men and women living in private households in England. These figures rise to 76 per cent and 81 per cent for men and women living in residential or nursing homes (Hirani & Malbut, 2000). Consequently, an increasing proportion of the work of health professionals is concerned with the management of persons with a chronic illness and disability and this workload is likely to increase as the population ages further. A detailed understanding of disability is therefore required to support the development of evidence-based management strategies able to optimise the functional abilities of people living with chronic conditions.

To understand disability first requires an understanding of what disability is, i.e. how disability is conceptualised. This is important because it influences the theoretical models used to understand it and shapes intervention policy.

What is Disability?

In the Disability Discrimination Act the UK government defines a disabled person as someone who has a physical or mental impairment that has a substantial and long-term adverse effect on his or her ability to carry out normal day-to-day activities. In this chapter disability refers to limitations in the ability to perform specific activities such as walking, dressing, climbing stairs and bathing. Multiple and diverse approaches to understanding disability and the process of disablement are available but three discourses dominate: the biomedical, the social and the psychological. Table 25.1 identifies the central tenets of each approach. The three models or theoretical approaches to disability vary in three key respects. First, how cause in relation to disability is attributed differs between the models. Second, each model identifies different intervention targets, derived from the model-specific causal pathways. Third, each intervention requires to be delivered by very disparate services or agencies. Psychological models, for example, identify cognitions as causal factors in disability, which implies that interventions should aim to change cognitions within individuals with disabilities and/or their families or caregivers as a means to reduce disability.

It can be seen from Table 25.1 that the three approaches vary widely in terms of cause, intervention target and delivery agent. Debates between the three approaches are plentiful within the literature, with much effort being given to attempts to overcome the dualism that is evident between the biomedical and social models. The biomedical approach is characterised by its conceptualisation of disability as the result of a biological dysfunction that is the property of the individual. In contrast, the social approach conceptualises disability as resulting from social oppression (Oliver, 1995).

The exclusive focus on pathology, evident in simple medical models of disability, reflects the diagnostic paradigm that remains central to biomedicine, which reduces disability to a series of categories of dysfunction of various body parts. This extreme biomedical approach ignores the social context and its role in disablement and reduces the person to an object of scientific enquiry. However, reductionism is also evident in the social approach of disability studies, where the focus is exclusively on the social causes of disability. Although impairment is viewed as a prerequisite for disability, it is afforded no causal status and disability is conceptualised as a consequence of social exclusion (Thomas, 2004). The result of this approach is to ignore the individual's corporeal status and to reduce the individual to a social construction.

The biomedical approach would require medical intervention targeted at the alleviation of impairment. This approach is problematical for chronic conditions, which are not amenable to curative treatment. In effect, if the impairment cannot be reduced or removed, then disability cannot be addressed. In contrast, the social view necessitates intervention at the level of society and would, for example, advocate investment in the environment to reduce its causal

Table 25.1 The central tenets of three models of disability

Model	Cause	Intervention	Services
Biomedical	Disease	Treat the disease	Health services
Social	Physical and/or social environment	Change environment	Government policies, societal values
Psychological	Cognitions and/or emotions and/or environment	Change cognitions and/or environment	Individual, families, social groups

role in disability. However, such an intervention strategy denies the important role played by medicine in the effective management of many chronic conditions, for example, pharmacological pain control strategies.

To an extent, these two conceptualisations of disability represent minority extreme positions. Models of disability are now available that present a more complex picture and are able to accommodate multiple factors, including pathology, personal beliefs, social structures and the environment (Jette, 2006). This shift from somewhat simplistic models to more elaborate comprehensive models is evidenced by the work of the World Health Organization (WHO) which has, over the course of the last 30 years, worked to develop a comprehensive model of disability.

International Classification of Impairments, Disability and Handicap (ICIDH)

The WHO published its first model of disability in 1980, the International Classification of Impairments, Disability and Handicap (ICIDH) (World Health Organization, 1980); although similar models are available elsewhere (Verbrugge & Jette 1994). The ICIDH (see Figure 25.1) exemplifies the impairment-based approach to disability. In this model disability results from impairment and handicap is viewed as the direct result of both disability and impairment. The model predicts that disability should be a simple function of impairment. However, there is much evidence to show that disability is not linearly related to pathology. For example, the extent of brain damage after stroke, or the volume of heart damage following a myocardial infarction, are poor predictors of subsequent disability (Johnston & Pollard, 2001); similarly,

the severity of radiographic joint damage in osteoarthritis fails to predict either disability or physical functioning (Salaffi et al., 1991). In effect, individuals function at levels that are inconsistent with the magnitude of their pathology. Furthermore, health professionals see patients who experience disability in the absence of any definable pathology. In addition, the ICIDH was criticised for the use of stigmatising language and this problem was compounded by the concepts of disability and handicap which were articulated as being properties of the individual person rather than a result of social, cultural and attitudinal environments (Bickenbach et al., 1999).

Finally, the ICIDH described unidirectional relationships between the three constructs. Impairment affected disability but within the model disability could not affect impairment, similarly, disability could affect handicap but not vice versa. As a consequence, the ICIDH was inconsistent with many chronic disease management and rehabilitation regimens. For example, people who smoke may experience intermittent claudication (muscle pain associated with reduced blood flow to the limbs due to narrowing of blood vessels, which causes ischaemic damage to surrounding tissue). Increased exercise, such as walking, is often recommended for this condition. Exercise is a disability-level intervention but the aim is to reduce the impairment of reduced blood flow and ischaemic damage via exercise-induced improvements in collateral blood flow. The ICIDH model described impairment, disability and handicap as a unidirectional ordered series that did not recognise reciprocal relationships between handicap, disability and impairment.

In light of the demonstrated limitations of the ICIDH, the WHO worked to develop a model that was able to account for more complex influences on disability. The result of this endeavour is the

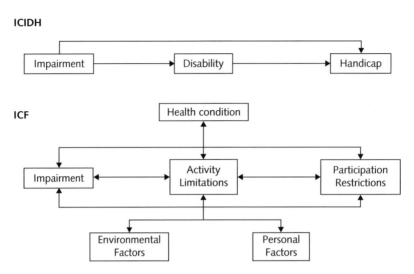

Figure 25.1   A schematic representation of the ICIDH (upper figure) and the ICF (lower figure)
Sources: World Health Organization (1980). *International classification of impairments, disabilities and handicaps.* Geneva: World Health Organization; World Health Organization (2001). *International classification of functioning, disability and health: ICF.* Geneva: World Health Organization.

International Classification of Functioning Disability and Health (ICF) (World Health Organization, 2001).

International Classification of Functioning Disability and Health (ICF)

The ICF (see Figure 25.1) is described as a classification system for health and disability, which can be used to inform the definition, measurement and policy formulations for health and disability. Three constructs, or health components, form the core of the model, namely, impairment ('problems in body functions or structure such as a significant deviation or loss'), activity limitations ('difficulties an individual may have in executing activities') and participation restrictions ('problems an individual may experience in involvement in life situations') (World Health Organization, 2001). However, the bidirectional relationships between the three constructs, together with the contextual factors, operate to reduce the role of impairment in disability. Rather, the ICF conceptualises disability as a property of all elements of the model (World Health Organization, 2001). For any particu-

lar health condition, the model sites disability at the intersection between three structures: body structures, person structures and social structures (Imrie, 2004). Consequently, a full understanding of disability will only be achieved by integrating knowledge across these three forms of analyses.

The ICF, therefore, is a more complex model of disability. Within the ICF the relationships between the three central components are reciprocal, rather than unidirectional. Although the ICF does not explicitly claim to be a causal model it should be possible to test implied casual relationships within the model. Accordingly, the ICF allows for impairment to give rise to activity limitations and participation restrictions, each of which can give rise to changes in pathology. For example, a rehabilitation regime that emphasises movement of the paralysed limb after a stroke may help promote changes in the central nervous system that allow undamaged parts of the brain to take over the control of that limb (Kopp *et al.*, 1999; Liepert *et al.*, 2000). Physiotherapy aimed at increasing activity in someone with arthritis can strengthen muscles, leading to improved strength and stability of the joint, i.e. reduced impairment, contributing to further improvements in activity (Talbot *et al.*, 2003).

Hence, within the ICF reductions in impairment can be achieved using interventions that target activity limitations. This is the opposite stream of causality to that found in biomedical models. Similarly, activity limitations may be reduced by changes in social participation, e.g. regular participation in some social event may afford the exercise which results in less walking limitations. Again, this is the opposite stream of causality to the biomedical model but is consistent with the social approach.

Also, the inclusion of contextual factors in the ICF recognises a role for both personal and environmental factors in disability. The WHO details the environmental factors, which are given in the form of assistive products and technologies; the natural and man-made environment; social services, systems and policies, all of which can act to influence the relationship between the components in the ICF (World Health Organization, 2001). The model therefore includes many of the issues of most importance to those who promote the social model of disability.

Psychology and Disability

Biomedical models of disability shaped the early input of psychology into the field of disability, in that, psychology focused on the treatment of the emotional sequelae of being disabled, rather than on the process of disablement itself. While this emotional treatment role remains, psychology has been increasingly involved in interventions to reduce disability per se and has addressed the issue of how disability is conceptualised and has developed and tested theoretical models of disability.

Psychological models of disability are themselves integrative in that they can be regarded as both individualistic and societal; disability is conceptualised as behaviour and behaviour is regarded, in part, as the result of an individual's cognitions and emotions. In this specific instance, the cognitions of interest are primarily a person's beliefs and knowledge relevant to their disability-related behaviour. Although, cognitions reside within an individual person they are shaped by the entire social and cultural milieu experienced by that individual. That is to say, cognitions are a means by which biomedical

or corporeal factors and societal and environmental factors are able to affect an individual's behaviour and hence disability.

The notion that disability can be understood as a form of behaviour enables theories of behaviour and behaviour change to be applied to further our understanding of the causes and correlates of disability and to effect reductions in disability. In a similar manner, Fordyce and colleagues conceptualised chronic pain in terms of behaviour, which enabled the design of interventions based on operant learning theory (Fordyce *et al.*, 1968a, 1968b). These effective interventions were perhaps the first demonstration of the power of the concept of pain-as-behaviour to generate positive change in disability without the need for preceding or concomitant reductions in impairment. We argue that conceptualising disability as behaviour has the same potential.

Modern psychological approaches to disability are likely to apply cognitive as well as operant models of behaviour. Cognitive models are motivational models of behaviour in which an individual's belief systems are predictive of and possibly cause their behaviour. Importantly for clinical practice, psychological theory not only identifies potential intervention targets to reduce disability, it also provides an evidence base on how best to intervene to effect behaviour change, thereby offering therapeutic approaches that do not depend on 'cure'. For example, psychological theory has been used to develop and improve self-management and rehabilitation regimes to reduce disability in several chronic conditions, including stroke, arthritis, heart disease, asthma, stroke and chronic pain (Foster *et al.*, 2007; Newman *et al.*, 2004; Riemsma *et al.*, 2003).

Measurement

To subject a theory to empirical test requires valid measures of the constructs in that theory (Jette *et al.*, 2003; Pollard *et al.*, 2006). Disability, when defined as behaviour, requires measures of those behaviours. Typically these are activities required for daily living, for example, bathing, walking, transfer to bed and chair. Standard measures of such behaviours are available, e.g. the Barthel index. There are four main methods of assessment of behaviour: self-report, proxy report, observation and objective measures (Powell *et al.*, 2007). Self-report measures typically use verbal response scales to enable respondents to indicate the degree of difficulty they have performing specified behaviours. Proxy reports are normally reports by caregivers on similar response scales. Observation requires a trained observer to record whether an individual can perform specified behaviours successfully. It is also possible to use objective electronic monitors to record behaviour, for example the use of pedometers and more sophisticated accelerometers to record activity. These devices tend to record movement rather than performance of specific behaviours, except for discriminating between walking, standing, sitting and lying.

Standard self-report measures, such as the Sickness Impact Profile or the SF-36, contain items which tap not only disability but also impairment and participation restrictions (Cieza *et al.*, 2002; Pollard *et al.*, 2006). For these measures to be useful in empirical investigation of the ICF, pure measures of the main constructs are necessary; otherwise spurious relationships between these constructs are likely to be observed. Many health-outcome measures also include items assessing disability and methods are available that enable 'pure' measures of disability to be obtained from existing health-outcome measures. Pure measures are currently available from the Sickness Impact Profile (Cieza *et al.*, 2002; Pollard & Johnston, 2001), as well as measures used in osteoarthritis (Brockow *et al.*, 2004; Pollard *et al.*, 2006; Weigl *et al.*, 2003), pain (Brockow *et al.*, 2004; Dixon *et al.*, 2007) and upper limb injury (Dixon *et al.*, 2008a; Drummond *et al.*, 2007).

Measures of health-related quality of life (HRQL) frequently include items assessing disability. However, HRQL is typically conceptualised as a global construct and does not provide a causal or explanatory model, therefore, process variables are unidentified. As a consequence it is not clear how interventions can be developed and tested within the quality-of-life paradigm. That is not to say that quality of life is not a useful or important outcome measure but conflating it with disability does not improve our understanding of disability or our ability to intervene to reduce disability.

Integrating Biomedical and Psychological Theory

The psychological, biomedical and social approaches to disability have all made valuable contributions to our understanding. However, it is possible to work to integrate across disciplines to develop an integrated model of disability that includes concepts central to biomedicine and psychology and address some of the key issues of concern to the social model.

It is possible to integrate the ICF with psychological models because both models conceptualise disability as behaviour. The ICF has several features that facilitate the integration with psychological theory. In the ICF, activity limitations are behaviour and participation restrictions may also be behaviour, for example, buttoning one's shirt is a discrete behaviour used as a measure of activity limitations and visiting friends is a complex series of behaviours used to index participation restrictions. The ICF is one of the first biomedical models of disability to support the concept of disability as behaviour. As such, the ICF invites psychological models of behaviour to contribute their predictive and explanatory power to disability.

The inclusion of the contextual construct in the ICF presents a further opportunity to integrate psychological theory. The WHO specifies the environmental component of the contextual factors construct in great detail. Many of these contextual factors, e.g. social support, are key elements in psychological theories. However, the personal factors component is less well specified but can be operationalised in the form of psychological theory.

The integration of psychological theory with the ICF potentially generates an improved model because it provides the ICF with process variables, i.e. it specifies *how* relationships occur. In its present form the ICF does not detail the processes via which the three central components are related. Indeed, the ICF has been criticised for lacking a clearly articulated theoretical base (Imrie, 2004). Consequently, the ICF is unable to provide information on how best to intervene to effect change in activity limitations or participation restrictions; it simply catalogues environmental factors that may impinge on both. The inclusion of psychological theory strengthens the theoretical basis of the ICF. It also facilitates clinical practice through the identification of key psychological processes that mediate between impairment, activity limitations and participation restrictions. Furthermore, psychology specifies the means by which these key psychological processes can be manipulated to effect positive change in behaviour (Michie *et al.*, 2008), in this case improvements in activity and participation, i.e. reductions in disability. Importantly, psychological theory enables the development of interventions that are not reliant on improvements in disease or impairment status to achieve reductions in disability.

Testing an Integrated Model of Disability: ICF Integrated with Social Cognitive Theory

A schematic representation of the integration of psychological theory, social cognitive theory (Bandura, 1997), with the ICF is shown in Figure 25.2 (see also Chapters 10 and 12, this volume). Other psychological models could be used. We have, for example, previously illustrated how the ICIDH could be integrated with the theory of planned behaviour (Johnston, 1994). The integrated models progress the ICF from a static taxonomy into a predictive and potentially causal model. The integrated model identifies factors that precede activity limitations: cognitions and impairments. Thus when integrated with the ICF, psychological models identify cognitions as potential intervention targets and predict that intervening to change the beliefs that predict disability will effect reductions in disability.

In this integrated model social cognitive theory is used to operationalise the personal factors component of the ICF. Whether or not the person has an impairment is of no *a priori* importance to the model. Rather, the experience of the impairment affects the person's beliefs in relation to a specific behaviour, such as climbing stairs and these beliefs then act to influence that behaviour. Impairment is given no special status above or beyond all other aspects of the person's life experience. That is not to say impairment is not an important influence on a person's activity status. It should be noted that the direct relationship between impairment and activity limitations is maintained in the integrated model. This model also recognises influences, other than beliefs, for example social structures and policies,

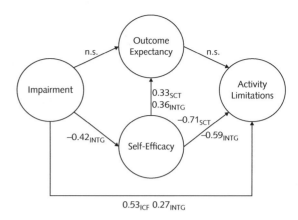

Figure 25.2   The integrated model

which may be related to disability. This integrated model provides a theoretical framework within which the evidence bases of medicine and psychology can not only be reconciled but contribute in a complementary manner to explaining and managing disability.

Figures indicate standardised path coefficients taken from a series of structural models representing the activity limitation of walking disability, in people awaiting joint replacement surgery. Subscripts identify the models from which the coefficient was derived: ICF = ICF model only; SCT = Social cognitive theory only; INTG = Integrated model. Only significant coefficients are shown, $p \leq 0.01$ throughout. The ICF model accounted for 28 per cent of the variance in activity limitations, compared to 53 per cent and 58 per cent variance for the social cognitive theory and integrated models, respectively.

The integrated model can be illustrated by consideration of a person with osteoarthritis of the hip. This person may experience joint stiffness (impairment), they might find it difficult to walk half a mile (activity limitations), which makes it difficult for them to reach their local cinema (participation restrictions). The integrated model suggests that the experience of joint stiffness may act to restrict walking and both joint stiffness and walking restrictions act to inhibit visits to the cinema. However, the integrated model also states that beliefs mediate between joint stiffness, walking and cinema visits. Within social cognitive theory, beliefs are viewed as causally related to behaviour (Bandura, 1997). There are three main constructs in the model, namely, self-efficacy (beliefs about one's ability to per-form a behaviour to achieve a desired goal), outcome expectancy (beliefs about the consequences of per-forming a behaviour) and personal goals. The model states that a person who is highly confident in their ability to walk, even in the face of impediments such as pain, uneven pavements and the journey to the cin-ema being uphill is more likely to walk than a person who has less confidence. The likelihood of the person walking is enhanced further if they anticipate positive consequences of the walk, for example feeling a sense of achievement or enjoying the film. Efficacy and expectancy beliefs affect proximal goals in the form of motivation toward walking. Equivalent beliefs mediate between walking and cinema visits. Consequently, walking can be promoted and hence disability reduced, by interventions that target cognitive change without the need to reduce impairment.

To illustrate, the integrated model can distinguish between two people, each with osteoarthritis and joint stiffness, one who feels confident they can walk despite stiffness, who is keen on cinema and expects to enjoy the film and the other who is less confident about walking, not so keen on cinema and whose partner will be supportive of them refusing the cinema trip.

Recent work has demonstrated that the integrated model is a more powerful predictor of mobility disabil-ity than either the ICF or psychological models alone in people awaiting hip or knee replacement surgery and in a community sample (Dixon et al., 2008b). Figure 25.2 also details the results of structural equation mod-elling analyses of the application of the integrated model to walking limitations in people awaiting joint surgery. In this sample, the ICF alone accounted for 28 per cent of the variance in walking limitations; social cognitive theory alone accounted for 48 per cent of the variance in walking limitations; but the integrated model accounted for 59 per cent of the variance. A proportion of the variance accounted for in each of the three models is likely to be shared method variance as all measures, including the measure of walking limita-tions, were self-report. The use of objective measures of behaviour typically reduces the predictive utility of social cognition models. However, self-report measures were used throughout; therefore, each model would likely have suffered to a similar degree. As a conse-quence, the comparative predictive utility of the three

models remains informative. Thus, it is possible to say that the biomedical and psychological models offer complementary explanatory power. The direct relation-ship between impairment, measured as joint pain and walking limitations was significant but self-efficacy sig-nificantly mediated this relationship. Impairment influ-enced self-efficacy, the negative structural paths indicat-ing less pain was associated with higher self-efficacy and higher self-efficacy was associated with less walking limitations. Impairment did not predict outcome expectancy and outcome expectancy was not predic-tive of walking limitations. Thus, in this sample, self-efficacy is the cognition that predicts disability and would be the obvious target for interventions to increase walking and thereby reduce mobility disability.

The integrated model can, therefore, identify fac-tors that account for differences in disability between people. The model suggests that disability could be reduced by interventions that increase self-efficacy. However, factors that distinguish between people might not necessarily be able to account for disability or changes in disability within an individual person. To be a suitable framework for the development of interventions the model needs to be able to identify the factors that explain individual-level behaviour change. There is developing evidence that different cognitions are predictive of activity limitations at the group and individual levels. For example, studies, which integrated the theory of planned behaviour with the ICF, have shown that intention to walk does not predict activity limitations in group studies but is predictive at the individual level (Quinn et al., 2008).

Experiments and Interventions

Experimental studies have shown that targeting con-trol-related cognitions can effect changes in disability. Control cognitions can be manipulated by very simple interventions, for example, patients attending a chro-nic pain clinic reported increased control cognitions after they were simply asked to talk about times when control had been high. Conversely, control cognitions were reduced in those patients asked about times when control had been low. In this randomised exper-imental study patients who received the increase con-trol cognitions intervention showed reduced disability measured objectively using a weight-lifting task. Patients who received the reduced control cognitions intervention showed increased disability on the same weight-lifting task (Fisher & Johnston, 1996).

Randomised controlled trials have also targeted disability in stroke patients. Stroke patients and their caregivers randomised to receive a workbook-based intervention designed to increase control cognitions demonstrated improved disability recovery, assessed by a performance measure, at six month follow-up compared to the control group. The workbook group also reported greater confidence in recovery but this did not mediate the effect of the intervention on actual recovery (Johnston et al., 2007).

Other studies have further focused on informal caregivers. Such an approach recognises the important role played by significant others in disability and recovery from disability. A randomised controlled trial trained caregivers in the key skills required for the day-to-day management of disabled stroke patients. The aim was to reduce the burden of stroke in both patients and their caregivers. At one-year follow-up the trained caregivers reported less caregiver burden, less anxiety and depression and higher quality of life compared to caregivers who did not receive the training. While patient mortality, institutionalisation and disability were not influenced by the training intervention, patients in the trained group reported less anxiety and depression and better quality of life (Kalra et al., 2004). Unfortunately, this study did not articulate the theoretical basis of the intervention and as a consequence, it is not possible to identify the process variables responsible for the observed positive effects on psychological well-being and lack of effect on disability. That said, an economic evaluation of the training programme indicated significant savings in the cost of care in the training group.

These data suggest that quite simple interventions, which directly target cognitions, can effect changes in disability in patients with what are generally considered difficult problems such as stroke or chronic intractable pain. Further, it is possible to broaden the target of interventions beyond individual patients. These interventions, which to date have been more complex, can successfully target patients and their caregivers or focus on informal caregivers more directly and effect changes in disability in patients and psychological well-being in both patients and caregivers.

Which of us is Disabled?

The disability-as-behaviour concept has the added advantage of acting to normalise disability because behaviour is measured on a continuum of performance. The performance ability of all individuals, even including elite athletes, regardless of their impairment status, will fall somewhere on the same continuum, i.e. everyone of us has activity limitations, but reach our limitations at different stages or in different environments. Thus, it is possible for people without impairments to be disabled or have activity limitations, for example, a person who is 1.5 metres tall would find their ability to take books out of a library severely limited if all the books were on shelves 2.5 metres from the floor compared with someone who is 2 metres tall. Whereas the opposite would be true if the activity were walking under a loft ceiling.

Therefore, the notion that there is a category distinction between those with disabilities and those without disabilities is entirely inconsistent with the disability-as-behaviour concept and, therefore, with the ICF, psychological theory and the integrated model. Consequently, the ICF and the integrated model provide an opportunity to move away from deficit-based models of disability, such as the ICIDH. The integrated model can focus on activity just as easily as activity limitations. This again acts to shift the emphasis away from the concept of impairment as the sole cause of disability. For example, the simple medical model assumes that a person with an impairment does not climb the stairs *because of their impairment*. At first sight this may seem a reasonable assumption, however, consider the opposite situation when applied to a person without an impairment – would it be reasonable to assume that they do climb the stairs because they do not have an impairment? This appears to be an unreasonable assumption and invites reconsideration of the notion that people with impairments do not do things because of their impairment. Perhaps the above individual with an impairment did not climb the stairs because they preferred to remain on the ground floor.

An impairment may influence behaviour, but to assume it causes behaviour is to remove personal agency from people with impairments. It should be emphasised that the integrated model does not 'blame' people with disabilities for those disabilities. The model is not consistent with the notion that people with disabilities are disabled simply because they lack motivation to be otherwise. Quite the opposite is the case, the integrated model accounts for activity and activity limitations in the same terms for all individuals. The behaviour of every person is influenced by biological, personal, social and environmental factors and those influences are unique to each individual. However, the extent of

the influence of each factor will vary between individuals; for example, the role of impairment relative to motivational factors in walking limitations are likely to be much different for a person with quadriplegia compared to the person with a stubbed toe. Indeed, as stated earlier, the ICF conceptualises disability as a property of all elements of the model (World Health Organization, 2001) and sites disability at the intersection between three structures; body structures, person structures and social structures (Imrie, 2004).

Acknowledgements

We would like to thank Professor Paul Dieppe, University of Plymouth, for his invaluable comments and input into the development of this chapter.

Discussion Points

1 Is integrating the biomedical, psychological and social models of disability the only way of accounting for all the factors that influence disability?
2 How might conceptualising disability as behaviour affect society's tendency to stigmatise people with disabilities?
3 Self-management interventions for people with chronic conditions often require input from multi-

disciplinary teams. How could the integrated model be used to support multidisciplinary working?
4 Disability is not something that happens to other people; the majority of us will experience some decline in the structure and function of our bodies as we age. How might your daily environment contribute to the functional limitations you will experience as you age?

Further Reading

Information about the WHO ICF can be found at: www.who.int/classifications/icf/en/. This site provides comprehensive information about the ICF and contains a great beginner's guide to the ICF: www.who.int/classifications/icf/training/icfbeginnersguide.pdf.

Barlow, J., Wright, C., Sheasby, J., Turner, A. & Hainsworth, J. (2002). Self-management approaches for people

with chronic conditions: a review. *Patient Education and Counseling, 48*, 177–187.

Kaplan, R.M. (1990). Behavior as the central outcome in health-care. *American Psychologist, 45*, 1211–1220.

Riemsma, R.P., Kirwan, J.R., Taal, E. & Rasker, H.J. (2003). Patient education for adults with rheumatoid arthritis. *Cochrane Database of Systematic Reviews* 2, CD003688.

References

Bandura, A. (1997). *Self-Efficacy: The Exercise of Control.* New York: W.H. Freeman.

Bickenbach, J.E., Chatterji, S., Badley, E.M. & Ustun, T.B. (1999). Models of disablement, universalism and the

International Classification of Impairments, Disabilities and Handicaps. *Social Science & Medicine, 48*, 1173–1187.

Brockow, T., Cieza, A., Kuhlow, H., Sigl, T., Franke, T., Harder, M. & Stucki, G. (2004). Identifying the concepts contained in outcome measures of clinical trials on musculoskeletal disorders and chronic widespread pain using the international classification of functioning, disability and health as a reference. *Journal of Rehabilitation Medicine, 36*, 30–36.

Cieza, A., Brockow, T., Ewart, T., Amman, E., Kolleritis, B., Chatterji, S. *et al.* (2002). Linking health-status measurements to the international classification of functioning, disability and health. *Journal of Rehabilitation Medicine, 34*, 205–210.

Dixon, D., Johnston, M., McQueen, M. & Court-Brown, C. (2008a). The Disabilities of the Arm, Shoulder and Hand Questionnaire (DASH) can measure the impairment, activity limitations and participation restriction constructs from the International Classification of Functioning, Disability and Health (ICF). *BMC Musculoskeletal Disorders, 9*.

Dixon, D., Johnston, M., Rowley, D. & Pollard, B. (2008b). Using the ICF and psychological models of behavior to predict mobility limitations. *Rehabilitation Psychology, 53*, 191–200.

Dixon, D., Pollard, B. & Johnston, M. (2007). What does the Chronic Pain Grade Questionnaire measure? *Pain, 130*, 249–253.

Drummond, A.S., Sampaio, R.F., Mancini, M.C., Kirkwood, R.N. & Stamm, T.A. (2007). Linking the disabilities of arm, shoulder and hand to the International Classification of Functioning, Disability and Health. *Journal of Hand Therapy, 20*, 336–343.

Fisher, K. & Johnston, M. (1996). Experimental manipulation of perceived control and its effect on disability. *Psychology & Health, 11*, 657–669.

Fordyce, W., Fowler, R.S., Lehmann, J.F. & Delateur, B.J. (1968a). Some implications of learning in problems of chronic pain. *Journal of Chronic Diseases, 21*, 179.

Fordyce, W.E., Fowler, R.S. & Delateur, B. (1968b). An application of behavior modification technique to a problem of chronic pain. *Behaviour Research and Therapy, 6*, 105–107.

Foster, G., Taylor, S.J.C., Eldridge, S.E., Ramsay, J. & Griffiths, C.J. (2007). Self-management education programmes by lay leaders for people with chronic conditions. *Cochrane Database of Systematic Reviews* 4, CD005108.

Hirani, H. & Malbut, K. (2000). *Health survey for England 2000: Disability among older people.* London: Stationery Office.

Imrie, R. (2004). Demystifying disability: a review of the International Classification of Functioning, Disability and Health. *Sociology of Health & Illness, 26*, 287–305.

Jette, A.M. (2006). Toward a common language for function, disability and health. *Physical Therapy, 86*, 726–734.

Jette, A.M., Haley, S.M. & Kooyoomjian, J.T. (2003). Are the ICF activity and participation dimensions distinct? *Journal of Rehabilitation Medicine, 35*, 145–149.

Johnston, M. (1994). Models of disability. *The Psychologist, 9*, 205–210.

Johnston, M., Bonetti, D., Joice, S., Pollard, B., Morrison, V., Francis, J.J. & MacWalter, R. (2007). Recovery from disability after stroke as a target for a behavioural intervention: Results of a randomised controlled trial. *Disability and Rehabilitation, 29*, 1117–1127.

Johnston, M. & Pollard, B. (2001). Consequences of disease: testing the WHO international classification of impairments, disabilities and handicaps (ICIDH) model. *Social Science & Medicine, 53*, 1261–1273.

Kalra, L., Evans, A., Perez, I., Melbourn, A., Patel, A., Knapp, M. & Donaldson, N. (2004). Training care givers of stroke patients: Randomised controlled trial. *British Medical Journal, 328*, 1099–1101.

Kopp, B., Kunkel, A., Muhlnickel, W., Villringer, K., Taub, E. & Flor, H. (1999). Plasticity in the motor system related to therapy-induced improvement of movement after stroke. *Neuroreport, 10*, 807–810.

Liepert, J., Bauder, H., Miltner, W.H.R., Taub, E. & Weiller, C. (2000). Treatment-induced cortical reorganization after stroke in humans. *Stroke, 31*, 1210–1216.

Michie, S., Johnston, M., Francis, J., Hardeman, W. & Eccles, M. (2008). From theory to intervention: mapping theoretically derived behavioural determinants to behaviour change techniques. *Applied Psychology: An International Review, 57*, 660–680.

Newman, S., Steed, L. & Mulligan, K. (2004). Self-management interventions for chronic illness. *Lancet, 364*, 1523–1537.

Oliver, M. (1995). *Understanding disability: From theory to practice.* London: Palgrave Macmillan.

Pollard, B. & Johnston, M. (2001). Problems with the Sickness Impact Profile: a theoretically based analysis and a proposal for a new method of implementation and scoring. *Social Science & Medicine, 52*, 921–934.

Pollard, B., Johnston, M. & Dieppe, P. (2006). What do osteoarthritis heath outcome instruments measure? Impairment, activity limitation or participation restriction? *Journal of Rheumatology, 33*, 757–763.

Powell, R., Johnston, M. & Johnston, D.W. (2007). Assessing walking limitations in stroke survivors: Are self-reports and proxy-reports interchangeable? *Rehabilitation Psychology, 52*, 177–183.

Quinn, F., Johnston, M. & Johnston, D.W. (2008). Does the TPB predict behaviour in one individual? A case study. *Psychology & Health, 23*, 218.

Riemsma, R.P., Kirwan, J.R., Taal, E. & Rasker, H.J. (2003). Patient education for adults with rheumatoid arthritis. *Cochrane Database of Systematic Reviews* 2, CD003688.

Salaffi, F., Cavalieri, F., Nolli, F. & Ferraccioli, G. (1991). Analysis of disability in knee osteoarthritis. Relationship with age, psychological variables, but not with radiographic score. *Journal of Rheumatology, 18*, 1581–1586.

Talbot, L.A., Gaines, J.M., Huynh, T.N. & Metter, E.J. (2003). A home-based pedometer-driven walking program to increase physical activity in older adults with osteoarthritis of the knee: a preliminary study. *Journal of the American Geriatrics Society, 51*, 387–392.

Thomas, C. (2004). How is disability understood? An examination of sociological approaches. *Disability & Society, 19*, 569–583.

Verbrugge, L.M. & Jette, A.M. (1994). The disablement process. *Social Science & Medicine, 38*, 1–14.

Weigl, M., Cieza, A., Harder, M., Kostanjsek, N. & Stucki, G. (2003). Linking osteoarthritis-specific health-status measures to the International Classification of Functioning, Disability and Health (ICF). *Osteoarthritis and Cartilage, 11*, 519–523.

World Health Organization (1980). *International classification of impairments, disabilities and handicaps.* Geneva: World Health Organization.

World Health Organization (2001). *International classification of functioning, disability and health: ICF.* Geneva: World Health Organization.

26

Quality of Life

Hannah McGee and Lena Ring

Chapter Outline

This chapter deals with the concepts of quality of life (QoL) and health-related quality of life (HRQoL). There has been an explosion of research on this topic in the past two decades. Much of the impetus for this research has come from applied questions, for instance comparing medical treatment regimes on HRQoL as well as other outcomes. This chapter overviews definitions, main uses of the concept, types of measures, recent developments, and the challenges and opportunities of this research area for health psychologists.

Key Concepts

Dimension-specific QoL
Disease- (or population-) specific QoL
Generic QoL
Health-related QoL
Individualised QoL
Proxy (or surrogate) ratings
Quality-adjusted life years (QALYs)
Response shift
Standard gamble techniques
Time trade-off techniques
Utility-based QoL

Definitions of Quality of Life

There are many definitions of QoL, from philosophical to pragmatic, with examples illustrating definitions from phenomenological to pragmatic approaches. At its most general and phenomenological:

> Quality of life is what the individual says it is (Joyce *et al.*, 1999)

Others identify the relative nature of QoL, e.g. QoL as a comparison between a present and an aspirational state:

> Quality of life measures the difference, or the gap, at a particular period of time, between the hopes and expectations of the individual and the individual's present experiences (Calman, 1984)

Another approach has been to acknowledge that it is not practical to assess all that is meant by QoL in health settings. The argument is that health interventions address health-related aspects of an individual's life and thus should be judged against the yard-stick of health-related quality of life (HRQoL). Then only health-related aspects of QoL (and not others such as economic status or environment) can be expected to change as a direct consequence of health interventions, as illustrated in this widely used definition:

> HRQoL is 'the value assigned to the duration of life as modified by the impairments, functional states, perceptions and social opportunities that are influenced by disease, injury, treatment or policy' (Patrick & Erickson, 1993)

Another HRQoL definition has a more clearly articulated role for the individual patient as the judge of his or her QoL:

> Quality of life in clinical medicine represents the functional effect of an illness and its consequent therapy upon a patient, as perceived by the patient (Schipper *et al.*, 1996)

The authors go on to specify four main components of QoL: physical and occupational functioning; psychological state; social interaction; and somatic sensation (symptoms). This is a typical formulation of QoL

from the HRQoL perspective. However, researchers who advocate both a more generic and individualised approach challenge the health-related focus by asking how external observers can determine what is health-related and what is not for an individual (Joyce *et al.*, 2003). For instance, income and environment would not typically be assessed by HRQoL instruments as they would be seen to be beyond the capacity of influence of health interventions. Yet ability to earn a reasonable income, financial demands of health care itself and ability to live independently in a safe and healthy environment may all be influenced by illness and health interventions. These factors in turn may not just vary by individual but also across cultures and countries. A World Health Organization (WHO) definition incorporates many of the features of previous definitions and acknowledges the interplay between health and other factors:

> QoL is an individual's perception of their position in life in the context of the culture and value systems in which they live and in relation to their goals and expectations, standards and concerns. It is a broad ranging concept affected in a complex way by a person's physical health, psychological state, level of independence and their relationships to salient features of their environment (WHOQoL Group, 1995)

It is interesting to note that some of the more vocal proponents of a wider and more individualised definition of QoL are those who work in disability and rehabilitation or in oncology and palliative care settings (Levack *et al.*, 2004). A problem in the general QoL area is that terminology is used inconsistently. In many situations HRQoL and QoL are used interchangeably. Bradley (2001) gives a clear outline of the difficulties in interpreting research results when different terms, definitions and types of measures are used interchangeably. While debate continues about definitions, one of the most notable characteristics across QoL-related studies is the relative scarcity of an explicit definition of QoL by authors in their publications (Taillefer *et al.*, 2003). In parallel, concepts such as life satisfaction, happiness, well-being and QoL are also used interchangeably. There is much to be gained from closer interaction on these issues with what is called the positive psychology movement (Seligman,

2002). Here a combined theory approach called authentic happiness takes pleasures, gratifications and meaningful life into account as separate aspects (Seligman, 2002). Further, Keyes and colleagues have shown that satisfaction/happiness (subjective well-being) and meaning/personal growth (psychological well-being) are two distinct but related concepts (Keyes, 2002). Research in the QoL area would be improved considerably if researchers made explicit their definition of QoL and related concepts and also how their definition relates to instrument selection for the study. Further collaborative research has been recommended (Camfield & Skerington, 2008).

The Concept of Quality of Life

While there is an extensive empirical literature on QoL, the conceptual and theoretical development is lacking (Joyce *et al.*, 2003). Most writing on QoL in the health setting considers the more pragmatic issue of 'how to measure' than 'what to measure'. From the philosophical perspective, two fundamental approaches underlie conceptualisation of QoL: 'needs' and 'wants' (see Hayry, 1991). The needs approach views QoL as the extent to which universal human needs are met. From this perspective, if the basic and universal needs are common to all people, then they can be identified objectively and without consulting about the relative value of various aspects of life with the individual to be assessed. Many HRQoL instruments conform to the needs approach, i.e. the themes are established independent of the person being assessed. The alternative wants approach proposes that it is the individual who determines his or her basic priorities ('wants') in terms of evaluating QoL. Measures reflecting this perspective allow for a definition of QoL using themes, questions or question weightings determined by the individual being assessed. The methodologies used to achieve the wants approach are individualised. They typically do not limit the focus of enquiry to health and they focus more on the individual's perception than on function. A typical 'wants' question is 'Are you satisfied with your ability to socialise and to meet other people?' whereas a needs question is 'How many times per week do you meet family or friends for social activities?'.

The wants approach to QoL assessment is more clearly psychological. An early influential research paper supports the relative nature of subjective assessments such as happiness and QoL. Brickman *et al.* (1978) compared major lottery winners with matched community controls and with accident victims who had become paralysed as a consequence of their accident. From a 'needs' perspective, the paralysed participants would be seen as automatically having poorer QoL with the ability to walk seen as a fundamental 'need'. Researchers found that participants in all three groups reported quite similar levels of current happiness. When asked to rate how happy they expected to be in the future, those levels became even more similar. This finding is understandable from the 'wants' perspective since individuals can have differing and changing perspectives on what is important in their lives. The authors of this research asked, 'Is happiness relative?' This is the challenge when considering assessment of QoL in the health setting.

Uses of the Concept of Quality of Life in Health Settings

The primary outcomes in health-care evaluation have traditionally been mortality and morbidity. Now there is a focus on identifying the impact of interventions on function and QoL. Measurement of aspects of QoL in health settings can be traced to work on performance status by Karnofsky and Burchenal (1947). They were the first to rate aspects other than physical health when evaluating the success of medical interventions. The Karnofsky performance index was an observer-rated measure to assess patients on a 0–100 scale (0 for 'dead' and 100 for 'no evidence of disease, able to carry out normal activity and to work'). A number of other performance status measures have been developed since that time, e.g. Spitzer *et al.*'s (1981) Quality of Life index is a multidimensional observer rating scale for cancer patients. QoL-related ratings by professionals continued to be the norm for some decades. Most attention focused on cancer treatment where the question of quality versus 'quantity' or duration of life was particularly evident with the emergence of partially effective treatments with very severe side effects. There was a gradual shift to asking patients themselves to provide information on aspects of their QoL. This was in part informed by research showing that physicians were not good judges of the QoL of their patients (Sprangers & Aaronson, 1992). Patients rated their QoL more positively than did both their doctors and their relatives. It is now considered standard practice to ask individuals to rate their own QoL. Indeed, in more recent times, the broader construct of patient-reported outcomes (PRO) has been introduced, reflecting this principle. QoL would thus be seen as one type of PRO.

Proxy or surrogate ratings are ratings about an individual's QoL provided by others – usually relatives or professionals. 'Proxy' or surrogate ratings by others are seen as only acceptable where individuals are unable to make judgements for themselves. In these cases, it is now more acceptable that relatives make such decisions than professionals. Most assessment concerns decisions about life-sustaining medical treatment preferences (Fagerlin et al., 2001).

While QoL-related research was first developed in the context of cancer research it has now spread to every area of health care. There are four main uses of QoL assessments in health settings:

- treatment comparisons in clinical trials;
- treatment choices in individual patient care;
- evaluations to determine the best uses of health-care resources; and
- general or patient population studies to evaluate QoL.

Clinical trials set outcome targets against which they evaluate the success of the intervention. The most important outcomes are called primary outcomes. QoL as used in clinical trials is usually considered a secondary outcome (Fayers & Machin, 2007). Where clinical outcomes, e.g. mortality following cardiac revascularisation, are the primary outcome, differences in QoL scores only become influential where two or more treatments achieve equivalent benefit on a primary outcome variable (Croog et al., 1986). QoL assessment is increasingly incorporated into clinical trials with influential groups such as the National Heart, Lung and Blood Institute in the US requiring most trials its funds to have a QoL component. In most of these studies, QoL is a secondary outcome.

There are some studies, e.g. in oncology, pain or heartburn, where QoL is the primary outcome of the study (Kulig et al., 2003; Shaw et al., 2001). The application of PRO outcomes such as HRQoL in clinical trials is a complex and developing field. The EMEA reflection paper and the FDA Draft PRO Guidance (Committee for Medicinal Products for Human Use, 2005; US Department of Health and Human Services Food and Drug Administration, 2006) have changed the regulatory landscape and the pharmaceutical industry is now adopting to new requirements for getting PROs approved as labelling or promotional claims (Patrick et al., 2007; Revicki et al., 2007). For example, there has been an increased focus on establishing content validity alongside evidence of the PRO instrument's psychometric properties.

Treatment choices in individual patient care can be influenced by QoL assessment (Higginson & Carr, 2001), for example by monitoring patient QoL in clinical practice. There are new computer-assisted data collection methods, which can be used on a routine basis (Davis et al., 2007; Hilarius et al., 2008). Knowledge of the clinical and QoL effects of different treatment options can help health-care professionals outline the choices available to patients and assist them in selecting the option which is best for them. Prostate cancer is one such problem for men – there are both surgical and hormonal treatment options with a balance of risks, benefits and side effects for the two options. Thus some men may opt for surgery, preferring to take an early surgical risk and a short period of postoperative discomfort, while others may find a monthly hormone injection with mild to moderate side effects to be more preferable. Information on QoL in this context can be useful to both professionals and patients when considering what to expect given certain health conditions and treatments. This kind of evidence to inform an individual professional or patient comes from studies of populations of patients who are experiencing the condition or treatment, i.e. a patient population assessment strategy. There is some evidence from cancer research that measuring QoL in the clinical context can improve communication and patient well-being (Velikova et al., 2004).

At the population level, research has evaluated QoL for the general public. The generic SF-36 instrument has been widely used in several countries (Alonso et al., 2005). However, more often measures have been used to determine the HRQoL of particular patient groups, e.g. patients with Parkinson's disease (Damiano *et al.*, 1999) or HIV (Clayson *et al.*, 2006). These studies increase our overall understanding of the psychosocial implications of particular health conditions and treatments and make it possible to compare QoL and/or health across countries and in relation to national norms.

Another consideration for QoL assessment is resource allocation in health care. In the context of scarce resources, every decision to provide a specific type of health intervention is a decision not to provide another. For instance a health service may recruit twice as many cardiac surgeons as orthopaedic surgeons. In this way different weightings are applied to the treatment of cardiac and orthopaedic disorders. While some health intervention decisions are about which treatment to provide to an individual patient (e.g. whether to treat anginal pain medically or surgically), many are taken about which treatments to fund across patients. Thus in the example of the recruitment of surgeons above, the decision is to focus more on surgical services for cardiac than on orthopaedic problems. These decisions have often been made in an arbitrary manner or in a manner influenced by the ability of certain individuals or professional groups to argue more successfully for resources. It is in this context that health economists argue that such decisions, and the rationale behind them, should be made explicit. One of the underlying principles of choice of health interventions to fund is value for money since treatments should provide the greatest benefit to the greatest number of people if they are to be selected for funding in public health systems. Interventions are seen as value for money depending on how they affect QoL and duration of life for a particular cost, i.e. quality adjusted life years (QALYs). A number of methods have been developed to assess QoL in a manner that assists health economic evaluation, which now are routinely used within the pharmaceutical industry.

Quality of Life Measurement Instruments

QoL instruments can be divided into five main categories: generic; disease or population specific; dimension specific; individualised; and utility (Garratt *et al.*, 2002). There are two databases that list available measures and their properties, i.e. the PROQOLID (www.proqolid. org) and the OLGA database (www.olga-qol.com). The different types of measures are outlined in Table 26.1 with illustrations focusing on cardiac-related QoL.

Generic measures

Generic measures of QoL (Coons *et al.*, 2000) can be used in general or disease-focused population studies. They are typically profile measures, i.e. they assess a number of dimensions of QoL but do not usually sum them into one single scale. The general assumption is that scores on separate dimensions, e.g. sleep and social function, cannot readily be added together in a meaningful way. Measures differ in the number and focus of the subscales and items included in their instruments. The three most commonly used generic instruments (Garratt *et al.*, 2002), are outlined in Table 26.2. These are all HRQoL instruments. The Functional Limitations Profile (FLP; an English adaptation of an American instrument – the Sickness Impact Profile) is an early and lengthy instrument that can be completed by any member of the population. Because of its length, selected subscales are sometimes used instead of the whole scale. Another long-established HRQoL measure is the Nottingham Health Profile (NHP). More recently the Short-Form 36 item scale has been developed from a large American study called the Medical Outcomes Study (MOS). The original aim of the study was to determine which factors influenced health-care use for those who had or did not have financial cover for such services. The SF-36 has become the most widely used HRQoL measure internationally and has been translated and validated in many languages (Stewart, 1989). The measures have differing strengths and weaknesses. The FLP is clearly very broad in its coverage but is also very long. It does not have a pain subscale. The NHP focuses on more severe levels of disability and thus is likely to be less sensitive to change in conditions where effects are in the milder range. Conversely, the SF-36 is more sensitive to lower levels of disability, but might still not be responsive enough in some settings.

Not all generic QoL assessment tools are health-related in focus. The World Health Organization has undertaken a major project to quantify QoL cross-culturally (Skevington *et al.*, 2004). Its aim was to assess if there are universal concepts and then to

Table 26.1   Typology of QoL instruments (examples relating to cardiac patients)

Type of instrument	Examples of instruments used in cardiac research
Generic: can be used across patient and general population groups	Short-Form 36 (SF-36) (McHorney et al., 1993, 1994; Ware & Sherbourne, 1992) Nottingham Health Profile (NHP) (Hunt et al., 1985)
Disease or population specific: focus on aspects of QoL relevant to particular health problems	Seattle Angina Questionnaire (SAQ) (Spertus et al., 1995) MacNew Heart Disease HRQL Questionnaire (MacNew) (Oldridge et al., 1991; Valenti et al., 1996) Minnesota Living with Heart Failure (MLHF) (Rector, 1987)
Dimension specific: focus on a particular component of QoL	Cardiac Depression Scale (Hare & Davis, 1996) Global Mood Scale (Denollet, 1993; Denollet & Brutsaert, 1995) Heart Patients' Psychological Questionnaire (Erdman et al., 1986) Hospital Anxiety and Depression Scale (Herrmann, 1997; Zigmond & Snaith, 1983)
Individualised: focus on aspects of life selected by the individual being assessed	Schedule for the Evaluation of Individual Quality of Life (SEIQoL) (Hickey et al., 1996; McGee et al., 1991; O'Boyle et al., 1992) Quality of Life Index (QLI-cardiac) (Ferrans & Power, 1985)
Utility: focus on hierarchy of preferences assigned by general population or patients for particular health states	EuroQoL (EQ-5D) (Kind, 1996) Quality of Well-being Scale (QWB) (Kaplan et al., 1993) Health Utilities Index (Horsman, 2003)

Table 26.2   Scale profiles of three commonly used generic HRQL questionnaires

Title	Functional Limitations Profile (FLP)	Nottingham Health Profile (NHP)	Medical Outcomes Study Short-Form 36 (SF-36)
Authors	Charlton et al., 1983	Hunt et al., 1985	Ware & Sherbourne, 1992
Number of items	136	38 (part 1)	36
Number of subscales	12	7 (part 2)	8
Subscale summary scores?	Physical Psychosocial	No	Physical component Mental health component
Total score?	Yes	No	No
Subscales	Ambulation	Energy	Physical functioning
	Body care and movement	Pain	Role limitations due to physical problems
	Mobility	Emotional reactions	Role limitations due to emotional problems
	Household management	Sleep	Social functioning
	Recreation and pastimes	Social isolation	Mental health
	Social interaction	Physical mobility	Energy/ vitality
	Emotion		Pain
	Alertness		General health perception
	Sleep and rest		
	Eating		
	Communication		
	Work		

Table 26.3 Scale profiles of three disease-specific quality of life questionnaires

Title	Arthritis Impact Measurement Scales (AIMS-2)*	EORTC Quality of Life Scale (30-item version) (EORTC-30)	Parkinson's Disease Questionnaire (PDQ)
Authors	Meenan et al., 1992.	Aaronson et al., 1993	Peto et al., 1995
Number of items	78	30	39
Number of subscales	12 (+ single items)	5 (+ 3 symptom subscales and single items)	8
Subscale summary scores?	No	No	No
Total score?	No	No	Yes
Subscales	Mobility level	Physical functioning	Mobility
	Walking and bending	Role functioning	Activities of daily living
	Hand and finger function	Cognitive functioning	Emotional well-being
	Arm function	Emotional functioning	Stigma
	Self-care tasks	General QoL	Social support
	Household tasks	Fatigue	Cognitions
	Social activities	Nausea and vomiting	
	Social support	Pain	
	Pain from arthritis		
	Work		
	Level of tension		
	Mood		

develop questions to operationalise these concepts in different cultures. Four universal themes were found: physical health; psychological well-being; social relationships; and environment. A 100-item questionnaire was developed based on conceptual equivalence in the different languages to assess QoL – the WHOQoL-100 – and more recently a 25-item briefer measure has become available (WHOQoL Group, 1998).

Disease-specific or population-specific measures

Disease- or population-specific QoL focuses on aspects of QoL seen as most relevant to particular health problems. There now exists a large body of research on instruments developed to measure aspects of QoL for specific diseases or populations.

Bowling (2001, 2005) has produced excellent summaries of many available instruments (Table 26.3). These instruments are developed to be sensitive to change in aspects of life believed to be most affected by the condition concerned and its treatments. For instance, mobility and pain is a focus in arthritis-related

instruments. Mobility is also an issue in a measure developed from patient interviews for Parkinson's disease but pain is not; stigma features more prominently for the Parkinson's disease group. The research challenge when using specific instruments is that it is never possible to determine how different a group is in function from the general population. This makes such assessment problematic from a health economic perspective. Hence, many studies combine specific and generic measures. The challenge when doing this of course is to have questionnaires which do not place excessive burden on participants because of their length. It may still be feasible and acceptable for patients especially now when electronic data-capturing methods are used more frequently (Gwaltney et al., 2008). Where QoL is an important variable, it is worth considering that many of the other assessments in clinical settings are complex (e.g. requiring laboratory assessment and specific equipment and training to assess and interpret) and that many of these will be repeated at regular intervals to monitor progress in the patient's condition. Indeed QoL assessment may be the only opportunity for the patient to provide his or her perspective on the success or otherwise of the treatment being provided.

A number of instruments have been developed to assess QoL in children (Clarke & Giser, 2004). These need to be appropriate for children of different age groups. Such work has been undertaken with asthma-specific instruments where three age-specific versions are available (Christie & French, 1994). In other situations, adult versions have been tested and adapted, usually for older children and adolescents (e.g. diabetes) (Skinner et al., 2006). Generic, health-related instruments have also been developed. The Child Health Questionnaire is one such measure (Landgraf et al., 1997). QoL in populations such as those with a learning disability provide an even more complex set of challenges than assessment in children (Herr & Weber, 1999).

Individualised measures

Individualised QoL focuses on aspects of life selected by the individual being assessed. Acknowledging the relative and variable nature of QoL across individuals and circumstances, a number of research teams have attempted to develop instruments to assess QoL which have a standardised framework but which allow individualisation in various aspects of the assessment (Fayers & Hays, 2005). Individualised measures can be generic or disease-specific.

Possibly the most individualised QoL assessment system is the Schedule for the Evaluation of Individual Quality of Life (SEIQoL) (McGee et al., 1991; O'Boyle et al., 1994) and its briefer direct weighting procedure (Browne et al., 1997; Hickey et al., 1996). The SEIQoL philosophy proposes that the definition of QoL is individual in nature, that the individual assesses his or her QoL on the basis of evaluation of current status on salient aspects of life and compared with his or her own set of standards concerning optimal function and that these discrete evaluations are combined in a unique formula based on the relative value of each aspect of life by the individual concerned. The SEIQoL attempts to make explicit this process. Individuals are asked to nominate the five aspects of their life which currently most contribute to their overall QoL. They then rate current function

on each aspect on visual analogue scales anchored as 'best possible' and 'worst possible'. Then individuals are asked to provide the QoL weights for their five nominated aspects of life by either a judgement analysis method or using the direct weighting procedure (SEIQoL-DW). Current status on each of the five life domains is multiplied by the relative weight of that domain and summed to make a 0–11 scale with higher scores indicating better QoL. Studies have shown that SEIQoL is more sensitive to change than generic or illness-related measures (O'Boyle et al., 1992). Further, health is not always listed as one of the salient aspects of QoL, even for groups with chronic health and there seems to be no correlation with physical functioning and individual quality of life (Clarke et al., 2001; Echteld et al., 2007; Neudert et al., 2004) and that QoL rated in this way can remain high in patients in palliative care settings (Fegg et al., 2005; Waldron et al., 1999).

A second individualised QoL instrument is the Patient Generated Index (PGI) (Martin et al., 2007; Ruta et al., 1994). The PGI can only be used in the context of a health condition. Patients are asked to name the five most important areas of life that are affected by their health condition. They then rate how badly affected each of these areas is on a rating scale of 0 (worst they can imagine) to 100 (no effect: exactly as they would like it to be). A sixth box is included to cover all other important aspects of life not already mentioned. They are then asked to 'spend' 60 points on these domains in any combination they choose but with the aim being to best improve their overall QoL. Levels are multiplied by the weighting scores to give an overall QoL score. PGI has been shown to be more responsive to health changes than generic instruments in a number of studies, e.g. back pain and sleep apnoea. SEIQoL and PGI represent ways in which QoL assessment can be individualised in health or other settings.

A number of other instruments include some level of individualisation (Fayers & Hays, 2005). For instance, the generic Quality of Life Index (QLI), the McMaster–Toronto Arthritis (MACTAR) Patient Function Preference Questionnaire (Tugwell et al., 1987) and the disease-specific Audit of Diabetes Dependent Quality of Life (ADDQoL) (Bradley et al., 1999).

Utility measures

Utility measures have been developed from a health economics perspective. These measures assess the value of health or other interventions in terms of a combination of increased QoL and length of life, i.e. quality-adjusted life years (QALYs). The challenge here is how to combine changes in length and quality of life, for instance how to compare a treatment for terminal cancer which extends life by 12 months but with severe nausea as a side effect with hip replacement surgery, a treatment for osteoarthritis which has no impact on length of life but results in reduced pain and increased mobility for those treated.

Quality-adjusted life years (QALYs) involve a calculation of the number of life years gained (or lost) because of illness or health intervention multiplied by the change in HRQoL of those treated. QALYs are usually calculated from population rather than individual data. HRQoL is rated from 1.0 (best possible life) to 0.0 (dead). Thus a treatment which lengthened life by five years and restored or maintained a person in perfect health ($5 \times 1.0 = 5.0$) would provide a health system gain of 5.0 QALYs. The cost per QALY can be calculated from the cost of the treatment and related costings in a traditional health economic calculation. Different treatments can thus be compared for the cost per QALY of the treatment (Normand, 1994). QALYs may also be compared across conditions.

The challenge in QALY assessment is how to determine the scores for the HRQoL ratings. Three methods have been used: the rating scale techniques; time trade-off; and standard gamble (Bennett & Torrance, 1996; Jenkinson & McGee, 1998; Morimoto & Fukui 2002). The standard gamble technique is considered to have the strongest methodological base for providing QALYs.

The rating scale is based on a visual analogue scale (VAS) scale where the respondent is asked to place a mark between 0–100 where 0 equals worst possible health or QoL and 100 equals best possible health or QoL. The corresponding number is then used as a proxy for QALYs, i.e. a mark at 80 means 0.8 QALY. This is the simplest and most feasible method for yielding QALYs.

Time trade-off techniques involve asking participants to ascertain how many years of perfect health they would be willing to sacrifice in order to be free of a chronic health condition. Various options are presented until equilibrium is reached – a point where the person sees the number of years of life lost as equivalent in value to the option of being able to live without the chronic condition. The HRQoL score is calculated as the ratio between the two options.

The standard gamble method provides the person with a choice between the certainty of a life with a chronic condition or a gamble. The gamble involves the chance to have perfect health restored or to die. Varying probabilities are presented until the person reaches equilibrium.

Further, several composite measures have been developed for yielding QALYs. One widely used measure, the EuroQol (EQ-5D) (Kind, 1996), uses assessment of five QoL-related dimensions (mobility, self-care, usual activity, pain and mood) by three levels (none, moderate or severe problem). A level or weighting of difficulty is assigned to each of these parameters. What differs in these methods from other means of calculating QoL or HRQoL is that the weightings used in many studies are weightings calculated from a validation population rather than the weightings of the individual being assessed. Critics of these methods argue that weights are assigned in an artificial context by general population samples who are not themselves experiencing the levels of ill-health described in the scenarios. On the other hand, the view is that the valuations do represent the public's rating of the severity of health conditions and thus their gauge against which to value the impact of interventions to improve health and QoL (Calvert et al., 2005).

Another problem with the health economic perspective on HRQoL is the inherent ageism in its formulation (Hirskyj, 2007). Any improvement in HRQoL will automatically indicate that the treatment is better value when provided to younger individuals. Criticisms of health economic approaches to HRQoL notwithstanding, the need for methods to inform explicit and objective criteria for societal spending on interventions to improve health is obvious. Today, the EQ-5D is routinely incorporated in pharmaceutical clinical trials since 'traditional' profile QoL scores cannot be used for economic evaluation. Several initiatives have evolved to construct algorithms for existing QoL or HRQoL instruments to convert their scale scores to QALYs to be usable in cost-effectiveness evaluation. This approach has been applied, for example, with the SF-36 and the Western Ontario and McMaster Universities Osteoarthritis Index: (WOMAC; Mortimer & Segal, 2008; Marshall *et al.*, 2008). This means that patient can fill out a standard HRQoL instrument and the answers can be converted to utilities which can be used in cost-effectiveness analysis.

Current Issues in Quality of Life Research

There is increasing evidence of construct dynamism in QoL, for instance QoL in populations with chronic disease can be as high or higher than that in healthy populations (e.g. Allison *et al.*, 1997). Similarly, there is evidence that individuals substantially reframe their perceptions in estimating past and present QoL over time (e.g. Bernhard *et al.*, 1999). Such reframing, or response shift (Schwarz & Sprangers, 2000), is probably integral to patient adaptation to disease and treatment. Response shift can occur as a result of:

- a change in one's internal standards of measurement (i.e. recalibration);
- a change in one's values (i.e. the importance of components constituting QoL); or
- a redefinition of QoL itself (i.e. reconceptualisation).

Methods of assessing response shift have been summarised by Schwartz & Sprangers (2000). It can also be argued that achieving a response shift may be a reasonable therapeutic aim in helping patients adapt to health-related challenges. This is in line with current suggestions in the positive psychology literature for using well-being therapy (Ruini & Fava, 2009).

Further, QoL assessments have primarily been used for research purposes in clinical trials but have had relatively little impact on clinical practice, even though monitoring patient QoL in clinical practice is likely to achieve better treatment outcomes, e.g. help to individualise care, enhance patient–physician communication, inform clinical decision making and improve patient outcomes, especially QoL itself. QoL information could enhance the clinical interview

which tends to focus primarily on physical symptoms and it could serve as the basis for joint doctor–patient decision making about treatment options. Some studies have explored the possibility of improving the care of patients by using systematic and continuing QoL assessments in clinical practice (Detmar *et al.*, 2000; Espallargues *et al.*, 2000; Greenhalgh & Meadows, 1999). Intervention studies in cancer patients have shown that providing patient-specific QoL information to the physician and the patient before an appointment is an effective means of improving patient–provider communication (Detmar *et al.*, 2002; Hilarius *et al.*, 2008; Velikova *et al.*, 2002). Developments in information technology mean that electronic, web-based or PDA/mobile phone QoL versions can now be used to overcome some of the difficulties of administration and scoring in clinical practice (Dale & Hugen, 2007; Davis, 2007; Velikova *et al.*, 2002). If QoL measures are to become a routine feature of clinical practice, they must be easy to use, highly reliable, valid and sensitive to change.

Population studies might make available new knowledge and although the meaning of QoL can differ across cultures, it may be possible to develop measures that can capture at least some elements of QoL across all cultures. The cross-cultural adaptation of an instrument involves both assessment of cultural and linguistic equivalence and evaluation of measurement properties (Bowden & Fox-Rushby, 2003; ISPOR Task Force, 2005). There is growing interest in applying cognitive aspects of survey methodology (CASM) techniques to existing instruments to investigate whether the cognitive processes employed by respondents, in reading, comprehending and interpreting questions and in formulating and providing answers, vary across cultures or with respect to other respondent characteristics. CASM provides techniques such as cognitive interviewing and linguistic analysis that help to elucidate the cognitive mechanisms underlying responses (McColl *et al.*, 2003). An appraisal model has been proposed by Rapkin and colleagues to aid in clarifying respondents' understanding of QoL assessments (Rapkin *et al.*, 2004). Further, recent studies are also looking into the link between QoL and genetics and have put forward the hypothesis regarding an individual QoL or happiness set-point (Diener *et al.*, 2006; Sprangers & Schwarz, 2008).

Questionnaire development

The level and organisation of activity in terms of questionnaire development and refinement in QoL is worth noting. In cancer research, the European Organisation for Research and Treatment of Cancer (EORTC) researchers has developed a core cancer HRQoL instrument (Sprangers et al., 1998). In rheumatology, a group called OMERACT (Outcome Measures in Rheumatoid Arthritis Clinical Trials) has also been working towards an agreed set of instruments for use across arthritis research. In cardiology, a consortium involving the Association for Cardiovascular Prevention and Rehabilitation and the European Health Psychology Society is developing a core heart-related QoL instrument across European languages (Oldridge et al., 2005). Further, the IMMPACT group (Initiative on Methods, Measurement and Pain Assessment in Clinical Trials) group has outlined recommendations for assessments in chronic pain patients (Turk et al., 2008). There are also consortiums involving academia, the pharmaceutical industry and governmental bodies like the US Federal Drug Administration (FDA) to develop new novel instruments, for example a Cancer-Related Fatigue Measurement Consortium.

Computerised adaptive testing (CAT) is a new method designed to make surveys much shorter, more precise and less expensive. Associated with CAT is the emerging statistical approach of item response theory (IRT), which is used instead of the 'classical' psychometric approach for constructing and calibrating generic and disease-specific HRQoL measures (Bjorner et al., 2007; Ware, 2003).

Recently there has been more focus on establishing content validity, partly as a consequence of the changing regulatory landscape but also as a reaction to a more patient-centred approach within health care. Further, the need to interpret one's results has been highlighted. Today the US FDA requires evidence of all PRO measures used for claim purposes to have established their minimal important differences (MIDs) (Marquis et al., 2004). Further, a combination of quantitative and qualitative methods can be used to develop and confirm the items/scales/concepts included in a QoL instrument using for example factor analysis and cognitive debriefing (Watt et al., 2008).

Conclusions

The value of QoL assessment is now widely accepted in health settings. Developing a common language around QoL can facilitate dialogue between physicians and social scientists (including health psychologists) about the experiences, both individually and collectively, of patients. It allows for the development of a greater understanding of the patient's experience of illness using a common language. While physicians may be interested in the overall profile of patients in research models such as randomised clinical trials or in knowledge to inform individual patient care, the same information can facilitate social scientists to develop theoretical models concerning issues such as changing perspectives on illness over time, over intervention and over culture.

The challenge for the coming decades is to find some reconciliation between these two perspectives. In this way QoL assessment can be better used to direct services at individual and societal levels while expanding our understanding of how QoL is developed, maintained and altered as necessary through the course of illness and health interventions.

Discussion Points

1 Can health-related quality of life be distinguished from quality of life per se?
   What factors can influence an individual's rating of quality of life?
2 Can surrogate assessment be called a 'quality of life' assessment of the individual being assessed?
3 Can quality of life and duration of life variables be validly combined as is done for health economic type evaluations of quality of life?
4 What is the value of quality of life assessment if individuals change what constitutes their quality of life over time?
5 What is the role of health psychologists advance the field of quality of life research?

Further Reading

Allison, P.J., Locker, D. & Feine, J.S. (1997). Quality of life: A dynamic construct. *Social Science & Medicine, 45,* 221–230. *Good summary of the complexities of QoL assessment.*

Bowling, A. (2001). *Measuring disease: A review of disease-specific quality of life scales* (2nd edn). Buckingham: Open University Press and Bowling, A. (2005). *Measuring health: A review of quality of life scales* (3rd edn). Buckingham: Open University Press. *Invaluable companion books including summaries of a large set of QoL-related instruments: descriptions, psychometric properties, key references and typical uses of the instruments.*

Bradley, C. (2001). Importance of differentiating health status from quality of life. *Lancet, 357,* 7–8. *Concise outline of the difficulties posed when using QoL instruments based on very different meanings of the concept. The problems are illustrated by a diabetes research example.*

Hayry, M. (1991). Measuring the quality of life: Why, how and what? *Theoretical Medicine, 12,* 97–116. *Excellent outline of the basic philosophical challenges underlying efforts to assess QoL.*

Joyce, C.R.B., O'Boyle, C.A. & McGee, H.M. (1999). *Individual quality of life: Approaches to conceptualisation and assessment.* Amsterdam: Harwood. *Detailed overview of diverse set of individualised methods of assessing QoL.*

Sprangers, M.A. & Aaronson, N.K. (1992). The role of health care providers and significant others in evaluating the quality of life of patients with chronic disease: A review. *Journal of Clinical Epidemiology, 45,* 743–760. *Demonstrates that physicians and relatives consistently view patient QoL as poorer than do patients themselves.*

Stewart, A.L., Greenfield, S., Hays, R.D., Wells, R.D., Rogers, W.H., Berry, S.D. *et al.* (1989). Functional status and well-being of patients with chronic conditions: Results from the Medical Outcomes Study. *Journal of the American Medical Association, 262,* 907–913. *Classic study using SF-36 to illustrate the differing HRQoL profile of patients with one of nine chronic health conditions.*

References

Aaronson, N.K., Ahmedzai, S. & Bergman, B. (1993). The European Organisation for Research and Treatment of Cancer QLQ-30: A quality of life instrument for use in international clinical trials in oncology. *Journal of the National Cancer Institute, 85,* 365–376.

Allison, P.J., Locker, D. & Feine, J.S. (1997). Quality of life: A dynamic construct. *Social Science & Medicine, 45,* 221–230.

Alonso, J., Ferrer, M., Gandek, B., Ware, J.E., Jr, Aaronson, N.K., Mosconi, P. *et al.* (2005). Health-related quality of life associated with chronic conditions in eight countries: Results from the International Quality of Life Assessment (IQOLA) Project. *Quality of Life Research, 13,* 283–298.

Bennett, K.J. & Torrance, G.W. (1996). In B. Spilker (Ed.) *Quality of life and pharmacoeconomics in clinical trials* (2nd edn, pp. 253–266). Philadelphia: Lippincott-Raven.

Bernhard, J., Huerny, C., Maibach, R., Herrrmann, R., Laffer, U. for the Swiss Group for Clinical Cancer Research. (1999). Quality of life as subjective experience: Reframing of perception in patients with colon cancer undergoing radical resection with or without chemotherapy. *Annals of Oncology, 10,* 775–782.

Bjorner, J.B., Chang, C.H., Thissen, D. & Reeve, B.B. (2007). Developing tailored instruments: Item banking and computerized adaptive assessment. *Quality of Life Research, 16,* 95–108.

Bowden, A. & Fox-Rushby, J.A. (2003). A systematic and critical review of the process of translation and adaptation of generic health-related quality of life measures in Africa, Asia, Eastern Europe, the Middle East, South America. *Social Science & Medicine, 57,* 1289–1306.

Bowling, A. (2001). *Measuring disease: A review of disease-specific quality of life scales* (2nd edn). Milton Keynes: Open University Press.

Bowling, A. (2005). *Measuring health: A review of quality of life scales* (3rd edn). Milton Keynes: Open University Press.

Bradley, C. (2001). Importance of differentiating health status from quality of life. *Lancet, 357,* 7–8.

Bradley, C., Todd, C., Gorton, T., Symonds, E., Martin, A. & Plowright, R. (1999). The development of an individualised questionnaire measure of perceived impact of diabetes on quality of life: The ADDQoL. *Quality of Life Research, 8,* 79–91.

Brickman, P., Coates, D.D. & Janoff-Bulman, C. (1978). Lottery winners and accident victims: Is happiness relative? *Journal of Personality and Social Psychology, 36,* 917–927.

Browne, J.P., O'Boyle, C.A., McGee, H.M., McDonald, N.J. & Joyce, C.R.B. (1997). Development of a direct weighting procedure for quality of life domains. *Quality of Life Research, 6,* 301–309.

Calman, K.C. (1984). The quality of life in cancer patients – An hypothesis. *Journal of Medical Ethics, 10,* 124–129.

Calvert, M.J., Freemantle, N. & Cleland J. (2005). The impact of heart failure on health-related quality of life acquired in the baseline phase of the CARE-HF study. *European Journal of Heart Failure, 7*, 243–251.

Camfield, L. & Skevington, S.M. (2008). On subjective well-being and quality of life. *Journal of Health Psychology, 13*, 764–775.

Charlton, J.R., Patrick, D.L. & Peach, H. (1983). Use of multivariate measures of disability in health surveys. *Journal of Epidemiology & Community Health, 37*, 296–304.

Christie, M. & French, D. (Eds.) (1994). *Assessment of quality of life in childhood asthma*. London: Harwood Academic.

Clarke, S.A. & Eiser, C. (2004). The measurement of health-related quality of life (QOL) in paediatric clinical trials: A systematic review. *Health and Quality of Life Outcomes, 22*, 66.

Clarke, S., Hickey, A., O'Boyle, C. & Hardiman, O. (2001). Assessing individual quality of life in amylotrophic lateral sclerosis. *Quality of Life Research, 10*, 117–122.

Clayson, D.J., Wild, D.J., Quarterman, P., Duprat-Lomon, I., Kubin, M. & Coons, S.J. (2006). A comparative review of health-related quality-of-life measures for use in HIV/AIDS clinical trials. *Pharmacoeconomics, 24*, 751–765.

Committee for Medicinal Products for Human Use (CHMP) (2005). Reflection paper on the regulatory guidance for the use of health-related quality of life (HRQL) measures in the evaluation of medicinal products, 27 July 2005. Doc. Ref. EMEA/CHMP/EWP/139391/2004.

Coons, S.J., Rao, S., Keininger, D.L. & Hays, R.D. (2000) A comparative review of generic quality-of-life instruments. *Pharmacoeconomics, 17*, 13–35.

Croog, S.H., Levine, S., Testa, M.A. et al. (1986). The effects of antihypertensive therapy on the quality of life. *New England Journal of Medicine, 314*, 1657–1664.

Dale, O. & Hagen, K.B. (2007). Despite technical problems personal digital assistants outperform pen and paper when collecting patient diary data. *Journal of Clinical Epidemiology, 60*, 8–17.

Damiano, A.M., Snyder, C., Strausser, B. & Willian, M.K. (1999). A review of health-related quality-of-life concepts and measures for Parkinson's disease. *Quality of Life Research, 8*, 235–243.

Davis, K., Yount, S., Del Ciello, K., Whalen, M., Khan, S., Bass, M. et al. (2007). An innovative symptom monitoring tool for people with advanced lung cancer: A pilot demonstration. *Journal of Support Oncology, 5*, 381–387.

Denollet, J. (1993). Emotional distress and fatigue in coronary heart disease: The Global Mood Scale (GMS). *Psychological Medicine, 23*, 111–121.

Denollet, J. & Brutsaert, D.L. (1995). Enhancing emotional well-being by comprehensive rehabilitation in patients with coronary heart disease. *European Heart Journal, 16*, 1070–1078.

Detmar, S.B., Aaronson, N.K., Wever, L.D. et al. (2000). How are you feeling? Who wants to know? Patients' and oncologists' preferences for discussing health-related quality-of-life issues. *Journal of Clinical Oncology, 18*, 3295–3301.

Detmar, S.B., Muller, M.J., Schornagel, J.H. et al. (2002). Health-related quality-of-life assessments and patient–physician communication: a randomized controlled trial. *Journal of the American Medical Association, 288*, 3027–3034.

Diener, E., Lucas, R.E., Scollon, C.N. (2006). Beyond the hedonic treadmill: Revising the adaptation theory of well-being. *American Psychologist, 61*, 305–314.

Echteld, M.A., van Zuylen, L., Bannink, M., Witkamp, E. & Van der Rijt, C.C. (2007). Changes in and correlates of individual quality of life in advanced cancer patients admitted to an academic unit for palliative care. *Palliative Medicine, 21*, 199–205.

Erdman, R., Duivenvoorden, H., Verhage, F., Krazemier, M. & Hugenholtz P. (1986). Predictability of beneficial effects in cardiac rehabilitation: A randomised clinical trial of psychosocial variables. *Journal of Cardiopulmonary Rehabilitation, 6*, 206–213.

Espallargues, M., Valderas, J.M. & Alonso, J. (2000). Provision of feedback on perceived health status to health care professionals: A systematic review of its impact. *Medical Care, 38*, 175–186.

Fagerlin, A., Ditto, P., Danks, J.H. & Houts, R.M. (2001). Projection in surrogate decisions about life-sustaining medical treatments. *Health Psychology, 20*, 166–175.

Fayers, P. & Hays, R.D. (Eds.) (2005). *Assessing quality of life in clinical trials: Methods and practice*. Oxford: Oxford University Press.

Fayers, P.M. & Machin, D. (2007). *Quality of life: The assessment, analysis and interpretation of patient-reported outcomes* (2nd edn). Chichester: Wiley.

Fegg, M.J., Wasner, M., Neudert, C. & Borasio, G.D. (2005) Personal values and individual quality of life in palliative care patients. *Journal of Pain Symptom Management, 30*, 154–159.

Ferrans, C.E. & Powers, M.J. (1985). Quality of life index: Development and psychometric properties. *Advances in Nursing Science, 8*, 15–24.

Garratt, A., Schmidt, L., Mackintosh, A. & Fitzpatrick, R. (2002). Quality of life measurement: Bibliographic study of patient assessed health outcome measures. *British Medical Journal, 324*, 1417–1421.

Greenhalgh, J. & Meadows, K. (1999). The effectiveness of the use of patient-based measures of health in routine practice in improving the process and outcomes of patient care: A literature review. *Journal of Evaluation in Clinical Practice, 5,* 401–416.

Gwaltney, C.J., Shields, A.L. & Shiffman, S. (2008). Equivalence of electronic and paper-and-pencil administration of patient-reported outcome measures: A meta-analytic review. *Value in Health, 11,* 322–333.

Hare, D. & Davis, C. (1996). Cardiac Depression Scale: Validation of a new depression scale for cardiac patients. *Journal of Psychosomatic Research, 40,* 379–386.

Hayry, M. (1991). Measuring the quality of life: Why, how and what? *Theoretical Medicine, 12,* 97–116.

Herr, S.S. & Weber, G. (Eds.) (1999). *Ageing, rights and quality of life. Prospects for older people with developmental difficulties.* Baltimore: Paul H. Brooks.

Herrmann, C. (1997). International experiences with the Hospital Anxiety and Depression Scale – A review of validation data and clinical results. *Journal of Psychosomatic Research, 42,* 17–41.

Hickey, A.M., Bury, G., O'Boyle, C.A., Bradley, F., O'Kelly, F.D. & Shannon, W. (1996). A new short-form individual quality of life measure (SEIQoL-DW): Application in a cohort of individuals with HIV/AIDS. *British Medical Journal, 313,* 29–33.

Higginson, I.J. & Carr, A.J. (2001). Using quality of life measures in the clinical setting. *British Medical Journal, 322,* 1297–1300.

Hilarius, D.L., Kloeg, P.H., Gundy, C.M. & Aaronson, N.K. (2008). Use of health-related quality-of-life assessments in daily clinical oncology nursing practice: A community hospital-based intervention study. *Cancer, 113,* 628–637.

Hirskyj, P. (2007). QALY: an ethical issue that dare not speak its name. *Nursing Ethics, 14,* 72–82.

Horsman, J., Furlong, W., Feeny, D. & Torrance, G. (2003) The Health Utilities Index (HUI(R)): Concepts, measurement properties and applications. *Health and Quality of Life Outcomes, 1,* 54.

Hunt, S., McEwan, J. & McKenna, S. (1985). Measuring health status: A new tool for clinicians and epidemiologists. *Journal of the Royal College of General Practitioners, 35,* 185–188.

ISPOR Task Force for Translation and Cultural Adaptation (2005). Principles of good practice for the translation and cultural adaptation process for Patient-Reported Outcomes (PRO) measures. *Value in Health, 8,* 95–104.

Jenkinson, C. & McGee, H.M. (1998). *Health status measurement. A brief but critical introduction.* Oxford: Radcliffe Medical Press.

Joyce, C.R.B., O'Boyle, C.A. & McGee, H.M. (1999). *Individual quality of life: Approaches to conceptualisation and assessment.* Amsterdam: Harwood.

Joyce, C.R.B., Hickey, A., McGee, H.M. & O'Boyle, C.A. (2003). A theory-based method for the evaluation of individual quality of life: The SEIQoL. *Quality of Life Research, 12,* 275–280.

Kaplan, R.M. anderson, J.P. & Ganaits, T.G. (1993). The quality of well-being scale: Rationale for a single quality of life index. In S.R. Walker & R.M. Rosser (Eds.) *Quality of life assessment: Key issues in the 1990s.* Dordrecht: Kluwer Academic.

Karnofsky, D.A. & Burchenal, J.H. (1947). The clinical evaluation of chemotherapeutic agents in cancer. In C.M. McLead (Ed.) *Evaluation of chemotherapeutic agents.* New York: Columbia University Press.

Keyes, C.L., Shmotkin, D. & Ryff, C.D. (2002) Optimizing well-being: The empirical encounter of two traditions. *Journal of Personality and Social Psychology, 82,* 1007–1022.

Kind, P. (1996). The EuroQol Instrument: an index of health-related quality of life. In B. Spilker (Ed.) *Quality of life and pharmacoeconomics in clinical trials* (2nd edn, pp. 191–202). Philadelphia: Lippincott-Raven.

Kulig, M., Leodolter, A., Vieth, M., Schulte, E., Jaspersen, D., Labenz, J. *et al.* (2003). Quality of life in relation to symptoms in patients with gastro-oesophageal reflux disease: An analysis based on the ProGERD initiative. *Alimentary Pharmacology & Therapeutics, 18,* 767–776.

Levack, P., Graham, J. & Kidd, J. (2004). Listen to the patient: Quality of life of patients with recently diagnosed malignant cord compression in relation to their disability. *Palliative Medicine, 18,* 594–601.

Landgraf, J.M., Abetz, L. & Ware, J.E. Jr (1997). *The Child Health Questionnaire (CHQ): A user's manual.* Boston, MA: The Health Institute.

Martin, F., Camfield, L., Rodham, K., Kliempt, P. & Ruta, D. (2007). Twelve years' experience with the Patient Generated Index (PGI) of quality of life: A graded structured review. *Quality of Life Research, 16,* 705–715.

Marshall, D., Pericak, D., Grootendorst, P., Gooch, K., Faris, P., Frank, C. *et al.* (2008). Validation of a prediction model to estimate health utilities index Mark 3 utility scores from WOMAC index scores in patients with osteoarthritis of the hip. *Value Health, 11,* 470–477.

Marquis, P., Chassany, O. & Abetz, L. (2004). A comprehensive strategy for the interpretation of quality-of-life data based on existing methods. *Value Health, 7,* 93–104.

McColl, E., Meadows, K. & Barofsky, I. (2003). Cognitive aspects of survey methodology and quality of life assessment. *Quality of Life Research, 12,* 217–218.

McGee, H.M., O'Boyle, C.A., Hickey, A.M., Joyce, C.R.B. & O'Malley, K. (1991). Assessing the quality of life of the individual: The SEIQoL with a healthy and a gastroenterology unit population. *Psychological Medicine, 21,* 749–759.

McHorney, C.A., Ware, J.E. Jr & Raczek, A. (1993). The MOS 36-Item Short-Form Health Survey (SF-36): II.

Psychometric and clinical tests of validity in measuring physical and mental health constructs. *Medical Care, 31,* 247–263.

McHorney, C.A., Ware, J.E. Jr, Lu, J.F.R. & Shelbourne, C.D. (1994). The MOS 36-Item Short-Form Health Survey [SF-36]: III. Tests of data quality, scaling assumptions and reliability across diverse patient groups. *Medical Care, 32,* 40–66.

Meenan, R.F., Mason, J.H. & Anderson, J. (1992). AIMS2: the content and properties of a revised and expanded Arthritis Impact Measurement Scales Health Status Questionnaire. *Arthritis & Rheumatism, 35,* 1–9.

Morimoto, T. & Fukui, T. (2002). Utilities measured by rating scale, time trade-off and standard gamble: review and reference for health care professionals. *Journal of Epidemiology, 12,* 160–178.

Mortimer, D. & Segal, L. (2008) Comparing the incomparable? A systematic review of competing techniques for converting descriptive measures of health status into QALY-weights. *Medical Decision Making, 28,* 66–89.

Neudert, C., Wasner, M. & Borasio, G.D. (2004) Individual quality of life is not correlated with health-related quality of life or physical function in patients with amyotrophic lateral sclerosis. *Journal of Palliative Medicine, 20,* 7551–7557.

Normand, C. (1994). Health care resource allocation and the management of renal failure. In H.M. McGee & C. Bradley (Eds.) *Quality of life following renal failure* (pp. 145–153). London: Harwood Academic.

O'Boyle, C.A., McGee, H.M., Hickey, A.M., O'Malley, K. & Joyce, C.R.B. (1992). Individual quality of life in patients undergoing hip replacement. *Lancet, 339,* 1088–1091.

O'Boyle, C.A., McGee, H.M. & Joyce, C.R.B. (1994). Quality of life: Assessing the individual. *Advances in Medical Sociology, 5,* 159–180.

Oldridge, N., Guyatt, G., Jones, N., Crowe, J., Singer, J., Feeny, D. *et al.* (1991). Effects on quality of life with comprehensive rehabilitation after acute myocardial infarction. *American Journal of Cardiology, 67,* 1084–1089.

Oldridge, N., Saner, H., McGee, H. for the HeartQoL Study Investigators. (2005). The Euro Cardio-QoL Project. An international study to develop a core heart disease health-related quality of life questionnaire, the Heart QoL. *European Journal of Cardiovascular Prevention and Rehabilitation, 12,* 87–94.

Patrick, D.L., Burke, L.B., Powers, J.H., Scott, J.A., Rock, E.P., Dawisha, S. *et al.* (2007). Patient-reported outcomes to support medical product labelling claims. FDA Perspective. *Value in Health, 10,* 125–137.

Patrick, D.L. & Erickson, P. (1993). *Health status and health policy. Quality of life in health care evaluation and resource allocation.* New York: Oxford University Press.

Peto, V., Jenkinson, C. & Greenhall, R. (1995). The development and validation of a short measure of functioning and well-being for individuals with Parkinson's disease. *Quality of Life Research, 4,* 241–248.

Rapkin, B.D. & Schwartz, C.E. (2004). Toward a theoretical model of quality-of-life appraisal: Implications of findings from studies of response shift. *Health and Quality of Life Outcomes, 15,* 14.

Rector, T.S., Kubo, S.H. & Cohn, J.N. (1987). Patients' self-assessment of their congestive heart failure: content, reliability and validity of a new measure, the Minnesota Living with Heart Failure questionnaire. *Heart Failure, 3,* 198–209.

Revicki, D.A., Gnanasakthy, A. & Weinfurt, K. (2007). Documenting the rationale and psychometric characteristics of patient reported outcomes for labelling and promotional claims: The PRO Evidence Dossier. *Quality of Life Research, 16,* 717–723.

Ruini, C. & Fava, G.A. (2009). Well-being therapy for generalized anxiety disorder. *Journal of Clinical Psychology.* [Epub ahead of print.]

Ruta, D.A., Garratt, A.M., Russell, I.T. & MacDonald, L.M. (1994). A new approach to the measurement of quality of life. The Patient-Generated Index. *Medical Care, 32,* 1109–1126.

Schipper, H., Clinch, J.J. & Olweny, C.L.M. (1996). Quality of life studies: Definitions and conceptual issues. In B. Spilker (Ed.) *Quality of life and pharmacoeconomics in clinical trials* (2nd edn, pp. 11–23). Philadelphia: Lippincott-Raven.

Schwartz, C.E. & Sprangers, M.A.G. (Eds.) (2000). *Adaptation to changing health. Response shift in quality-of-life research.* Washington, DC: American Psychological Association.

Seligman, M.E. (2002). *Authentic Happiness. Using the new positive psychology to realize your potential for lasting fulfilment.* London: Nicholas Brealey.

Shaw, M.J., Talley, N.J., Beebe, T.J., Rockwood, T., Carlsson, R., Adlis, S. *et al.* (2001). Initial validation of a diagnostic questionnaire for gastroesophageal reflux disease. *American Journal of Gastroenterology, 96,* 52–57.

Skevington, S.M., Sartorius, N. & Amir, M. (2004). Developing methods for assessing quality of life in different cultural settings. The history of the WHOQoL instruments. *Social Psychiatry & Psychiatric Epidemiology, 39,* 1–8.

Skinner, T.C., Hoey, H., McGee, H.M., Skovlund, S.E. for the Hvidore Study Group on Childhood Diabetes. (2006). A short form of the Diabetes Quality of Life for Youth questionnaire: Exploratory and confirmatory analysis in a sample of 2,077 young people with diabetes mellitus. *Diabetologia, 49,* 621–628.

Spertus, J.A., Winder, J.A., Dewhurst, T.A., Deyo, R.A., Prodzinski, J., McDonell, M. *et al.* (1995). Development and evaluation of the Seattle Angina Questionnaire: A new functional status measure for coronary artery disease. *Journal of the American College of Cardiology, 25*, 333–341.

Spitzer, W.O., Dobson, A.J. & Hall, J. (1981). Measuring the quality of life of cancer patients: A concise QL index for use by physicians. *Journal of Chronic Diseases, 34*, 585–597.

Sprangers, M.A. & Aaronson, N.K. (1992). The role of health care providers and significant others in evaluating the quality of life of patients with chronic disease: A review. *Journal of Clinical Epidemiology, 45*, 743–760.

Sprangers, M.A., Cull, A., Groenvold, M., Bjordal, K., Blazeby, J. & Aaronson, N.K. (1998). The European Organization for Research and Treatment of Cancer approach to developing questionnaire modules: an update and overview. EORTC Quality of Life Study Group. *Quality of Life Research, 7*, 291–300.

Sprangers, M.A. & Schwartz, C.E. (2008). Reflections on changeability versus stability of health-related quality of life: Distinguishing between its environmental and genetic components. *Health and Quality of Life Outcomes, 2*, 89.

Stewart, A.L., Greenfield, S., Hays, R.D., Wells, R.D., Rogers, W.H., Berry, S.D. *et al.* (1989). Functional status and well-being of patients with chronic conditions: Results from the Medical Outcomes Study. *Journal of the American Medical Association, 262*, 907–913.

Taillefer, M.-C., Dupuis, G., Roberge, M.-A. & Le May, S. (2003). Health-related quality of life models: Systemic review of the literature. *Social Indicators Research, 64*, 293–323.

Tugwell, P., Bombardier, C., Buchanan, W.W. *et al.* (1987). The MACTAR Patient Preference Disability Questionnaire. *Journal of Rheumatology, 1*, 446–451.

Turk, D.C., Dworkin, R.H., McDermott, M.P., Bellamy, N., Burke, L.B., Chandler, J.M. *et al.* (2008) Analyzing multiple endpoints in clinical trials of pain treatments: IMMPACT recommendations. *Pain* [Epub ahead of print.]

US Department of Health and Human Services Food and Drug Administration (2006). *Guidance for Industry: Patient-reported outcome measures: Use in medical product development to support labelling claims.* Center for Drug Evaluation and Research (CDER), Center for Biologics Evaluation and Research (CBER), Center for Devices and Radiological Health (CDRH).

Valenti, L., Lim, L., Heller, R.F. & Knapp, J. (1996). An improved questionnaire for assessing quality of life after myocardial infarction. *Quality of Life Research, 5*, 151–161.

Velikova, G., Brown, J.M., Smith, A.B. *et al.* (2002). Computer-based quality of life questionnaires may contribute to doctor-patient interactions in oncology. *British Journal of Cancer, 86*, 51–59.

Velikova, G., Booth, L., Smith, A.B., Brown, P.M., Lynch, P., Brown, J.M. & Selby, P.J. (2004). Measuring quality of life in routine oncology practice improves communication and patient well-being: a randomized controlled trial. *Journal of Clinical Oncology, 22*, 714–724.

Waldron, D., O'Boyle, C.A., Kearney, M., Moriarty, M. & Carney, D. (1999). Quality of life measurement in advanced cancer: Assessing the individual. *Journal of Clinical Oncology, 17*, 3603–3611.

Ware, J.E. Jr (2003). Conceptualization and measurement of health-related quality of life: Comments on an evolving field. *Archives of Physical Medicine & Rehabilitation, 84*, S43–S51.

Ware, J.E. Jr & Sherbourne, C.D. (1992). The MOS 36-item Short-Form Health Survey (SF-36). I. Conceptual framework and item selection. *Medical Care, 30*, 473–483.

Watt, T., Rasmussen, Å.K., Groenvold, M., Bjorner, J.B., Watt, S.H., Bonnema S.J. *et al.* (2008). Improving a newly developed patient-reported outcome for thyroid patients, using cognitive interviewing. *Quality of Life Research, 17*, 1009–1017.

WHOQoL Group (1995). The World Health Organization Quality of Life assessment (WHOQoL): Position paper from the World Health Organization. *Social Science & Medicine, 41*, 1403–1409.

WHOQoL Group (1998). Development of the World Health Organization WHOQoL-BREF quality of life assessment. *Psychological Medicine, 28*, 551–558.

Zigmond, A.S. & Snaith, R.P. (1983). The hospital anxiety and depression scale. *Acta Psychiatrica Scandinavica, 67*, 361–370.

Part V

Lifespan, Gender and Sociocultural Perspectives

27

Sociocultural Aspects of Health and Illness

Ayse K. Uskul

Chapter Outline

This chapter will provide a summary of sociocultural differences observed in various aspects of health and illness, drawing on evidence from medical anthropology and health psychology. It will then introduce a theoretical framework borrowed from cultural psychology, one frequently adopted when examining cultural differences in areas such as social behaviour, cognition and emotion, but rarely implemented when examining cultural differences in the domain of health and illness. This section will be followed by some recent research originating from the area of illness cognitions, health communication and coping (use of social support), which adopts this framework to understand cultural differences.

Key Concepts

Culture
Culture and health
   communication
Culture and illness
   representations
Culture and social support
Individualism–collectivism

Introduction

The biomedical view of health, characterised by a focus on physical mechanisms and diseases featuring a reductionist point of view which defines health as the absence of disease (e.g. Suls & Walston, 2003) has long been replaced by a view that emphasises the role played by sociocultural forces in the shaping of health (and illness) and related psychological experiences (Engel, 1977; Taylor, 1978). In 1948, the World Health Organization (WHO) defined health as 'a complete state of physical, mental and social well-being and not merely the absence of disease or infirmity', calling attention to the complexity and multidimensionality of the concept. Adding *social well-being* to the definition opened the way to conceptualising the individual as a social being, part of a bigger entity than his/her own body. Later, WHO (World Health Organization, 1982) referred to the importance of sociocultural factors by endorsing the following view:

> If actions are to be effective in the prevention of diseases and in the promotion of health and well-being, they must be based on an understanding of culture, tradition, beliefs and patterns of family interaction (p. 4).

This shift in the definition of health and the factors responsible for disease prevention and health promotion is mirrored in a shift in the study of health and illness in disciplines such as psychology which traditionally focused on the individual as the unit of analysis and the force primarily responsible for avoiding disease and promoting well-being. In more recent psychological approaches to health and illness, the individual is increasingly viewed as part of a larger network of forces significantly influenced by his/her sociocultural environment. This approach has clear implications for models used in health psychology such as social cognitive and behavioural models of health and health promotion.

Traditionally, medical anthropologists have displayed an interest in the role of sociocultural factors in health and illness. They have extensively examined how illness is conceptualised and treated differently across cultures (e.g. Helman, 1994; Kleinman, 1980). For their part, medical sociologists have been interested in the effects of larger societal structures or institutions, such as medical delivery systems, on health and illness (e.g. Bird *et al.*, 2000). Now, psychologists are asking research questions that incorporate sociocultural variables into health and illness, investigating them in groups from different sociocultural backgrounds. This is encouraging for the field of health psychology: cross-cultural work can help researchers test their theories and assumptions in different cultural environments and practitioners in the field can be equipped with the knowledge to interact with individuals of different cultural backgrounds, a much-needed skill in a globalising world.

Culture, Health and Illness

This section provides a brief overview of research conducted to examine cross-cultural differences or similarities in areas relevant to health psychology: the experience of different medical conditions such as menopause and pain, health-care seeking, and doctor–patient relationship. While the literature on the role of sociocultural factors in health and illness is by no means limited to this list, the goal is to draw attention to the sociocultural nature of health and illness and to issues typically considered individually driven.

Culturally construed and experienced medical conditions: menopause and pain

Our sociocultural environments shape our psychology regarding health and illness – that is, how we think of, feel about and act upon our physical states. Perhaps more striking is that individuals' (reported) physical experiences seem to also be shaped by their sociocultural environments. The experience of menopause is an example of how previously universally defined physical signs of a certain stage of the life cycle may actually vary, depending on cultural characteristics. For example, Lock (1986) observed that Japanese women view menopause as a natural life-cycle transition in which the biological marker of cessation of menstruation is not considered to be of great importance. The reporting of symptoms was also different in Japan than in the West. Japanese women reported fewer symptoms and symptoms such as hot flushes or sudden perspiration were experienced very infrequently, whereas these were among the most commonly reported by Western women. Lock explains the general Japanese experience of menopause by referring to women's place in Japanese society and how menopause is viewed historically by both medical and lay persons.

Another sample of culturally shaped physical experiences comes from studies showing whether and when people complain of pain (Clark & Clark, 1980; Lipton & Marbach, 1984; Mechanic, 1963; Poliakoff, 1993; Zborowski, 1952, 1969; Zola, 1966). For example, Zborowski (1952) examined experience of pain among three groups of patients: Italian Americans, Jewish Americans and mainly Protestant 'Old Americans'. Both Jewish and Italian Americans tended to be more emotional in response to pain and to exaggerate their pain experience, leading some physicians to conclude that these groups had a lower threshold of pain. However, this emotional display, although similar in these two groups, was based on different attitudes towards pain. The Italians were mainly concerned with the immediacy of the pain experience, especially the pain sensation itself. They complained a great deal, drawing attention to their suffering by groaning, crying or moaning, but once they were given analgesics, they rapidly forgot their suffering and returned to their normal behaviour. The anxieties of the Italian patients centred on the effects of the experience upon their immediate situation, such as their occupation or economic situation. By contrast, Jewish patients were mainly concerned with the meaning and significance of the pain in relation to their health and welfare and eventually, the welfare of their families. Their anxieties were concentrated on the implications of the pain experience on the future. Old Americans also tended to be future-oriented, but unlike Jews, they were rather optimistic. When in pain, however, they tended to withdraw socially, while both Jews and Italians showed a preference for the social company of their relatives.

Zborowski (1952) points out that a cultural group's expectations and acceptance of pain as a 'normal' part of life will determine whether it is seen as a clinical problem which requires a clinical solution. For example, in Poland, labour pains are both expected and accepted by women giving birth, while in the USA they are not accepted and analgesia is frequently demanded. How one reacts to pain-killers may differ as well. Not all cultures are equally willing to use 'pain-killing' medication. Poliakoff (1993) suggests that many Chinese people fear that such medication will give them a feeling of being out of control; thus, they are reluctant to use them. Moreover, some people may accept pain as their due. For instance, Hindus who believe they are facing death may wish to do so 'clear-headed' rather than sedated and that negative feelings, such as pain, may be attributed to wrongs that they have committed in the past (Poliakoff, 1993). As these examples demonstrate, cognitive, emotional and behavioural responses to pain depend on cultural experiences and learning.

Culture and health-care seeking

Extensive literature in the domain of health-care seeking reveals that those from different sociocultural backgrounds tend to differ in the extent to which they delay seeking medical help. For example, studies show that being a member of an ethnic minority group can add to delay (e.g. Bottorff et al., 1998; Dibble et al., 1997; Stein et al., 1991; Vernon et al., 1985; Vernon et al., 1992). Black women tend to have more advanced breast cancer when detected and, as a consequence, have poorer survival rates than white women once the cancer is detected (Bain et al., 1986; Long, 1993; Nemcek, 1990; Polednak, 1986; Shapiro et al., 1982). Hispanic women also have later-staged tumours and decreased survival rates (e.g. Westbrook et al., 1975; Samet et al., 1988). A Canadian National Population Health Survey has revealed the importance of sociocultural background in breast cancer related detection strategies: Canadian women are less likely to have mammograms if they are single, have less education, are unemployed and are immigrants from South America, Central America, the Caribbean, Africa or Asia (Gentleman & Lee, 1997).

Cultural differences in delay in health-care seeking are attributed to a diverse set of factors, ranging from knowledge and beliefs regarding causes of the disease, associated symptoms, curability and consequences to trust in physicians (for a review on delay in seeking help for breast cancer symptoms see Uskul, 2001). Factors of a more sociocultural nature have also been considered. For example, in the realm of breast cancer, studies reveal that women's place in the society can shape their help-seeking behaviour by determining their priorities. In several studies, Chinese women indicate concern about potential or actual disruptions in carrying out their responsibilities in the event of breast cancer symptoms (Facione *et al.*, 2000; Lee *et al.*, 1996; Mo, 1992); in the end, these are factors influencing whether medical help is sought. Similarly, South-Asian societies focus on how women should act, how they should fulfil their responsibilities towards their families and how they should maintain their proper place in the community; these too may lead to their decision to put others first and delay engagement in health-care behaviours (e.g. Bhakta *et al.*, 1995; Bottorf *et al.*, 1998).

Culture and doctor–patient relationships

Some cultural norms heavily regulate gender relationships even in a health-care setting such as a hospital. Studies show that female members of some cultural groups may be reluctant to be examined by male physicians and even the anticipation of this happening may contribute to delays in or complete avoidance of health-care seeking (Facione *et al.*, 2000; Pillsbury, 1978; Uskul & Ahmad, 2003). In these cultural groups, being examined by a female physician can mitigate the embarrassment (Bhakta *et al.*, 1995). Some Asian women, although they had been in North America for a while and knew the language, indicated that they may choose to access traditional Chinese medicine because the traditional Chinese doctor examines the patient without asking her to take her clothes off (Facione *et al.*, 2000).

The physician–patient relationship might also prove difficult if one thinks that one's beliefs do not fit with the medical beliefs endorsed by physicians. Bhopal (1986), who has explored causal beliefs and illness among Punjabis, observes that South Asians who associate their symptoms with traditional or folk beliefs may be reluctant to seek medical advice because they perceive that health-care providers lack cultural sensitivity.

A Framework for Understanding Cultural Differences in Psychology of Health and Illness

Cross-cultural variations of a given psychological phenomenon are commonly attributed to *culture*. Because culture can be very broadly defined as a set of structures and institutions, values, traditions and ways of engaging with the social and non-social world that are transmitted across generations (e.g. Shweder & LeVine, 1984), the term lacks the conceptual specificity required for predictions of when and how culture shapes health and illness-related psychological experiences (Oyserman & Uskul, 2008). Therefore, psychologists have proposed features of cultures to be used as organising constructs (e.g. tight vs. loose cultures, Triandis, 1995; masculine vs. feminine, high vs. low power distance, high vs. low uncertainty avoidance cultures, Hofstede, 1980; survival vs. self-expression, Inglehart 1997). The most commonly used constructs to account for observed cultural differences and similarities in human psychology are *individualism* and *collectivism* (e.g. Hofstede, 1980; Kagitcibasi, 1997; Kashima, 2001; Oyserman *et al.*, 2002; Triandis, 1995). These constructs have been particularly useful in helping understand cultural differences as to how people view the self and relationships with social others. As argued below, these differences are important in understanding cultural differences in health and illness-related experiences.

In *individualistic* cultures, such as the United Kingdom or the United States, the dominant model of the self is an independent self characterised by self-defining attributes which serve to fulfil personal autonomy and self-expression (Hofstede, 1980; Kagitcibasi, 1994; Markus & Kitayama, 1991; Oyserman *et al.*, 2002; Schwartz, 1990; Triandis, 1995). People are seen as agentic and thus responsible for their own decisions and actions. Moreover, in cultures shaped by individualism, individuals favour promotion over prevention, focusing on the positive outcomes they hope to approach rather than the negative outcomes they hope to avoid (Elliot *et al.*, 2001; Lee *et al.*, 2000; Lockwood *et al.*, 2005). Relationships are seen as freely chosen and easy to enter and exit (Adams, 2005; Adams & Plaut, 2003).

By contrast, in *collectivistic* cultures, such as many East Asian cultures, the dominant model is an interdependent self embedded within the social context and defined by social relations and memberships in groups (Markus & Kitayama, 1991; Shweder & Bourne, 1984; Triandis, 1995). People are seen as relational or communal and their decisions and actions as heavily influenced by social, mutual obligations and the fulfilment of in-group expectations (Hofstede, 1980; Kagitcibasi, 1994; Oyserman *et al.*, 2002; Schwartz, 1990; Triandis, 1995). In such cultures, individuals tend to be motivated to fit in with their group and maintain social harmony (Markus & Kitayama, 1991); they focus on their responsibilities and obligations while trying to avoid behaviours that might cause social disruptions or disappoint significant others (Heine *et al.*, 1999; Kitayama & Uchida, 2005; Markus & Kitayama, 1991). They favour prevention over promotion in their motivational strategies, focusing on the negative outcomes they hope to avoid rather than the positive outcomes they wish to approach (Elliot *et al.*, 2001; Lee *et al.*, 2000; Lockwood *et al.*, 2005). Relationships are seen as less voluntary and more difficult to leave (Adams, 2005).

These cultural differences in the views of the self and relationships have implications for how health and illness are experienced and acted upon. Individualism, on the one hand, is likely to make individuals focus on the physical body and wellness; thus, having a healthy body can be characterised as a goal within an individualistic frame. In literature focusing explicitly on American individualism, the health–individualism linkage is evident; sociologists Rose (1996) and Lock (1999) link the American cultural focus on wellness, avoidance of illness and improvement of health with the American cultural focus on self-actualisation and personal responsibility. Psychologists Crawford (1984) and Baumeister (1997) link Americans' desire to maintain their health with their desire be autonomous individuals. Collectivism, on the other hand, is likely to posit illness as a to-be-avoided breakdown in one's abilities to carry out obligations (Uskul & Hynie, 2007; Uskul & Oyserman 2010). Having a healthy body can be characterised as a resource that facilitates fitting into the social order

within a collectivistic frame. Thus, for collectivists, the desire to avoid the negative social obligation consequences of ill-health is likely to matter.

Individualism–Collectivism, Health and Illness

Although the theoretical framework presented above has been extensively used to explain cultural differences with regard to social, cognitive and affective cultural differences in many domains of human psychology, its use has been somewhat limited in the area of psychology of health and illness. This section summarises the existing research which implicitly or explicitly uses an individualism–collectivism framework to cross-culturally test models of illness cognition, health communication, and coping.

Culture and illness representations

According to the self-regulation model of illness cognition and behaviour (Leventhal *et al.*, 1984), illness representations are organised sets of beliefs regarding illness labels or diagnoses and associated symptoms (identity), the factors or conditions believed to have caused the illness (cause), the expected duration of the illness (timeline), the expected effects of an illness on physical, social and psychological well-being (consequences), and the extent to which the illness can be cured or controlled through treatment measures and behaviours (control/cure). Adopting this framework, one could hypothesise that different components of illness representations endorsed by individuals of collectivistic cultural backgrounds will likely include other factors in addition to or different from the individual or biological ones; these will be embedded in the larger network of forces of which individuals are part. What these forces are will depend on the nature of collectivism adopted in different cultures. A limited number of studies show that illness representations are highly linked with a culture's philosophical and spiritual orientations which shape individuals' connectedness with social others and the surrounding physical world.

In cultures that emphasise the separation of individuals from their social and physical environments, physiological processes of illness are given greater weight and are typically seen as separate from the social and physical environments in which individuals are embedded (e.g. Landrine & Kolonoff, 2001). In cultures emphasising the connectedness of individuals with their social and physical environments, physiological processes of illness are given lesser weight and illness beliefs are shaped by holistic worldviews connecting relational, collective and physical forces. For example, Maori in New Zealand identify spiritual, mental, physical and family well-being as interrelated dimensions of health; they believe that a break down in one of these dimensions is likely to cause illness (Durie, 1994).

In India, metaphysical beliefs, that is, belief in Karma, God and spirits, are understood to be important determinants of many events in one's life, including illness and suffering (Kohli & Dalal, 1998). Karma holds that good and bad deeds accumulate through a series of lives and people face the consequences; physical suffering is typically attributed to one's misdeeds in this and/or previous lives. God is an external agent who controls reward and punishment, not always according to what one deserves. The belief in fate implies that all life events are predestined and one can do little to alter them. In studies with Indian patients, Kohli and Dalal (1998) show that belief in fate and God's will is negatively correlated with perceived controllability, implying that those who attribute their illness to fate and God's will perceive little control over the course of the illness. Patients who believe God's will to be the cause of their illness show greater perceived recovery; patients who perceive bodily weakness as the cause of their illness are less effective in dealing with the crisis and their psychological recovery is poor. As seen in these studies and others (e.g. Agrawal & Dalal, 1992; Dalal & Singh, 1992; Lau et al., 1989) perceived causality can vary dramatically as a function of cultural features; the network of forces in which individuals are embedded can have a significant bearing on responses to illness.

A study by Westbrook et al. (1994) examines the causal attributions for mid-life deafness among Anglo, Chinese, German, Greek, Italian and Arabic communities and compares these attributions with biomedical explanations. They ask health practitioners from these cultures to give causes that they believe members of their own cultural community will use to explain deafness. The predicted causes are the following: God's will, chance, stress and tension, temperament, poor health, upsetting event and evil eye. The most frequently mentioned causes differ between cultures, but more interestingly, all differ from the specialists' expectations.

Collectivism has been shown to be associated with an interpretation of ill-health in terms of social responsibility and desire to avoid the failure to properly fulfil social obligations (Uskul & Hynie, 2007). In a study involving recall of a time when one was ill, participants rating themselves as relational and collective are more concerned with the social consequences of health problems, such as being a burden to and unable to fulfil responsibilities towards loved ones (Uskul & Hynie, 2007). They are also more likely to report socially engaged emotions (emotions that motivate one to restore harmony in a relationship by compensating for harm done or repaying a debt, e.g. shame and embarrassment) about their illness rather than socially disengaged emotions (emotions that make salient one's inner attributes which are set in a social context, e.g. anger and frustration, see Kitayama et al., 2006). Thus, one's sense of separation or connectedness with social others is associated with how illness consequences are represented and the emotional responses evoked by these consequences.

As seen in these examples, cross-cultural studies in illness representations point to clear differences in how beliefs about causes and consequences of different diseases are formed and responded to. Studies undertaken in the West show that causal beliefs are embedded in the physical and social world; in a collectivistic world, however, metaphysical beliefs and relationships with others are integral to an individual's worldview. In short, the health-care process is likely to be facilitated if attention is paid to patients' culturally shaped appraisals of their symptoms, the assumptions they make about the causes and how responses to medical advice are conditioned by the culturally shaped theories they use to understand their bodily responses. Understanding the illness theories used by patients offers the potential for improved communication, better treatment and enhanced adherence to medical advice.

Culture, health communication and persuasion

As summarised in the previous section, individualistic and collectivistic cultural perspectives provide a useful framework for understanding cultural representations of health and illness. Following from this, studies testing the effectiveness of health communications targeting an audience of diverse cultural backgrounds have begun to incorporate messages congruent with the audience's prevalent cultural frame. The underlying assumption is that if health communications match culturally salient characteristics, messages will feel more relevant and therefore will more likely influence judgement about appropriate behaviour. Indeed, research shows that messages are more persuasive when there is a match between the recipient's cognitive (e.g. Petty *et al.*, 2000; Williams-Piehota *et al.*, 2005) or motivational (e.g. Cesario *et al.*, 2004; Mann *et al.*, 2004; Sherman *et al.*, 2006) characteristics and the content or framing of the message.

Research also suggests that matching health communications to motivational strategies adopted at varying levels by different cultural groups is a way to influence health behaviour change. Recent work by Uskul *et al.* (2009) on the use of dental floss tests the hypothesis that health messages will be more persuasive if they are congruent with the cultural patterns of promotion or prevention predominant in Western (individualistic) and Eastern (collectivistic) cultures. They draw on the literature suggesting that health messages congruent with a person's predominant motivational orientation are more effective than messages that are not (Mann *et al.*, 2004; Sherman *et al.*, 2006; Updegraff *et al.*, 2007). On the one hand, individuals who are predominantly approach-oriented (i.e. those who focus on the positive outcomes they hope to approach) report flossing more and are more generally persuaded in terms of attitudes and intentions when presented with a gain-framed health message about flossing (i.e. a message framed to convey the benefits of health-promoting behaviours). On the other hand, individuals who are predominantly avoidance-oriented (i.e. those who focus on the negative outcomes they hope to avoid) report flossing more and are more generally persuaded in terms of attitudes and intentions when presented with a loss-framed

health message about flossing (i.e. a message framed to convey the costs associated with failing to perform a health-promoting behaviour; see Sherman *et al.*, 2008, for a review).

Uskul and colleagues (2009) show that the individualistic white British participants are more persuaded (i.e. have more positive attitudes and stronger intentions to floss) when they receive the gain-framed message than when they receive the loss-framed message. By contrast, the collectivistic East Asian participants are more persuaded when they receive the loss-framed message than the gain-framed message. Furthermore, they demonstrate that cultural differences in the effectiveness of gain- and loss-framed messages in a dental health domain are mediated by a match between individuals' motivational orientation and the message frame. Thus, the interplay of individual difference factors (motivational orientation), sociocultural factors (cultural background) and situational factors (message frame) is likely to influence important factors related to health behaviour change, including attitudes towards and intentions to perform the health behaviour.

Studies that attempt to match message content to independent or interdependent aspects of the self of members of cultural groups yield somewhat inconsistent results. A study involving Mexican immigrant or African American participants (Murray-Johnson *et al.*, 2001) finds some effects when messages are matched to collectivism: Mexican immigrant participants and those who rate themselves as collectivistic find an AIDS message more frightening when it focuses on family-related consequences of AIDS. Some effects are found when messages are matched to individualism: African American participants and those who rate themselves as individualistic find the AIDS message more frightening when it focuses on self-related consequences of AIDS. Match results are found only for self-rated fear evoked by the message; no effects are observed for attitudes towards AIDS prevention or for intentions to prevent the risk of HIV infection. In other studies with African American participants, however, messages incorporating interdependent and not independent content are rated more favourably, thus showing the opposite effect to Murray-Johnson and colleagues' (2001) findings (e.g. Herek *et al.*, 1998; Kreuter *et al.*, 2004).

To address these inconsistencies, Uskul and Oyserman (2010) have employed a culturally informed social cognition framework (e.g. Oyserman & Lee, 2008; Oyserman & Sorensen, 2009) which suggests that what comes to mind at a given moment depends on the available situational cues and momentary cues can increase salience of cultural frames in information processing. They test the effectiveness of culturally matched health messages after making salient the dominant cultural frame using priming procedures. Specifically, they test the hypothesis that messages will be more persuasive when the message frame fits the dominant cultural frame. They find that matching health messages to salient cultural frames increases persuasiveness; further, culturally relevant messages are more persuasive if they come after being reminded of one's cultural frame. Individualist European Americans primed to focus on individualism are more persuaded by health messages associating health behaviour with negative physical consequences for the self, whereas collectivistic Asian Americans primed to focus on collectivism are more persuaded by health messages associating health behaviour with negative social consequences. Thus, message effectiveness can be increased by reminding potential listeners of their relevant cultural orientation. These findings also support the notion that the physical body and consequences for its well-being are perceived as part of the bounded self within an individualistic framework but that health appeals intending to improve health by focusing on the physical body are unlikely to be convincing when the self is socially embedded, as within a collectivistic framework.

Culture and coping

How people cope with health problems differs across cultural groups. Cultural differences, particularly in the use of social support have been shown in studies comparing individuals of Asian, European American and Asian American backgrounds (for a review, see Kim et al., 2008). Studies using various methods and samples from different groups with Asian heritage (Chinese, Japanese, Korean and Vietnamese) have consistently found that Asians and Asian Americans seek less social support than European Americans (Kim et al., 2006; Taylor et al., 2004).

Studies conducted to examine the underlying reasons for cultural differences in social support seeking show that Asian Americans are more concerned that seeking support will cause them to lose face, to disrupt group harmony and to be criticised by others; these relationship concerns seem to discourage them from drawing social support from their social networks. Other potential factors such as the availability of unsolicited support and independence concerns are not related to their use of social support to cope (Kim et al., 2006; Taylor et al., 2004).

Given the positive effects of social support seeking on physical well-being in the form of reduced levels of depression or anxiety during stressful times (Fleming et al., 1982), positive adjustment to a series of diseases such as diabetes and cancer (e.g. Holahan et al., 1997; Stone et al., 1999) and faster recovery speed from illness (e.g. House et al., 1988), the finding that individuals of Asian origin tend to seek less social support than their European American counterparts may be worrying. Research, however, shows that while Asian groups tend to avoid explicit patterns of social support seeking, which involve the explicit disclosure and sharing of stressful events typically adopted by individuals in Western cultures, they benefit from implicit social support (the emotional comfort that one can attain from one's relationships without discussing problems caused by stressful events), without potential concerns about the relational implications.

This interaction between cultural group and social support has been shown in a number of studies, including one demonstrating the beneficial effects of culturally appropriate forms of social support and the harmful effects of culturally inappropriate forms of social support at the physiological level (Taylor et al., 2007). An online diary study shows that European Americans report using explicit social support in coping with their daily stressors to a greater extent than do Koreans; Koreans report using implicit social support to a greater extent than do European Americans (Kim et al., 2008). These findings point to the importance of exploring the meanings and associated benefits of social support in different cultural groups.

A recent set of studies underlines the need to test findings in Western groups against those in groups of other cultural backgrounds. Uchida et al. (2008) explored the relationship between emotional support and well-being and physical health. In their initial study of college students, a positive effect of perceived emotional support on subjective well-being was found to be weak among European Americans; it disappeared when self-esteem is statistically controlled. In contrast, among Japanese and Filipinos perceived emotional support positively predicted subjective well-being, even after self-esteem is controlled. The authors replicated these findings in a second study with an adult sample using different well-being and physical health measures; in this study, perceived emotional support positively predicted well-being and health for Japanese adults, but such effects are virtually absent for American adults. As these studies show, culture moderates the impact of perceived emotional support on well-being and physical health.

Conclusion

Sociocultural environments play an important role in how health and illness are experienced. Psychological responses to physical experiences such menopause or pain, understandings of causes and consequences of disease, effectiveness of health messages, use of social support and its impact on physiological responses and many others, vary as a function of the characteristics of the sociocultural environments into which individuals are socialised. Evidence suggests that sociocultural factors can shape psychological constructs such as illness cognitions, attitudes and intentions – key constructs in such models of illness and health behaviour as the self-regulation model of illness cognition and behaviour (Leventhal *et al.*, 1984) and the theory of planned behaviour (Ajzen & Fishbein, 1980). To date, most health and illness models in psychology are designed and tested in a Western cultural context and are therefore likely to be biased. More research is certainly required as the incorporation of sociocultural factors into existing health models can contribute to a comprehensive understanding of the moderating factors that determine how illness cognitions are shaped or when behaviour is likely to change. It is time to collate the vast amount of knowledge accumulated in the hitherto disconnected subfields of cultural and health psychology and to explore the degree to which theories and models developed in the West can be used to understand health and illness-related psychological experiences elsewhere.

Discussion Points

1   What are some theoretical and practical implications of taking into account sociocultural factors in the study of health and illness?
2   The chapter introduces one theoretical framework commonly used to understand cultural differences and similarities in psychological phenomena. It also refers to other organising frameworks. Choose one of these alternative frameworks and discuss how it might be useful in making sense of cultural differences in the experience of pain.
3   Identify from the existing literature a health behaviour that has been reported to show varia-
tion across cultural groups. Discuss how this variation might be explained in reference to individualism–collectivism framework.
4   Discuss how a culturally informed social cognition framework can be applied in real-life settings in the domain of health communication.
5   Imagine you are a Western physician working in a Western country with many patients of East Asian background. What would be some of the issues that you would attend to in interacting with those patients?

Further Reading

Beardslee, L.M. (1994). Medical diagnosis and treatment across cultures. In W. J. Lonner & R. Malpass (Eds.) *Psychology and culture* (pp. 279–284). Boston: Allyn & Bacon.

Harkness, S. & Super, C.M. (1994). Culture and psychopathology. In M. Lewis & S. Miller (Eds.) *Handbook of developmental psychopathology* (pp. 289–313). New York: Plenum.

Helman, C. (2007). *Culture, health and illness.* London: Hodder & Arnold.

Kazarian, S.S. & Evans, D.R. (2001). *Handbook of cultural health psychology.* San Diego, CA: Academic Press.

Kitayama, S. & Cohen, D. (2007). *Handbook of cultural psychology.* New York: Guilford Press.

Maclachlan, M. (1997). *Culture and health: Psychological perspectives on problems and practice.* Chichester: Wiley.

Taylor, S.E., Welch, W., Kim, H.S. & Sherman, D.K. (2007). Cultural differences in the impact of social support on psychological and biological stress responses. *Psychological Science, 18,* 831–837.

Uskul, A.K., Sherman, D. & Fitzgibbon, J. (2009). The cultural congruency effect: Culture, regulatory focus and the effectiveness of gain- vs. loss-framed health messages. *Journal of Experimental Social Psychology, 45,* 535–541.

Winkelman, M. (2008). *Culture and health: Applying medical anthropology.* San Francisco: Jossey-Bass.

Zborowski, M. (1952). Cultural components in responses to pain. *Journal of Social Issues, 8,* 16–30.

References

Adams, G. (2005). The cultural grounding of personal relationship: Enemyship in North American and West African worlds. *Journal of Personality and Social Psychology, 88,* 948–968.

Adams, G. & Plaut, V.C. (2003). The cultural grounding of personal relationship: Friendship in North American and West African worlds. *Personal Relationships, 10,* 333–348.

Agrawal, M. & Dalal, A.K. (1996). Beliefs about the world and recovery from myocardial infarction. *Journal of Social Psychology, 133,* 385–394.

Ajzen, I. & Fishbein, M. (1980). *Understanding attitudes and predicting social behavior.* Englewood Cliffs, NJ: Prentice-Hall.

Bain, R.P., Greenberg, R.S. & Whitaker, J.P. (1986). Racial differences in survival of women with breast cancer. *Journal of Chronic Diseases, 39,* 631–642.

Baumeister R.F. (1997). The self and society: Changes, problems and opportunities. In R.D. Ashmore & L. Jussim (Eds.) *Self and identity: Fundamental issues* (Rutgers Series on Self and Social Identity, Vol. 1, pp. 191–217). New York: Oxford University Press.

Bhakta, P., Donnelly, P. & Mayberry, J. (1995). Management of breast disease in Asian women. *Professional Nursing, 11,* 187–189.

Bhopal, R.S. (1986). Asians' knowledge and behaviour on preventive health issues: Smoking, alcohol, heart disease, pregnancy, rickets, malaria prophylaxis and surma. *Community Medicine, 8,* 315–321.

Bird, C.E., Conrad, P. & Fremont, A.M. (2000). *Handbook of medical sociology* (5th edn). Upper Saddle River, NJ: Prentice Hall.

Bottorff, J.L., Johnson, J.L., Bhagat, R., Grewal, S., Balneaves, L.G., Clarke, H. & Hilton B.A. (1998). Beliefs related to breast health practices: The perceptions of South Asian women living in Canada. *Social Science & Medicine, 47,* 2075–2085.

Cesario, J., Grant, H. & Higgins, T. E. (2004). Regulatory fit and persuasion: Transfer from 'Feeling right'. *Journal of Personality and Social Psychology, 86,* 388–404.

Clark, W.C. & Clark, S.B. (1980). Pain responses in Nepalese porters. *Science, 209,* 410–412.

Crawford, R. (1984). A cultural account of health: self-control, release and the social body. In J. McKinlay (ED.), *Issues in the political economy of health care* (pp. 60–103). London: Tavistock.

Dalal, A.K. & Singh, A.K. (1992). Role of causal and recovery beliefs in the psychological adjustment to a chronic disease. *Psychology & Health, 6,* 193–203.

Dibble, S.L., Vanoni, J.M. & Miaskowski, C. (1997). Women's attitudes toward breast cancer screening procedures: Differences by ethnicity. *Women's Health Issues, 7,* 47–54.

Durie, M.H. (1994). Maori perspectives of health and illness. In J. Spicer, A. Trlin & J.A. Walton (Eds.) *Social dimensions of health and disease: New Zealand perspectives* (pp. 194–203). Palmerston North, NZ: Dunmore Press.

Elliot, A.J., Chirkov, V.I., Kim, Y. & Sheldon, K.M. (2001). A cross cultural analysis of avoidance (relative to approach) personal goals. *Psychological Science, 12,* 505–510.

Engel, G.L. (1977). The need for a new medical model: a challenge for biomedicine. *Science, 196,* 129–136.

Facione, N.C., Giancarlo, C. & Chan, L. (2000). Perceived risk and help-seeking behavior for breast cancer. A Chinese-American perspective. *Cancer Nursing, 23,* 258–267.

Fleming, R., Baum, A., Gisriel, M.M. & Gatchel, R.J. (1982). Mediating influences of social support on stress at Three Mile Island. *Journal of Human Stress, 8,* 14–22.

Gentleman, J.F. & Lee, J. (1997). Who doesn't get a mammography? *Health Reports* (Statistic Canada, Catalogue 82-003-XPB), *9,* 20–28.

Heine, S.J., Lehman, D.R., Markus, H.R. & Kitayama, S. (1999). Is there a universal need for positive self-regard? *Psychological Review, 106,* 766–794.

Helman, C. (1994). *Culture, health and illness.* London: Butterworth-Heinemann.

Herek, G., Gillis, J., Glunt, E., Lewis, J., Welton, D. & Capitanio, J. (1998). Culturally sensitive AIDS education videos for African American audiences: Effects of source, message, receiver and context. *American Journal of Community Psychology, 26,* 705–743.

Hofstede, G. (1980). *Culture's consequences.* Beverly Hills, CA: Sage.

Holahan, C.J., Moos, R.H., Holahan, C.K. & Brennan, P.L. (1997). Social context, coping strategies and depressive symptoms: An expanded model with cardiac patients. *Journal of Personality and Social Psychology, 72,* 918–928.

House, J.S., Landis, K.R. & Umberson, D. (1988). Social relationships and health. *Science, 241,* 540–545.

Inglehart, R. (1997). *Modernization and post-modernization: Cultural, economic and political change in 43 societies.* Princeton: Princeton University Press.

Kagitcibasi, C. (1994). A critical appraisal of individualism and collectivism: Toward a new formulation. In U. Kim, H.C. Triandis, C. Kagitcibasi, S.-C. Choi & G. Yoon (Eds.) *Individualism and collectivism: Theory, method and applications* (pp. 52–65). Thousand Oaks, CA: Sage.

Kagitcibasi, C. (1997). Individualism and collectivism. In J. Berry, M. Segall & C. Kagitcibasi (Eds.) *Handbook of cross-cultural psychology* (Vol. 3, 2nd edn, pp. 1–49). Needham Heights, MA: Allyn & Bacon.

Kashima, Y. (2001). Culture and social cognition: Toward a social psychology of cultural dynamics. In D. Matsumoto (Ed.) *The handbook of culture and psychology* (pp. 325–360). New York: Oxford University Press.

Kim, H.S., Sherman, D.K. & Taylor, S.E. (2008). Culture and social support. *American Psychologist, 63,* 518–526.

Kim, H.S., Sherman, D.K., Ko, D. & Taylor, S.E. (2006). Pursuit of happiness and pursuit of harmony: Culture, relationships and social support seeking. *Personality and Social Psychology Bulletin, 32,* 1595–1607.

Kitayama, S. & Uchida, Y. (2005). Interdependent agency: An alternative system for action. In R.M. Sorrentino, D. Cohen, J.M. Olson & M.P. Zanna (Eds.) *Cultural and social behavior: The Ontario Symposium* (Vol. 10, pp. 137–164). Mahwah, NJ: Erlbaum.

Kitayama, S., Mesquita, B. & Karasawa, M. (2006). Cultural affordances and emotional experience: Socially engaging and disengaging emotions in Japan and the United States. *Journal of Personality and Social Psychology, 91,* 890–903.

Kleinman, A. (1980). *Patients and healers in the context of culture: An exploration of the borderland between anthropology, medicine and psychiatry.* Berkeley, CA: University of California Press.

Kohli, N. & Dalal, A.K. (1998). Culture as a factor in causal understanding of illness: A study of cancer patients, *Psychology & Developing Societies, 10,* 115–129.

Kreuter, M., Skinner, C., Steger-May, K., Holt, C., Bucholtz, D., Clark, E. & Haire-Joshu, D. (2004). Response to

behaviorally vs. culturally tailored cancer communication among African American women. *American Journal of Health Behavior, 28,* 195–207.

Landrine, H. & Klonoff, E.A. (2001). Cultural diversity and health psychology. In A. Baum, T.A. Reverson & J.E. Singer (Eds.) *Handbook of health psychology* (pp. 851–892). Mahwah, NJ: Erlbaum.

Lau, R.R., Bernard, T.M. & Hartman, K.A. (1989). Further explorations of common-sense representations of common illness. *Health Psychology, 8,* 195–219.

Lee, A.Y., Aaker, J.L. & Gardner, W.K. (2000). The pleasures and pains of distinct self-construals: The role of interdependence in regulatory focus. *Journal of Personality and Social Psychology, 78,* 1122–1134.

Lee, M. & Lee, F. &. Stewart, S. (1996). Pathways to early breast and cervical detection for Chinese-American women. *Health Education Quarterly, 23,* 76–88.

Leventhal, H., Nerenz, D.R. & Steele, D.J. (1984). Illness representations and coping with health threats. In A. Baum, S.E. Taylor & J.E. Singer (Ed.) *Handbook of psychology and health* (pp. 219–252). Hillsdale, NJ: Erlbaum.

Lipton, J.A. & Marbach, J.J. (1984). Ethnicity and the pain experience. *Social Science & Medicine, 19,* 1279–1298.

Lock, M. (1986). Ambiguities of aging: Japanese experience and perceptions of menopause. *Culture, Medicine and Psychiatry, 10,* 23–46.

Lock, M. (1999). The politics of health, identity and culture. In R. Contrada & R. Ashmore (Eds.) *Self, social identity and physical health.* New York: Oxford University Press.

Lockwood, P., Marshall, T. & Sadler, P. (2005). Promoting success or preventing failure: Cultural differences in motivation by positive and negative role models. *Personality and Social Psychology Bulletin, 31,* 379–392.

Long, E. (1993). Breast cancer in African-American women: Review of the literature. *Cancer Nursing, 16,* 1–24.

Mann, T.L., Sherman, D.K. & Updegraff, J.A. (2004). Dispositional motivations and message framing: A test of the congruency hypothesis in college students. *Health Psychology, 23,* 330–334.

Markus, H. & Kitayama, S. (1991). Culture and the self: Implications for cognition, emotion and motivation. *Psychological Review, 98,* 224–253.

Mechanic, D. (1963). Religion, religiosity and illness behavior: The special case of the Jews. *Human Organization, 22,* 202–208.

Mo, B. (1992). Modesty, sexuality and breast health in Chinese-American women. *Western Journal of Medicine, 157,* 260–264.

Murray-Johnson, L., Witte, K., Liu, W. & Hubbell, A. (2001). Addressing cultural orientation in fear appeals: promoting AIDS-protective behaviors among Hispanic immigrants and African-American adolescents and American and Taiwanese college students. *Journal of Health Communication, 6,* 335–358.

Nemcek, M.A. (1990). Health beliefs and breast examination among black women. *Health Values, 14,* 41–52.

Oyserman, D. & Lee, S.W.S. (2008). Does culture influence what and how we think? Effects of priming individualism and collectivism. *Psychological Bulletin, 134,* 311–342.

Oyserman, D. & Sorensen, N. (2009). Understanding cultural syndrome effects on what and how we think: a situated cognition model. In C. Chiu, R. Jr. Wyer & Y. Hong (Eds) *Problems and solutions in cross-cultural theory, research and application* (pp. 23–50). New York: Psychology Press.

Oyserman, D. & Uskul, A.K. (2008). Individualism and collectivism: societal-level processes with implications for individual-level and society-level outcomes. In F. van de Vijver, D. van Hemert & Y. Poortinga (Eds.) *Multilevel analysis of individuals and cultures* (pp. 145–173). Mahwah, NJ: Erlbaum.

Oyserman, D., Coon, H. & Kemmelmeier, M. (2002). Rethinking individualism and collectivism: Evaluation of theoretical assumptions and meta-analyses. *Psychological Bulletin, 128,* 3–73.

Petty, R., Wheeler, S. & Bizer, G. (2000). Attitude functions and persuasion: An elaboration likelihood approach to matched versus mismatched messages. In G. Maio & J. Olson (Eds.) *Why we evaluate: Functions of Attitudes* (pp. 133–162). Mahwah, NJ: Erlbaum.

Pillsbury, B. (1978). Convalescence of Chinese women after childbirth. *Social Science & Medicine, 12,* 111–122.

Polednak, A.P. (1986). Breast cancer in black and white women in New York State. Case distribution and incidence rates by clinical stage at diagnosis. *Cancer, 58,* 807–815.

Poliakoff, M. (1993). Cancer and cultural attitudes. In R. Masi, L. Mensah & K.A. McLeod (Eds.) *Health and Cultures: Policies, professional practice and education.* New York: Mosaic Press.

Rose, N. (1996). Identity, geneology, history. In S. Hall & P. duGay (Eds.) *Questions of cultural identity* (pp. 128–150). London: Sage.

Samet, J.M., Hunt, W.C., Lerchen, M.L. & Goodwin, J. S. (1988). Delay in seeking care for cancer symptoms: A population-based study of elderly New Mexicans. *Journal of the National Cancer Institute, 80,* 432–438.

Schwartz, S. (1990). Individualism–collectivism: Critique and proposed refinements. *Journal of Cross-Cultural Psychology, 21,* 139–157.

Shapiro, S., Venet, W., Strax, P., Venet, L. & Roeser, R. (1982). Prospects for eliminating racial differences in breast cancer survival rates. *American Journal of Public Health, 72,* 1142–1145.

Sherman, D.K., Mann, T.L. & Updegraff, J.A. (2006). Approach/avoidance orientation, message framing and health behaviour: Understanding the congruency effect. *Motivation and Emotion, 30,* 165–169.

Sherman, D.K., Updegraff, J.A. & Mann, T. (2008). Improving oral health behaviour: a social psychological approach. *Journal of the American Dental Association, 139,* 1382–1387.

Shweder, R.A. & Bourne, L. (1984). Does the concept of the person vary cross-culturally? In R.A. Shweder & R. LeVine (Eds.) *Culture theory: Essays on mind, self, and emotion* (pp. 158–199). Cambridge: Cambridge University Press.

Shweder, R. & LeVine, R. (Eds.) (1984). *Culture Theory: Essays on mind, self and emotion.* Cambridge: Cambridge University Press.

Stein, J.A., Fox, S.A. & Murata, P.J. (1991). The influence of ethnicity, socio-economic status and psychological barriers on use of mammography. *Journal of Health and Social Behaviour, 32,* 101–113.

Stone, A.A., Mezzacappa, E.S., Donatone, B.A. & Gonder, M. (1999). Psychosocial stress and social support are associated with prostatespecific antigen levels in men: Results from a community screening program. *Health Psychology, 18,* 482–486.

Suls, J. & Wallston, K.A. (2003). Introduction. In J. Suls & K.A. Wallston (Eds.) *Social psychological foundations of health and illness* (pp. x–xx). Oxford: Blackwell Publishing.

Taylor, S. (1978). A developing role of social psychology in medicine and medical practice. *Personality and Social Psychology Bulletin, 4,* 515–524.

Taylor, S.E., Sherman, D.K., Kim, H.S., Jarcho, J., Takagi, K. & Dunagan, M.S. (2004). Culture and social support: Who seeks it and why? *Journal of Personality and Social Psychology, 87,* 354–362.

Taylor, S.E., Welch, W., Kim, H.S. & Sherman, D.K. (2007). Cultural differences in the impact of social support on psychological and biological stress responses. *Psychological Science, 18,* 831–837.

Triandis, H. (1995). *Individualism and Collectivism.* Boulder, CO: Westview Press.

Uchida, Y., Kitayama, S., Mesquita, B., Reyes, J.A.S. & Morling, B. (2008). Is perceived emotional support beneficial? Well-being and health in independent and interdependent cultures. *Personality and Social Psychology Bulletin, 34,* 741–754.

Updegraff, J.A., Sherman, D.K., Luyster, F.S. & Mann, T.L. (2007). Understanding how tailored communications work: the effects of message quality and congruency on perceptions of health messages. *Journal of Experimental Social Psychology, 43,* 249–257.

Uskul, A.K. (2001). *Sociocultural determinants of delay in seeking medical help for breast cancer symptoms.* At www.cehip.org/menujs.html.

Uskul, A.K. & Ahmad. F. (2003). Physician–patient interaction: A gynaecology clinic in Turkey. *Social Science & Medicine, 57,* 205–215.

Uskul, A.K. & Hynie, M. (2007). Self-construal and concerns elicited by imagined and real health problems. *Journal of Applied Social Psychology, 37,* 2156–2189.

Uskul, A.K. & Oyserman, D. (2010). When message-frame fits salient cultural-frame, messages feel more persuasive. *Psychology & Health, 25,* 321–337.

Uskul, A.K., Sherman, D. & Fitzgibbon, J. (2009). The cultural congruency effect: Culture, regulatory focus and the effectiveness of gain- vs. loss-framed health messages. *Journal of Experimental Social Psychology, 45,* 535–541.

Vernon, S.W., Tilley, B.C., Neale, A.V. & Steinfeldt, L. (1985). Ethnicity, survival and delay in seeking treatment for symptoms of breast cancer. *Cancer, 55,* 1563–1571.

Vernon, S.W., Vogel, V.G., Halabi, S., Jackson, G.L, Lundy, R.O., Peters, G.N. *et al.* (1992). Breast cancer screening behaviours and attitudes in three racial/ethnic groups. *Cancer, 69,* 165–174.

Westbrook, K.C., Brown, B.W. & McBride, C.M. (1975). Breast cancer: A critical review of a patient sample with a ten-year follow-up. *Southern Medical Journal, 68,* 543–548.

Westbrook, M., Legge, V. & Pennay, M. (1994). Causal attributions for deafness in a multicultural society. *Psychology & Health, 10,* 17–31.

Williams-Piehota, P., Pizarro, J., Schneider, T.R., Mowad, L. & Salovey, P. (2005). Matching health messages to monitor-blunter coping styles to motivate screening mammography. *Health Psychology, 24,* 58–67.

World Health Organization (1982). *Medium term programme.* Geneva: World Health Organization.

Zborowski, M. (1952). Cultural components in responses to pain. *Journal of Social Issues, 8,* 16–30.

Zborowski, M. (1969). *People in Pain.* San Francisco: Jossey-Bass.

Zola, I.K. (1966). Culture and symptoms: An analysis of patient's presenting complaints. *American Sociological Review, 31,* 615–630.

28

Gender, Health and Illness

Myra S. Hunter and Magdalene Rosairo

Chapter Outline	Key Concepts
Women and men differ in terms of their biology (sex differences), their access to and control over resources and their decision-making power in the family and community, as well as the roles and responsibilities that society assigns to them (gender differences). In this chapter we describe the impact of gender upon life expectancy and experience of illness and discuss the psychosocial, cultural and biological explanations for these differences. Psychological processes are then discussed including symptom perception, health beliefs and health-related behaviours, with examples from health psychology research.	Alcohol Cognition Culture Diet Exercise Gender Gender roles Health beliefs Health promotion Health-related behaviour Help seeking Illness Illness representations Life expectancy Risk taking Sex differences Smoking Symptom perception

Introduction

Gender and sex, often interacting with socioeconomic circumstances, influence exposure to health risks, access to health information and services, health outcomes and the social and economic consequences of ill-health (Ostlin *et al.*, 2007). It is now generally accepted that biological differences cannot solely account for gender differences in health and that social and cultural influences on men and women's experience and behaviour and social constructions of gender play a crucial role (Lee & Owens, 2002; Ussher, 1997).

Health researchers have been criticised for investigating men and neglecting women, thus reinforcing assumptions that men's experiences are the norm and women's are not. Women's health activists and researchers have worked to improve women's health in relation to reproduction and sexuality, women roles and social disadvantages, including access to employment, domestic violence and sexual abuse and in relation to increased information and choice over health decisions. The medicalisation of women's bodies and the social discourses of being female are being researched and challenged (Hunter & O'Dea, 1997; Malson, 1997; Stoppard, 1997). While men have been studied as the norm, they have been relatively neglected in research on the health impacts of male gender roles (Lee & Owens, 2002). We will argue that being either male or female confers both advantages and disadvantages to health.

Gender and Life Expectancy

'Women get sick and men die' (Nathanson, 1977). This well-known quote reflects the general finding that in industrialised societies men die earlier than women, but that women have poorer health than men (Bird & Rieker, 2008; Macintyre *et al.*, 1996). In the UK, men have a shorter life expectancy than women, by approximately six years, although this is decreasing, largely because men's life expectancy is rising at a faster rate than women's (Brettingham, 2005). The average gap in life expectancy is approximately seven years in developed countries. However, in developing countries the average gender gap is only three years. The largest differences are in Russia (13 years) and the Ukraine (12 years), while there are no differences in

Bangladesh or Nepal and in Afghanistan men have a one-year advantage over women in life expectancy. The global differences in life expectancy tend to be linked to socioeconomic disadvantage affecting access to education, health care and nutrition, as well as rates of infant death and maternal mortality. Neonatal deaths are consistently more common among boys than girls. While boys outnumber girls in all countries, by the age of 30–35 women start to outnumber men and this trend continues to the extent that the numbers of elderly women greatly outnumber elderly men in most countries (Kinsella & Gist, 1998).

Gender and Illness

In general adult women tend to report more symptoms and chronic health problems than men, but the direction and magnitude of differences in morbidity has been found to vary considerably (Macintyre *et al.*, 1996). It is also important to remember that the main diseases affecting men and women are broadly fairly similar, for example cardiovascular disease, cancers, musculoskeletal problems, diabetes, mental illness, sensory impairments, infectious diseases and their sequaelae (World Health Organization, 2003a). Cardiovascular disease (CVD) is the main cause of death of older people, regardless of gender, across the world (World Health Organization, 2003a), but there are some clinically relevant differences for men and women in the prevalence of CVD, its presentation, management and outcome. A significant factor in the gender difference in mortality is that men typically have an earlier onset of heart disease than women. In the USA for example almost three-quarters of those who die of heart attacks before the age of 65 are men. The gender difference in mortality from CVD decreases with age, particularly after the menopause, which has been partly explained by the protective effects of oestrogen. However, an analysis of age-related trends in CVD suggests a deceleration in the death rate of men with age rather than an increase in that of women, suggesting that environmental or behavioural factors are important determinants of CVD in both men and women (Lawlor *et al.*, 2002). Moreover, results from prospective studies of the long-term effects of hormone therapy (HT) found increased risk of stroke with HT and therefore it is not recommended for prevention of CVD (Wenger, 2004). Women tend to experience longer stays in hospital and suffer greater pain and disability secondary to heart disease (Rabi & Cox, 2007). Despite this, health services such as cardiac rehabilitation tend to be modelled around men's rather than women's needs (White *et al.*, 2007).

Male mortality rates for cancer are some 30–50 per cent higher than for females; a figure mostly driven by lung cancer in men, but female lung cancer is on the increase which may be partly due to increased smoking among young women (World Health Organization, 2003a). In the UK, in 2006 there were 19,600 male and 14,550 female deaths from lung cancer. Lung (20 per cent), breast (17 per cent) and colorectal (10 per cent) were the most common causes of cancer death for women, while for men, lung (24 per cent), prostate (12 per cent) and colorectal (11 per cent) cancers were the most common causes of death (Office of National Statistics, www.statistics.gov.uk, 2006). Interestingly, there has been a decrease in breast cancer rates following the reduction of HT use during the past five years (Parkin, 2009). Throat cancer is more prevalent for men than for women, with almost 1800 male compared with 394 female new cases diagnosed in the UK in 2005, which is likely to be explained by differences in smoking and alcohol use. Cervical cancer remains the cancer most commonly associated with mortality for women in the developing world (World Health Organization, 2003a); while in the UK cervical cancer rates have halved since the cervical screening programme was set up in 1985 (Kmietowicz, 2009).

Women have a higher incidence of diabetes and tend to suffer disproportionately from acute diabetes-related complications (Coker & Shumaker, 2003; Grodstein *et al.*, 2001). Musculoskeletal problems, for example, osteoarthritis and osteoporosis, are also more common in older women than men (World Health Organization, 2003a).

Although it is beyond the scope of this chapter to focus on the extensive literature relating to mental health, there is evidence that although there are no large differences in the overall incidence or prevalence rates of major psychological disorders, adult women experience substantially higher rates of anxiety and depression than men, whereas men experience higher rates of substance abuse, antisocial behaviour and suicide (see Bird & Rieker, 2008).

Biological Explanations

Until relatively recently, gender differences in health have typically been explained in terms of sex or biological differences. Reproductive differences between men and women do have important implications for mortality; it is estimated that approximately half a million women die each year as a direct consequence of pregnancy and childbirth (Doyal, 2001). Male infant mortality is higher than that of females (Reddy *et al.*, 1992), such that although 5 per cent more boys are born in the world, given similar care, women survive better at all ages, including before birth (Craft, 1997a). Biological differences obviously influence sites of diseases, such as cancers and also include a range of genetic, hormonal and metabolic influences.

Differences in oestrogen levels might influence the onset of coronary heart disease by reducing clotting tendencies and reducing cholesterol levels, while testosterone increases platelet aggregation (McGill & Stern, 1979). Women appear to have greater resistance to infections (Davey *et al.*, 2001) and studies of stress responses have found that men typically show greater stress hormone, blood pressure and cholesterol rises in response to laboratory stressors than women (Matthew & Stoney, 1988). Tremblay *et al.* (2007) note that the Y chromosome (in men) may contribute to differences in blood pressure and stress responses between men and women, while the X chromosome is hypothesised to play a role in hypertension, cardiovascular malformations, renal disease and Turner syndrome. Sex differences in the experience of pain have been widely reported, with females generally reporting more frequent clinical pain and demonstrating greater pain sensitivity. However, age, menstrual phase, anxiety and depression, as well as the testing environment and the modality of the noxious stimuli have also been found to influence pain reports (Hurley & Adams, 2008). Gender differences may be partially mediated by anxiety (Jones & Zachariae, 2004). A study by Edwards *et al.* (2004) suggested that catastrophising might mediate the sex difference in clinical pain ratings but not the much larger sex differences in pain threshold and tolerance, found in experimental settings.

Responses to pain therapies also differ between men and women, although whether these differences are related to physiological mechanisms, gender or both has not been clarified (Pinn, 2007). Awareness of the possible differences between males and females in response to pain is the only clinical recommendation that can be made (Hurley & Adams, 2008).

Sociocultural Explanations

Gender differences include socially constructed roles, behaviours, activities and attributes that a given society considers appropriate for men and women. In most societies women are not treated as equals with men and this inevitably affects their health. Stereotypically, 'feminine' behaviour is characterised by passivity, subservience, emotionality, physical weakness, being caring and uncompetitive. Gender roles lead to inequalities in income and wealth and result in women being more vulnerable to poverty, having heavy burdens of work, often combining employment with domestic duties and childrearing (Doyal, 2001). The link between poverty and ill-health is well established (Smith *et al.*, 1990). In addition, women are subject to domestic violence and rape to a greater extent than men, which cuts across socioeconomic, religious and ethnic lines (Craft, 1997b). Until recently little attention has been given to the impact of gender on men's health. 'Masculinity' is essentially characterised by toughness, unemotionality, physical competence, competitiveness and aggression. The development of a male identity often requires the taking of risks that are hazardous to health, which may result in accidents and violence and making unhealthy behavioural and lifestyle choices. For both genders there are more contemporary egalitarian models, such as the 'new man' for men, but these roles are often negatively valued and for both genders individual choices are constrained by social pressures (Lee & Owens, 2002).

Gender roles tend to be fairly fluid and vary over time. For example, the average age of having a first child is rising in developed countries and relatively more younger women are smoking and drinking heavily (Brettingham, 2005; Hunter & Orth-Gomer, 2003). Working and employment conditions typically vary by sex, from country to country. Men have many more fatal injuries and more occupational accidents than women (World Health Organization, 2004). Many societies accept that males can be asked to do more dangerous jobs, which may involve exposure to chemicals, ionising radiation, toxic contamination and high temperatures, which may be hazardous to male reproductive health. There is also evidence to suggest that men tend to adopt more health-damaging behaviours such as smoking and drinking in response to job stress than women (Murphy & Bennett, 2005). The proportion of women in the paid workforce is increasing rapidly in many countries (Brettingham, 2005), with women making up 42 per cent of the estimated global workforce (World Health Organization, 2004). Globally, women are more likely to occupy lower socioeconomic positions, for example undertaking domestic work or work from home which tends to be less regulated (Craft, 1997b). Nevertheless, in general, being employed tends to be associated with better health.

Depression is more common in women than men and overall the evidence suggests that psychosocial factors play a more important role in these differences than do biological or genetic factors (Piccinelli & Wilkinson, 2000). Women are more at risk of childhood sexual abuse and are more likely to be subject to domestic violence than men. Although women do not consistently experience more stressful life events in adulthood, their reaction to life events, particularly those relating to children and relationships, may have particular significance and negative impact upon them (Nazroo *et al.*, 1997). While having several social roles tends to be protective to health, having too few or too many roles that conflict or are overwhelming may be damaging to health and well-being. Having roles that are undervalued may be a risk factor for mental health; it appears to be the quality of the roles that are important. The gender difference in health between men and women is most apparent during the 'reproductive years' and lessens after the age of 50–55 years (O'Dea *et al.*, 1999). Interestingly, when psychosocial differences were controlled in a study of civil servants, the rates of depression were similar in both sexes (Jenkins, 1985). In summary, the causes of the gender difference in depression are likely to be multifactorial but the evidence does suggest that these are mainly psychosocial. Although the focus of this chapter is on physical health, well-being and mood have important influences upon perception and management of health and illness.

Gender not only affects experience of illness and what we are likely to die from, but also affects our perceptions of illness and health beliefs, the extent to which we practise unhealthy and risky behaviours, engagement with health-promoting behaviours and consultation with physicians, (Murphy & Bennett, 2005; Reddy et al., 1992).

Symptom and Illness Perceptions

Gijsbers van Wijk and Kolk (1996) suggest that gender differences in symptom perception might explain higher levels of female morbidity and the higher rates of health-care utilisation typically seen among women (Kapur et al., 2004; Gijsbers van Wijk et al., 1995). According to their symptom perception model, the higher morbidity and help seeking in women might be understood in terms of a relative excess of somatic information, being influenced by the female reproductive role, disadvantageous social position, a female proclivity to selectively attend to the body, a female preference for somatic attributional style or a greater willingness to report symptoms. In addition, they proposed that negative affectivity might result in selective attention to the body.

There is some evidence to support the model, but findings have not been consistent across populations. For example, comparing student and patient groups, female patients have been found to selectively attend to their bodies and score highly for negative affect, while female students were more likely to attribute physical symptoms to psychological causes. Only female students (not female patients) reported reduced external information compared to men and it was only for 'somatisation' that both female students and patients scored highly, indicating a greater tendency to experience and report somatic symptoms in general. In addition, low levels of external information, coupled with low levels of positive mood and high levels of negative mood, have been associated with increased symptom reporting (Gijsbers van Wijk & Kolk, 1997; Gijsbers van Wijk et al., 1999). Negative affect has frequently been associated with increased symptom reports (Kolk et al., 2002; Watson &

Pennebaker, 1989) and might mediate gender differences in physical symptoms reported. For example, Piccinelli and Simon (1997) found a strong correlation between somatic symptoms and emotional distress (anxiety and depression) for both sexes, but females tended to report more somatic symptoms at each level of emotional distress.

It is also likely that gender socialisation processes could encourage men to be stoical (Reddy et al., 1992; Zakowski et al., 2003), but might encourage women to attend to bodily sensations, particularly through 'medicalisation' of the female body and through their increased likelihood of being carers for others (Gijsbers van Wijk & Kolk, 1997).

The observed female excess of health morbidity is predominantly associated with less severe and more subjectively reported health problems and is typically found in non-clinical populations (Gijsbers van Wijk & Kolk, 1997). The difference is also more apparent when symptoms are retrospectively reported (Kolk et al., 2003). Interestingly, there is some evidence to suggest that men and women are equally likely to report severe symptoms and that men may actually report more symptoms in the presence of identified illness or disease (Arber & Cooper, 1999; Macintyre, 1993). Therefore the direction and magnitude of differences in symptom perception appears to vary according to the type and severity of symptoms as well as the population sampled.

Gender differences in illness perceptions have been explored among cardiac patients. Aalto et al. (2005) compared women and men with coronary heart disease (CHD) and found that men were more likely to attribute their condition to risk behaviours and internal factors, such as their own attitude or behaviour, while women were more likely to perceive stress or genes as causes. Women also perceived more symptoms to be associated with CHD (and more non-CHD related symptoms). Compared with men, women regarded their illness as less controllable but reported fewer severe consequences of CHD. In a similar study of acute coronary syndrome patients (Grace et al., 2005), women perceived a more chronic course and more cyclical episodes than men, while men perceived greater personal control and treatability than women. The impact of such gender differences in patients' beliefs and expectations upon adjustment and health-related behaviours warrants further research.

Health Beliefs and Health-Related Behaviours

In general, men tend to engage in more negative health-related behaviours than women and similarly fewer men than women engage in positive health-related behaviours (Gijsbers van Wijk *et al.*, 1995; Reddy *et al.*, 1992). Men are more likely to hold beliefs that relate to perceived invulnerability to risk and personal control over health; they are less likely to believe that they are at risk of an illness, while, in fact, they are more at risk of becoming ill (Courtenay, 2000). Men have been found to have significantly poorer dietary practice (Baker & Wardle, 2003), engage in fewer preventative behaviours, have poorer medical adherence, engage in riskier substance use practices and to report riskier health-related beliefs than women (Courtenay *et al.*, 2002). These findings are noteworthy since more men than women reported their overall health behaviour as good or excellent, despite obviously greater risk. These behaviours are closely linked to gender roles – men engaging in stoical and risky behaviour to 'prove' their masculinity – behaviours which are likely to be more common among men in the poorest communities (Doyal, 2001).

According to Johnston and Dixon (2008), 48 per cent of deaths in USA are attributable to behaviour. It is estimated that 70 per cent of cancers have behavioural factors as causes and lack of adherence to recommended treatments has significant impact on outcomes (Doll & Peto, 1981). Behavioural risk factors for health include alcohol use, smoking, dietary behaviours and physical activity.

Alcohol

One of the few universal gender differences in human social behaviour relates to alcohol consumption (Holmila & Raitsalo, 2005), although the sizes of gender differences vary between societies. After smoking, drinking alcohol is the second biggest risk factor in cancer of the throat and mouth. Cirrhosis of the liver can lead to liver cancer and for women, alcohol intake can increase risk of breast cancer. On average, men drink more frequently, consume a higher volume of alcohol and drink to a greater level of intoxication than women (Reddy *et al.*, 1992). It has been suggested that in many cultures, alcohol is one of the more powerful symbols of gender role. However, there is growing evidence of convergence in male and female drinking patterns in developed countries, possibly related to changes in women's lives, such as increased employment outside of the home, more freedom as individual consumers, stress caused by dual roles outside of and within the home, 'contagion' from men and women working together (see Holmila & Raitsalo, 2005).

Smoking

In 2002, tobacco killed 4.83 million people worldwide, a sharp increase from previous estimates (World Health Organization, 2003b). Cigarette smoking is a major cause of lung cancer and of heart disease and is associated with decreased fertility, premature labour, low birthweight infants, cervical cancer, early menopause and bone fractures (World Health Organization, 2003b). Tobacco use is particularly prevalent among men and boys – being male is the greatest predictor of use in most countries. The overall prevalence of tobacco use, globally, is four times higher for men than women (World Health Organization, 2003b). Men smoke more per day, inhale more deeply and are less likely to smoke low tar and nicotine cigarettes (Reddy *et al.*, 1992; Waldron, 1986). There are likely to be interactions between smoking and risk factors that vary between males and females, due to physiological differences (for example, females develop lung cancer at lower levels of smoking but have better prognosis) or differences in environmental exposure, for example asbestos exposure and cigarette smoking interact to increase the risk of lung cancer in men, partly because many more men are exposed to asbestos (Waldron, 1986).

The smoking gap between men and women is greatest in the Western Pacific region and smallest in the Americas and European regions. In the UK the proportion of male smokers decreased from 51 per cent in 1974, to 28 per cent in 2002, whilst the decline for women has been slower (41 per cent to 26 per cent). It has been suggested that changing norms may make women and girls particularly vulnerable, with increased autonomy and role changes being associated with greater uptake and also through the exploitation of 'psychosocial aspirations' by the tobacco industry in product promotion (World Health Organization,

2003b). Men and women may smoke for different reasons, such as to control weight gain or as a buffer against negative feelings in women, or to enhance positive feelings in men (World Health Organization, 2003b). Interestingly, UK government antismoking campaigns have not been as successful in cutting the number of female smokers as male smokers, suggesting a gender difference in reaction to such initiatives (Brettingham, 2005).

Diet

Men are more likely to snack daily than women and to avoid breakfast, to be less flexible in their diet and less aware of role of dietary factors in health and disease (Reddy et al., 1992). In a UK study, men were found to consume fewer servings of fruit and vegetables per day than women and had less healthy food preferences than women (Baker & Wardle, 2003). There is some evidence that these preferences and behaviours are established in adolescence (Reynolds et al., 1999). Young women develop a greater interest in healthy diets and lower calorie foods and their nutritional knowledge is greater than men's. In a study of sex differences in diet in older adults, Baker and Wardle (2003) found that men's poor nutritional knowledge (about dietary recommendations and the links between diet and disease) was a more significant predictor of eating behaviour than attitudes and preferences. Women are more likely to take responsibility for family food shopping than men and are exposed to more health information. Health promotion strategies need to target nutritional knowledge in men.

There are also gender differences in weight and obesity (Dasgupta et al., 2007). While, in general, women are more aware of healthy eating, they are also encouraged by female gender stereotypes to be thin and concerned with physical appearance, which can result in body image dissatisfaction, eating disorders and an increase in cosmetic surgery in many Western cultures. Men are more likely to be overweight than women, but these differences vary considerably depending on social and ethnic background. For example in the USA, white and Mexican Americans have a higher prevalence of men classed as 'overweight' than women, while black American women are more likely to be classed as overweight. This finding is also the case in the UK where black women have a higher risk of obesity independent of socioeconomic status (Evans et al., 2001). Wardle et al. (2002) found that risk of obesity was greater among both men and women with fewer years of education and lower socioeconomic status. However, for occupational status there was a gender differences in that higher occupational status reduced risk for women but not for men. The association between education and obesity again suggests that a focus on improving educational opportunities for both sexes, as well as health promotion initiatives, possibly targeting lower socioeconomic groups, might increase nutritional knowledge and activity levels.

Exercise

One of the few health-related behaviours that men engage in more than women is exercise; women are generally less physically active than men (Dasgupta et al., 2007; Lee & Russell, 2003). For men, physical activity is arguably concordant with masculine gender stereotypes, which promote physical prowess and strength. It has been noted that women still spend more time on household tasks, having less leisure time than men (Hunter & Orth-Gomer, 2003) and that women with children, in particular, are less likely to participate in formal exercise activity (Bergman et al., 2003). Physical activity is associated with physical and emotional well-being and there is evidence that, for older women, maintaining or adopting moderate physical exercise is beneficial, whereas reducing the amount of exercise taken is associated with negative changes in emotional well-being (Lee & Russell, 2003). Health promotion interventions suggest that starting moderate levels of exercise during mid-life can be beneficial to both men and women. For example, an 'exercise on prescription' brief primary care intervention (nurse counselling based on motivational interviewing with telephone follow-up) for women aged 40–74 led to significant increases in physical activity and improved quality of life (Lawton et al., 2008). In a recent study, 50-year-old men who had increased their physical activity during mid-life benefited from a reduction in mortality similar to that of men who had exercised consistently during their lives (Byberg et al., 2009).

Risk-Taking Behaviour

Men have a general tendency to engage in riskier activities than women (Reddy *et al.*, 1992). Masculinity is associated with risk-taking behaviour, acceptance of risk and disregard for pain and injury. Almost three times as many males as females die from road traffic injuries globally (World Health Organization, 2002), partly because more men drive than women but also as a result of high-risk behaviour patterns when driving (World Health Organization, 2002). Alcohol use, combined with risky behaviour, contributes to the higher rate of fatality and injury and it has been found that men are more likely than women to be driving or walking under the influence of alcohol (World Health Organization, 2002). However, for women, their smaller stature appears to place them at increased risk of bodily injuries from a similar crash force (World Health Organization, 2002).

'Ideals of masculinity associated with risk taking and sexual conquest' increase men's vulnerability to HIV and other sexually transmitted infections (Jewkes *et al.*, 2003). In almost all cultures, masculinity is associated with virility and sexual potency (World Health Organization, 2003c). Women, in turn, can be made vulnerable by social norms defining acceptable behaviour and economic dependence and are more likely to have risky sexual practices imposed on them (Dunkle et al, 2004; Logan *et al.*, 2002). Risky sexual practices increase exposure to sexually transmitted infections (STIs) and HIV, and sexual violence leads to increased risk of HIV, through rape and through fear of violence if attempts are made to negotiate safe sexual practices. Minority females are disproportionately affected by HIV, with higher rates among African American and Hispanic females (Logan *et al.*, 2002). It has been suggested that African American men may conform to more traditional gender roles (Logan *et al.*, 2002). Women who have lower levels of education and socio-economic status, married to older partners and in relationships with a gender power imbalance, may be at increased risk of STIs and HIV (Boer & Mashamba, 2007; Dunkle *et al.*, 2004). The previously seen gap in HIV prevalence rates between men and women has narrowed, so that by the end of 2002, almost 50 per cent of adults living with HIV/AIDS globally were female and in Sub-Saharan Africa, 58 per cent of HIV positive adults are female (World Health Organization, 2003c).

Help Seeking

In the UK, women are twice as likely as men to consult doctors and the difference is greater for socially disadvantaged groups (Kapur *et al.*, 2004). Men tend to make less use of general health checks and screening than women (Thorogood *et al.*, 1993) and often seek help for symptoms late in an illness episode, sometimes with fatal results (Dearnaly, 1994). For men, the perception of symptoms as a threat to masculinity may delay help seeking (Gascoigne *et al.*, 1999; Tudiver & Talbot, 1999), while women may be more willing to accept they have health problems and to disclose and seek help for them than men.

Men are less likely to restrict activity or stay in bed when unwell, to practise self-examination and to participate in health screening (Courtenay, 2000). There are strong social pressures for men to struggle on when ill and to deny symptoms. Illness is often seen as sign of weakness and this has been cited as a reason for delay in self-referral (Gascoigne *et al.*, 1999). There is some evidence that the gender of the health provider can make a difference. For example, Henderson and Weisman (2001) found that men were more likely to discuss sensitive topics with female doctors. Men who score highly on tests of traditional masculinity have been found to have greater difficulty in expressing emotions. This tendency in some men might inhibit opportunities for social support, which in turn can impact on immune functioning (see Pennebaker, 1997). Similarly, social support provided by women has been found to reduce blood pressure and heart rate for men and women, whereas support provided by men had little impact on their partners (Glynn *et al.*, 1999). Thus men appear to gain from partner's support and might therefore have less need to seek help from services. Conversely women tend to seek support from a wider network of friends and family (Hann *et al.*, 2002). Although married men may avoid seeking help, they may still attend earlier than unmarried men, who may not be encouraged by partners. This might explain why married men have higher survival rates than single men for many cancers

(Kravdal, 2001). Attitudes are likely to vary considerably between different age cohorts; for example different life experiences and expectations might enable younger men to resist social pressures to struggle on when ill or to view illness as a sign of weakness, or to deny symptoms that might reflect negatively on their masculine image (Connell, 1995; Goldscheier, 1990).

Conclusions

Many sex differences, for example in heart disease and in longevity, are believed to be biologically determined. This brief overview of gender, health and illness provides numerous examples of the importance of psychosocial and cultural influences on health, particularly health-related behaviours and therefore offers opportunities for the development of health psychology interventions. These behaviours are strongly influenced by sociocultural norms of male and female gendered behaviour, which have powerful impacts on both men's and women's health. For example, men are more likely to adopt behaviours which are detrimental to their health and women may be damaged by the actions of male partners who are following the scripts of masculinity (Doyal, 2001). Multidisciplinary research might usefully explore how these social expectations are negotiated and challenged in different communities. Socioeconomic status and ethnicity have been found to interact with gender in a number of studies. Gender-specific and culturally appropriate health promotion and disease prevention interventions are needed. Too many campaigns are addressed to women reinforcing the notion that they are responsible for the health and well-being of others. Recognising gender inequalities in research in health psychology is crucial when designing health promotional strategies. If gender differences are ignored, the effectiveness of the interventions may be adversely affected and existing gender biases in health research, policy and services are likely to be reinforced.

Discussion Points

1   What are the main gender differences in health?
2   'Women get sick and men die' (Nathanson, 1997). Discuss this paradox.
3   List the range of biological, psychological and social factors that might influence gender differences in health.
4   Consider the social and cultural factors that impact on health and life expectancy worldwide. What might diminish gender differences in health in developing countries?
5   Describe the male and female gender stereotyped beliefs that might influence help-seeking behaviour.
6   Should health promotion interventions be gender specific in order to maximise behaviour change? Discuss with examples from health psychology research.

Further Reading

Baker, A.H. & Wardle, J. (2003). Sex differences in fruit and vegetable intake in older adults. *Appetite, 40*, 269–275.

Bird, C. & Rieker, P. (2008). *Gender and health. The effects of constrained choices and social policies.* New York: Cambridge University Press.

Boer, H. & Mashamba, M.T. (2007). Gender power imbalance and differential psychosocial correlates of intended condom use among male and female adolescents from Venda, South Africa. *British Journal of Health Psychology, 12*, 51–63.

Courtenay, W.H. (2000). Constructions of masculinity and their influence on men's well-being: a theory of gender and health. *Social Science & Medicine, 50*, 1385–1401.

Courtenay, W.H., McCreary, D.R. & Merighi, J.R. (2002). Gender and ethnic differences in health beliefs and behaviours. *Journal of Health Psychology, 7*, 219–231.

Craft, N. (1997). Women's health: women's health is a global issue. *British Medical Journal, 315*, 1154–1157.

Gijsbers van Wijk, C.M.T. & Kolk, A.M. (1997). Sex differences in physical symptoms: the contribution of symptom perception theory. *Social Science & Medicine, 45*, 231–246.

Lee, C. & Owens, R.G. (2002). *The psychology of men's health.* Buckingham: Open University Press.

References

Aalto, A-M., Heijmans, M., Weinman, J. & Aro, A.R. (2005). Illness perceptions in coronary heart disease: sociodemographic, illness-related and psychosocial correlates. *Journal of Psychosomatic Research, 58,* 393–402.

Arber, S. & Cooper, H. (1999). Gender differences in health in later life: the new paradox. *Social Science & Medicine, 48,* 61–76.

Baker, A.H. & Wardle, J. (2003). Sex differences in fruit and vegetable intake in older adults. *Appetite, 40,* 269–275.

Bergman, B., Ahmad, F. & Stewart, D.E. (2003). Physician health, stress and gender at a university hospital. *Journal of Psychosomatic Research, 54,* 171–178.

Bird, C. & Rieker, P. (2008). *Gender and health. The effects of constrained choices and social policies.* New York: Cambridge University Press.

Boer, H. & Mashamba, M.T. (2007). Gender power imbalance and differential psychosocial correlates of intended condom use among male and female adolescents from Venda, South Africa. *British Journal of Health Psychology, 12,* 51–63.

Brettingham, M. (2005). Men's life expectancy is catching up with women's. *British Medical Journal, 331,* 656.

Byberg, L., Melhus, H., Gedeorg, R., Dundstrom, J., Ahlbom, A., Zethelius, B. *et al.* (2009). Total mortality after changes in leisure time physical activity in 50 year old men: 35 year follow-up of population based cohort. *British Medical Journal, 338,* b688.

Coker, L.H. & Shumaker, S.A. (2003). Type 2 diabetes mellitus and cognition: an understudied issue in women's health. *Journal of Psychosomatic Research, 54,* 129–139.

Connell, R.W. (1995). *Masculinities.* Sydney: Allen & Unwin.

Courtenay, W.H. (2000). Constructions of masculinity and their influence on men's well-being: a theory of gender and health. *Social Science & Medicine, 50,* 1385–1401.

Courtenay, W.H., McCreary, D.R. & Merighi, J.R. (2002). Gender and ethnic differences in health beliefs and behaviours. *Journal of Health Psychology, 7,* 219–231.

Craft, N. (1997a). Women's health: life span: conception to adolescence. *British Medical Journal, 315,* 1227–1230.

Craft, N. (1997b). Women's health: women's health is a global issue. *British Medical Journal, 315,* 1154–1157.

Dasgupta, K., Kirkland, S., Rabi, D. & Takalakis, K. (2007). Cardiovascular risk factors in women and men. *Canadian Medical Association Journal, 176,* S12–S21.

Davey, B., Halliday, T. & Hirst, M. (2001). *Human biology and health: An evolutionary approach.* Milton Keynes: Open University Press.

Dearnaly, D.P. (1994). Current issues in cancer: Cancer of the prostate. *British Medical Journal, 308,* 780–784.

Doll, R. & Peto, R. (1981). The causes of cancer: quantitative estimates of avoidable risks of cancer in the United States today. *Journal National Cancer Institute, 66,* 1191–1308.

Doyal, L. (2001) Sex, gender and health: the need for a new approach. *British Medical Journal, 323,* 1061–1063.

Dunkle, K.L., Jewkes, R.K., Brown, H.C., Gray, G.E., McIntyre, J.A. & Harlow, S.D. (2004). Gender-based violence, relationship power and risk of HIV infection in women attending antenatal clinics in South Africa. *Lancet, 363,* 1415–1421.

Edwards, R., Haythornthwaite, J., Sullivan, M. & Fillingim, R. (2005). Catastrophizing as a mediator of sex differences in pain: differential effects for daily pain versus laboratory-induced pain. *Pain, 111,* 335–341.

Evans, P., Primatesta, P. & Prior, P. (2001). *Health Survey for England '99. The health of minority ethnic groups.* London: HMSO.

Gascoigne, P., Mason, M.D. & Roberts, E. (1999). Factors affecting presentation and delay in patients with testicular cancer. *Psycho-Oncology, 8,* 144–154.

Gijsbers van Wijk, C.M.T., Huisman, H. & Kolk, A.M. (1999). Gender differences in physical symptoms and illness behaviour. *Social Science & Medicine, 49,* 1061–1074.

Gijsbers van Wijk, C.M.T. & Kolk, A.M. (1996). Psychometric evaluation of symptom perception related measures. *Personality and Individual Differences, 20,* 55–70.

Gijsbers van Wijk, C.M.T. & Kolk, A.M. (1997). Sex differences in physical symptoms: the contribution of symptom perception theory. *Social Science & Medicine, 45,* 231–246.

Gijsbers van Wijk, C.M.T., Kolk, A.M., van den Bosch, W.J.H.M. & van den Hoogen, H.J.M. (1995). Male and female health problems in general practice: the differential impact of social position and social roles. *Social Science & Medicine, 40,* 597–611.

Glynn, L., Christenfield, N. & Gerin W. (1999). Gender and social support and cardiovascular responses to stress. *Psychosomatic Medicine, 6,* 234–242.

Goldscheier, F.K. (1990). The aging of the gender revolution: what do we know and what do we need to know? *Research on Aging, 12,* 531–545.

Grace, S.L., Krepostman, S., Brooks, D., Arthur, H., Scholey, P., Suskin, N. *et al.* (2005). Illness perceptions among cardiac patients: relation to depressive symptomatology and sex. *Journal of Psychosomatic Research, 59,* 153–160.

Grodstein, F., Manson, J.E. & Stampfer, M.J. (2001). Postmenopausal hormone use and secondary prevention of coronary events in the nurses' health study: a prospective, observational study. *Annals of Internal Medicine, 135,* 1–8.

Hann, D., Baker, F., Dennison, M., Gesme, D., Redign, D., Flynn, T. *et al.* (2002). The influence of social support on depressive symptoms in cancer patients: age and gender differences. *Journal of Psychosomatic Research, 52*, 279–283.

Henderson, J.T. & Weisman, C.S. (2001). Physician gender effects on preventive screening and counseling: an analysis of male and female patients' health care experiences. *Medical Care, 39*, 1281–1292.

Holmila, M. & Raitsalo, K. (2005). Gender differences in drinking: why do they still exist? *Addiction, 1000*, 1763–1769.

Hunter, M.S. & O'Dea, I. (1997). Menopause: bodily changes and multiple meanings. In J.M. Ussher (Ed.) *Body talk* (pp. 199–222). London: Routledge.

Hunter, M.S. & Orth-Gomer, K. (2003). Women's health. *Journal of Psychosomatic Research, 54*, 99–101.

Hurley, R.W. & Adams, M.C.B. (2008). Sex, gender and pain: an overview of a complex field. *Anesthesia & Analgesia, 107*, 309–317.

Jenkins, R. (1985). Sex differences in minor psychiatric morbidity. *Psychological Medicine Monograph, 7*, 1–53.

Jewkes, R.K., Levin, J.B. & Penn-Kekana, L.A. (2003). Gender inequalities, intimate partner violence and HIV preventive practices: findings of a South African cross-sectional study. *Social Science & Medicine, 56*, 125–134.

Johnston, M. & Dixon, D. (2008). Current issues and new directions in psychology and health: What happened to behaviour in the decade of behaviour. *Psychology & Health, 23*, 509–513.

Jones, A. & Zachariae, R. (2004). Investigation of the interactive effects of gender and psychological factors on pain response. *British Journal of Health Psychology, 9*, 405–418.

Kapur, N., Hunt, I., Lunt, M., McBeth, J., Creed, F. & Macfarlane, G. (2004). Psychosocial and illness related predictors of consultation rates in primary care: a cohort study. *Psychological Medicine, 34*, 719–728.

Kinsella, K. & Gist, Y.J. (1998). *Gender and Aging*. US Census Bureau, Official Statistics, IB/98-2, 1–7.

Kmietowicz, Z. (2009). Screening has halved incidence of cervical cancer in UK. *British Medical Journal, 338*, b807.

Kolk A.M.M., Hanewald, G.J.F.P., Schagen, S. & Gijsbers van Wijk, C.M.T. (2002). Predicting medically unexplained physical symptoms and health care utilization. A symptom-perception approach. *Journal of Psychosomatic Research, 52*, 35–44.

Kolk, A.M., Hanewald, G.J.F.P., Schagen, S. & Gijsbers van Wijk, C.M.T. (2003). A symptom perception approach to common physical symptoms. *Social Science & Medicine, 57*, 2343–2354.

Kravdal, O. (2001). The impact of marital status on cancer survival. *Social Science & Medicine, 52*, 357–368.

Lawlor, D.A., Ebrahim. S. & Smith. G.D. (2002). Role of endogenous oestrogen in aetiology of coronary heart disease: analysis of age related trends in coronary heart disease and breast cancer in England and Wales and Japan. *British Medical Journal, 325,* 311–312.

Lawton, B.A., Rose, S.B., Elley, C.R., Dowell, A.C., Fenton, A. & Moyes S.A. (2008). Exercise on prescription for women aged 40–74 recruited through primary care: two year randomised controlled trial. *British Medical Journal, 337,* a2509.

Lee, C. & Owens, R.G. (2002). *The psychology of men's health.* Buckingham: Open University Press.

Lee, C. & Russell, A. (2003). Effects of physical activity on emotional well-being among older Australian women: cross-sectional and longitudinal analyses. *Journal of Psychosomatic Research, 54,* 155–160.

Logan, T.K., Cole, J. & Leukefeld, C. (2002). Women, sex and HIV: social and contextual factors, meta-analysis of published interventions and implications for practice and research. *Psychological Bulletin, 128*, 851–885.

Macintyre, S. (1993). Gender differences in the perception of common cold symptoms. *Social Science & Medicine, 36*, 15–20.

Macintyre, S., Hunt, K. & Sweeting, H. (1996). Gender differences in health: are things really as simple as they seem? *Social Science & Medicine, 42*, 617–624.

Malson, H. (1997). Anorexic bodies and the discursive production of feminine excess. In J.M. Ussher (Ed.) *Body talk* (pp. 223–245). London: Routledge.

Matthew, R.A. & Stoney, C.M. (1988). Influence of sex and age on cardiovascular responses during stress. *Psychosomatic Medicine, 50*, 46–56.

McGill, H. & Stern, M. (1979). Sex and atherosclerosis. *Atherosclerosis Review, 4*, 157–248.

Murphy, S. & Bennett, P. (2005). Lifespan and gender. Cross-cultural perspectives in health psychology. In S. Sutton, A. Baum & M. Johnston (Eds.) *Health psychology* (pp. 241–269). London: Sage.

Nathanson, C.A. (1977). Sex, illness and medical care. A review of data, theory and method. *Social Science & Medicine, 11*, 13–25.

Nazroo, J.Y., Edwards, A.C. & Brown, G.W. (1997). Gender differences in the onset of depression following a shared life event: a study of couples. *Psychosomatic Medicine, 27*, 9–19.

O'Dea, I., Hunter, M.S. & Anjou, S. (1999). Life satisfaction and health-related quality of life (SF-36) of middle-aged men and women. *Climacteric, 2*, 131–140.

Ostlin P., Eckermann, E., Mishra, U.S., Nkowane, M. & Wallstam, E. (2007). Gender and health promotion: A multisectorial approach. *Health Promotion International, 21*, 25–35.

Parkin, D.M. (2009). Is the recent fall in incidence of post-menopausal breast cancer in UK related to changes in use of hormone replacement therapy? *European Journal of Cancer*, doi:10.1016/j.ejca.2009.01.016.

Pennebaker, J.W. (1997). *Opening up: The healing power of expressing emotions*. New York: Guilford Press.

Piccinelli, M. & Simon, G. (1997). Gender and cross-cultural differences in somatic symptoms associated with emotional distress. An international study in primary care. *Psychological Medicine, 27*, 433–444.

Piccinelli, M. & Wilkinson, G. (2000). Gender differences in depression: critical review. *British Journal of Psychiatry, 1777*, 468–492.

Pinn, V.W. (2007). Sex and gender factors in medical studies. Implications for health and clinical practice. *Journal of the American Medical Association, 289*, 397–400.

Rabi, D. & Cox, J. (2007). Burden of cardiovascular disease in women and men. *Canadian Medical Association Journal, 176*, S1–S4.

Reddy, D.M., Fleming, R. & Adesso, V.J. (1992). Gender and health. In S. Maes, H. Leventhal & M. Johnston (Eds.) *International review of health psychology* (pp. 3–33). Chichester: Wiley.

Reynolds, K.D., Baranowski, T., Bishop, D.B., Farris, R.P., Binkley, D., Nicklas, T.A. & Elmer, P.J. (1999). Patterns in child and adolescent consumption of fruit and vegetables: effects of gender and ethnicity across four sites. *Journal of American College of Nutrition, 18*, 248–254.

Smith, D.V, Bartley, M. & Blane, D. (1990). The Black Report on socioeconomic inequalities in health 10 years on. *British Medical Journal, 301*, 18–25.

Stoppard, J.M. (1997). Women's bodies, women's lives and depression: towards a reconciliation of material and discursive accounts. In J.M. Ussher (Ed.) *Body talk* (pp. 10–32). London: Routledge.

Thorogood, M., Coulter, A., Jones, L., Yudkin, P., Muir, J. & Mant, D. (1993). Factors affecting response to an invitation to attend general health check. *Journal of Epidemiology & Community Health, 47*, 224–228.

Tremblay, J., Petrovich, M. & Hamet, P. (2007). Genetic and sex determinants of hypertension and CVD. *Canadian Medical Association Journal, 176*, S23–S26.

Tudiver, F. & Talbot, Y. (1991). Why don't men seek help? Family physicians' perspectives on help-seeking behavior in men. *Journal of Family Practice, 48*, 472.

Ussher, J.M. (1997). *Fantasies of femininity: Reframing the boundaries of sex*. New Brunswick: Rutgers University Press.

Waldron, I. (1986). The contribution of smoking to sex differences in mortality. *Public Health Reports, 101*, 163–173.

Wardle, J., Waller, J. & Jarvis, M.J.J. (2002). Sex differences in the association of socioeconomic status with obesity. *American Journal of Public Health, 92*, 1299–1304.

Watson, D. & Pennebaker, J.W. (1989). Health complaints, stress and distress: exploring the central role of negative affectivity. *Psychological Review, 26*, 641–646.

Wenger, N.K. (2004). You've come a long way baby: cardiovascular health and disease in women, problems and prospects. *Circulation, 109*, 558–560.

White, J., Hunter, M.S. & Holltum., S. (2007). How do women experience myocardial infarction? A qualitative exploration of illness perceptions, adjustment and coping. *Psychology, Health & Medicine, 12*, 278–288.

World Health Organization (2002). *Gender and road traffic injuries*. Geneva: World Health Organization.

World Health Organization (2003a). *Gender, health and ageing*. Geneva: World Health Organization.

World Health Organization (2003b). *Gender, health and tobacco*. Geneva: World Health Organization.

World Health Organization (2003c). *Gender and HIV/AIDS*. Geneva: World Health Organization.

World Health Organization (2004). *Gender, health and work*. Geneva: World Health Organization.

Zakowski, S.G., Harris, C., Krueger, N., Laubmeier, K.K., Garrett, S., Flanigan, R. & Johnson, P. (2003). Social barriers to emotional expression and their relations to distress in male and female cancer patients. *British Journal of Health Psychology, 8*, 271–286.

29

Developmental and Family Factors

Emily Arden-Close and Christine Eiser

Chapter Outline

This chapter will provide an overview of two major topics. The first section will focus on children's perceptions and experience of illness in themselves and their families. It will review evidence from studies examining the psychological impact of illness as well as those which have evaluated interventions to improve outcome. The second section focuses on the role of the family in illness. This covers ways in which couples cope with illness and the impact of support provided. This section also examines the impact on the family of a child's illness and the role of interventions in facilitating coping and outcomes.

Key Concepts

Developmental theory
Dyadic coping
Protective buffering
Resiliency

Children's Perceptions of Illness

There are a number of situations in which it is important to understand children's views about health and illness. The first is when children themselves are ill. Approximately 12–15 per cent of children experience chronic or life-threatening conditions such as cancer, cystic fibrosis or diabetes. Children must accept the restrictions associated with the disease and some responsibility for managing their own treatment. Any involvement of children in their own care requires them to have some knowledge of the condition and awareness of the implications of non-adherence to treatment. The challenge is to impart the information at an appropriate time and in an age-appropriate manner.

Second, new health technologies mean that it is increasingly possible to identify children at risk of inherited conditions, many of which are severe and not treatable. The potential benefits of early screening need to take into account the value of early diagnosis and treatment as well as the child's ability to understand the implications for future health. Involving children in health-care decisions of this kind requires considerable sensitivity and again, ability to put information in a way that children understand.

The third situation is when a child's parent or sibling is ill. In these cases, healthy children can feel neglected by parents and harbour concerns about the nature of the illness (is it contagious?) and their personal responsibility (did I do something wrong?). Here also, children need an explanation about the nature of illness, its cause, timeline and implications.

Considerable attention has been directed to understanding how children's concerns change with age. A key assumption is that if it is possible to identify systematic changes associated with age, it should be possible to 'match' illness information to the child's needs. We therefore begin by considering the evidence regarding how children's understanding of illness changes with age or experience. This is followed by an account of how children's understanding of illness is important in the three situations described above. Finally we consider some of the implications of the work for interventions and their evaluation.

Developmental changes in children's understanding of illness

Early work tended to emphasise the 'cuteness' of children's thinking. Children may use creative language to describe pain (e.g. 'There's a demon in your belly' (Perrin & Gerrity, 1981) and 'elephants dancing on my head' (Harbeck & Peterson, 1992)).

Bibace and Walsh (1981) and Perrin and Gerrity (1981) utilised ideas from general developmental theory (Piaget & Inhelder, 1969) to describe three stages of thought characteristic of children's views about illness. In the *pre-operational* stage (2–7 years), explanations focus on magic or superstition. In the *concrete-operational* stage, children are able to distinguish between internal and external determinants of illness. This phase includes *contamination*, where children believe the cause of illness to be external to themselves but understand links between germs and possible effects on their body and *internalisation*. Children understand how the cause of illness can be internal (e.g. 'bad' cells multiply and overcome 'good' cells). By 11 years, children enter the *formal-operational* stage and accept physiological explanations of illness that increasingly accommodate scientific theory.

Several studies provided broad support for the above schema, describing how children's views of death, medical treatment (Steward & Steward, 1991) and AIDS follow the developmental sequence outlined above. For example, children's perceptions of vulnerability to AIDS decrease with age and cognitive development. Five year olds believe AIDS is contracted merely through proximity and 9 to 10 year olds think it is transmitted through casual contact (Osborne *et al.*, 1993).

During the 1980s and 1990s, these ideas formed the basis of most empirical research. However, a number of limitations became apparent, including the failure to specify how transitions between stages occurred and, importantly, to take into account how the child's experience affected development. Evidence began to emerge that children's illness experience could affect their understanding (Crisp *et al.*, 1996).

Furthermore, even very young children were shown to have much more sophisticated knowledge than previously thought (Carey, 1985; Hergenrather & Rabinowitz, 1991). Children's understanding of illness does not take place in isolation but reflects a much wider system of beliefs. Thus, we should not focus on the relatively narrow issue of how children understand illness, but on the wider context of real-life experience and growth in general biological knowledge.

This awareness that children are more able to understand issues surrounding cause and implications of illness coincided with other work showing they desired information about their own illness. Kendrick *et al.* (1986) showed how children with cancer who were not told about their illness tried to elicit information from whomever they could, including other children in the ward and on occasions, hospital cleaners.

When a child is ill

Between 10 and 30 per cent of children under 16 years experience a chronic disease (Newacheck & Taylor, 1992). These conditions frequently require children to assume responsibility for many aspects of their own care. For example, those with diabetes need to test their blood sugar and inject insulin. Given that one of the goals of medical care for chronic disease is to foster self-efficacy, considerable research has looked at children's knowledge of their disease and treatment (assuming that knowledgeable children will manage their illness and its treatment better). Most work suggests that children are insufficiently informed about their disease, to the detriment of self-care (Veldtman *et al.*, 2000).

Many interventions aim to reduce stress and improve well-being in children with chronic illness, or generally manage stress, including drawing (Rollins, 2005) and art therapies (Favara-Scacco *et al.*, 2001). Other interventions are directed at specific issues, such as managing treatment-related pain (hypnosis, Liossi & Hatira, 2003; music therapy, Barrera *et al.*, 2002). Although many interventions are well meaning, they are often poorly evaluated, or require specific expertise (e.g. music therapy) that is not widely available. Given the often disappointing results, there has been a call for more theoretically driven interventions (Hampson *et al.*, 2001). The social cognition models (Chapter 10, this volume) and models of illness cognition (Chapter 12, this volume) are good examples of the types of theoretical approach which can provide the basis for such interventions.

Information and communication technologies have opened up new possibilities in the field of health care (Suzuki & Beale 2006). For young people, internet services or chat rooms offer a relatively cheap method to increase symptom management self-efficacy. Also, mobile phone based symptom management systems can be useful in the remote monitoring of chemotherapy-related toxicity (Kearney *et al.*, 2006). Video games have been created for teenagers and young adults in order to increase self-efficacy and knowledge as well as adherence to treatment regimens (Kato, 2008).

Genetic testing

New health technologies have created a range of challenging new situations for children and their families. Genetic testing enables identification of risk of an inherited disorder in a healthy child. Where no medical intervention is available for those at risk, guidelines encourage decisions about testing to be left until the child is old enough to make an informed choice (Borry *et al.*, 2006). However, in practice most parents want to know their children's carrier status, sometimes before they reach the age of majority, leading to tensions with health-care professionals (Borry *et al.*, 2005).

Requests by parents for screening raise complex ethical issues, including distressing psychological consequences of a positive test result and the issue of the parent's right to know versus the child's personal autonomy. Testing children for untreatable adult-onset conditions can lead to parental anxiety about how and when to disclose carrier status to the child. Health professionals generally encourage disclosure of genetic predisposition occasionally and gradually over the years (Clarke & Gaffe, 2008).

Before testing for inherited genetic disorders, it is important to ensure the family understand the implications of a positive test result (Borry *et al.*, 2006). All three aspects of psychosocial maturity (responsibility, temperance and perspective) continue to develop during mid to late adolescence, stabilising after 19 years (Cauffman & Steinberg, 2000). Thus, even 18 year olds may lack sufficient maturity to make informed decisions regarding screening (Richards, 2006). Risk information is often given in terms of probabilities, such as, 'your risk of developing breast cancer later in life is 10 per cent', which may be difficult to understand.

What does research therefore tell us about how children understand about causes and prevention of disease or indeed genetics? Richards and Ponder (1996) emphasise the need to take a 'bottom-up' approach based on pre-existing understanding and focus on the conflicts between this and the scientific position, rather than the more traditional 'top-down' approach that begins with the scientific assumptions and attempts to provide a simplified account. This approach is also likely to be of value when explaining illness to newly diagnosed children.

When a parent or sibling is ill

Parents Approximately 5–15 per cent of children and adolescents have a parent diagnosed with a chronic disease (Worsham *et al.*, 1997). Chronic parental illness is a threat to daily routines as well as compromising parents' availability to their children (Hoke, 2001). Given that approximately 30 per cent of women with breast cancer have one or more school-aged or adolescent children living at home (Lewis *et al.*, 1993), most research has involved these women. The consequences of other parental illnesses, or implications of paternal rather than maternal illness, have not systematically been investigated.

Some general conclusions can be made regarding how children's age affects their responses to parental illness. Younger children are more likely to turn to the healthy parent, whereas adolescents are more likely to rely on friends for social and emotional support (Romer *et al.*, 2002). Younger children are also more likely to show their distress through behavioural problems, whereas adolescents are more likely to be anxious or depressed (Osborn, 2007).

There is in fact, considerable evidence that adolescents are particularly at risk for psychological distress (Compas *et al.*, 1996; Welch *et al.*, 1996), especially adolescent daughters (Compas *et al.*, 1994), among whom there is an increased incidence of post-traumatic stress disorder (PTSD: Huizinga *et al.*, 2005). Adolescent daughters of mothers with cancer report the highest levels of psychological symptoms (i.e. anxiety and depression) of all age groups (Compas *et al.*, 1996; Grant & Compas, 1995; Osborn, 2007). They are old enough to understand the possible implications of the disease and may resent the increased

demands placed on them (Hoke, 2001; Welch *et al.*, 1996). This is likely to be magnified in diseases where there is a significant hereditary component (e.g. some breast cancers). However, despite the difficulties faced by adolescents when a parent is ill, some report good social, academic and family adjustment. Family, friends and the school system are important in providing a sense of normality (Eiser, 1993).

Siblings Diagnosis of a chronic illness in a child can significantly impact on healthy siblings (Eiser, 1993). Changes in parental behaviour and care by a substitute caregiver are likely to distress younger children (Kleiber *et al.*, 1995), while older siblings often have to assume parental responsibilities (McMahon *et al.*, 2001), including housework and care of younger children.

Interrupted school attendance, lower achievement and problem behaviour have been identified (Eiser, 1993). Depression associated with fear about the sibling's health (Montgomery *et al.*, 2002), feelings of guilt, isolation and resentment or rivalry towards the ill child (Sparacino *et al.*, 1997) have also been noted. A meta-analysis of 50 studies (cancer: 10; diabetes: 6) concluded there was a detrimental effect on psychological functioning, peer activities and cognitive development, which was more pronounced for internalising behaviours (e.g. anxiety and depression) than externalising behaviours (e.g. behaviour problems and aggression) (Sharpe & Rossiter, 2002). Diseases such as cancer, diabetes and bowel disease, which require intensive treatment regimens that restrict school and play activities, had a greater impact on sibling function. Conditions requiring fewer lifestyle changes had less effect on psychological functioning among siblings.

A number of interventions have been developed to facilitate adjustment in children and adolescents with a chronically ill sibling or parent (Beardslee *et al.*, 1993). Such interventions are generally based on the hypothesis that children require developmentally appropriate knowledge. Targeted information about the illness or group discussions or activities soon after diagnosis may be useful to reduce stress in siblings of childhood cancer patients (Lähteenmäki, 2004).

Spath (2007) identified a number of methodological limitations with family-based interventions. Satisfaction with the intervention was often taken as a measure of effectiveness and very few studies utilised outcome measures with established reliability. Few studies reported a power calculation, many appear under-powered and levels of retention varied considerably (Houtzager *et al.*, 2001). Random assignment to intervention and control groups was often not achieved. Finally, as already discussed in relation to interventions for sick children, very few were based on theoretical models.

Conclusions

Improvements in treatment for many chronic and life-threatening conditions mean that children now live longer than in the past. However, although many achieve excellent quality of life, others have to accept significantly compromised 'normal' life. Helping children achieve a good quality of life in addition to increased longevity requires sensitive communication and empathy. When children themselves are ill, they need information to empower self-management of their illness and facilitate treatment-related decisions. When parents or siblings are ill, they need information to allay their fears and help them offer practical help wherever possible.

In medicine, there has been a significant move away from the idea that doctors should make decisions for patients. The emphasis is on shared decision making, so that patients are able to make decisions about their own care. This approach is also integral to care of children as adults. Current legislation emphasises that all individuals have a right to information about their illness and opportunities to make treatment-related decisions. Further, empirical work emphasises how far children are comfortable with this responsibility (Alderson & Montgomery, 1996).

In some situations, including when a parent or sibling is ill, there has been a tendency to rely on parents as informants about how their children are affected. This is partly practical; sometimes children are too young to answer for themselves and therefore parents are asked how they think their child is reacting. It is also more difficult to arrange for a child to provide the information, since they are unlikely to attend hospital and parents often want to 'protect' the child from potentially upsetting information. However, parents and children do not always agree about these issues and therefore information should be elicited from children whenever possible.

The Role of the Family in Health and Illness

The family plays a significant role in promoting positive attitudes and health behaviours among individual family members. This applies to all families in the promotion and maintenance of health behaviours related to smoking, drinking and eating a balanced diet (Padula & Sullivan, 2006). In addition, families play a critical role when an individual is diagnosed with a chronic or life-limiting illness. While the patient must live with the physical pain, the whole family experiences the emotional trauma and disturbances in their everyday lives. This section focuses first on the impact of chronic illness on couples and second on how the diagnosis of chronic illness in a child affects their parents. This complements the work described in the previous section concerning the impact of parent or sibling illness on children.

The impact of a chronic illness on the patient's family is dependent on the specific condition. Where illnesses involve significant daily management, (e.g. diabetes or coronary heart disease), the family is important in helping cope with the necessary lifestyle changes (Gallant, 2003). Illnesses that involve cognitive and communicative impairments (e.g. Alzheimer's disease, Parkinson's disease) pose a specific challenge. Families must watch the slow demise of the patient, knowing there is nothing that can be done, but constant vigilance is needed to ensure individual safety. Other illnesses can impact on sexual functioning, leading to marital strain and declines in intimacy and connectedness.

Impact of chronic illness on couples

In recent years, there has been a shift from an individualistic to a dyadic perspective on stress and coping, which focuses on how couples interact as they deal with stressors (Bodenmann, 2005). In this context, there are three ways of appraising stressful events: individual; indirect relational (where one member of the dyad experiences stress as a side effect of the other person's stress); and shared. The coping congruence approach holds that congruence in coping (both partners using the same coping strategy) is associated with less distress than incongruence. However, more recent evidence suggests that adjustment may depend on whether the dyad as a unit uses appropriate coping strategies, rather than whether the individuals use similar coping strategies (Badr, 2004; Ben-Zur et al., 2001). Alternative approaches where patient perceptions of partner involvement are assessed directly have also been suggested (e.g. Manne et al., 1999a). Patients adjust better when they perceive the partner is offering support and collaboration rather than control.

Berg and Upchurch (2007) proposed a developmental-contextual model of dyadic coping, which emphasises lifespan developmental and temporal processes. Dyadic coping is viewed as the first line of coping for couples dealing with stressful events. This changes across the adult lifespan and is influenced by sociocultural context (culture and gender), proximal context (marital quality, nature of the illness) and across adult development. Appraisals (regarding illness representations, illness ownership and specific stressful events) and coping change over time as the couple deal with stressors such as initial symptom identification, treatment and daily management. Dyadic coping can be viewed as a continuum involving the following stages: non-involvement of the partner (the person perceives he/she is coping individually); support (the partner provides emotional/instrumental support); collaboration (joint problem solving); and control (the partner dominates the actions of the other) (Berg et al., 1998).

Patient and partner distress   Partners experience many difficulties. Some are emotional: uncertainty about treatment outcome, helplessness and isolation (Coe & Kluka, 1988; Zahlis & Shands, 1991). Others are more practical: providing care and support (both practical and emotional) and changing role responsibilities (Zahlis & Shands, 1991), coping with the partner's emotional distress (Northouse, 1989) and obtaining information and support from medical professionals (Coe & Kluka, 1988). These stressors place the healthy partner at risk of psychological distress and physical disorders. Partners of cancer patients report greater mood disturbance than other relatives (Cassileth et al., 1985), particularly during the initial phases of treatment, as well as during recurrent and late stages (Blanchard et al., 1997).

Women experience more distress than men, regardless of whether they are patient or partner (Hagedoorn et al., 2008). Nevertheless, distress reactions in both partner and patient appear to be closely linked across all phases of the illness (Hagedoorn et al., 2008; Manne, 1998). Couples who are distressed at diagnosis often remain distressed over time (Northouse et al., 2000).

Implications of partner support   Partner support increases motivation to seek more aggressive treatment and may buffer management of the psychological stresses and physiological changes of disease progression. Certainly, emotional support and marital satisfaction are associated with better psychological adjustment to the illness (Giese-Davis et al., 2000). However, partners can show a variety of unsupportive responses to a diagnosis of a chronic illness, including excessive worry and pessimism, underestimating the severity of the illness, avoiding and withdrawing from the patient, criticising the patient's coping strategies, communicating disinterest in patient concerns and changing the topic when the patient is talking about the illness (Manne et al., 1997). Unsupportive responses may precipitate more psychological distress than supportive responses as they adversely affect coping strategies (Lepore et al., 2000). Unsupportive behaviour increases negative mood (Manne et al., 1999b) and decreases coping efficacy due to undermining feelings of control (Manne & Glassman, 2000).

One common coping strategy used by partners of patients with chronic illness is protective buffering (Manne et al., 1997), which includes hiding concerns, denying worries, concealing discouraging information and preventing the patient from thinking about their illness. This is commonly used when caring for patients with reduced life expectancy and older patients, due to their greater functional needs (Kuijer et al., 2000) and used more by women with ill partners than men (Coyne & Smith 1991). Protective buffering has been associated with more distress in male survivors of myocardial infarction (Coyne & Smith 1991) and is associated with lower marital quality, particularly in patients experiencing high levels of psychological distress and those with high levels of physical impairment (Hagedoorn et al., 2000).

Recent evidence from qualitative studies suggests that viewing the illness as a couple-related stressor is an important determinant of marital quality (Kayser et al., 2007; Skerrett, 1998). A recent study demonstrated that more 'we talk' by the spouse predicted reductions in symptoms and general health improvements among patients with heart failure (Rohrbaugh et al., 2008). Open communication between couples is important to promote a united outlook and enhance manageability. More constructive communication (discussion of issues, expression of feelings) has been associated with lower levels of distress and higher relationship satisfaction in breast cancer patients at nine months follow-up (Manne et al., 2006).

Interventions   Couple-focused interventions appear to be more effective than interventions for patients alone (Martire, 2005) and have also been associated with reduced depressive symptoms in partners (Martire et al., 2004). Interventions that focus on relationship issues reduce depressive symptoms in patients, possibly through helping the partner to be more supportive and less critical (Martire et al., 2004). Similarly, a couple-focused group intervention for women with breast cancer and their partners was most beneficial for women who initially perceived their partners as unsupportive (Manne et al., 2005).

Impact of a child's diagnosis on parents

Diagnosis of a chronic disease or health condition in children can have a significant impact on family functioning. Parents experience a number of stressors including altered parenting roles, separations from the child, adjustment to the medical system and general uncertainty regarding the child's prognosis (Brown et al., 2008; Hughes & McCollum, 1994). Often the mother is identified as the primary caregiver, with responsibility for making and keeping health-care appointments and administering medications, in addition to household chores and caring for the family (Steele et al., 2003). This burden of care remains relatively stable throughout the illness and may have significant physiological effects, leading to health problems in the caregiver (Epel et al., 2004). Chronic illness in the family can also cause a significant financial burden, with families typically reporting deterioration in finances or job loss as a result of the child's illness (Eiser & Upton, 2007; Montgomery et al., 2002).

Adjustment and distress experienced   Diagnosis of childhood illness requires adaptation to a new way of life (Jerrett & Costello, 1996), which can affect parents

both physically (need to perform time-consuming therapies) and psychologically (changing lifestyle). With time, most families regain a sense of control through managing their time, the illness and information and gaining awareness of their daily environment (Gravelle, 1997). However, this is fragile and heightened uncertainty can easily be triggered by routine medical appointments, minor symptoms, changes in the child's therapeutic regimen and evidence of negative outcomes for other siblings (Cohen, 1995).

Increased levels of depression and anxiety are often reported at diagnosis (Barrera et al., 2004). Particularly high levels of distress have been reported in mothers of children with cancer, compared to both fathers of children with cancer (Sloper, 2000) and mothers of children with acute illnesses (Barrera et al., 2004). Parents of children with cancer are at risk for increased post-traumatic stress symptoms (Kazak et al., 2004; Manne et al., 2002), which have been related to long-term adjustment difficulties (Kazak & Barakat, 1997). In addition, parents' adaptation can have a significant impact on the health of both the ill child (Johnston & Marder, 1994) and any siblings (Cohen et al., 1995). Although levels of distress decline over the first year following diagnosis (Grootenhuis & Last, 1997; Steele et al., 2003), heightened distress can persist until 18 months post-diagnosis (Manne et al., 2004). Family adjustment at diagnosis is a significant predictor of long-term adaptation (Best et al., 2002).

Despite the obvious problems facing families with a child with serious illness, positive effects including re-evaluation of goals, increased closeness within the family and stronger marital relationships can also occur (Grootenhuis & Last, 1997). Factors that may contribute to a positive outcome include social support, open and frequent communication about disease, maintaining hope and being optimistic.

In an attempt to integrate the various factors identified as contributing to family adjustment, Varni and Wallander (1988) proposed that maternal adjustment was predicted by intrapersonal factors (severity of disease, functional independence and child temperament); interpersonal factors (mother temperament and coping style) and socioecological factors (marital and family functioning, socioeconomic status, service utilisation). Families with a chronically ill child are exposed to increased numbers of stressful situations and adjustment is dependent on successful management of these stressful situations. The model is one of the first to take a coping perspective rather than emphasise the difficulties families experience and emphasises that interventions need to focus on promoting active coping.

The resiliency model of family stress, adjustment and adaptation (McCubbin & McCubbin, 1996) assumes that: (i) stress is a predictable aspect of family life; (ii) families develop strengths and competences to protect them and facilitate recovery from expected and unexpected events; (iii) families benefit from a network of relationships in the community, especially during crises; (iv) families search for an outlook on life that will give them a shared purpose to move forward; (v) when faced with stressors, families seek to restore order. Dealing with a stressor involves two phases. First, in the adjustment phase, the family relies on established patterns of functioning with only minor changes. If this is insufficient to adjust to the situation, the family is considered to be in crisis. In the adaptation stage, accumulation of demands created by the stressful event from all areas of work and family life increase the family's vulnerability. Resiliency factors include newly established patterns of family functioning, social support and engaging in new coping and problem-solving strategies. The eventual outcome is defined as one in which individual members are functioning well and the family has a sense of harmony in carrying out tasks and relationships with the community. This is a dynamic state, however, as another stressor can create a new crisis. This theory is useful in suggesting differences in family adaptation to stressors and has been used to identify six resiliency factors in parents of children with cancer (McCubbin et al., 2002). These include: the ability of the family to mobilise quickly at the time of diagnosis; support from the health-care team; extended family; community; workplace; and changes in family appraisal.

Interventions Interventions have mostly focused on mothers of children with cancer. For example, Kazak et al. (2005) conducted a pilot randomised controlled trial to understand how beliefs about cancer and its treatment influence caregivers and help family members anticipate the impact of cancer on the family over time. This was effective in reducing state anxiety in primary caregivers and decreasing post-traumatic stress symptoms in both primary and secondary caregivers, relative to controls. Methodological limitations parallel those identified earlier.

Conclusions

This section has reviewed research to date on the role of the family in health and illness, with a focus on health promotion, the impact of chronic illness on couples and the impact of a child's illness on their parents. Most work to date has been descriptive and has facilitated identification of correlates of familial distress. The recent move to a dyadic coping perspective has enhanced this work, enabling understanding of the ways in which coping strategies complement each other. Patients benefit most from support and collaborative engagement in their care. Having a family member diagnosed with a chronic illness is a traumatic experience, although positive outcomes have also been identified.

Further research needs to identify correlates of distress in parents of children with chronic illness and to determine how levels of distress vary across the lifespan. The design and evaluation of theory-based interventions is also essential, in order to identify the processes underlying successful methods. Finally, much of this work has considerable implications for practice, but sadly often remains 'hidden' in academic journals. Wider dissemination to include government and health service initiatives is vital.

Discussion Points

1 How far does children's understanding of illness depend on (i) their age or (ii) illness experience?
2 Who should decide whether or not young children should be tested for inherited genetic disorders?

3 Why do women experience more distress than men when one partner is diagnosed with a chronic illness?
4 What type of psychological interventions may be most effective for (i) children with a chronic

illness; (ii) couples where one partner has a chronic illness; (iii) parents of children with a chronic illness?

5 How might theoretical models inform the development of interventions to improve quality of life in (i) children or (ii) adults with diabetes?

Further Reading

Berg, C.A. & Upchurch, R. (2007). A developmental-contextual model of couples coping with chronic illness across the adult life span. *Psychological Bulletin, 133,* 920–954.
Cauffman E. & Steinberg, L. (2000). (Im)maturity of judgment in adolescence: Why adolescents may be less culpable than adults. *Behavioral Sciences & the Law, 18,* 741–760.
Clarke, A.J. & Gaffe, C. (2008) Challenges in the genetic testing of children for familial cancers. *Archives of Disease in Childhood, 93,* 911–914.
Eiser, C. (1993). *Growing up with a chronic disease: The impact on children and their families.* London: Jessica Kingsley.
Kazak, A.E., Simms, S., Alderfer, M.A., Rourke, M.T., Crump, T., McClure, K. *et al.* (2005). Feasibility and preliminary outcomes from a pilot study of a brief psychological

intervention for families of children newly diagnosed with cancer. *Journal of Pediatric Psychology, 30,* 644–655.
Rohrbaugh, M.J., Mehl, M.R., Shoham, V., Reilly, E.S. & Ewy, G.A. (2008). Prognostic significance of spouse we talk in couples coping with heart failure. *Journal of Consulting and Clinical Psychology, 76,* 781–789.
Varni, J.W. & Wallander, J.L. (1988) Pediatric chronic disabilities: Hemophilia and spina bifida as examples. In D. Routh (Ed.) *Handbook of pediatric psychology* (pp. 190–221). New York, Guilford Press.
Worsham, N., Compas, B. & Ey, S. (1997). Children's coping with parental illness. In S. Wolichik & I. Sandler (Eds.) *Handbook of children's coping: Linking theory and intervention* (pp. 195–213). New York: Plenum Press.

References

Alderson P. & Montgomery, J. (1996). What about me? *Health Service Journal,* 11 April, 22–24.
Badr, H. (2004). Coping in marital dyads: A contextual perspective on the role of gender and health. *Personal Relationships, 11,* 197–211.
Barrera, M., D'Agostino, N.M., Gibson, J., Gilbert, T., Weksberg, R. & Malkin, D. (2004). Predictors and mediators of psychological adjustment in mothers of children newly diagnosed with cancer. *Psycho-Oncology, 13,* 620–641.
Barrera M.E., Rykov, M.H. & Doyle, S.L. (2002). The effects of interactive music therapy on hospitalized children with cancer: A pilot study. *Psycho-Oncology, 11,* 379–388.
Beardslee, W.R., Salt, P., Porterfield, K., Rothberg, P.C., Van De Velde, P., Swatling, S. *et al.* (1993). Comparison of preventive interventions for families with parental affective disorders. *Journal of the American Academy of Child & Adolescent Psychiatry, 32,* 254–263.
Ben-Zur, H., Gilbar, O. & Lev, S. (2001). Coping with breast cancer: Patient, spouse and dyad models. *Psychosomatic Medicine, 63,* 32–39.
Berg, C.A., Meegan, S.P. & DeViney, F.P. (1998). A social contextual model of coping with everyday problems across the life span. *International Journal of Behavioral Development, 22,* 239–261.
Berg, C.A. & Upchurch, R. (2007). A developmental-contextual model of couples coping with chronic illness across the adult life span. *Psychological Bulletin, 133,* 920–954.

Best, M., Streisand, R., Catania, L., Kazak, Anne E. (2001). Parental distress during pediatric leukemia and post-traumatic stress symptoms (PTSS) after treatment ends. *Journal of Pediatric Psychology, 26,* 299–307.
Bibace, R. & Walsh, M.E. (1981). Children's conceptions of illness. In R. Bibace & M.E. Walsh (Eds.) *New directions for child development: Children's conceptions of health, illness and bodily functions.* San Fransisco: Jossey-Bass.
Blanchard, C.G., Albrecht, T.L. & Ruckdeschel, J.C. (1997). The crisis of cancer: Psychological impact on family caregivers. *Oncology, 11,* 189–194.
Bodenmann, G. (2005). Dyadic coping and its significance for marital functioning. In T.A. Revenson, K. Kayser & G. Bodenmann (Eds.) *Couples coping with stress: Emerging perspectives on dyadic coping* (pp. 33–50). Washington, DC: American Psychological Association.
Borry, P., Fryns, J.P., Schotsmans, P. & Dierickx, K. (2005). Attitudes towards carrier testing in minors: A systematic review. *Genetic Counseling, 16,* 341–352.
Borry, P., Fryns, J.P., Schotsmans, P. & Dierickx, K. (2006). Carrier testing in minors: A systematic review of guidelines and position papers. *European Journal of Human Genetics, 14,* 133–138.
Brown, R.T., Wiener, L., Kupst, M.J., Brennan, T., Behrman, R., Compas, B.E. *et al.* (2008). Single parents of children with chronic illness: An understudied phenomenon. *Journal of Pediatric Psychology, 33,* 408–421.

Carey, S. (1985). *Conceptual change in childhood.* Massachusetts: MIT.

Cassileth, B., Lusk, E., Brown, L. & Cross, P. (1985). Psychosocial status of cancer patients and next of kin: Normative data from the Profile of Mood States. *Journal of Psychosocial Oncology, 3,* 99–105.

Cauffman E. & Steinberg, L. (2000). (Im)maturity of judgment in adolescence: Why adolescents may be less culpable than adults. *Behavioral Sciences & the Law, 18,* 741–760.

Clarke, A.J. & Gaffe, C. (2008). Challenges in the genetic testing of children for familial cancers. *Archives of Disease in Childhood, 93,* 911–914.

Coe, M. & Kluka, S. (1988). Concerns of clients and spouses regarding ostomy surgery for cancer. *Journal of Enterostomal Therapy, 15,* 232–239.

Cohen, F.L., Nehring, W.M., Malm, K.C. & Harris, D.M. (1995). Family experiences when a child is HIV-positive: Reports of natural and foster parents. *Pediatric Nursing, 21,* 248–254.

Cohen, M.H. (1995). The triggers of heightened uncertainty in chronic life-threatening childhood illness. *Qualitative Health Research, 5,* 63–77.

Compas, B.E., Worsham, N.L., Epping-Jordan, J.E., Grant, K.E., Mirealt, G., Howell, D.C. & Malcarne, V.L. (1994). When mom or dad has cancer: Markers of psychological distress in cancer patients, partners and children. *Health Psychology, 13,* 507–515.

Compas, B.E., Worsham, N.L., Ey, S. & Howell, D.C. (1996). When mom or dad has cancer: II. Coping, cognitive appraisals and psychological distress in children of cancer patients. *Health Psychology, 15,* 167–175.

Coyne, J.C. & Smith, D.A.F. (1991). Couples coping with a myocardial infarction – a contextual perspective on wives' distress. *Journal of Personality and Social Psychology, 61,* 404–412.

Crisp, J., Ungerer, J.A. & Goodnow, J.J. (1996). The impact of experience on children's understanding of illness. *Journal of Pediatric Psychology, 21,* 57–72.

Eiser, C. (1993). *Growing up with a chronic disease: The impact on children and their families.* London: Jessica Kingsley.

Eiser, C. & Upton, P. (2007). Costs of caring for a child with cancer: A questionnaire survey. *Child Care, Health & Development, 33,* 455–459.

Epel, E.S., Blackburn, E.H., Dhabhar, F.S., Adler, N.E., Morrow, J.D. & Cawthon, R.M. (2004). Accelerated telomere shortening in response to life stress. *Proceedings of the National Academy of Sciences of the USA, 101,* 17312–17315.

Favara-Scacco, C., Smirne, G., Schiliro, G. & Di Cataldo, A. (2001). Art therapy as support for children with leukaemia during painful procedures. *Medical and Pediatric Oncology, 36,* 474–480.

Gallant, M.P. (2003). The influence of social support on chronic illness self-management: A review and directions for research. *Health Education & Behavior, 30,* 170–195.

Giese-Davis, J., Weibel, D. & Spiegel, D. (2000). Quality of couples' relationship and adjustment to metastatic breast cancer. *Journal of Family Psychology, 14,* 251–266.

Grant, K.E. & Compas, B.E. (1995). Stress and anxious-depressed symptoms among adolescents: Searching for mechanisms of risk. *Journal of Consulting and Clinical Psychology, 63,* 1015–1021.

Gravelle, A.M. (1997). Caring for a child with a progressive illness during the complex chronic phase: Parents' experience of facing adversity. *Journal of Advanced Nursing, 25,* 738–745.

Grootenhuis, M.A. & Last, B.F. (1997). Adjustment and coping by parents of children with cancer: A review of the literature. *Supportive Care in Cancer, 5,* 466–484.

Hagedoorn, M., Kuijer, R.G., Buunk, B.P., Dejong, G.M., Wobbes, T. & Sanderman, R. (2000). Marital satisfaction in patients with cancer: Does support from intimate partners benefit those who need it the most? *Health Psychology, 19,* 274–282.

Hagedoorn, M., Sanderman, R., Bolks, H.N., Tuinstra, J. & Coyne, J.C. (2008). Distress in couples coping with cancer: A meta-analysis and critical review of role and gender effects. *Psychological Bulletin, 134,* 1–30.

Hampson, S.E., Skinner, T.C., Hart, J., Storey, L., Gage, H., Foxcroft, D., *et al.* (2001). Effects of educational and psychosocial interventions for adolescents with diabetes mellitus: Systematic review. *Health Technology Assessment, 5,* 1–79.

Harbeck, C. & Peterson, L. (1992). Elephants dancing on my head: A developmental approach to children's concepts of specific pains. *Child Development, 63,* 138–149.

Hergenrather, J. & Rabinowitz, M. (1991). Age-related differences in the organisation of children's knowledge of illness. *Developmental Psychology, 27,* 952–959.

Hoke, L.A. (2001). Psychosocial adjustment in children of mothers with breast cancer. *Psycho-Oncology, 10,* 361–369.

Houtzager, B.A., Grootenhuis, M.A. & Last, B.F. (1999). Adjustment of siblings to childhood cancer: A literature review. *Supportive Care in Cancer, 7,* 302–320.

Hughes, M. & McCollum, J. (1994). Neonatal intensive care: Mothers' and fathers' perceptions of what is stressful. *Journal of Early Intervention, 18,* 258–268.

Huizinga, G.A., Visser, A., van der Graaf, W.T.A. *et al.* (2005). Stress response symptoms in adolescent and young adult children of parents diagnosed with cancer. *European Journal of Cancer, 41,* 288–295.

Jerrett, M.D. & Costello, E.A. (1996). Gaining control: Parents' experiences of accommodating children's asthma. *Clinical Nursing Research, 5,* 294–308.

Johnston, C.E. & Marder, L.R. (1994). Parenting the child with a chronic condition: An emotional experience. *Pediatric Nursing, 20*, 611–614.

Kato, P.M. (2008). A video game improves behavioral outcomes in adolescents and young adults with cancer: A randomized controlled trial. *Pediatrics, 122*, 305–317.

Kayser, K., Watson, L.E. & Andrade, J.T. (2007). Cancer as a 'We-disease': Examining the process of coping from a relational perspective. *Families, Systems & Health, 25,* 404–418.

Kazak, A.E., Alderfer, M., Rourke, M.T., Simms, S., Streissand, R. & Grossman, J.R. (2004). Posttraumatic stress disorder (PTSD) and posttraumatic stress symptoms (PTSS) in families of adolescent childhood cancer survivors. *Journal of Pediatric Psychology, 29*, 211–219.

Kazak, A.E. & Barakat, L.P. (1997). Brief report: Parenting stress and quality of life during treatment for childhood leukemia predicts child and parent adjustment after treatment ends. *Journal of Pediatric Psychology, 22*, 749–758.

Kazak, A.E., Simms, S., Alderfer, M.A., Rourke, M.T., Crump, T., McClure, K. *et al.* (2005). Feasibility and preliminary outcomes from a pilot study of a brief psychological intervention for families of children newly diagnosed with cancer. *Journal of Pediatric Psychology, 30*, 644–655.

Kearney, N., Kidd, L., Miller, M., Sage, M., Khorrami, J., McGee, M. *et al.* (2006). Utilising handheld computers to monitor and support patients receiving chemotherapy: Results of a UK-based feasibility study. *Supportive Care in Cancer, 14*, 742–752.

Kendrick, C., Culling, J., Oakhill, T. & Mott, M. (1986) Children's understanding of their illness and its treatment within a paediatic oncology unit. *Association of Child Psychology and Psychiatry, 8*, 16–20.

Kleiber, C., Montgomery, L.A. & Craft-Rosenberg, M. (1995). Information needs of the siblings of critically ill children. *Children's Health Care, 24*, 47–60.

Kuijer, R., Ybema, J., Buunk, B.P. & DeJong, M. (2000). Active engagement, protective buffering and overprotection. *Journal of Social and Clinical Psychology, 19*, 256–275.

Lähteenmäki P.M., Sioblom, J., Korhonen, T. & Salmi, T.T. (2004). The siblings of childhood cancer patients need early support: A follow-up study over the first year. *Archives of Disease in Childhood, 89*, 1008–1013.

Lepore, S.J., Ragan, J.D. & Jones, S. (2000). Talking facilitates cognitive-emotional processes of adaptation to an acute stressor. *Journal of Personality and Social Psychology, 78*, 499–508.

Lewis, F.M., Hammond, M.A. & Woods N. F. (1993) The family's functioning with newly diagnosed breast cancer in the mother: The development of an explanatory model. *Journal of Behavioral Medicine, 16*, 351–370.

Liossi, C. & Hatira, P. (2003). Clinical hypnosis in the alleviation of procedure-related pain in pediatric oncology patients. *International Journal of Clinical & Experimental Hypnosis, 51*, 4–28.

Manne, S.L. (1998). Cancer in the marital context: A review of the literature. *Cancer Investigation, 16*, 188–202.

Manne, S.L., DuHamel, K., Nereo, N., Ostroff, J., Parsons, S., Martini, R. *et al.* (2002). Predictors of PTSD in mothers of children undergoing bone marrow transplantation: The role of cognitive and social processes. *Journal of Pediatric Psychology, 27*, 607–617.

Manne, S.L., DuHamel, K., Ostroff, J., Parsons, S., Martini, D.R., Williams, S.E. *et al.* (2004). Anxiety, depressive and posttraumatic stress disorders among mothers of pediatric survivors of hematopoietic stem cell transplantation. *Pediatrics, 113*, 1700–1708.

Manne, S. & Glassman, M. (2000). Perceived control, coping efficacy and avoidance coping as mediators between spouses' unsupportive behaviors and cancer patients' psychological distress. *Health Psychology, 19*, 155–164.

Manne, S.L., Ostroff, J.S., Norton, T.R., Fox, K., Goldstein, L. & Grana, G. (2006). Cancer-related relationship communication in couples coping with early stage breast cancer. *Psycho-Oncology, 15*, 234–247.

Manne, S.L., Ostroff, J., Winkel, G., Fox, K., Grana, G. & Miller, E. (2005). Couple-focused group intervention for women with early stage breast cancer. *Journal of Consulting and Clinical Psychology, 73*, 646.

Manne, S.L., Alfieri, T., Taylor, K.L. & Dougherty, J. (1999a). Spousal negative responses to cancer patients: The role of social restriction, spouse mood and relationship satisfaction. *Journal of Consulting and Clinical Psychology, 67*, 352–361.

Manne, S.L., Pape, S.J., Taylor, K.L. & Dougherty, J. (1999b). Spouse support, coping and mood among individuals with cancer. *Annals of Behavioral Medicine, 21*, 111–121.

Manne, S.L., Taylor, K.L., Dougherty, J. & Kemeny, N. (1997). Supportive and negative responses in the partner relationship: Their association with psychological adjustment among individuals with cancer. *Journal of Behavioral Medicine, 20*, 101–125.

Martire, L.M. (2005). The 'relative' efficacy of involving family in psychosocial interventions for chronic illness: Are there added benefits to patients and family members. *Families, Systems & Health, 23*, 312–328.

Martire, L.M., Lustig, A.P., Schulz, R., Miller, G.E. & Helgeson, V.S. (2004). Is it beneficial to involve a family member? A meta-analysis of psychosocial interventions for chronic illness. *Health Psychology, 23*, 599–611.

McCubbin, M., Balling, K., Possin, P., Frierdich, S. & Bryne, B. (2002). Family resiliency in childhood cancer. *Family Relations, 51*, 103–111.

McCubbin, M. & McCubbin, H. (1996). Resiliency in families: A conceptual model of family adjustment and adaptation in response to stress and crisis. In H. McCubbin, A. Thompson & M. McCubbin (Eds.) *Family assessment: Resiliency, coping and adaptation – inventories for research and practice* (pp. 1–64). Madison: University of Wisconsin.

McMahon, M.A., Noll, R.B., Michaud, L.J. & Johnson, J.C. (2001). Sibling adjustment to pediatric traumatic brain injury: A case-controlled pilot study. *Journal of Head Trauma Rehabilitation, 16,* 587–594.

Montgomery, V., Oliver, R., Reisner, A. & Fallat, M.E. (2002). The effect of severe traumatic brain injury on the family. *Journal of Trauma, 52,* 1121–1124.

Newacheck, P.W. & Taylor, W.R. (1992). Childhood chronic illness: Prevalence, severity and impact. *American Journal of Public Health, 82,* 364–371.

Northouse, L.L. (1989). The impact of breast cancer on patients and husbands. *Cancer Nursing, 12,* 276–284.

Northouse, L.L., Mood, D., Templin, T., Mellon, S. & George, T. (2000). Couples' patterns of adjustment to colon cancer. *Social Science & Medicine, 50,* 271–284.

Osborn, T. (2007). The psychosocial impact of parental cancer on children and adolescents: A systematic review. *Psycho-Oncology, 16,* 101–126.

Osborne, M.L., Kistner, J.A. & Helgemo, B. (1993). Developmental progression in children's knowledge of AIDS: Implications for education and attitudinal change. *Journal of Pediatric Psychology, 18,* 177–192.

Padula, C.A. & Sullivan, M. (2006). Long-term married couples' health promotion behaviors: Identifying factors that impact decision-making. *Journal of Gerontology Nursing, 32,* 37–47.

Perrin, E.C. & Gerrity, P.S. (1981). There's a demon in your belly: Children's understanding of illness. *Pediatrics, 67,* 841–849.

Piaget, J. & Inhelder, B. (1969). *The psychology of the child.* New York: Basic Books.

Richards, F.H. (2006). Maturity of judgement in decision making for predictive testing for nontreatable adult-onset neurogenetic conditions: A case against predictive testing of minors. *Clinical Genetics, 70,* 396–401.

Richards, M. & Ponder, M. (1996). Lay understanding of genetics: A test of a hypothesis. *Journal of Medical Genetics, 33,* 1032–1036.

Rohrbaugh, M.J., Mehl, M.R., Shoham, V., Reilly, E.S. & Ewy, G.A. (2008). Prognostic significance of spouse we talk in couples coping with heart failure. *Journal of Consulting and Clinical Psychology, 76,* 781–789.

Rollins, J.A. (2005). Tell me about it: Drawing as a communication tool for children with cancer. *Journal of Pediatric Oncology Nursing, 22,* 203–221.

Romer, G., Barkman, C., Schulte-Markwort, M., Thomalia, G. & Riedesser, P. (2002). Children of somatically ill parents: A methodological review. *Clinical Child Psychology and Psychiatry, 7,* 17–38.

Sharpe, D & Rossiter, L. (2002). Siblings of children with a chronic illness: A meta-analysis. *Journal of Pediatric Psychology, 27,* 699–710.

Skerrett, K. (1998). Couple adjustment to the experience of breast cancer. *Families, Systems & Health, 16,* 281–298.

Sloper, P. (2000). Predictors of distress in parents of children with cancer: A prospective study. *Journal of Pediatric Psychology, 25,* 79–91.

Sparacino, P.S., Tong, E.M., Messias, D.K., Foote, D., Chesla, C.A. & Gilliss, C.L. (1997). The dilemmas of parents of adolescents and young adults with congenital heart disease. *Heart & Lung, 26,* 187–195.

Spath, M. (2007). Children facing a family member's acute illness: A review of intervention studies. *International Journal of Nursing Studies, 44,* 834–844.

Steele, R.G., Long, A., Reddy, K.A., Luhr, M. & Phipps, S. (2003). Changes in maternal distress and child-rearing strategies across treatment for pediatric cancer. *Journal of Pediatric Psychology, 28,* 447–452.

Steward, M.S. & Steward, D.S. (1981). Children's conceptions of medical procedures. In R. Bibace & M. Walsh (Eds.) *Children's conceptions of health, illness and bodily functions* (pp. 67–84). San Francisco: Jossey-Bass.

Suzuki, L. & Beale, I. (2006). Personal web home pages of adolescents with cancer: Self-presentation, information dissemination and interpersonal connection. *Journal of Pediatric Oncology Nursing, 23,* 152–161.

Varni, J.W. & Wallander, J.L. (1988) Pediatric chronic disabilities: Hemophilia and spina bifida as examples. In D. Routh (Ed.) *Handbook of pediatric psychology* (pp. 190–221). New York: Guilford Press.

Veldtman, G.R., Matley, S.L., Kendall, L., Quirk, J., Gibbs, J.L., Parsons, J.M. & Hewison, J. (2000). Illness understanding in children and adolescents with heart disease. *Heart, 84,* 395–397.

Welch, A.S., Wadsworth, M.E. & Compas, B.E. (1996). Adjustment of children and adolescents to parental cancer. *Cancer, 77,* 1409–1418.

Worsham, N., Compas, B. & Ey, S. (1997). Children's coping with parental illness. In S. Wolichik & I. Sandler (Eds.) *Handbook of children's coping: Linking theory and intervention* (pp. 195–213). New York: Plenum Press.

Zahlis, E.H. & Shands, M.E. (1991). Breast cancer: Demands of illness on the patient's partner. *Journal of Psychosocial Oncology, 9,* 75–93.

30

Ageing, Health and Illness

Frank Penedo, Madeline Hernandez and Jason Dahn

Chapter Outline

The central part of this chapter will provide an examination of the main ways in which ageing impacts on health, disease and well-being. It begins with a brief summary of the demography of ageing and a consideration of some of the myths and realities associated with the process of ageing. Following this, there is an overview of the impact of ageing on health status, functioning and outcome in a range of major diseases. There is then a more in-depth consideration of the nature and determinants of emotional well-being in older age and the development of specific interventions in that context. The final part of the chapter considers the effects of retirement on well-being and identifies some key issues associated with successful ageing.

Key Concepts

Common chronic
   conditions in later life
Emotional well-being and
   ageing
Myths and realities of
   ageing
Primary vs. secondary
   ageing processes
Psychological interventions
   in older adults
Retirement and role
   transitions
Successful ageing

Introduction

Demographics of ageing

In 2006, about 37 million men and women in the US were age 65 or older and accounted for 12 per cent of the population. Worldwide, by the year 2050 one out of every ten people will be age 65 or older reflecting a doubling in the elderly population of the world (US Census Bureau, 2009). Over the next 20 years, older adults in the US will reach 72 million and will represent nearly 20 per cent of the total US population. Moreover, by 2050, it is expected that there will be 5.3 million individuals over the age of 85 living in the US (Federal Interagency Forum on Aging-Related Statistics, 2008). The older population will also grow more diverse in the US. Currently about 81 per cent of the older adult population in the US is non-Hispanic white. Projections show that by the year 2050, this rate will drop to 61 per cent and 39 per cent of older adults will be members of an ethnic minority with Hispanics and African Americans comprising the largest ethnic groups, respectively. Most men and women over the age of 65 are married; however, the majority of women aged 75 and older are widowed. Life expectancy is expected to continue to rise with individuals living to about 87 years of age (Horiuchi, 2000). Women continue to show greater longevity than men and blacks continue to show significantly lower life expectancy rates; however, blacks that survive to age 85 show a slight life expectancy advantage over non-Hispanic whites. Cardiovascular disease continues to be the leading cause of death among people age 65 and older, followed by cancer, cerebrovascular disease, chronic lower respiratory infections and Alzheimer's disease. While deaths attributed to heart disease have steadily declined over the past several decades, deaths attributed to cancer and other leading causes of death have remained fairly stable. Today, older adults are retiring with higher education levels (76 per cent hold a high school diploma) and higher income (about 65 per cent report middle or high income) than ever before. Consequently, currently retired older adults represent the wealthiest cohort of retirees in history. In regard to living arrangement, older men are more likely than older women to be married and live with a spouse and wid-owhood is more common among older women than men (Federal Interagency Forum on Aging-Related Statistics, 2008). Furthermore, about 5 per cent of those 65 and older lived in a nursing home or institution.

Myths and realities of ageing

Older adults are often stereotyped as a critically limited subgroup of the population that suffers from severe limitations in social, physical and functional capacity. While this perception likely represents our own fears of ageing, it significantly misrepresents the realities for a considerable majority of older adults. When we think of growing old, our images of ageing include living in a nursing home with a significant physical disability while experiencing intellectual decline. Additionally, we are more likely to perceive the older population as more conservative and not receptive to new ideas and to some extent, we experience guilt based on the belief that we provided better care for older adults in the past. On the other hand, we are likely to view older adults as wiser and more religious, perhaps as a result of their numerous life experiences and advanced age, respectively (US Department of Health and Human Services, Administration on Aging, 2008).

The ageing process does impact a variety of facets of daily life; however, these age-related changes tend to be gradual and do not interfere with living a productive and satisfying life. The majority of older adults live with spouses/partners, family or independently (i.e., only 5 per cent reside in nursing homes) and remain employed (30 per cent) or active as volunteers (30 per cent). Additionally, less than 10 per cent have a significant limiting physical disability that interferes with their capacity to carry out activities of daily living (US Department of Health and Human Services, Administration on Aging, 2008). While there are a range of normative cognitive changes that occur with ageing (e.g. declining processing speed), older adults tend to easily compensate with minor adjustments such that there are few perceptible decrements in overall functioning. Ageing does necessitate adjustment to change; however, these changes are often subtle and occur over many decades. In marked contrast, at the age of 85, older adults do begin to experience significant disability with about 50 per cent of this subgroup needing help with daily activities and about 25 per cent living in a nursing home or assisted care facility (Federal Interagency Forum on Aging-Related Statistics, 2008).

Health, Disease and Disability

One of the many challenges involved in understanding both physical and psychosocial aspects of adult development and ageing is that traditionally the field of ageing has been data rich but theory poor. There is an overabundance of cross-sectional studies and few sound causal models that clearly delineate determinants of the ageing process that have been proposed and empirically evaluated in well-controlled prospective studies. Additionally, there has been a lack of integrative theory in the presence of an exponential growth in research that has not allowed adequate time for integration of research findings (Birren & Birren, 1990). Nonetheless, it is clear that ageing is associated with a variety of age-related changes.

Primary ageing changes are viewed as changes intrinsic to the ageing process that are ultimately irreversible, that is, normal, usual or healthy ageing such as developing wrinkles and grey hair. In contrast, secondary ageing involves changes caused by illness that are correlated with age but are preventable or reversible such as cardiovascular disease or cancer. A final pattern, tertiary ageing, involves changes that occur precipitously in older age and immediately precede death leading to a complete shutdown of body systems (Birren & Cunningham, 1985). The ageing process involves several age-related physical changes that impact the nervous, cardiovascular, respiratory, endocrine and immune systems, as well as sensory organs. A discussion of these system changes is beyond the scope of this chapter. Nonetheless, below we describe several chronic conditions within the context of ageing.

The impact of ageing on physical health status is highly variable and understanding individual differences in ageing is quite challenging given the multiple and complex factors that are involved in the ageing process (e.g. genetics, health behaviours, environmental exposure to toxins, psychosocial factors (Belsky, 1997)). Although ageing is not synonymous with

disease, most chronic conditions typically manifest in later life (e.g. cardiovascular disease, cancer). Older adults report lower levels of health control, self-efficacy and self-esteem (Schieman & Campbell, 2001) although only 18 per cent to 27 per cent rate their health status as 'fair' or 'poor'. A similar percentage (26 per cent) between the ages of 65–74 report being limited in activities by a chronic health condition and this increases to 45 per cent for those over age 75. Nonetheless, older adult's self-ratings of well-being indicate that the majority of this group perceives themselves in 'good health'.

Heart disease is the leading cause of death for older adults in the US and is followed by cancer, cerebrovascular disease, lung disease, pneumonia and influenza and finally diabetes-related complications. In older adults, disability is caused primarily by arthritis, accounting for one-third of cases, followed by heart disease, hypertension and diabetes-related complications (Federal Interagency Forum on Aging-Related Statistics, 2008). Depression and disability are consistent independent predictors of mortality (Shulz et al., 2000) even after controlling for medical and socioeconomic factors.

Management of chronic disease can diminish quality of life (QoL), reduce opportunities for social interaction and alter illness-related perceptions. The impact of chronic disease is both physical and psychological, affecting an individual's actual functioning as well as their perceptions of health and functioning. Perceived overall health has been shown to predict mortality and declines with increasing co-morbid conditions (Kaplan et al., 1996). In a community sample of older adults, pain was found to be persistent over time and to have a strong longitudinal association to depression (Chou, 2007), suggesting a reciprocal relationship and being indicative of a poor prognosis. The treatments for many of the diseases of later life serve to manage the disease process rather than cure it and as a consequence, individuals must cope as best they can with the resources available to them.

Cardiovascular disease. As a result of atherosclerosis and blockage of the arteries, several conditions can lead to critical and often lethal cardiovascular events. For example, ischaemic heart disease is most common in older adults with about 12 per cent of women and 20 per cent of men having had an episode in their lifetime. In this condition, the heart muscle cells receive insufficient oxygen due to blockage of the arteries and in severe cases it can lead to congestive heart failure. Other conditions associated with lack of adequate blood flow and oxygen to the heart include angina and in extreme cases where blood flow drops significantly below normal levels, cells in the heart muscle die creating a myocardial infarction. Other common conditions in older adults associated with lack of blood flow to the brain due to conditions such as artherosclerosis include cerebrovascular disease where complete cutoff of blood flow to an area of the brain can lead to a cerebrovascular accident (CVA) or stroke with consequences ranging in severity from unnoticed to severe impairment. As individuals age, they also experience increases in blood pressure. Severe increases in blood pressure are diagnosed as hypertension and are primarily due to structural changes in the heart and the arteries. Older adults with hypertension are three times more likely to die from cardiovascular disease (Topol, 2006).

Cancer. Cancer risk for some of the most common cancers is positively and significantly associated with ageing. In fact, over 50 per cent of women diagnosed with breast cancer and about 80 per cent of men diagnosed with prostate cancer are age 65 or older (American Cancer Society, 2009). Age-related biological processes are related to the development and progression of cancer. For example, age-related changes in the immune system such as a decreased capacity to identify and kill tumour cells are one possible risk factor (Anisimov, 2007). While the most effective way to prevent dying from cancer involves engaging in recommended screening practices and changes in lifestyle, older adults do not generally undergo adequate screenings or receive recommendations for lifestyle modification (Hurria & Balducci, 2009). Some work has shown that older cancer survivors may be at a psychosocial disadvantage due to other age-related stressors such as co-morbidities and financial limitations. Among older adults with cancer, uncontrolled cancer symptoms have been associated with greater depression, sleep disturbance and service utilisation and less social interactions (Ferrel *et al.*, 1998).

HIV/AIDS. Adults over the age of 50 account for about 15 per cent of reported AIDS cases. About 88 per cent of these cases occur between the ages of 50 and 65 and over the past decade, HIV/AIDS rates have grown twice as fast in the older population (Centers for Disease Control and Prevention, 2007). Men who have sex with men continue to be the highest risk group in this population with ethnic minorities accounting for about 60 per cent of all cases. Heterosexual men and women are the fastest growing subgroup and in general, older adults are less likely to request testing for HIV or be tested by a physician since there are various similarities between HIV/AIDS symptoms and geriatric problems (Linsk, 2000). Among older adults, more HIV is produced and more CD4 T-lymphocytes are infected and destroyed. There is also impaired replacement of naive CD-4 T-cells and less effective anti-HIV immunity (Adler *et al.*, 1997). Furthermore, older adults are at greater risk of HIV/AIDS progression, have a greater number of opportunistic infections and show higher HIV/AIDS-related mortality rates relative to younger individuals (Rozance, 1996; Skiest *et al.*, 1997).

Respiratory disease. In older adults, smoking and pollution are the most common causes of chronic obstructive pulmonary disease (COPD). In COPD, bronchial tubes become blocked and abnormal tissue develops (National Institutes of Health, 2006). These changes significantly compromise ability to breathe and engage in normal everyday activities such as walking. Smoking has been directly linked to the development of emphysema in older adults. In this debilitating condition, irreversible damage to the air sacs in the lungs compromise CO_2 to O_2 exchange leading to compromised breathing capacity (Karrasch *et al.*, 2008).

Cognitive processing, memory and intelligence. Processing speed is one of the most significant cognitive processing changes observed in older adults (Dywan *et al.*, 1992). Encoding speed or how rapidly storage occurs is decreased in older adults, particularly when processing visual information. Such decreases in visual processing explain why older adults are slower in responding to stimuli and may be associated with memory difficulties (Vaughn & Hartman, 2009). Older adults also have more difficulty encoding complex stimuli. The more complex the task, the greater the decrements we see in older adults. One argument that has been proposed is that older adults have more difficulty inhibiting irrelevant stimuli. Older adults also show significant decrements in psychomotor speed. In fact, the only universally accepted behavioural age-related change is reduced psychomotor speed (Whitbourne, 2005) and reaction time, particularly in complex tasks. Reduced processing speed and a deficit in the inhibition of irrelevant information are also associated with age-related deficits in memory. Independent of organic disorders such as Alzheimer's, there are small changes in various types of memory capacities. For example, semantic memory for familiar words, procedural memory for tasks such as riding a bicycle and autobiographical memory for details of a personal event remain fairly intact (Rabitt, 1996). In contrast, we see some challenges in episodic memory tasks such as recalling word lists and working memory functions. In addition to cognitive processing speed and memory changes, we see several age-related changes in intellectual functioning. Most of the work evaluating intelligence in later life has focused on evaluating fluid, crystallised and general intelligence throughout the lifespan. Generally, studies show that crystallised capacity (i.e. language capacity, knowledge of mathematics and rules of formal logic) increases throughout the lifespan, while fluid capacity (i.e. ability to integrate and analyse new information, inductive reasoning) begins to decrease around the late teens. In the Seattle Longitudinal Study (Schaie, 2005) investigators showed that generally, abilities continue to improve throughout our 30s and 40s with significant stability in intellectual abilities until the 60s and no significant declines until the late 70s.

Sexual function. Significant changes in sexual functioning are observed in both men and women as we age. Among older men, some of the physical changes include a longer time to develop an erection, less firm erections that are only complete at orgasm, more rapid loss of erection after orgasm, less ejaculatory power or contractions and a longer resolution period. In older women, there is change in the shape and flexibility of the vagina, decreased vaginal lubrication, less clitoral and labia swelling, less breast engorgement and less contractions. Co-morbidities in diseases more common in older age such as diabetes, heart disease and hypertension and associated pharmacological treatments, have been associated with compromised sexual dysfunction among men. In contrast, among older women, lack of interest, inability to achieve an orgasm

and not finding sex pleasurable has been related to sexual dysfunction. In general, findings among older women suggest that psychological factors are more important than menopausal status, age or medical issues in predicting sexual dysfunction (Rheaume & Mitty, 2008).

Ageing, Mental Health and Quality of Life

Emotional well-being in later life

Older adults are more likely to experience a series of psychosocial stressors that may render them more vulnerable to compromises in emotional well-being and overall quality of life (QoL). Life transitions such as retirement and widowhood can present a significant emotional and psychological burden to older adults. For example, someone who retires without adequate financial resources can experience financial burdens that can compromise overall functioning. For some individuals, retirement may also lead to a sense of lack of productivity and low self-efficacy. Similarly, the experience of widowhood can be highly variable depending on several factors (e.g. long-term illness) and for some older adults, losing a spouse can present a significant burden. Some older adults may also experience social isolation related to factors such as relocation of other family members and the death of close friends. Chronic illness and caregiving burdens can also create a psychosocial disadvantage for the older adult (Nokes, 1996).

Prevalence of mental health conditions

About 20 per cent of adults age 55 or older meet diagnostic criteria for a mental disorder (Gatz et al., 1990) and older adults have the highest suicide rate of any age group. Anxiety disorder is the most common diagnosis in older adults (11.4 per cent) followed by simple phobia (7.3 per cent), any mood disorder (4.4 per cent), agoraphobia (4.1 per cent) and major depressive disorder (3.8 per cent; Cavanaugh & Blanchard-Fields, 2006). The emotional well-being of this population can be further compromised by challenges more commonly encountered in the older population such as multiple pathologies and co-morbidities, atypical or non-specific presentation of illness, delay in reporting emotional problems, underreporting of symptoms and polypharmacy (Lemme, 1999). About 13 per cent of adults age 65–74 and 19 per cent of those 85 and older in the US report at least four significant symptoms of major depression (Federal Interagency Forum on Aging-Related Statistics, 2008). Furthermore, depression rates are lower in older males than females. Some have argued that among the older population, symptoms that include social withdrawal, loss of interest, sense of hopelessness and a loss of appetite reflect a 'depletion syndrome' that may more adequately represent depression as a mental disorder in this population (Lemme, 1999). Additionally, late-onset depression or a mild or moderate depression that first appears after the age of 60 has been associated with several risk factors including being a widow, less than a high school education, having physical impairments and heavy alcohol use (Blazer, 2003). In general, older adults may be underdiagnosed for depression, as they are less likely to report depressive symptoms or be adequately assessed by physicians for mental health conditions (Fiske et al., 2009). Furthermore, older adults being treated in clinical setting for medical conditions or who are living in long-term care facilities report up to 20 per cent and 50 per cent rates, respectively, of depressive symptoms (Wagenaar et al., 2003).

About 20 per cent of older adults report significant symptoms of anxiety (Sampson, 2009) typically associated with generalised anxiety. Panic disorder or the experience of physical symptoms involving extreme shortness of breath, pounding heart and the belief that death is imminent is rare among older adults (about 0.5 per cent). Specific phobias or social phobias are more common, however. For example, some studies have reported up to 7 per cent of the older adult population meets criteria for fear of a specific situation or object (Pontillo et al., 2002). Social phobias are less common with 1 per cent prevalence in older adults although about 13 per cent experience related symptoms. Obsessions or repetitive thoughts and compulsions, a condition known as obsessive-compulsive disorder, is also rare with about 0.8 per cent prevalence. Post-traumatic stress disorder (PTSD) rates are about 1 per cent in the general older adult population.

However, rates are as high as 19 per cent for an ageing cohort of Vietnam veterans (Averill & Beck, 2000). Psychotic disorders such as schizophrenia are very rare among older adults (0.2 per cent prevalence). This disorder typically manifests before age 40 and has a highly variable course with about 25 per cent remission rates. A form of schizophrenia termed late-onset schizophrenia can occur among adults over the age of 45 and persist through the 60s. Individuals who develop this disorder tend to be more paranoid, have less cognitive impairment and respond better to antipsychotic medications (Howard et al., 2000). Finally, while suicide rates among teenagers and young adults (15–24 years old) have doubled over the past 60 years, suicide rates have dropped among older adults over the same time period. However, older adult suicide rates among those aged 80–84 is 27 per 100,000, whereas it is about 15 per 100,000 for young adults age 15 to 24. One reason for higher rates among older adults is that older individuals have a higher success rate, as they are more likely to use lethal means to take their lives (Centers for Disease Control and Prevention, 2009).

Generally, older adults have lower rates of substance use disorders relative to younger individuals. About 0.6 per cent report marijuana use and less than 1 per cent report any cocaine use. However, among older adults who receive emergency medical attention, alcohol dependence rates are about 10–15 per cent. About two-thirds of older adults who are alcohol dependent began drinking earlier in life. Individuals 65 and older have the highest rates of alcohol-related hospital admissions and alcohol use among the elderly is highly related to depression and liver damage. Additionally, cognitive function in older adults decreases more after an alcoholic drink and less alcohol is needed to reach legal limits of blood alcohol concentration. One possibility for greater impairment in cognitive function may be that the liver does not metabolise alcohol as rapidly in older adults (US Department of Health and Human Services, 1999).

Psychological interventions, emotional well-being and physical health

Mental health disorders may lead to or exacerbate physical conditions in older adults via multiple cognitive, behavioural and physiological pathways

(Frasure-Smith *et al.*, 1993; McEwen, 1998). For example, depression has been associated with poor medical treatment adherence thus compromising an older adult's capacity to take care of him or herself (Mackin & Arean, 2007). Similarly, depression is associated with social isolation, an impaired capacity to rally social support networks and impaired physiological function such as suppressed immunity (Fiske *et al.*, 2009). Several factors such as multiple pathologies and atypical presentations can complicate mental health assessment and treatment in older populations. Nonetheless, once a mental health disorder such as depression or anxiety is identified, it can be successfully treated. In a meta-analysis of psychological interventions for the treatment of depression in later life, researchers have shown efficacy of cognitive behavioural approaches in reducing depressive symptoms and the magnitude of the effect is equal to antidepressant medications (Schneider, 1993; Scogin & McElreth, 1994). For depression and anxiety, relaxation training and cognitive behavioural therapy has also shown successful treatment rates in older populations (e.g. Stanley *et al.*, 2009). Work has shown that generally, older adults are likely to be very compliant with psychotherapeutic treatment although they move at a slower pace and change occurs in smaller increments over time. Older adults are also more likely to digress and provide more anecdotal and detailed accounts (Sprenkel, 1999). Nonetheless, studies support that psychotherapy and behavioural interventions are effective in older populations (Gatz *et al.*, 1998).

Adapting psychosocial interventions for older populations

Some work has focused on adapting group-based psychosocial interventions for older adults by providing a slowly paced presentation, using multimodal didactic techniques and providing memory aids such as audiotapes of the intervention (Zeiss & Steffen, 1996). Over the past several decades, the number of older adults participating in support groups and psychosocial interventions has been growing likely due to a declining number of family support networks (e.g. fewer children or grandchildren), job mobility, retirement and relocation. Cognitive behavioural treatments have shown to be effective in older adults. Consistent

findings support the efficacy of individual and group interventions using cognitive behavioural therapy in improving QoL and there is some evidence of health benefits from these interventions (Scogin *et al.*, 2007).

Investigators have developed a transtheoretical framework that guides changes that are needed for delivering psychological interventions among older populations. The contextual, cohort-based, maturity, specific challenge model (Knight, 1996) draws upon lifespan developmental psychology, social gerontology and clinical psychology. This model is not a specific therapy system but a framework for adapting any therapy system to work with older adults. The model proposes that reasons for changing therapy for older adults are not due to developmental differences but to context and cohort effects and specific challenges common in later life. For example, when considering delivering a psychosocial intervention, the setting or context where the older adult resides such as retirement communities, long-term care settings, hospitals or outpatient medical settings needs to be considered. Similarly, the specific cohort is important. For instance, earlier born cohorts have different skills, values and life experiences that may guide the intervention content. Finally, specific challenges that require knowledge and therapeutic skills about a specific medical condition, financial situation or familial issue specific to the challenges of ageing need to be considered. Taking these factors into consideration allows for the development and delivery of specifically targeted interventions that are sensitive to the needs of the older adult population targeted.

Psychological and behavioural interventions and quality of life

About 75 per cent of people age 65 and older rate their overall health as good to excellent. At age 85 or older, this rate drops to about 65 per cent. In contrast, 42 per cent of the 65 and older population reports at least one functional limitation and 12 per cent of this group reported difficulty in performing an instrumental activity of daily living (IADL). Nonetheless, rates of functional limitations have decreased over the past 15 years and generally, older adults report good-to-excellent quality of life (Federal Interagency Forum on Aging-Related Statistics, 2008). While there is some debate as to how to conceptualise QoL, most studies assess this construct as the level of satisfaction in general functioning domains that include social, emotional, physical employment and family functioning. Life stressors can affect all domains of QoL as they can lead to social isolation, anxiety, depression and can have a direct (e.g. compromised immunity) and indirect (e.g. risk behaviours) effect on physical health status and disruptions in work and interpersonal relations (Shih, 2008). Therefore, a significant amount of work has been aimed at establishing the efficacy of psychological and behavioural interventions in improving QoL and over all health status in older populations. Furthermore, the leading causes of death in the US have behavioural implications that may be modifiable via interventions. For example, diet, smoking and stress have been implicated as risk factors for heart disease and cancer (e.g. Jensen et al., 2008). Furthermore, several psychosocial processes are known to impact disease course and to some extent, influence health outcomes and survival. Social support as opposed to isolation, emotional expression rather than emotional inhibition and adaptive and active coping styles instead of passive compliance have all been associated with slowed disease course and better health outcomes across several conditions (Cruess et al., 2004). Psychosocial and behavioural interventions typically target intrapersonal (e.g. coping style, appraisals), interpersonal (e.g. social support) and behavioural (e.g. treatment adherence, risk reduction) factors in an effort to modify these factors and subsequently improve QoL.

Chronic disease interventions

Among cancer survivors, several studies suggest that group-based psychosocial interventions can improve QoL and physical functioning among older cancer survivors (e.g. Andersen et al., 2008; Penedo et al., 2007). Some of these studies have been specifically developed for older adults with cancer. Penedo and colleagues (Molton et al., 2008; Penedo et al., 2008) adapted a group-based cognitive behavioural stress management intervention for older prostate cancer survivors and have reported intervention-associated improvements in general and disease-specific QoL

outcomes including sexual functioning. Recently Andersen and colleagues (Andersen et al., 2008) reported that a cognitive behavioural group based intervention that targeted coping skills, stress management and treatment adherence improved QoL and survival among women treated for regional breast cancer. Although this latter study was not specifically tailored for older adults, a significant proportion of participants were over age 60. Similar findings have been reported in interventions delivered to primarily older men with malignant melanoma (Fawzy et al., 2003). Group-based stress management interventions have also been successful in reducing distress among middle-aged and older adults living with HIV/AIDS (Penedo et al., 2003).

Caregiving interventions

Dementia caregivers show increased risk of coronary heart disease (von Kanel et al., 2008) even after controlling for a multitude of risk factors including smoking history, alcohol intake, body mass index, medical history and menopausal status. The authors suggest that the increased risk of CHD may be the result of immune and endocrine alterations that are caused by caregiving distress. A significant amount of work has focused on establishing the efficacy of psychosocial interventions in improving QoL and physiological function, particularly immune function (Penedo & Dahn, 2005), among caregivers of chronically ill older adults. For example, among older dementia caregivers participating in an intervention to strengthen psychological resources and facilitate management of behavioural problems showed stronger immune proliferative responses to mitogens from baseline to post-intervention and then again at six-month follow-up. In a study with relatively younger caregivers (mean age = 54), participants in a structured stress management programme reported less depression, anxiety, fatigue and confusion. In addition, they demonstrated significantly increased natural killer cell activity. Using an antibody response model, Vedhara et al. (1999) showed that distressed elderly caregivers who participated in a cognitive behavioural stress management intervention demonstrated enhanced antibody responses to influenza vaccination relative to a control group of caregivers and a non-caregiving control group.

Retirement

The concept of retirement is closely associated with ageing. Retirement marks the end of an individual's work career and unlike other normative age-graded events such as graduation and marriage, retirement may carry some ambivalence. The concept of retirement is also highly variable across older populations and partly dependent on factors such as financial resources at age of retirement and reasons for retirement (i.e. voluntary vs. forced). About 30 per cent of older adults never retire and about 15 per cent re-enter the workforce after retirement. Today, older adults are retiring with higher education levels and higher income. Consequently, currently retired older adults represent the wealthiest cohort of retirees in history. Older adults who are not in institutions fall within a high- or medium-income category and about 30 per cent are in the low-income category and about 10 per cent meet criteria for poverty (Federal Interagency Forum on Aging-Related Statistics, 2008).

Although some suggest that loss of the work role as a result of retirement can cause changes in physical and mental health there is no evidence that supports these changes (Ekerdt, 1987). An alternative view suggests that retirement does not lead to serious disruptions in the individual's sense of identity, social connections or productivity. The continuity theory of retirement proposes that retirees maintain previous goals, activities and relationships and that older adults view retirement as another stage in their careers (Atchley, 2000). Therefore, it has been suggested that the notion that retirement confers a downturn in health that increases risk of mortality is a myth. The fact that older adults who are in poor health and have more psychological problems are more likely to retire contributes to this myth (Hannson et al., 1997), as mortality is associated with poor physical and mental health, not retirement. Actually, some have shown that retirement may actually improve physical and emotional well-being (Crowley, 1985). Nonetheless, about 30 per cent of retirees view retirement as a stressful event and some have shown that factors such as retiring early, reason for retirement and less than two years of planning for retirement are associated with poor adjustment. Additionally, low retirement self-efficacy, a perceived inability to make a smooth transition and negative self-appraisals has been related to greater retirement anxiety (Van Soling & Henkens, 2008).

Successful Ageing

Successful ageing is typically measured by indices of health, finances and social relations. More adults are reaching age 65 in better physical and mental health than ever before. Improved diet, physical fitness and health care are attributed to improvements in the health status of older adults (Federal Interagency Forum on Aging-Related Statistics, 2008). However, 'normal' or primary ageing involves some physical declines such as decreased mobility and sensory abilities, slower reaction time, mild memory deficits and decreased pulmonary and immune function (Rowe & Kahn, 1987). Some have proposed a continuum perspective of successful ageing where at one extreme we can eliminate ageing through specific treatments or interventions and at the other extreme, we face inevitable ageing with few opportunities to postpone or stop the negative effects. In the middle of this continuum, we find successful ageing where we can ameliorate the disease and disability associated with ageing through lifestyle choices. A more balanced view as proposed by the McArthur Model of Successful Ageing proposes three interactive components which include: (a) absence of disabling disease and the disability associated with the disease or no significant physical impairment; (b) maintaining high cognitive and physical function thus allowing the individual to be active and competent; and (c) engagement with life as reflected by involvement in productive activities and involvement with others (Rowe & Kahn, 1998). It is important to note that not ageing is not a component of successful ageing. That is, to age successfully still involves growing old. Much knowledge has been gained over the past several decades on the ageing process and we now know that growing old is not filled with depression and despair and that the few personality changes that do take place in late life are typically in the positive direction (Costa et al., 2008). However, we typically view successful agers as exceptions rather than the rule and this misrepresentation of the ageing experience is partly due to the social indicator model.

We tend to assess successful ageing by evaluating individuals on a series of demographic and social variables such as age, gender, marital status and income. By these standards alone, older individuals are in a disadvantage, particularly in age, income, health and marital status.

Since low income, widowhood and poor health are all associated with poor mental health status, we assume that older adults facing these difficulties would have a difficult time in later life (Rowe & Kahn, 1997). However, we consistently find that older adults maintain relatively high levels of psychological well-being (Costa *et al.*, 2008). This phenomenon is referred to as the paradox of well-being and suggests that despite difficult circumstances, people in later life feel good about themselves and their situations. Therefore, successful ageing is the norm rather than the exception and older Americans describe themselves as being 'very' or 'pretty' happy. This experience is consistent in other countries and cultures and reflects a high level of subjective well-being. Subjective well-being typically consists of three components that include positive affect, negative affect and life satisfaction (Diener *et al.*, 1997). Research has shown that the relationship between subjective well-being and age varies as a function of gender, personality and marital satisfaction (Junowitz, 2000). The extent to which an individual can adapt to life circumstances and age-related social, emotional and physical changes also plays a key role in subjective well-being. That is, the ability to integrate negative life experiences into who they are as individuals through a process referred to as identity assimilation helps improve and maintain self-esteem and well-being in later life. Additionally, older adults engage in a process where they develop a narrative or 'life story' of their lives that emphasises the positive and fosters well-being. Collectively, this adaptation and assimilation of life and age-related challenges fosters better QoL and subjective well-being in older populations.

Concluding Remarks

We often stereotype older adults as frail, isolated, living in a nursing home and disengaged from active lifestyles. The reality is that most older adults, particularly those between the ages of 65 and 85, are living independently and free of chronic diseases with major debilitating effects. Additionally, about one-third of the 65 and older population remains active in the workforce, while another third continues to work on a part-time or volunteer basis. There is a distinction between primary or 'normal' ageing processes that tend to be typical and universal (e.g. reduced processing speed) and abnormal processes which are more common in later life. These 'atypical' or secondary ageing processes involve chronic conditions that are preventable or reversible such as cardiovascular disease. Although ageing is not synonymous with disease, there is clearly a strong positive association with growing old and developing major chronic conditions such as cancer and cardiovascular disease. Most disability in older age is caused by arthritis and older adults report low levels of self-efficacy over their medical conditions. Moreover, ageing is associated with cognitive declines typically represented by a 'slowing down' in processing speed and reaction time. Paradoxically, most older adults also perceive themselves in good health. Physical health conditions can also impact emotional well-being.

Older adults are more likely to experience common and unique psychosocial stressors such as social isolation, financial burden, caregiving burden and chronic diseases that may render them at a psychosocial disadvantage and at risk for compromises in emotional well-being. Symptoms of anxiety and depression are common in later life and the older adult population suffers from the highest suicide rate. Generally, however, older adults experience relatively good emotional well-being and evidence suggests that morbidity of mental health disorders earlier in life typically account for mental health challenges in later life. A growing number of studies are documenting the efficacy of psychosocial interventions in older adults across multiple outcomes including emotional well-being, quality of life and to some extent physical health. Typically, psychosocial interventions involve group-based cognitive behavioural therapies. While the mechanisms of change in these interventions are fairly similar to those applied to younger populations, several adaptations such as a slower pace of presentation, multimodal didactic approaches and more room for reminiscence facilitate delivery of these interventions. Psychosocial interventions have also been effective in improving physiological function (e.g. immunocompetence) and physical functioning.

Retirement is closely related to ageing and highly variable across individuals. For some, it marks the end of a productive and satisfying work role, while for others, it is associated with financial burdens and isolation. There is no substantial evidence suggested that retirement is associated with faster mortality. In fact, currently retired older adults represent the most educated and wealthiest cohort of retirees. Nonetheless, about 30 per cent of individuals view retirement as a stressful transition but most adapt

relatively well. Early approaches at successful ageing used indices of socioeconomic status and health and thus presented a distorted picture or concept of what it means to age successfully. Although not synonymous with ageing, older age is associated with chronic conditions and financial limitations. A more balanced approach at measuring successful ageing such as the McArthur model proposes three interactive components that include absence of disabling disease, maintaining high cognitive and physical function to remain active and competent, and engagement in life. Using these components, successful ageing is the rule rather than the exception for most older adults.

Discussion Points

1   Think about how some of the myths of ageing might influence both the attitudes of health-care professionals and the quality of health-care delivery for older adults.
2   To what extent are the age-related changes in health primary and irreversible or secondary and potentially preventable?
3   Which psychosocial stressors are more common in older age and how do they impact on well-being?

4   How can an understanding of the factors involved in successful ageing be helpful to health psychologists?
5   How can an understanding of health psychology contribute to the development of interventions to promote the maintenance of good health and well-being in older age?

Further Reading

Cavanaugh, J.C. & Blanchard-Fields, F. (Eds.) (2006). *Adult development and aging* (5th edn, pp. 114–153). Belmont, CA: Thomson Wadsworth.

Fiske, A., Wetherell, J.L. & Gatz, M. (2009). Depression in older adults. *Annual Review of Clinical Psychology, 5,* 363–389.

Mackin, R.S. & Arean, P.A. (2007). Cognitive and psychiatric predictors of medical treatment adherence among older adults in primary care clinics. *International Journal of Geriatric Psychiatry, 22*(1), 55–60.

Molton, I., Siegel, S., Penedo, F.J., Dahn, J.R., Kinsinger, D., Traeger, L.N. *et al.* (2008). Promoting recovery of sexual functioning after radical prostatectomy with group-based stress management: The role of interpersonal sensitivity. *Journal of Psychosomatic Research, 64*(5), 527–536.

Rowe, J.W. & Kahn, R.L. (1997). Successful aging. *Gerontologist, 37*(4), 433–440.

Scogin, F., Morthland, M., Kaufman, A., Burgio, L., Chaplin, W. & Kong, G. (2007). Improving quality of life in diverse rural older adults: A randomized trial of a psychological treatment. *Psychology and Aging, 22*(4), 657–665.

Shih, M. (2008). Health-related quality of life among adults with serious psychological distress and chronic medical conditions. *Quality of Life Research, 17*(4), 521–528.

Stanley, M.A., Wilson, N.J., Novy, D.M., Rhoades, H.M., Wagener, P.D., Greisinger, A.J. *et al.* (2009). Cognitive behavior therapy for generalized anxiety disorder among older adults in primary care: A randomized clinical trial. *Journal of the American Medical Association, 301*(14), 487.

Van Soling, H. & Henkens, K. (2008). Adjustment to and satisfaction with retirement: Two of a kind? *Psychological Aging, 23*(2), 422–434.

Whitbourne, S.K. (2005). *Adult development and aging: Biopsychosocial Perspectives* (2nd edn, pp. 176–204). New York: Wiley.

References

Adler, W.H., Baskar, P.V., Chrest, F.J., Dorsey-Cooper, B., Winchurch, R. & Nagel, J.E. (1997). HIV infection and aging: Mechanisms to explain the accelerated rate of progression in the older patient. *Mechanisms of Ageing Development, 96*, 137–155.

American Cancer Society. (2009). *Cancer facts and figures 2008*. Atlanta: American Cancer Society.

Andersen, B.L., Yang, H.C., Farrar, W.B., Golden-Kreutz, D.M., Emery, C.F., Thornton, L.M. *et al.* (2008). Psychological intervention improves survival for breast cancer patients: A randomized clinical trial. *Cancer, 113(*12), 3450–3458.

Anisimov, V.N. (2007). Biology of aging and cancer. *Cancer Control, 14*(1), 23–31.

Atchley, R.C. (2000). *Social forces and aging: An introduction to social gerontology* (9th edn, pp. 91–130). New York: Wadsworth.

Averill, P.M. & Beck, J.G. (2000). Posttraumatic stress disorder in older adults: A conceptual review. *Journal of Anxiety Disorder, 14*(2), 133–156.

Belsky, J. (1997). *The adult experience*. St. Paul, MN: West Publishing.

Birren, J.E. & Birren, B. (1990). The concepts, models and history of the psychology of aging. In J.E. Birren & K.W. Schaie (Eds.) *Handbook of the psychology of aging* (pp. 216–231). New York: Academic Press.

Birren, J.E. & Cunningham, W.R. (1985). Research on the psychology of aging: principles, concepts and theory. In J.E. Birren & K.W. Schaie (Eds.) *The handbook of the psychology of aging* (pp. 3–34). New York: Van Nostrand Reinhold.

Blazer, D.G. (2003). Depression in late life: Review and commentary. *Journal of Gerontology, 58*(3), 249–265.

Cavanaugh, J.C. & Blanchard-Fields, F. (Eds.) (2006). *Adult development and aging* (5th edn, pp. 114–153). Belmont, CA: Thomson Wadsworth.

Centers for Disease Control and Prevention (2007). *HIV/AIDS surveillance report, 2007.* (Vol. 19). Atlanta, GA: US Department of Health and Humans Services, Centers for Disease Control.

Centers for Disease Control and Prevention (2009). *Elderly suicide fact sheet*. At www.suicidology.org/web/guest/stats-and-tools/fact-sheets.

Chou, K. (2007). Reciprocal relationship between pain and depression in older adults: Evidence from the English longitudinal study of ageing. *Journal of Affective Disorders, 102*, 115–123.

Costa P.T., Yang, J. & McCrae, R.R. (2008). Aging and personality traits: Generalizations and clinical implications. In I.H. Nordhus, G.R., VandenBos, S. Ber & P. Fromholt (Eds.) *Clinical geropsychology* (pp. 33–48). Washington, DC: American Psychological Association.

Crowley, J.E. (1985). Longitudinal effects of retirement on men's psychological and physical well-being. In H.S. Parnes (Ed.) *Retirement among American men* (pp. 147–173). Lexington, MA: D.C. Heath.

Cruess, D.G., Schneiderman, N., Antoni, M.H. & Penedo, F. (2004). Biobehavioral bases of disease processes. In T.J. Boll (Ed.) *Handbook of clinical health psychology models and perspectives in health psychology* (Vol. 3, pp. 31–79). Washington, DC: American Psychological Association.

Diener, E., Suh, E. & Oishi, S. (1997). Recent findings on subjective well-being. *Indian Journal of Clinical Psychology, 24*, 25–41.

Dywan, J., Segalowitz, S.J. & Unsal, A. (1992). Speed of information processing, health and cognitive performance in older adults. *Developmental Neuropsychology, 8*, 473–490.

Ekerdt, D.J. (1987). Why the notion persists that retirement harms health. *Gerontologist, 27*, 454–457.

Fawzy, F.I., Canada, A.L. & Fawzy, N.W. (2003). Malignant melanoma: Effects of a brief, structured psychiatric intervention on survival and recurrence at 10-year follow-up. *Archives of General* Psychiatry, *60*, 100–103.

Federal Interagency Forum on Aging-Related Statistics (2008). *Older Americans 2008: Key indicators of well-being*. Washington, DC: US Government Printing Office.

Ferrell, B.R., Ferrell, B., Weston, R.E., Rapkin, B.D., Potts, R.G., Smith, M.Y. *et al.* (1998). Persons with special needs. In J.C. Holland (Ed.) *Psycho-Oncology* (pp. 839–877). New York: Oxford University Press.

Fiske, A., Wetherell, J.L. & Gatz, M. (2009). Depression in older adults. *Annual Review of Clinical Psychology, 5*, 363–389.

Frasure-Smith, N., Lesperance, F. & Talajic, M. (1993). Depression following myocardial infarction: Impact on 6-month survival. *Journal of the American Medical Association, 270*, 1819–1825.

Gatz, M., Fiske, A., Kaskie, B., Kasl-Godley, J.E., McCallum, T.J. & Wetherell, J.L. (1998). Empirically validated psychological treatments for older adults. *Journal of Mental Health and Aging, 4*(1), 9–46.

Gatz, M., Kasl-Godley, J.E. & Karel, M. (1990). The concepts, models and history of the psychology of aging. In J.E. Birren & K.W. Schaie (Eds.) *Handbook of the psychology of aging* (pp. 365–382). New York: Academic Press.

Hansson, R.O., DeKoekkoek, P.D., Neese, W.M. & Patterson, D.W. (1997). Successful aging at work: Annual review,

1992–1996: The older worker and transitions to retirement. *Journal of Vocational Behavior, 51*, 202–233.

Horiuchi, S. (2000). Greater lifetime expectation. *Nature, 405*, 744–745.

Howard, R., Rabins, P.V., Seeman, M.V., Jeste, D.V. & the International Late-Onset Schizophrenia Group. (2000). Late onset schizophrenia and very-late-onset schizophrenia-like psychosis: An international consensus. *American Journal of Psychiatry, 157*, 172–178.

Hurria, A. & Balducci, L. (Eds.) (2009). *Geriatric oncology: Treatment, assessment and management.* New York: Springer.

Jensen, M.K., Chiuve, S.E., Rimm, E.B., Dethlefsen, C., Tjonneland, A., Joensen, A.M. & Overvad, D. (2008). Obesity, behavioral lifestyle factors and risk of acute coronary events. *Circulation, 117*(24), 3062–3069.

Junowitz, D.J. (2000). Effects of health and personality on subjective well-being in older adults. *Dissertation Abstracts International: Section B: The Sciences and Engineering, 61*, 563.

Kaplan, G.A., Goldber, D.E., Everson, S.A., Cohen, R.D., Salonen, R., Tuomilehto, J. & Salonen, J. (1996). Perceived health status and morbidity and mortality: Evidence from the Kuopio ischaemic heart disease risk factor study. *International Journal of Epidemiology, 25*, 259–265.

Karrasch, S., Holz, O. & Jorres, R. A. (2008). Aging and induced sescence as factors in the pathogenesis of lung emphysema. *Respiratory Medicine, 102*, 1215–1230.

Knight, B. (1996). Overview of psychotherapy with the elderly: The contextual, cohort-based, maturity specific challenge model. In S. Zarit & R. Knight (Eds.) *Effective clinical interventions in a life stage context: A guide to psychotherapy and aging* (pp. 17–34). Washington, DC: American Psychological Association.

Lemme, B.H. (1999). *Development in adulthood* (2nd edn, pp. 376–439). Boston, MA: Allyn & Bacon.

Linsk, N.L. (2000). HIV among older adults: age specific issues in prevention and treatment. *AIDS Reader, 10*, 430–440.

Mackin, R.S. & Arean, P.A. (2007). Cognitive and psychiatric predictors of medical treatment adherence among older adults in primary care clinics. *International Journal of Geriatric Psychiatry, 22*(1), 55–60.

McEwen, B.S. (1998). Protective and damaging effects of stress mediators. *New England Journal of Medicine, 338*(3), 171–179.

Molton, I., Siegel, S., Penedo, F.J., Dahn, J.R., Kinsinger, D., Traeger, L.N. *et al.* (2008). Promoting recovery of sexual functioning after radical prostatectomy with group-based stress management: The role of interpersonal sensitivity. *Journal of Psychosomatic Research, 64*(5), 527–536.

National Institutes of Health. National Heart, Lung and Blood Institute. (2006). *COPD: Are you at risk?* (NIH publication no. 07-5840). At www.nhlbi.nih.gov/health/public/lung/copd/campaign-materials/pub/copd-atrisk.pdf.

Nokes, K. (Ed.) (1996). *HIV/AIDS and the older adult.* Washington, DC: Taylor & Francis.

Penedo, F.J., Antoni, M.H. & Schneiderman, N. (2008). *Cognitive-behavioral stress management for prostate cancer recovery: Facilitator guide.* New York: Oxford University Press.

Penedo, F.J. & Dahn, J.R. (2005). Psychoneuroimmunology and Ageing. In K. Vedhara & M. Irwin (Eds.) *Human psychoneuroimmunology* (pp. 81–106). Oxford: Oxford University Press.

Penedo, F.J., Molton, I., Dahn, J.R., Scanlon, B., Costa, P. & Schneiderman, N. (2003). *CBSM reduces psychological distress in middle-aged and older adults living with HIV/AIDS.* Poster presentation at the Annual Meeting of the Society of Behavioral Medicine, Salt Lake City, Utah.

Penedo, F.J., Traeger, L., Dahn, J., Molton, I., Schneiderman, N. & Antoni, M.H. (2007). Cognitive behavioral stress management intervention improves quality of life in Spanish monolingual Hispanic men treated for localized prostate cancer: Effects of a randomized controlled trial. *International Journal of Behavioral Medicine, 14*(3), 164–172.

Pontillo, D., Lang, A. & Stein, M. (2002). Management and treatment of anxiety disorders in the older patient. *Journal of Clinical Geriatrics, 10*, 38–49.

Rabitt, P. (1996). Speed of processing and ageing. In R.R. Woods (Ed.) *Handbook of the clinical psychology of ageing* (pp. 59–72). Chichester: Wiley.

Rheaume, C. & Mitty, E. (2008). Sexuality and intimacy in older adults. *Geriatric Nursing, 29*(5), 342–349.

Rowe, J.W. & Kahn, R.L. (1987). Human aging: Usual and successful. *Science, 237*, 143–149.

Rowe, J.W. & Kahn, R.L. (1997). Successful aging. *Gerontologist, 37*(4), 433–440.

Rowe, J.W. & Kahn, R.L. (1998). Successful aging. *Aging, 10*(2), 142–144.

Rozance, C.P. (1996). HIV and AIDS in older adults. *Infectious Disease Clinical Practice, 5*, 193–197.

Sampson, S. & Anxiety Disorders Association of America (2009). *New thinking on anxiety and aging: Anxiety disorders common in the elderly.* At www.adaa.org/ADAA per cent-20web per cent20fin/articles/aging.pdf.

Schaie, K.W. (2005). *Developmental influences on adult intelligence: The Seattle Longitudinal Study.* New York: Oxford University Press.

Schieman, S. & Campbell, J.E. (2001). Age variations in personal agency and self-esteem: The context of physical disability. *Journal of Aging and Health, 13*, 155–185.

Schneider, L.S. (1993). Efficacy of treatment for geropsychiatric patients with severe mental illness. *Psychopharmacology Bulletin, 29*(4), 501–524.

Scogin, F. & McElreth, L. (1994). Efficacy of psychosocial treatments of geriatric depression: A quantitative review. *Journal of Consulting and Clinical Psychology, 62*, 69–74.

Scogin, F., Morthland, M., Kaufman, A., Burgio, L., Chaplin, W. & Kong, G. (2007). Improving quality of life in diverse rural older adults: a randomized trial of a psychological treatment. *Psychology and Aging, 22*(4), 657–665.

Shih, M. (2008). Health-related quality of life among adults with serious psychological distress and chronic medical conditions. *Quality of Life Research, 17*(4), 521–528.

Shulz, R., Beach, S.R., Ives, D.G., Martire, L.M., Ariyo, A.A. & Kop, W. (2000). Association between depression and mortality in older adults: The cardiovascular health study. *Archives of Internal Medicine, 160*, 1761–1768.

Skiest, D.J., Rubinstein, E., Carley, N., Gioiella, L. & Lyons, R. (1996). The importance of comorbidity in HIV-infected patients over 55: A retrospective case-control study. *American Journal of Medicine, 101*, 605–611.

Sprenkel, D.G. (1999). Therapeutic issues and strategies in group therapy with older men. In M. Duffy (Ed.) *Handbook of counseling and psychotherapy with older adults* (pp. 214–227). New York: Wiley.

Stanley, M.A., Wilson, N.J., Novy, D.M., Rhoades, H.M., Wagener, P.D., Greisinger, A.J. *et al.* (2009). Cognitive behavior therapy for generalized anxiety disorder among older adults in primary care: A randomized clinical trial. *Journal of the American Medical Association, 301*(14), 487.

Topol, E.J. (Ed.) (2006). *Textbook of cardiovascular medicine* (3rd edn, pp. 561–581). Philadelphia: Lippincott, Williams & Wilkins.

US Census Bureau (2009). *Unprecedented global aging examined in new census bureau report commissioned by the National Institute of Aging.* Press release. At www.census.gov/Press-Release/www/releases/archives/aging_population/013988.html.

US Department of Health and Human Services, Administration on Aging. (2008). *A profile of older Americans.* Washington, DC: US Department of Health and Human Services.

US Department of Health and Human Services. (1999). *Mental health: A report of the Surgeon General.* Rockville, MD: US Department of Health and Human Services.

Van Soling, H. & Henkens, K. (2008). Adjustment to and satisfaction with retirement: Two of a kind? *Psychological Aging, 23*(2), 422–434.

Vaughn, L. & Hartman, M. (2009). Aging and visual short-term memory: Effects of object type and information load. *Aging, Neuropsychology, and Cognition, 22*, 1–20.

Vedhara, K., Cox, N.K., Wilcock, G.K., Perks, P., Hunt, M. anderson, S. *et al.* (1999). Chronic stress in elderly carers of dementia patients and antibody response to influenza vaccination. *Lancet, 353*(9153), 627–631.

Von Kanel, R., Mausbach, B.T., Patterson, T.L., Dimsdale, J.E., Aschbacher, K., Mills, P.J. *et al.* (2008). Increased Framingham coronary heart disease risk score in dementia caregivers relative to non-caregiving controls. *Gerontology, 54*, 131–137.

Wagenaar, D., Colenda, C.C., Kreft, M., Sawade, J., Gardiner, J. & Poverejan, E. (2003). Treating depression in nursing homes: Practice guidelines in the real world. *Journal of the American Osteopathic Association, 103*(10), 465–469.

Whitbourne, S.K. (2005). *Adult development and aging: Biopsychosocial Perspectives* (2nd edn, pp. 176–204). New York: Wiley.

Zeiss, A.M. & Steffen, A.M. (1996). Interdisciplinary health care teams: The basic unit of geriatric care. In L.L. Carstensen & B.A. Edelstein (Eds.) *The practical handbook of clinical gerontology* (pp. 423–450). Thousand Oaks, CA: Sage.

31

Palliative and End-of-Life Care

Sue Hall and Sheila Payne

Chapter Outline

People reaching the end of life experience a range of physical and psychological problems. This chapter focuses on some of the important end-of-life issues and their psychological impact on these people and their families. It begins with an explanation of some of the terminology used in this area, the main causes of death and the most prevalent symptoms. It then focuses on the prevalence and causes of psychological, spiritual and existential distress and the importance of maintaining dignity at the end of life, along with examples of therapies aimed at fostering a sense of dignity and reducing distress. This is followed by sections on the impact on family carers and bereavement, coping, advance care planning and communication on end-of-life issues. The chapter concludes with a summary including some potential roles for psychologists in end-of-life care.

Key Concepts

Cancer
Communication
Coping
Depression
Dignity
Dignity therapy
End of life
Existential distress
Expressive writing
Palliative care
Psychological distress
Spirituality
Supportive-expressive
   group therapy
Symptoms
Terminal care

Introduction

Although there is an increasing number of psychologists working with health-care professionals and their patients at various stages of their illness trajectories, relatively few work with people reaching the end of life and their families (Nydegger, 2008). However, many of the issues for people reaching the end of life are of a psychosocial nature and psychologists have much to offer in this field (Professional Practice Board of the British Psychological Society, 2008).

What is palliative and end-of-life care?

Palliative and end-of-life care are important public health issues. Palliative care is concerned with reducing the suffering, maintaining the dignity and quality of life and addressing the care needs of people at the end of their lives. It is about the management of physical symptoms and psychological, social and spiritual problems, coordination and continuity of care in different settings and across the disease trajectory, and interdisciplinary and cross-sectional teamwork involving staff from different health-care professions as well as volunteer services. It includes carers, both in their role as partners in the team and as family members, who require care and support (Radbruch, 2008). Palliative care affirms life and views dying as a normal process and aims to achieve a 'good death' and neither to hasten nor prolong it.

The rapid development of hospices and the recognition of the success of their work in the past 40 years has been extraordinary. The term 'hospice care' first came into use in the 1960s when Dame Cicely Saunders founded St Christopher's Hospice in London to care for dying people with a focus on those with incurable cancer. Hospice care is now no longer provided only in buildings known as hospices, or only for people with incurable cancer. The term can be used for people with other life-threatening illnesses and those being cared for at home. In some countries such as the USA, hospice care is largely home care, however, the term 'hospice' is not appropriate in French-speaking countries as it implies custodial care. Terms such as 'palliative care', 'hospice care' 'terminal care' or 'end-of-life care' are often used interchangeably in the literature. Since 1975, the term 'palliative care' has increasingly been used to describe hospice-type services. Up to the 1980s most hospice and palliative care services described the care they gave as 'terminal'. However, in some countries, such as the UK, the term 'terminal' was thought to be a barrier to health professionals referring patients, and also to patients accepting such care. There is also a movement towards offering such care earlier on in the disease trajectory, rather than only in the dying phase, therefore, the term 'palliative care' is increasingly used. 'Terminal' care is often used when it is clear that a person is in a progressive state of decline and this is an important part of palliative care. 'End-of-life care' is increasingly used in the UK as an alternative to palliative care to encompass the last few years of life and it extends to all dying people whatever their diagnosis (Department of Health, 2008).

Causes of death

Traditionally within the UK, palliative care has focused on the needs of people with advanced cancer and their families. However, more people die from non-cancer diseases. The top five predicted causes of death for 2020 are: (i) ischaemic heart disease; (ii) cerebrovascular disease (including stroke); (iii) chronic obstructive pulmonary disease,; (iv) lower respiratory infections; and (v) lung, trachea and bronchial cancer (Murray & Lopez, 1997). The principles of palliative can also apply to these and other patients with progressive life-threatening or advanced diseases such as HIV/AIDS, renal or liver failure, neurogenerative and sickle cell diseases.

Symptoms at the end of life

People reaching the end of life experience a range of symptoms. Some of these, such as anorexia and breathlessness, can be complex and frightening. A Canadian study found a high prevalence of physical and psychological symptoms in both people with metastatic cancer and patients with end-stage diseases (Tranmer et al., 2003). Overall the most prevalent physical symptoms were lack of energy (84 per cent), dry mouth (81 per cent), drowsiness (70 per cent), pain (63 per cent), cough and shortness of breath (both 62 per cent). Worry was the most prevalent psychological symptom (70 per cent), followed by difficulty in sleeping (59 per cent) and feeling sad (53 per cent). The two groups differed on physical, but not on psychological symptoms. For example, people with cancer experienced more pain while those with other diseases experienced more breathlessness. Chapter 24, this volume, focuses on the management of pain.

Distress at the End of Life

Psychological distress

From a psychological perspective, dying creates a dual crisis: coping with current ill-health (living the life left) and simultaneously making meaning of the life lived. A systematic and evidence-based review of the psychological issues experienced by patients at the end of life describes the normal coping responses, the epidemiology of common psychiatric disorders, approaches to the clinical assessment of psychological distress and therapeutic approaches to common psychological problems at the end of life (Block, 2006). There are many sources of distress for people reaching the end of life. These include grief about current and anticipated losses, concerns about being a burden, fear and uncertainty about the future, unresolved issues from the past and concerns about loved ones. Worries about family members are a major feature of life-threatening illness for most patients (Greisinger et al., 1997). Other stressors include problems with work, finances, housing, transportation and legal matters.

Psychological distress is common in people reaching the end of life. Although distress can have a major impact on the individual and their family, such problems often remain undetected and under-treated. This may be due to the normalisation of distress by patients and a lack of awareness and skill by clinicians in identifying and differentiating distress from appropriate sadness (Thekkumpurath et al., 2008). The assessment of distress in people reaching the end of life can be a challenge. For example, some of the common physical symptoms they experience, such as fatigue, sleep and appetite problems and loss of concentration and energy, are also used to diagnose depression. Untreated distress has an impact on quality of life, physical symptoms such as pain, physical functioning, role and social functioning and on families.

Most studies of the prevalence of distress in palliative care populations have focused on depression (Thekkumpurath et al., 2008). However, a systematic review of the prevalence of depression in advanced disease found that studies used widely different methodologies and had markedly different results (Hotopf et al., 2002). A high proportion of people reported depression as a symptom when this was assessed using a single question (median 40.5 per cent). The median prevalence in those using the Hospital Anxiety and Depression Scale was lower at 29 per cent and even lower when psychiatric interviews were used (15 per cent). The studies were heterogeneous in terms of the patients studied, the assessments made and the definition of depression used, which led to wide variations in the prevalence reported. Although there is considerable overlap between anxiety and depression, anxiety disorders are less prevalent than depression (LeFevre et al., 1999). Anxiety is often seen as a natural consequence of becoming aware of mortality. Although low levels of anxiety can trigger adaptation and coping responses, high levels of anxiety are problematic and can interfere with functioning and information processing. Depression and anxiety are seen as potentially treatable, even at the end of life.

Treatment of psychological distress includes medication, supportive psychotherapy and patient and family education (Block, 2006). A systematic review of the treatment of depression in palliative care identified only three randomised control trials (RCTs) assessing pharmacological treatments for depressants and none assessing psychotherapy specifically addressing depression (Ly et al., 2002). The authors concluded that there were too few adequate studies to draw clear conclusions about the management of depression in advanced disease. Psychotherapies not focusing specifically on depression are described later in this chapter.

Spiritual and existential distress

The importance of spiritual care at the end of life was emphasised by Dame Cicely Saunders, the founder of the modern hospice movement, who introduced the idea that suffering was the result of psychological, social and spiritual factors as well as physical symptoms. She used the multidimensional concept of 'total pain' to describe how life-threatening illness can impact on individuals and suggested that holistic care was necessary to treat pain effectively. Spiritual and existential issues can have an important impact on the well-being of people reaching the end of life, for example, finding a sense of purpose and meaning in life and in an illness is associated with an ability to tolerate psychosocial symptoms and satisfaction with quality of life (Brady et al., 1999). Poor spiritual well-being is associated with a desire for hastened death, hopelessness and suicidal ideation (McClain et al., 2003) and loss of meaning in life is often cited by doctors caring for the dying as a reason as to why patients requested assisted suicide (Meier et al., 1998). Consequently, there has been an increasing emphasis on the importance of spiritual care as an essential part of holistic care, especially in palliative care and nursing.

There are many definitions of spirituality and it is clear that the construct is broader than religion. Kearney and Mount (2000) distinguish 'the spiritual' from 'religion', where the spirit is a dimension of personhood and religion is a construct of human making. A comprehensive review of the health literature documented 92 definitions of spirituality. These were categorised under seven themes: (i) relationship to God, a spiritual being, a Higher Power, or a reality greater than the self; (ii) not of the self; (iii) transcendence or connectedness unrelated to a belief in a higher being; (iv) existential, not material world; (v) meaning and purpose in life; (vi) life force of the person, integrating aspect of the person; and (vii) summative definitions that combined multiple themes (Unruh et al., 2002). Another review concluded that there was some consensus in the literature that existential questions played an important role in spiritual pain, but some disagreement concerning the inclusion of a dimension related to faith (Lemay & Wilson, 2008).

Several studies have explored the spiritual needs of patients. For example, Murray and colleagues (Murray et al., 2004) conducted a qualitative study of 20 people dying of lung cancer or heart failure and their informal carers in Scotland. They found spiritual concerns were important to many patients in both groups, both early and later in the illness progression. They felt a need for love, meaning and purpose and sometime transcendence, regardless of whether or not they held religious beliefs. Signs of spiritual needs included feeling that life

was not worthwhile and asking 'what have I done to deserve this?'. Signs of spiritual well-being included inner peace and harmony and finding meaning. Patients and carers were often reluctant to raise spiritual issues with 'busy' health professionals and some sought to disguise their spiritual distress. In a study of 248 ethnically diverse cancer patients in the USA 51 per cent wanted help in overcoming fears, 42 per cent in finding hope, 40 per cent in finding meaning in life, 39 per cent finding spiritual resources and 25 per cent having someone to talk with about the meaning of life and death (Moadel et al., 1999). People who were recently diagnosed, unmarried, Hispanic or African American were more likely to report five or more such needs. In view of the increasing diversity of populations in many countries, this study emphasises the importance of developing interventions which acknowledge the distinctive spiritual beliefs, images and meanings valued in different cultures. Cross-cultural perspectives on illness are covered in more detail in Chapter 27, this volume.

Dignity

Maintaining dignity is given a high priority in health and social care strategy documents in most European countries and is an overarching value or goal of palliative care. The term dignity has been highly politicised and is frequently used to justify various end-of-life care practices and policies (Chochinov, 2006). For some, the term 'dying with dignity' is synonymous with the right to assisted suicide and euthanasia. A survey of doctors conducted in the USA found that loss of dignity was cited in 53 per cent of cases where prescriptions had been written for the purpose of hastening death (Meier et al., 1998). Although there is a great deal of rhetoric around dignity, there is no agreed definition. A brief review of the studies exploring the concept of dignity from a nursing perspective showed a wide range of definitions and themes relating to the construct, however, a common theme was respecting a patient as a person (Franklin et al., 2006).

One approach to dignity-oriented care provision, which focuses specifically on the terminally ill, is Chochinov's dignity conserving model (Chochinov et al., 2002). The model (Figure 31.1) was developed in Canada from interviews with 50 patients with

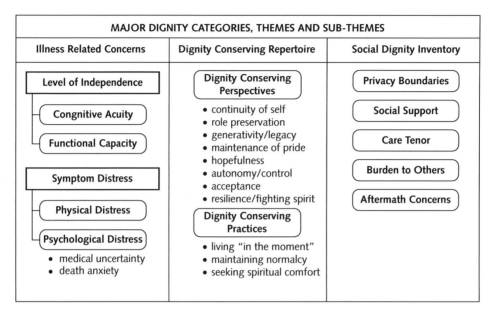

Figure 31.1   The dignity model
Source: Chochinov, H.M., Hack, T., McClement, S., Kristjanson, L. & Harlos, M. (2002). Dignity in the terminally ill: a developing empirical model. *Social Science & Medicine, 54,* 433–443. Elsevier.

advanced cancer focusing on what supports and what undermines their dignity. The three major categories (illness-related concerns, dignity-conserving repertoire, social aspects of the illness experience) refer to broad issues that determine how individuals experience a sense of dignity as death approaches. Each has several themes and sub-themes. The main categories of this dignity model were broadly supported in a study of older people in care homes (Hall, Longhurst & Higginson, 2009). The dignity model provides direction for how to develop interventions that enhance a sense of dignity (Chochinov, 2006) and has provided the framework for psychotherapy (described in the following section) to help promote a sense of dignity and reduce psychological and spiritual distress for people reaching the end of life (Chochinov *et al.*, 2005).

Therapies to Reduce Psychological and Existential Distress

Conventional psychological therapies may have limited applications for patients who are very sick or dying. Having little time left, fatigue and cognitive problems due to the illness or its treatment make providing intensive and long-term psychotherapy difficult. Furthermore, there have also been relatively few RCTs to provide an evidence base for interventions to reduce psychological and spiritual distress at the end of life. For example, although it has been suggested that incorporating analytically informed therapy into psychotherapy during the last weeks of life can be beneficial for people reaching the end of life (Macleod, 2009), no RCT of such interventions has been published. A review of eight manualised interventions to treat existential distress in life-threatening illness found that only one, supportive-expressive group therapy, met the criteria for a 'probably efficacious' treatment (Lemay & Wilson, 2008). There was an absence of evidence to support the remaining seven. Furthermore, six of the eight interventions were group therapies, which limited their application to ambulatory patients who were still well enough to take part. In their review, LeMay and Wilson highlight some of the challenges to conducting research in this area and some of the shortcomings in published research. These included problems with recruitment and attrition, data analysis, follow-up assessments, confounding variables and the operationalisation of outcomes. One obvious problem is that patients often have many physical symptoms and sometimes high levels of distress which may affect their willingness to participate. Attrition rates are often high as patients become too ill or die before participation in the study is completed.

Supportive-expressive group therapy

The aim of supportive-expressive group therapy is to provide patients with advanced cancer who are having difficulty adjusting to their illness with a supportive environment where they can be helped to adjust to the demands of their illness, learn to live life as fully and authentically as possible, improve their quality of life and possibly slow the progression of their disease (Spiegel & Spira, 1991). Members of the group are encouraged to interact within and outside the sessions to learn from each other's experiences and to share their thoughts and emotions about their cancer and their concerns about death. Over the course of the therapy, participants are also taught techniques such as self-hypnosis and breath awareness to help them gain control of symptoms. The therapy is fairly intensive and long term (over a year or more), involving 90-minute weekly sessions. Lemay and Wilson's review (2008) identified RCTs, which suggested that long-term supportive-expressive group therapy may reduce distress in women with metastatic breast cancer who have elevated levels of distress at baseline and who receive treatment for a year. The therapy has not, however, been shown to increase survival. A short-term approach held over a period of 12 weeks has been developed (Classen et al., 1993), although evidence as to the efficacy of this version is mixed.

Dignity therapy

In contrast to supportive-expressive group therapy, which would not be accessible to patients who are very ill or very close to the end of life, dignity therapy (Chochinov et al., 2005) is brief and can be delivered at the bedside by a trained health-care professional to people who are very close to death. This individualised therapy aims to address physical, psychosocial, existential and spiritual domains of concern or dis-

tress. The therapy is informed by an empirical model of dignity at the end of life (described in the section on dignity). It comprises an interview with a trained therapist (usually a nurse or other health-care professional) covering important aspects of the individual's life, the times they felt most alive, characteristics they would like their families to know and remember about them, important roles adopted during their lives, concerns that have been left unsaid and any advice or messages for their loved ones. The interview is recorded, promptly transcribed, edited and the resulting document is returned to the patient, who can then revise it if they wish. Much of the benefit of this therapy is thought to derive from creating this lasting legacy document, which individuals can share with or bequeath to people of their choosing. Thus, dignity therapy aims to help both people who are dying and those they leave behind. A preliminary evaluation of dignity therapy conducted with hospice patients in Canada produced positive findings for patients (Chochinov et al., 2005) and their families (McClement et al., 2007). A randomised controlled trial of dignity therapy for hospice patients is currently underway in Canada, Australia and the USA and a Phase II pilot study is being conducted with older people in care homes in the UK (Hall, Chochinov et al., 2009). A small trial assessing the feasibility of delivering dignity therapy using videophone has been conducted (Passik et al., 2004).

Expressive writing

Another intervention which has attracted some attention in health psychology, and seemed promising for people with advanced cancer, is expressive writing (Pennebaker, 1999). This involves people writing about their most upsetting and traumatic experiences. Although a preliminary study of expressive writing in patients with advanced renal cancer showed no impact of the intervention on symptom distress, perceived stress or mood, there was a positive impact on sleep disturbances (deMoor et al., 2002). This prompted Bruera and colleagues (Bruera et al., 2008) to conduct a pilot study with patients with advanced cancer receiving palliative care. They asked patients in the intervention group to write about their most traumatic and upsetting experiences, important things about which they had deepest feelings and thoughts and an event or experience that they had not talked about with others in detail. The researchers felt that the study could be considered successful if 80 per cent of patients completed four writing sessions during the two-week study period. They suggest that their rapid accrual of patients into the study demonstrates patient interest in taking part in such studies. However, although the majority of patients were able to complete the baseline measures, only two of the 24 completed the two-week study (one in the intervention and one in the control group). Furthermore an analysis of the writing they returned to the research team found that most patients wrote relatively little, they often gave chronological accounts of their illness and/or talked about positive aspects and rarely expressed emotions. The study closed early. The authors felt that much of the problem was due to patients becoming ill or being hospitalised. They suggest studies of expressive writing in a palliative care setting are not feasible without major modifications of the methods, including recruiting patients who are less ill.

Carers

People in close relationships, be they within the family network or friends, are crucial to supporting and providing care to people in the final phase of life. They share the illness experience and provide vital care including psychological support, domestic and physical tasks. Most carers manage very well and draw upon the support of family members and wider social networks, but there is evidence that vicarious suffering – witnessing the physical and mental deterioration of the ill person – is profoundly distressing (Payne & Hudson, 2009). Caregiving within palliative care contexts is arguably especially demanding because of the sense of imminent loss and the demands of caring for a patient with unpredictable and high dependency needs. Many carers do not identify with the label 'carers', as they regard caregiving as a normal part of complex patterns of reciprocal relationships that are characteristic of most family, kinship and friendship systems. Thus, most caregiving is enmeshed in the normal web of mutual dependencies, responsibilities, demands and rewards that make up everyday family life (Grande et al., 2009).

It is estimated that there are approximately 500,000 people providing such care in the UK at any point, with up to 100 million in Europe. The impact of their financial contribution to providing care is estimated to be greater than the budget spent on professional nursing services in each country. While there is relatively poor data, it is known that carers of dying people are predominantly female, older people and are spouses of the cared-for person. Undertaking a caregiving role can impact on their physical health (e.g. back strain), psychological health (e.g. depression, anxiety), social interactions (e.g. more isolated), finances (e.g. loss of income, promotion prospects, pension) and wider engagement with society. There are a number of theoretical models that conceptualise the caregiver experience including psychological models that focus on carer strain and deficits, stress and coping models that emphasise individual appraisal and coping, and social systems approaches that look at broader aspects of society and the social position of carers (Payne & Hudson, 2009). In the past there has been a tendency to focus on the negative demands of care provision with little recognition of the rewards including self-esteem, mutually loving relationships and sense of fulfilling a family obligation. This has shifted discourses in the literature from vulnerability to resilience, although neither fully account for caring experience nor adequately indicate the types of support required (Payne, 2007). A systematic review has indicated few well-validated interventions to support carers (Harding & Higginson, 2003).

Bereavement

The experience of loss is challenging at all times of life, and perhaps one of the most difficult losses is the death of a significant family member or friend. While grief is a normal response to loss, it is recognised that for many individuals grief can be acutely distressing and impair normal functioning. Many hospices provide bereavement care for families of their patients (Field et al., 2007). A national survey of hospice bereavement support services in the UK demonstrated a diversity of activities, mostly focused on providing information, psychological and social support rather than practical interventions. Most support was provided by trained volunteers rather than professionals – usually nurses and social workers, with very little input from psychologists. Support is generally offered to all bereaved people who need to opt in to services, rather than screening to identify those at most risk of poor psychological outcomes. Grief counselling is widely available in the community but there is inconsistent evidence about its efficacy (Larson & Hoyt, 2007).

Coping

Despite the many sources of distress for people at the end of life, many cope with their illness and its prognosis. Coping has an important role in understanding people's responses to illness. One in-depth qualitative study explored the coping strategies used by people receiving palliative care for advanced cancer (Sand *et al.*, 2009). All 20 participants were aware that they were dying, and their efforts to cope with this were symbolised as a cognitive and emotional pendulum swinging between extremes of life and death. During swings of the pendulum people used any means available to cope: their own resources, other people, animals, nature, a transcendent power, hope, imagination and magical thinking. They strove to maintain their links to life and shielded themselves against negative emotions due to impending death using coping strategies such as togetherness, involvement hope and continuance (Figure 31.2).

The results of research examining the association between coping styles and outcomes for people reaching the end of life are equivocal. For example, 'fighting spirit' was thought to reduce the likelihood of cancer recurrence and mortality, however, a meta-analytic review found no evidence to support this (Petticrew *et al.*, 2002). Although avoidance and denial are often thought of as maladaptive coping styles, they can also be adaptive. Avoidance can reduce stress, allowing people to come to terms with their condition before developing more effective coping strategies and denial can allow people to enjoy the times when they are feeling relatively well. However, as people become iller, their ability to process information can decline which can limit their coping resources. Research with family carers of older people dying of heart failure indicates that they use a range of coping strategies to deal with

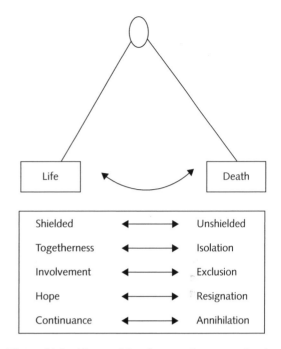

Figure 31.2 The pendulum between factors associated with life and death
Source: Sand, L., Olsson, M. & Strang, P. (2009). Coping strategies in the presence of one's own impending death from cancer. *Journal of Pain and Symptom Management, 37,* 13–22. Elsevier.

the everyday demands of their situation (Barnes *et al.*, 2006).

Advance Care Planning

There is a growing recognition that patients should have greater opportunity to plan their future end-of-life care, a process known as advance care planning. This may lead to the completion of an advance directive or 'living will', where an adult makes an advance decision to refuse a specific medical treatment or procedure should they lose capacity to make such decisions in the future. Such discussions are a chance for individuals and their families to discuss a wide range of issues, including: their concerns, important values or personal goals of care; understanding about their illness and prognosis; and their preferences for types of care or treatment that may be beneficial in the future and the availability of these. Plans can include where patients are cared for and eventually die and funeral plans. An advance care plan not only provides valuable information for patient choice, but can also be helpful in keeping open dialogue between care providers, patients and their families. This is a time when patients and their families may need psychological support.

Although many people welcome the opportunity to make such plans, some feel unable or not ready to do so (Barnes *et al.*, 2007). This focus group study conducted in the UK, involving 22 palliative care and oncology patients, relatives and user group members found that the timing of the discussion was important (not at the time of diagnosis or active treatment), and the person initiating discussion should be skilled in responding to the patient's cues and avoid destroying hope. Participants felt that advance decisions to refuse treatment should be part of a broader discussion of end-of-life issues rather than the focus of the discussion and that people should be given the opportunity to change their minds in the future. Although some people felt that the opportunity to make choices regarding end of life could maintain a sense of control, there was some concern that such discussions could have a detrimental effect on the doctor–patient relationship. It is particularly important to take into account differences in culture, religion and value positions.

Communication

In end-of-life care, especially palliative care, effective communication with patients, caregivers and family is of vital importance (Gordon *et al.*, 2007) as the communication of information, predictions and prognosis can have a major impact on their current and future behaviour, as well as potentially on treatment and illness outcomes. People reaching the end of life and their families often have 'difficult' questions for health-care professionals, for example about their symptoms and prognosis, the process of dying and the choices they have to make. These questions need to be answered sensitively and honestly while at the same time bearing in mind the capability of people to understand and manage the information they are requesting.

Conversations with patients and their families about dying almost always results in some degree of discomfort or awkwardness. This can be attributed to

three main sources: those related to society; those related to individual patients; and those relating to health-care professionals (Buckman, 1998). Difficulties related to society arise from the social denial of death resulting from lack of experience of death in the family, raised expectations of life and health due to the constant bombardment of news of apparently miraculous cures, and the changing role of religion. Difficulties relating to individuals focus their fears of dying (fear of physical, psychological symptoms, existential concerns, worries about treatment, financial problems and loss of social status). Health-care professionals can be distressed by interviews with dying patients. Their concerns include being blamed, not having the necessary skills and their emotional reactions and those of their patients. Studies focusing on giving 'bad news' to patients highlight the importance of: preparing well; being empathetic, sympathetic, compassionate; encouraging and validating emotions; and arranging a follow-up (Gordon *et al.*, 2007).

Conclusions

People reaching the end of life can experience many problems: physical, psychological and social. They and their families are often expected to make difficult decisions involving sensitive discussion with the people involved in their care. Although many people cope with these problems, psychological and existential distress is common and conventional therapies may have limited application for patients who are sick and dying. Although psychologists have much to offer in the field of palliative and end-of-life care it has been suggested that what they have to offer is not as visible and as available as it could be (Nydegger, 2008). Health psychology is a discipline which is firmly rooted in research and theoretical understanding. Since the knowledge and skills base which a psychologist brings to end-of-life care is both broad (e.g. the ability to understand and apply several different models and approaches) and deep (e.g. expertise in specific models of therapy and research) (Professional Practice Board of the British Psychological Society, 2008), they have much to offer in the area of palliative and end-of-life care. This can be clearly seen in other chapters of this book, for example, those covering symptom perceptions (Chapter 13), stress, health and illness (Chapter 19), illness cognitions (Chapter 12), pain (Chapter 24), coping (Chapter 21), social support (Chapter 22), quality of life (Chapter 26), psychological interventions in chronic illness (Chapter 16) and ageing, health and illness (Chapter 30).

Discussion Points

1 Is it possible to have a good death?
2 List the possible sources of distress for people reaching the end of life?
3 What is spiritual distress and how is it different from psychological distress?
4 What does the term dignity mean to you? Is it something deep within you or is it something that can be taken away or fostered by others?
5 Discuss how possible interventions to reduce psychological distress might be useful for people reaching the end of life? Would they need to be adapted for this group and how?
6 What end-of-life issues are patients and their families likely to need to discuss with health-care professionals? What particular communication skills are needed to do this sensitively and effectively?
7 What types of support are most likely to be perceived as helpful to family carers and those who are bereaved?

Further Reading

Block, S.D. 2006. Psychological issues in end-of-life care. *Journal of Palliative Medicine*, 9, 751–772.

Chochinov, H.M., Hack, T., Hassard, T., Kristjanson, L.J., McClement, S. & Harlos, M. (2005). Dignity therapy: a novel psychotherapeutic intervention for patients near the end of life. *Journal of Clinocal Oncology*, 23, 5520–5525.

Hudson, P. & Payne, S. (Eds.) (2008). *Family carers and palliative care*. Oxford: Oxford University Press.

LeMay, K. & Wilson, K.G. (2008). Treatment of existential distress in life threatening illness: a review of manualized interventions. *Clinical Psychology Review*, 28, 472–493.

Lloyd Williams, M. (Ed.) (2008). *Psychosocial issues in palliative care* (2nd edn). Oxford: Oxford University Press.

Ly, K.L., Chidgey, J., Addington-Hall, J. & Hotopf, M. (2002). Depression in palliative care: a systematic review. Part 2. Treatment. *Palliative Medicine*, 16, 279–284.

Professional Practice Board of the British Psychological Society (2008). *The role of psychology in end of life care*. Leicester: British Psychological Society.

References

Barnes, K., Jones, L., Tookman, A. & King, M. (2007). Acceptability of an advance care planning interview schedule: a focus group study. *Palliative Medicine, 21,* 23–28.

Barnes, S., Gott, M., Payne, S., Parker, C., Seamark, D., Gariballa, S. *et al.* (2006). Characteristics and views of family carers of older people with heart failure. *Intenational Journal of Palliative Nursing, 12,* 380–389.

Block, S.D. (2006). Psychological issues in end-of-life care. *Journal of Palliative Medicine, 9,* 751–772.

Brady, M.J., Peterman, A.H., Fitchett, G., Mo, M. & Cella, D. (1999). A case for including spirituality in quality of life measurement in oncology. *Psycho-Oncology, 8,* 417–428.

Bruera, E., Willey, J., Cohen, M. & Palmer, J.L. (2008). Expressive writing in patients receiving palliative care: a feasibility study. *Journal of Palliative Medicine, 11,* 15–19.

Buckman, R. (1998). Communication in palliative care: a practical guide. In D. Doyle, G.W.C. Hanks & N. MacDonald (Eds.) *Oxford textbook of palliative medicine* (2nd edn, pp. 141–156). Oxford: Oxford Medical Publishers.

Chochinov, H.M. (2006). Dying, dignity and new horizons in palliative end-of-life care. *CA: A Cancer Journal for Clinicians, 56,* 84–103.

Chochinov, H.M., Hack, T., Hassard, T., Kristjanson, L.J., McClement, S. & Harlos, M. (2005). Dignity therapy: a novel psychotherapeutic intervention for patients near the end of life. *Journal of Clinical Oncology, 23,* 5520–5525.

Chochinov, H.M., Hack, T., McClement, S., Kristjanson, L. & Harlos, M. (2002). Dignity in the terminally ill: a developing empirical model. *Social Science & Medicine, 54,* 433–443.

Classen, C., Diamond, S., Soleman, A., Fobair, P., Spira, J. & Spiers, J. (1993). *Brief supportive-expressive group therapy for women with primary breast cancer: A treatment manual.* Stanford, CA: Stanford University School of Medicine.

deMoor C., Sterner, J., Hall, M., Warneke, C., Gilani, Z., Amato, R. *et al.* (2002). A pilot study of the effects of expressive writing on psychological and behavioral adjustment in patients enrolled in a Phase II trial of vaccine therapy for metastatic renal cell carcinoma. *Health Psychology, 21,* 615–619.

Department of Health (2008). *End of life care strategy – Promoting high quality care for all adults at the end of life.* London: Department of Health.

Field, D., Payne, S., Relf, M. & Reid, D. (2007). Some issues in the provision of adult bereavement support by UK hospices. *Social Science & Medicine, 64,* 428–438.

Franklin, L.L., Ternestedt, B.M. & Nordenfelt, L. (2006). Views on dignity of elderly nursing home residents. *Nursing Ethics, 13,* 130–146.

Gordon, M., Buchman, D. & Buchman, S.H. (2007). 'Bad news' communication in palliative care: a challenge and key to succcess. *Annals of Long-Term Care, 15,* 32–35.

Grande, G., Stajduhar, K., Aoun, S., Toye, C., Funk, L., Addington-Hall, J. *et al.* (2009). Supporting lay carers in end of life care: current gaps and future priorities. *Palliative Medicine, 23,* 339–344.

Greisinger, A.J., Lorimor, R.J., Aday, L.A., Winn, R.J. & Baile, W.F. (1997). Terminally ill cancer patients. Their most important concerns. *Cancer Practitioner, 5,* 147–154.

Hall, S., Chochinov, H., Murray, S., Harding, R., Richardson, A. & Higginson, I.J. (2009). Assessing the feasibility, acceptability and potential effectiveness of dignity therapy for older people in care homes: Study Protocol. *BMC Geriatrics, 9.*

Hall, S., Longhurst, S. & Higginson, I. (2009). Living and dying with dignity: a qualitative study of the views of older people in nursing homes. *Age and Ageing, 38,* 411–416.

Harding, R. & Higginson, I.J. (2003). What is the best way to help caregivers in cancer and palliative care? A systematic literature review of interventions and their effectiveness. *Palliative Medicine, 17,* 63–74.

Hotopf, M., Chidgey, J., Addington-Hall, J. & Ly, K.L. (2002). Depression in advanced disease: a systematic review. Part 1. Prevalence and case finding. *Palliative Medicine, 16,* 81–97.

Kearney, M. & Mount, B. (2000). Spiritual care of the dying patient. In H.M. Cochinov & W. Reitbart (Eds.) *Handbook of psychiatry in palliative medicine* (pp. 357–373). New York: Oxford University Press.

Larson, D.G. & Hoyt, W.T. (2007). What has become of grief counselling? An evaluation of the empirical foundations of the new pessimism. *Professional Psychology: Research and Practice, 38,* 347–355.

LeFevre, P., Devereux, J., Smith, S., Lawrie, S.M. & Cornbleet, M. (1999). Screening for psychiatric illness in the palliative care inpatient setting: a comparison between the Hospital Anxiety and Depression Scale and the General Health Questionnaire-12. *Palliatiative Medicine, 13,* 399–407.

Lemay, K. & Wilson, K.G. (2008). Treatment of existential distress in life threatening illness: a review of manualized interventions. *Clinical Psychology Review, 28,* 472–493.

Ly, K.L., Chidgey, J., Addington-Hall, J. & Hotopf, M. (2002). Depression in palliative care: a systematic review. Part 2. Treatment. *Palliative Medicine, 16,* 279–284.

Macleod, A.D. (2009). Psychotherapy at the end of life: psychdynamic contributions. *Progress in Palliative Care, 17,* 1–10.

McClain, C.S., Rosenfeld, B. & Breitbart, W. (2003). Effect of spiritual well-being on end-of-life despair in terminally-ill cancer patients. *Lancet, 361,* 1603–1607.

McClement, S., Chochinov, H.M., Hack, T., Hassard, T., Kristjanson, L.J. & Harlos, M. (2007). Dignity therapy: family member perspectives. *Journal of Palliative Medicine, 10,* 1076–1082.

Meier, D.E., Emmons, C.A., Wallenstein, S., Quill, T., Morrison, R.S. & Cassel, C.K. (1998). A national survey of physician–assisted suicide and euthanasia in the United States. *New England Journal of Medicine, 338,* 1193–1201.

Moadel, A., Morgan, C., Fatone, A., Grennan, J., Carter, J., Laruffa, G. *et al.* (1999). Seeking meaning and hope: self-reported spiritual and existential needs among an ethnically-diverse cancer patient population. *Psycho-Oncology, 8,* 378–385.

Murray, C.J. & Lopez, A.D. (1997). Alternative projections of mortality and disability by cause 1990–2020: Global Burden of Disease Study. *Lancet, 349,* 1498–1504.

Murray, S.A., Kendall, M., Boyd, K., Worth, A. & Benton, T.F. (2004). Exploring the spiritual needs of people dying of lung cancer or heart failure: a prospective qualitative interview study of patients and their carers. *Palliative Medicine, 18,* 39–45.

Nydegger, R. (2008). Psychologists and hospice: where we are and where we can be. *Professional Psychology: Research and Practice, 39,* 459–463.

Passik, S.D., Kirsh, K.L., Leibee, S., Kaplan, L.S., Love, C., Napier, E. *et al.* (2004). A feasibility study of dignity psychotherapy delivered via telemedicine. *Palliative & Supportive Care, 2,* 149–155.

Payne, S. (2007). Resilient carers and caregivers. In B. Monroe & D. Oliviere (Eds.) *Resilience in palliative care – Achievement in adversity* (pp. 83–97). Oxford: Oxford University Press.

Payne, S. & Hudson, P. (2009). European Association for Palliative Care Task Force on Family Carers. *European Journal of Palliative Care, 16,* 77–81.

Pennebaker, J.W. (1999). The effects of traumatic disclosure on physical and mental health: the values of writing and talking about upsetting events. *International Journal of Emergency Mental Health, 1,* 9–18.

Petticrew, M., Bell, R. & Hunter, D. (2002). Influence of psychological coping on survival and recurrence in people with cancer: systematic review. *British Medical Journal, 325,* 1066.

Professional Practice Board of the British Psychological Society (2008). *The role of psychology in end of life care.* Leicester: British Psychological Society.

Radbruch, L. (2008). Palliative care in Europe: experiences and the future. *European Journal of Palliative Care, 15,* 186–189.

Sand, L., Olsson, M. & Strang, P. (2009). Coping strategies in the presence of one's own impending death from cancer. *Journal of Pain and Symptom Management, 37,* 13–22.

Spiegel, D. & Spira, J. (1991). *Supportive-expressive group therapy: A treatment manual of psychosocail intervention for women with recurrent breast cancer.* Stanford, CA: Stanford University School of Medicine.

Thekkumpurath, P., Venkateswaran, C., Kumar, M. & Bennett, M.I. (2008). Screening for psychological distress in palliative care: a systematic review. *Journal of Pain and Symptom Management, 36,* 520–528.

Tranmer, J.E., Heyland, D., Dudgeon, D., Groll, D., Squires-Graham, M. & Coulson, K. (2003). Measuring the symptom experience of seriously ill cancer and noncancer hospitalized patients near the end of life with the memorial symptom assessment scale. *Journal of Pain and Symptom Management, 25,* 420–429.

Unruh, A.M., Versnel, J. & Kerr, N. (2002). Spirituality unplugged: a review of commonalities and contentions and a resolution. *Canadian Journal of Occupational Therapy, 69,* 5–19.

Index

Printed and bound in the UK by
CPI Antony Rowe, Eastbourne